Global Business Today

Postscript

Global Business Today

Postscript 2002
Second Edition

Charles W. L. Hill
University of Washington

McGraw-Hill
Irwin

Boston   Burr Ridge, IL   Dubuque, IA   Madison, WI   New York   San Francisco   St. Louis
Bangkok   Bogotá   Caracas   Kuala Lumpur   Lisbon   London   Madrid   Mexico City
Milan   Montreal   New Delhi   Santiago   Seoul   Singapore   Sydney   Taipei   Toronto

McGraw-Hill Higher Education

A Division of The **McGraw-Hill** Companies

GLOBAL BUSINESS TODAY, POSTSCRIPT 2002

Some ancillaries, including electronic and print components, may not be available to customers outside the United States.

This book is printed on acid-free paper.

1 2 3 4 5 6 7 8 9 0 VNH/VNH 0 9 8 7 6 5 4 3 2 1

ISBN   0-07-249957-5

Publisher: *John E. Biernat*
Sponsoring editor: *Marianne Rutter*
Developmental editor II: *Christine Scheid*
Marketing manager: *Lisa Nicks*
Project manager: *Jim Labeots*
Production supervisor: *Debra R. Sylvester*
Media technology producer: *Jenny R. Williams*
Senior designer: *Jennifer McQueen*
Cover image: *Copyright © 2000 PhotoDisc, Inc. All rights reserved.*
Interior design: *Crispin Prebys*
Printer: *Von Hoffman Press, Inc.*
Typeface: *10/12 Baskerville*
Compositor: *York Graphic Services, Inc*

Library of Congress Cataloging-in-Publication Data

Hill, Charles W. L.
   Global Business Today, Postscript 2002 / Charles W. L. Hill / 2nd ed.
      p.   cm.
   ISBN 0-07-249957-5
   Includes Index
   1. International finance.   2. Financial crisis.   3. International
trade.   4. Foreign exchange.   5. Foreign exchange–Management.   I. Title.
HG3881.H488   2002
658.049– dc21   2001031281

www.mhhe.com

Introduction

One key task of the author of any text that deals with international business is to keep the content as current as possible. This is difficult given that the world around us is constantly changing. In this postscript, we review important developments that have occurred since the manuscript for the second edition of this book was sent to the publishers, and we discuss the implications of these developments for international business.

One development has been the continuing globalization of the world economy. Here we update the statistics contained in this book on the growth of world trade and foreign direct investment. A second important development was the breakdown of the World Trade Organization meetings in Seattle in December 1999 in the face of protests from various groups opposed to globalization. In this postscript we examine why these talks failed and what this means for the WTO. A third development was the decision to allow China to enter the World Trade Organization. A fourth development has been the rebound of Asian economies from the 1997–98 financial crises. A fifth development has been the poor performance of the euro, the currency unit that has been used by 11 of the 15 nations of the European Union since January 1999. By late 2000, the euro had depreciated by as much as 20 percent against the US dollar since its introduction, and this postscript examines why. A sixth development has been the surge in world oil prices to levels not seen since the early 1980s. In this postscript we examine why this has occurred, and we discuss the implications for the global economy. Finally, to mark the first year of a new millenium, the postscript closes with a review of the economic and political achievements of the 20th century and a discussion of the outlook for the early years of the 21st century.

Globalization of the World Economy

As discussed in Chapter 1, for half a century global trade has expanded much faster than global output. Between 1950 and 1999 the volume of world trade increased twentyfold, while the inflation-adjusted value of world gross domestic product (GDP) increased a little over 6.3 times. The late 1990s and first part of 2000 were no exception to this long-term trend. In 1998 and 1999, the volume of global trade in merchandised products expanded at 5 percent a year compounded, while world GDP grew at 2 percent in 1998 and 2.5 percent in 1999.[1]

For the first nine months of 2000, the volume of world trade surged to a near record 12 percent annual rate. While a slowdown in the last quarter of 2000 was expected to bring the total growth in the volume of world trade to about 10 percent for the year, this is still well above historic norms and far in excess of the estimated 4.5 percent expansion in world GDP. There are three reasons for the particularly strong growth in world trade in 2000. First, robust economic growth in the world's largest economy, the United States, resulted in high demand for imports, which grew at an annual rate of 20 percent during the first nine months of 2000. By comparison, US exports grew at an annual rate of 14 percent over the same period. As a result, in mid-2000, the US trade deficit hit a record $400 billion, amounting to about 4.5 percent of GDP. Second, the continuing recovery of Asian countries from the 1997–98 financial crisis helped to fuel growth in world trade. The value of Asia's imports and exports rose at a 27 percent annual rate in the first nine months of 2000 (these figures exclude China and Japan). Third, spurred by continued rapid economic growth, the value of China's trade expanded by more than one-third in the first nine months of 2000. Japan, too, registered a large expansion in international trade, which increased by 23 percent over the same period.[2]

The strong continuation of the long-term growth in the volume of international trade signals that the global economy is continuing to become ever more tightly integrated. As global trade grows faster than global GDP, national economies are becoming increasingly intertwined, depending on each other for an ever-larger percentage of goods and services. As this development unfolds, globalization is accelerating with global markets and global production systems replacing national markets and national production systems. The economic theories reviewed in Chapter 4 suggest this development is beneficial, with greater trade translating into increased efficiency in the world economy, income gains in countries involved in the global trading system, and greater global economic growth.

A similar trend toward globalization can be seen in the data on foreign direct investment (FDI) flows. According to the most recent figures from the United Nations, 1999 saw foreign direct investment outflows hit record levels.[3] During 1999, enterprises resident in one country invested some $860 billion in productive assets in another country. This was up from $732 billion in 1998. Provisional data suggest foreign direct investment outflows will exceed $1 trillion in 2000. To put this in perspective, in 1980 the value of foreign direct investment was just $60 billion, and in 1990 it was $210 billion.[4]

The rapid expansion of FDI suggests two things. First, individual enterprises are increasingly building global production systems, dispersing various activities to those locations in the world where they can be produced most efficiently. Second, the data imply that enterprises are entering each other's markets in an attempt to create and exploit emerging global markets for the goods and services they produce. The most recent data also suggest a sharp rise in the volume and value of cross-border mergers and acquisitions. Mergers and acquisitions, rather than building operations from the ground up, are becoming the favored mode for entering foreign markets. In 1999, for example, the value of completed cross-border mergers and acquisitions rose to $720 billion and involved about 6,000 transactions, up from $100 billion in 1987.[5]

As a result of foreign direct investment activity, there are now some 63,000 multinational companies in the world with about 700,000 foreign affiliates. Their growing importance in the world economy can be measured by their share of foreign direct investment stock in world GDP, which increased from 2 percent in 1980 to 14 percent at the start of 2000.[6]

Despite this rapid growth, recent data show that foreign direct investment remains highly concentrated, with most of the flows occurring between a limited group of nations. In 1999, some 10 developed countries received 70 percent of all FDI inflows, and 10 developing nations accounted for 80 percent of all the flows into that group. The usual suspects figured prominently among this select group including the United States (the largest recipient of FDI and the second largest source), the United Kingdom (the largest source), France, Germany, the Netherlands, China, and Mexico. A similar though less dramatic pattern can be seen in the trade data, where 10 countries accounted for 58 percent of the value of world trade in 1999.

Both the trade and foreign direct investment data suggest that we are witnessing not so much the globalization of the world economy as the rapid integration of the economies of a select club of developed and developing nations. The poorer nations of the world continue to be left on the sidelines in the headlong rush toward global economic integration. Africa, for example, accounted for a little over 1 percent of all FDI in 1999 and about 2 percent of all international trade flows. In a recent report, the World Bank focused on this issue, noting that one-sixth of the world's people produce 78 percent of the world's goods and services and receive 78 percent of the world's income, an average of $70 a day. But, three-fifths of the world's people in the 61 poorest countries receive 6 percent of the world's income, or less than $2 a day on average.[7]

This continuing disparity suggests that one of the biggest challenges facing global economic institutions such as the World Trade Organization, the World Bank, the International Monetary Fund, and the United Nations is to bring the poorer nations of the world into the global economic system of the 21st century. The exclusion of the majority of the world's population from the global economic system represents an enormous waste of resources, to say nothing of the suffering implied by the continued existence of extreme poverty. Moreover, if the lot of the poor does not improve, the growing division between the rich and poor nations of the world could lead to geopolitical conflicts that impinge on the economic prosperity of the developed world.

The critical question is how to engage the world's poorer nations in the global economic system. The material contained in Chapters 2, 4, 6, and 9 suggests introducing democratic political institutions, reducing corruption, protecting property rights, deregulating markets, privatizing state-owned enterprises, and liberalizing regulations governing foreign trade and foreign direct investment will all help the poorer nations of the world raise their economic growth rates and promote engagement in the world economy. However, some in the developed and developing world disagree with this assessment. Those who hold this contrary view made their presence felt in November 1999, when they helped to derail talks sponsored by the World Trade Organization that were aimed at initiating a new round of negotiations to reduce barriers to international trade and foreign direct investment.

The World Trade Organization: Recent Developments

The World Trade Organization (WTO) is the multinational institution that polices the global trading system, resolving trade disputes between member nations (see Chapter 5 for details). The WTO also coordinates efforts to further reduce barriers to cross-border trade and investment. With 140 countries on its membership roster as of November 30, 2000, and another 29–including China, the Russian Federation, and Saudi Arabia–negotiating their membership into the organization, the WTO is at the forefront of efforts to promote global free trade. Established in 1995, the WTO replaced the General Agreement on Tariffs and Trade (GATT), which had been overseeing world trade since 1947. The experience of the last few years suggests that the policing and enforcement mechanisms of the WTO are working well. Between 1995 and late 2000, some 213 trade disputes between member countries were brought to the WTO.[8] This record compares with a total of 196 cases that were handled by the GATT over almost half a century. Of the cases brought to the WTO, some three-quarters had been resolved by late 2000 following informal consultations between the countries in dispute. Resolving the remainder involved more formal dispute resolution procedures, but these have been largely successful. In general, the countries involved have adopted the WTO's recommendations. Only a handful of cases so far have yet to be resolved by the WTO.

The fact that countries are using the WTO represents an important vote of confidence in the organization's dispute resolution procedures. Reflecting this success, in its 1999 annual report the WTO noted:

> The state of the world trading system is generally sound . . . there were no major trade policy reversals in 1998 and 1999 and . . . there is no evidence of a return to protectionist measures. On the contrary, a number of countries have undertaken concrete measures to further liberalize their economic and trade regimes.[9]

However, the tone of this report, released in November 1999, was to sound overly optimistic given events that occurred in Seattle just a few days later.

The World Trade Organization in Seattle

At the end of November 1999, representatives from the WTO's member states met in Seattle. The goal of the meeting was to launch a new round of talks—dubbed "the millennium round"—aimed at further reducing barriers to cross-border trade and investment. This round of talks was to be the ninth since 1947, when the forerunner of the WTO, the General Agreement on Tariffs and Trade (GATT), was established (see Chapter 5 for details). Since 1947, the GATT and then the WTO have substantially lowered barriers to cross-border trade. Under the auspices of the GATT and WTO, the average tariff rate on manufactured products imported into developed nations has fallen from over 20 percent of value in 1950, to 3.4 percent today. As barriers tumbled, the volume of international trade expanded dramatically, increasing twentyfold between 1950 and 1999. Many economists argued that this surge in trade was one of the engines of world economic growth in the second half of the 20th century. As explained in Chapter 4, free trade allows countries to specialize in the production of goods and services that they can produce most efficiently, while importing those goods and services that they produce less efficiently. By increasing the efficiency of resource utilization, economic theory predicts that free trade will boost economic growth and real incomes in all countries that participate in a free trade agreement. The experience of the past 50 years seems to bear this theory out.

Given this background, when the WTO convened in Seattle, expectations were high that after the normal amount of haggling, posturing, and last-minute brinkmanship, the talks would yield agreement on major goals for the next round of talks, which were scheduled to begin soon after. Prominent on the agenda was an attempt to get the assembled countries to agree to work toward the reduction of barriers to cross-border trade in agricultural products and cross-border trade and investment in services. These expectations were dashed on the rocks of a hard and unexpected reality. On December 3, 1999, the talks ended without any agreement being reached. Inside the meeting rooms, the problem was an inability to reach consensus on the primary goals for the next round of talks. A major stumbling block was friction between the United States and the European Union over whether to endorse the aim of ultimately eliminating subsidies to farmer exporters. The United States wanted the elimination of such subsidies to be a priority. The EU, with its politically powerful farm lobby and long history of farm subsidies, was unwilling to take this step. Another stumbling block was related to efforts by the United States to write "basic labor rights" into the law of the world trading system. The United States wanted the WTO to allow governments to impose tariffs on goods imported from countries that did not abide by what the United States saw as fair labor practices. Representatives from developing nations reacted angrily to this proposal, suggesting it was simply an attempt by the United States to find a legal way of restricting imports from poorer nations.

However, while the disputes inside the meeting rooms were acrimonious, it was events outside that captured the attention of the world press. Originally, the choice of Seattle as the host city for the WTO meetings seemed auspicious. The Seattle region was one of the export powerhouses of the United States and was home to two of the largest multinationals in the country: Boeing and Microsoft. Also, Washington state, in which Seattle is located, has the highest ratio of exports per capita in the United States, with agricultural products and timber supplementing its high-tech aerospace and software exports. Surely there were few cities in the world that would be more open to the idea of free trade.

The calculation went spectacularly amiss. The WTO talks proved to be a lightning rod for a diverse collection of organizations from environmentalists and human rights groups to labor unions. For various reasons, these groups are opposed to free trade. All these organizations argue that the WTO is an undemocratic institution that was usurping the national sovereignty of member states and making important decisions behind closed doors. They took advantage of the Seattle meetings to voice their opposition, which the world press duly recorded. Environmentalists express concern about the impact that free trade in agricultural products might have on the rate of global deforestation. They argue that lower tariffs on imports of lumber from developing nations will stimulate demand and accelerate the rate at which virgin forests are logged, particularly in nations such as Malaysia and Indonesia. They also point to the adverse impact that some WTO rulings have had on environmental policies. For example, the WTO recently blocked a US rule that ordered fisherman to equip shrimp nets with a device that allows endangered sea turtles to escape. The WTO found the rule discriminated against foreign importers who lacked such nets.[10] Environmentalist argued that the rule was necessary to protect the turtles from extinction.

Human rights activists see WTO rules as outlawing the ability of nations to stop imports from countries where child labor is used or working conditions are hazardous. Similarly, labor unions oppose trade laws that allow imports from low-wage countries and result in a loss of jobs in high-wage countries. They buttress their position by arguing that American workers are losing their jobs to imports from developing nations that do not have adequate labor standards.

Supporters of the WTO and free trade are quick to dismiss these concerns. They have repeatedly pointed out that the WTO exists to serve the interests of its member states, not subvert them. The WTO lacks the ability to force any member nation to take an action that it is opposed to. The WTO can allow member nations to impose retaliatory tariffs on countries that do not abide by WTO rules, but that is the limit of its power. Furthermore, supporters argue, rich countries pass strict environmental laws and laws governing labor standards, not poor ones. In their view, free trade, by raising living standards in developing nations, will be followed by the passage of such laws in these nations. Using trade regulations to try to impose such practices on developing nations, they believe, will produce a self-defeating backlash.

Many representatives from developing nations, which make up about 105 of the WTO's 140 members, also reject the position taken by environmentalists and advocates of human and labor rights. Poor countries, which depend on exports to boost their economic growth rates and pull their way out of poverty, fear that rich countries will use environmental concerns, human rights, and labor-related issues to erect barriers to the products of the developing world. They believe that attempts to incorporate language about the environment or labor standards in future trade agreements will amount to little more than trade barriers by another name.[11] If this were to occur, they argue that the effect would be to trap developing nations in a grinding cycle of poverty and debt.

However, such pro-trade arguments fell on deaf ears. As the WTO representatives gathered in Seattle, environmentalists, human rights activists, and labor unions marched in the streets. Some of the more radical elements in these organizations together with anarchists who were philosophically opposed to "global capitalism" and "the rape of the world by multinationals" succeeded not only in shutting down the opening ceremonies of the WTO but also in sparking violence in the normally peaceful streets of Seattle. Against the wishes of the vast majority of protesters, a number of demonstrators engaged in property damage and looting. The police responded with tear gas, rubber bullets, pepper spray, and baton charges. When it was all over, 600 demonstrators had been arrested, millions of dollars in property damage had been done to downtown Seattle, and the global news media had their headline: WTO talks collapse amid violent demonstrations.

The question that now must be asked is whether the events in Seattle portray an end to half a century of trade liberalization, or whether they represent nothing more than a bump in the road. On the one hand, history suggests the WTO will ultimately get the next round of talks under way. After all, the last round of global trade talks, the Uruguay Round, also took several years to initiate.

On the other hand, there is a sense that Seattle may have been a watershed. In the past, previous trade talks were pursued in relative obscurity with only interested economists, politicians, and businesspeople paying much attention. Seattle demonstrated, however, that the issues surrounding the global trend toward free trade have suddenly moved to center stage in the popular consciousness. The debate on the merits of free trade and globalization has become mainstream. Whether further liberalization occurs, therefore, may depend on the importance that popular opinion in countries such as the United States attaches to issues such as human rights and labor standards, job security, environmental policies, and national sovereignty. It will also depend on the ability of advocates of free trade to articulate in a clear and compelling manner the argument that in the long run, free trade is the best way of promoting adequate labor standards, of providing more jobs, and of protecting the environment. Much of the media coverage surrounding the Seattle conference made it clear that the merits of free trade are not well understood, while the perceived drawbacks are easy to identify and make for good press copy. Exactly how this debate will play out remains to be seen, but given recent trends it would not be surprising if labor rights and environmental considerations played a much larger role in the next round of global trade talks when they finally get started (which despite the breakdown of the Seattle meeting, seem likely to occur within the next two to three years).

China and the World Trade Organization

China has been trying to join the WTO, and the GATT before it, for 14 years. Within China, membership in the WTO is seen as a necessary component of the country's long march toward a fully functioning market economy. Over the past 20 years the value of China's exports to the rest of the world have climbed by 15 percent per year on average, while imports have grown at an annual rate of 13 percent.[12] The growth in international trade has helped China to expand its economy at 8 percent annually for the past decade. China is now the world's seventh largest economy and with the addition of Hong Kong, its fourth largest exporter.

China's leaders believe that further gains from trade will require membership in the WTO. They understand that this will not be a painless process. Joining the WTO will require China to dismantle many trade barriers that currently protect local industry from foreign competition. They are calculating that such short-term pain will be quickly outweighed by long-term gains as foreign competition forces China's producers to become more efficient and as trade with other nations expands.

Historically, one of the biggest roadblocks to China's accession to the WTO has been the United States. The United States is China's largest trading partner, accounting for $70 billion of exports in 1999. With its large population and rapid economic growth, China also holds out the promise of being a very important market for US producers. For years, however, influential political forces in the United States have opposed China's entry into the WTO on the grounds that the country has scant respect for human rights, labor standards, and intellectual property rights (China is one of the largest consumers of pirated computer software).

Despite domestic opposition, the Clinton administration in the United States supported greater economic engagement with China. This administration repeatedly argued that greater economic freedom in China would be followed by greater political freedom and greater respect for human rights. Accordingly, in November 1999, after a difficult series of negotiations, the Clinton administration and China signed a bilateral trade agreement. The agreement resolved a series of outstanding trade issues between the two countries and set down schedules for phasing out tariff and nontariff barriers. In return for Chinese cooperation, the United States agreed to support China's application to join the WTO. China's bid to enter the WTO was further strengthened in mid-2000, when the European Union negotiated a bilateral trade agreement with China, effectively removing EU objections to China's entry into the WTO. A further signal of US support was given in September 2000 when the US Senate voted to normalize trade relations with China. By doing so, the United States signaled its intention to stop linking trade deals with China to human rights issues. This vote, coming as it did almost a year after the protests in Seattle, seemed to signal that political consensus in the United States was still in favor of pursuing a pro-trade agenda.

With these endorsements in hand, China was in the final stages of negotiating entry into the WTO as of late 2000. The process is now being held up by forces inside the country. There is unease in China about the impact that entry into the WTO will have on farmers and workers in inefficient enterprises, particularly those based in state-supported industries. Entry into the WTO will hurt producers in inefficient sectors, although it will be a tremendous boon to producers in more efficient sectors. Although the objections from internal forces are not trivial, it still seems likely that China will join the World Trade Organization sometime in 2001.

Asia Rebounds from Financial Crisis

When this edition of *Global Business* went to press, many Southeast Asian countries were still struggling to come to grips with the financial crisis that rocked the region in 1997 and 1998. This crisis, which is described in Chapter 9, was caused by a combination of excess investment; too much industrial capacity; excessive debt, much of it denominated in dollars; and asset inflation, particularly in property. As the crisis spread throughout Asia in 1997 and 1998, several countries saw the value of their currencies fall by as much as 80 percent against the US dollar, while their stock markets registered similar declines. Following the crash, these countries were plunged into a deep recession. Worst hit were Indonesia, Thailand, Malaysia, and South Korea.

The International Monetary Fund stepped in to help many of these countries, committing over $110 billion in short-term loans to South Korea, Thailand, and Indonesia. To access this money, these countries had to agree to implement tight macroeconomic policies, deregulate their economies, and reform their domestic banking systems. The IMF came in for substantial criticism at the time. Some critics claimed the conditions applied to its loans were too tough and would make the situation worse. Others argued that the IMF should not bail out Asia's troubled economies and by extension the banks that had engaged in excessive lending (see Chapter 9 for details). Despite mounting criticism, the IMF stuck to its course. Two years later, the signs are that doing so was the correct decision.

The apparent strength and speed of the recovery in Asian has surprised most observers. Thailand's gross domestic product, which fell 10.2 percent in 1998, rebounded by 4.2 percent in 1999 and 5.0 percent in 2000. For Indonesia, the corresponding figures are -13.0 percent and 4.0 percent; for Malaysia, -7.5 percent, 5.6 percent, and 6 percent; for South Korea, -6.7 percent, a stunning 10.7 percent, and 8.8 percent.[13] The region's stock markets staged an even more impressive rebound, led by the South Korean stock market, which surged over 80 percent during 1999.[14] The recovery has continued into 2000. For the region as a whole, growth looks likely to come in at 6.7 percent in 2000, and the International Monetary Fund is forecasting growth of 6.6 percent in 2001.

There are a number of reasons for this strong recovery. Perhaps the most important factor was that while Asia slumped, the American economy continued to boom. A strong American economy consumed exports from Asia, which, following the 1997–98 collapse of Asian currencies, were far less expensive than they had been a year earlier. Also helping to lift demand in the beleaguered Asian economies was the beginning of a recovery in Japan, which had been mired in a recession for much of the 1990s. Continued economic growth throughout much of Western Europe also helped to create demand for Asian exports. Thus, export-led growth helped to pull Asia's economies off the floor. Across the region, exports in 1999 were 15 percent ahead of those in 1998 by value.[15] The export-led expansion continued throughout 2000.

A second reason for the strong recovery was that after some initial belt-tightening at the insistence of the IMF, the region's countries relaxed their restrictive fiscal policies, boosting government spending on infrastructure projects and reducing taxes.[16] This fiscal stimulus helped to pump demand into the region's economies. However, there has been a price to pay for this stimulus. South Korea, Indonesia, Malaysia, and Thailand are now all running budget deficits that are equivalent to about 5 to 6 percent of their GDP. This will not matter much if tax revenues start to grow in line with the recovery in domestic demand, but it is important for government's in the region to limit their fiscal spending. Otherwise, the recovery might be choked by too much government debt and higher domestic interest rates.

As the combination of strong export demand and fiscal stimulus raised economic growth, companies across the region begin to rebuild their inventories. These had been run down to very low levels during the height of the 1997–98 financial crisis. In turn, inventory buildups have played a leading role in the economic rebound, particularly in heavily industrialized South Korea. Also important has been growth in intraregional trade, which accounts for half of all trade in the region.

Despite the impressive rebound, problems still remain in the region's economies. Following the crisis there were calls for substantial structural reforms, including a removal of barriers to foreign investment, a reduction in government spending, a halt to government direction of corporate investment, widespread reform of the national banking systems, and the breakup of indebted companies, particularly the South Korean *chaebol* (see Chapter 9 for details). Although progress has been made on all these fronts, the pace of structural reform has been slower than many economists and the IMF would like to see.

For example, while there have been clear moves to reform the region's troubled banking systems, there are still far too many weak banks and nonperforming loans

(loans where the debtor has defaulted on the repayment of debt). In Thailand about 35 percent of bank loans remained nonperforming by October 2000, and in Indonesia political problems have slowed the pace of debt restructuring.[17] The high level of nonperforming loans means that credit is still tight, making it difficult for enterprises in the region to borrow money to fund new investments. Although this has had little effect so far given the excess industrial capacity in the region, as demand continues to expand companies will need to borrow money to fund investments in new capacity. If they cannot do so, the recovery may stall.

Some banks have been sold to foreign companies, troubled banks have been forced to merge, barriers to foreign investment have been lowered, and there has been less government involvement in corporate investment decisions. In South Korea, the government has also pushed with some success for the breakup or restructuring of the nation's industrial groups (the *chaebol*). The government's case was helped by financial troubles at Daewoo, one of the largest *chaebol,* which is effectively bankrupt and is selling many of its assets.

For Asia to continue to rebound, analysts argue that governments must continue to push forward with these much-needed structural reforms and they must strengthen domestic banking systems. They also point out that although the region's economic recovery in 1999 and 2000 looked impressive, this recovery was from the depths of a severe slump. It is far too early to declare victory. The region's recovery may stall if economic growth in the United States slows, as looks possible in 2001, or if Japan fails to sustain its tentative economic recovery and slumps back into a recession. A slowdown in the United States would halt Asia's export-led recovery and reexpose the structural weaknesses in the region. Also of concern would be a financial crisis in China, the region's largest economy. China escaped the 1997–98 crisis, but concerns remain that China's economy is vulnerable to the kind of currency debacle that hit other Asian states in 1997.

The Trials and Tribulations of the Euro

The euro, born January 1, 1999, is the common currency unit now used by 11 of the 15 nations of the European Union (EU). The 11 states are members of what is often referred to as the euro zone. For now three EU countries, Britain, Denmark, and Sweden, are still sitting on the sidelines, although there are indications that Britain and Sweden may join before 2002. Supporters of the euro claimed that its introduction would facilitate the development of EU-wide markets and force European enterprises to become more efficient. They also believed that ultimately the euro would vie with the US dollar in importance as a reserve currency for many of the world's major nations. Detractors argued that adopting the euro meant that member nations would have to give up control over monetary policy to an untested European Central Bank (ECB). They claimed that the ECB would be vulnerable to political pressures and might adopt monetary policy in the euro zone that would lead to price inflation (see Chapter 7 for details of these arguments).

In the first two years of its existence, the euro did not live up to the expectations of all its supporters. In January 1999, the euro was trading at 1 euro = $1.17. By late November of that year, the value of the euro had slumped to 1 = $1. Although it recovered slightly in December, by the end of the year the euro had still lost 15 percent of its value against the US dollar and was also down significantly against the Japanese yen. The slide continued in 2000, and by fall the euro was trading at 0.88 = $1, representing a decline against the dollar of more than 20 percent.

Critics were quick to claim that the fall in the euro demonstrated the lack of confidence the foreign exchange market has in the ability of the ECB to manage monetary policy. However, there are no signs that the ECB is mismanaging monetary policy in the euro zone.[18] Inflationary pressures seem to be under control, the ECB seems to have managed interest rates with some skill, and there is no sign that the ECB is bowing to political pressure. Rather, the decline in the value of the euro can be attributed to two other factors: the growth differential and the interest rate differential between the United States and the European Union.[19]

With regard to the growth differential, while the US economy has continued to expand at a robust rate since January 1999, the EU economy showed more moderate growth. In 1999, the US economy grew at a 4.2 percent annual rate, while the EU economy grew at a slower 2.4 percent. A big drag on the EU economy in 1999 was Germany, the largest national economy in the euro zone accounting for one-third of all output. Germany's economy grew by 1.6 percent in 1999. The weakness in Germany can be partly attributed to inflexible labor markets, which have kept labor costs high and hindered the international competitiveness of German enterprises. In addition, Germany was more exposed than other EU nations to Eastern European economies. When Eastern Europe was hard hit in 1997–98, German industry suffered more than most. Although 2000 looks to have been better for Europe, with the EU nations set to grow by 3.5 percent over the full year, the US economy grew by an even stronger 5.2 percent. Yet again, Germany was the drag on the EU economy. Although Germany is coming to grips with its internal problems and a recovery in Eastern Europe has helped, at 2.9 percent Germany still registered the lowest growth rate among all major EU economies in 2000.

With relatively slow growth in Europe, much of it attributable to problems in Germany, investors have been hesitant to hold euro-denominated assets, particularly when the returns to holding dollar-denominated assets, such as US stocks, has been so much greater. The healthy US economy and the long boom in the US stock market drew investment money away from Europe and into the United States. The perception that the US economy was strong led to a surge in foreign direct investment into the United States. Both of these factors helped to bid up the price of the dollar relative to the euro.

The interest rate differential between the United States and the euro zone countries has exacerbated this trend. In a world where capital is internationally mobile, interest rate differentials can play a large role in explaining short-term exchange rate movements. In the United States, the Federal Reserve Board raised interest rates in 1999 and early 2000 in an attempt to slow the rapidly expanding US economy, which was beginning to show signs of inflationary pressures. As a consequence, the differential between the long-term interest rates on dollar- and euro-denominated government bonds widened from 0.5 percent in January 1999 to 1.6 percent in August 2000. Not surprisingly, capital flowed to the United States and away from the euro zone to gain the benefits of higher U.S. interest rates. As that occurred, the euro continued to depreciate against the dollar.

While this situation created the impression that the euro has not been the success that was originally hoped for, there are some silver linings to these clouds. For one thing, the depreciation in the value of the euro against the dollar, and to a lesser extent the Japanese yen, has helped make EU enterprises more competitive in the global marketplace. This has been translated into growing exports and a growing surplus on the current account of the balance of payments in the euro zone (i.e., a trade surplus). According to the IMF, the current account surplus in the euro zone will amount to 0.9 percent of GDP in 2000 and is forecasted to reach 1.3 percent of GDP in 2001. In contrast, the United States has been running a current account deficit (a trade deficit) amounting to 4.2 percent of GDP in 2000 and was expected to run the same again in 2001.

Also, there are now signs that the US economy is slowing, causing the Federal Reserve Board to lower interest rates in the United States. This has reduced the interest rate differential between the United States and euro zone and could slow or reverse the flow of money from Europe to the United States. Furthermore, if the slowdown in the United States is steep enough, investors may take money out of US stocks, and foreign businesses may slow their rate of investment in the United States. If these trends occur, the euro may recover much of the ground it has lost against the dollar. In sum, the recent weakness of the euro seems to owe more to short-term capital flows than it does to long-term problems in the euro zone or to any mismanagement by the ECB. It is certainly too early to write off the euro. It would not be surprising if the euro strengthened against the dollar in 2001.

Gyrations in the Global Oil Market

Sharp gyrations in the price of oil have always had an effect on the global economy. In 1973, and then again in 1979, a fourfold increase in the price of oil to around $34 a barrel ushered in a global economic slowdown and spurred price inflation in many oil-importing nations. In large part, the Organization of Petroleum Exporting Countries (OPEC) engineered the oil price rises of the 1970s. OPEC is a cartel between 11 major oil produces in the developing world, including Saudi Arabia, Iran, Iraq, Venezuela, and Nigeria. OPEC currently supplies about 40 percent of the world's oil, and some 78 percent of the world's proven reserves are located in OPEC nations. OPEC operates by establishing production quotas between its member nations, thereby influencing the price of oil in the world market (the lower the quotas, the higher the price). In the 1970s, OPEC increased the price of oil to punish oil-importing nations in the West who supported Israel, the legitimacy of which was questioned by many of OPEC's Arab members. However, OPEC members discovered that high prices stimulated more drilling for oil outside of OPEC. By the mid-1980s new supplies of oil appeared from areas outside of OPEC's control, such as Alaska and the North Sea. These supplies drove down oil prices to $12 a barrel and led many to predict that the heyday of the cartel was past.

During much of the 1990s oil prices rose steadily, reaching $25 a barrel by mid-1997. The reason for this steady price increase was solid economic growth in the developed and developing world and a commensurate rise in global oil consumption. Then the Asian economic crisis hit. Because many Asian nations were major oil importers, the crisis quickly translated into a fall in global demand for oil. With supply again exceeding demand, prices collapsed to $10 a barrel by December 1998. This price collapse hurt many OPEC nations hard, but it was relatively short lived. Prices started to recover slowly in 1999, and in 2000 they surged, hitting $34 by mid-2000, the highest level since 1979.

The sharp increase in the price of oil during 1999 and 2000 can be explained by several factors. First, the recovery of Asian economies from the 1997–98 financial crisis led to an increase in demand from those nations. Second, strong economic growth in the United States, the world's largest economy, resulted in increased demand for oil imports. Third, in the aftermath of the price collapse of 1998, many oil companies outside of OPEC had sharply reduced their plans for new drilling and new refining capacity. As a result, when global demand bounced back in 1999, they

price increase

1. Asian recovery

2. U.S. growth

3. outside OPEC nation reduce drilling plans

4.
OPEC
agreements to
limit production

global
tax
increase=
price increase

were left without sufficient supply to meet the increased demand. Fourth, OPEC reached agreements in 1998 and 1999 to limit production of oil in order to help oil prices recover from their 1998 lows. These agreements were more successful than most observers expected, with the majority of OPEC nations sticking to their production quotas. As a result, with supply constrained, prices surged as global demand for oil rebounded during 1999 and 2000.

The tripling of oil prices since late 1998 has had a number of effects on the global economy. One way to think of the price increases is as a global tax increase. By raising the price that consumers must pay for energy, the oil price increase has reduced the funds consumers have to spend on other goods and services. This has helped keep global economic growth below the levels that might otherwise have been attained. Second, because oil is such an important input into economic activity, the oil price increase is somewhat inflationary. To keep inflation in check, monetary authorities, such as the US Federal Reserve Board, have had to keep interest rates higher than they might otherwise have been. Again, this too has meant lower economic growth. Third, the rise in oil prices has meant deterioration in the trade balance for many oil-importing nations. In 2000, for example, the US trade deficit rose to a record $400 billion, or 4.2 percent of GDP. The increase in the price of oil imports was an important factor in this. Finally, because oil is priced and paid for in US dollars, the rise in the price of oil has resulted in a flow of dollars into the coffers of OPEC nations. Often referred to as "petrodollars," this inflow has helped these nations to pay down government debt and to strengthen their foreign currency reserves, and it has generated a budget surplus in several OPEC countries. Some of this new cash is being used to fund increased government spending in oil-producing nations, leading to higher economic growth there, but much of it is being recycled into foreign investments, particularly US government bonds.

In sum, although OPEC oil producers have benefited, the net effect of the oil price increase has been to slow global economic activity, increase inflationary pressures, and deteriorate the balance of trade of oil-importing nations. The price rise has certainly awakened memories of the 1970s. In Europe, the rapid increase in the price of gasoline led to spontaneous protests by consumers against high government gas taxes, which account for as much as 80 percent of the price of gasoline. In the United States, President Clinton authorized a limited release of 30 million barrels from the country's strategic petroleum reserve in an attempt to reduce prices (with global demand running at over 75 million barrels a day, this action was little more than symbolic). However, it is important to keep things in perspective. In real terms, the price of oil today is still substantially below its price in 1978. Factoring in inflation, the price would have to rise to $60 a barrel for it to be at the same level we saw in 1978, and no one expects that. Also, due to economic growth, oil is not as important a factor as it once was in overall economic activity. For example, in the United States, oil consumption accounted for 4 percent of economic output in 1973 and 6 percent in 1979, but it represented just 1.9 percent in 2000.[20]

Still, the price increase has raised concerns that the world is too dependent on OPEC. While OPEC seems intent on managing production so that oil prices stay in the $25 to $30 range, analysts worry that political instability in the Middle East, particularly Iran or Iraq, could disrupt supply and lead to further price increases. Of particular concern is Iraq's Saddam Hussein, who is capable of turning off Iraq's oil supply in order to hurt the West even if it produces hardship for his own people. Although Iraqi oil represents only 3 to 4 percent of world supply, in the global oil market, supply and demand is finely balanced. The sudden halting of supply would have a dramatic upward effect on prices. In the long run the position of OPEC is likely to get stronger. Although OPEC currently accounts for only about 40 percent of global production, by 2020 it could account for over 50 percent, increasing its ability to manipulate global oil prices and, in the worst-case scenario, do harm to the global economy. For this reason, it is important to keep an eye on developments in the global oil market and within OPEC.

International Business in the New Millennium

With the dawn of a new millennium, it seems worthwhile reflecting on how far the world has come over the past hundred years and what the next few years might hold for the global economy and for international business.

A Hundred Years of Progress

The past hundred years have in many ways seen remarkable progress. A person born at the beginning of the 1900s in the United States, then the world's richest country, entered a world in which few had access to running water, electricity, or the telephone. The automobile had only recently been invented and was still the plaything of the rich. Aircraft, radio, penicillin, television, computers, and the Internet all lay in the future. Average life expectancy was 47.3 years. Many people were infirm by the age of 40. There were 75 million people in the country and 1.65 billion people on the planet, up from 980 million in 1800. Income per capita was less than $400. The United States was a continental economy in which international business and international trade played a limited role in economic activity, but that role was starting to expand.

A person born at the beginning of 2000 in the United States entered a dramatically different world. Life expectancy had risen to 77 years, the consequence of a revolution in health care. Income per capita was $30,000. Automobiles, aircraft, antibiotics, computers, television, cell phones, and Internet connections were common. There were now over 6 billion people in the world and 270 million in the United States. There had been a dramatic expansion in both industrial output and in international trade. World trade had expanded twentyfold and world output sixfold since 1950.[21]

The world was a much more democratic place. In 1900, there were 55 sovereign nations, another 55 national entities that were governed by colonial and imperial systems, and 20 protectorates under the sway or protection of foreign powers. A mere 12.4 percent of the world's people lived under some form of democratic government, although suffrage was generally limited to males. By 2000, the great imperial empires had disappeared and the world had 192 sovereign nations. Freedom House, an organization that tracks the spread of democratic freedoms, classified some 85 of these nations, or 44.3 percent, as "free." In 2000 55 percent of the world's population was living in democratic states, a greater proportion than at any other time in history.[22]

Market-based economic systems were also at a high-water mark around the globe. During the 20th century, rival philosophies of political economy, including fascism and communism, had fallen by the wayside. The "free world" had won a hot war against fascism (World War II) and a cold war against communism. Liberal democracy, with its emphasis on market-based economic systems, was the ascendant ideology. Even the last great Communist state, China, had embraced market-based systems, making its claim to be a "Communist" country ring hollow. Clearly, this was a world in which international business could thrive, as indeed it was.

However, the 20th century was not one of smooth progress. There were two world wars and hundreds of minor ones that claimed some 37 million lives. Worse still, several Communist governments exhibited an appalling proclivity to murder their own people. Some 62 million civilians were killed in the Soviet Union between 1917 and 1991, 35 million in China between 1949 and 1990, and 1.5 million in a spasm of brutality in Cambodia. There was mass genocide in Turkey, Nazi Germany, Rwanda, and Bosnia. The Japanese killed some 6 million civilians in occupied territories during World War II. Overall, governments during the 20th century killed some 170 million civilians.[23] Atomic bombs were dropped on Hiroshima and Nagasaki. There was the influenza pandemic of 1918, which left 20 million people dead around the world (in contrast, 8.5 million soldiers lost their lives during World War I). There was the still unfolding AIDS pandemic, which had claimed 16 million lives by 2000 and left 36 million infected with the HIV virus worldwide.[24] There was the Great Depression of the 1930s, during which the average American saw his income fall by more than half. For much of the 20th century most of the world lived under totalitarian dictatorships. Only in the last decade, since the 1989 collapse of communism in Eastern Europe, has the balance of the world's population lived in democratic states. Moreover, for all of the progress of the 20th century, much of the world's population still lives in conditions that have more in common with the United States of 1900 than that of 2000. The GNP per capita of India with its 1 billion people, for example, is only about $400 a year. Despite dramatic economic growth, China's 1.2 billion people have a GNP per capita of less than $900.

Reasons for Optimism

Looking forward, there are plenty of reasons for optimism, but the history of the 20th century also teaches us to expect reversals and uneven progress. Although correctly predicting the future is impossible, one can argue that if current trends hold, living standards around the world will continue to improve. There are several reasons for expecting this. First, the prevailing economic ideology of the globe, with its emphasis on market-based systems, is likely to be supportive of the capitalist mode of production. In turn, as explained in Chapter 2, market-based systems beget innovations in products and processes, and innovations are the fuel of economic progress.

Second, the prevailing economic ideology is also supportive of removing barriers to cross-border trade and investment. Even without any further reductions in such barriers, the relatively low level of such barriers today seems likely to ensure that the trend toward the globalization of product and capital markets will continue. In turn, the efficiency gains that flow from global markets will constitute a rising tide that lifts all economic boats.

Third, as noted above, for the first time in history the majority of the world's population now lives in democratic states. The trend toward greater democracy seems to be firmly in place. Over the past 15 years, new democracies have sprung up throughout Latin America and Eastern Europe. There are signs that democracy may be gaining a foothold in parts of Africa, and several Asian countries, such as South Korea, have become far more democratic in recent decades. History teaches us that democracies rarely start wars, a fact that bodes well for the future.

Fourth, current advances in computing and communications technology, if maintained for two more decades, promise to vastly improve the efficiency of global markets and global business. Communications technology has always been a major driver of economic progress. The Gutenberg press, postal services, the telegraph, the telephone, and most recently the Internet have all lowered the costs of bringing together buyers and sellers—of making markets work—realizing substantial efficiency gains in the process. The Internet, because of its global reach, rapid growth, and potential for transmitting huge bundles of information at almost zero cost, will have a particularly dramatic impact in the near future. In 1990, fewer than 1 million users were connected to the Internet. By late 1999, the Internet had about 150 million users. By the year 2003 there may be well over 350 million users.[25] In July 1993, some 1.8 million host computers were connected to the Internet (host computers host the Web pages of local users). By July 1999, the number of host computers had increased to 56.3 million and the number is still growing rapidly.[26] The Internet and World Wide Web promise to develop into the information backbone of tomorrow's global economy. From virtually nothing in 1994, the value of transactions occurring on the Web has increased at an exponential rate, hitting $98.4 billion 1999. According to a recent report issued by the US Department of Commerce, this figure could well reach $300 billion in the United States alone by 2003.[27] Other estimates suggest that it could reach as much as $1.3 trillion by the same year.[28] Already, companies such as Dell Computer are booking over $5 million a day in Web-based sales, while Internet equipment giant Cisco Systems books more than 80 percent of its total sales online. It seems highly likely that Internet-based commercial transactions will become an integral part of the global economy in the near future. The resulting gains in efficiency could provide a huge boost to global economic growth. By extension, any international business that does not incorporate the Internet into its business processes will probably lose market share to those that do.

Future Challenges

Having laid out the reasons for being optimistic about the near future, it would be naïve not to highlight some potential problems that might stall global economic growth in the coming decades, or at least present international businesses with some significant challenges. One possibility is that a combination of continued population growth, poverty in some less developed nations, and environmental degradation might lead to an ideological backlash against the global move toward free markets and the capitalist mode of production. The protest against the World Trade Organization in Seattle, was discussed earlier in this postscript, might portend the leading edge of such a backlash.

Current estimates suggest that global population will continue to expand from 6 billion today to between 9 and 11 billion by 2100. Much of this growth is predicted to occur in the poorer nations of the world, many of which have yet to share in the economic benefits of global capitalism.[29] Environmentalists argue that population pressure puts stress on the environment, ranging from deforestation and soil erosion to air pollution and global warming.[30] As we saw at the recent World Trade Organization meetings, there will certainly be those who maintain that the adoption of free market economics and free trade are causes of such problems.

Naturally, one could counter that the relationship is not this simple. By creating wealth and incentives for enterprises to produce technological innovations, the free market system and free trade could make it easier for the world to cope with problems of pollution and population growth. While pollution levels are rising in the world's poorer countries, they have been falling in developed nations. In the United States, for example, the concentration of carbon monoxide and sulphur dioxide pollutants in the atmosphere decreased by 60 percent between 1978 and 1997, while lead concentrations decreased by 98 percent—and these reductions have occurred against a background of sustained economic expansion.[31] These figures are a testament to the ability of rich countries to take steps that limit the adverse environmental impact of economic development. However, this somewhat subtle argument is not an easy one for many to accept and often falls on deaf ears. It seems possible that a backlash of sorts could take place. The collapse of communism has created something of an ideological vacuum into which a political movement opposed to unfettered free markets might step; and a movement advocating greater regulation of markets and trade to protect the environment could fit the bill.

If such a movement does arise, it may create many challenges for international businesses, including limits to cross-border trade and investment, government regulation of business activities, consumer revolts, and the imposition of "pollution taxes." For a foretaste of what might come, one only has to look at the recent unhappy experience of Monsanto. Using recombinant DNA technology, Monsanto has genetically engineered certain types of seed corn so that they produce proteins that function as natural insecticides or so they are resistant to Roundup, a popular herbicide sold by Monsanto. Seeds engineered in this manner reduce the need to use insecticides and herbicides, thereby lowering farmers' costs and boosting crop yields. Monsanto thought the world would welcome its innovations, which it believed were environmentally beneficial. Its genetically altered seeds, such as soybeans, have become extremely popular among farmers not only in the United States, but also in many other countries including Brazil, India, and China.

In Europe, however, environmentalists have mounted a vigorous and largely successful campaign against Monsanto's products, arguing that genetically altered crops might lead to "genetic pollution." According to environmentalists, one possibility is that insects might soon become resistant to the "natural insecticides" produced by Monsanto's genetically modified seed corn. Thus, in the long run, Monsanto's products might actually end up creating "superbugs" that damage crop yields, not improve them. There is also a vague fear that genetic engineering, because it "upsets the natural order of things," might lead to serious problems that have yet to be identified, such as cancer. While these argument lack scientific support, consumers and politicians across Europe have been receptive to them. Responding to pressure from consumers, many European supermarkets will no longer stock genetically modified foods. The European Union has banned the importation of some genetically modified crops, even though this probably violates World Trade Organization rules. This backlash has effectively reduced Monsanto's ability to sell its products in a market of more than 350 million people, costing the company significant revenues.[32]

Another challenge to globalization and international business might arise from the fear that rapid globalization will drive down the wage rates of workers in developed nations, who will see their jobs "exported" to low-wage locations in the developing world. This fear has long underlay the opposition of labor unions to free trade. Populist politicians on both the left and right frequently articulate this argument. These politicians call for "fair trade"—meaning tariff barriers on imports from low-wage countries to protect inefficient domestic producers—as opposed to "free trade." If the argument gains wider support, it could lead to a partial retreat from free market ideology and an increase in trade barriers. To buttress their case, those who make this argument point to the evidence on growing wage inequality in developed nations. For example, a Federal Reserve study found that in the seven years up until 1996, the earnings of the best paid 10 percent of US workers rose in real terms by 0.6 percent annually while the earnings of the 10 percent at the bottom of the heap fell by 8 percent. In some areas the fall was much greater. In New York City, the real wages of the worst paid 10 percent dropped by 27 percent over this time period.[33] However, it seems unlikely that this growing inequality is due to globalization. In the United States, for example, only 13 percent of GNP can be attributed to international trade, and only one-fifth of that, or some 2.6 percent, is trade with developing nations. Most of America's trade is with high-wage countries such as Japan, Canada, and the nations of Europe. Given this, it is difficult to argue that international trade is the cause of growing income inequality.

Also, recent research suggests the evidence of growing income inequality may be suspect. Robert Lerman of the Urban Institute has taken a close look at the data. He believes that the finding of inequality is based on inappropriate calculations of wage rates. Reviewing the data using a different methodology, Lerman has found that far from increasing income inequality, an index of wage rate inequality for all workers actually fell by 5.5 percent between 1987 and 1994.[34] If future research supports Lerman's finding, the argument that globalization leads to growing income inequality may lose much of its punch. During the last few years of the 1990s, the income of the worst paid 10 percent of the population has actually risen twice as fast as that of the average worker, suggesting that the high employment levels of these years have triggered a rise in the income of the lowest paid.[35]

A final challenge to globalization and international business might arise if the economic gap between the wealthy nations of the world and the poorest nations continues to widen. Despite all the benefits associated with globalization, over the past hundred years or so the gap between the rich and poor nations of the world has gotten wider. In 1870 the average income per capita in the world's 17 richest nations was 2.4 times that of all other countries. In 1990, the same group was 4.5 times as rich as the rest.[36] While recent history has shown that some of the world's poorer nations are capable of rapid periods of economic growth—witness the transformation that has occurred in some Southeast Asian nations such as South Korea, Thailand, and Malaysia—there also appear to be strong forces for stagnation among the world's poorest nations. A quarter of the countries with a GDP per capita of less than $1,000 in 1960 had growth rates of less than zero from 1960 to 1995, and a third had growth rates of less than 0.05 percent.[37]

Although the reasons for economic stagnation vary, several factors stand out. Many of the world's poorest countries have suffered from totalitarian governments, economic policies that destroyed wealth rather than facilitated its creation, and scant protection for property rights and war. Such factors certainly help explain why countries such as Afghanistan, Cambodia, Cuba, Haiti, Iraq, Libya, Nigeria, Sudan, Vietnam, and Zaire have failed to improve the economic lot of their citizens during recent decades. A complicating factor is that many of these countries have rapidly expanding populations. Without a major change in government, population growth may exacerbate their problems.

It is an open question as to whether such states will prove to be a destabilizing influence in the economy of the 21st century. They may lash out at their neighbors, as Iraq did in the 1991 Gulf War; export their people to other nations, as Haiti and Vietnam have done; or sponsor extensive terrorist activities, as Libya has done. If such geopolitical events do come to pass, there may be significant fallout for the global economy and international businesses. The task for the world community is to find ways to bring these countries into the global trading system so they can share in the prosperity that has been and will be created.

Notes

1. World Trade Organization, *International Trade Statistics, 2000* (Geneva: WTO Secretariat, November 30, 2000).

2. Ibid.

3. United Nations, *World Investment Report, 2000* (New York and Geneva: United Nations, October 2000).

4. United Nations, "Global Foreign Direct Investment to Exceed $1 Trillion," UN press release TAD/1926, October 3, 2000.

5. Ibid.

6. United Nations, *World Investment Report 2000.*

7. World Bank, *World Development Report, 2000-2001* (Oxford: Oxford University Press, 2000).

8. *Annual Report by the Director General. Overview of developments in the international trading environment* (Geneva: World Trade Organization, November 22, 2000).

9. *World Trade Organization 1999 Annual Report* (Geneva: WTO, 1999).

10. Jim Carlton, "Greens Target WTO Plan for Lumber," *The Wall Street Journal,* November 24, 1999, p. A2.

11. Kari Huus, "WTO Summit Leaves Only Discontent," **MSNBC,** December 3, 1999, www.msnbc.com.

12. "China and the WTO: The Real Leap Forward," *The Economist,* November 20, 1999, pp. 25–26.

13. International Monetary Fund, *World Economic Outlook* (Washington, DC: IMF, October 2000).

14. J. Sprague, "Asia's Big Comeback," *Asiaweek,* January 7, 2000, pp. 104–5.

15. J. Fenby, "Awakening Stirs Fears of False Dawn," *The Observer,* October 24, 1999, p. 4.

16. "On Their Feet Again?" *The Economist,* August 21, 1999, pp. 16–18.

17. International Monetary Fund, *World Economic Outlook.*

18. "The Confused Muddle," *The Economist,* December 11, 1999, pp. 44–45; and "Currency Crossroads," *The Economist,* December 4, 1999, pp. 17–18.

19. International Monetary Fund, *World Economic Outlook.*

20. J. Maggs, "Over a Barrel," *The National Journal,* November 4, 2000.

21. **World Trade Organization,** *1999 Annual Report.*

22. **Freedom House,** "Freedom in the World: The Annual Survey of Political Rights and Civil Liberties, 1999–2000," http://freedomhouse.org.

23. These figures are from "Freedom's Journey: A Survey of the 20th Century. On the Yellow Brick Road," *The Economist,* September 11, 1999, p. 7.

24. D. Brown, "New Cases of HIV Decline in Africa for the First Time," *Washington Post,* November 29, 2000, p. A3.

25. Data compiled from various sources and listed at http://cyberatlas.internet.com.

26. Data on number of host computer can be found at http://www.nw.com/zone/WWW/report.html.

27. V. Houlder, "Fear and Enterprise as the Net Closes In," *Financial Times,* May 20, 1998, p. 18.

28. Data estimates from http://cyberatlas.internet.com.

29. Malcom Potts, "The Unmet Need for Family Planning," **Scientific America,** January 2000, pp. 88–93.

30. A. J. McMichael, **Planetary Overload** (Cambridge: Cambridge University Press, 1993).

31. These figures are from "Freedom's Journey: A Survey of the 20th Century. Our Durable Planet," **The Economist,** September 11, 1999, p. 30.

32. Tom Rhodes, "Bitter Harvest. The Real Story of Monsanto and GM Food," **Sunday Times,** August 22, 1999.

33. "A Survey of Pay. Winner and Losers," **The Economist,** May 8, 1999, pp. 5–8.

34. See Robert Lerman, *Is Earnings Inequality Really Increasing? Economic Restructuring and the Job Market. Brief No.* 1 (Washington, DC: Urban Institute, March 1997).

35. "A Survey of Pay. Winner and Losers."

36. Lant Pritchett, "Divergence, Big Time," **Journal of Economic Perspectives** 11 no., 3, (Summer 1997), pp. 3–18.

37. Ibid.

Global Business Today

Second Edition

McGraw-Hill Advanced Topics in Global Management

UNITED KINGDOM (THE INSÉAD GLOBAL MANAGEMENT SERIES)

Dutra and Manzoni
Process Re-Engineering, Organizational Change and Performance Improvement

El Kahal
Business in Europe

Goddard & Demirag
Financial Management for International Business

Hayes et al.
Principles of Auditing: An International Perspective

Lasserre and Schütte
Strategy and Management in Asia Pacific

Walter and Smith
Global Capital Markets and Banking

CANADA

Beamish / Woodcock
Strategic Management: Text, Readings and Cases, 5/e

McShane
Canadian Organizational Behaviour

AUSTRALIA

Clark
Human Resource Management

Deery
Industrial Relations: A Contemporary Analysis

Hughes
Management Skills Series
    Managing Information
    Managing Operations—Customer Service
    Managing Operations—Productivity
    Managing Operations—Innovations
    Managing Operations—Change
    Managing Effective Working Relationships
    Managing and Developing Teams
    Managing and Organising Work for Goal Achievement
    Managing Performance and Goal Achievement
    Managing Grievances and Disputes
    Managing People—Workplace Practice
    Managing People—Recruitment, Selection and Induction
    Managing Group Problem Solving and Decision Making
    Managing People—Training and Development

McKenna
New Management

Meredith
Managing Finance

Page
Applied Business and Management Research

Travaglione
Human Resource Strategies

UNITED STATES

Ball/McCulloch
International Business—The Challenge of Global Competition, 7/e

Bartlett, Ghoshal
Transnational Management: Text, Cases, and Readings in Cross-Border Management, 3/e

Beamish, Morrison, Rosenzweig, Inkpen
International Management, Text and Cases, 4/e

de la Torre, Doz, Devinney
Managing the Global Corporation, 2/e

Hill
Global Business Today, 2/e

Hill
International Business—Competing in the Global Marketplace, 3/e

Hodgetts and Luthans
International Management, 4/e

Global Business Today

Second Edition

Charles W. L. Hill
University of Washington

Boston   Burr Ridge, IL   Dubuque, IA   Madison, WI   New York   San Francisco   St. Louis
Bangkok   Bogotá   Caracas   Lisbon   London   Madrid
Mexico City   Milan   New Delhi   Seoul   Singapore   Sydney   Taipei   Toronto

McGraw-Hill Higher Education

A Division of The McGraw·Hill Companies

GLOBAL BUSINESS TODAY

Published by Irwin/McGraw-Hill, an imprint of The McGraw-Hill Companies, Inc. 1221 Avenue of the Americas, New York, NY, 10020. Copyright © 2001, 1998, by The McGraw-Hill Companies, Inc. All rights reserved. No part of this publication may be reproduced or distributed in any form or by any means, or stored in a data base or retrieval system, without the prior written consent of The McGraw-Hill Companies, Inc., including, but not limited to, in any network or other electronic storage or transmission, or broadcast for distance learning.

Some ancillaries, including electronic and print components, may not be available to customers outside the United States.

This book is printed on acid-free paper.

1 2 3 4 5 6 7 8 9 0 VNH/VNH 0 9 8 7 6 5 4 3 2 1 0

ISBN 0-07-232055-9

Senior vice president and editorial director: *Robin J. Zwettler*
Publisher: *John E. Biernat*
Executive editor: *Jennifer Roche*
Developmental editor: *Christine Scheid*
Senior marketing manager: *Ellen Cleary*
Project manager: *Christine A. Vaughan*
Senior production supervisor: *Lori Koetters*
Senior designer: *Jennifer McQueen Hollingsworth*
Senior photo research coordinator: *Keri Johnson*
Supplement coordinator: *Rose M. Range*
Senior new media project manager: *Barb Block*
Cover image: Copyright © 2000 PhotoDisc, Inc. All rights reserved.
Interior design: *Crispin Prebys*
Compositor: *York Graphic Services, Inc.*
Typeface: *10/12 Baskerville*
Printer: *Von Hoffmann Press, Inc.*

Library of Congress Cataloging-in-Publication Data

Hill, Charles W. L.
    Global business today / Charles W. L. Hill. – 2nd ed.
      p. cm.
    Includes bibliographical references and index.
    ISBN 0-07-232055-9
      1. International business enterprises – Management. 2. International trade.
    3. Investments, Foreign. 4. Capital market. I. Title.

HD62.4.H548 2001
658'.049 – dc21   00-026734

www.mhhe.com

For June and Mike Hill, my parents

About the Author

Charles W. L. Hill is the Hughes M. Blake Professor of International Business at the School of Business, University of Washington. Professor Hill received his Ph.D. in industrial organization economics in 1983 from the University of Manchester's Institute of Science and Technology (UMIST) in Great Britain. In addition to the University of Washington, he has served on the faculties of UMIST, Texas A&M University, and Michigan State University.

Professor Hill has published over 40 articles in peer-reviewed academic journals. He has also

published two college textbooks, one on strategic management and the other on international business.

Professor Hill serves on the editorial boards of several academic journals and previously served as consulting editor at the *Academy of Management Review.*

Professor Hill teaches in the MBA and executive MBA programs at the University of Washington and has received awards for teaching excellence in both programs. He has also taught on several customized executive programs.

Brief Contents

Glossary

Notes

Index

Contents

Preface

Global Business Today is intended for the first international business course at the undergraduate level. My goal in writing this book has been to set the standard for international business textbooks: I have attempted to write a book that (1) is comprehensive and up-to-date, (2) goes beyond an uncritical presentation and shallow explanation of the body of knowledge, (3) maintains a tight, integrated flow between chapters, (4) focuses managerial implications, and (5) makes important theories accessible and interesting to students.

COMPREHENSIVE AND UP-TO-DATE

To be comprehensive, an international business textbook must:

- Explain how and why the world's countries differ.

- Present a thorough review of the economics and politics of international trade and investment.

- Explain the functions and forms of the global monetary system.

- Examine the strategies and structures of international businesses.

- Assess the special roles of an international business's various functions.

This textbook does all these things. Too many other textbooks pay scant attention to the strategies and structures of international businesses and to the implications of international business for firms' various functions. This omission is a serious deficiency because the students in these international business courses will soon be international managers, and they will be expected to understand the implications of international business for their organization's strategy, structure, and functions. This book pays close attention to these issues.

Comprehensiveness and relevance also require coverage of the major theories. Although many international business textbooks do a reasonable job of reviewing long-established theories (e.g., the theory of comparative advantage and Vernon's product life-cycle theory) they tend to ignore such important newer work as:

- The new trade theory and strategic trade policy.

- Michael Porter's theory of the competitive advantage of nations.

- Robert Reich's work on national competitive advantage.

- The new growth theory championed by Paul Romer and Gene Grossman.

- The work of Douglass North and others on national institu-

tional structures and the protection of property rights.

- Samuel Huntington's discussion of the geopolitical implications of the new world order.

- The market imperfections approach to foreign direct investment that has grown out of Ronald Coase and Oliver Williamson's work on transaction cost economics.

- Bartlett and Ghoshal's research on the transnational corporation.

- The writings of C. K. Prahalad and Gary Hamel on core competencies, global competition, and global strategic alliances.

The failure of many books to discuss such work is a deficiency considering how influential these theories have become, not just in academic circles but also in the world at large. A major proponent of strategic trade policy, Laura Tyson, served as chairperson of President Clinton's Council of Economic Advisors. Robert Reich served as secretary of Labor in the Clinton administration. Ronald Coase won the 1992 Nobel Prize in economics, giving the market imperfections approach new respectability. Two years later, Douglass North won the Nobel Prize in economics for his work showing how a nation's economic history influences its contemporary institutions and property rights regime.

Huntington's work is regarded as being very influential in political circles. The work of Bartlett, Ghoshal, Hamel, and Prahalad is having an important impact on business practices.

I have incorporated all relevant state-of-the-art work at the appropriate points in this book. For example, in Chapter 2, "Country Differences in Political Economy," reference is made to the new growth theory, the work of North and others on national institutional structures and property rights, and Huntington's work on the geopolitical implications of the new world order. In Chapter 4, "International Trade Theory," in addition to such standard theories as the theory of comparative advantage and the Heckscher-Ohlin theory, there is detailed discussion of the new trade theory and Porter's theory of national competitive advantage. In Chapter 5, "The Political Economy of International Trade," the pros and cons of strategic trade policy are discussed. In Chapter 6, "Foreign Direct Investment," the market imperfections approach is reviewed. Chapter 10, which deals with the strategy of international business, draws extensively on the work of Bartlett, Ghoshal, Hamel, and Prahalad.

In light of the fast-changing nature of the international business environment, every effort is made to ensure that the book is as up-to-date as possible when it goes to press. In the past 10 years many significant events have shaped the world of international business. The Uruguay Round of GATT negotiations was successfully concluded in 1995 and the World Trade Organization was established. The European Union moved forward with its post-1992 agenda to achieve a closer economic and monetary union, and on January 1, 1999, introduced a common currency unit, the euro. The North American Free Trade Agreement became law, and Chile indicated its desire to become the next member of the free trade area. The Asia-Pacific Economic Cooperation forum (APEC) emerged as the kernel of a possible future free trade area.

The former Communist states of Eastern Europe and Asia continued on the road to economic and political reform. As they did, the euphoric mood that followed the collapse of communism in 1989 was slowly replaced with a growing sense of realism about the hard path ahead for many of these countries. The global money market continued its meteoric growth. By 1999 over $1.5 trillion per day was flowing across national borders. The size of such flows fueled concern about the ability of short-term speculative shifts in global capital markets to destabilize the world economy. These fears were fanned by the dramatic wave of financial crises that swept through several Asian nations in 1997 and hit Russia and Brazil in 1998. All these nations saw catastrophic plunges in the value of their currencies on the foreign exchange market and in their stock markets. The International Monetary Fund stepped into the breach to stabilize the situation and help these economies restructure.

The World Wide Web emerged from nowhere to become the backbone of an emerging global network for electronic commerce. By 2001 some 350 million people worldwide were expected to have Internet connections, and the value of transactions executed over the Web was predicted to exceed $1.3 billion in the United States alone.

The world continued to become more global with cross-border trade and investment growing much faster than world output. The world's most populous nation, China, continued to grow its economy at a rapid rate. New multinationals continued to emerge from developing nations in addition to the world's established industrial powers. And increasingly, the globalization of the world economy affected firms of all sizes, from the very large to the very small.

Reflecting this rapid pace change, I have tried to ensure that all material and statistics are as up-to-date as possible as of 2000. However, being absolutely up-to-date is impossible because change is always with us. What is current today may be outdated tomorrow. Accordingly, I have established a home page for this book on the World Wide Web at **www.mhhe.com/hillgbt2e.** From this home page the reader can access regular updates of chapter material and reports on topical developments that are relevant to students of international business. I hope readers find this a useful addition to the support material for this book.

BEYOND UNCRITICAL PRESENTATION AND SHALLOW EXPLANATION

Many issues in international business are complex and thus necessitate considerations of pros and cons. To demonstrate this to students, I have adopted a critical approach that presents the arguments for and against economic theories, government policies, business strategies, organizational structures, and so on.

I have attempted to explain the complexities of the many theories and phenomena unique to international business so the student might fully comprehend the statements of a theory or the reasons a phenomenon is the way it is. These theories and phenomena are typically explained in more depth in this book than they are in competing textbooks, the rationale being that a shallow explanation is little better than no explanation. In international business, a little knowledge is a dangerous thing.

INTEGRATED PROGRESSION OF TOPICS

Many textbooks lack a tight, integrated flow of topics from chapter to chapter. In this book students are told in Chapter 1 how the book's topics are related to each other. Integration has been achieved by organizing the material so that each chapter builds on the material of the previous ones in a logical fashion.

Part 1, Chapter 1 provides an overview of the key issues to be addressed and explains the plan of the book.

Part 2, Chapters 2 and 3, focuses on national differences in political economy and culture. Most international business textbooks place this material at a later point, but I believe it is vital to discuss national differences first. After all, many of the central issues in international trade and investment, the global monetary system, international business strategy and structure, and international business operations arise out of national differences in political economy and culture. To fully understand these issues, students must first appreciate the differences in countries and cultures.

Part 3, Chapters 4 through 7, investigates the political economy of international trade and investment. The purpose of this part is to describe and explain the trade and investment environment in which international business occurs.

Part 4, Chapters 8 and 9, describes and explains the global monetary system, laying out in detail the monetary framework in which international business transactions are conducted.

Part 5, Chapters 10 through 14, shifts attention from the environment to the firm. Here the book examines the strategies and structures that firms adopt to compete effectively in the international business environment. These chapters explain how firms can perform their key functions—manufacturing, marketing, R&D, and human resource management—to compete and succeed in the international business environment.

Throughout the book, the relationship of new material to topics discussed in earlier chapters is pointed out to the students to reinforce their understanding of how the material comprises an integrated whole.

FOCUS ON MANAGERIAL IMPLICATIONS

Many international business textbooks fail to discuss the implications of the various topics for the actual practice of international business. This does not serve the needs of business school students who will soon be practicing managers. Accordingly, the usefulness of this book's material in the practice of international business is discussed explicitly. In particular, at the end of each chapter in Parts 2, 3, and 4—where the focus is on the environment of international business, as opposed to particular firms—is a section titled "Implications for Business." In this section, the managerial implications of the material discussed in the chapter are clearly explained. For example, Chapter 4, "International Trade Theory," ends with a detailed discussion of the various trade theories' implications for international business management.

In addition, each chapter begins with a case that illustrates the relevance of chapter material for the practice of international business. Chapter 2, "Country Differences in Political Economy," for example, opens with a case that describes Brazil's privatization efforts.

I have also added a closing case to each chapter. These cases are also designed to illustrate the relevance of chapter material for the practice of international business. The closing case to Chapter 2, for example, describes the problems General Electric has had trying to establish profitable operations in Hungary. As the case makes clear, these problems are rooted in the political economy of Hungary and in General Electric's initial failure to fully appreciate the impact that political economy has on business operations. Each closing case is followed by a list of discussion questions, which facilitates the use of these cases as a vehicle for in-class case discussion and analysis.

Management Focus

Another tool that I have used to address managerial implications are "Management Focus" boxes. There is at least one "Management Focus" in each chapter. Like the opening case, the purpose of these boxes is to illustrate the relevance of chapter material for the practice of international business. The "Management Focus" in Chapter 2, for example, looks at Microsoft's battle against software piracy in China. This fits in well with a section of the chapter that looks at the protection of intellectual property rights in different countries.

ACCESSIBLE AND INTERESTING

The international business arena is fascinating and exciting, and I have tried to communicate my enthusiasm for it to the student. Learning is easier and better if the subject matter is communicated in an interesting, informative, and accessible manner. One technique I have used to achieve this is weaving anecdotes into the narrative of the text—stories that illustrate theory. The opening cases and focus boxes are also used to make the theory being discussed in the text both accessible and interesting.

Country Focus

Each chapter has two kinds of focus boxes—a "Management Focus" (see previous page) and a "Country Focus." "Country Focus" boxes provide background on the political, economic, social, or cultural aspects of countries grappling with an international business issue. In Chapter 2, for example, the "Country Focus" discusses the changing political economy in India. I refer to and utilize opening cases and boxed material in the main body of the text. The idea is to show students real-world examples of the issues being discussed in the text.

Could You Do This? Entrepreneurial Peer Profiles

Helena Czepiec of California State Polytechnic University, Pomona, has written five new peer profiles of students that she has taught that have utilized their entrepreneurial drive and moved into the international business arena. Located at the end of each part, these profiles are designed to give students inspiration based on what their peers have accomplished.

Just how accessible and interesting this book is will be revealed by time and student feedback. I am confident, however, that this book is far more accessible to students than its competitors. For those of you who view such a bold claim with skepticism, I urge you to read the sections in Chapter 1 on the globalization of the world economy, the changing nature of international business, and how international business is different.

WHAT'S NEW IN THE SECOND EDITION

The success of the first edition of *Global Business Today* was based in part on the incorporation of lead-ing-edge research into the text, the use of up-to-date examples and statistics to illustrate global trends and enterprise strategy, and the discussion of current events within the context of the appropriate theory. Building on these strengths, my goals for the second revision have been threefold:

1 Incorporate new insights from recent scholarly research wherever appropriate.

2 Make sure the content of the text covers all appropriate issues.

3 Make sure the text is as up-to-date as possible with regard to current events, statistics, and examples.

Often these goals have overlapped. For example, the global financial crisis that started in Asia in 1997 and spread to Russia in 1998 is relevant both because it is a current event of great significance to international business and because it has sparked a furious debate between scholars as to the appropriate role of the IMF. Thus, in Chapter 9, I outline the causes and consequences of the recent Asian and Russian financial crises, and I discuss the current debate between scholars such as Jeffrey Sachs and Stanley Fisher over the role of the IMF in such crises.

As part of the revision process, changes have been made to every chapter in the book. The following are examples.

Chapter 1, "Globalization," has been rewritten around the theme of globalization. All the statistics pertaining to globalization (such as the growth of world trade, output, and foreign direct investment) have been updated to incorporate the most recently available data. A new section deals with the debate between scholars on the merits and drawbacks of globalization. This debate is concerned with the impact of globalization on job security, income levels, labor policies, the environment, and national sovereignty.

Chapter 2, "National Differences in Political Economy," includes a new section titled "States in Transition." This section discusses the nature of the economic transformation, or liberalization, now being pursued by numerous states around the world, including many former Communist nations. The section discusses deregulation and privatization in greater depth than hitherto. Also new to this chapter is a discussion of Samuel Huntington's influential work on the clash of civilizations and the new world order. Huntington rejects the popular view, best articulated by Francis Fukuyama in *The End of History,* that we are moving toward a universal global civilization based on Western liberal ideology. Instead, Huntington paints a picture of a world divided between different civilizations, some of which are potentially opposed to Western ideology. If Huntington is correct, the implications for international business are profound.

Chapter 5, "The Political Economy of International Trade," has been significantly updated to reflect the recent activities of the World Trade Organization (WTO). This includes a discussion of the record of the WTO in resolving trade disputes between nations as well as a discussion of recent multinational agreements, brokered by the WTO, to liberalize cross-border trade and investment in financial services and telecommunications.

Chapter 7, "Regional Economic Integration," has been updated to reflect recent developments in the European Union, including the move toward monetary union, which began to take effect January 1, 1999. The chapter also contains an expanded and updated discussion of the effects of the 1993 North American Free Trade Agreement (NAFTA) and the South American free trade pact,

MERCOSUR. Recent research has shed new light on the magnitude of the effects of NAFTA and MERCOSUR. The chapter also updates the evolution of other moves toward regional economic integration, including the Asia-Pacific Economic Cooperation forum (APEC).

Chapter 9, "The Global Monetary System," includes new material that reviews the causes and consequences of the recent financial crises in Asia and Russia. The response of the International Monetary Fund to these crises has been discussed in light of the debate between scholars such as Jeffrey Sachs and Stanley Fisher as to the appropriate role of the IMF.

Chapter 12, "Global Marketing and Product Development," has been extensively rewritten and extended to enhance its contribution to the text. A new section deals with market segmentation in global markets. The discussion of pricing strategy has been expanded to incorporate recent research on multipoint pricing by international businesses. The section on new product development has been significantly expanded to incorporate new research and discuss additional issues. Additional areas covered include how best to integrate different functions and manage cross-functional product development teams in a globally dispersed enterprise, and where to locate R&D activities in a firm's global value chain.

NEW!! Another Perspective

Developed and written by Jeanne McNett of Assumption College and co-chair of the Academy of Management International Management Division Teaching Committee, these boxes are designed to give students an idea of how the surrounding material applies to and affects them or simply more infor-

mation on a nearby topic. They are sometimes narrative, but can also contain a few probing questions or even a trip to the Internet.

NEW!! Internet Exercises

Although the Internet exercises are not a new feature, they have been updated by Veronica Horton of the University of Akron. These exercises have been written to not only extend the ideas presented in the text, but also to develop the notion of e-commerce as an important component in the global business environment. Each chapter has four exercises. Two can be found in the printed text, and two additional exercises can be found with the student resources on the website.

INSTRUCTOR SUPPORT MATERIAL

Instructor's Manual/Test Bank–0-07-232056-7

The instructor's manual, prepared by Veronica Horton of the University of Akron, and test bank, prepared and updated by Bruce Barringer of the University of Central Florida, contain chapter overviews, teaching suggestions, lecture notes, and video notes. The test bank portion for this edition contains approximately 90 questions per chapter.

Computerized Testing for Windows–0-07-239058-1

A computerized version of the test bank allows the instructor to generate random tests and to add his or her own questions.

PowerPoint®– 0-07-239060-3

The PowerPoint slides, by Jeanne McNett of Assumption College,

contain a blend of material from the text and also new material, amounting to approximately 15–20 slides per chapter.

Video Collection– 0-07-239059-X

This edition will also include an improved video collection, consisting of NBC News footage and original business documentaries for each chapter. For a comprehensive line-up of video selections for each chapter, please visit our website (**www.mhhe.com/hillgbt2e**) for complete details.

Online Instructor Resources: www.mhhe.com/hillgbt2e

Adopters of *Global Business Today* will have access to a password-protected book website that provides coverage of the latest in online news and links relating to selected companies, countries, and situations referenced in the text. Other online and downloadable teaching resources will also be available.

STUDENT RESOURCES

Global Business Plan Project and Resource CD–0-07-239062-X

Designed to help students gain experience in conducting research and applying text concepts to the real world of international business, the resources on this CD are organized around a series of activities, created by Les Dlabay of Lake Forest College, which guide students step-by-step through the development of their own global business plan. As students work through the activities, they can link to hypertext chapters from the book, view related video clips, or launch to the book website and Internet.

Online Student Resources: www.mhhe.com/hillgbt2e

Students can use a variety of information and study aids including the new Online Learning Center, featuring the **e-Learning Session.** The e-Learning Session is an interactive tool that includes quizzes, essential terms, links to other material on the Internet, and video clips. Students will also have access to chapter study questions and Internet applications; Internet exploration questions tied to each chapter; a business jargon dictionary; and an online Web directory containing links to websites of international organizations, news agencies, companies, and countries.

Rand McNally's New Millennium World Atlas Deluxe CD-ROM

Ask your sales representative for more information on how to package the Rand McNally CD-ROM with the text for your students.

By clicking on points of interest on this interactive world atlas, students can quickly access over 800 articles on world cultures, cities, and science, as well as 237 country profiles and links to specific Internet sites. Special tools such as Notebook, Map Customization, Global Find, Compare Maps, and Compare Facts allow you to access, manipulate, customize, organize, save, and print the content information.

ACKNOWLEDGMENTS

Numerous people deserve to be thanked for their assistance in preparing this book. First, thank you to all the people at Irwin/McGraw-Hill who have worked with me on this project:

Jennifer Roche, Executive editor

Christine Scheid, Development editor

Amy Hill, Senior project manager

Jennifer Hollingsworth, Senior designer

Lori Koetters, Senior production supervisor

Keri Johnson, Senior photo research coordinator

Second, my thanks go to the reviewers, who provided good feedback that helped shape this book.

Michael Cicero, Highline Community College

Carolina Gomez, Towson University

Veronica Horton, University of Akron

Thomas W. Lloyd, Westmoreland County Community College

Jeanne McNett, Assumption College

Francine Newth, Providence College

Doug Ross, Towson University

Thank you also to reviewers and focus group participants who provided feedback on previous editions:

Hal Babson, Columbus State Community College

Doug Copeland, Johnson County Community College

Fred Ellis, Richland Community College

Jim Fatina, Harper College

Thomas Fletcher Grooms, Northwood University

Marty Hanson, Black Hawk College

Neila A. Holland, Richland College

John Kapoor, College of DuPage

Robert Ridich, Lincoln Land Community College

Third, I would like to thank my MBA research assistants, Maria Gonzalez and Maureen Kibelsted, for their assistance in preparing this manuscript. And last, but by no means least, I would like to thank my wife, Alexandra, and my daughters, Elizabeth, Charlotte, and Michelle, for their support and for giving me the strength to write this book.

Charles W. L. Hill

one

Chapter

Globalization

Opening Case   The Emerging Global Telecommunications Industry

A generation ago, telecommunications markets around the world could be characterized by a number of stylized facts. Most nations had a dominant telecommunications provider: AT&T in the United States, British Telecom in Britain, Deutsche Telekom in Germany, NTT in Japan, Telebras in Brazil, and so on. That provider was often state owned, and even when it wasn't, its operations were tightly regulated by the state. Cross-border competition between telecommunications providers was

Estimates from the World Trade Organization (WTO) suggest that the price for international telephone calls should fall by 80% over 3–5 years as competition increases. Soon it will cost no more to place a call halfway around the world than it does to call next door. What do you think will be the effect on the price of cell phones, such as these on sale in Tokyo?

Learning Objectives

1 Understand what is meant by the term "globalization."

2 Be familiar with the main causes of globalization.

3 Understand why globalization is now proceeding at a rapid rate.

4 Appreciate how changing international trade patterns, foreign direct investment flows, differences in economic growth rates among countries, and the rise of new multinational corporations are all changing the nature of the world economy.

5 Have a good grasp of the main arguments in the debate over the impact of globalization on job security, income levels, labor and environmental policies, and national sovereignty.

6 Appreciate that the process of globalization is giving rise to numerous opportunities and challenges that business managers must confront.

---

all but nonexistent. Typically, regulations prohibited foreign firms from entering a country's telecommunications market and competing with the domestic carrier. Most of the traffic carried by telecommunications firms was voice traffic, almost all of it was carried over copper wires, and most telecommunications firms charged their customers a hefty premium to make long-distance and international calls.

A generation later, the landscape is radically different. Telecommunications markets around the world have been deregulated. New competitors have emerged to take on the dominant providers. State-owned monopolies have been privatized, including British Telecom and Deutsche Telekom. Several dominant telecommunications firms, state owned or otherwise, have been broken up into smaller companies. For example, in 1998 Brazil's state-owned telecommunications monopoly, Telebras, was privatized and broken up into 12 smaller companies that are allowed to compete with each other. New wireless technologies have facilitated the emergence of competitors such as Orange and Vodafone in Britain, which now compete head-to-head with the former state monopoly, British Telecom. Thanks to the Internet, the volume of data traffic (e.g., Web graphics) is growing much more rapidly than that of voice traffic. By 2005, the volume of data traffic may be triple that of voice. Much of this data traffic is being *prices falling*

transmitted over new all-digital networks that utilize fiber optics, Internet protocols, digital switches, and photons to send data around the world at the speed of light.

Telecommunications firms are investing billions of dollars in digital networks to handle this traffic. To cap it all, under a 1997 agreement brokered by the World Trade Organization, 68 countries accounting for more than 90 percent of the world's telecommunications revenues have agreed to start opening their telecommunications markets to foreign competition and to abide by common rules for fair competition in telecommunications. Most of the world's biggest markets, including the United States, European Union, and Japan, were fully liberalized and open to foreign competition on January 1, 1998.

The consequences of these changes are becoming apparent. A global market for telecommunications services is rapidly emerging. Telecommunications companies are entering each other's markets. Prices are falling, both in the international market where prices have long been kept artificially high by a lack of competition and in the wireless market, which is rapidly becoming price competitive with traditional wire-line telecommunications services. Estimates

from the World Trade Organization suggest that the price for international telephone calls should fall by 80 percent over three to five years as competition increases, saving consumers $1,000 billion.

As competition intensifies, national telecommunications companies are entering into marketing alliances and joint ventures with one another in an attempt to offer multinational companies a single global telecommunications provider for all their international voice and data needs. In July 1998, AT&T and British Telecom announced they would merge most of their international operations into a jointly owned company that will have $10 billion in revenues. The venture will serve the global telecommunications needs of multinational corporations, enabling workers in Manhattan to communicate as easily with computer systems in New Delhi, say, as with colleagues in New Jersey. AT&T and British Telecom estimate that the market for providing international communications services to large and medium-sized business customers will expand from $36 billion in 1998 to $180 billion in 2007. Other companies that are working together on a global basis include MCI-WorldCom, the number two long-distance car-

rier in the United States, and Telefonica of Spain, which is also Latin America's biggest telecommunications carrier. The Sprint Corporation, the number three long-distance carrier in the United States, is partly owned by Deutsche Telekom and France Telecom. Together this trio is positioning itself to compete with the WorldCom/Telefonica and AT&T/BT ventures to gain the business of multinational customers in the brave new world of global telecommunications. A similar trend toward cross-border consolidation is occurring in the wireless arena. In a 1999 transaction, Britain's Vodafone acquired the large American wireless service provider Air Touch to build a transatlantic wireless service colossus. In November 1999, Vodafone continued its expansion thrust with a $128 billion takeover offer for Mannesmann AG, Germany's largest wireless service company. Reflecting on these trends, many observers believe that in a few years the global telecommunications markets will be dominated by a handful of transnational corporations. These companies will compete around the world and offer customers a bundle of wireline, wireless, and Internet services at a much lower cost than those available today.[1]

Introduction

A fundamental shift is occurring in the world economy. We are moving progressively further away from a world in which national economies were relatively isolated from each other by barriers to cross-border trade and investment, distance, time zones, language, and national differences in government regulation, culture, and business systems and toward a world in which national economies are merging into an interdependent global economic system. Commonly referred to as **globalization,** the trend toward a more integrated global economic system has been in place for many years. However, the rate at which this shift is occurring has been accelerating recently, and it looks set to continue to do so during the early years of this millennium.

The global telecommunications industry, which was profiled in the opening case, is one industry at the forefront of this development. A decade ago most national telecommunications markets were dominated by state-owned monopolies and isolated from each other by substantial barriers to cross-border trade and investment.

globalization The trend toward a more integrated global economic system.

This is rapidly becoming a thing of the past. A global telecommunications market is emerging. In this new market, prices are being bargained down as telecommunications providers compete with one another around the world for residential and business customers. The big winners are those customers, who should see the price of telecommunications services plummet, saving them billions of dollars.

The rapidly emerging global economy raises a multitude of issues for businesses both large and small. It creates opportunities to expand revenues, drive down costs, and boost profits. For example, companies can take advantage of the falling cost and enhanced functionality of global telecommunications services to more easily establish global markets for their products. Ten years ago no one would have thought that a small British company based in Stafford would have built a global market for its products by utilizing the Internet, but that is exactly what Bridgewater Pottery has done.[2] Bridgewater has traditionally sold premium pottery through exclusive distribution channels, but the company found it difficult and laborious to identify new retail outlets. Bridgewater established an Internet presence in 1997 and is now conducting business in other countries that could not be reached through existing distribution channels or reached cost-effectively. Bridgewater is not alone; thousands of companies around the world are using the new global communications infrastructure to build global markets for their products. As I sit in Seattle writing this book, I do so using an ergonomic computer mouse that was designed by a former farmer in Norway who found that repeated computer use gave him carpal tunnel syndrome. The farmer designed a mouse that alleviates his problem, started a company to manufacture it, and has now sold the mouse to consumers worldwide, using the Internet as his distribution channel.[3]

While the emerging global economy creates opportunities such as this for new entrepreneurs and established businesses around the world, it also presents challenges and threats that yesterday's business managers did not have to deal with. Managers now routinely have to decide how best to expand into a foreign market. Should they export to that market from their home base; should they invest in production facilities in that market, producing locally to sell locally; or should they produce in a third country where the cost of production is favorable and export from that base to other foreign markets and perhaps to their home market? Managers have to decide whether and how to customize their product offerings, marketing policies, human resource practices, and business strategies to deal with national differences in culture, language, business practices, and government regulation. And managers have to decide how to deal with the threat posed by efficient foreign competitors entering their home market.

The opening case provides us with an example of how service providers in the telecommunications industry are positioning themselves to cope with this new global reality. Companies such as AT&T and British Telecom, which for years had a monopoly within their protected national markets, are now competing with other telecommunications service providers for the business of consumers. As the case tells us, AT&T and British Telecom have formed a joint venture to enhance their chances of capturing the business of those multinational corporations that prefer a single telecommunications provider for their worldwide operations (and most do). Other competitors, such as MCI-WorldCom and Telefonica of Spain, have entered into more loosely structured marketing alliances in an attempt to achieve the same basic goal. These companies are experimenting with different strategies in order to better compete and prosper in the emerging global marketplace. Only time will tell which strategy makes most sense. Such strategic experimentation is occurring in a range of industries as firms struggle to come to grips with the new realities of global markets and competition.

Against the background of rapid globalization, this book explains how and why globalization is occurring and explores in some detail the impact that globalization has on the firm and its management. In this introductory chapter we discuss what we mean by globalization, review the main drivers of globalization, look at the changing profile of firms that do business outside their national borders, highlight concerns raised by critics of globalization, and explore the challenges that globalization holds for managers within an international business.

What Is Globalization?

As used in this book, globalization refers to the shift toward a more integrated and interdependent world economy. Globalization has two main components: the globalization of markets and the globalization of production.

The Globalization of Markets

globalization of markets The merging of historically distinct and separate national markets into one huge global marketplace.

The **globalization of markets** refers to the merging of historically distinct and separate national markets into one huge global marketplace. Some argue that the tastes and preference of consumers in different nations are beginning to converge on a global norm, helping to create a global market.[4] The global acceptance of consumer products such as Citicorp credit cards, Coca-Cola, Levi's jeans, Sony Walkmans and Discmans, Nintendo game players, and McDonald's hamburgers is frequently held up as a prototypical example of this trend. Firms such as Citicorp, Coca-Cola, McDonald's, Sony, and Levi Strauss are more than just benefactors of this trend, they are also facilitators of it. By offering a standardized product worldwide, they are helping to *create* a global market. A company does not have to be the size of these multinational giants to facilitate and benefit from the globalization of markets. For example, in the United States the number of small companies with fewer than 100 employees that export goods and services tripled between 1987 and 1997 to reach 209,455. Nearly 97 percent of US companies that export are small firms. Companies with fewer than 20 employees accounted for 65 percent of all US exporting firms in 1997. Small businesses now account for about one-third of all exports from the United States, up sharply from a decade earlier. Between 1993 and 1997 the value of exports from small businesses increased by about 300 percent. Many of these small exporters are targeting emerging markets. Thus, small business were responsible for close to 40 percent of the goods exported to China and Hong Kong in the late 1990s.[5]

Despite the global prevalence of Citicorp credit cards, Coca-Cola, Sony PlayStations, Levi's blue jeans, and McDonald's hamburgers, it is important not to push too far the view that national markets are giving way to a global market. As we shall see in later chapters, *very* significant differences still exist among national markets along many relevant dimensions, including consumer tastes and preferences, distribution channels, culturally embedded value systems, and the like. For many products, these differences frequently require that marketing strategies, product features, and operating practices be customized to best match conditions in a country. Thus, for example, automobile companies will promote varying car models in different countries depending on a range of factors such as local fuel costs, income levels, traffic congestion, and cultural values.

Currently the most global of markets are for industrial goods and materials that serve a universal need the world over. These include the markets for commodities such as aluminum, oil, and wheat; the markets for industrial products such as microprocessors, DRAMs (computer memory chips), and commercial jet aircraft; and

Significant differences still exist in natl mkts

the markets for financial assets from US Treasury bills to Eurobonds and futures on the Nikkei Index or the Mexican peso.

An important feature of many global markets—whether they be in consumer goods, industrial materials, or financial services—is that the same firms frequently confront each other as competitors in nation after nation. Coca-Cola's rivalry with Pepsi is a global one, as are the rivalries between Ford and Toyota, Boeing and Airbus, Caterpillar and Komatsu, and Nintendo and Sony. If one firm moves into a nation that is unserved by its rivals, those rivals are sure to follow lest their competitor gain an advantage.[6] These firms bring with them the assets that have served them well in other markets, creating a certain degree of homogeneity across markets. As rivals following rivals around the world, these multinational enterprises emerge as an important driver of the convergence of different national markets into a single, and increasingly homogenous, global marketplace. In an increasing number of industries it is no longer meaningful to talk about "the German market," "the American market," "the Brazilian market," or the Japanese market"; for many firms there is only the global market.

The Globalization of Production

The **globalization of production** refers to the tendency among firms to source goods and services from different locations around the globe to take advantage of national differences in the cost and quality of factors of production (such as labor, energy, land, and capital). By doing so, companies hope to lower their overall cost structure and/or improve the quality or functionality of their product offering, thereby allowing them to compete more effectively against their rivals. Consider Boeing Company's latest commercial jet airliner, the 777. The 777 contains 132,500 major component parts that are produced around the world by 545 suppliers. Eight Japanese suppliers make parts for the fuselage, doors, and wings; a supplier in Singapore makes the doors for the nose landing gear; three suppliers in Italy manufacture wing flaps; and so on.[7] Part of Boeing's rationale for outsourcing so much production to foreign suppliers is that these suppliers are the best in the world at performing their particular activity. (Boeing also outsources some production to foreign countries to increase the chance that it will win significant orders from airlines based in that country.) Having a *global web* of suppliers results in a better final product, which enhances the chances of Boeing's winning a greater share of total orders for aircraft than its global rival, Airbus.

The global dispersal of productive activities is not limited to giants such as Boeing. Many much smaller firms are also getting into the act. Consider Swan Optical, a US-based manufacturer and distributor of eyewear. With sales revenues only in the $20 to $30 million range, Swan is hardly a giant, yet Swan manufactures its eyewear in low-cost factories in Hong Kong and China that it jointly owns with a Hong Kong-based partner. Swan also has a minority stake in eyewear design houses in Japan, France, and Italy. Swan Optical has dispersed its manufacturing and design processes to different locations around the world to take advantage of the favorable skill base and cost structure found in other countries. Foreign investments in Hong Kong and then China have helped Swan to lower its cost structure, while investments in Japan, France, and Italy have helped it to produce designer eyewear for which it can charge a premium price. By dispersing its manufacturing and design activities, Swan has established a competitive advantage for itself in the global marketplace for eyewear, just as Boeing has tried to do by dispersing some of its activities to other countries.[8]

Robert Reich, former secretary of labor in the Clinton administration, has argued that, as a consequence of the trend exemplified by Boeing and Swan Optical, in many industries it is becoming irrelevant to talk about American products,

globalization of production The sourcing of goods and services from different locations around the globe to take advantage of national differences in the cost and quality of factors of production.

Japanese products, German products, or Korean products. Increasingly, according to Reich, the outsourcing of productive activities to different suppliers results in the creation of products that are global in nature; that is, "global products."[9] As with the globalization of markets, one must be careful not to push the concept of the globalization of production too far. As we will see in later chapters, substantial impediments still exist to the optimal dispersion of productive activities to different locations around the globe. These impediments include formal and informal barriers to trade between countries, barriers to foreign direct investment, transportation costs, and issues associated with economic and political risk.

Nevertheless, we are traveling down the road toward a future characterized by the increased globalization of markets and production. Modern firms are important actors in this drama, fostering by their very actions increased globalization. These firms, however, are merely responding in an efficient manner to changing conditions in their operating environment. In the next section, we look at the main drivers of globalization.

Drivers of Globalization

Two macro factors underlie the trend toward greater globalization. The first is the decline in barriers to the free flow of goods, services, and capital that has occurred since the end of World War II. The second factor is technological change, particularly the dramatic developments that have occurred in recent years in communications, information processing, and transportation.

Declining Trade and Investment Barriers

During the 1920s and 1930s many of the nation-states of the world erected formidable barriers to international trade and foreign direct investment. **International trade** occurs when a firm exports goods or services to consumers in another country. **Foreign direct investment** occurs when a firm invests resources in business activities outside its home country. Many barriers to international trade took the form of high tariffs on imports of manufactured goods. Such tariffs aimed to protect domestic industries from "foreign competition." One consequence, however, was "beggar thy neighbor" retaliatory trade policies; countries progressively raised trade barriers against each other. Ultimately, this depressed world demand and contributed to the Great Depression of the 1930s.

Having learned from this experience, after World War II, the advanced industrial nations of the West—under US leadership—committed themselves to removing barriers to the free flow of goods, services, and capital between nations.[10] This goal was enshrined in the treaty known as the **General Agreement on Tariffs and Trade (GATT).** Under the umbrella of GATT, there have been eight rounds of negotiations between member states, which now number more than 130. The most recent round of negotiations, known as the Uruguay Round, was completed in December 1993. The Uruguay Round further reduced trade barriers; extended GATT to cover services as well as manufactured goods; provided enhanced protection for patents, trademarks, and copyrights; and established the **World Trade Organization (WTO)** to police the international trading system.[11] Table 1.1 summarizes the impact of GATT agreements on average tariff rates for manufactured goods. As can be seen, average tariff rates have fallen significantly since 1950 and under the Uruguay agreement hit 3.9 percent in 2000.

In addition to reducing trade barriers, many countries have also been progressively removing restrictions on barriers to foreign direct investment (FDI). According to the United Nations, between 1991 and 1996 more than 100 countries made

Table 1.1

Average Tariff Rates on Manufactured Products as Percent of Value

	1913	1950	1990	2000*
France	21	18	5.9	3.9
Germany	20	26	5.9	3.9
Italy	18	25	5.9	3.9
Japan	30	–	5.3	3.9
Holland	5	11	5.9	3.9
Sweden	20	9	4.4	3.9
Britain	–	23	5.9	3.9
United States	44	14	4.8	3.9

*Rates for 2000 based on full implementation of Uruguay agreement.

Source: "Who Wants to Be a Giant?" *The Economist,* June 24, 1995, pp. 3–4.

599 changes in legislation governing FDI. Some 95 percent of these changes involved liberalizing a country's foreign investment regulations to make it easier for foreign companies to enter the markets. Governments' desire to facilitate FDI has also been reflected in a dramatic increase in the number of bilateral investment treaties designed to protect and promote investment between two countries. As of January 1, 1997, there were 1,330 such treaties in the world involving 162 countries, a threefold increase in five years.[12] During 1997, the latest year for which data are available, 76 countries made 151 changes in FDI regulatory regimes, 89 percent of them creating a more favorable environment for FDI.[13]

Such trends facilitate both the globalization of markets and the globalization of production. The lowering of barriers to international trade enables firms to view the world, rather than a single country, as their market. The lowering of trade *and* investment barriers also allows firms to base individual production activities at the optimal site for that activity, serving the world market from that location. Thus, a firm might design a product in one country, produce component parts in two other countries, assemble the product in yet another country, and then export the finished product around the world.

There is plenty of evidence that the lowering of trade barriers has facilitated the globalization of production. According to data from the World Trade Organization, the volume of world trade has grown consistently faster than the volume of world output since 1950.[14] Over this period, world trade has expanded almost 20-fold, far outstripping world output, which has grown sixfold. Thus, exports now account for 26.4 percent of global production, up from 8 percent in 1950. As suggested by Figure 1.1, the growth in world trade has continued to outpace the growth in world output during the 1990s.

This implies two things. First, more firms are doing what Boeing does with the 777 and dispersing production to different locations around the globe to drive down costs and increase quality. Second, the economies of the world's nations are becoming more closely intertwined. As trade expands, nations are becoming increasingly dependent on each other for important goods and services.

Evidence also suggests that foreign direct investment (FDI) is playing an increasing role in the global economy as firms ranging in size from Boeing to Swan Optical increase their cross-border investments. The average yearly *outflow* of FDI increased from about $25 billion in 1975 to a record $644 billion in 1998.[15] Not

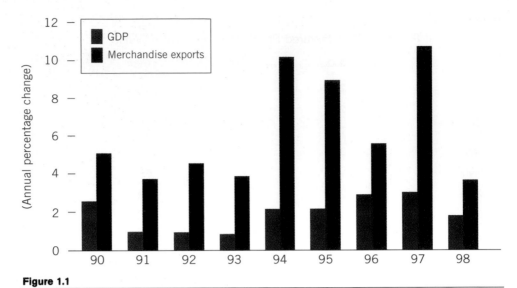

Figure 1.1

The Growth of World Trade and World Output, 1990–1998
Source: World Trade Organization, *International Trade Trends and Statistics,* 1999.

only did the flow of FDI accelerate during the 1980s and 1990s, but it also accelerated faster than the growth in world trade. Between 1984 and 1998 the total flow of FDI from all countries increased by over 1,000 percent, while world trade grew by 91 percent and world output by 27 percent.[16] By 1997 the global stock of FDI exceeded $3.5 trillion. By 1998 some 60,000 parent companies with more than 500,000 affiliates in foreign markets collectively produced an estimated $11 trillion in global sales, or 25 percent of global output.[17] The major investors have been US, Japanese, and Western European companies investing in Europe, Asia (particularly China), and the United States.

Finally, the globalization of markets and production—and the resulting growth of world trade, foreign direct investment, and imports—all imply that firms around the globe are finding their home markets under attack from foreign competitors. This is true in Japan, where US companies such as Texas Instruments, Procter & Gamble, and Merrill Lynch are expanding their presence. It is true in the United States, where the Nordic telecommunications equipment companies, Nokia and Ericsson, have taken market share away from Motorola. And it is true in Europe where the once-dominant Dutch company Philips Electronics NV has seen its market share in the consumer electronics industry taken by Japan's JVC, Matsushita, and Sony. The growing integration of the world economy into a single, huge marketplace is increasing the intensity of competition in a wide range of manufacturing and service industries.

But we cannot take declining trade barriers for granted. As we shall see in the following chapters, demands for "protection" from foreign competitors are still often heard in countries around the world, including the United States. Although a return to the "beggar thy neighbor" trade policies of the 1920s and 1930s is unlikely, it is not clear whether the political majority in the industrialized world favors further reductions in trade barriers. This was highlighted at a December 1999 meeting of the World Trade Organization held in Seattle. The meeting was intended to launch a new round of talks aimed at further reductions in cross-border barriers to trade and investment. However, demonstrations from trade unions, environmentalists, and human rights groups delayed the opening meetings of the WTO. The demonstrations focused world attention on the strength of opposition to further liberalization of cross-border trade.

When they did meet, delegates from the 132 member states of the WTO were unable to reach any agreements, and the talks ended without an agenda for a new round of trade negotiations. If trade barriers decline no further for the time being, this may slow the rapid globalization of both markets and production.

The Role of Technological Change

While the lowering of trade barriers made globalization of markets and production a theoretical possibility, technological change has made it a tangible reality. Since the end of World War II, there have been major advances in communications, information processing, and transportation technology, including the explosive emergence of the Internet and World Wide Web. In the words of Renato Ruggiero, director-general of the World Trade Organization,

> Telecommunications is creating a global audience. Transport is creating a global village. From Buenos Aires to Boston to Beijing, ordinary people are watching MTV, they're wearing Levi's jeans, and they're listening to Sony Walkmans as they commute to work.[18]

MICROPROCESSORS AND TELECOMMUNICATIONS Perhaps the single most important innovation has been development of the microprocessor, which enabled the explosive growth of high-power, low-cost computing, vastly increasing the amount of information that can be processed by individuals and firms. The microprocessor underlies many recent advances in telecommunications technology. Over the past 30 years global communications have been revolutionized by developments in satellite, optical fiber, and wireless technology, and now the Internet and the World Wide Web. These technologies rely on the microprocessor to encode, transmit, and decode the information that flows along these electronic highways. Plus, the cost of microprocessors continues to fall while their power increases (a phenomenon known as **Moore's Law,** which predicts that the power of microprocessor technology doubles, and its costs of production fall in half, every 18 months).[19] As this happens, the costs of global communications plummet, which lowers the costs of coordinating and controlling a global organization.

Moore's Law Prediction that the power of microprocessor technology doubles and its costs of production fall in half every 18 months.

THE INTERNET AND WORLD WIDE WEB The phenomenal recent growth of the Internet and the associated World Wide Web (which utilizes the Internet to communicate between World Wide Web sites) is the latest expression of this development. In 1990, fewer than 1 million users were connected to the Internet. By late 1999 the Internet had about 180 million users, of which some 110 million were in the United States. In addition, some 18 million Japanese used the Internet regularly, 14 million Britons, 13 million Canadians, 12 million Germans, 6 million Chinese, and 6 million Brazilians. By the year 2003 there may be well over 350 million users of the Internet.[20] In July 1993, some 1.8 million host computers were connected to the Internet (host computers host the Web pages of local users). By July

Perhaps the single most important innovation affecting globalization has been the development of the microprocessor, shown here being manufactured by two technicians. Not only has it enabled the explosive growth of high-power, low-cost computing, but it has vastly increased the amount of information that can be processed by individuals and firms.

1999, the number of host computers had increased to 56.3 million, and the number is still growing rapidly.[21]

The Internet and World Wide Web promise to develop into the information backbone of tomorrow's global economy. From virtually nothing in 1994, the value of transactions taking place on the Web has increased at an exponential rate, hitting $98.4 billion in 1999. According to a recent report issued by the US Department of Commerce, this figure could reach $300 billion in the United States alone by 2003.[22] Other estimates suggest it could reach as much as $1.3 trillion by the same year.[23] Already, companies such as Dell Computer are booking over $54 million a day in Web-based sales, and Internet equipment giant Cisco Systems books more than 80 percent of its total sales on-line.

e-commerce
Web-based electronic commerce.

Included in this expanding volume of Web-based electronic commerce—or **e-commerce** as it is commonly called—is a growing percentage of cross-border transactions. Viewed globally, the Web is emerging as the great equalizer. It is a powerful dislocating force that rolls back some constraints of location, scale, and time zones. The Web allows businesses, both small and large, to expand their global presence at a lower cost than ever before. One example is a small California-based start-up, Cardiac Science, which makes defibrillators and heart monitors. In 1996, Cardiac Science was itching to break into international markets but had little idea of how to establish an international presence. By 1998, the company was selling to customers in 46 countries and foreign sales accounted for 85 percent of its $1.2 million revenues. Although some of this business was developed through conventional export channels, a growing percentage of it came from hits to the company's website, which according to the company's CEO, "attracts international business people like bees to honey."[24] The Web makes it much easier for buyers and sellers to find each other, wherever they may be located and however large or small they might be.

To facilitate the creation of the global electronic marketplace, many on-line commerce and media companies are moving into the global arena. For example, the three largest American on-line companies, AOL, Amazon.com, and Yahoo!, are establishing overseas properties. They are aided by World Trade Organization rules, which currently prohibit countries from placing a tax on cross-border sales executed via the Web. The accompanying "Management Focus" looks at how one major on-line company, Yahoo!, is rapidly building a global presence. Others can be expected to quickly follow its lead.

TRANSPORTATION TECHNOLOGY In addition to developments in communications technology, several major innovations in transportation technology have occurred since World War II. In economic terms, the most important are the development of commercial jet aircraft and superfreighters and the introduction of containerization, which greatly simplifies transshipment from one mode of transport to another. The advent of commercial jet travel, by reducing the time needed to get from one location to another, has effectively shrunk the globe (see Figure 1.2). Because of jet travel, in terms of travel time New York is now "closer" to Tokyo than it was to Philadelphia in the Colonial days.

Containerization has revolutionized the transportation business, significantly lowering the costs of shipping goods over long distances. Before containerization, moving goods from one mode of transport to another was a very labor-intensive, lengthy, and costly process. It could take several hundred longshoremen days to unload a ship and reload goods onto trucks and trains for delivery to their next and/or final destinations. With the advent of widespread containerization in the 1970s and 1980, the whole process could be executed by a handful of longshoremen in a couple of days. Since 1980, the world's containership fleet has more than quadrupled, reflecting in part the growing volume of international trade and in part the switch to this mode of transportation. Transportation costs have plummeted because of the

1500–1840

Best average speed of horse-drawn coaches
and sailing ships, 10 mph.

1850–1930

Steam locomotives average 65 mph.
Steam ships average 36 mph.

1950s

Propeller aircraft
300–400 mph.

1960s

Jet passenger aircraft
500–700 mph.

Figure 1.2

The Shrinking Globe
Source: P. Dicken, *Global Shift* (New York: Guilford Press, 1992), p. 104.

efficiency gains associated with containerization, making it much more economical
to ship goods around the globe, thereby driving the globalization of markets and
production. In the United States, for example, the cost of shipping freight per ton
mile on railroads has fallen from 3 cents in 1985 to 2.4 cents in 1997, largely as a
result of efficiency gains from the widespread use of containers.[25]

IMPLICATIONS FOR THE GLOBALIZATION OF PRODUCTION   Due to containerization, the transportation costs associated with the globalization of production have declined. Because of the technological innovations discussed above, the real costs of information processing and communication have fallen dramatically in the past two
decades. This makes it possible for a firm to manage a globally dispersed production

In 1993, Jerry Yang and David Filo, two graduate engineering students at Stanford University, decided to post their list of favorite websites on Yang's home page. They dubbed the site "Jerry's Guide to the World Wide Web." Almost by accident, they had created one of the first Web directories. In doing so, they had solved a pressing need: how to find things on the Web. In 1994, they changed the name of the directory to Yahoo! (http://www.yahoo.com).

to building Yahoo! into a business. One of their first hires, Srinija Srinivasan, or "ontological yahoo" as she is known within the company, refined and developed the classification scheme that has become the hallmark of Yahoo!'s Web directory. Yang and Filo's business model was to derive revenues from renting advertising space on the pages of the fast-growing directory.

To expand the business, however, they needed capital to fund

pany that listed 200,000 websites under 20,000 different categories and was being used by 800,000 people per day. This, however, was just the beginning. In conjunction with Yang and Filo, Koogle crafted a vision of Yahoo! as a global media company whose principal asset would be a major Internet gateway, or portal, that would enable anyone wherever they lived to connect with anything or anybody. Koogle's ambition was to transform Ya-

Global Yahoo!

Filo and Yang insist they selected the name because they considered themselves "yahoos."

By late 1994, Yahoo! was drawing over 100,000 people a day. The directory had outgrown the limited capacity of the Stanford site, and Yahoo! was borrowing server space from Netscape. Yang and Filo had decided to put their graduate studies on hold while they turned their attention

investments in servers, software development, and classification personnel. A solution came in the form of an investment from a Silicon Valley venture capital firm. As part of the investment package, Sequoia required Yang and Filo to hire an experienced CEO. The man chosen for the job was Tim Koogle, a 45-year-old engineer with 15 years' experience in the management of high-technology firms.

By mid-1996, Koogle was heading a publicly traded com-

hoo!'s simple directory service into a conduit for bringing together globally dispersed buyers and sellers, thereby facilitating commercial transactions over the Web (e-commerce). In this vision, Yahoo! would continue to generate revenues from the sale of advertising space on its directory pages, but it would also garner significant revenues from e-commerce transactions by taking a small slice of each transaction executed over its service.

system. A worldwide communications network has become essential for many international businesses. For example, Texas Instruments (TI), the US electronics firm, has approximately 50 plants in 19 countries. A satellite-based communications system allows TI to coordinate, on a global scale, its production planning, cost accounting, financial planning, marketing, customer service, and personnel management. The system consists of more than 300 remote entry terminals, 8,000 inquiry terminals, and 140 mainframe computers. The system enables managers of TI's worldwide operations to send vast amounts of information to each other instantaneously and to implement tight coordination between the firm's different plants and activities.[26]

500 Engineers, 13 Time Zones, 3 Continents

Lucent Technologies is creating a new fiber optic switch in its Bell Labs division. Called the Bandwidth Manager, this switch is a global product whose development illustrates a global team approach. Its *distributed development* (a term used to describe a dispersed global team) involved light-wave science from Lucent's plant north of Boston, cross-connect products from a New Jersey plant, timing devices from the Netherlands, and optics from Germany. In addition, the test engineers were in India, so the project operated on a 24-hour schedule. (*The Wall Street Journal,* April 23, 1999)

The service, Yahoo! Store (http://store.yahoo.com), enables businesses to quickly create, publish, and manage secure on-line stores to market goods and services. After launching their store, merchants are included in searches on Yahoo! Shopping.

To make this vision a reality, Yahoo! had to become one of the most useful and well-known locations on the Web—in short, it had to become a global megabrand. A directory alone would not suffice, no matter how useful. To increase traffic Yahoo! added features that increased its appeal. It supplemented the directory with compelling content. It allowed registered users to use Yahoo!'s service to perform tasks such as sending e-mail, keeping appointment calendars, or tracking investments.

To build brand awareness, Yahoo! spent heavily on radio and television ads. To expand the reach of the service, Yahoo! opened services around the world and posted local-language versions of Yahoo!'s Web directory.

An example is Yahoo! Brazil, which began service in June 1999. Yahoo! Brazil includes more than 12,000 Brazilian websites, as well as other Portu- guese websites, organized into 14 easy-to-use categories by a team of native Brazilian Web surfers.

Yahoo! also began to work with content providers and merchants to build their on-line presence, and by extension to increase the value of Yahoo!'s site to users who could access the content and merchants through Yahoo!. Simultaneously, Yahoo! has been working with a number of banks in different countries to facilitate on-line bill paying and to allow bank customers to monitor their accounts on-line. Yahoo! also increased its value to advertisers by enabling them to better target their advertising message to certain demographics.

The results of this strategy have been spectacular. During September 1999, more than 105 million unique users visited Yahoo!'s network of global properties, up from 50 million the previous year and 26 million in 1997.

Some 80 million of these were registered with Yahoo!. These users were accessing 385 million Yahoo! pages per day in September 1999. By the end of 1999, some 7,000 merchants were selling products over Yahoo! Shopping, up from 3,500 in December 1998. At the same time, there were 21 Yahoo!'s outside the United States, including the most recent addition, Yahoo! China. Independent third-party research ranked Yahoo! the number one Web network in the United States, United Kingdom, Germany, France, Italy, Spain, Japan, and Korea. Yahoo! could be accessed in 16 languages. The company's revenues had grown from $21.5 million in 1996 to a projected $500 million in 1999. Meanwhile, Yahoo!'s stock price soared from $5 a share in 1996 to a high of $282 a share in late 1999, effectively valuing Yahoo! at a staggering $72 billion and making Yang and Filo billionaires.[27]

Another US electronics firm, Hewlett-Packard, also uses satellite communications and information processing technologies to link its worldwide operations. Hewlett-Packard has new-product development teams composed of individuals based in different countries (e.g., Japan, the United States, Great Britain, and Germany). When developing new products, these individuals use videoconferencing technologies to "meet" on a weekly basis. They also communicate with each other daily via telephone, electronic mail, and fax. Communication technologies have enabled Hewlett-Packard to increase the integration of its globally dispersed operations and to reduce the time needed for developing new products.[28]

In addition to communications and information processing technology, the development of commercial jet aircraft has helped knit the worldwide operations of many international businesses. Using jet travel, an American manager need spend a day at most traveling to European or Asian operations, enabling the manager to oversee a globally dispersed production system.

IMPLICATIONS FOR THE GLOBALIZATION OF MARKETS In addition to the globalization of production, technological innovations have also facilitated the globalization of markets. As noted above, low-cost transportation has made it more economical to ship products around the world. Low-cost global communications networks such as the World Wide Web are helping to create electronic global marketplaces. In addition, low-cost jet travel has resulted in the mass movement of people between countries. This has reduced the cultural distance between countries and is bringing about some convergence of consumer tastes and preferences. At the same time, global communications networks and global media are creating a worldwide culture. Television networks such as CNN, MTV, and HBO are now received in many countries around the world, and Hollywood films are shown the world over. In any society the media are primary conveyors of culture; as global media develop, we can expect the evolution of something akin to a global culture. A logical result of this evolution is the emergence of global markets for consumer products. It is now as easy to find a McDonald's restaurant in Tokyo as it is in New York, to buy a Sony PlayStation in Rio as it is in Berlin, and to buy Gap jeans in Paris as it is in San Francisco.

But we must be careful not to overemphasize this trend. While modern communications and transportation technologies are ushering in the "global village," very significant national differences remain in culture, consumer preferences, and the ways in which business is conducted. A firm that ignores differences between countries does so at its peril. We shall stress this point repeatedly throughout this book and elaborate on it in later chapters.

The Changing Demographics of the Global Economy

Accompanying the trend toward globalization has been a dramatic change in the demographics of the global economy over the past 30 years or so. As late as the 1960s four stylized facts described the demographics of the global economy. The first was US dominance in the world economy and world trade picture. The second was US dominance in world foreign direct investment. The third fact was the dominance of large, multinational US firms on the international business scene. The fourth was that roughly half the globe—the centrally planned economies of the Communist world—was off-limits to Western international businesses. As will be explained below, all four of these facts either have changed or are now changing rapidly.

The Changing World Output and World Trade Picture

In the early 1960s the United States was still by far the world's dominant industrial power. In 1963, for example, the United States accounted for 40.3 percent of world output. By 1997, the United States accounted for only 20.8 percent (see Table 1.2). The United States was not the only developed nation to see its relative standing slip. The same occurred to Germany, France, and the United Kingdom, all nations that were among the first to industrialize. This decline in the US position was not an absolute decline because the US economy grew at a relatively robust average annual rate of close to 3.0 percent in the 1963–97 period (the economies of Germany, France, and the United Kingdom also grew). Rather, it was a relative decline, reflecting the faster economic growth of several other economies, particularly in Asia. For example, as can be seen from Table 1.2, over the 1963–97 time period, Japan's share of world output increased from 5.5 percent to 8.3 percent. Other countries that markedly increased their share of world output included China, Thailand, Malaysia,

Table 1.2

The Changing Pattern of World Output and Trade

Country	Share of World Output, 1963	Share of World Output, 1997†	Share of World Exports, 1998
United States	40.3%	20.8%	12.7%
Japan	5.5	8.3	7.26
Germany*	9.7	4.8	10.0
France	6.3	3.5	5.7
United Kingdom	6.5	3.2	5.1
Italy	3.4	3.2	4.5
Canada	3	1.7	4.0
China‡	NA	11.3	3.4
South Korea	NA	1.7	2.45

*1963 figure for Germany refers to the former West Germany.
†Output is measured by gross national product. The 1997 estimates are based on purchasing power parity (PPP) statistics that adjust GNP for differences in prices (the cost of living) between countries.
‡The Chinese figures are somewhat suspect. When calculated using unadjusted GNP data, China's share of world output shrinks to 3.1 percent. Thus, China's high share of world output on a PPP basis is partly due to the relatively low cost of living in China.

Source: Export data from World Trade Organization, *Annual Report, 1999 and Statistics, 1996* (Geneva: WTO, 1996). World output data from *CIA factbook,* 1999.

Taiwan, and South Korea. By virtue of its huge population and rapid industrialization, China in particular is emerging as an economic colossus.

By the end of the 1980s the US position as the world's leading exporter was threatened. Over the past 30 years US dominance in export markets has waned as Japan, Germany, and a number of newly industrialized countries such as South Korea and China have taken a larger share of world exports. During the 1960s the United States routinely accounted for 20 percent of world exports of manufactured goods. Table 1.2 also reports manufacturing exports as a percentage of the world total in 1998. As can be seen, the US share of world exports of manufactured goods had slipped to 12.6 percent by 1998. But despite the fall, the United States still remained the world's largest exporter, ahead of Germany and Japan.

In 1997 and 1998 the dynamic economies of the Asian Pacific region were hit by a serious financial crisis that slowed their economic growth rates. Despite this, their powerful growth may continue over the long run, as will that of several other important emerging economies in Latin America (e.g., Brazil) and Eastern Europe (e.g., Poland). Thus, a further *relative* decline in the share of world output and world exports accounted for by the United States and other long-established nations seems likely. This is not a bad thing. The relative decline of the United States reflects the growing economic development and industrialization of the world economy, as opposed to any absolute decline in the health of the US economy, which in the late 1990s was stronger than it had ever been.

Most forecasts for 20 years into the future predict a rapid rise in the share of world output accounted for by developing nations such as China, India, Indonesia, Thailand, South Korea, and Brazil and a commensurate decline in the share enjoyed by rich industrialized countries such as Britain, Germany, Japan, and the United States. The World Bank, for example, has estimated that if current trends continue, by 2020

shift in economic geography.

the Chinese economy could be 40 percent larger than that of the United States, while India's economy will be larger than that of Germany. The bank also estimates that today's developing nations may account for over 60 percent of world economic activity by 2020, while today's rich nations, which currently account for over 55 percent of world economic activity, may account for only about 38 percent.[29] These forecasts suggest that a dramatic shift in the economic geography of the world is under way. For international businesses, the implications of this changing economic geography are clear; many of tomorrow's economic opportunities may be found in the developing nations of the world, and many of tomorrow's most capable competitors will probably also emerge from these regions.

The Changing Foreign Direct Investment Picture

Reflecting the dominance of the United States in the global economy, US firms accounted for 66.3 percent of worldwide foreign direct investment flows in the 1960s. British firms were second, accounting for 10.5 percent, while Japanese firms were a distant eighth, with only 2 percent. The dominance of US firms was so great that books were written in Europe about the economic threat posed to Europe by US corporations.[30] Several European governments, most notably that of France, talked of limiting inward investment by US firms.

However, as the barriers to the free flow of goods, services, and capital fell, and as other countries increased their shares of world output, non-US firms increasingly began to invest across national borders. The motivation for much of this foreign direct investment by non-US firms was the desire to disperse production activities to optimal locations and to build a direct presence in major foreign markets. For example, during the 1970s and 1980s European and Japanese firms began to shift labor-intensive manufacturing operations from their home markets to developing nations where labor costs were lower. In addition many Japanese firms have invested in North America and Europe, often as a hedge against unfavorable currency movements and the possible imposition of trade barriers. Toyota, the Japanese automobile company, rapidly increased its investment in automobile production facilities in the United States and Britain during the late 1980s and early 1990s. These investments were driven by Toyota's belief that an increasingly strong Japanese yen would price Japanese automobile exports out of foreign markets, so production in the most important foreign markets, as opposed to exports from Japan, made sense. Toyota also undertook these investments to head off growing political pressures in the United States and Europe to restrict Japanese automobile exports into those markets.

stock of foreign direct investment The total cumulative value of foreign investments in a country.

Figure 1.3 shows the changes from 1980 to 1997 in the percentage of stock of foreign direct investment owned by companies in the United States, Britain, Japan, Germany, France, and the Netherlands, the six most important sources of such investment. (The **stock of foreign direct investment** refers to the total cumulative value of foreign investments.) Figure 1.3 also shows the stock accounted for by firms from other developed nations and firms from developing economies. As can be seen, the share of the total stock accounted for by US firms declined substantially from about 44 percent in 1980 to 25 percent in 1997. Meanwhile, the shares accounted for by Japan, France, other developed nations, and the world's developing nations all increased markedly. The rise in the share owned by developing nations reflects a small but growing trend for firms from these countries, such as South Korea, to invest outside their borders. In 1997 firms based in developing nations accounted for 9.7 percent of the stock of foreign direct investment, up from only 1.2 percent in 1980.

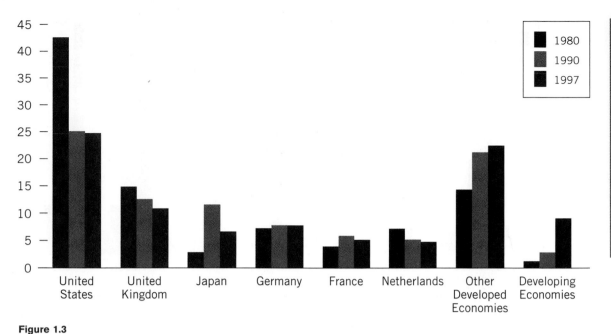

Figure 1.3

Percentage Share of Total FDI Stock, 1980–1997
Source: Data from *World Investment Report, 1998* (New York: United Nations, 1998).

Figure 1.4 illustrates another important trend: the increasing incidence of cross-border investments directed at developing rather than rich industrialized nations. Figure 1.4 details recent changes in the annual inflows of foreign direct investment (the **flow of foreign direct investment** refers to amounts invested across national borders each year). Notable in Figure 1.4 is the increase in the share of foreign direct investment inflows accounted for by developing countries during the 1990s and the commensurate decline in the share of inflows directed at developed nations. In 1997, foreign direct investment inflows into developing nations hit a record $149 billion, or 37 percent of the total, up from just $42 billion in 1991, or 26 percent of the total. Among developing nations, China has received the greatest volume of inward FDI in recent years. China took a record $45 billion of the investment that went to developing nations in 1997. Other developing nations receiving a large amount of FDI in 1997 included Indonesia, Malaysia, the Philippines, Thailand, and Mexico. At the other end of the spectrum, the smallest 100 recipient countries accounted for just 1 percent of all FDI inflows.[31] Foreign investment into developing nations is focused on a relatively small group of countries that are currently experiencing rapid industrialization and economic growth. Businesses investing in these nations are positioning themselves to be active participants in those areas of the world that are expected to grow most rapidly over the next quarter of a century.

flow of foreign direct investment The amount of money invested across national borders.

The Changing Nature of the Multinational Enterprise

A **multinational enterprise** is any business that has productive activities in two or more countries. Since the 1960s, there have been two notable trends in the demographics of the multinational enterprise. The first has been the rise of non-US multinationals, particularly Japanese multinationals. The second is the growth of mini-multinationals.

multinational enterprise Any business that has productive activities in two or more countries.

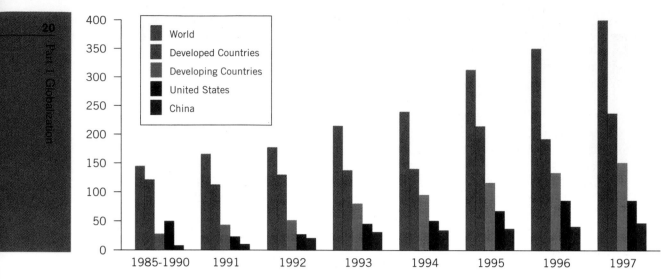

Figure 1.4

FDI Inflows, 1985–1997 (in US$ billions)

Source: United Nations, *World Investment Report 1997* (New York: United Nations, 1997). The 1997 data are from a November 8, 1998, UN press release, TAD/1861.

NON-US MULTINATIONALS   In the 1960s global business activity was dominated by large US multinational corporations. With US firms accounting for about two-thirds of foreign direct investment during the 1960s, one would expect most multinationals to be US enterprises. According to Table 1.3, in 1973 48.5 percent of the world's 260 largest multinationals were US firms. The second-largest source country was Great Britain, with 18.8 percent of the largest multinationals. Japan accounted for only 3.5 percent of the world's largest multinationals at the time. The large number of US multinationals reflected US economic dominance in the three decades after World War II, while the large number of British multinationals reflected that country's industrial dominance in the early decades of the 20th century.

By 1997, however, things had shifted significantly. In that year US firms accounted for 32.4 percent of the world's 500 largest multinationals, followed by Japan with 25.2 percent. France was a distant third with 8.4 percent. Although the two sets of figures in Table 1.3 are not strictly comparable (the 1973 figures are based on the largest 260 firms, and the 1997 figures are based on the largest 500 firms), they illustrate the trend. The globalization of the world economy, together with Japan's

Table 1.3

The National Composition of the Largest Multinationals

	Of the Top 260 in 1973	Of the Top 500 in 1997
United States	126 (48.5%)	162 (32.4%)
Japan	9 (3.5)	126 (25.2)
Britain	49 (18.8)	34 (6.8)
France	19 (7.3)	42 (8.4)
Germany	21 (8.1)	41 (8.2)

Source: The 1973 figures from Hood and Young, *The Economics of the Multinational Enterprise* (New York: Longman, 1979). The 1997 figures from "The Global 500," *Fortune,* August 4, 1997, pp. 130–31.

rise to the top rank of economic powers, has resulted in a relative decline in the dominance of US (and to a lesser extent British) firms in the global marketplace.

In the future, we can reasonably expect the growth of new multinational enterprises from the world's developing nations. As the accompanying "Country Focus" demonstrates, there is already a strong tendency for South Korean firms to invest outside their national borders. The South Koreans may soon be followed by firms from countries such as Mexico, China, Russia, and Brazil.

THE RISE OF MINI-MULTINATIONALS   Another trend in international business has been the growth of medium-size and small multinationals (mini-multinationals). When people think of international businesses they tend to think of firms such as Exxon, General Motors, Ford, Fuji, Kodak, Matsushita, Procter & Gamble, Sony, and Unilever—large, complex multinational corporations with operations that span the globe. Although most international trade and investment is still conducted by large firms, many medium-size and small businesses are increasingly involved in international trade and investment, such as Swan Optical and Cardiac Science.

Consider Lubricating Systems, Inc., of Kent, Washington. Lubricating Systems, which manufactures lubricating fluids for machine tools, employs 25 people and generates sales of $6.5 million. It is hardly a large, complex multinational, yet more than $2 million of the company's sales are generated by exports to a score of countries from Japan to Israel and the United Arab Emirates. Lubricating Systems also has set up a joint venture with a German company to serve the European market.[32] Consider also Lixi, Inc., a small US manufacturer of industrial X-ray equipment; 70 percent of Lixi's $4.5 million in revenues come from exports to Japan.[33] Or take G. W. Barth, a manufacturer of cocoa-bean roasting machinery based in Ludwigsburg, Germany. Employing just 65 people, this small company has captured 70 percent of the global market for cocoa-bean roasting machines.[34] International business is conducted not just by large firms but also by medium-size and small enterprises.

The Changing World Order

Between 1989 and 1991 a series of remarkable democratic revolutions swept the Communist world. For reasons that are explored in more detail in Chapter 2, in country after country throughout Eastern Europe and eventually in the Soviet Union itself, Communist governments collapsed. The Soviet Union is now history, having been replaced by 15 independent republics. Czechoslovakia has divided itself into two states, while Yugoslavia has dissolved into a bloody civil war among its five successor states.

Many of the former Communist nations of Europe and Asia seem to share a commitment to democratic politics and free market economics. If this continues, the opportunities for international businesses may be enormous. For the best part of half a century these countries were essentially closed to Western international businesses. Now they present a host of export and investment opportunities. Just how this will play itself out over the next 10 to 20 years is difficult to say. The economies of most of the former Communist states are in very poor condition, and their continued commitment to democracy and free market economics cannot be taken for granted. Disturbing signs of growing unrest and totalitarian tendencies are seen in many Eastern European states. Thus, the risks involved in doing business in such countries are very high, but so may be the returns.

In addition to these changes, more quiet revolutions have been occurring in China and Latin America. Their implications for international businesses may be just as profound as the collapse of communism in Eastern Europe. China suppressed its own prodemocracy movement in the bloody Tiananmen Square massacre of 1989.

In the forefront of South Korea's emergence as a modern industrial economy over the past 25 years have been the diversified business groups known as the *chaebol.* Samsung, the largest of the *chaebol,* had 1998 revenues of $72 billion and is involved in a range of industries including electronics (it is the world's largest manufacturer of memory chips for computers), automobiles, shipbuilding, aerospace, and machinery. Samsung is closely followed in size by three other major *chaebol,* Hyundai,

Korea have risen sharply, nullifying important sources of the *chaebol's* competitive advantage in the global economy. An analysis of national competitiveness by the Swiss-based International Institute of Management Development (IMD) ranked South Korea 24th out of 41 developed and developing nations, just behind Thailand and Chile and just ahead of Spain and Mexico (the three top countries were the United States, Singapore, and Japan).

seas, establishing factories in countries where direct labor costs are lower and employee productivity is higher than in South Korea. In 1996, for example, Daewoo expanded its investment in a videotape recorder plant in Northern Ireland partly to take advantage of lower labor costs. The average $1,300 monthly wage at Daewoo's video recorder plant in Kumi, South Korea, was higher than the $1,200 it paid workers at a similar factory in Antrim, Northern Ireland, plus the output per

South Korea's New Multinationals

LG (Lucky Goldstar), and Daewoo. Together with six smaller *chaebol,* these large diversified industrial groups collectively account for about one-quarter of South Korea's gross national product.

Historically, South Korea's *chaebol* took advantage of low labor costs to export a variety of goods to industrialized countries. In recent years, however, the costs of both land and labor in South

Unlike Japanese enterprises, with which the South Koreans are often compared, several of the *chaebol* suffer from relatively poor product quality and inferior product design. Thus, they have been unable to respond to higher costs by moving their exported products upmarket and raising prices (as did many Japanese enterprises). Rather, in an attempt to maintain their competitive position, the *chaebol* have responded to rising costs at home by expanding over-

employee was 20 percent higher at the Irish plant.

Another reason for foreign investment by the *chaebol* has been to acquire foreign-owned entities that have the quality, design, engineering know-how, or market presence that the *chaebol* lack. For example, in early 1995 Samsung acquired 40 percent of AST, one of the largest manufacturers of personal computers in the United States, for $378 million. Simi-

Despite this, China seems to be moving progressively toward greater free market reforms. The southern Chinese province of Guangong, where these reforms have been pushed the furthest, now frequently ranks as the fastest-growing economy in the world.[35] If what is now occurring in southern China continues, particularly if it spreads throughout the country, China may move from Third World to industrial superpower status even more rapidly than Japan did. If China's GDP per capita grows by an average of 6 percent to 7 percent, which is slower than the 8 percent growth rate achieved during the last decade, then by 2020 this nation of 1.5 billion people could boast an average income per capita of about $13,000, roughly equivalent to that of Spain today. The potential consequences for Western international business are enormous. China represents a huge and largely untapped market. Between 1983 and 1997 annual foreign direct investment in China increased from less than $2 billion to $45 billion. China's new firms are proving to be capable competitors, and they will probably take global market share away from Western and Japanese enterprises. Thus, the changes in China are creating both opportunities and threats for established international businesses.

In Latin America, both democracy and free market reforms also seem to have taken hold. For decades most Latin American countries were ruled by dictators, many of whom seemed to view Western international businesses as instruments of imperialist domination. Accordingly, they restricted direct investment by foreign

Quangong fastest growing economy in the world

larly, Hyundai Electronics Industries, a subsidiary of Hyundai, the second-largest *chaebol*, recently acquired US computer diskmaker Maxtor for $165 million and a semiconductor division of AT&T for $340 million. Daewoo, meanwhile, has been acquiring automobile plants in Eastern Europe, Vietnam, and Brazil as part of its strategy to become a major supplier of automobiles to developing nations and to use that low-cost base to export to the developed world.

A third rationale for foreign expansion by South Korea's *chaebol* has been to placate foreign governments that have expressed concerns about the rising tide of Korean imports into their economies. This has been particularly notable in Western Europe, where lawsuits have been filed with the European Commission claiming that South Korean firms have been dumping products in the European market—selling them at a price below their cost of production—in an attempt to gain market share and drive European firms out of business.

South Korean firms are increasingly trying to sidestep such charges by setting up production facilities in Europe. For example, a recent complaint against Samsung and Hyundai by European manufacturers of earthmoving equipment triggered direct investments by both *chaebol* in facilities to manufacture the equipment in Europe.

Spurred on by such forces, foreign direct investment by South Korea's *chaebol* has accelerated rapidly in recent years. In 1987 South Korean firms invested a little over $300 million in foreign establishments. By 1990 the figure had risen to $1.5 billion, in 1994 the figure hit $2.5 billion, and in 1997 it reached a record $4.19 billion. Since 1985, about 50 percent of this investment has been directed at other Asian countries, 30 percent at North America, and 15 percent at Europe. However, the 1997–98 financial crisis, which hit South Korea hard, led to a temporary slowdown in this foreign investment activity. Many of the *chaebol* find themselves with

too much debt and too much excess capacity to contemplate further investments on the scale of those undertaken in the mid-1990s. Many of the largest *chaebol* are now true multinationals. In 1996, for example, the United Nations ranked Daewoo as the 52nd-largest multinational in the world. Samsung now has over 305 foreign subsidiaries located in 65 countries. Most observers expect the country's economy to recover from the 1997–98 financial crisis and when it does, it seems likely that the drive to invest outside the country's borders will accelerate again.[36]

firms. In addition, the poorly managed economies of Latin America were characterized by low growth, high debt, and hyperinflation—all of which discouraged investment by international businesses. All this seems to be changing. Throughout most of Latin America, debt and inflation are down, governments are selling state-owned enterprises to private investors, foreign investment is welcomed, and the region's economies are growing rapidly. These changes have increased the attractiveness of Latin America, both as a market for exports and as a site for foreign direct investment. At the same time, given the long history of economic mismanagement in Latin America, there is no guarantee that these favorable trends will continue. As in the case of Eastern Europe, substantial opportunities are accompanied by substantial risks.

Substantial opportunities accompanied by substantial risks

The Global Economy of the 21st Century

The last quarter of the 20th century experienced rapid changes in the global economy. Barriers to the free flow of goods, services, and capital came down. The volume of cross-border trade and investment grew more rapidly than global output, indicating that national economies were becoming more closely integrated into a single, interdependent, global economic system. As their economies advanced, more nations joined the ranks of the developed world. A generation ago, South Korea and

integration barriers down.

23

Taiwan were viewed as second-tier developing nations. Now they boast powerful economies, and their firms are major players in many global industries from ship-building and steel to electronics and chemicals. The move toward a global economy was further strengthened by the widespread adoption of liberal economic policies by countries that for two generations or more were firmly opposed to them. Thus, following the normative prescriptions of liberal economic ideology, we saw the privatization of state-owned businesses, widespread deregulation, markets opened to more competition, and increased commitment to removing barriers to cross-border trade and investment. This suggests that over the next few decades, countries such as the Czech Republic, Poland, Brazil, China, and South Africa may build powerful market-oriented economies. Current trends suggest that the world is moving rapidly toward an economic system that is more favorable to international business.

But it is always hazardous to take established trends and use them to predict the future. The world may be moving toward a more global economic system, but globalization is not inevitable. Countries may pull back from the recent commitment to liberal economic ideology if their experiences do not match their expectations. There are signs, for example, of a retreat from liberal economic ideology in Russia. Russia has experienced considerable economic pain as it tries to shift from a centrally planned economy to a market economy. If Russia's hesitation were to become more permanent and widespread, the liberal vision of a more prosperous global economy based on free market principles might not come to pass as quickly as many hope.

Greater globalization brings its own risks. This was starkly demonstrated in 1997 and 1998 when a financial crisis in Thailand spread first to other East Asian nations and then in 1998 to Russia and Brazil. Ultimately the crisis threatened to plunge the economies of the developed world, including the United States, into a recession. We explore the causes and consequences of this and other similar global financial crises in Chapter 9. Even from a purely economic perspective, globalization is not all good. The opportunities for doing business in a global economy may be significantly enhanced, but the risks associated with global financial contagion are also greater. But, as explained later in this book, firms can exploit the opportunities associated with globalization while at the same time reduce the risks through appropriate hedging strategies.

The Globalization Debate: Prosperity or Impoverishment?

Is the shift toward a more integrated and interdependent global economy a good thing? Many influential economists, politicians, and business leaders seem to think so. They argue that falling barriers to international trade and investment are the twin engines driving the global economy toward greater prosperity. They argue that increased international trade and cross-border investment will result in lower prices for goods and services. They believe that globalization stimulates economic growth, raises the incomes of consumers, and helps to create jobs in all countries that participate in the global trading system.

The arguments of those who support globalization are not without foundation. These arguments are covered in detail in Chapters 4, 5, and 6. As we shall see in these chapters, there are good theoretical reasons for believing that declining barriers to international trade and investment do stimulate economic growth, create jobs, and raise income levels. As described in Chapters 5 and 6, there is also considerable evidence to support the predictions of this theory. However, despite the existence of a compelling body of theory and evidence, globalization has its critics.[37] This was

Demonstrators at the WTO meeting in Seattle in December 1999 began looting and rioting in the city's downtown area. Why do you think they felt that kind of behavior was necessary? The sign in the photo reads, "Labor says WTO Ends Democracy." Why do you think they think this is so?
© AFP/CORBIS.

made clear in December 1999 when protesters disrupted meetings of the World Trade Organization in Seattle and drew worldwide attention to their concerns. Here we briefly review the main themes of the debate. In later chapters we elaborate on many points mentioned below.

Globalization, Jobs, and Incomes

One frequently voiced concern is that the removal of barriers to international trade actually destroys manufacturing jobs in wealthy advanced economies such as the United States and United Kingdom. Critics argue that reducing trade barriers allows firms to move manufacturing activities offshore to countries where wage rates are much lower.[38] Bartlett and Steele, two journalists for the *Philadelphia Inquirer* who have gained notoriety for their attacks on free trade, cite the case of Harwood Industries, a US clothing manufacturer, that closed its US operations, where it paid workers $9 per hour, and shifted manufacturing to Honduras, where textile workers receive 48 cents per hour.[39] Because of moves like this, argue Bartlett and Steele, the wage rates of poorer Americans have fallen significantly over the past 25 years.

Supporters of globalization reply that critics such as Bartlett and Steele miss the essential point about free trade—the benefits outweigh the costs.[40] They argue that free trade results in countries specializing in the production of those goods and services that they can produce most efficiently, while importing goods that they cannot produce as efficiently from other countries. When a country embraces free trade there is always some dislocation—lost textile jobs at Harwood Industries, for example—but

the whole economy is better off as a result. According to this view, it makes little sense for the United States to produce textiles at home when they can be produced at a lower cost in Honduras or China (which, unlike Honduras, is a major source of US textile imports). Importing textiles from China leads to lower prices for clothes in the United States, which enables US consumers to spend more of their money on other items. At the same time, the increased income generated in China from textile exports increases income levels in that country, which helps the Chinese to purchase more products produced in the United States, such as Boeing jets, Intel-based computers, Microsoft software, and Motorola cellular telephones. In this manner, globalization supporters argue that free trade benefits all countries that adhere to a free trade regime.

Some supporters of globalization do concede that the wage rate enjoyed by unskilled workers in many advanced economies has declined in recent years.[41] For example, data from the Organization of Economic Cooperation and Development suggest that between 1980 and 1995 the lowest 10 percent of American workers saw a drop in their real wages (adjusted for inflation) of about 20 percent, while the top 10 percent enjoyed a real pay increase of around 10 percent.[42] Similar trends can be seen in many other countries. However, while critics of globalization argue that the decline in unskilled wage rates is due to the migration of low-wage manufacturing jobs offshore, and a corresponding reduction in demand for unskilled workers, supporters of globalization see a more complex picture. They maintain that the declining real wage rates of unskilled workers owes far more to a technology-induced shift within advanced economies away from jobs where the only qualification was a willingness to turn up for work every day and toward jobs that require employees to possess significant education and skills. They point out that within many advanced economies there is a shortage of highly skilled workers and an excess supply of unskilled workers. Thus, growing income inequality is a result of the wages for skilled workers being bid up by the labor market and the wages for unskilled workers being discounted. If one agrees with this logic, a solution to the problem of declining incomes is to be found not in limiting free trade and globalization, but in increasing society's investment in education to reduce the supply of unskilled workers.[43]

Recent research, however, suggests that the evidence of growing income inequality may be suspect. Robert Lerman of the Urban Institute believes that the finding of inequality is based on inappropriate calculations of wage rates. Reviewing the data using a different methodology, Lerman has found that far from increasing income inequality, an index of wage rate inequality for all workers actually fell by 5.5 percent between 1987 and 1994.[44] If future research supports this finding, the argument that globalization leads to growing income inequality may lose much of its punch.

Globalization, Labor Policies, and the Environment

A second source of concern is that free trade encourages firms from advanced nations to move manufacturing facilities offshore to less developed countries that lack adequate regulations to protect labor and the environment from abuse by the unscrupulous.[45] Adhering to labor and environmental regulations significantly increases the costs of manufacturing enterprises and puts them at a competitive disadvantage in the global marketplace compared to firms based in developing nations that do not have to comply with such regulations. Firms deal with this cost disadvantage, so the theory goes, by moving production facilities to nations that do not have such

burdensome regulations or by failing to enforce the regulations they have on their books. If this is the case, one might expect free trade to lead to an increase in pollution and result in firms from advanced nations exploiting the labor of less developed nations.[46] This argument was used repeatedly by those who opposed the 1994 formation of the North American Free Trade Agreement (NAFTA) between Canada, Mexico, and the United States. The vision they painted was one of US manufacturing firms moving to Mexico in droves so that they would be free to pollute the environment, employ child labor, and ignore workplace safety and health issues, all in the name of higher profits.[47]

Supporters of free trade and greater globalization express serious doubts about this scenario. They point out that tougher environmental regulations and stricter labor standards go hand in hand with economic progress. In general, as countries get richer, they enact tougher environmental and labor regulations. Because free trade enables developing countries to increase their economic growth rates and become richer, this should lead to the introduction of tougher environmental and labor laws. In this view, the critics of free trade have got it backward—free trade does not lead to more pollution and labor exploitation, it leads to less. Supporters of free trade point out that it is possible to tie free trade agreements to the implementation of tougher environmental and labor laws in less developed countries. NAFTA, for example, was passed only after agreements had been negotiated that committed Mexico to tougher enforcement of environmental protection regulations. Thus, supporters of free trade argue that factories based in Mexico are now cleaner than they would have been without the passage of NAFTA.[48]

Free trade supporters also argue that business firms are not the amoral organizations that critics suggest. While there may be a few rotten apples, the vast majority of businesses are staffed by managers who are committed to behave in an ethical manner and would be unlikely to move production offshore just so they could pump more pollution into the atmosphere or exploit labor. Furthermore, the relationship between pollution, labor exploitation, and production costs may not be that suggested by critics. A well-treated labor force is generally a productive workforce, and it is productivity rather than base wage rates that often has the greatest influence on costs. Given this, in the vast majority of cases the vision of greedy managers who shift production to low-wage countries to "exploit" their labor forces may be misplaced.

Globalization and National Sovereignty

A final concern voiced by critics of globalization is that in today's increasingly interdependent global economy, economic power is shifting away from national governments and toward supranational organizations such as the World Trade Organization, the European Union, and the United Nations. As perceived by critics, unelected bureaucrats now can sometimes impose policies on the democratically elected governments of nation-states, thereby undermining the sovereignty of those states. The ability of the national state to control its own destiny is being limited, critics say.[49]

The World Trade Organization is a favorite target of those who attack the rush toward a global economy. The WTO was founded in 1994 to police the world trading system established by the GATT. The WTO arbitrates trade disputes between the 130 or so states that are signatories to the GATT. The WTO arbitration panel can issue a ruling instructing a member state to change trade policies that violate GATT regulations. If the violator refuses to comply with the ruling,

the WTO allows other states to impose appropriate trade sanctions on the transgressor. As a result, according to US environmentalist and consumer rights advocate Ralph Nader:

> Under the new system, many decisions that affect billions of people are no longer made by local or national governments but instead, if challenged by any WTO member nation, would be deferred to a group of unelected bureaucrats sitting behind closed doors in Geneva (which is where the headquarters of the WTO are located). The bureaucrats can decide whether or not people in California can prevent the destruction of the last virgin forests or determine if carcinogenic pesticides can be banned from their foods; or whether European countries have the right to ban dangerous biotech hormones in meat. . . . At risk is the very basis of democracy and accountable decision making.[50]

In contrast to Nader's rhetoric, many economists and politicians maintain that the power of supranational organizations such as the WTO is limited to what nation-states collectively agree to grant. They argue that bodies such as the United Nations and the WTO exist to serve the collective interests of member states, not to subvert those interests. Supporters of supranational organizations point out that the power of these bodies rests largely on their ability to *persuade* member states to follow a certain action. If these bodies fail to serve the collective interests of member states, those states will withdraw their support, and the supranational organization will quickly collapse. In this view then, real power still resides with individual nation-states, not supranational organizations.

Managing in the Global Marketplace

international business Any business that engages in international trade or investment.

Much of this book is concerned with the challenges of managing in an international business. An **international business** is any firm that engages in international trade or investment. A firm does not have to become a multinational enterprise, investing directly in operations in other countries, to engage in international business, although multinational enterprises are international businesses. All a firm has to do is start to export products or import products from other countries. As the world shifts toward a truly integrated global economy, more firms, both large and small, are becoming international businesses. What does this mean for managers within an international business?

As their organizations increasingly engage in cross-border trade and investment, managers need to recognize that managing an international business differs from managing a purely domestic business in many ways. At the most fundamental level, the differences arise from the simple fact that countries are different. Countries differ in their cultures, political systems, economic systems, legal systems, and levels of economic development. Despite all the talk about the emerging global village, and despite the trend toward globalization of markets and production, as we shall see in this book many of these differences are very profound and enduring.

Differences among countries require that an international business vary its practices country by country. Marketing a product in Brazil may require a different approach from marketing the product in Germany; managing US workers might require different skills than managing Japanese workers; maintaining close relations with a particular level of government may be very important in Mexico and

Procter & Gamble entered the Japanese market in 1972 and was the first company to introduce disposable diapers into Japan, soon commanding an 80 percent share of the market. This had all the makings of a great success story; except that by 1985 P&G's share of the disposable diaper market had slipped to 8 percent, the company had

who headed P&G's Japanese subsidiary failed to appreciate that what worked in America would not work in Japan.

When it launched its bath soap in Japan, P&G used TV advertising that showed a Japanese woman relaxing in a luxurious bath of soap bubbles, while her husband walked in and asked her about the soap. This same adver-

that were more in tune with the tastes of Japanese consumers. The company was quickly rewarded with a 30 percent share of the market, all taken at P&G's expense.

Realizing that a lack of international business literacy among many of the Americans that worked in its Japanese operation had contributed to the debacle in

Procter & Gamble in Japan

failed repeatedly to establish a strong position in the Japanese laundry detergent and personal care product markets, and its Japanese subsidiary was reportedly losing $40 million per year. The central problem: P&G had simply transferred its marketing strategies and products to Japan without customizing them to account for local cultural differences. The American managers

tisement had worked well in the United States and Europe, but in Japan, where it was culturally frowned on for a man to walk in on a woman having a bath, even if she is his wife, it was a huge flop.

P&G's Japanese competitors soon took advantage of the company's cultural myopia. In the diaper market, for example, Kao took market share from P&G by developing a line of trim-fit diapers

that country, P&G now appoints local nationals to key management positions in many foreign subsidiaries.[51]

---

irrelevant in Great Britain; the business strategy pursued in Canada might not work in South Korea; and so on. Managers in an international business must not only be sensitive to these differences, but they must also adopt the appropriate policies and strategies for coping with them. Much of this book is devoted to explaining the sources of these differences and the methods for coping with them successfully. The accompanying "Management Focus," which reviews Procter & Gamble's experience in Japan, shows what happens when managers don't consider country differences.

A further way in which international business differs from domestic business is the greater complexity of managing an international business. A manager in an international business is confronted with a range of issues that the manager in a domestic business never confronts. An international business must decide where in the world to site its production activities to minimize costs and to maximize value added. Then it must decide how best to coordinate and control its globally dispersed production activities (which, as we shall see later in the

ANOTHER PERSPECTIVE

No Longer Exotic, International Is a Given
In a global economy, we can find ourselves working for a foreign company in many different ways. We could take an overseas assignment with a US company or a foreign one. Or we could work with a foreign company in the United States. Or we could work in a US company with foreign workers as our company globalizes. The point is, international business is no longer an exotic luxury. Our economy is globalizing and understanding how that happens will help us build our careers. As former US Secretary of Labor Robert Reich put it, "Who is us?" and "Who is them?" The differences are no longer clear. That's one good reason to study international business.

greater complexity

book, is not a trivial problem). An international business also must decide which foreign markets to enter and which to avoid. It must choose the appropriate mode for entering a particular foreign country. Is it best to export its product to the foreign country? Should the company allow a local firm to produce its product under license in that country? Should the firm enter into a joint venture with a local business to produce its product in that country? Or should the firm set up a wholly owned subsidiary to serve the market in that country? As we shall see, the choice of entry mode is critical because it has major implications for the long-term health of the firm.

Another way international business is different is that it involves transactions across national borders. An international business must operate within the framework of the international trading and investment system. Managers in an international business must also deal with government restrictions on international trade and investment. They must find ways to work within the limits imposed by specific governmental interventions. As this book explains, even though many governments are nominally committed to free trade, their interventions to regulate cross-border trade and investment are substantial. Managers within international businesses must develop strategies and policies for dealing with such interventions.

Cross-border transactions also require that money be converted from the firm's home currency into a foreign currency and vice versa. Because currency exchange rates vary in response to changing economic conditions, an international business must develop policies for dealing with exchange rate movements. A firm that adopts a wrong policy can lose large amounts of money, and a firm that adopts the right policy can increase the profitability of its international transactions.

In sum, managing an international business is different from managing a purely domestic business for at least four reasons: (1) countries are different, (2) the range of problems confronted by a manager in an international business is wider and the problems are more complex than those confronted by a manager in a domestic business, (3) an international business must find ways to work within the limits imposed by government intervention in the international trade and investment system, and (4) international transactions involve converting money into different currencies. In this book we examine all these issues, paying close attention to the different strategies and policies that managers pursue to deal with the various challenges created when a firm becomes an international business. By the time you have completed this book, you should have a good grasp of the issues that international business managers have to grapple with on a daily basis, and you should be familiar with the range of strategies and operating policies that managers can adopt to compete more effectively in today's rapidly emerging global economy.

Key Terms

Summary

This chapter sets the scene for the rest of the book. We have seen how the world economy is becoming more global, we have reviewed the main drivers of globalization and argued that they seem to be thrusting nation-states toward a more tightly integrated global economy, we have looked at how the nature of international business is changing in response to the changing global economy, we have discussed some concerns raised by rapid globalization, and we have reviewed implications of rapid globalization for individual managers. These major points were made in the chapter:

1 Over the past two decades we have witnessed the globalization of markets and production.

2 The globalization of markets implies that national markets are merging into one huge market-place. However, it is important not to push this view too far.

3 The globalization of production implies that firms are basing individual productive activities at the optimal world locations for the particular activities. As a consequence, it is increasingly irrelevant to talk about "American" products, "Japanese" products, or "German" products, since these are being replaced by "global" products.

4 Two factors seem to underlie the trend toward globalization: declining trade barriers and changes in communication, information, and transportation technologies.

5 Since the end of World War II there has been a significant lowering of barriers to the free flow of goods, services, and capital. More than anything else, this has facilitated the trend toward the globalization of production and has enabled firms to view the world as a single market.

6 As a consequence of the globalization of production and markets, in the 1990s, world trade has grown faster than world output, foreign direct investment has surged, imports have penetrated more deeply into the world's industrial nations, and competitive pressures have increased in many industries.

7 The development of the microprocessor and related developments in communications and information processing technology have helped firms to link their worldwide operations via sophisticated information networks. Jet air travel, by shrinking travel time, has also facilitated the worldwide operations of international businesses. These changes have enabled firms to achieve tight coordination of their worldwide operations and to view the world as a single market.

8 Over the past three decades a number of dramatic changes have occurred in the nature of international business. In the 1960s, the US economy was dominant in the world, US firms accounted for most of the foreign direct investment in the world economy, US firms dominated the list of large multinationals, and roughly half the world—the centrally planned economies of the Communist world—was closed to Western businesses.

9 By the mid-1990s, the US share of world output had been cut in half, with major shares of world output being accounted for by Western European and Southeast Asian economies. The US share of worldwide foreign direct investment had also fallen by about two-thirds. US multinationals were facing competition from a large number of Japanese and European multinationals. In addition, mini-multinationals emerged.

10 The most dramatic environmental trend has been the collapse of Communist power in Eastern Europe, which has created enormous long-run opportunities for international businesses. In addition, the move toward free market economies in China and Latin America is creating opportunities (and threats) for Western international businesses.

11 The benefits and costs of the emerging global economy are being hotly debated among businesspeople, economists, and politicians.

The debate focuses on the impact of globalization on jobs, wages, the environment, working conditions, and national sovereignty.

12 Managing an international business is different from managing a domestic business for at least four reasons: (*i*) countries are different, (*ii*) the range of problems confronted by a manager in an international business is wider and the problems more complex than those confronted by a manager in a domestic business, (*iii*) managers in an international business must find ways to work within the limits imposed by governments' intervention in the international trade and investment system, and (*iv*) international transactions involve converting money into different currencies.

Critical Thinking and Discussion Questions

1 Describe the shifts in the world economy over the past 30 years. What are the implications of these shifts for international businesses based in

- Britain?
- North America?
- Hong Kong?

2 "The study of international business is fine if you are going to work in a large multinational enterprise, but it has no relevance for individuals who are going to work in small firms." Critically evaluate this statement.

3 How have changes in technology contributed to the globalization of markets and of production? Would the globalization of production and markets have been possible without these technological changes?

4 How might the Internet and the associated World Wide Web affect international business activity and the globalization of the world economy?

5 If current trends continue, China may emerge as the world's largest economy by 2020. Discuss the possible implications of such a development for

- The world trading system.
- The world monetary system.
- The business strategy of today's European and US-based global corporations.

6 "Ultimately, the study of international business is no different from the study of domestic business. Thus, there is no point in having a separate course on international business." Evaluate this statement.

Internet Exercises

1 While the Internet and e-commerce have been the business buzzwords recently, cross-border e-commerce and international online expansion are sure to be the focus of attention in the new millennium. The world is experiencing a technological revolution unlike any before. The Internet not only makes it relatively easy for companies to set up shop, but it also allows them to become instantly global. With this capability comes a host of issues including questions related to consumer privacy, trade barriers, and the speed of change.

Is the Internet the driver of globalization? Go on-line and "buy" a pair of jeans, a bike, and some industrial bearings. "Buy" the products from three different countries. Record where you bought the products, and how long it took you to find them. Also, maintain records related to what information companies requested from you as you shopped. Now consider purchasing the same three items in a traditional way. What does your on-line shopping experience demonstrate about the global economy? As the marketing manager for an international consumer products company, how can/ should you respond to the Internet. Is your response any different if you are the marketing manager of an industrial products multinational company? What effect has the Internet had on you as a consumer?

2 The massive at a recent international trade conference in a major city in the Midwest was that it has never been easier nor more crucial for companies to expand into foreign markets. Today, competitive forces from around the world are a major driving force in the globalization of markets, as are the complementary effects of the emergence of new markets, better-informed consumers, and the technology explosion. Exports and/or other forms of international activity were deemed vital to the success of companies. A major theme at the conference revolved around how the Internet can be a useful tool in both finding new markets and promoting products and/or services in foreign countries. In the past, com-

panies seeking information on foreign markets often faced a lengthy process. Today, however, many governments have websites providing prospective market entrants with a wealth of information. In addition, numerous trade intermediaries from around the world are also advertising their services via the Internet.

Go to **www.ita.doc.gov/exportmatch** and also to **http://** **infoserve2ita.doc.gov/tic.nsf.** Consider the information available to companies seeking to invest in, or export to, the United States. Similarly, examine the resources available to American companies seeking assistance in expanding into foreign markets. Discuss the role of the Internet in the global marketplace. Specifically, do you feel that the availability of resources on-line makes it easier for companies to find receptive environments for their products or services? Will, and if so how, the availability of information, and the fact that companies may be more knowledgeable about foreign markets, affect companies' bargaining power with host governments? Similarly, does the fact that governments can easily learn about companies influence the relationship between the two players?

33

Citigroup—Building a Global Financial Services Giant

In the largest merger ever in the financial services business, Citicorp joined forces with Travelers Group in the autumn of 1998. The combined group has revenues of close to $50 billion, assets in excess of $700 billion, and global reach. Before the merger, Travelers Group was the largest property-casualty and life insurance business in the United States. In addition, Travelers had considerable investment banking, retail brokerage, and asset management operations. Travelers' insurance operations were almost exclusively domestic in their focus, although its investment banking and asset management business had some foreign exposure.

Citicorp was one of the world's most global banks. Citicorp had two main legs to its business—corporate banking activities and consumer banking activities. The corporate banking side of Citicorp focused on providing a range of financial services to 20,000 corporations in 75 emerging economies and 22 developed economies. This business, which always had an international focus, generated revenues of $8.0 billion in 1997, more than half of which came from activities in the world's emerging economies. However, the rapid growth of Citicorp's global consumer banking business captured the attention of many observers. The consumer banking business focuses on providing basic financial services to individuals, including checking accounts, credit cards, and personal loans. In 1997 this business served 50 million consumers in 56 countries through a global network of 1,200 retail branches and generated revenues of $15 billion.

The merger talks were initiated by Travelers CEO Sandy Weill. Given the rapid globalization of the world economy, Weill believed it was important for Travelers to start selling its insurance products in foreign countries. Until recently, the barriers to cross-border trade and investment in financial services would have made this a difficult proposition. However, under the terms of a deal brokered by the World Trade Organization in December 1997, more than 100 countries agreed to open their banking, insurance, and securities markets to foreign competition. The deal, which took effect March 1, 1999, included all developed nations and many developing nations. The deal allowed insurance companies such as Travelers to sell their products in foreign markets for the first time. To take advantage of this opportunity, however, Travelers needed a global retail distribution system, which is where Citicorp came in. For the past 20 years, the central strategy of Citicorp has been to build just such a distribution channel.

The architect of Citicorp's global retail banking strategy was longtime CEO John Reed (Reed is now co-CEO of Citigroup, a position he shares with Weill). Reed has been on a quest to establish "Citicorp" as a global brand, in effect positioning the bank as the Coca-Cola or McDonald's of financial services. The basic belief underpinning Reed's consumer banking strategy is that people everywhere have the same financial needs—needs that broaden as they pass through various life stages and levels of affluence. At the outset customers need the basics—a checking account, a credit card, and perhaps a loan for college. As they mature financially customers add a mortgage, car loan, and investments (and insurance). As they accumulate wealth, portfolio management and estate planning become priorities. Citicorp aimed to provide these services to customers around the globe in a standardized fashion, in much the same way as McDonald's provides the same basic menu of fast food to consumers everywhere. With the merger with Travelers now complete, the company will push this concept further, cross-selling insurance products and asset management services through its global retail distribution system.

Reed believes that global demographic, economic, and political forces strongly favor such a strategy. In the developed world, aging populations are buying more financial services. In the rapidly growing economies of many developing nations, Citigroup is targeting the emerging middle classes, whose needs for consumer banking services and insurance are rising with their affluence. This world view got Citicorp into many developing economies years ahead of its slowly awakening rivals. As a result, Citigroup is today the largest credit card issuer in Asia and Latin America, with 7 million cards issued in Asia and 9 million in Latin America. As for political forces, the worldwide movement toward greater deregulation of financial services allowed Citigroup to set up consumer banking operations in countries that only a decade ago did not allow foreign banks into their markets. Examples in the fast-growing Asian region include India, Indonesia, Japan, Taiwan, Vietnam, and the biggest potential prize of them all, China.

A key element of Citigroup's global strategy for its consumer bank is the standardization of operations around the globe. This has found its most visible expression in the so-called model branch. Originally designed in Chile and refined in Athens, the idea is to give Citigroup's mobile customers the same retail experience everywhere in the world, from the greeter by the door to the standard blue sign overhead to the ATM machine to the gilded doorway through which the retail-elite "Citi-Gold" customers pass to meet with their "personal financial executives." By the end of 1997 this model branch was in place at 600 of the company's 1,200 retail locations and it was being rapidly introduced elsewhere. Another element of standardization, less obvious to customers, is Citigroup's emphasis on the uniformity of a range of back-office systems across its branches, including the systems to manage checking and savings accounts, mutual fund investments, and so on. According to Citigroup, this uniformity makes it easier for the company to roll out branches in a new market. Citigroup has also taken advantage of its global reach to centralize aspects of its operations to realize cost savings from economies of scale. Take Citigroup's growing European credit card business as an example. All credit cards are manufactured in Nevada. Printing and mailing are done in the Netherlands and data processing in South Dakota. Within each country, credit card operations are limited to marketing people and two staff units, customer service and collections.[52]

CASE DISCUSSION QUESTIONS

1 What was the rationale for the merger between Travelers Group and Citicorp? How will this merger create value for (a) the stockholders of Citigroup and (b) the customers of Citigroup's global retail bank?

2 In 1997 the World Trade Organization brokered an agreement to liberalize cross-border trade and investment in global financial services. What do you think the impact of this deal will be on competition in national markets? What would you expect to see occur?

Polywogs is a woman-owned and run company that designs and distributes upscale children's sweaters. The sweaters are manufactured in the Philippines but sold throughout the United States in department and specialty stores. It is the creation of Yolanda C. De Wit, originally from the Philippines, and her American-born partner Ann E. Meyers. The two women met while working together at a sweater distributorship. Yolanda was a manager and

sacrifice and held lots of risk. Yolanda at the time was a nontraditional student, a mother of two, who had returned to college to get an MBA. She needed to finish the degree, find a job to support herself, and fund a new business. Ann, also a mother of two, had a successful track record of launching a children's apparel line that generated sales of over $1 million in two years but at another company.

With $15,000 raised from family and friends, Yolanda and

who oversees the network of eight sales representatives, attends trade shows, and creates the marketing plan.

The business has grown from that initial $50,000 order to annual sales of a quarter million, even though Yolanda lives in California and Ann in Connecticut. In fact, Ann's move has been opportune because the market for sweaters is so much better in the East.

Polywogs specializes in distinctive sweaters made from natural

Polywogs—Children's Togs

Ann was a designer who had taken an entry-level job as Yolanda's assistant.

They started Polywogs out of desperation after each had lost her job. "After being unemployed for several months, I decided that the solution to never being jobless again was to become self-employed," Yolanda stated. Ann was in a similar situation and state of mind. However, despite their strong personal commitment, starting the business required lots of

Ann jumped in. They secured their first order for $50,000 within a few months. From the beginning, Yolanda has been in charge of administration, operation, and finance. She is responsible for coordinating with manufacturers for the production and importation of the finished product, order processing, and shipping the merchandise. Ann designs the children's collection created four times a year. She is also the national sales manager,

fibers for boys and girls from newborn to 14 years old. There are 24 million children in the United States in this age range. "All we want to capture is a little niche," Yolanda stated.

Although there are many factors for success in the apparel business, one of the most critical is the reliability of the supplier. "We are better off specializing in sweaters because we have a dependable manufacturer in the Philippines," Yolanda said.

It is important to get the shipment on time because the sweaters and designs are so seasonal. Yolanda recalls how they were once forced to heavily discount a Christmas sweater that did not arrive until November. The sweaters also must be produced to exact specifications. If the retailers have agreed to purchase a particular sample, they will not accept changes in the design or construction as one supplier the company was investigating proposed. The supplier must also be willing to produce in small volume to match their incoming orders.

Most children's sweaters are imported because their production is so labor intensive that manufacturing in the United States has declined. According to 1994 Bureau of Census foreign trade statistics, total imports for cotton and knit sweaters was 84,228 dozens versus 5,668 dozens of domestic production.

Unable to find a domestic manufacturer who could meet her requirements, Yolanda located the nephew of a former supplier in the Philippines with whom she had worked and kept in contact for 15 years. Her communication skills continue to be essential as she must now stay in daily contact with her supplier by phone or fax and visit at least once a year.

"Speaking Tagalog is useful because there are always things you cannot express as clearly in a foreign language," Yolanda stressed. However, her English-only partner often gets a quicker response to a fax because as the designer she is seen as the linchpin on which both Polywogs' and its supplier's mutual growth depends.

Currently the price of a Polywogs sweater is about $20 wholesale and $40 retail. The average landed cost per sweater is about 55 percent of the selling price. Competitive lines sell for 10 percent to 50 percent more.

The company already ships to about 300 customers across the continental United States and Hawaii through eight sales representatives and their showrooms.

Because of limited funds Polywogs has restricted its promotion to retailers. The company sends out flyers twice a year to 2,000 retailers announcing its sweater collections. Polywogs is also part of a virtual on-line trade show for apparel manufacturers. It exhibits at one trade show a year in New York. "We have lots of ideas for contacting television wardrobe decision makers or negotiating for product placement on magazine covers," Yolanda speculated about possible promotional efforts.

In the future, Polywogs must continue to keep its overhead low and its inventories lean and to raise more capital. It must find ways to increase sales volume while operating within these constraints. However, Yolanda is optimistic. "This is something we really want to do and so we will find a way."

two

Country Differences in Political Economy

Brazilian Privatization

In the middle years of the 20th century, Latin American governments took many private companies into state ownership. This wave of nationalizations reflected a populist ideology that was interlaced with socialist, nationalist, and sometimes fascist rhetoric. Supported by strong trade unions, particularly in Argentina and to some extent in Brazil, politicians advocated taking private enterprises into public ownership so they could be run "for the

Brazil's Embraer, the only manufacturer of jet aircraft in Latin America, went from a reputation for solid engineering, to state ownership and a loss of $310 million in 1994. Following privatization in 1994, a new management team in 1996, and increased sales in 1997, the company seems to be turning itself around. What are other benefits that an airline manufacturer could reap due to privatization?

Learning Objectives

1. Understand how the political systems of countries differ.

2. Understand how the economic systems of countries differ.

3. Understand how the legal systems of countries differ.

4. Understand how political, economic, and legal systems collectively influence a country's ability to achieve meaningful economic progress.

5. Be familiar with the main changes that are currently reshaping the political, economic, and legal systems of many nation-states.

6. Appreciate how a country's political, economic, and legal systems influence the benefits, costs, and risks associated with doing business in that country.

7. Be conversant with the ethical issues that can arise when doing business in a nation in which the political and legal systems do not support basic human rights.

benefit of the state and its citizens, rather than the enrichment of a small capitalist elite."

However, by the early 1990s it was clear that inefficient management, political manipulation, and, in some cases, corruption had turned many state-owned enterprises into national liabilities. An example was Brazil's Embraer, the only manufacturer of jet aircraft in Latin America. Founded by a military regime in 1969, Embraer developed a repu-

tation for solid engineering. Unfortunately, no one at Embraer, protected by public ownership from the need to account for its performance to private investors, seemed to care about costs or customers. As a result, in 1994 Embraer lost $310 million on sales of only $253 million.

At the same time, the winds of change were also blowing through many of the world's economies. Communism was collapsing in Eastern Europe, socialism was in retreat

throughout much of the rest of the world, and free market economics was clearly on the ascendancy. Against this background, the Latin American political establishment moved sharply toward free market economics. This shift in political and economic ideology expressed itself through the privatization of many state-owned enterprises.

In Brazil, the privatization program began slowly and quietly, but it has recently accelerated. Around

70 state-owned enterprises were sold to private investors between 1990 and 1996 for a total take of $14.9 billion. In 1997, Brazil sold over $20 billion of state-owned assets, including Companhia Vale do Rio Doce (CVRD), the world's largest iron ore producer. In 1998, Brazil sold a further $30 billion worth of state assets, including Telebras, Brazil's telecommunications company, which was broken up into four companies.

Evidence suggests these privatizations are having the desired effects on the companies involved. Following its privatization in December 1994, Embraer reduced its payroll from 12,700 to 3,600 in 1996 as the new management team struggled to turn the company around. But as new orders began to flow in, the company in 1997 added 1,100 employees to handle increased sales. Another example concerns Brazil's formerly state-owned steel industry. In 1990 the state-owned monopoly employed 115,000 people and produced 22.6 million tons of steel, or 196 tons per employee. Between 1991 and 1993, the company was sold as six separate companies for $8.2 billion. In 1996 the six successor private companies produced 25.2 million tons of steel with only 65,000 employees, or 388 tons per employee, a striking increase in employee productivity. Along similar lines, the private owners of CVRD expected to cut operating costs by at least 20 percent.

The benefits of privatization are not limited to improvements in efficiency, important as that is. The Brazilian government is also opening up the sale of state-owned assets to foreign investors and allowing foreign companies to set up their own enterprises in industries formerly controlled by state monopolies, such as steel, electric power generation, and telecommunications. Private investment, much from foreign sources, has surged and much of it was targeted toward basic infrastructure. Excluding telecommunications, infrastructure projects worth $190 billion were planned between 1997 and 2000. This compares to a total spending of only $10 billion between 1993 and 1996. Such an investment will have a significant impact on the growth rate of Brazil's economy.[1]

Introduction

As noted in Chapter 1, international business is much more complicated than domestic business because countries differ in many ways. Countries have different political systems, economic systems, and legal systems. Cultural practices can vary dramatically from country to country, as can the education and skill level of the population, and different countries are at varying stages of economic development. All these differences have major implications for international business. They have a profound impact on the benefits, costs, and risks associated with doing business in different countries; on the management of operations in different countries; and on the strategies that international firms should pursue in different countries. This chapter and the next develop an awareness of and appreciation for the significance of country differences in political, economic, and legal system and national culture. Other functions of these chapters are to describe how the political, economic, legal, and cultural systems of many of the world's nation-states are evolving and to discuss the implications of these changes on international business.

The opening case illustrates the changes occurring in the political and economic systems of one nation, Brazil. As in many other countries, over the last decade political and economic ideology in Brazil has shifted toward a free market orientation. Two consequences of this ideological shift—the adoption of an aggressive privatization program and the opening of the Brazilian economy to foreign investors—are transforming Brazil's economy. These changes are creating enormous opportunities for foreign investors, who for the first time in recent history can now invest in many sectors of Brazil's expanding economy. For example, in 1997 the US-based telecommunications company BellSouth paid $2.45 billion to the Brazilian government for a license to install and market a wireless phone network in Brazil's largest city, Sao Paulo. Since there are only 12 telephone lines per 100 people in Sao Paulo, BellSouth believes that a huge untapped market exists.[2]

In this chapter we focus on how the political, economic, and legal systems of countries differ. We refer to these systems as constituting the **political economy** of a country. The political, economic, and legal systems of a country are not independent of each other. They interact and influence each other, and in doing so they affect the level of economic well-being. In addition to reviewing these systems, we also explore how differences in political economy influence the benefits, costs, and risks associated with doing business in different countries and how they affect management practice and strategy. In the next chapter we will look at how differences in culture influence international business. What we should bear in mind is that the political economy and culture of a nation are not independent of each other. As will become apparent in Chapter 3, culture can exert an impact on political economy. The converse can also hold true.

political economy Political, economic, and legal systems of a country.

41

Political Systems

The economic and legal systems of a country are often shaped by its political system.[3] As such, we need to understand the nature of different political systems before discussing the economic and legal systems. By **political system** we mean the system of government in a nation. Political systems can be assessed according to two *related* dimensions. The first is the degree to which they emphasize collectivism as opposed to individualism. The second dimension is the degree to which they are democratic or totalitarian. These dimensions are interrelated; systems that emphasize collectivism tend to be totalitarian, while systems that place a high value on individualism tend to be democratic. However, there is a gray area in the middle. It is possible to have democratic societies that emphasize a mix of collectivism and individualism, and totalitarian societies that are not collectivist.

political system System of government in a nation.

Collectivism and Individualism

The term **collectivism** refers to a system that stresses the primacy of collective goals over individual goals.[4] When collectivism is practiced, the needs of society as a whole are generally viewed as being more important than individual freedoms. In such circumstances, an individual's right to do something may be restricted on the grounds that it runs counter to "the good of society" or to "the common good." Advocacy of collectivism can be traced to the ancient Greek philosopher Plato (427–347 BC), who in the *Republic* argued that individual rights should be sacrificed for the good of the majority and that property should be owned in common. In modern times the collectivist mantle has been picked up by socialists.

collectivism Political system that stresses the primacy of collective goals over individual goals.

SOCIALISM Socialists trace their intellectual roots to Karl Marx (1818–1883). Marx's basic argument is that in a capitalist society that does not restrict individual freedoms, the few benefit at the expense of the many. While successful capitalists accumulate considerable wealth, Marx postulated that the wages earned by the majority of workers in a capitalist society will be forced down to subsistence levels. Marx argued that capitalists expropriate for their own use the value created by workers, while paying workers only subsistence wages in return. According to Marx, the pay of workers does not reflect the full value of their labor. To correct this perceived wrong, Marx advocated state ownership of the basic means of production, distribution, and exchange (i.e., businesses). He argued that if the state owned the means of production, the state could ensure that workers were fully compensated for their labor. Thus, the idea is to manage state-owned enterprise to benefit society as a whole, rather than individual capitalists.[5]

In the early 20th century, the socialist ideology split into two broad camps. On the one hand were the **communists** who believed that socialism could be achieved

communists Followers of socialist ideology who believe that socialism can be achieved only through violent revolution and totalitarian dictatorship.

social democrats Followers of socialist ideology who commit themselves to achieving socialism through democratic means.

only through violent revolution and totalitarian dictatorship. On the other hand were the **social democrats** who committed themselves to achieving socialism by democratic means, and who turned their back on violent revolution and dictatorship. Both versions of socialism have waxed and waned during the 20th century.

The Communist Party version of socialism reached its high point in the late 1970s, when the majority of the world's population lived in Communist states. The countries under Communist rule at that time included the former Soviet Union; its Eastern European client nations (e.g., Poland, Czechoslovakia, Hungary); China; the Southeast Asian nations of Cambodia, Laos, and Vietnam; various African nations (e.g., Angola, Mozambique); and the Latin American nations of Cuba and Nicaragua. By the mid-1990s, however, communism was in retreat worldwide. The Soviet Union had collapsed and had been replaced by a collection of 15 republics, most of which were at least nominally structured as democracies. Communism was swept out of Eastern Europe by the largely bloodless revolutions of 1989. Many believe it is only a matter of time before Communism collapses in China, the last major Communist power left. Although China is still nominally a Communist state and substantial limits to individual political freedom exist, in the economic sphere the country has moved away from strict adherence to communist ideology.[6]

Social democracy also seems to have passed its high-water mark, although the ideology may prove to be more enduring than communism. Social democracy's greatest influence has been in a number of democratic Western nations including Australia, Britain, France, Germany, Norway, Spain, and Sweden, where Social Democratic parties have held political power. Social democracy also has had an important influence in India and Brazil. Consistent with their Marxist roots, many Social Democratic governments nationalized private companies in certain industries, transforming them into state-owned enterprises to be run for the "public good rather than private profit." In Britain, for example, by the end of the 1970s state-owned companies had a monopoly in the telecommunications, electricity, gas, coal, railway, and shipbuilding industries as well as substantial interests in the oil, airline, auto, and steel industries.

However, experience has demonstrated that state ownership of the means of production often runs counter to the public interest. In many countries the performance of state-owned companies has been poor (for an example, see the opening case on Brazil). Protected from significant competition by their monopoly position and guaranteed government financial support, many state-owned companies became increasingly inefficient. In the end, individuals found themselves having to pay for the luxury of state ownership through higher prices and higher taxes. Many Social Democratic parties in a number of Western democracies were voted out of office in the late 1970s and early 1980s. They were succeeded by political parties, such as Britain's Conservative Party and Germany's Christian Democratic Party, that were more committed to free market economics. These parties sold state-owned enterprises to private investors (referred to as privatization). In Britain the Conservative government sold the state's interests in telecommunications, electricity, gas, shipbuilding, oil, airlines, autos, and steel to private investors. Even when Social Democratic parties have regained power, as in Britain in 1997 when the left-leaning Labor Party won control of the government, they now seem to be committed to greater private ownership.

individualism Political philosophy that an individual should have freedom in his or her economic and political pursuits.

INDIVIDUALISM   Individualism is the opposite of collectivism. In a political sense, **individualism** refers to a philosophy that an individual should have freedom in his or her economic and political pursuits. In contrast to collectivism, individualism stresses that the interests of the individual should take precedence over the interests of the state. Like collectivism, however, individualism can be traced to an ancient Greek philosopher, in this case Plato's disciple Aristotle (384–322 BC). In contrast

More on Aristotle

Aristotle believed that the means of production should be privately owned. In addition, he argued that the abolition of private property would lead to moral harm, because without private property, there would be neither need nor ability to exercise generosity. "The abolition of private property will mean that no man will be seen to be liberal and no man will ever do any act of liberality; for only in the use of money is liberality made effective." (*The Politics,* Book 2, Chapter 5, translated by T. A. Sinclair.)

to Plato, Aristotle argued that individual diversity and private ownership are desirable. In a passage that might have been taken from a speech by Margaret Thatcher or Ronald Reagan, he argued that private property is more highly productive than communal property and will thus make for progress. According to Aristotle, communal property receives little care, whereas property that is owned by an individual will receive the greatest care and therefore be most productive.

After sinking into oblivion for nearly two millennia, individualism was reborn as an influential political philosophy in the Protestant trading nations of England and the Netherlands during the 16th century. The philosophy was refined in the work of a number of British philosophers including David Hume (1711–1776), Adam Smith (1723–1790), and John Stuart Mill (1806–1873). The philosophy of individualism influenced those in the American colonies who sought independence from Britain. Individualism underlies the ideas expressed in the Declaration of Independence. In more recent years the philosophy has been championed by several Nobel Prize-winning economists, including Milton Friedman, Friedrich von Hayek, and James Buchanan.

Individualism is built on two central tenets. The first is an emphasis on the importance of guaranteeing individual freedom and self-expression. As John Stuart Mill put it

> The sole end for which mankind are warranted, individually or collectively, in interfering with the liberty of action of any of their number is self-protection. . . . The only purpose for which power can be rightfully exercised over any member of a civilized community, against his will, is to prevent harm to others. His own good, either physical or moral, is not a sufficient warrant. . . . The only part of the conduct of any one, for which he is amenable to society, is that which concerns others. In the part which merely concerns himself, his independence is, of right, absolute. Over himself, over his own body and mind, the individual is sovereign.[7]

The second tenet of individualism is that the welfare of society is best served by letting people pursue their own economic self-interest, as opposed to having some collective body (such as government) trying to dictate what is in society's best interest. Or as Adam Smith put it in a famous passage from the *Wealth of Nations,* an individual who intends his own gain is

> led by an invisible hand to promote an end which was no part of his intention. Nor is it always worse for the society that it was no part of it. By pursuing his own interest he frequently promotes that of the society more effectually than when he really intends to promote it. I have never known much good done by those who effect to trade for the public good.[8]

The central message of individualism, therefore, is that individual economic and political freedoms are the ground rules on which a society should be based. This puts individualism in direct conflict with collectivism. Collectivism asserts the primacy of the collective over the individual, while individualism asserts just the opposite. This underlying ideological conflict has shaped much of the recent history of the world. The Cold War, for example, was essentially a war between collectivism, championed by the now-defunct Soviet Union, and individualism, championed by the United States.

In practical terms, individualism translates into an advocacy for democratic political systems and free market economics. Since the late 1980s the waning of collectivism has been matched by the ascendancy of individualism. A wave of democratic ideals and free market economics is sweeping away socialism and communism worldwide. Recent changes go beyond the revolutions in Eastern Europe and the former Soviet Union to include a move toward greater individualism in Latin America and in some of the social democratic states of the West (e.g., Britain and Sweden). Individualism has not won the long battle with collectivism, but as a guiding political philosophy, individualism is on the rise. This represents good news for international business because the pro-business and pro-free trade values of individualism create a favorable environment within which international business can thrive.

Democracy and Totalitarianism

Democracy and totalitarianism are at different ends of a political dimension. **Democracy** refers to a political system in which government is by the people, exercised either directly or through elected representatives. **Totalitarianism** is a form of government in which one person or political party exercises control over all spheres of human life, and opposing political parties are prohibited. The democratic–totalitarian dimension is not independent of the collectivism–individualism dimension. Democracy and individualism go hand in hand, as do the communist version of collectivism and totalitarianism. However, gray areas exist; it is possible to have a democratic state where collective values predominate, and it is possible to have a totalitarian state that is hostile to collectivism and in which some degree of economic individualism is encouraged. For example, Chile in the 1980s was ruled by a totalitarian military dictatorship that encouraged economic freedom but not political freedom.

DEMOCRACY   The pure form of democracy, as originally practiced by several city-states in ancient Greece, is based on a belief that citizens should be directly involved in decision making. In complex advanced societies with populations in the tens or hundreds of millions, this is impractical. Most modern democratic states practice what is commonly referred to as **representative democracy.** In a representative democracy, citizens periodically elect individuals to represent them. These elected representatives then form a government, which makes decisions on behalf of the electorate. A representative democracy rests on the assumption that if elected representatives fail to perform this job adequately, they can and will be voted down at the next election.

To guarantee that elected representatives can be held accountable for their actions by the electorate, an ideal representative democracy has constitutional safeguards. These include (1) an individual's right to freedom of expression, opinion, and organization; (2) a free media; (3) regular elections in which all eligible citizens are allowed to vote; (4) universal adult suffrage; (5) limited terms for elected representatives; (6) a fair court system that is independent from the political system; (7) a nonpolitical state bureaucracy; (8) a nonpolitical police force and armed service; and (9) relatively free access to state information.[9]

TOTALITARIANISM   Totalitarian countries deny citizens all the constitutional guarantees on which representative democracies are built. In most totalitarian states, political repression is widespread and those who question the right of the rulers to rule find themselves imprisoned, or worse.

democracy Political system in which government is by the people, exercised either directly or through elected representatives.

totalitarianism Form of government in which one person or political party exercises absolute control over all spheres of human life and in which opposing political parties are prohibited.

representative democracy Political system in which citizens periodically elect individuals to represent them.

There are four major forms of totalitarianism in the world today. Until recently the most widespread was **communist totalitarianism.** As discussed earlier, communism is a version of collectivism that advocates that socialism can be achieved only through totalitarian dictatorship. Communism, however, is in decline worldwide and many of the old Communist dictatorships have collapsed since 1989. The major exceptions to this trend (so far) are China, Vietnam, Laos, North Korea, and Cuba, although in all these nations the Communist Party's monopoly on political power is under attack.

A second form of totalitarianism might be labeled **theocratic totalitarianism.** Theocratic totalitarianism exists where political power is monopolized by a party, group, or individual that governs according to religious principles. The most common form of theocratic totalitarianism is based on Islam. It is exemplified by countries such as Iran and Saudi Arabia, where the laws of the state are based on Islamic principles and both religious and political expression are restricted.

A third form of totalitarianism might be referred to as **tribal totalitarianism.** Tribal totalitarianism is found mainly in African countries such as Zimbabwe, Tanzania, Uganda, and Kenya. The borders of most African states reflect the administrative boundaries drawn by the old European colonial powers, rather than tribal realities. Consequently, the typical African country contains a number of tribes. Tribal totalitarianism occurs when a political party that represents the interests of a particular tribe (and not always the majority tribe) monopolizes power. Such one-party states still exist in Africa.

A fourth major form of totalitarianism might be described as **right-wing totalitarianism.** Right-wing totalitarianism generally permits individual economic freedom but restricts individual political freedom on the grounds that it would lead to the rise of communism. One common feature of most right-wing dictatorships is an overt hostility to socialist or communist ideas. Many right-wing totalitarian governments are backed by the military, and the government may even be made up of military officers. Until the early 1980s right-wing dictatorships, many of which were military dictatorships, were common throughout Latin America. They were also found in several Asian countries, particularly South Korea, Taiwan, Singapore, Indonesia, and the Philippines. Since the early 1980s, however, this form of government has been in retreat. The majority of Latin American countries are now genuine multiparty democracies, while significant political freedoms have been granted to the political opposition in countries such as South Korea, Taiwan, and the Philippines.

communist totalitarianism Form of totalitarianism that advocates achieving socialism through totalitarian dictatorship.

theocratic totalitarianism Form of totalitarianism in which political power is monopolized by a party, group, or individual that governs according to religious principles.

tribal totalitarianism Form of totalitarianism found mainly in Africa in which a political party that represents the interests of a particular tribe monopolizes power.

right-wing totalitarianism Form of totalitarianism in which individual economic freedom is allowed but individual political freedom is restricted on the grounds that it could lead to communism.

Economic Systems

It should be clear from the previous section that there is a connection between political ideology and economic systems. In countries where individual goals are given primacy over collective goals, we are more likely to find free market economic systems. In contrast, in countries where collective goals are given preeminence, the state may control many enterprises, and markets in such countries are likely to be restricted rather than free. We can identify four broad types of economic system—a market economy, a command economy, a mixed economy, and a state-directed economy.

Market Economy

In a pure **market economy** all productive activities are privately owned. The goods and services produced and the quantity produced are not dictated by anyone. Rather, production is determined by the interaction of supply and demand and signaled to

market economy Economic system in which the interaction of supply and demand determines the quantity in which goods and services are produced.

producers through the price system. If demand for a product exceeds supply, prices will rise, signaling producers to produce more. If supply exceeds demand, prices will fall, signaling producers to produce less. Consumers are sovereign. The purchasing patterns of consumers, as signaled to producers through the mechanism of the price system, determine what is produced and in what quantity.

For a market to work in this manner, there must be no restrictions on supply. A restriction on supply occurs when a market is monopolized by a single firm. In such circumstances, rather than increasing output in response to increased demand, a monopolist might restrict output and let prices rise. This allows the monopolist to make a greater profit margin on each unit it sells. Although this is good for the monopolist, it is bad for the consumer, who has to pay higher prices, and it is probably bad for the welfare of society. Because a monopolist has no competitors, it has no incentive to search for ways to lower its production costs. Rather, it can simply pass on cost increases to consumers in the form of higher prices. The net result is that the monopolist is likely to become increasingly inefficient, producing high-priced, low-quality goods, while society suffers as a consequence.

Given the dangers inherent in monopoly, government's role in a market economy is to encourage vigorous competition among private producers. Governments do this by outlawing monopolies and restrictive business practices designed to monopolize a market (antitrust laws serve this function in the United States). Private ownership also encourages vigorous competition and economic efficiency. Private ownership ensures that entrepreneurs have a right to the profits generated by their efforts. This gives entrepreneurs an incentive to search for better ways of serving consumer needs, by introducing new products, developing more efficient production processes, bettering marketing and aftersales service, or managing their businesses more efficiently than their competitors. In turn, the constant improvement in product and process that results from such an incentive has been argued to stimulate economic growth and development.[10]

Costs in a Command Economy

Kentucky Fried Chicken entered Beijing, China, in 1986 in a joint venture with the city government of Beijing. The flagship store is located on Tiananmen Square, just across from Mao's Tomb. The American side brought the restaurant concept, methods, and management skills to the venture, while the Chinese side supplied the real estate, the labor, the chicken and other inputs. Imagine the American managers' confusion and then astonishment when, as they negotiated prices for chicken supplies, the Chinese through their translator told them they could pay whatever they would like for the chickens. To the Chinese business managers, who ran a centralized, state enterprise in a command economy, the concept of cost had a quite different meaning than it did for the American managers. The Chinese learned about costs in a demand-led model very quickly, though!

Command Economy

command economy
Economic system in which the goods and services produced, the quantity in which they are produced, and the prices at which they are sold are all planned by the government.

In a pure **command economy** the goods and services that a country produces, the quantity in which they are produced, and the prices at which they are sold are all *planned* by the government. Consistent with the collectivist ideology, the objective of a command economy is for government to allocate resources for "the good of society." In addition, in a *pure* command economy all businesses are state owned so the government can direct them to make investments that are in the best interests of the nation as a whole, rather than in the interests of private individuals.

Historically, command economies were found in communist countries where collectivist goals were given priority over individual goals. Since the demise of communism in the late 1980s, the number of command economies has fallen dramatically. Some elements of a command economy were also evident in a number of democratic nations led by socialist-inclined governments. France and India both experimented with extensive government planning and state ownership, but government planning has fallen into disfavor in both countries.

While the objective of a command economy is to mobilize economic resources for the public good, in practice the opposite seems to occur. In a command economy, state-owned enterprises cannot go out of business so they have little incentive to control costs and be efficient. Also, the abolition of private ownership removes the incentive for individuals to look for better ways of serving consumer needs; hence, command economies lack dynamism and innovation. Instead of growing and becoming more prosperous, they tend to be characterized by economic stagnation.

Mixed Economy

In between market economies and command economies can be found mixed economies. In a **mixed economy** certain sectors of the economy are left to private ownership and free market mechanisms, while there is significant state ownership and government planning in other sectors. Mixed economies are relatively common in Western Europe; although they are becoming less so. France, Italy, and Sweden can all be classified as mixed economies. The governments intervene in those sectors where private ownership is believed to not be in the best interests of society. For example, Britain and Sweden both have extensive state-owned health systems that provide free universal health care to all citizens (it is paid for through higher taxes). Both countries believe government has a moral obligation to provide for the health of its citizens. One consequence is that private ownership of health care operations is very restricted in both countries.

In mixed economies governments also tend to take into state ownership troubled firms whose continued operation is believed to be vital to national interests. The French automobile company, Renault, until recently was state owned. The government took over the company when it ran into serious financial problems. The French government reasoned that the social costs of the unemployment that might result if Renault collapsed were unacceptable, so it nationalized the company to save it from bankruptcy. Renault's competitors weren't thrilled by this move, since they had to compete with a company whose costs were subsidized by the state.

State-Directed Economy

A **state-directed economy** is one in which the state plays a significant role in directing the investment activities of private enterprise through "industrial policy" and in otherwise regulating business activity in accordance with national goals. Japan and South Korea are frequently cited as examples of state-directed economies. A state-directed economy differs from a mixed economy in that the state does not routinely take private enterprises into public ownership. Instead, it nurtures private enterprise but directs investments made by private firms in accordance with the goals of its industrial policy. For example, in the early 1970s the Japanese Ministry of International Trade and Industry (MITI) targeted the semiconductor industry as the focus of Japanese investment.[11] Industrial policy often takes the form of state subsidies to private enterprises to encourage them to build sales in industries deemed

mixed economy Economy in which some sectors are left to private ownership and free market mechanisms while others are state-owned and controlled.

state-directed economy Economy in which the state plays a significant role in directing the investment activities of private enterprise through "industrial policy" and in otherwise regulating business activity in accordance with national goals.

to be of strategic value for the nation's economic development. Thus, the Japanese government subsidized research and development (R&D) investments made by Japanese semiconductor companies. It also used direct administrative pressure to persuade several companies to enter the industry. In addition, Japanese semiconductor companies were protected from foreign competition by import barriers and restrictions on the ability of foreigners to establish operations in Japan.

The intellectual foundation for a state-directed economy is based on the so-called *infant industry argument* (which we shall study in greater depth in Chapter 5). This argument suggests that in some industries, economies of scale are so large and incumbent firms from developed nations have such an advantage that it is difficult for new firms from developing nations to establish themselves. Industrial policy is seen as a way to overcome this economic disadvantage. It also is argued that state-directed industrial policy may allow a country to establish a leading position in a newly emerging industry where scale economies will ultimately be of great importance. (This argument is at the core of the *new trade theory,* which we review in Chapter 4.)

Critics of state-directed economies question whether government bureaucrats can make better decisions about the allocation of investment capital than the market mechanism can. For a long time, the economic success of Japan and South Korea allowed advocates of state involvement to dismiss such criticisms.[12] However, a decade of stagnant growth in Japan coupled with the 1997 implosion of the South Korean economy have bolstered these criticisms. The South Korean collapse, in particular, has been widely attributed to uneconomic investments by South Korean companies in industries that the government deemed to be of national importance, such as semiconductors.

Legal Systems

legal system The rules, or laws, that regulate behavior and the processes by which the laws of a country are enforced and through which redress of grievances is obtained.

The **legal system** of a country refers to the system of rules, or laws, that regulate behavior and the processes by which the laws of a country are enforced and through which redress for grievances is obtained. A country's legal system is of immense importance to international business. Laws regulate business practice, define the manner in which business transactions are to be executed, and set down the rights and obligations of those involved in business transactions. Countries' legal environments differ in significant ways. As we shall see, differences in legal systems can have an important impact on the attractiveness of a country as an investment site and/or market.

Like the economic system of a country, the legal system is influenced by the prevailing political system. The government defines the legal framework within which firms do business; often the laws that regulate business are a reflection of the rulers' dominant political ideology. For example, collectivist-inclined totalitarian states tend to enact laws that restrict private enterprise, while the laws in democratic states where individualism is the dominant political philosophy tend to be pro-private enterprise and pro-consumer.

The variations in the structure of law is a massive topic that warrants its own textbook. Here we do not attempt to give a full description of the variations in legal systems. Rather, we will focus on three issues that illustrate how legal systems can vary among countries and how such variations can affect international business. First, we look at the laws governing property rights with particular reference to patents, copyrights, and trademarks. Second, we look at laws covering product safety and product liability. Third, we look at country differences in contract law.

Property Rights

In a legal sense the term *property* refers to a resource over which an individual or business holds a legal title; that is, a resource that is owned. **Property rights** refer to the bundle of legal rights over the *use* to which a resource is put and over the *use* made of any income that may be derived from that resource.[13] Countries differ significantly in the extent to which their legal systems protect property rights. Although almost all countries have laws that protect property rights, many countries fail to enforce these laws, and property rights are routinely violated. Property rights can be violated in two ways—through private action and through public action.

49

PRIVATE ACTION   Private action refers to theft, piracy, blackmail, and the like by private individuals or groups. While theft occurs in all countries, a weak legal system allows for a much higher level of criminal action in some countries than in others. Russia's chaotic legal system in the post-Communist era, coupled with a weak police force and judicial system, offers both domestic and foreign businesses scant protection from blackmail by the "Russian Mafia." Successful business owners often must pay "protection money" to the Mafia or face violent retribution, including bombings and assassinations. (About 500 contract killings of businessmen occurred in 1995 and again in 1996.)[14] For example, Ivan Kivelidi, a banker and founder of the Russian Business Roundtable, was murdered by poison applied to the rim of his coffee cup. Vladislav Listiev, the head of Russia's largest nationwide TV network, announced in 1996 that he was going to remove unsavory elements (i.e., Mafia) from the network. Soon afterward he was gunned down by professional assassins outside his apartment building.[15] And in perhaps the most disturbing case, American businessman Paul Tatum was assassinated in late 1996 after a Moscow hotel joint venture that he was involved in turned sour.[16]

Russia is not alone in having Mafia problems. The Mafia has a long history in the United States, and in Japan the local version of the Mafia, known as the *yakuza,* runs protection rackets, particularly in the food and entertainment industries.[17] However, there is an enormous difference between the magnitude of such activity in Russia and its limited impact in Japan and the United States. This difference arises because the legal enforcement apparatus, such as the police and court system, is so weak in Russia. Many other countries have problems similar or even greater than those being experienced by Russia. In Somalia, for example, the breakdown of law and order in 1993 and 1994 was so complete that even United Nations food relief convoys proceeding to famine areas under armed guard were held up by bandits.

PUBLIC ACTION   Public action to violate property rights occurs when public officials, such as politicians and government bureaucrats, extort income or resources from property holders. This can be done through a number of mechanisms including excessive taxation, requiring expensive licenses or permits from property holders, taking assets into state ownership without compensating the owners (as occurred to the assets of numerous US firms in Iran after the 1979 revolution), or demanding bribes from businesses in return for the rights to operate in a country, industry, or location.[18] For example, the government of the late Ferdinand Marcos in the Philippines was famous for demanding bribes from foreign businesses wishing to operate in that country.[19]

Another example of such activity surfaced in mid-February 1994. The *Sunday Times* of Britain ran an article alleging that a £1 billion ($750 million) sale of defense equipment by British companies to Malaysia was secured only after bribes had been paid to Malaysian government officials and after the British Overseas Development Administration (ODA) had agreed to approve a £234 million grant to the

Malaysian government for a hydroelectric dam of dubious economic value (according to the *Sunday Times*). The clear implication was that UK officials, in their enthusiasm to see British companies win a large defense contract, had yielded to pressures from "corrupt" Malaysian officials for bribes—both personal and in the form of the £234 million development grant.[20]

The Protection of Intellectual Property

Intellectual property refers to property, such as computer software, a screenplay, a music score, or the chemical formula for a new drug, that is the product of intellectual activity. It is possible to establish ownership rights over intellectual property through patents, copyrights, and trademarks. A **patent** grants the inventor of a new product or process exclusive rights to the manufacture, use, or sale of that invention. **Copyrights** are the exclusive legal rights of authors, composers, playwrights, artists, and publishers to publish and dispose of their work as they see fit. **Trademarks** are designs and names, often officially registered, by which merchants or manufacturers designate and differentiate their products (e.g., Christian Dior clothes).

The philosophy behind intellectual property laws is to reward the originator of an invention, book, song, clothing design, restaurant chain, and the like, for his or her idea and effort. As such, they stimulate innovation and creative work. They provide an incentive for people to search for novel ways of doing things and they reward creativity. Consider innovation in the pharmaceutical industry. A patent will grant the inventor of a new drug a 17-year monopoly in production of that drug. This gives pharmaceutical firms an incentive to undertake the expensive, difficult, and time-consuming research required to generate new drugs (on average it costs $150 million in R&D and takes 12 years to get a new drug on the market). Without the guarantees provided by patents, it is unlikely that companies would commit themselves to extensive basic research.[21]

The protection of intellectual property rights differs greatly from country to country. While many countries have stringent intellectual property regulations on their books, *enforcement* of these regulations has often been lax. This has been the case even among countries that have signed important international agreements to protect intellectual property, such as the **Paris Convention for the Protection of Industrial Property,** which 96 countries are party to. Weak

Piracy in countries like China and Thailand can be the result of weak enforcement of the protection of intellectual property rights. In this photo, a man in Thailand destroys thousands of counterfeit Winnie-the-Poohs. Why do you think the demand for these goods in these countries is so high as to make pirating a lucrative business?
© AFP/CORBIS.

enforcement encourages the piracy of intellectual property. China and Thailand have been among the worst offenders in Asia. For example, local bookstores in China commonly maintain a section that is off-limits to foreigners; it ostensibly is reserved for sensitive political literature, but it more often displays illegally copied textbooks. Pirated computer software is also widely available in China. Similarly, the streets of Bangkok, the capital of Thailand, are lined with stands selling pirated copies of Rolex watches, Levi blue jeans, videotapes, and computer software.

The computer software industry suffers the most from lax enforcement of intellectual property rights. Estimates suggest that violations of intellectual property rights cost computer software companies revenues equal to $11 billion in 1998.[22] According to the Business Software Alliance, a software industry association, in 1998 38 percent of all software applications used in the world were pirated. The 10 countries with the highest dollar losses due to software piracy were (in rank order): the United States, China, Japan, Germany, the United Kingdom, France, Brazil, Italy, Canada, and Russia. Total losses for these countries were $7.3 billion, or 67 percent of worldwide losses. The study estimates that more than 9 in 10 business software applications in Vietnam (97 percent), China (95 percent), Indonesia (92 percent), and Russia (92 percent) were pirated. The piracy rate in the United States is estimated to be 25 percent.

Music recordings represent another area where piracy is rampant. According to one estimate, nearly 200 million illegal compact disks are stamped each year, almost 60 percent of them from China. The International Federation of the Phonographic Industry claims its members lose $2.2 billion annually to pirates.[23]

International businesses have a number of possible responses to such violations. Firms can lobby their respective governments to push for international agreements to ensure that intellectual property rights are protected by law and that the law is enforced. The accompanying "Management Focus," which looks at how Microsoft urged the US government to insist that other countries abide by stricter intellectual property laws, gives an example of such lobbying.

Partly as a result of such actions, international laws are being strengthened. As we shall see in Chapter 5, the most recent world trade agreement extends the scope of the **General Agreement on Tariffs and Trade (GATT)** to cover intellectual property. Under the new agreement, as of 1995 a council of the newly created **World Trade Organization (WTO)** oversees the enforcement of much stricter intellectual property regulations. These regulations oblige WTO members to grant and enforce patents lasting at least 20 years and copyrights lasting 50 years. Rich countries must comply with the rules within a year. Poor countries, in which such protection has generally been much weaker, have 5 years' grace, and the very poorest have 10 years.[24] (For further details, see Chapter 5.)

One problem with these new regulations, however, is that the world's biggest violator—China—is not yet a member of the WTO and is not obliged to adhere to the agreement. However, following pressure from the US government that included the threat of trade sanctions, the Chinese government in 1996 agreed to enforce its existing intellectual property rights regulations. (In China, as in many countries, the problem is not a lack of laws; the problem is that the existing laws are not enforced.) During 1996 Chinese officials closed 19 counterfeit CD-ROM factories with a capacity of 30 to 50 million units a year. Still, according to the Business Software Alliance, a further 21 counterfeit CD-ROM factories were operating in China as of late 1996.[25]

In addition to lobbying their governments, firms may want to stay out of countries where intellectual property laws are lax rather than risk having their ideas stolen by local entrepreneurs. Firms also need to ensure that pirated copies of their products, produced in countries where intellectual property laws are lax, do not turn up

General Agreement on Tariffs and Trade Treaty designed to remove barriers to the free flow of goods, services, and capital between nations; often referred to as GATT.

World Trade Organization Agency established at the Uruguay Round in 1993 to police the international trading system.

Microsoft, the world's biggest personal computer software company, developed MS-DOS and then Windows, respectively the operating system and graphical user interface that now reside on over 90 percent of the world's personal computers. In addition, Microsoft has a slew of best-selling applications software, including its office and back-office suites. An integral part of Mi-

achieve this goal, the company has to overcome a very serious obstacle—software piracy. Over 95 percent of the software used in China in 1998 was pirated. Microsoft is a prime target of this activity. Most Microsoft products used in China are illegal copies made and then sold with no payment to Microsoft. Microsoft executives don't have to go far to see the problem. Just a few blocks

cracy to find cheap software solutions. Thus, much of the government uses pirated software, Microsoft claims.

To make matters worse, China is becoming a mass exporter of counterfeit software. The Hong Kong customs seized a shipment of 2,200 such disks enroute from China to Belgium.

The problem arises because the Chinese judicial authorities do

Microsoft Battles Software Piracy in China

crosoft's international strategy has been expansion into mainland China, where 5 million personal computers were sold in 1998. With a population of 1.5 billion, China represents a potentially huge market for Microsoft.

Microsoft's goal is to increase Chinese sales from nothing in 1994 to $200 million by 2002. However, before it can

from the company's Hong Kong office is a tiny shop that offers CD-ROMs, each crammed with dozens of computer programs that collectively are worth about $20,000. The asking price is about 500 Hong Kong dollars, or $52! China's government is believed to be one of the worst offenders. Microsoft's lawyers complain that Beijing doesn't yet budget for software purchases, forcing its cash-strapped bureau-

not enforce their own laws. Microsoft found this out when it first tried to use China's judicial system to sue software pirates. Microsoft pressed officials in China's southern province of Guangdong to raid a manufacturer who was producing counterfeit holograms that Microsoft used to authenticate its software manuals. The Chinese authorities prosecuted the counterfeit manufacturer, acknowledged that a copyright viola-

in their home market or in third countries. The US computer software giant Microsoft, for example, discovered that pirated Microsoft software, produced illegally in Thailand, was being sold worldwide as the real thing (including in the United States). In addition, Microsoft has encountered significant problems with pirated software in China, which is discussed in the "Management Focus."

Product Safety and Product Liability

Product safety laws set standards to which a product must adhere. Product liability involves holding a firm and its officers responsible when their product causes injury, death, or damage. Product liability can be much greater if a product does not conform to required safety standards. There are both civil and criminal product liability laws. Civil laws call for payment and money damages. Criminal liability laws result in fines or imprisonment. Both civil and criminal liability laws are probably more extensive in the United States than in any other country; although many other Western nations also have comprehensive liability laws. Liability laws are typically least extensive in less developed nations.

In the United States a boom in product liability suits and awards has resulted in a dramatic increase in the cost of liability insurance. In turn, many business executives

tion had occurred, but awarded Microsoft only $2,600 and fined the pirating company $3,000!

To compete with pirated software, Microsoft in October 1994 reduced the price of its Chinese software by as much as 200 percent. This action may have had little impact because the programs are still priced at $100 to $200, compared to $5 to $20 for an illegal copy of the same software.

Yet another company tactic has been to lobby the US government to pressure Chinese authorities to start enforcing their own laws. As part of its lobbying effort, Microsoft has engaged in its own version of "guerrilla warfare," digging through trash bins, paying locals to spy, even posing as money-grubbing businessmen to collect evidence of piracy, which is then passed along to US trade officials. The tactic has worked because the US government currently has some leverage over China. China wishes to join the new World Trade Organization and views US support as

crucial. The United States has said it will not support Chinese membership unless China starts enforcing its intellectual property laws. This demand was backed by a threat to impose tariffs of $1.08 billion on Chinese exports unless China agreed to stricter enforcement. After a tense standoff, the Chinese backed down and acquiesced to US demands in February 1995. The Chinese government agreed to start enforcing its intellectual property rights laws, to crack down on factories that the United States identified as pirating US goods, to respect US trademarks, including Microsoft's, and to instruct Chinese government ministries to stop using pirated software.

To supplement these actions, Microsoft announced it would work with the Chinese Ministry of Electronics to develop a Chinese version of the Windows operating system. Microsoft's logic is that the best way to stop the Chinese government from using pirated software is to go into business with it. Once the government has

a stake in maximizing sales of legitimate Microsoft products, the company reckons it will also have a strong incentive to crack down on sales of counterfeit software.

In a sign that Microsoft is making limited headway against the piracy problem in China, a Beijing court in March 1999 awarded Microsoft approximately 800,000 yuan ($744,720) in compensation after two Chinese companies were found guilty of copyright infringement. This was the first time Microsoft had pursued a software piracy case in a mainland Chinese court. Although small in terms of the monetary compensation, the victory may signal the beginning of a trend in China.[26]

argue that the high costs of liability insurance make American businesses less competitive in the global marketplace.[27] The competitiveness issue apart, differences in product safety and liability laws raise an important ethical issue for firms doing business abroad. When the product safety laws are tougher in a firm's home country than in a foreign country, and/or when liability laws are more lax, should a firm doing business in that foreign country adhere to the more relaxed local standards, or should it adhere to the standards of its home country? While the ethical thing to do is undoubtedly to adhere to home country standards, firms have been known to take advantage of lax safety and liability laws to do business in a manner that would not be allowed back home.

Contract Law

A contract is a document that specifies the conditions under which an exchange is to occur and details the rights and obligations of the parties to a contract. Many business transactions are regulated by some form of contract. Contract law is the body of law that governs contract enforcement. The parties to an agreement normally resort to contract law when one party believes the other has violated either the letter or the spirit of an agreement.

common law system
Legal system that evolved in England over hundreds of years and is now found in Britain's former colonies, including the United States; based on tradition, precedent, and custom.

civil law system Legal system based on a detailed set of laws, organized into codes, that is used in more than 80 countries, including Germany, France, Japan, and Russia.

Contract law can differ significantly among countries, and as such it affects the kind of contracts that an international business will want to use to safeguard its position should a contract dispute arise. The main differences can be traced to differences in legal tradition. Two main legal traditions exist in the world today—the **common law system** and the **civil law system.** The common law system evolved in England over hundreds of years. It is now found in most of Britain's former colonies, including the United States. Common law is based on tradition, precedent, and custom. When law courts interpret common law, they do so with regard to these characteristics. Civil law is based on a very detailed set of laws organized into codes. Among other things, these codes define the laws that govern business transactions. When law courts interpret civil law, they do so with regard to these codes. More than 80 countries, including Germany, France, Japan, and Russia, operate with a civil law system. Because common law tends to be relatively ill-specified, contracts drafted under a common law framework tend to be very detailed, spelling out all contingencies. In civil law systems, however, contracts tend to be much shorter and less specific because many of the issues typically covered in a common law contract are already covered in a civil code.

The Determinants of Economic Development

One reason for studying the political, economic, and legal systems in the world is that collectively these different systems can have a profound impact on the level of a country's economic development, and on the attractiveness of a country as a possible market and/or production location. Here we look first at how countries differ in their level of development. Then we look at how political economy affects economic progress.

Differences in Economic Development

Countries have dramatically different levels of economic development. One common measure of economic development is a country's gross national product (GNP) per head of population. GNP is often regarded as a yardstick for the economic activity of a country; it measures the total value of the goods and services produced annually. Map 2.1 summarizes the GNP per head of the world's nations in 1998. Japan, Sweden, Switzerland, and the United States are among the richest on this measure, while the large countries of China and India are among the poorest. Switzerland, for example, had a 1998 GNP per head of $40,080, but China achieved only $750 and India, $430. The world's poorest country, Ethiopia, had a GNP per head of only $100, compared to $29,340 in the United States.[28]

GNP per head figures can be misleading because they don't consider differences in the cost of living. For example, while the 1998 GNP per head in Switzerland of $40,808 exceeded that of the United States, which was $29,340, the higher cost of living in Switzerland meant that American citizens could afford more goods and services than Swiss citizens. GNP per capita can be adjusted to account for differences in purchasing power. Referred to as a purchasing power parity (PPP) adjustment, this adjustment allows for a more direct comparison of living standards. The base for the adjustment is the cost of living in the United States. Thus, under a PPP adjustment, the GNP of the United States remains at $29,340, whereas that of Switzerland falls to $26,620. Map 2.2 summarizes the PPP adjusted GNP per capita in 1998 for the nations of the world.

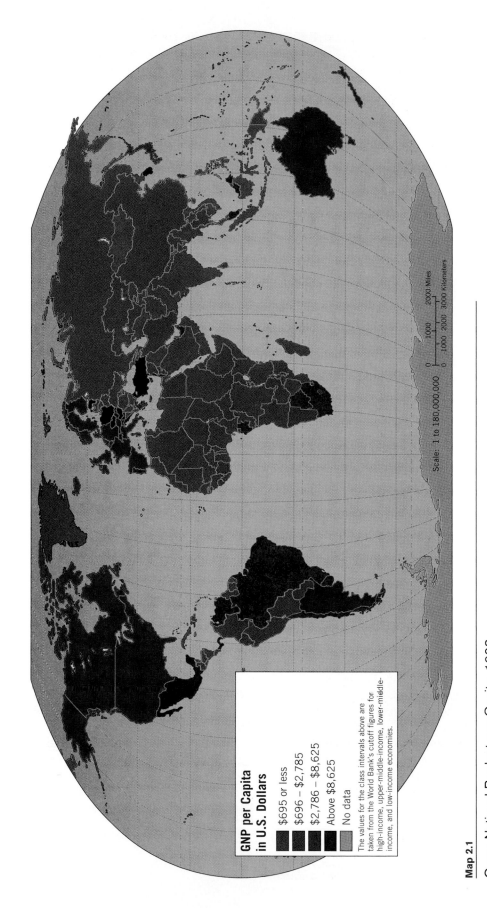

**GNP per Capita
in U.S. Dollars**

■ $695 or less
■ $696 – $2,785
■ $2,786 – $8,625
■ Above $8,625
▨ No data

The values for the class intervals above are
taken from the World Bank's cutoff figures for
high-income, upper-middle-income, lower-middle-
income, and low-income economies.

Scale: 1 to 180,000,000

2000 Miles

1000

0   1000   2000   3000 Kilometers

Map 2.1

Gross National Product per Capita, 1998
Source: *World Development Indicators, 1998.* Reprinted with permission of the World Bank.

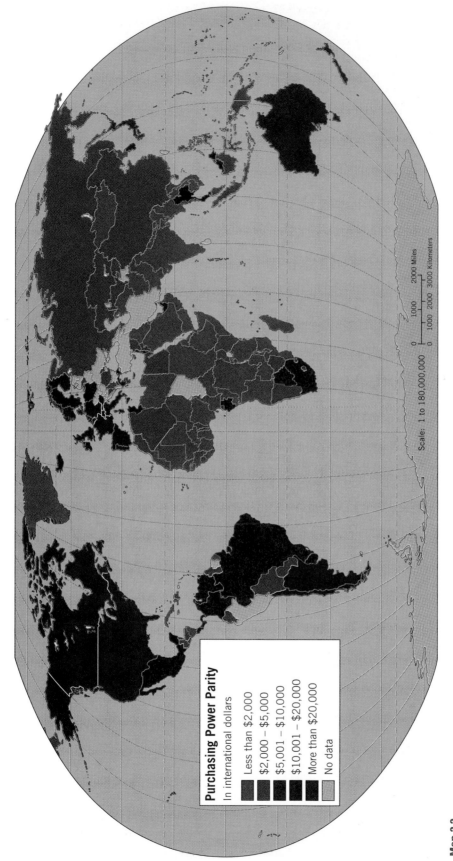

Map 2.2

Purchasing Power Parity in 1998

Source: World Development Indicators, 1998. Reprinted with permission of the World Bank.

Purchasing Power Parity

In international dollars

- Less than $2,000
- $2,000 – $5,000
- $5,001 – $10,000
- $10,001 – $20,000
- More than $20,000
- No data

Scale: 1 to 180,000,000

0   1000   2000 Miles

0   1000   2000   3000 Kilometers

There are striking differences in the standard of living in different countries. PPP data suggest the average Indian citizen can afford to consume only 5.7 percent of the goods and services consumed by the average US citizen (the PPP adjusted GNP for India is $1,700). One might conclude that, despite having a population of close to 1 billion, India is unlikely to be a lucrative market for the consumer products produced by many Western international businesses. However, this is not the correct conclusion because India has a fairly wealthy middle class, despite its many very poor people.

The GNP and PPP data discussed so far give a static picture of development. They tell us, for example, that China is poorer than the United States, but they do not tell us if China is closing the gap. To assess this, we have to look at economic growth rates. Map 2.3 summarizes the growth rate in GNP for 1990 to 1998. Although countries such as China and India are very poor, their economies are growing more rapidly than those of many advanced nations. Thus, in time they may become advanced nations themselves and huge markets for international businesses. Given their potential, it may be good advice for international businesses to get a foothold in these markets now. Even though their current contribution to an international firm's revenues might be small, their future contributions could be much larger.

A number of other indicators can also be used to assess a country's economic development and its likely growth rate. These include literacy rates, the number of people per doctor, infant mortality rates, life expectancy, calorie (food) consumption per head, car ownership per 1,000 people, and education spending as a percentage of GNP. To estimate the impact of such factors on the quality of life in a country, the United Nations developed the **Human Development Index.** This index is based on three measures: life expectancy, literacy rates, and whether average incomes, based on PPP estimates, are sufficient to meet the basic needs of life in a country (adequate food, shelter, and health care). The Human Development Index is scaled from 0 to 100. Countries scoring less than 50 are classified as having low human development (the quality of life is poor), those scoring from 50 to 80 are classified as having medium human development, while those countries that score above 80 are classified as having high human development. Map 2.4 summarizes the Human Development Index scores for 1995, the most recent year for which data are available.

Human Development Index United Nations-developed index based on life expectancy, literacy rates, and whether average incomes are sufficient to meet the basic needs of life in a country.

Political Economy and Economic Progress

It is often argued that a country's economic development is a function of its economic and political systems. What then is the nature of the relationship between political economy and economic progress? This question has been the subject of debate among academics and policy makers for years. Despite the long debate, this remains a question for which it is not possible to give an unambiguous answer. However, it is possible to untangle the main threads of the academic arguments and make a few generalizations as to the nature of the relationship between political economy and economic progress.

INNOVATION IS THE ENGINE OF GROWTH There is general agreement that innovation is the engine of long-run economic growth.[29] Those who make this argument define **innovation** broadly to include not just new products, but also new processes, new organizations, new management practices, and new strategies. Thus, Toys 'Я' Us's strategy of establishing large warehouse-type toy stores and then engaging in heavy advertising and price discounting to sell the merchandise can be classified as an innovation because Toys R Us was the first company to pursue this strategy. One can conclude that if a country's economy is to sustain long-run economic growth, the business environment within that country must be conducive to the production of innovations.

innovation Process through which people create new products, new processes, new organizations, new management practices, and new strategies.

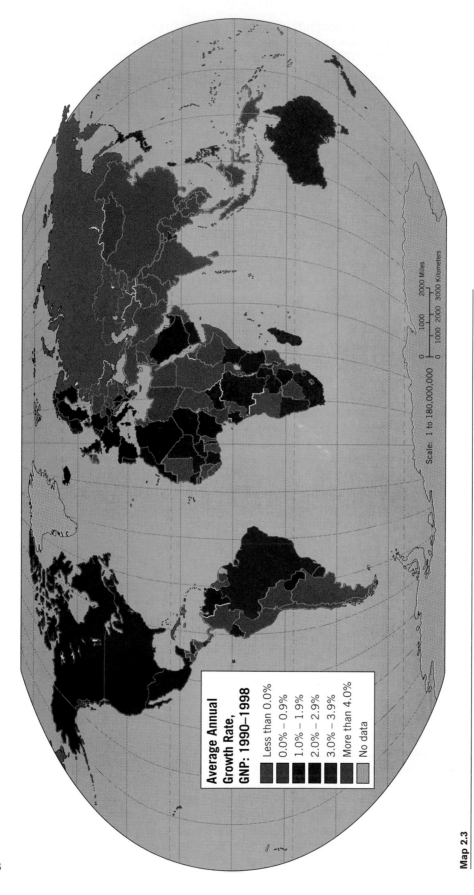

Map 2.3

Growth in Gross National Product, 1990–98

Source: *World Development Report 1999/2000.* Reprinted with permission of Oxford University Press.

Average Annual Growth Rate, GNP: 1990–1998

- Less than 0.0%
- 0.0% – 0.9%
- 1.0% – 1.9%
- 2.0% – 2.9%
- 3.0% – 3.9%
- More than 4.0%
- No data

Scale: 1 to 180,000,000

0   1000   2000 Miles

0   1000   2000   3000 Kilometers

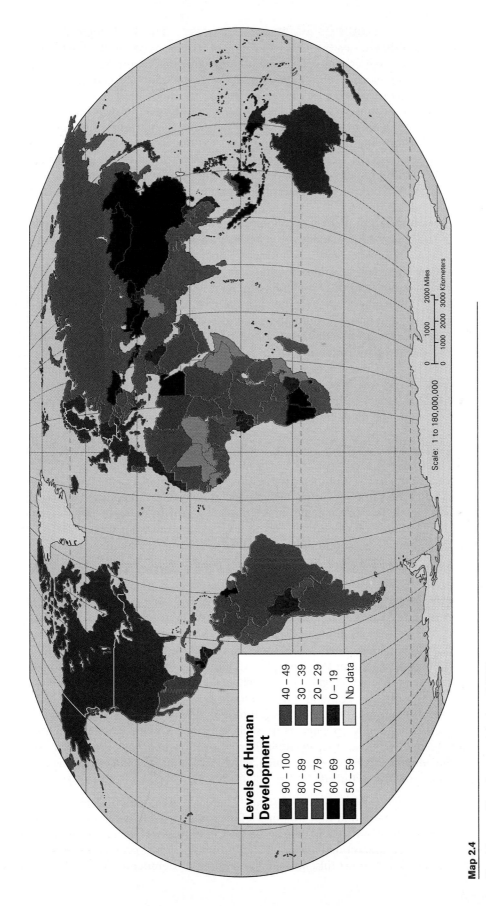

Map 2.4

The Human Development Index, 1995

Source: From *Student Atlas of World Geography, 1st edition,* by John Allen. Copyright 1999 by The McGraw-Hill Companies, Inc. Reprinted by permission of Dushkin/McGraw-Hill. Data from *Human Development Report 1998* by the United Nations Development Programme. Copyright 1998 by the United Nations Development Programme. Used by permission of Oxford University Press, Inc.

Levels of Human
Development

90 – 100
80 – 89
70 – 79
60 – 69
50 – 59
40 – 49
30 – 39
20 – 29
0 – 19
No data

Scale: 1 to 180,000,000

0   1000   2000 Miles
0   1000   2000   3000 Kilometers

INNOVATION REQUIRES A MARKET ECONOMY   This leads logically to a further question: What does a business environment require to be conducive to innovation? Those who have considered this issue highlight the advantages of a market economy in this regard.[30] It has been argued that the economic freedom associated with a market economy creates greater incentives for innovation than either a planned or a mixed economy. In a market economy any individual who has an innovative idea is free to try to make money from that idea by starting a business (by engaging in entrepreneurial activity). Similarly, existing businesses are free to improve their operations through innovation. To the extent that they are successful, both individual entrepreneurs and established businesses can reap rewards in the form of high profits. Thus, there are enormous incentives to develop innovations in market economies.

In contrast, in a planned economy the state owns all means of production. Consequently there is no incentive for entrepreneurial individuals to develop valuable new innovations because it is the state, rather than the individual, that captures all the gains. The lack of economic freedom and incentives for innovation was probably a main factor in the economic stagnation of so many former Communists states and led ultimately to their collapse at the end of the 1980s. Similar stagnation occurred in many mixed economies in sectors where the state had a monopoly (such as health care and telecommunications in Britain). This stagnation provided the impetus for the privatization of state-owned enterprises in many mixed economies during the mid-1980s and today. (**Privatization** refers to the selling of state-owned enterprises to private investors.)

privatization
Process of selling state-owned enterprises to private investors.

A study of 102 countries over a 20-year period revealed a strong relationship between economic freedom (as provided by a market economy) and economic growth.[31] This study found that the more economic freedom a country had between 1975 and 1995, the more economic growth it achieved and the richer its citizens became. The 6 countries that had persistently high ratings of economic freedom from 1975 to 1995 (Hong Kong, Switzerland, Singapore, the United States, Canada, and Germany) were also all in the top 10 in terms of economic growth rates. In contrast, no country with a persistently low rating achieved a respectable growth rate. For the 16 countries for which the index of economic freedom declined the most during the 1975–95 period, average annual gross domestic product *fell* at an annual rate of 0.6 percent.

INNOVATION REQUIRES STRONG PROPERTY RIGHTS   Strong legal protection of property rights is also necessary for a business environment to be conducive to innovation and economic growth.[32] Both individuals and businesses must be given the opportunity to profit from innovative ideas. Without strong property rights protection, businesses and individuals run the risk that the profits from their innovative efforts will be expropriated, either by criminal elements or by the state itself. The state can expropriate the profits from innovation through legal means, such as excessive taxation, or through illegal means, such as demands from state bureaucrats for kickbacks in return for granting a license to do business. According to the Nobel Prize-winning economist Douglass North, throughout history many governments have displayed a tendency to engage in such behavior. When property rights are not adequately enforced, the incentives for innovation and entrepreneurial activity are reduced—since the profits from such activity are "stolen"—and hence the rate of economic growth is reduced.

THE REQUIRED POLITICAL SYSTEM   There is a great deal of debate as to the kind of political system that best supports a functioning market economy with strong protection for property rights.[33] We in the West tend to associate a representative democracy with a market economy strong property rights protection, and economic progress. Building on this, we tend to argue that democracy is good for growth.[34]

Although Hong Kong switched from a British colony to Chinese sovereignty in 1997, its economy still displays democratic influence. This shopping district street in Hong Kong could be mistaken for a big city street in the U.S. What do you think are some of the reasons that places like Hong Kong, Singapore, and Taiwan have flourished, while others in Eastern Europe, the former Soviet Union, and India have not?

However, several totalitarian regimes have fostered a market economy and strong property rights protection and experienced rapid economic growth. The examples include four of the fastest-growing economies of the past 30 years—South Korea, Taiwan, Singapore, and Hong Kong—all of which have grown faster than the Western democracies. All these economies had one thing in common for at least the first period of their economic takeoff—undemocratic governments! At the same time, countries with stable democratic governments, such as India, experienced sluggish economic growth for long periods.

Commenting on this issue in 1992, Lee Kuan Yew, Singapore's leader for many years, told an audience, "I do not believe that democracy necessarily leads to development. I believe that a country needs to develop discipline more than democracy. The exuberance of democracy leads to undisciplined and disorderly conduct which is inimical to development."[35] Others have argued that many of the current problems in Eastern Europe and the states of the former Soviet Union are due to the fact that democracy arrived before economic reform, making it more difficult for elected governments to introduce the policies that, while painful in the short run, were needed to promote rapid economic growth. Some argue that Russia got its political and economic reforms the wrong way round, unlike China, which maintains a totalitarian government but has moved rapidly toward a market economy.

However, those who argue for the value of a totalitarian regime miss an important point—if dictators made countries rich, then much of Africa, Asia, and Latin America should have been growing rapidly for the past 40 years, and this has not been the case. Only a certain kind of totalitarian regime can promote economic growth. It must be a dictatorship that is committed to a free market system and strong protection of property rights. Also, there is no guarantee that a dictatorship will continue to pursue such progressive policies. Many dictators are tempted to use the state apparatus to further their own private ends, in which cases property rights are often violated and economic growth stalls. Given this, it seems likely that democratic regimes are far more conducive to long-term economic growth than a dictatorship, even a benevolent one. Only in a well-functioning, mature democracy are property rights truly secure.[36]

ECONOMIC PROGRESS BEGETS DEMOCRACY   While it is possible to argue that democracy is not a prerequisite for the establishment of a free market economy in which property rights are protected, subsequent economic growth often leads to the establishment of a democratic regime. Several of the fastest-growing Asian economies have recently adopted more democratic governments, including South Korea and Taiwan. Thus, while democracy may not always be the cause of initial economic progress, it seems to be one of the consequences of that progress.

A strong belief that economic progress leads to the adoption of a democratic regime underlies the fairly permissive attitude that many Western governments have adopted toward human rights in China. Although China has a totalitarian government in which human rights are abused, many Western countries have hesitated to criticize the country too much for fear that this might hamper the country's march toward a free market system. The belief is that once China has a free market system, democracy will follow. Whether this optimistic vision comes to pass remains to be seen. Nevertheless, such a vision was an important factor in the US government's 1996 decision to grant China most-favored-nation trading status (which makes it easier for Chinese firms to sell products in the United States) despite reports of widespread human rights abuses in China.

Other Determinants of Development: Geography and Education

While a country's political and economic systems are probably the big locomotive driving its rate of economic development, other factors are also important. One that has received some attention recently is geography.[37] One argument, which goes back to Adam Smith, is that geography can influence economic policy and hence economic growth rates. For example, the influential Harvard University economist Jeffrey Sachs has argued,

> Throughout history, coastal states, with their long engagements in international trade, have been more supportive of market institutions than landlocked states, which have tended to organize themselves as hierarchical (and often military) societies. Mountainous states, as a result of physical isolation, have often neglected market based trade. Temperate climes have generally supported higher densities of population and thus a more extensive division of labor than tropical regions.[38]

His point is that by virtue of favorable geography, certain societies were more likely to engage in trade than others and were thus more likely to be open to and develop market-based economic systems, which would promote faster economic growth. He also argues that irrespective of the economic and political institutions a country adopts, adverse geographical conditions, such as the high rate of disease, poor soil, and hostile climate that afflicts many tropical countries, can hamper development.

Along with colleagues at Harvard's Institute for International Development, Sachs tested for the impact of geography on a country's economic growth rate between 1965 and 1990. He found that landlocked countries grew more slowly than coastal economies, and that being entirely landlocked reduced a country's annual growth rate by roughly 0.7 percent a year. He also found that tropical countries grew 1.3 percent more slowly each year than countries in the temperate zone.

Education emerges as another important determinant of economic development. The general assertion is that nations that invest more in education will have higher growth rates. The theory behind this assertion is that an educated population is more productive. Anecdotal evidence suggests this is the case. For example, in 1960 Pakistanis and South Koreans were about as rich as each other. However, just 30 percent of Pakistani children were enrolled in primary schools, but 94 percent of South Koreans were. By the mid-1980s, South Korea's GNP per person was three times that of Pakistan's.[39] A survey of 14 statistical studies that looked at the relationship between a country's investment in education and its subsequent growth rate concluded that investment in education had a positive and statistically significant impact on a country's economic growth rate.[40] Similarly, the work by Sachs discussed above suggests that investments in education help explain why several countries in Southeast Asia, such as Indonesia, Malaysia, and Singapore, have been able to overcome the disadvantages associated with their tropical geography and grow far more rapidly than tropical nations in Africa and Latin America.

States in Transition

Since the late 1980s there have been major changes in the political economy of many nation-states. Two trends have been evident. First, during the late 1980s and early 1990s a wave of democratic revolutions swept the world. Totalitarian governments collapsed, replaced by democratically elected governments that were typically more committed to free market capitalism than their predecessors had been. The change was most dramatic in Eastern Europe, where the collapse of communism brought an end to the Cold War and led to the breakup of the Soviet Union, but similar changes occurred throughout the world during the same period. Much of Asia, Latin America, and Africa saw a shift toward greater democracy. Second, there has been a strong move away from centrally planned and mixed economies and toward a free market economic model. Here we look at the spread of democracy, and then turn our attention to the spread of free market economics.

The Spread of Democracy

A notable development of the past 15 years or so has been the spread of democracy (and by extension, the decline of totalitarianism). Map 2.5 reports data on the extent of totalitarianism in the world as determined by Freedom House.[41] This map charts political freedom in 1997, on a scale from 1 for the highest degree of political freedom to 7 for the lowest. Among the criteria that Freedom House uses to determine ratings for political freedom are the following:

- Free and fair elections of the head of state and legislative representatives.
- Fair electoral laws, equal campaigning opportunities, and fair polling.
- The right to organize into different political parties.
- A parliament with effective power.
- A significant opposition that has a realistic chance of gaining power.
- Freedom from domination by the military, foreign powers, totalitarian parties, religious hierarchies, or any other powerful group.
- A reasonable amount of self-determination for cultural, ethnic, and religious minorities.

Factors contributing to a low rating (i.e., to totalitarianism) include military or foreign control, the denial of self-determination to major population groups, a lack of

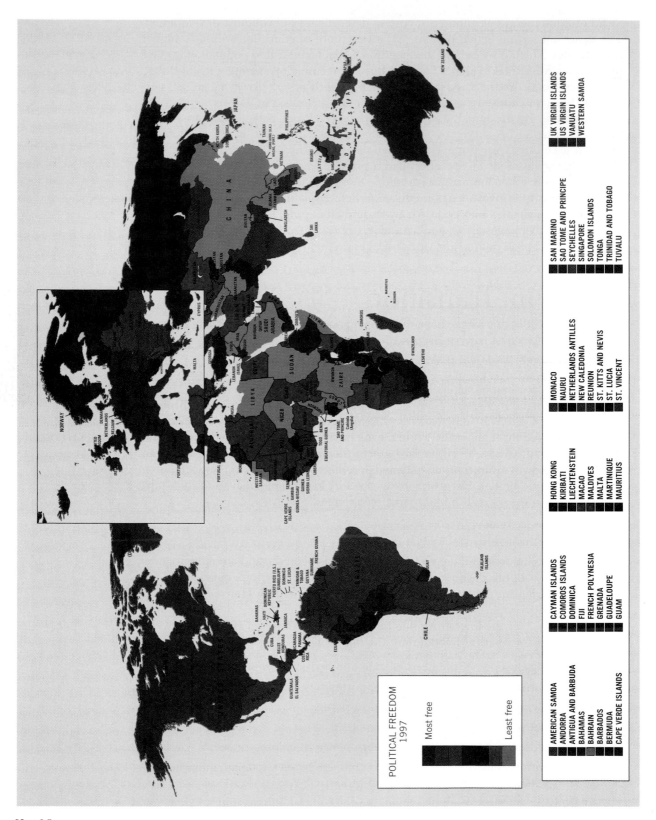

Map 2.5

Political Freedom in 1997

decentralized political power, and an absence of democratic elections. As 1998 drew to a close, 88 of the world's 191 countries (46 percent) were rated as free, meaning they maintain a high degree of political and economic freedom and respect basic civil liberties. This was the largest number of free countries on record. Almost 55 percent of the world's population now lives under democratic rule. Many of these new democracies are to be found in Eastern Europe and Latin America, although there have also been some notable gains for democracy in Africa, such as in South Africa.

There are three main reasons for the spread of democracy.[42] First, many totalitarian regimes failed to deliver economic progress to most of their populations. The collapse of communism in Eastern Europe, for example, was precipitated by the growing gulf between the vibrant and wealthy economies of the West and the stagnant economies of the Communist East. In looking for alternatives to the socialist model, the people in these countries must have noticed that most of the world's strongest economies were governed by representative democracies. Today, the economic success of many of the newer democracies, such as Poland and the Czech Republic in the former Communist bloc, the Philippines and Taiwan in Asia, and Chile in Latin America, has helped strengthen the case for democracy as a key component of successful economic advancement.

Second, the spread of new information and communications technologies, including shortwave radio, satellite television, fax machines, desktop publishing, and now the Internet, has broken down a nation's ability to control access to uncensored information. These technologies have created new conduits for the spread of democratic ideals and information from free societies. In 1989 the collapse of East Germany's Communist government was in part due to unrest among a population who for years had been exposed via TV to the affluent lifestyles of West Germans. Today the Internet is allowing democratic ideals to penetrate closed societies as never before. In response, some governments have tried to restrict access to the Internet; for example, China limits access to government employees and those affiliated with universities.[43]

Third, in many countries the economic advances of the past 25 years have led to the emergence of increasingly prosperous middle and working classes, which have pushed for democratic reforms. This was a factor in the democratic transformation of South Korea. Entrepreneurs and other business leaders, eager to protect their property rights and ensure the dispassionate enforcement of contracts, are another force that has been pressing for more accountable and open government.

It would be naive to conclude that the global spread of democracy will continue unchallenged. There have already been several reversals. In the former Soviet republic of Belarus, for example, the president, Alexander Lukashenko, has dissolved a democratically elected parliament and harassed the press. In the African nation of Niger, a military coup deposed a democratically elected government. In Asia, Singapore's Lee Kuan Yew and China's Marxist-Leninist leaders continue to advocate the virtues of authoritarian paths to democracy and to denounce Western democracies as an unacceptable model.

China, the Internet, and the World Trade Organization

As China prepares to enter the World Trade Organization, the required reduction in trade barriers presents Chinese leaders with difficult choices. One concern of American Internet service providers is access to the Chinese market. When their government can no longer block their access to the Internet, Chinese citizens will be able to get information openly and freely. Their government will have lost a measure of control. Is this one of the large steps toward a more democratic government?

Plus, there are still large parts of the world where democracy is rare. In Africa just 18 states, one-third of those on the continent, are electoral democracies. Among the 12 countries that are full or associated members of the Commonwealth of Independent States (i.e., the republics of the former Soviet Union minus the Baltic states) only four are electoral democracies. And there are no democracies in the Arab world.

Universal Civilization or a Clash of Civilizations?

The end of the Cold War and the "new world order" that followed the collapse of communism in Eastern Europe and the former Soviet Union, along with the collapse of many authoritarian regimes in Latin America, have spurred intense speculation about the future shape of global geopolitics. On the one hand, authors such as Francis Fukuyama have argued, "We may be witnessing . . . the end of history as such: that is, the end point of mankind's ideological evolution and the universalization of Western liberal democracy as the final form of human government."[44] Fukuyama argues that the war of ideas may be at an end, and that liberal democracy has triumphed.

Others have questioned Fukuyama's vision of a more harmonious world dominated by a universal civilization characterized by democratic regimes and free market capitalism. In a controversial book, the influential political scientist Samuel Huntington argues there is no "universal" civilization based on widespread acceptance of Western liberal democratic ideals.[45] Huntington maintains that while many societies may be modernizing, in the sense that they have adopted the material paraphernalia of the modern world, from automobiles to Coca-Cola and MTV, they are not becoming more Western. On the contrary, Huntington theorizes that the process of modernization in non-Western societies can result in a retreat toward the traditional. For example, he says this about the resurgence of Islam in many traditionally Muslim societies:

> The Islamic resurgence is both a product of and an effort to come to grips with modernization. Its underlying causes are those generally responsible for indigenization trends in non-Western societies: urbanization, social mobilization, higher levels of literacy and education, intensified communication and media consumption, and expanded interaction with Western and other cultures. These developments undermine traditional village and clan ties and create alienation and an identity crisis. Islamist symbols, commitments, and beliefs meet these psychological needs, and Islamist welfare organizations, the social, cultural, and economic needs of Muslims caught in the process of modernization. Muslims feel a need to return to Islamic ideas, practices, and institutions to provide the compass and the motor of modernization.[46]

He portrays the rise of Islamic fundamentalism as a response to the alienation produced by modernization.

In contrast to Fukuyama, Huntington sees a world that is split into different civilizations, each of which has its own value systems and ideology. In addition to Western civilization, Huntington sees the emergence of strong Islamic and Chinese civilizations, as well as civilizations based on Japan, Africa, Latin America, Eastern Orthodox Christianity (Russian), and Hinduism (Indian). Moreover, Huntington sees the civilizations as headed for conflict, particularly along the "fault lines" that separate them, such as Bosnia (where Muslims and Orthodox Christians have clashed), Kashmir (where Muslims and Hindus clash), and the Sudan (where a bloody war between Christians and Muslims has persisted for decades). Figure 2.1 summarizes his views as to which civilizations are most likely to conflict in the future. Hunting-

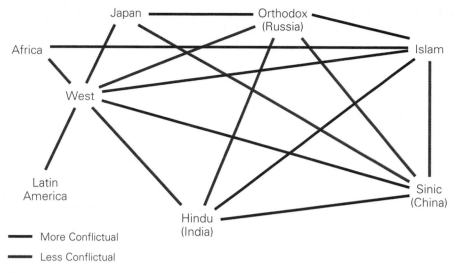

- ————— More Conflictual
- ——— Less Conflictual

Figure 2.1
The Global Politics of Civilizations
Reprinted with permission of Simon & Schuster from *The Clash of Civilizations and the Remaking of World Order* by Samuel P. Huntington. Copyright ©1996 by Samuel P. Huntington.

ton predicts conflict between the West and Islam and between the West and China. His predications are based on an analysis of the different value systems and ideology of these civilizations, which in his view tend to bring them into conflict with each other.

If Huntington's views are even partly correct, they have important implications for international business. They suggest many countries may be increasingly difficult places in which to do business, either because they suffer violent conflicts or because they are part of a civilization that is in conflict with that of an enterprise's home country. Remember, however, that Huntington's views are speculative. More likely, perhaps, is the evolution of a global political system that is positioned somewhere between Fukuyama's universal global civilization based on liberal democratic ideals and Huntington's vision of a fractured world. That would still be a world, however, in which geopolitical forces periodically limit the ability of business enterprises to operate in certain foreign countries.

The Spread of Market-Based Systems

Paralleling the spread of democracy, many countries have tried to transform their economic systems from centrally planned command economies to market-based economies. More than 30 countries that were in the former Soviet Union or the Eastern European Communist bloc are now shifting their economies. A complete list of countries would also include Asian states such as China and Vietnam, as well as African countries such as Angola, Ethiopia, and Mozambique.[47] There has been a similar shift away from a mixed economy. Many states in Asia, Latin America, and Western Europe have sold state-owned businesses to private investors (privatization) and deregulated their economies to promote greater competition. The accompanying "Country Focus" details India's changes.

The underlying rationale for economic transformation has been the same the world over. In general, command and mixed economies failed to deliver the kind of sustained economic performance that was achieved by countries adopting market-based

After gaining independence from Britain in 1947, India adopted a democratic system of government. The economic system that developed in India was a mixed economy characterized by a heavy dose of state enterprise and planning. This system placed major constraints around the growth of the private sector. Private companies could expand only with government permission. Under this system, derisively

ment of a healthy private sector was also stunted by production quotas and high tariffs on imports. Access to foreign exchange was limited, investment by foreign firms was restricted, land use was strictly controlled, and prices were routinely managed by the government, as opposed to being determined by market forces.

By the early 1990s it was clear that after 40 years of near

tation; and only 2.3 percent of the population had a household income in excess of $2,484. The World Bank estimated that some 40 percent of the world's desperately poor lived in India.

In 1991 the lack of progress led the government of Prime Minister P.V. Narasimha Rao to embark on an ambitious economic reform program. Much of the industrial licensing system was dismantled, and several areas once

The Changing Political Economy of India

dubbed the "License Raj," private companies often had to wait months for government approval of routine business activities, such as expanding production or hiring a new director. It could take years to get permission to diversify into a new product. Also, much of heavy industry, such as auto, chemical, and steel production, was reserved for state-owned enterprises. The develop-

stagnation this system was incapable of delivering the economic progress that many Southeast Asian nations had started to enjoy. In 1994 India had an economy that was smaller than Belgium's, despite having a population of 950 million. Its GDP per head was a paltry $310; less than half the population could read; only 6 million had access to telephones; only 14 percent had access to clean sani-

closed to the private sector were opened up, including electricity generation, parts of the oil industry, steelmaking, air transport, and some areas in the telecommunications industry. Foreign investment, formerly allowed only grudgingly and subject to arbitrary ceilings, was suddenly welcomed. Approval is now automatic for foreign equity stakes of up to 51 percent in an Indian enterprise,

systems, such as the United States, Switzerland, Hong Kong, and Taiwan. As a consequence, more states have gravitated toward the market-based model.

Map 2.6 illustrates the spread of market-based economic systems. This map is based on data from the Heritage Foundation, a conservative US research foundation, which constructed an index of economic freedom based on 10 indicators such as the extent to which the government intervenes in the economy, trade policy, the degree to which property rights are protected, foreign investment regulations, and taxation rules. A country can score between 1 (most free) and 5 (least free) on each indicators. The lower a country's average score across all 10 indicators, the more closely its economy represents the pure market model. According to the 1999 index, which is summarized in Map 2.6, the world's freest economies are (in rank order) Hong Kong, Singapore, Bahrain, New Zealand, Switzerland, the United States, Ireland, Luxembourg, Taiwan, and the United Kingdom. Japan is ranked 12, South Korea checks in at 28, France at 34, Indonesia at 65, Brazil at 90, Russia at 106, India at 120, China at 124, while the command economies of Cuba and North Korea prop up the bottom of the rankings.[48]

Economic freedom as shown in Map 2.6 does not necessarily equate with political freedom, as detailed in Map 2.5. For example, the top three countries in the Her-

and 100 percent foreign ownership is now allowed under certain circumstances. The government announced plans to privatize many of India's state-owned businesses. Raw materials and many industrial goods can now be freely imported, and the maximum tariff that can be levied on imports has been reduced from 400 percent to 65 percent. The top rate of income tax has also been cut, and corporate tax was reduced from 57.5 percent down to 46 percent in 1994 and then to 35 percent in 1997.

By some measures, the response was impressive. The economy expanded at an annual rate of almost 5 percent between 1992 and 1996, exports began to grow at a respectable pace (they were up 20 percent between 1993 and 1994), and corporate profits jumped. Delivery trucks loaded with once-banned foreign products, such as Ruffles potato chips and Nestlé Crunch bars, rumble over India's potholed highways. Advertisements for AT&T's communications solutions can be seen on New Delhi streets, signs of an upcoming liberalization of the telecommunications industry. Foreign investment, which is a good indicator of foreign companies' perceptions about the health of the Indian economy, surged from $150 million in 1991 to an estimated $3.5 billion in 1998.

However, India has still not achieved the kind of free market economic system now found in many Western nations. The reform process is being fought by many bureaucrats and politicians. Several Western companies now investing in India have painful memories of the 1970s when India nationalized the assets of foreign companies on terms that were tantamount to confiscation. Such memories are one reason why companies such as IBM, Coca-Cola, and Mobil have kept their investment modest. Other foreign companies have made major investment commitments to India only after securing special guarantees. For example, AES Corporation, a power-generating company based in Virginia, concluded a deal to build power stations in India, but only after the Indian government agreed to give guarantees that it would pay for power delivered to Indian electric utilities if the utilities defaulted.

Despite ambitious plans, India's privatization program has proceeded slowly. By 1997 the government had sold equity stakes in about 40 companies to private investors, including state-owned telecommunications, steel, and electronics enterprises. However, India still has about 245 state-owned companies, which are engaged in activities ranging from baking bread to making railway carriages. Many outside observers believe the government needs to accelerate its privatization program if it is to continue to attract foreign capital.[49]

itage Foundation index, Hong Kong, Singapore, and Bahrain, are not politically free. Hong Kong was reabsorbed into Communist China in 1997, and the first thing Beijing did was to shut down Hong Kong's freely elected legislature. Singapore is ranked as only "partly free" on Freedom House's index of political freedom due to practices such as widespread press censorship, while Bahrain is classified as "least free" due to the monopolization of political power by a hereditary monarchy (see Map 2.5).

The Nature of Economic Transformation

The shift toward a market-based economic system typically entails a number of steps. These include deregulation, privatization, and the creation of a legal system to safeguard property rights. We shall review each before looking at the track record of states engaged in economic transformation.

DEREGULATION **Deregulation** involves removing legal restrictions to the free play of markets, the establishment of private enterprises, and the manner in which private enterprises operate. For example, before the collapse of communism, the governments in most command economies exercised tight control over prices and outputs, setting both through detailed state planning. They also prohibited private

deregulation Removing legal restrictions to the free play of markets, the establishment of private enterprises, and the manner in which private enterprises operate.

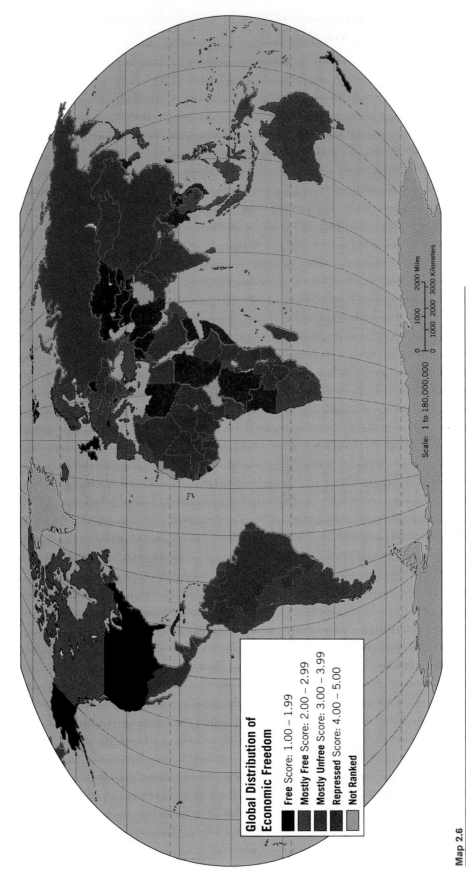

Map 2.6

Global Distribution of Economic Freedom

Source: *1999 Index of Economic Freedom*, The Heritage Foundation. Reprinted by permission of The Heritage Foundation.

Global Distribution of Economic Freedom

■ Free Score: 1.00 – 1.99
■ Mostly Free Score: 2.00 – 2.99
■ Mostly Unfree Score: 3.00 – 3.99
■ Repressed Score: 4.00 – 5.00
■ Not Ranked

Scale: 1 to 180,000,000

0   1000   2000 Miles
0 1000 2000 3000 Kilometers

enterprises from operating in most sectors of the economy. Deregulation in these cases involved the removal of price controls, thereby allowing prices to be set by the interplay between demand and supply, and the abolition of laws regulating the establishment and operation of private enterprises.

In mixed economies, deregulation has involved the abolition of laws that either prohibited private enterprises from competing in certain sectors of the economy or regulated the manner in which they operated. For example, as outlined in the "Country Focus" feature on India, deregulation there has involved reforming the industrial licensing system that made it difficult to establish private enterprises; opening areas that were once closed to the private sector such as electricity generation, parts of the oil industry, steelmaking, air transport, and some areas of the telecommunications industry; and removing restrictions to foreign investment. The Japanese government is trying to abolish some of the 11,000 regulations and 10,000 administrative guidelines that regulate and restrict private enterprise in that economy. For example, if a private enterprise wants to open a retail store with floor space of more than 1,000 square meters, it must first gain the consent of a government advisory panel charged with limiting the influence on local shop owners against which the new retail store wants to compete! In addition, the average large retailer must file more than 150 documents to gain permission to sell everyday items such as meat, tofu, and electric appliances. In an effort to unravel such restrictions, the Japanese government plans to deregulate a diverse range of industries including power generation, gasoline retailing, financial services, retail, telecommunications, and transportation.[50] How quickly this can be achieved, however, depends on the ability of a weak government to impose its wishes on Japan's traditionally powerful civil service bureaucracies, which can be expected to resist any attempt to diminish their influence on the economy.

PRIVATIZATION   Hand in hand with deregulation has been a sharp increase in privatization during the 1990s. Privatization involves transferring the ownership of state property into the hands of private individuals, frequently by the sale of state assets through an auction.[51] Privatization is seen as a way to unlock gains in economic efficiency by giving new private owners a powerful incentive—the reward of greater profits—to search for increases in productivity, to enter new markets, and to exit failing ones.

The privatization movement started in Britain in the early 1980s when then-Prime Minister Margaret Thatcher started to sell state-owned assets, such as the British telephone company, British Telecom (BT). In a pattern that has been repeated around the world, this sale was linked with the deregulation of the British telecommunications industry. By allowing other firms to compete head-to-head with BT, deregulation ensured that privatization did not simply replace a state-owned monopoly with a private monopoly.

The opening case to this chapter details the extent of privatization in Brazil, and the "Country Focus" discusses privatization in India. As these two examples suggest, privatization has become a worldwide movement. In Africa, for example, Mozambique and Zambia are leading the way with very ambitious privatization plans. Zambia has put over 145 state-owned companies up for sale, while Mozambique has sold scores of enterprises, ranging from tea plantations to a chocolate factory. The most dramatic privatization programs, however, have occurred in the economies of the former Soviet Union and its Eastern European satellite states. There huge changes in the ownership of economic assets have been engineered by privatization programs. In the Czech Republic, for example, three-quarters of all state-owned enterprises were privatized between 1989 and 1996, pushing the share of gross domestic product accounted for by the private sector up from 11 percent in 1989 to 60 percent in 1995.

In Russia, where the private sector had been almost completely repressed before 1989, 50 percent of GDP was in private hands by 1995. And in Poland the private sector accounted for 59 percent of GDP in 1995, up from 20 percent in 1989.[52] However, Poland also illustrates how far some of these countries still have to travel, for despite an aggressive privatization program, Poland still had 4,000 state-owned enterprises that dominate the heavy industry, mining, and transportation sectors.

LEGAL SYSTEMS As noted earlier in this chapter, a well-functioning market economy requires laws protecting private property rights and providing mechanisms for contract enforcement. Without a legal system that protects property rights, and without the machinery to enforce that system, the incentive to engage in economic activity can be reduced substantially by private and public entities, including organized crime, that expropriate the profits generated by private-sector entrepreneurs. As noted earlier, this has become a problem in many former Communist states, such as Russia, where organized crime has penetrated deeply into the fabric of many business enterprises. When communism collapsed many of these countries lacked the legal structure required to protect property rights, all property having been held by the state. Although many states have made big strides toward putting the required system in place, it will be many more years before the legal system is functioning as smoothly as it does in the West. For example, in most Eastern European nations the title to urban and agricultural property is often uncertain because of incomplete and inaccurate records, multiple pledges on the same property, and unsettled claims resulting from demands for restitution from owners in the pre-Communist era. While most countries have improved their commercial codes, institutional weaknesses still undermine contract enforcement. Court capacity is often inadequate, and procedures for resolving contract disputes out of court are often inadequate or poorly developed.[53]

THE ROCKY ROAD The road that must be traveled to reach a market-based economic system is often rocky.[54] This has been particularly true for the states of Eastern Europe in the post-Communist era. In this region, the move toward greater political and economic freedom has been accompanied by economic and political chaos.[55] Most Eastern European states began to liberalize their economies in the heady days of the early 1990s. They dismantled decades of price controls, allowed widespread private ownership of businesses, and permitted much greater competition. Most also planned to sell state-owned enterprises to private investors. However, given the vast number of such enterprises and how inefficient many were, and thus unappealing to private investors, most privatization efforts moved forward slowly. Many inefficient state-owned enterprises found that they could not survive without a guaranteed market. The newly democratic governments often continued to support these enterprises in an attempt to stave off massive unemployment. The resulting subsidies to state-owned enterprises led to ballooning budget deficits that were typically financed by printing money. The tendency of governments to print money, along with the lack of price controls, often led to hyperinflation. In 1993 the inflation rate was 21 percent in Hungary, 38 percent in Poland, 841 percent in Russia, and a staggering 10,000 percent in the Ukraine.[56] Since then, however, many governments have instituted tight monetary policies and reduced their inflation rates. By 1995, for example, Russia's inflation rate was less than 7 percent a month.

Collapsing output was another consequence of the shift toward a market economy as inefficient state-owned enterprises failed to find buyers for their goods. Real gross domestic product fell dramatically in many post-Communist states in the 1990–94 period. However, the corner has been turned in a number of countries. Poland, the Czech Republic, and Hungary now all boast growing economies and relatively low inflation. But countries such as Russia and the Ukraine still find themselves grappling with major economic problems.

A study by the World Bank suggests that the post-Communist nations that have been most successful at transforming their economies were those that followed an economic policy described as "shock therapy." In these countries—which include the Czech Republic, Hungary, and Poland—prices and trade were liberated quickly, inflation was held in check by tight monetary policy, and the privatization of state-owned industries was implemented rapidly. Among the 26 economies of Eastern Europe and the former Soviet Union, the World Bank found a strong positive correlation between the imposition of such "shock therapy" and subsequent economic growth. Speedy reformers suffered smaller falls in output and returned to growth more quickly than those such as Russia and the Ukraine that moved more slowly.[57]

Implications

The global changes in political and economic systems discussed above have several implications for international business. It would seem that the ideological conflict between collectivism and individualism that so defined the 20th century is winding down. The free market ideology of the West has won the Cold War and has never been more widespread. Although command economies still remain, and although totalitarian dictatorships can still be found, the tide is running in favor of free markets and democracy.

The implications for business are enormous. For nearly 50 years half the world was off-limits to Western businesses. Now all that is changing. Many of the national markets of Eastern Europe, Latin America, Africa, and Asia may still be undeveloped and impoverished, but they are potentially enormous. With a population of 1.2 billion, the Chinese market is potentially bigger than that of the United States, the European Union, and Japan combined! Similarly India, with its 950 million people, is a potentially huge market. Latin America has another 400 million potential consumers. It is unlikely that China, Russia, Poland, or any of the other states now moving toward a free market system will attain the living standards of the West soon. Nevertheless, the potential is so large that companies need to consider making inroads now.

However, just as the upside potential is large, so are the risks. There is no guarantee that democracy will thrive in Eastern Europe particularly if these states have to grapple with severe economic setbacks. Totalitarian dictatorships could return, although they are unlikely to be of the Communist variety. Although the bipolar world of the Cold War era has vanished, it may be replaced by a multipolar world dominated by a number of civilizations. In such a world, much of the economic promise inherent in the global shift toward market-based economic systems may evaporate in the face of conflicts between civilizations. While the long-term potential for economic gain from investment in the world's new market economies is large, the risks associated with any such investment are also substantial. It would be foolish to ignore these.

Implications for Business

The implications for international business of the material discussed in this chapter fall into two broad categories. First, the political, economic, and legal environment of a country clearly influences the *attractiveness* of that country as a market and/or investment site. The benefits, costs, and risks associated with doing business in a country are in part a function of that country's political, economic, and legal systems. Second, the political, economic, and legal systems of a country can raise important *ethical issues* that have implications for international business. Here we consider each of these issues.

Attractiveness

The overall attractiveness of a country as a market and/or investment site depends on balancing the likely long-term benefits of doing business in that country against the likely costs and risks. Below we consider the determinants of benefits, costs, and risks.

BENEFITS   In a general sense the long-run monetary benefits of doing business in a country are a function of the size of the market, the present wealth (purchasing power) of consumers in that market, and the likely future wealth of consumers. While some markets are very large when measured in number of consumers (e.g., China and India), low living standards may imply limited purchasing power and, therefore, a relatively small market when measured in economic terms. While international businesses need to be aware of this distinction, they also need to keep in mind the likely future prospects of a country. In 1960, for example, South Korea was viewed as just another impoverished Third World nation. By 1996 it was the world's 11th largest economy, measured in terms of GDP. International firms that recognized South Korea's potential in 1960 and began to do business in that country may have reaped greater benefits than those that wrote-off South Korea.

By identifying and investing early in a potential future economic star, international firms may be able to build up brand loyalty and experience in that country. These will pay substantial dividends if that country achieves sustained high economic growth rates. Late entrants may find that they lack the brand loyalty and business experience necessary to achieve a significant presence in the market. In the language of business strategy, early entrants into potential future economic stars may be able to reap substantial **first-mover advantages,** while late entrants may fall victim to **late-mover disadvantages.**[58] (First-mover advantages are the benefits that accrue to early entrants into a market. Late-mover disadvantages are the handicap that late entrants might suffer.)

Two factors that are reasonably good predictors of a country's future economic prospects are its economic system and property rights regime. In this chapter we have seen that countries with free market economies in which property rights are protected tend to achieve greater economic growth rates than command economies and/or economies where property rights are poorly protected. A country's economic system, property rights regime, and market size (in terms of population) probably constitute reasonably good indicators of the potential long-run benefits of doing business in a country.[59]

COSTS   The costs of doing business in a country are determined by a number of political, economic, and legal factors. With regard to political factors, the costs can be increased by a need to pay off the politically powerful to be allowed by the government to do business in that country. The need to pay what are essentially bribes generally is greater in closed totalitarian states than in open democratic societies where politicians are held accountable by the electorate. Whether a company should pay bribes in return for market access should be determined on the basis of the legal and ethical implications of such action. We discuss this consideration below.

With regard to economic factors, one important variable is the sophistication of a country's economy. It may be more costly to do business in relatively primitive or undeveloped economies because of the lack of infrastructure and supporting businesses. At the extreme, an international firm may have to provide its own infrastructure and supporting business if it wishes to do business in a country, which obviously raises costs. For example, when McDonald's decided to open its first restaurant in Moscow, it found that to serve food and drink indistinguishable from that served in McDonald's restaurants elsewhere, it had to vertically integrate backward to supply its own

first-mover advantages Advantages that accrue to early entrants into a business market.

late-mover disadvantages Handicap suffered by late entrants into a business market.

needs. The quality of Russian-grown potatoes and meat was too poor. Thus, to protect the quality of its product, McDonald's set up its own dairy farms, cattle ranches, vegetable plots, and food processing plants in Russia. This raised the costs of doing business in Russia, relative to the costs in more sophisticated economies where high-quality inputs could be purchased on the open market.

As for legal factors, it can be more costly to do business in a country where local laws and regulations set strict standards regarding product safety, safety in the workplace, environmental pollution, and the like (since adhering to such regulations is costly). It can also be more costly to do business in a country such as the United States, where the absence of a cap on damage awards has meant spiraling liability insurance rates. It can be more costly to do business in a country that lacks well-established laws for regulating business practice (as is the case in many of the former Communist nations). Without a well-developed body of business contract law, international firms may find there is no satisfactory way to resolve contract disputes and so face large losses from contract violations. Similarly, local laws that fail to adequately protect intellectual property can lead to the "theft" of an international business's intellectual property and thus to lost income (see the "Management Focus" on Microsoft).

RISKS   As with costs, the risks of doing business in a country are determined by a number of political, economic, and legal factors. On the political front, there is the issue of **political risk.** Political risk has been defined as *the likelihood that political forces will cause drastic changes in a country's business environment that adversely affects the profit and other goals of a particular business enterprise.*[60] Political risk tends to be greater in countries experiencing social unrest and disorder or in countries where the underlying nature of society means the likelihood of social unrest is high. Social unrest typically finds expression in strikes, demonstrations, terrorism, and violent conflict. Such unrest is more likely to be found in countries that contain more than one ethnic nationality, where competing ideologies are battling for political control, where economic mismanagement has created high inflation and falling living standards, or where "fault lines" between civilizations are straddled, such as Bosnia.

Social unrest can result in abrupt changes in government and government policy or in protracted civil strife. Such strife tends to have negative economic implications, which may affect the profit goals of business enterprises. For example, in the aftermath of the 1979 Islamic revolution in Iran, the Iranian assets of numerous US companies were seized by the new Iranian government without compensation. Similarly, the violent disintegration of the Yugoslavian federation into warring states, including Bosnia, Croatia, and Serbia, precipitated a collapse in the local economies and, consequently, a collapse in the profitability of investments in those countries.

On the economic front, **economic risks** arise from economic mismanagement by the government of a country. Economic risks can be defined as *the likelihood that economic mismanagement will cause drastic changes in a country's business environment that adversely affect the profit and other goals of a particular business enterprise.* Economic risks are not independent of political risk. Economic mismanagement may give rise to significant social unrest and hence political risk. One visible indicator of economic mismanagement tends to be a country's inflation rate. Another tends to be the level of business and government debt. In Asian states such as Indonesia, Thailand, and South Korea, businesses increased their debt rapidly during the 1990s, often at the bequest of the government, which was encouraging them to invest in industries deemed to be of "strategic importance" to the country. The result was overinvestment, with more industrial (factories) and commercial capacity (office space) being built than could be justified by demand conditions. Many of these investments, turned out to be uneconomic.

political risk
Likelihood that political forces will cause drastic changes in a country's business environment that adversely affect the profit and other goals of a business enterprise.

economic risk Likelihood that economic mismanagement will cause drastic changes in a country's business environment that adversely affect the profit and other goals of a business enterprise.

The borrowers were unable to generate the profits required to meet their debt payment obligations. In turn, the banks that had lent money to these businesses suddenly found that they had a rapid increase in nonperforming loans on their books. Foreign investors, believing that many local companies and banks might go bankrupt, pulled their money out of these countries, selling local stocks, bonds, and currency. This action precipitated the 1997–98 financial crisis in Southeast Asia. The crisis included a precipitous decline in the value of Asian stock markets, which in some cases exceed 70 percent; a similar collapse in the value of many Asian currencies against the US dollar; an implosion of local demand; and a severe economic recession that will affect many Asian countries for years. In short, economic risks were rising throughout Southeast Asia during the 1990s. Astute foreign businesses and investors, seeing this situation, would have limited their exposure in this part of the world in advance of the collapse. More naive businesses and investors would have lost their shirts!

On the legal front, risks arise when a country's legal system fails to provide adequate safeguards in the case of contract violations or to provide for the protection of property rights. When legal safeguards are weak, firms are more likely to break contracts and/or steal intellectual property if they perceive it as being in their interests to do so. Thus, **legal risks** might be defined as *the likelihood that a trading partner will opportunistically break a contract or expropriate property rights.* When legal risks are high, an international business might hesitate to enter into a long-term contract or joint venture with a firm in that country. For example, in the 1970s when the Indian government enacted a law requiring all foreign investors to enter into joint ventures with Indian companies, US companies such as IBM and Coca-Cola closed their investments in India. They did this because they believed the Indian legal system did not adequately protect intellectual property rights. Thus, the danger existed that the Indian partners of IBM and Coca-Cola might expropriate the intellectual property of the American companies, which for both IBM and Coca-Cola amounted to the core of their competitive advantage.

legal risk Likelihood that a trading partner will opportunistically break a contract or expropriate property rights.

OVERALL ATTRACTIVENESS The overall attractiveness of a country as a potential market and/or investment site for an international business depends on balancing the benefits, costs, and risks associated with doing business in that country. The costs and risks associated with doing business in a foreign country are typically lower in economically advanced and politically stable democratic nations, and they generally are greater in less developed and politically unstable nations. The calculus is complicated, however, by the fact that the potential *long-run* benefits bear little relationship to a nation's current stage of economic development or political stability. Rather, they depend on likely future economic growth rates. In turn, economic growth appears to be a function of a free market system and a country's capacity for growth (which may be greater in less developed nations). This one to the conclusion that, other things being equal, the benefit–cost–risk trade-off is likely to be most favorable in politically stable developed and developing nations that have free market systems where there is not a dramatic upsurge in either inflation rates or private sector debt. It is likely to be least favorable in politically unstable developing nations that operate with a mixed or command economy or in developing nations where speculative financial bubbles have led to excess borrowing.

Ethical Issues

Country differences give rise to important and contentious ethical issues. Three important issues that have been the focus of much debate in recent years are *(i)* the ethics of doing business in nations that violate human rights, *(ii)* the ethics of doing business in countries with very lax labor and environmental regulations, and *(iii)* the ethics of corruption.

ETHICS AND HUMAN RIGHTS   One major ethical dilemma facing firms from democratic nations is whether they should do business in totalitarian countries that routinely violate the human rights of their citizens (such as China). There are two sides to this issue.

Some argue that investing in totalitarian countries provides comfort to dictators and props up repressive regimes that abuse basic human rights. For instance, Human Rights Watch, an organization that promotes the protection of basic human rights around the world, has argued that the progressive trade policies adopted by Western nations toward China has done little to encourage the Chinese to limit human rights abuses.[61] According to Human Rights Watch, the Chinese government stepped up its repression of political dissidents in 1996 after the Clinton administration removed human rights as a factor in determining China's trade status with the United States. Critics such as Human Rights Watch argue that many repressive regimes would collapse and be replaced by more democratically inclined governments if investment by Western firms and support of Western governments were removed. In recent years, firms that have invested in Chile, China, Iraq, and South Africa have all been the direct targets of such criticisms. The 1994 dismantling of the apartheid system in South Africa has been credited to economic sanctions by Western nations, including a lack of investment by Western firms. This, say those who argue against investment in totalitarian countries, is proof that investment boycotts can work (although decades of US-led investment boycotts against Cuba and Iran, among other countries, have failed to have a similar impact).

In contrast, there are those who argue that investment by a Western firm can help change a totalitarian country from within by raising the level of economic development. They note that economic well-being and political freedoms often go hand in hand. Thus, when arguing against attempts to apply trade sanctions to China in the wake of the violent 1989 government crackdown on prodemocracy demonstrators, the Bush administration claimed that US firms should continue to be allowed to invest in mainland China because greater political freedoms would follow the resulting economic growth. The Clinton administration used similar logic as the basis for its 1996 decision to decouple human rights issues from trade policy considerations.

Because both positions have merit, it is difficult to arrive at a general statement of what firms should do. Unless mandated by government (as in the case of investment in South Africa) each firm must make its own judgments about the ethical implications of investment in totalitarian states on a case-by-case basis. The more repressive the regime, however, and the less amenable it seems to be to change, the greater the case for not investing.

ETHICS AND REGULATIONS   A second important ethical issue is whether an international firm should adhere to the same standards of product safety, work safety, and environmental protection that are required in its home country. This is of particular concern to many firms based in Western nations, where such standards are among the toughest in the world. Should Western firms investing in less developed countries adhere to tough Western standards, even though local regulations don't require them to do so? This issue has taken on added importance after revelations that Western enterprises have been using child labor or very poorly paid "sweatshop" labor in developing nations. Companies criticized for using sweatshop labor include the Gap, Disney, Wal-Mart, and Nike.[62]

Again there is no easy answer. While the argument for adhering to Western standards might seem strong, on closer examination the issue becomes more complicated. What if adhering to Western standards would make the foreign investment unprofitable, thereby denying the foreign country much-needed jobs? What then is the ethical thing to do? As with many ethical dilemmas, there is no easy answer. Each case needs to be assessed on its own merits.

Foreign Corrupt Practices Act US law enacted in 1977 that prohibits US companies from making "corrupt" payments to foreign officials for the purpose of obtaining or retaining business.

ETHICS AND CORRUPTION   A final ethical issue concerns bribes and corruption. Should an international business pay bribes to corrupt government officials in order to gain market access to a foreign country? To most Westerners bribery seems to be a corrupt and morally repugnant way of doing business, so the answer might initially be no. Some countries have laws that prohibit their citizens from paying bribes to foreign government officials in return for economic favors. In the United States, for example, the **Foreign Corrupt Practices Act** of 1977 prohibits US companies from making "corrupt" payments to foreign officials for the purpose of obtaining or retaining business. Many developed nations lack similar laws. Trade and finance ministers from the member states of the Organization for Economic Cooperation and Development (the OECD), an association of the world's 20 most powerful economies, are working on a convention that would oblige member states to make the bribery of foreign public officials a criminal offense.

However, in many parts of the world payoffs to government officials are a part of life. One can argue that not investing if bribes are required ignores the fact that such investment can bring substantial benefits to the local populace in terms of income and jobs. The practice of giving bribes, although a little evil, may be the price that must be paid to do a greater good (assuming the investment creates jobs where none existed before and assuming that the practice is not illegal). This kind of reasoning has been advocated by several economists, who suggest that in the context of cumbersome regulations in developing countries, corruption may actually improve efficiency and help growth! These economists theorize that in a country where political structures distort or limit the workings of the market mechanism, corruption in the form of black marketeering, smuggling, and making side payments to government bureaucrats to "speed up" approval for business investments may actually enhance welfare.[63]

However, other economists have argued that corruption can reduce the returns on business investment.[64] In a country where corruption is common, the profits from a business activity may be siphoned off by unproductive bureaucrats who demand side payments for granting the enterprise permission to operate. This reduces the incentive for businesses to invest and may hamper a country's economic growth rate. A recent study by one economist of the connection between corruption and growth in 70 countries found that corruption had a significant negative impact on a country's economic growth rate.[65]

Given the debate and the complexity of this issue, one again might conclude that generalization is difficult. Yes, corruption is bad, and yes, it may hurt a country's economic development, but yes, there are cases where side payments to government officials can remove the bureaucratic barriers to investments that create jobs. However, this pragmatic stance ignores, that corruption tends to "corrupt" both the bribe giver and the bribe taker. Corruption feeds on itself, and once an individual has started to walk down the road of corruption, pulling back will be difficult. If this is so, it strengthens the moral case for never engaging in corruption, no matter how compelling the benefits might seem to be.

Key Terms

Summary

This chapter reviewed how the political, economic, and legal systems of different countries vary. We noted that the potential benefits, costs, and risks of doing business in a country are a function of its political, economic, and legal systems. More specifically:

1 Political systems can be assessed according to two dimensions: the degree to which they emphasize collectivism as opposed to individualism, and the degree to which they are democratic or totalitarian.

2 Collectivism is an ideology that views the needs of society as being more important than the needs of the individual. Collectivism translates into an advocacy for state intervention in economic activity and, in the case of communism, a totalitarian dictatorship.

3 Individualism is an ideology that emphasizes the primacy of individuals' freedom in the political, economic, and cultural realms. Individualism translates into an advocacy for democratic ideals and free market economics.

4 Democracy and totalitarianism are at different ends of a political spectrum. In a representative democracy, citizens periodically elect individuals to represent them and political freedoms are guaranteed by a constitution. In a totalitarian state, political power is monopolized by a party, group, or individual, and basic political freedoms are denied to citizens.

5 There are four broad types of economic system: a market economy, a command economy, a mixed economy, and a state-directed economy. In a market economy prices are free of any controls and private ownership is predominant. In a command economy prices are set by central planners, productive assets are owned by the state, and private ownership is forbidden. A mixed economy has elements of both a market economy and a command economy. In a state-directed economy the state plays a significant role in directing the investment activities of private enterprise through "industrial policy" and in otherwise regulating business activity in accordance with national goals.

6 Differences in the structure of law between countries can have important implications for international business. The degree to which property rights are protected can vary dramatically as can product safety and product liability legislation and the nature of contract law.

7 The rate of economic progress in a country seems to depend on the extent to which that country has a well-functioning market economy in which property rights are protected.

8 Many countries are now in transition. There is a shift away from totalitarian governments and command or mixed economic systems and toward democratic political institutions and free market economic systems.

9 It is not clear, however, that we are witnessing the emergence of a universal global civilization based on democratic institutions and free market capitalism. It is

possible that the bipolar world of the Cold War era may ultimately be replaced by a multipolar world of ideologically divergent civilizations.

10 The attractiveness of a country as a market and/or investment site depends on balancing the likely long-run benefits of doing business in that country against the likely costs and risks.

11 The benefits of doing business in a country are a function of the size of the market (population), its present wealth (purchasing power), and its future growth prospects. By investing early in countries that are currently poor but are growing rapidly, firms can gain first-mover advantages that will pay back substantial dividends in the future.

12 The costs of doing business in a country tend to be greater in those countries where political payoffs are required to gain market access, where supporting infrastructure is lacking or underdeveloped, and where adhering to local laws and regulations is costly.

13 The risks of doing business in a country tend to be greater in countries that are politically unstable, are subject to economic mismanagement, and have inadequate safeguards to protect against contract violations or the loss of property rights.

14 Country differences give rise to several ethical dilemmas. These including (i) should a firm do business in a repressive totalitarian state, (ii) should a firm conform to its home product, workplace, and environmental standards when they are not required by host country laws, and (iii) should a firm pay bribes to government officials in order to gain market access?

Critical Thinking and Discussion Questions

1 Free market economies stimulate greater economic growth, whereas state-directed economies stifle growth! Discuss.

2 A democratic political system is essential for *sustained* economic progress. Discuss.

3 During the late 1980s and early 1990s, China was routinely cited by various international organizations such as Amnesty International and Freedom Watch for major human rights violations, including torture, beatings, imprisonment, and executions of political dissidents. Despite this, in the mid-1990s China was the recipient of record levels of foreign direct investment, mainly from firms based in democratic societies such as the United States, Japan, and Germany. Evaluate this trend from an ethical perspective. If you were the chief executive officer (CEO) of a firm that had the option of making a potentially very profitable investment in China, what would you do?

4 You are the CEO of a company that has to choose between making a $100 million investment in either Russia or the Czech Republic. Both investments promise the same long-term return, so your choice of which investment to make is driven by considerations of risk. Assess the various risks of doing business in each of these nations. Which investment would you favor and why?

Internet Exercises

1 A key component in the globalization of the world economy involves the transfer of intellectual material across borders. Access to new ideas and information is an important means of development in most economies. Today, thanks to the Internet, the flow of information is much easier; intellectual ideas and property can be exchanged across borders almost instantaneously. Companies operating on-line, such as bookseller Amazon.com, are facilitating this flow of ideas, and in turn the globalization of the world economy.

Published materials, especially in the form of books, are an important part of the exchange of new ideas. In the past, because publishers or agents held the rights to books, consumers in countries where legitimate copes of a book were unavailable had very limited access to foreign books. For example, Kitty Kelly's book *The Royals* was initially banned in Great Britain, although it was readily available in the United States. Today, however, because companies such as Amazon.com have websites that are accessible to anyone anywhere with a computer and a modem, these barriers have disappeared. Consumers who want a particular book can simply order it on-line. Go to **www.amazon.com** and click on the Option for the company's foreign sites. Explore the bookseller's international sites and compare the titles that are available, particularly those that are listed among the best-sellers. What similarities do you find? What do your findings imply in terms of the globalization of the world economy and the transfer of intellectual property?

2 The previous exercise examined the role of on-line booksellers in the transfer of intellectual property. On-line booksellers have made the exchange of published materials from around the world open to nearly everyone. This phenomenon threatens to challenge governments' ability to restrict the flow of ideas, a critical component of some governments' philosophies. Even in locations where the rights for translated versions of books have not been sold, English versions are now available through the Internet.

Go to **www.barnesandnoble. com.** Examine the company's non-US sites and explore the politically oriented as well as the pop culture books that are currently top sellers. Search for books that are available in multiple locations either in the local language or in the original language. Consider what role English, now often referred to as the universal language, has in the globalization of markets. Then, consider the role of English in the exchange of political ideas. In your opinion, will markets and governments be brought closer together because of these flows of intellectual property? What effect will the newest form of published material, electronic books, have on the process?

General Electric in Hungary

In the heady days of late 1989 when Communist regimes were disintegrating across Eastern Europe, General Electric Company (GE) launched a major expansion in Hungary with the $150 million acquisition of a 51 percent interest in Tungsram. A manufacturer of lighting products, Tungsram was widely regarded as one of Hungary's industrial gems. GE was attracted to Tungsram by Hungary's low wage rates and by the possibility of using the company to export lighting products to Western Europe. Like many other Western companies, GE believed that Hungary's shift from a totalitarian Communist country with a state-owned and planned economic system to a politically democratic country with a largely free market economic system would create enormous long-term business opportunities.

At the time, many observers believed that General Electric would show other Western companies how to turn enterprises once run by Communist Party hacks into capitalist moneymakers. GE promptly transferred some of its best management to Tungsram and waited for the miracle to happen. The miracle was slow in coming. As losses mounted General Electric faced the reality of what happens when grand expectations collide with the grim realities of an embedded culture of waste, inefficiency, and indifference about customers and quality.

The American managers complained that the Hungarians were lackadaisical; the Hungarians thought the Americans pushy. The company's aggressive management system depended on communication between workers and managers; the old Communist system had forbidden this, and changing attitudes at Tungsram proved difficult. The Americans wanted strong sales and marketing functions that would pamper customers; used to life in a centrally planned economy, the Hungarians believed that these things took care of themselves. Hungarians expected GE to deliver Western-style wages, but GE came to Hungary to take advantage of the country's low wages.

In retrospect, GE managers admit they underestimated how long it would take to turn Tungsram around—and how much it would cost. As Charles Pipper, Tungsram's American general manager, said, "Human engineering was much more difficult than product engineering." GE believes it has turned the corner. However, getting to this point meant laying off half of Tungsram's 20,000 employees, in-cluding two out of every three managers. It also meant an additional $440 million investment in new plant and equipment and in retraining the employees and managers that remained. By 1997 the investments seemed to be paying off. Despite a 50 percent cut in the workforce, production volume was double the 1989 level.[66]

CASE DISCUSSION QUESTIONS

1 What does GE's experience in Hungary tell you about the relationships among economic systems, political systems, and national culture?

2 Given the problems GE experienced with Tungsram, in retrospect might it have chosen a better strategy to attack the Western European lighting products market?

3 How important to the economic development of Hungary are investments like that undertaken by GE? What benefits does GE bring to Hungary?

4 If Tungsram had continued under local ownership, what do you think would have been the fate of the company?

three

Differences
in Culture

Chapter

Opening Case   A Scotsman
at Mazda

In 1996 a small earthquake hit Japan—Henry Wallace, a Scotsman, was appointed head of Hiroshima-based Mazda, Japan's fifth-largest auto manufacturer. Although Mazda had a proud history as one of Japan's more innovative automobile manufacturers, the company seemed to have lost its way in the 1990s. With Japan mired in a prolonged recession, Mazda saw its domestic sales shrink. At the same time, the company was unable to expand its

When Scotsman Henry Wallace was appointed as head of Mazda, several Japanese employees of the company thought that many of the company's organizational practices and relationships would be adversely affected. After all, these practices and relationships are influenced by the country's cultural traditions, something a foreigner would know little about and have trouble understanding. Four years later, Wallace is making improvements to Mazda's performance and repeatedly emphasizes that he is not trying to dismantle the traditional supplier network, or *keiretsu*.

Learning Objectives

1 Understand that substantial differences between societies arise from cultural differences.

2 Know what is meant by the term *culture*.

3 Appreciate that cultures vary because of differences in social structure, religion, language, education, economic philosophy, and political philosophy.

4 Understand the relationship between culture and the values found in the workplace.

5 Appreciate that culture is not a constant, but changes over time.

6 Appreciate that much of the change in contemporary social culture is being driven by economic advancement, technological change, and globalization.

7 Understand the implications for international business management of differences among cultures.

---

international sales to make up for the shortfall. From the peak of 1.4 million units in 1990, Mazda's sales had slumped to 770,000 units in 1995. In the fiscal year ending in March 1995 the company lost the equivalent of $710 million, and in the year ending March 1996 it managed a thin profit of $2.7 million. This poor performance was too much for its major shareholder, the Ford Motor Company of the United States. Ford responded by increas-

ing its stake in Mazda to 33.4 percent with a $500 million investment and placing one of its own, Wallace, as president.

Wallace, who before moving to Mazda had been the president of Ford's Venezuela operation, was the first foreigner to head a major Japanese company. The appointment was greeted with some trepidation in Hiroshima. Like many Japanese companies, Mazda's organization practices and business

relationships had been influenced by the country's cultural traditions. The company honored the practice of lifetime employment. Internal promotions were based primarily on seniority. Decision making was consensus-based, and there was an emphasis on harmony and a reluctance to create discord within the management group. Mazda also had long-standing "family-like" relationships with an extensive network of local suppliers.

Many in Hiroshima feared that Wallace's appointment would signal an end to all this. How would Wallace's decisions affect a community where 40 percent of the workforce depended directly or indirectly on Mazda? Would lifetime employment be replaced by American-style layoffs? How would Wallace function in a society and company that valued long-term relationships, trust, and reciprocal obligations? Would Wallace break decades long commitments to local suppliers and instead purchase more parts from overseas? The head of one small Hiroshima supplier noted, "If the president were Japanese he would have some sympathy towards us. He would think, 'You have been working hard for Mazda, even in times of difficulties, so we will support you.' He would take care so that as many companies as possible would survive."

Others worried about what would happen to Mazda's consensus-based decision making. When the Japanese have a meeting, "only those who are opposed to a proposal speak," noted Takeshi Morikawa, the president of Mazda's workers union, in an interview. "If you are for an idea, you keep quiet. But Ford people speak, even if they are for an idea. They ask questions, or they speak about why they are for the idea. So at some meetings the Japanese think that foreigners are dominating the floor too much . . . In Japan, asking about details can seem to be an attack on the integrity of the person. Just look into my eyes and then you will know. So the questioning process to a Japanese is a problem. They don't understand it."

Another concern centered on whether a man whose command of Japanese was highly imperfect could possibly understand the cultural context within which business decisions were made in Japan.

Wallace also admitted to having concerns, particularly with communication. As he observed in a 1996 interview, "In the West we have this direct communication. But in Japan it's indirect communication. Very often you are left to draw your own conclusions . . . It's particularly difficult to have brainstorming sessions. When you have to go through an interpreter, all you get back is the answer to your question. You don't get back the wider view."

Eighteen months into his job, Wallace seemed to be making progress improving Mazda's performance, while simultaneously easing some fears that followed his appointment. A clear strategy had been articulated where none existed before. The workforce had been reduced, but through attrition rather than layoffs and the lifetime employment system remains intact. Some suppliers were cut as orders for parts were shifted to lower-cost sources overseas, but the shift was not as dramatic as many feared it might be. Wallace repeatedly emphasized that he was not trying to dismantle the traditional supplier network, or keiretsu. Several unprofitable models were discontinued, and more attention was focused on marketing and market research than had historically been the case at Mazda. Big changes also occurred in the internal management structure and decision-making processes. Merit became a much more important basis for promotions, while decision making shifted away from the old consensus-based system and toward a system characterized by more spirited debate.

Wallace also noted that being Western was an advantage. Because foreigners are always expected to act differently, Wallace was able to cross the lines of Japan's hierarchical business world in ways that would be more difficult for a Japanese president. For example, the day after he was appointed president Wallace asked the leaders of Mazda's union to talk with him, an action that was unprecedented at Mazda. Wallace also took the unusual step of sharing confidential strategic information with the union leaders in order to win their cooperation—a move that so far has been successful.[1]

Introduction

International business is different from domestic business because countries are different. In Chapter 2 we saw how national differences in political, economic, and legal systems influence the benefits, costs, and risks associated with doing business in different countries. In this chapter we will explore how differences in culture across *and* within countries can affect international business. Two themes run through this chapter.

The first theme is that cross-cultural literacy is required to successfully conduct business in a variety of countries. By cross-cultural literacy, we mean an understanding of how cultural differences across *and* within nations can affect the way in which business is practiced. In these days of global communications, rapid transportation, and global markets, when the era of the global village seems just around the corner, it is easy to forget just how different various cultures really are. Under-

Continued

86

neath the veneer of modernism, deep cultural differences often remain. Westerners in general, and Americans in particular, are prone to jump to the conclusion that because people from other parts of the world also wear blue jeans, listen to Western popular music, eat at McDonald's, and drink Coca-Cola, they also accept the basic tenets of Western (or American) culture. Just because someone has adopted the symbols of modern consumer society does not mean they have also adopted Western value systems. Many of the "Islamic militants" who invaded the American embassy in Iran after the revolution that ousted the pro-Western shah wore blue jeans, but they certainly showed no love of American values.

Japan is another example. The Japanese have embraced the products of modern society, but as the opening case demonstrates, the country's long-standing cultural traditions continue to have an important impact on many aspects of Japanese life, including the organization and management principles of enterprises such as Mazda. However, the opening case also illustrates that a sophisticated manager who is willing to work within the constraints of traditional values can change some of those management principles. Despite his lack of Japanese language skills, Henry Wallace displayed a sensitivity for important culturally grounded institutions in Japan, such as lifetime employment and reciprocal relationships with suppliers. A less sophisticated Western manager might have pushed for large-scale American-style layoffs or cut out most local suppliers to source components from lower-cost Asian countries. Such actions might have provoked a counterproductive backlash. Wallace seems to have understood the importance of honoring traditional commitments. At the same time, he used his position as a foreigner to push for important changes. He appears to be changing the consensus-based decision-making process within Mazda, and he has been able to cross some barriers that a native-born Japanese might find difficult, such as the barrier between management and labor. Wallace, therefore, illustrates how cross-cultural literacy can be a valuable asset in a foreign country.

A second theme found in this chapter is that a relationship may exist between culture and the costs of doing business in a country or region. It can be argued that the culture of some countries (or regions) is supportive of the capitalist mode of production and lowers the costs of doing business there. Cultural factors can help firms based in such countries to achieve a competitive advantage in the world economy. For example, some observers have argued that cultural factors have helped to lower the costs of doing business in Japan.[2] This may have helped some Japanese businesses achieve a competitive advantage in the world economy. By the same token, cultural factors can sometimes raise the costs of doing business. For example, firms based in Britain, a culture that historically experienced class conflict, found it difficult to achieve cooperation between management and labor, resulting in many industrial disputes. This raised the costs of doing business in Britain, relative to the costs of doing business in countries such as Switzerland, Norway, Germany, or Japan, where class conflict was historically less prevalent.

ANOTHER PERSPECTIVE

A Relationship between Culture and the Cost of Doing Business

Think about the strategic advantage that an American-based multinational corporation might be able to build by drawing on the experience and cultural knowledge of its corporate managers whose home culture is similar to that of the targeted foreign market. For example, a manager of Greek origin might reduce the MNC's cost of doing business in Bulgaria.

We open this chapter with a general discussion of what culture actually is. Then we focus on how differences in social structure, religion, language, and education influence the culture of a country. The implications of these differences will be highlighted throughout the chapter and summarized in a section at the end.

What Is Culture?

Scholars have never been able to agree on a simple definition of culture. In the 1870s the anthropologist Edward Tylor defined culture as "that complex whole which includes knowledge, belief, art, morals, law, custom, and other capabilities acquired by man as a member of society."[3] Since then hundreds of other definitions have been offered. Geert Hofstede, an expert on cross-cultural differences and management, defined culture as "the collective programming of the mind which distinguishes the members of one human group from another . . . Culture, in this sense, includes systems of values; and values are among the building blocks of culture."[4] Another definition of culture comes from sociologists Zvi Namenwirth and Robert Weber who see culture as "a system of ideas" and argue that these ideas constitute "a design for living."[5]

Here we follow both Hofstede and Namenwirth and Weber by viewing **culture** as *a system of values and norms that are shared among a group of people and that when taken together constitute a design for living.* By **values** we mean abstract ideas about what a group believes to be good, right, and desirable. Values are shared assumptions about how things ought to be.[6] By **norms** we mean the social rules and guidelines that prescribe appropriate behavior in particular situations. We shall use the term **society** to refer to a group of people who share a common set of values and norms. While a *society* may be equivalent to a country, some countries harbor several societies (i.e., they support multiple cultures) and some societies embrace more than one country.

Values and Norms

Values form the bedrock of a culture. They provide the context within which a society's norms are established and justified. They may include a society's attitudes toward such concepts as individual freedom, democracy, truth, justice, honesty, loyalty, social obligations, collective responsibility, the role of women, love, sex, marriage, and so on. Values are not just abstract concepts; they are invested with considerable emotional significance. People argue, fight, and even die over values such as "freedom." Values also often are reflected in the political and economic system of a society. As we saw in Chapter 2, democratic free market capitalism is a reflection of a philosophical value system that emphasizes individual freedom.

Norms are the social rules that govern the actions of people toward one another. Norms can be subdivided further into two major categories: *folkways* and *mores*. **Folkways** are the routine conventions of everyday life. Generally, folkways are actions of little moral significance. Rather, folkways are social conventions concerning things such as the appropriate dress code in a particular situation, good social manners, eating with the correct utensils, neighborly behavior, and the like. While folkways define the way people are expected to behave, violation of folkways is not normally serious. People who violate folkways may be thought of as eccentric, or ill-mannered, but they are not usually considered to be evil or bad. In many countries foreigners may be initially excused for violating folkways.

A good example of folkways concern attitudes toward time in different countries. In the United States people are very time-conscious. Americans tend to arrive a few minutes early for business appointments. When invited for dinner to someone's home, it is considered polite to arrive on time or just a few minutes late. In other countries the concept of time can be very different. It is not necessarily a breach of etiquette to arrive a little late for a business appointment; it might even be considered more impolite to arrive early. As for dinner invitations, arriving on time for a

culture System of values and norms that are shared among a group of people and that when taken together constitute a design for living.

values Abstract ideas about what a group believes to be good, right, and desirable.

norms Social rules and guidelines that prescribe appropriate behavior in particular situations.

society Group of people who share a common set of values and norms.

folkways Routine conventions of everyday life.

dinner engagement can be very bad manners. In Britain, for example, when someone says, "Come for dinner at 7 PM," what he means is "Come for dinner at 7:30 to 8 PM." The guest who arrives at 7 PM is likely to find an unprepared and embarrassed host. Similarly, when an Argentinean says, "Come for dinner anytime after 8 PM," what she means is don't come at 8 PM—it's far too early!

Mores are norms that are central to the functioning of a society and to its social life. They have much greater significance than folkways. Accordingly, the violation of mores can bring serious retribution. Mores include such factors as indictments against theft, adultery, incest, and cannibalism. In many societies certain mores have been enacted into law. Thus, all advanced societies have laws against theft, incest, and cannibalism. However, there are also many differences between cultures as to what is perceived as mores. In America, for example, drinking alcohol is widely accepted, but in Saudi Arabia the consumption of alcohol is viewed as violating important social mores and is punishable by imprisonment (as some Western citizens working in Saudi Arabia have discovered).

mores Norms that are seen as central to the functioning of a society and to its social life.

Culture, Society, and the Nation-State

We have defined a society as a group of people that share a common set of values and norms; that is, people bound together by a common culture. But there is *not* a strict one-to-one correspondence between a society and a nation-state. Nation-states are political creations. They may contain a single culture or several distinct cultures. While the French nation can be thought of as the political embodiment of French culture, the nation of Canada has at least three cultures—an Anglo culture, a French-speaking "Quebecois" culture, and a native American culture. Similarly in many African nations there are important cultural differences among tribal groups, a fact that was driven home in a horrific fashion in the early 1990s when the nation of Rwanda dissolved into a bloody civil war between two tribes, the Tutsi and Hutus. Nor is Africa alone in this regard. India, with its nearly 1 billion inhabitants and rich history, is composed of many distinct cultural groups. During the Gulf War the prevailing view presented to Western audiences was that Iraq was a homogenous Arab nation. But in the chaos that followed the war it became apparent that Iraq was composed of several different societies, each with its own culture. In the north are the Kurds, who do not view themselves as Arabs and who have their own distinct history and traditions. There are two Arab societies, the Shiites in the south and the Sunnis, who populate the middle of the country and who rule Iraq (the terms *Shiites* and *Sunnis* refer to different sects within the religion of Islam). Moreover, among the southern Sunnis is another distinct society of 500,000 "marsh Arabs" who live at the confluence of the Tigris and Euphrates rivers pursuing a way of life that dates back 5,000 years.[7]

At the other end of the scale, we can speak of cultures that embrace several nations. Several scholars, for example, argue that we can speak of an Islamic society or culture that is shared by the citizens of many different nations in the Middle East, Asia, and Africa. As you will recall from the last chapter, this view of expansive cultures that embrace several nations underpins Samuel Huntington's view of a world that is fragmented into different civilizations including Western, Islamic, and Chinese civilizations.[8]

To complicate things further, it is also possible to talk about culture at different levels. It is reasonable to talk about "American society" and "American culture," but we must recognize that there are several societies within America, each with its own culture. One can talk about African-American culture, Cajun culture, Chinese-American culture, Hispanic culture, Indian culture, Irish-American culture, and Southern culture.

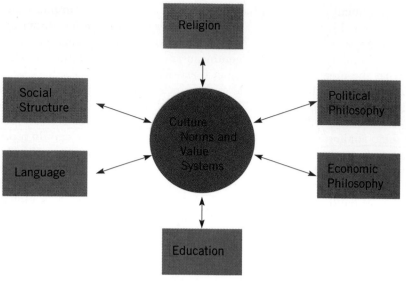

Figure 3.1

The Determinants of Culture

The point is that the relationship between culture and country is often ambiguous. One cannot always characterize a country as having a single homogenous culture, and even when one can, one must also often recognize that the national culture is a mosaic of subcultures, many of which can be quite distinct.

The Determinants of Culture

The values and norms of a culture do not emerge fully formed. They are the evolutionary product of a number of factors at work in a society. These factors include the prevailing political and economic philosophy, the social structure of a society, and the dominant religion, language, and education (see Figure 3.1). We discussed political and economic philosophy in Chapter 2. Such philosophy clearly influences the value systems of a society. Below we will discuss the influence of social structure, religion, language, and education. Remember that the chain of causation runs both ways. While factors such as social structure and religion clearly influence the values and norms of a society, it is also true that the values and norms of a society can influence social structure and religion.

Social Structure

A society's "social structure" refers to its basic social organization. Although there are many aspects of social structure, two main dimensions stand out when explaining differences between cultures. The first is the degree to which the basic unit of social organization is the individual, as opposed to the group. Western societies tend to emphasize the primacy of the individual, while groups tend to figure much larger in many other societies. The second dimension is the degree to which a society is stratified into classes or castes. Some societies are characterized by a relatively high degree of social stratification and relatively low mobility between strata (e.g., Indian), while other societies are characterized by a low degree of social stratification and high mobility between strata (e.g., the United States).

We are involved in *groups* almost every day of our lives: the friends with whom you go out on the weekend, your study groups, your classmates for this course, people at your job with whom you work closely. © PhotoDisc.

Individuals and Groups

A **group** is an association of two or more individuals who have a shared sense of identity and who interact with each other in structured ways on the basis of a common set of expectations about each other's behavior.[9] Human social life is group life. Individuals are involved in families, work groups, social groups, recreational groups, and so on. However, while groups are found in all societies, societies differ according to the degree to which the group is viewed as the primary means of social organization.[10] In some societies individual attributes and achievements are viewed as being more important than group membership, while in other societies the reverse is true.

THE INDIVIDUAL   In Chapter 2 we discussed individualism as a political philosophy. However, individualism is more than just an abstract political philosophy. The individual is the basic building block of social organization in many Western societies. This is reflected not just in the political and economic organization of society, but also in the way in which people perceive themselves and relate to each other in social and business settings. The value systems of many Western societies, for example, emphasize individual achievement. The social standing of an individual is not so much a function of whom they work for, as of their individual performance in whatever work setting they choose for themselves.

The emphasis placed on individual performance in many Western societies is both beneficial and harmful. In the United States, for example, the emphasis placed on individual performance finds expression in an admiration of rugged individualism and entrepreneurship. One benefit of this is the high level of entrepreneurial activity in the United States and other Western societies. New products and new ways of doing business (e.g., personal computers, photocopiers, computer software, biotechnology, supermarkets, and discount retail stores) have repeatedly been created in the United States by entrepreneurial individuals. One can argue that the dynamism of the US economy owes much to the philosophy of individualism.

group Association of two or more individuals who have a shared sense of identity and who interact with each other in structured ways on the basis of a common set of expectations about each other's behavior.

But the philosophy of individualism also finds expression in a high degree of managerial mobility between companies, and this is not always a good thing. While moving from company to company may be good for individual managers, who are trying to build impressive resumes, it is not necessarily good for American companies. The lack of loyalty and commitment to an individual company, and the tendency to move on when a better offer comes along, can result in the creation of managers that have good general skills but lack the in-depth knowledge, experience, and network of interpersonal contacts that come from years of working in the same company. Company-specific experience, knowledge, and personal contacts are all good things because they may increase the ability of a manager to perform his or her job effectively. A manager may draw on past experience, knowledge, and a network of contacts to find solutions to current problems. American companies may suffer if their managers lack these things.

The emphasis on individualism also may make it difficult to build teams within an organization to perform collective tasks. If individuals are always competing with each other, it may prove difficult for them to cooperate. A study by the Massachusetts Institute of Technology of US competitiveness concluded that a failure to achieve cooperation both within a company (e.g., between functions; between management and labor) and between companies (e.g., between a firm and its suppliers) is hurting US firms in the global economy. Given the emphasis on individualism in the American value system, this failure is not surprising.[11] The emphasis on individualism in the United States, while helping to create a dynamic entrepreneurial economy, may also raise the costs of doing business because of its adverse impact on managerial mobility and cooperation.

There is one positive aspect of high managerial mobility. Moving from firm to firm exposes executives to different ways of doing business. The ability to compare business practices helps US executives identify how good practices and techniques developed in one firm might be profitably applied to other firms.

THE GROUP In contrast to the Western emphasis on the individual, in many other societies the group is the primary unit of social organization. In Japan, for example, the social status of an individual is determined as much by the standing of the group to which he or she belongs as by his or her individual performance.[12] In traditional Japanese society the group was the family or village to which an individual belonged. Today the group has frequently come to be associated with the work team or business organization to which an individual belongs. In a now classic study of Japanese society, Nakane noted how this expresses itself in everyday life:

> When a Japanese faces the outside (confronts another person) and affixes some position to himself socially he is inclined to give precedence to institution over kind of occupation. Rather than saying, "I am a type setter" or "I am a filing clerk," he is likely to say "I am from B Publishing Group" or "I belong to S company."[13]

Nakane also observed that the primacy of the group to which an individual belongs often evolves into a deeply emotional attachment in which identification with the group becomes all important in one's life. One central value of Japanese culture is the importance attached to group membership. This may benefit businesses. Strong identification with the group is argued to create pressures for mutual self-help and collective action. If the worth of an individual is linked to the achievements of the group (e.g., firm), as Nakane maintains is the case in Japan, this creates a strong incentive for individual members of the group to work together for the common good. The failures of cooperation that the MIT study found in many American firms may not be a problem in Japanese firms. Some argue that the competitive advantage of

Japanese enterprises in the global economy is based partly on their ability to achieve close cooperation between individuals within a company and between companies. This finds expression in the widespread diffusion of self-managing work teams within Japanese organizations, the close cooperation that has often been observed between different functions within Japanese companies (e.g., between manufacturing, marketing, and R&D), and the cooperation between a company and its suppliers on issues such as design, quality control, and inventory reduction.[14] In all of these cases, cooperation is driven by the need to improve the performance of the group (i.e., the business firm) to which individuals belong.

The primacy of the value of group identification in cultures such as Japan can also be expected to discourage managers and workers from moving from company to company. In Japan lifetime employment in one company is the norm in certain sectors of the economy (estimates suggest that between 20 and 40 percent of all Japanese employees have formal or informal lifetime employment guarantees). One result of the lifetime employment system is that managers and workers build up knowledge, experience, and a network of interpersonal business contacts over the years. These things can help managers perform their jobs more effectively and assist them in achieving cooperation with others.

However, the primacy of the group is not always beneficial. Just as US society is characterized by dynamism and entrepreneurship, reflecting the primacy of values associated with individualism, some argue that Japanese society is characterized by a corresponding lack of dynamism and entrepreneurship. For cultural reasons the United States may continue to be more successful than Japan at pioneering radically new products and new ways of doing business.

Social Stratification

All societies are stratified on a hierarchical basis into social categories—that is, into **social strata.** These strata are typically defined on the basis of characteristics such as family background, occupation, and income. Individuals are born into a particular stratum. They become a member of the social category to which their parents belong. Individuals born into a stratum toward the top of the social hierarchy tend to have better *life chances* than individuals born into a stratum toward the bottom of the hierarchy. They are likely to have a better education, better health, a better standard of living, and better work opportunities. Although all societies are stratified to some degree, societies differ from each other in two related ways that are of interest to us here. First, they differ with regard to the degree of *mobility* between social strata, and second, they differ with regard to the *significance* attached to social strata in business contexts.

SOCIAL MOBILITY   The term **social mobility** refers to the extent to which individuals can move out of the stratum into which they are born. Social mobility varies significantly from society to society. The most rigid system of stratification is a caste system. A **caste system** is a *closed system of stratification* in which social position is determined by the family into which a person is born, and change in that position is usually not possible during an individual's lifetime (i.e., social mobility

social strata Social categories in a society defined on the basis of characteristics such as family background, occupation, and income.

social mobility Extent to which individuals can move out of the strata into which they are born.

caste system Closed system of stratification in which social position is determined by the family into which a person is born, and change in that position is usually not possible during an individual's lifetime.

is very limited). Often a caste position carries with it a specific occupation. Members of one caste might be shoemakers, members of another might be butchers, and so on. These occupations are embedded in the caste and passed down through the family to succeeding generations. Although the number of societies with caste systems diminished rapidly during the 20th century, one major example still remains: India has four main castes and several thousand subcastes. Even though the caste system was officially abolished in 1949, two years after India became independent, the caste system is still a powerful force in rural Indian society where occupation and marital opportunities are still partly related to caste.

class system
Form of open social stratification in which the position a person has by birth can be changed through his or her achievements or luck.

A **class system** is a less rigid form of social stratification in which social mobility is possible. A class system is a form of *open stratification* in which the position a person has by birth can be changed through his or her own achievements and/or luck. Individuals born into a class at the bottom of the hierarchy can work their way up, while individuals born into a class at the top of the hierarchy can slip down.

While many societies have class systems, social mobility within a class system varies from society to society. For example, some sociologists have argued that Britain has a more rigid class structure than certain other Western societies, such as the United States.[15] Historically, British society was divided into three main classes; the *upper class,* which was made up of individuals whose families for generations had wealth, prestige, and occasionally power; the *middle class,* whose members were involved in professional, managerial, and clerical occupations; and the *working class,* whose members earned their living from manual occupations. The middle class was further subdivided into the *upper-middle class*, whose members were involved in important managerial occupations and the prestigious professions (e.g., lawyers, accountants, doctors), and the *lower-middle class,* whose members were involved in clerical work (e.g., bank tellers) and the less prestigious professions (e.g., schoolteachers).

The British class system was noted for the extent of divergence between the life chances of members of different classes. The upper and upper-middle classes typically send their children to a select group of private schools, where they don't mix with lower-class children and where they pick up the speech accents and social norms that mark them as being from the higher strata of society. These same private schools have also had close ties with the most prestigious universities, such as Oxford and Cambridge. Until recently Oxford and Cambridge guaranteed a certain number of places for the graduates of these private schools. Having been to a prestigious university, the offspring of the upper and upper-middle classes then had an excellent chance of being offered a prestigious job in companies, banks, brokerage firms, and law firms that were run by members of the upper and upper-middle classes.

In contrast, the members of the British working and lower-middle classes typically went to state schools. The majority left at age 16, and those that went on to higher education found it more difficult to get accepted at the best universities. When they did, they found that their lower-class accent and lack of social skills marked them as being from a lower social stratum, which made it more difficult for them to get access to the most prestigious jobs.

As a result of these factors, the class system in Britain tended to perpetuate itself from generation to generation, and mobility was limited. Although upward mobility was always possible, it could not normally be achieved in one generation. While an individual from a working-class background may have established an income level that was consistent with membership of the upper-middle class, he or she may not have been accepted as such by others of that class due to accent and background. However, by sending his or her offspring to the "right kind of school," the individual could ensure that his or her children are accepted.

According to many politicians and popular commentators, modern British society is now rapidly leaving this class structure behind and moving toward a society without classes. However, sociologists continue to dispute this and present evidence to the contrary. For example, a recent study reported that in 1994, state schools in the London suburb of Islington, which has a population of 175,000, had only 79 candidates for university, while one prestigious private school alone, Eton, sent more than that number to Oxford and Cambridge.[16] This, according to the study's authors, implies that "money still begets money." They argue that a good school means a good university, a good university means a good job, and "merit" has only a limited chance of elbowing its way into this tight little circle.

The class system in the United States is less extreme than in Britain and mobility is greater. Like Britain, the United States has its own upper, middle, and working classes. However, class membership is determined principally by individual economic achievements, as opposed to background and schooling. Thus, individuals can, by their own economic achievement, move smoothly from the working class to the upper class in their own lifetimes. In American society successful individuals from humble origins are highly respected.

SIGNIFICANCE   The stratification of a society is significant if it affects the operation of a business. In American society, the high degree of social mobility and the emphasis on individualism limits the impact of class background on business operations. The same is true in Japan, where most people perceive themselves to be middle class. In a country such as Britain, however, the relative lack of class mobility and the differences between classes have resulted in the emergence of class consciousness. **Class consciousness** refers to a condition where people tend to perceive themselves in terms of their class background, and this shapes their relationships with members of other classes.

This has been played out in British society in a traditional hostility between upper-middle-class managers and their working-class employees. Mutual antagonism and lack of respect historically made it difficult to achieve cooperation between management and labor in many British companies and resulted in many industrial disputes. However, the number of such disputes has declined dramatically in the past two decades, which bolsters the arguments of those who claim that Britain is moving toward a society without classes. An antagonistic relationship between management and labor, and the resulting lack of cooperation and high level of industrial disruption, tends to raise the costs of production in countries characterized by significant class divisions. This can make it more difficult for companies based in such countries to establish a competitive advantage in the global economy.

Religious and Ethical Systems

Religion may be defined as a system of shared beliefs and rituals that are concerned with the realm of the sacred.[17] **Ethical systems** refer to moral principles, or values, that are used to guide and shape behavior. Most of the world's ethical systems are the product of religions. Thus, we can talk about Christian ethics and Islamic ethics. However, a major exception to the principle that ethical systems are grounded in religion is Confucianism. Confucian ethics play an important part in influencing behavior and shaping culture in parts of Asia, and particularly China, Japan, and Korea, yet it is incorrect to characterize Confucianism as a religion.

The relationship among religion, ethics, and society is subtle, complex, and profound. While there are thousands of different religions in the world, four dominate: Christianity, Islam, Hinduism, and Buddhism (see Map 3.1). We review each of these,

class consciousness
Condition where people perceive themselves in terms of their class background, and this shapes their relationships with members of other classes.

religion System of shared beliefs and rituals that are concerned with the realm of the sacred.

ethical systems Sets of moral principles, or values, that are used to guide and shape behavior.

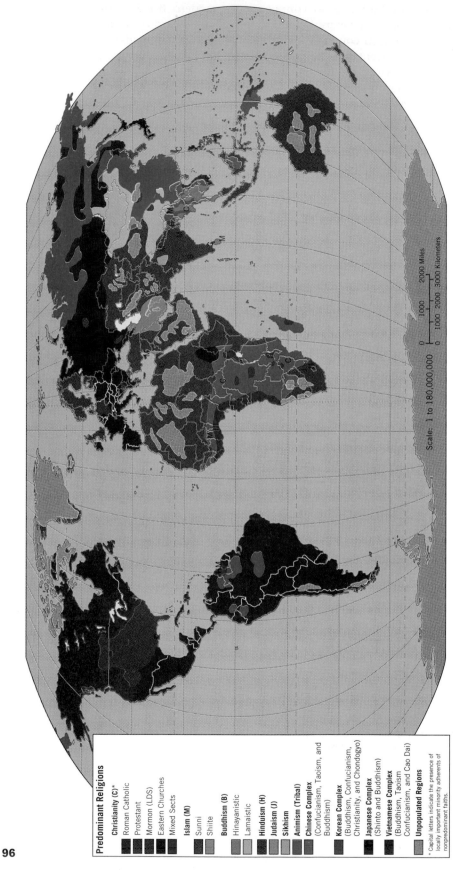

Predominant Religions

Christianity (C)*
Roman Catholic
Protestant
Mormon (LDS)
Eastern Churches
Mixed Sects

Islam (M)
Sunni
Shiite

Buddhism (B)
Hinayanistic
Lamaistic

Hinduism (H)

Judaism (J)

Sikhism

Animism (Tribal)

Chinese Complex
(Confucianism, Taoism, and
Buddhism)

Korean Complex
(Buddhism, Confucianism,
Christianity, and Chondogyo)

Japanese Complex
(Shinto and Buddhism)

Vietnamese Complex
(Buddhism, Taoism
Confucianism, and Cao Dai)

Unpopulated Regions

* Capital letters indicate the presence of
locally important minority adherents of
nonpredominant faiths.

Scale: 1 to 180,000,000

0   1000   2000 Miles
0   1000   2000   3000 Kilometers

Map 3.1

World Religions

Source: From *Student Atlas of World Geography, 1st edition*, by John Allen. Copyright 1999 by The McGraw-Hill Companies, Inc. Reprinted by permission of Dushkin/McGraw-Hill.

along with Confucianism, focusing primarily on their business implications. Perhaps the most important business implications of religion center on the extent to which different religions shape attitudes toward work and entrepreneurship and the degree to which the religious ethics of a society affect the costs of doing business in a country.

Christianity

Christianity is probably the most widely practiced religion in the world. About 20 percent of the world's people identify themselves as Christians. The vast majority of Christians live in Europe and the Americas, although their numbers are growing rapidly in Africa. Christianity grew out of Judaism. Like Judaism it is a monotheistic religion (monotheism is the belief in one god). A religious division in the 11th century led to the establishment of two major Christian organizations: the Roman Catholic church and the Orthodox church. Today the Roman Catholic church accounts for more than half of all Christians, most of whom are found in Southern Europe and Latin America. The Orthodox church, while less influential, is still of major importance in several countries (e.g., Greece and Russia). In the 16th century the Reformation led to a further split with Rome; the result was the establishment of Protestantism. The nonconformist nature of Protestantism has facilitated the emergence of numerous denominations under the Protestant umbrella (e.g., Baptist, Methodist, Calvinist).

ECONOMIC IMPLICATIONS OF CHRISTIANITY: THE PROTESTANT WORK ETHIC

Some sociologists have argued that of the two main branches of Christianity—Catholicism and Protestantism—the latter has the most important economic implications. In 1904 a German sociologist, Max Weber, made a connection between Protestant ethics and "the spirit of capitalism" that has since become famous.[18] Weber noted that capitalism emerged in Western Europe and that in Western Europe

> [b]usiness leaders and owners of capital, as well as the higher grades of skilled labor, and even more the higher technically and commercially trained personnel of modern enterprises, are overwhelmingly Protestant.[19]

According to Weber, there was a relationship between Protestantism and the emergence of modern capitalism. Weber argued that Protestant ethics emphasize the importance of hard work and wealth creation (for the glory of God) and frugality (abstinence from worldly pleasures). According to Weber, this was just the kind of value system needed to facilitate the development of capitalism. Protestants worked hard and systematically to accumulate wealth. However, their ascetic beliefs suggested that rather than consuming this wealth by indulging in worldly pleasures, they should reinvest it in the expansion of capitalist enterprises. Thus, the combination of hard work and the accumulation of capital, which could be used to finance investment and expansion, paved the way for the development of capitalism in Western Europe and in the United States. Weber argued that the Catholic promise of salvation in the next world, rather than this world, did not foster the same kind of work ethic.

There is also another way in which Protestantism may have encouraged the development of capitalism. By breaking away from the hierarchical domination of religious and social life that characterized the Catholic church for much of its history, Protestantism gave individuals more freedom to develop their own relationship with God. The emphasis on individual religious freedom may have paved the way for the subsequent emphasis on individual economic and political freedoms and the development of individualism as an economic and political philosophy. As we saw in Chapter 2, such a philosophy forms the bedrock upon which entrepreneurial free market capitalism is based.

Islam

With close to 1 billion adherents, Islam is the second largest of the world's major religions. Islam dates back to 610 AD when the Prophet Muhammad began spreading the word. Adherents of Islam are referred to as Muslims. Muslims constitute a majority in over 35 countries and inhabit a nearly contiguous stretch of land from the northwest coast of Africa, through the Middle East, to China and Malaysia.

Islam has roots in both Judaism and Christianity (Islam views Jesus Christ as one of God's prophets). Like Christianity and Judaism, Islam is a monotheistic religion. The central principle of Islam is that there is no god but the one true omnipotent God. Islam requires unconditional acceptance of the uniqueness, power, and authority of God and the understanding that the objective of life is to fulfill the dictates of His will in the hope of admission to paradise. According to Islam, worldly gain and temporal power are an illusion. Those who pursue riches on earth may gain them, but those who forgo worldly ambitions to seek the favor of Allah may gain the greater treasure—entry into paradise. Other major principles of Islam include (1) honoring and respecting parents, (2) respecting the rights of others, (3) being generous but not a squanderer, (4) avoiding killing except for justifiable causes, (5) not committing adultery, (6) dealing justly and equitably with others, (7) being of pure heart and mind, (8) safeguarding the possessions of orphans, and (9) being humble and unpretentious.[20] There are obvious parallels here with many of the central principles of both Judaism and Christianity.

Islam is an all-embracing way of life governing the totality of a Muslim's being.[21] As God's surrogate in this world, a Muslim is circumscribed by religious principles—by a code of conduct for interpersonal relations—in his or her social and economic activities. Religion is paramount in all areas of life. The Muslim lives in a social structure that is shaped by Islamic values and norms of moral conduct. The ritual nature of everyday life in a Muslim country is striking to a Western visitor. Muslim ritual requires prayer five times a day (it is not unusual for business meetings to be put on hold while the Muslim participants engage in their daily prayer ritual), dictates that women should be dressed in a certain manner and subordinate to men, and forbids the consumption of either pig meat or alcohol.

ISLAMIC FUNDAMENTALISM   The past two decades have witnessed a surge in what is often referred to as "Islamic fundamentalism."[22] In the West, Islamic fundamentalism is often associated in the media with militants, terrorists, and violent upheavals, such as the bloody conflict in Algeria or the killing of foreign tourists in Egypt. This characterization is at best a half-truth. Just as Christian fundamentalists are motivated by sincere and deeply held religious values firmly rooted in their faith, so are Islamic fundamentalists. The violence that the Western media associates with Islamic fundamentalism is perpetrated by a very small minority of fundamentalists and explicitly repudiated by many.

The rise of fundamentalism in part is a response to the social pressures created by the move toward modernization and by the influence of Western ideas, such as liberal democracy, materialism, and equal rights for women, and by Western attitudes toward sex, marriage, and alcohol. In many Muslim countries modernization has been accompanied by a growing gap between a rich urban minority and an impoverished urban and rural majority. For the impoverished majority, modernization has offered little in the way of tangible economic progress while threatening the traditional value system. Thus, for a Muslim who cherishes his traditions and feels that his identity is jeopardized by the encroachment of alien Western values, Islamic fundamentalism has become his cultural anchor.

Fundamentalists demand a rigid commitment to traditional religious beliefs and rituals. The result has been a marked increase in the use of symbolic gestures that confirm Islamic values. Women are again wearing floor-length, long-sleeve dresses and covering their hair; religious studies have increased in universities; the publication of religious tracts has increased; more religious orations are heard in public.[23] The sentiments of some fundamentalist groups are increasingly anti-Western. Rightly or wrongly, Western influence is blamed for a range of social ills, and the actions of many fundamentalists are directed against Western governments, cultural symbols, businesses, and even individuals.

In several Muslim countries, fundamentalists have gained political power and have used this to try to make Islamic law (as set down in the Koran, the bible of Islam) the law of the land. There are good grounds for this in Islam. There is technically no distinction between church and state in Islam. Islam is not just a religion; it is also the source of law, a guide to statecraft, and an arbiter of social behavior. Muslims believe that every human endeavor is within the purview of the faith—and this includes political activity—because the only purpose of any activity is to do God's will.[24] This view is also shared by some Christian fundamentalists.

The fundamentalists have been most successful in Iran, where a fundamentalist party has held power since 1979, but they also have a considerable and growing influence in many other countries, such as Algeria, Egypt, Pakistan, and Saudi Arabia. The accompanying "Country Focus" profiles the rise of Islamic fundamentalism in Saudi Arabia. If fundamentalist forces gain power in Saudi Arabia, they may turn away from the West in general and the United States in particular, a longtime ally. Given the importance of Saudi Arabia as a source for oil, the economic ramifications of such a shift in geopolitics are clearly serious.

ECONOMIC IMPLICATIONS OF ISLAM Some quite explicit economic principles are set down in the Koran.[25] Many of the economic principles of Islam are pro-free enterprise. The Koran speaks approvingly of free enterprise and of earning *legitimate* profit through trade and commerce (the Prophet Muhammad was once a trader). The protection of private property is also embedded within Islam, although Islam does assert that all property is a favor from Allah (God), who created and so owns everything. Those who hold property are entitled to receive profits from it and are regarded as trustees, rather than as owners in the Western sense of the word. Those who hold property are admonished to use it in a righteous, socially beneficial, and prudent manner. This reflects Islam's concern with social justice. Islam is critical of those who earn profit through the exploitation of others. In the Islamic view of the world, man is part of a collective in which the wealthy and successful have obligations to help the disadvantaged. In Muslim countries it is fine to earn a profit, as long as that profit is justly earned and not based on the exploitation of others for one's own advantage. It also helps if those making profits undertake charitable acts to help the poor. Furthermore, Islam stresses the importance of living up to contractual obligations, of keeping one's word, and of abstaining from deception.

Given the Islamic proclivity to favor market-based systems, Muslim countries are likely to be receptive to international businesses as long as those businesses behave in a manner that is consistent with Islamic ethics. Businesses that are perceived as making an unjust profit through the exploitation of others, by deception, or by breaking contractual obligations are unlikely to be welcomed in an Islamic state. In addition, in Islamic states where fundamentalism is on the rise, it is also likely that hostility to Western-owned business will be increasing.

The desert kingdom of Saudi Arabia is a new nation. It was a loosely governed area inhabited by 7 million members of numerous Bedouin tribes when King Abdel-Aziz unified the country by conquest and intermarriage in 1935. His descendants—the House of Saudi—still rule what remains a monarchy with few democratic institutions. The majority of Saudis are Sunnis, although a Shiite minority lives on the eastern coast. Saudi Arabia has long been thought of as a close ally of the West. Western governments have gone out of their way to curry the favor of Saudi Arabia, a cynic might say because the country sits on top of more than a quarter of the world's oil reserves—oil that the West needs to keep its industrial machinery humming. In the 1970s and early 1980s high oil

As oil revenues and government spending shrunk, the Saudis began to experience unemployment and social unrest. This has led Islamic fundamentalists to question the legitimacy of the rule of the House of Saudi. The irony of the current predicament is that the House of Saudi has always seen itself as the guardian of traditional Islamic values. The legitimacy of the royal family has been based in part on the backing of the *ulema,* an influential group of Islamic scholars, and the country's laws have always been based on Islamic principles. Still, dissident members of the *ulema* have united with hard-line Islamic radicals—a group that includes preachers, professors, students, and marginalized city dwellers—to criticize the ruling family. These radicals

its fundamentalist opponents may prove to be a costly error for the government. As the governments of Algeria and Egypt have recently discovered, fundamentalists seem to draw strength from repression.

Another source of dissent has been lingering resentment among the radicals to the government's decision to allow 500,000 Western troops onto Saudi soil during the Gulf War. The fact that Saudi Arabia was on the winning side during the war apparently matters less to the fundamentalists than the "dishonor" associated with having to rely on outsiders, and Western ones at that, to protect Saudi sovereignty.

In November 1995, the dissent became violent when a car stuffed with 250 pounds of explosives blew up at a base in

Islamic Dissent in Saudi Arabia

prices turned Saudi Arabia into one of the world's richest countries when measured by GDP per capita. This oil wealth supported a spending spree on basic infrastructure that gave the country the trappings of a modern state. Nevertheless, traditional tribal values remained just below the surface.

The spending spree is now over for the 21 million inhabitants. The high oil prices that sustained Saudi spending collapsed in 1985 and have yet to recover. Also, while Saudi Arabia was on the winning side in the Gulf War, the cost of financing the war drained the treasury. As a consequence, government spending has been declining sharply since 1991. In 1994, the Saudi government announced it would cut spending by 20 percent.

tend to be anti-Western, anti-Shiite, and highly critical of the ruling family. Their opposition is based not just on economic problems, but also on a perception that the House of Saudi has been corrupted by its wealth and has monopolized political power.

The sermons of radical preachers denounce a Judeo-Christian conspiracy against Islam and criticize Western values and lifestyles. In September 1994, one of the best-known radical preachers, Sheik Salman al-Audah, was asked by the government to sign a gag order. He refused, published the order, and was arrested. Hundreds of his followers were also arrested when they protested by taking to the streets of Buraida, a fundamentalist stronghold. Harassing, arresting and sometimes torturing

Riyadh where US military personnel helped train their Saudi counterparts. The blast killed 5 Americans and wounded 34. In May 1996, the Saudi government beheaded four "Muslim extremists" that the government claimed confessed to the bombing, though no trial was held and Saudi officials denied US investigators access to the men. Less than a month later, a huge truck bomb tore the face off a US military apartment tower outside of Dhahran, killing 19 more US military personnel and wounding 200 others. Since then things have quieted down in Saudi Arabia, but there is growing concern that dissent is growing and may come to a head.[26]

Islam prohibits the payment or receipt of interest, which is considered usury. To the devout Muslim, acceptance of interest payments is seen as a very grave sin. Practitioners of the black art of usury are warned on the pain of hellfire to abstain; the giver and the taker are equally damned. This is not just a matter of theology; in several Islamic states it is also becoming a matter of law. In 1992, for example, Pakistan's federal Shariat Court, the highest Islamic law-making body in the country, pronounced interest to be un-Islamic and therefore illegal and demanded that the government amend all financial laws accordingly.[27]

Rigid adherence to this particular Islamic law could wreak havoc with a country's financial and banking system, raising the costs of doing business and scaring away international businesses and investors. To skirt the ban on interest, Islamic banks have been experimenting with a profit-sharing system to replace interest on borrowed or lent money. When an Islamic bank lends money to a business, rather than charging interest on the loan, it takes a share in the profits derived from the investment. Similarly, when a business (or individual) deposits money at an Islamic bank in a savings account, the deposit is treated as an equity investment in whatever activity the bank uses the capital for. Thus, the depositor receives a share in the profit from the bank's investment (as opposed to interest payments). Some Muslims claim this is a more efficient system than the Western banking system because it encourages both long-term savings and long-term investment. However, there is no hard evidence of this, and many believe that the Islamic banking system is less efficient than a conventional Western banking system.

Hinduism

Hinduism has approximately 500 million adherents, most of them in the Indian subcontinent. Hinduism began in the Indus Valley in India more than 4,000 years ago, making it the world's oldest major religion. Unlike Christianity and Islam, its founding is not linked to a particular person. Nor does it have an officially sanctioned sacred book such as the Bible or the Koran. Hindus believe there is a moral force in society that requires the acceptance of certain responsibilities, called *dharma*. Hindus believe in *reincarnation,* rebirth into a different body after death. Hindus also believe in *karma,* the spiritual progression of each person's soul. A person's *karma* is affected by the way he or she lives. The moral state of an individual's *karma* determines the challenges that person will face in the next life. By perfecting the soul in each new life, Hindus believe that an individual can eventually achieve *nirvana,* a state of complete spiritual perfection that renders reincarnation no longer necessary. Many Hindus believe that the way to achieve nirvana is to lead an ascetic lifestyle of material and physical self-denial, devoting life to a spiritual rather than material quest.

ECONOMIC IMPLICATIONS OF HINDUISM   Max Weber, who is famous for expounding on the Protestant work ethic, also argued that the ascetic principles embedded in Hinduism do not encourage the entrepreneurial activity in pursuit of wealth creation that we find in Protestantism.[28] According to Weber, traditional Hindu values emphasize that individuals should not be judged by their material achievements, but by their spiritual achievements. Hindus perceive the pursuit of material well-being as making the attainment of nirvana more difficult. Given the emphasis on an ascetic lifestyle, Weber thought that devout Hindus would be less likely to engage in entrepreneurial activity than devout Protestants.

Mahatma Gandhi, the famous Indian nationalist and spiritual leader, was the embodiment of Hindu asceticism. It has been argued that the values of Hindu asceticism and self-reliance that Gandhi advocated hampered the economic development of postindependence India.[29] But one must be careful not to read too much into Weber's arguments. Today there are millions of hardworking entrepreneurs in India who form the economic backbone of a rapidly growing economy.

Hinduism also supports India's caste system. The concept of mobility between castes within an individual's lifetime makes no sense to Hindus. Hindus see mobility between castes as something that is achieved through spiritual progression and reincarnation. People can be reborn into a higher caste in their next life if they achieve spiritual development in this life. In so far as the caste system limits the opportunities for otherwise able individuals to adopt positions of responsibility and influence in society, the economic consequences of this religious belief are bound to be negative. For example, able individuals may find their route to the higher levels of the business blocked simply because they come from a lower caste. Also, individuals may get promoted to higher positions within a firm as much because of their caste background as because of their ability.

Buddhism

Buddhism was founded in India in the sixth century BC by Siddhartha Gautama, an Indian prince who renounced his wealth to pursue an ascetic lifestyle and spiritual perfection. Siddhartha achieved nirvana, but decided to remain on earth to teach his followers how they too could achieve this spiritual enlightenment. Siddhartha became known as the Buddha (which means "the awakened one"). Today Buddhism has 250 million followers, most of whom are found in Central and Southeast Asia, China, Korea, and Japan. According to Buddhism, life is comprised of suffering. Misery is everywhere and originates in people's desires for pleasure. These desires can be curbed by systematically following the "Noble Eightfold Path," which emphasizes right seeing, thinking, speech, action, living, effort, mindfulness, and meditation. Unlike Hinduism, Buddhism does not support the caste system. Nor does Buddhism advocate the extreme ascetic behavior that is encouraged by Hinduism. Nevertheless, like Hindus, Buddhists stress the afterlife and spiritual achievement, rather than involvement in this world.

The emphasis on wealth creation that is embedded in Protestantism is not found in Buddhism. Thus, in Buddhist societies we do not see the same kind of cultural stress on entrepreneurial behavior that we see in the Protestant West. On the other hand, unlike Hinduism, Buddhism's lack of support for the caste system and extreme ascetic behavior suggests that a Buddhist society may represent a more fertile ground for entrepreneurial activity than a Hindu culture.

Confucianism

Confucianism was founded in the fifth century BC by K'ung-Fu-tzu, more generally known as Confucius. For more than 2,000 years until the 1949 Communist revolution, Confucianism was the official ethical system of China. While observance of Confucian ethics has been weakened in China since 1949, more than 150 million people still follow the teachings of Confucius, principally in China, Korea, and Japan. Confucianism teaches the importance of attaining personal salvation through right action. Confucianism is built around a comprehensive ethical code that sets down guidelines for relationships with others. High moral and ethical conduct and loyalty to others are central to Confucianism. Unlike religions, Confucianism is not concerned with the supernatural and has little to say about the concept of a supreme being or an afterlife.

ECONOMIC IMPLICATIONS OF CONFUCIANISM Some people maintain that Confucianism may have economic implications as profound as those found in Protestantism, although they are of a different nature.[30] The basic thesis of those who take this position is that the influence of Confucian ethics on the cultures of Japan, South Korea, and Taiwan lowers the costs of doing business in those countries, explaining their economic success. Three values that are central to the Confucian system of ethics are of particular interest: loyalty, reciprocal obligations, and honesty in dealings with others.

In Confucian thought loyalty to one's superiors is regarded as a sacred duty—an absolute obligation that is necessary for religious salvation. In modern organizations based in Confucian cultures, the bonds of loyalty that bind employees to the heads of their organization can reduce the conflict between management and labor that we find in class-conscious societies such as Britain. Cooperation between management and labor can be achieved at a lower cost in a culture where the virtue of loyalty is emphasized.

However, this loyalty to one's superiors is not blind loyalty. The concept of reciprocal obligations also comes into play. Confucian ethics stress that superiors are obliged to reward the loyalty of their subordinates by bestowing blessings on them. If these "blessings" are not forthcoming, then neither will be the loyalty. This Confucian ethic exhibits itself in the concept of lifetime employment in Japanese organizations. The employees of a Japanese company are loyal to the leaders of the organization, and in return the leaders bestow on them the "blessing" of lifetime employment. The business implications of this practice were addressed earlier in this chapter when we were discussing the importance of group identification in Japanese society. The lack of mobility between companies implied by the lifetime employment system suggests that managers and workers over the years build up knowledge, experience, and a network of interpersonal business contacts. All these things can help managers and workers perform their jobs more effectively and assist them in achieving cooperation with others in the organization. One result is improving the company's economic performance.

A third concept found in Confucian ethics is the importance attached to honesty. Confucian thinkers emphasize that although dishonest behavior may yield short-term benefits for the transgressor, in the long run dishonesty does not pay. The importance attached to honesty in dealings with others has major economic implications. Business costs are lowered when companies can trust each other not to break contracts. There is no need to employ expensive lawyers to resolve contract disputes. In addition, when companies adhere to Confucian ethics, they can trust each other not to violate the terms of cooperative agreements. Thus, the costs of achieving cooperation between companies may be lowered in societies such as Japan (relative to societies such as the United States where trust is less pervasive). For example, it has been argued that the close ties between the automobile companies and their component part suppliers in Japan are facilitated by a combination of trust and reciprocal obligations. These close ties allow the auto companies and their suppliers to work together on inventory reduction, quality control, and design, giving Japanese auto companies a competitive advantage.[31]

Language

One obvious way in which countries differ is language. By language, we mean both the spoken and the unspoken means of communication. Language is one of the defining characteristics of a culture.

Spoken Language

Language enables people to communicate with each other, but it does far more than this. The nature of a language also structures the way we perceive the world. The language of a society can direct the attention of its members to certain features of the world rather than to others. The classic illustration of this is that the English language has one word for snow, while the language of the Inuit (Eskimos) lacks a general term for it. Instead, because distinguishing different forms of snow is so important in the lives of the Inuit, they have 24 words that describe different types of snow (e.g., powder snow, falling snow, wet snow, drifting snow).[32]

Because language shapes the way people perceive the world, it also helps define culture. In countries with more than one language, one also often finds more than one culture. In Canada, for example, there is an English-speaking culture and a French-speaking culture. Tensions between the two run quite high, with a substantial proportion of the French-speaking minority demanding independence from a Canada "dominated by English speakers." The same phenomenon can be observed in other countries. For example, Belgium is divided into Flemish and French speakers, and tensions between the two groups exist; in Spain a Basque-speaking minority with its own distinctive culture has been agitating for independence from the Spanish-speaking majority for decades; on the Mediterranean island of Cyprus the culturally diverse Greek- and Turkish-speaking populations of the island engaged in open conflict in the 1970s, and the island is now partitioned into two halves. While it does not necessarily follow that language differences create cultural differences and, therefore, separatist pressures (witness the harmony in Switzerland, where four languages are spoken), there seems to be a tendency in this direction.

Chinese is the "mother tongue" of the largest number of people, followed by English and Hindi, which is spoken in India. However, the most widely spoken language in the world is English, followed by French, Spanish, and Chinese (many people speak English as a second language). English is increasingly becoming the language of international business. When Japanese and German businesspeople get together to do business, they will almost certainly communicate in English. However, while English is widely used, learning the local language has its advantages. For one thing, most people prefer to converse in their own language, and speaking the local language can build rapport, which may be very important for a business deal.

International businesses that do not understand the local language can make major blunders through improper translation. For example, Sunbeam Corporation used the English words for its "Mist-Stick" mist-producing hair-curling iron when it entered the German market, only to discover after an expensive advertising campaign that "mist" means "excrement" in German. In another example, General Motors was troubled by the lack of enthusiasm among Puerto Rican dealers for its newly introduced Chevrolet Nova. When literally translated into Spanish, "Nova" meant star. However, when spoken it sounded like "no va," which in Spanish means "it doesn't go." General Motors changed the name of the car to Caribe.[33]

Unspoken Language

Unspoken language refers to nonverbal communication. We all communicate with each other through nonverbal cues. The raising of eyebrows is a sign of recognition in most cultures, while a smile is a sign of joy. Many nonverbal cues, however, are culturally bound. A failure to understand the nonverbal cues of another culture can lead to miscommunication. For example, making a circle with the thumb and the forefinger is a friendly gesture in the United States, but it is a vulgar sexual invitation in Greece and Turkey. Similarly, while most Americans and Europeans use the "thumbs-up" gesture to indicate that "it's all right," in Greece the gesture is obscene.

Another aspect of nonverbal communication is personal space, which is the comfortable amount of distance between people who are talking to each other. In the United States, the customary distance adopted by parties in a business discussion is five to eight feet. In Latin America it is three to five feet. Consequently, many North Americans unconsciously feel that Latin Americans are "invading their personal space" and can be seen backing away from them during a conversation. In turn, the Latin American may interpret such backing away as aloofness. The result can be a regrettable lack of rapport between two businesspeople from different cultures.

Education

Formal education plays a key role in a society. Formal education is the medium through which individuals learn many of the language, conceptual, and mathematical skills that are indispensable in a modern society. Formal education also supplements the family's role in socializing the young into the values and norms of a society. Values and norms are taught both directly and indirectly. Schools generally teach basic facts about the social and political nature of a society. They also tend to focus on the fundamental obligations of citizenship. Cultural norms are also taught indirectly at school. Respect for others, obedience to authority, honesty, neatness, being on time, and so on, are all part of the hidden curriculum of schools. The use of a grading system also teaches children the value of personal achievement and competition.[34]

From an international business perspective, one important aspect of education is the role it plays as a determinant of national competitive advantage.[35] The availability of a pool of skilled and educated human resources seems to be a major determinant of the likely economic success of a country. Such a pool of skilled and educated people is the product of a good national education system. In analyzing the competitive success of Japan since 1945, for example, Michael Porter notes that after the war Japan had almost nothing except for a pool of skilled and educated human resources.

> With a long tradition of respect for education that borders on reverence, Japan possessed a large pool of literate, educated, and increasingly skilled human resources . . . Japan has benefited from a large pool of trained engineers. Japanese universities graduate many more engineers per capita than in the United States . . . A first-rate primary and secondary education system in Japan operates based on high standards and emphasizes math and science. Primary and secondary education is highly competitive . . . Japanese education provides most students all over Japan with a sound education for later education and training. A Japanese high school graduate knows as much about math as most American college graduates.[36]

Porter's point is that Japan's excellent education system was an important factor explaining the country's postwar economic success. Not only is a good education system a determinant of national competitive advantage, but it is also an important factor guiding the location choices of international businesses. It would make little sense to base production facilities that require highly skilled labor in a country where the education system was so poor that a skilled labor pool wasn't available, no matter how attractive the country might seem on other dimensions. But it might make sense to base production operations that require only unskilled labor in such a country.

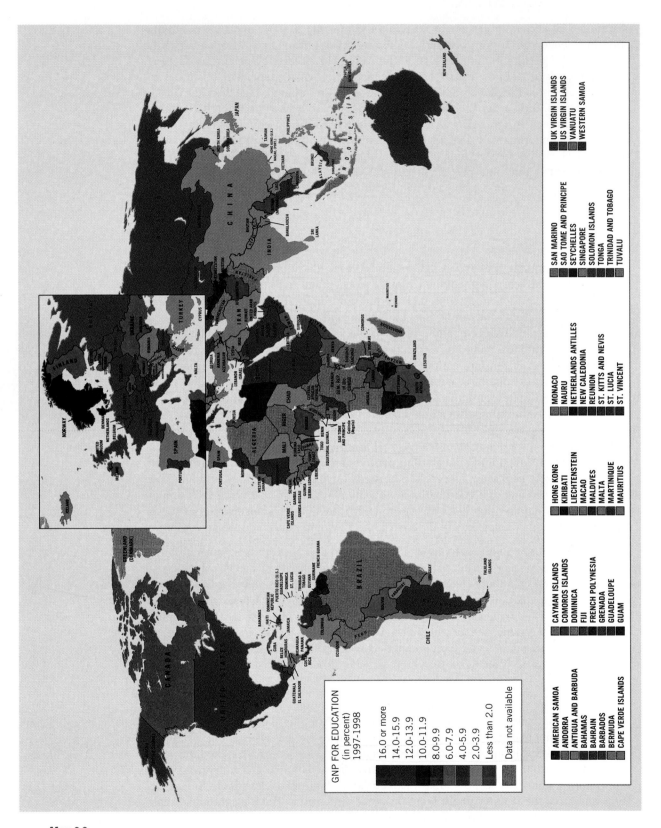

GNP FOR EDUCATION
(in percent)
1997-1998

16.0 or more
14.0-15.9
12.0-13.9
10.0-11.9
8.0-9.9
6.0-7.9
4.0-5.9
2.0-3.9
Less than 2.0

Data not available

AMERICAN SAMOA
ANDORRA
ANTIGUA AND BARBUDA
BAHAMAS
BAHRAIN
BARBADOS
BERMUDA
CAPE VERDE ISLANDS

CAYMAN ISLANDS
COMOROS ISLANDS
DOMINICA
FIJI
FRENCH POLYNESIA
GRENADA
GUADELOUPE
GUAM

HONG KONG
KIRIBATI
LIECHTENSTEIN
MACAO
MALDIVES
MALTA
MARTNIQUE
MAURITIUS

MONACO
NAURU
NETHERLANDS ANTILLES
NEW CALEDONIA
REUNION
ST. KITTS AND NEVIS
ST. LUCIA
ST. VINCENT

SAN MARINO
SAO TOME AND PRINCIPE
SEYCHELLES
SINGAPORE
SOLOMON ISLANDS
TONGA
TRINIDAD AND TOBAGO
TUVALU

UK VIRGIN ISLANDS
US VIRGIN ISLANDS
VANUATU
WESTERN SAMOA

Map 3.2

Percentage of Gross National Product (GNP) Spent on Education
World Development Report 1998/99. Reprinted with permission of the World Bank.

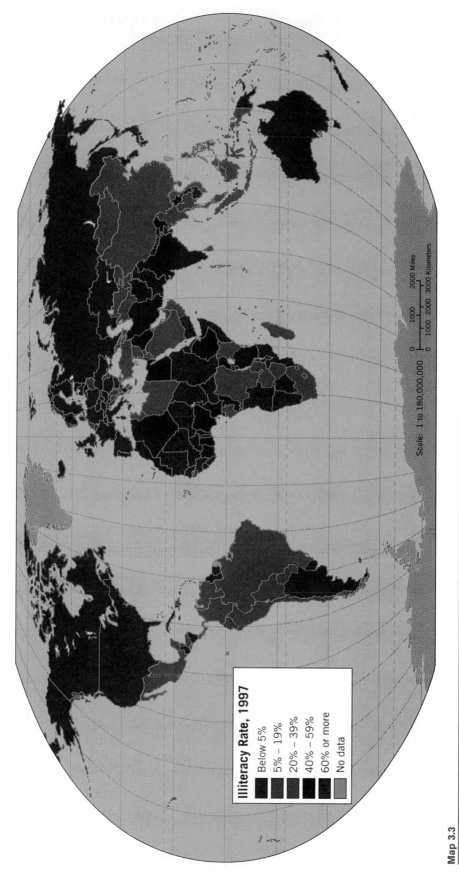

Map 3.3

Illiteracy Rates

Source: From *Student Atlas of World Geography, 1st edition*, by John Allen. Copyright 1999 by The McGraw-Hill Companies, Inc. Reprinted by permission of Dushkin/McGraw-Hill.

Illiteracy Rate, 1997

- Below 5%
- 5% – 19%
- 20% – 39%
- 40% – 59%
- 60% or more
- No data

Scale: 1 to 180,000,000

0   1000   2000 Miles

0   1000   2000   3000 Kilometers

The general education level of a country is also a good index of the products that might sell in a country and of the type of promotional material that should be used. For example, a country such as Pakistan where 73.8 percent of the population is illiterate is unlikely to be a good market for popular books. Promotional material containing written descriptions of mass marketed products are unlikely to have an effect in a country where almost three-quarters of the population cannot read. It is far better to use pictorial promotions in such circumstances.

Maps 3.2 and 3.3 provide some important data on education worldwide. Map 3.2 shows the percentage of a country's GNP that is devoted to education. Map 3.3 shows illiteracy rates. Although there is not a perfect one-to-one correspondence between the percentage of GNP devoted to education and the quality of education, the overall level of spending indicates a country's commitment to education. The United States spends more of its GNP on education than many other advanced industrialized nations, including Germany and Japan. Despite this, the quality of US education is often argued to be inferior to that offered in many other industrialized countries.

Culture and the Workplace

For an international business with operations in different countries a question of considerable importance is *how does a society's culture affect workplace values?* The question points to the need to vary management process and practices according to the culture's work-related values. For example, if the United States and France have different cultures, and if these cultures result in different work-related values, it might make sense for an international business with operations in both the United States and France to vary its management process and practices.

Hofstede's Model

Probably the most famous study of how culture relates to values in the workplace was undertaken by Geert Hofstede.[37] As part of his job as a psychologist for IBM, Hofstede collected data on employee attitudes and values for more than 100,000 individuals from 1967 to 1973. The data enabled him to compare dimensions of culture across 40 countries. Hofstede isolated four dimensions that he claimed summarized different cultures. These were power distance, uncertainty avoidance, individualism versus collectivism, and masculinity versus femininity.

Online View of a New Culture

Visit the online versions of some English-language daily newspapers in major foreign cities to get a sense of their cultures and their markets. Look at the ads and business names. Check out the classifieds. A good list link is at: **http://www. geocities.com/Hollywood/Boulevard/1529/ newspapers.html**.

In addition, check out the Nation (Nairobi, Kenya) at: **http://www.nationaudio.com/News/ DailyNation/Today**.

Hofstede's **power distance** dimension focused on how a society deals with the inequity in people's physical and intellectual capabilities. According to Hofstede, high power distance cultures were found in countries that let inequalities grow over time into inequalities of power and wealth. Low power distance cultures were found in societies that tried to play down such inequalities as much as possible.

The **individualism versus collectivism** dimension focused on the relationship between the individual and his or her fellows. In individualistic societies the ties between individuals were loose and individual achievement and freedom were highly valued. In societies where collectivism was emphasized the ties between individuals were tight. In such societies people were born into collectives, such as extended families, and everyone was supposed to look after the interest of his or her collective.

power distance Describes how a society deals with the inequity in people's physical and intellectual capabilities.

individualism versus collectivism Describes the relationship between the individual and his or her fellows.

Hofstede's **uncertainty avoidance** dimension measured the extent to which cultures socialized their members into accepting ambiguous situations and tolerating uncertainty. Members of high uncertainty avoidance cultures placed a premium on job security, career patterns, retirement benefits, and so on. They also had a strong need for rules and regulations; the manager was expected to issue clear instructions, and subordinates' initiatives were tightly controlled. Lower uncertainty avoidance cultures were characterized by a greater readiness to take risks and less emotional resistance to change.

Hofstede's **masculinity versus femininity** dimension looked at the relationship between gender and work roles. In masculine cultures sex roles were sharply differentiated and traditional "masculine values," such as achievement and the exercise of power, determined cultural ideals. In feminine cultures sex roles were less sharply distinguished, and little differentiation was made between men and women in the same job.

For each of these four dimensions Hofstede created an index score, which ranged from 0 to 100 and scored high for high individualism, high power distance, high uncertainty avoidance, and high masculinity. He averaged the score for all employees from a given country. Table 3.1 summarizes this data for 20 countries. The data show

uncertainty avoidance Measures the extent to which cultures socialized their members into accepting ambiguous situations and tolerating uncertainty.

masculinity versus femininity Describes the relationship between gender and work roles.

Table 3.1

Work-Related Values for 20 Selected Countries

	Power Distance	Uncertainty Avoidance	Individualism	Masculinity
Argentina	49	86	46	56
Australia	36	51	90	61
Brazil	69	76	38	49
Canada	39	48	80	52
Denmark	18	23	74	16
France	68	86	71	43
Germany (F.R.)	35	65	67	66
Great Britain	35	35	89	66
Indonesia	78	48	14	46
India	77	40	48	56
Israel	13	81	54	47
Japan	54	92	46	95
Mexico	81	82	30	69
Netherlands	38	53	80	14
Panama	95	86	11	44
Spain	57	86	51	42
Sweden	31	29	71	5
Thailand	64	64	20	34
Turkey	66	85	37	45
United States	40	46	91	62

Source: G. Hofstede, *Culture's Consequences,* Copyright ©1980 by Sage Publications. Reprinted by permission of Sage Publications, Inc.

that Western nations such as the United States, Canada, and Britain score high on the individualism scale and low on the power distance scale. At the other extreme are a group of Latin American and Asian countries that emphasize collectivism over individualism and score high on the power distance scale. Table 3.1 also reveals that Japan is a country with a culture of strong uncertainty avoidance and high masculinity. This characterization fits the standard stereotype of Japan as a country that is male dominant and where uncertainty avoidance exhibits itself in lifetime employment. Sweden and Denmark stand out as countries that have both low uncertainty avoidance and low masculinity (high emphasis on "feminine" values).

Evaluating Hofstede's Model

Many of Hofstede's findings are consistent with standard Western stereotypes about cultural differences. For example, the finding Americans are more individualistic and egalitarian than the Japanese (they have a lower power distance), who in turn are more individualistic and egalitarian than Mexicans, might strike many people as being reasonably valid. Similarly, many might agree that Latin countries such as Mexico place a higher emphasis on masculine value—they are machismo cultures—than the Nordic countries of Denmark and Sweden.

However, one should be careful about reading too much into Hofstede's research. For all of its fame, it is deficient in a number of important respects.[38] First, Hofstede assumes there is a one-to-one correspondence between culture and the nation-state, but as we saw earlier, many countries have more than one culture. Hofstede's results do not capture this distinction. Second, the research may have been culturally bound. The research team was composed of Europeans and Americans. The questions they asked of IBM employees and their analysis of the answers may have been shaped by their own cultural biases and concerns. So it is perhaps not surprising that Hofstede's results confirm Western stereotypes, since it was Westerners who undertook the research!

Third, Hofstede's subjects worked not only within a single industry, the computer industry, but also within a company, IBM. At the time IBM was renowned for its own strong corporate culture and employee selection procedures. It is possible, therefore, that the values of IBM employees are different in important respects from the values that underlie the cultures from which those employees came. Also, certain social classes (such as unskilled manual workers) were excluded from Hofstede's sample. A final caution is that Hofstede's work now looks dated. Cultures do not stand still, they evolve, albeit slowly. What was a reasonable characterization in the 1960s and 1970s may not be so today.

Still, just as it should not be accepted without question, Hofstede's work should not be dismissed entirely either. Several other scholars have also found strong evidence that differences in culture affect values and practices in the workplace.[39] The work by Hofstede and others represents a starting point for managers trying to figure out how cultures differ and what that might mean for management practices. Managers should use the results with caution, for they are not necessarily accurate.

Cultural Change

Culture is not a constant; it evolves over time, although changes in value systems can be slow and painful. In the 1960s, for example, American values toward the role of women, love, sex, and marriage changed significantly. Much of the social turmoil of that time reflected these changes. Similarly, today the value systems of many ex-Communist states, such as Russia, are undergoing significant changes as those countries move away from values that emphasize collectivism and toward those that emphasize individualism. Social turmoil is an inevitable outcome.

Some claim that a major cultural shift is now occurring in Japan, with a move toward greater individualism.[40] The model Japanese office worker, or salaryman, is pictured as being loyal to his boss and the organization to the point of giving up evenings, weekends, and vacations to serve the organization, which is the collective of which he is a member. However, a new generation of office workers does not seem to fit this model. It is claimed that an individual from the new generation

> is more direct than the traditional Japanese. He acts more like a Westerner, a gaijian. He does not live for the company, and will move on if he gets the offer of a better job. He is not keen on overtime, especially if he has a date with a girl. He has is own plans for his free time, and they may not include drinking or playing golf with the boss.[41]

A more detailed example of the changes occurring in Japan is given in the accompanying "Management Focus," which looks at the impact of Japan's changing culture on Hitachi Ltd.

The Hitachi example reviewed in the "Management Focus" points to two forces that may result in cultural change—economic advancement and globalization. Several studies have suggested that both these forces may be important factors in societal change.[42] For example, there is evidence that economic progress is accompanied by a shift in values away from collectivism and toward individualism.[43] Thus, as Japan has become richer, the cultural stress placed on collectivism has declined and greater individualism is being witnessed. If the Hitachi example is any guide, one reason for this shift may be that richer societies exhibit less need for social and material support structures built on collectives, whether the collective is the extended family or the paternalistic company. People are better able to take care of their own needs. As a result, the importance attached to collectivism declines, while greater economic freedoms lead directly to an increase in opportunities for expressing individualism.

Some have argued that the rise of global corporations, whose products can be found around the world, has created the conditions for the merging of cultures and a reduction in cultural variation. Do you think that this is so? Or could globalization of companies and products foster a shift towards and a reemphasis of a culture's roots and customs?
Paul Chelsey/Tony Stone Images.

Hitachi was founded in 1911 by Namihei Odaira, who named his company after the town in which it was based. By 1965 Hitachi was one of the giants of Japanese industry, with its sales accounting for more than 1 percent of Japan's gross national product. In many ways, Hitachi was a typical Japanese company. New recruits were lectured on Odaira's reverence for *wa,* or harmony. Managers and workers, dressed in identical uniforms, were tirelessly punctual and trusted each other like brothers. Decision making was characterized by the consensus model, typical of Japanese

bathhouse. In the evenings employees saw the same colleagues in the same company bars. Their wives shopped at the company store. The company even provided a wedding hall and funeral parlor.

Today two forces are affecting Japan's culture—prosperity and globalization. Both are leading to changes at Hitachi. Over the past four decades Japan has become one of the world's richest countries. At Hitachi, prosperity means that nobody sleeps two to a room in the company dormitory anymore. Since the 1960s employees have been moving "outside the fence," away from the company

leisure is an opportunity for individualism, not a prop for workplace harmony.

Like many other Japanese companies Hitachi is now a global enterprise with worldwide operations. Japanese society also has become more international in recent years. In this new environment, top management states bluntly that monoculture firms will not survive. In 1991 Hitachi set up a department to educate executives in other cultures. This department deliberately downplays the old notions of harmony and consensus decision making. Hitachi is also sending increasing numbers of its executives

*Hitachi and Japan's Changing Culture**

corporations, where managers consulted juniors exhaustively before making a decision. And the lifetime employment system was instituted at Hitachi.

According to old Hitachi hands, the harmony and togetherness owed as much to poverty as it did to anything else. Many employees and their families were housed in company dormitories because they could afford nothing else. Younger employees slept two to a room, and all ate their meals communally in the company cafeteria. Because public facilities were few, everyone went to the company

dormitories. Prosperity has brought more entertainment and leisure options. The company bathhouse has given way to private bathhouses. The choice between a French restaurant and an Indian restaurant divides one employee from the next. Hobbies are more diverse. There are cars, drinking, bonsai gardening, bands; before it was only drinking in company bars. Employees spend more time with their families; the biological family is replacing the company family as the anchor of social life. Companies such as Hitachi used to provide for all aspects of employees' lives. Now

for prolonged postings overseas, and it is starting to bring foreign managers to Japan. The foreign experience has encouraged senior managers to seek firmer leadership in Japan—to shift away from the old consensus decision-making model—and Hitachi's top executives have encouraged this trend.[44]

The culture may also change as societies become richer because economic progress affects a number of other factors, which in turn impact on culture. For example, increased urbanization and improvements in the quality and availability of education are both functions of economic progress, and both can lead to declining emphasis on the traditional values associated with poor rural societies.

Some have argued that advances in transportation and communication technologies, the dramatic increase in trade in goods and services that we have witnessed since World War II, and the rise of global corporations such as Hitachi, Disney, Microsoft, and Levi Strauss, whose products and operations can be found around the globe, are creating the conditions for the merging of cultures.[45] With McDonald's fast food in China, Levis in India, Sony Walkmans in South Africa, and MTV everywhere helping to foster a ubiquitous youth culture, some argue that the conditions have been created for reduced cultural variation across societies. At the same time, one must not ignore important countertrends, such as the shift toward Islamic fundamentalism in several Muslim countries, the separatist movement in Quebec, or the continuing ethnic strains and separatist movements in Russia. Such countertrends are often a reaction to the pressures for cultural convergence discussed here. In an increasingly modern and materialistic world, some societies are trying to reemphasize their cultural roots and uniqueness.

Implications for Business

International business is different from national business because countries and societies are different. In this chapter we have seen just how different societies can be. Societies differ because their cultures vary. Their cultures are different because of profound differences in social structure, religion, language, education, economic philosophy, and political philosophy. Two important implications for international business flow from these differences. The first is the need to develop cross-cultural literacy. There is a need to appreciate not only that cultural differences exist, but also to appreciate what such differences mean for international business. A second implication for international business centers on the connections among culture, the costs of doing business in a country, and national competitive advantage. There may be a link between culture and national competitive advantage. In this section, we will explore both of these issues in greater detail.

Cross-Cultural Literacy

One of the biggest dangers confronting a company that goes abroad for the first time is the danger of being ill-informed. International businesses that are ill-informed about the practices of another culture are unlikely to succeed. Doing business in different cultures requires adaptation to conform with the value systems and norms of that culture. Adaptation can embrace all aspects of an international firm's operations in a foreign country. The way in which deals are negotiated, the appropriate incentive pay systems for salespeople, the structure of the organization, the name of a product, the relations between management and labor, the manner in which the product is promoted, and so on, are all sensitive to cultural differences. What works in one culture might not work in another.

To combat the danger of being ill-informed, international business should consider employing local citizens. Businesses must also ensure that home country executives are cosmopolitan enough to understand how differences in culture affect the practice of international business. Multinational companies can build a cadre of cosmopolitan executives by transferring managers overseas at regular intervals to expose them to different cultures. Hitachi is taking this approach as it transforms itself from a Japanese company into a global company (see the "Management Focus" for details).

An international business must also be constantly on guard against the dangers of **ethnocentric behavior.** Ethnocentrism is a belief in the superiority of one's own ethnic group or culture. Hand in hand with ethnocentrism goes a disregard or contempt for the culture of other countries. Unfortunately ethnocentrism is prevalent; many Americans are guilty of it, as are many French people, Japanese people, British people, and so on. International businesses must be on continual guard against it.

ethnocentric behavior
Acting on the belief in the superiority of one's own ethnic group or culture.

Culture and Competitive Advantage

One theme that continually surfaced in this chapter is the relationship between culture and national competitive advantage. The value systems and norms of a country influence the costs of doing business in that country. The costs of doing business in a country influence the ability of firms based in that culture to establish a competitive advantage in the global marketplace. For example, we have seen how attitudes toward cooperation between management and labor, toward work, and toward the payment of interest are influenced by social structure and religion. It can be argued that the class-based conflict between workers and management that we find in British society raises the costs of doing business in that culture in so far as it leads to industrial disruption. This factor will tend to work against British firms, relative to say Japanese firms, where the importance of group identification minimizes conflict between management and labor. Similarly, we have seen how the ascetic "other worldly" ethics of Hinduism may not be as supportive of capitalism as the ethics embedded in Protestantism and Confucianism. We have also alluded to the possibility that the constraints on a country's banking system contained in Islamic laws on interest payments may put enterprises based in Islamic countries at a competitive disadvantage by raising the costs of doing business.

Some scholars have argued that the culture of modern Japan lowers the costs of doing business in that country, relative to the costs of doing business in most Western nations. Japan's emphasis on group affiliation, loyalty, reciprocal obligations, honesty, and education all boost the competitiveness of Japanese companies. Group affiliation and loyalty encourage individuals to identify strongly with the companies in which they work. This fosters an ethic of hard work and cooperation between management and labor "for the good of the company." Similarly, the concepts of reciprocal obligations and honesty help foster trust between companies and their suppliers. This encourages them to enter into long-term relationships with each other to work on factors such as inventory reduction, quality control, and design—all of which improve an organization's competitiveness. This level of cooperation has often been lacking in the West, where the relationships between a company and its suppliers tend to be short term and structured around competitive bidding, rather than based on long-term mutual commitments. In addition, the availability of a pool of highly skilled labor, particularly engineers, has helped Japanese enterprises develop cost-reducing process innovations that have boosted their productivity.[46] Thus, cultural factors may help explain the competitive advantage enjoyed by many Japanese businesses in the global marketplace and the rise of Japan as an economic power during the second half of the 20th century.

But it can also be argued that the culture of Japanese society is less supportive of entrepreneurial activity than, say, American society. Entrepreneurial activity is a product of an individualistic mind-set, and individualism is not a characteristic that the Japanese are known for. This may help explain why American enterprises, rather than Japanese corporations, dominate industries where entrepreneurship and innovation are highly valued, such as computer software and biotechnology.

For the international business, the connection between culture and competitive advantage is important for two reasons. First, the connection suggests which countries are likely to produce the most viable competitors. For example, US enterprises are likely to see continued growth in aggressive, cost-efficient competitors from Pacific Rim nations with a combination of free market economics, Confucian ideology, group-oriented social structures, and advanced education systems (e.g., South Korea, Taiwan, Japan, and increasingly China).

Second, the connection between culture and competitive advantage has important implications for the choice of countries in which to locate production facilities and do business. Consider the hypothetical case of a company deciding whether to locate a production facility in country A or B. Both countries are characterized by low labor costs and good access to world markets. Both countries are of roughly the same size (in terms of population) and both are at a similar stage of economic development. In country A the education system is undeveloped, the society is characterized by a marked stratification between the upper and lower classes, the dominant religion stresses the importance of reincarnation, and there are three major linguistic groups. In country B the education system is well-developed, there is a lack of social stratification, group identification is stressed by the culture, the dominant religion stresses the virtue of hard work, and there is only one linguistic group. Which country makes the best investment site?

Obviously country B does. The culture of country B is supportive of the capitalist mode of production and social harmony, whereas the culture of country A is not. In country A conflict between management and labor and between different language groups can be expected to lead to social and industrial disruption, thereby raising the costs of doing business. The lack of a good education system and the dominance of a religion that stresses ascetic behavior as a way of achieving advancement in the next life can also be expected to work against the attainment of business goals.

The same kind of comparison could be made for an international business trying to decide in which country to push its products. Again, country B would be the logical choice because cultural factors suggest that in the long-run country B is most likely to achieve the greatest level of economic growth. The culture of country A may produce economic stagnation.

Key Terms

Summary

We looked at the nature of social culture and implications for business practice. The following points have been made in the chapter:

1 Culture is that complex whole that includes knowledge, belief, art, morals, law, custom, and other capabilities acquired by people as members of society.

2 Values and norms are the central components of a culture. Values are abstract ideals about what a society believes to be good, right, and desirable. Norms are social rules and guidelines that prescribe appropriate behavior in particular situations.

3 Values and norms are influenced by political and economic philosophy, social structure, religion, language, and education.

4 The social structure of a society refers to its basic social organization. Social structures differ along two main dimensions: the individual-group dimension and the stratification dimension.

5 In some societies the individual is the basic building block of social organization. In these societies individual achievements are emphasized above all else. In other societies the group is the basic building block of social organization. In these societies group membership and group achievements are emphasized.

6 All societies are stratified into different classes. Class-conscious societies are characterized by low social mobility and a high degree of stratification. Less class-conscious societies are characterized by high social mobility and a low degree of stratification.

7 Religion may be defined as a system of shared beliefs and rituals that are concerned with the realm of the sacred. Ethical systems refer to a set of moral principles, or values, that are used to guide and shape behavior. The world's major religions are Christianity, Islam, Hinduism, and Buddhism. Although not a religion, Confucianism has an impact on behavior that is as profound as that of many religions. The values of different religious and ethical systems have implications for business practice.

8 Language is one defining characteristic of a culture. It has both a spoken and an unspoken dimension. In countries with more than one spoken language we tend to find more than one culture.

9 Formal education is the medium through which individuals learn skills and are socialized into the values and norms of a society. Education plays an important role in the determination of national competitive advantage.

10 Geert Hofstede studied how culture relates to values in the workplace. Hofstede isolated four dimensions that he claimed summarized different cultures: power distance, uncertainty avoidance, individualism versus collectivism, and masculinity versus femininity.

11 Culture is not a constant; it evolves over time. Economic progress and globalization are two important engines of cultural change.

12 One danger confronting a company that goes abroad for the first time is being ill-informed. To develop cross-cultural literacy international businesses need to employ host country nationals, build a cadre of cosmopolitan executives, and guard against the dangers of ethnocentric behavior.

13 The value systems and norms of a country can affect the costs of doing business in that country.

Critical Thinking and Discussion Questions

1 Outline why the culture of a country might influence the costs of doing business in that country. Illustrate your answer with examples.

2 Do you think business practices in an Islamic country are likely to differ from business practices in the United States, and if so how?

3 What are the implications of differences in the dominant religion and/or ethical system of a country for international business?

4 Choose two countries that appear to be culturally diverse. Compare the cultures of those countries and then indicate how cultural differences influence (a) the costs of doing business in each country, (b) the likely future economic development of that country, and (c) business practices.

Internet Exercises

1 Nestlé, the world's largest food company, is headquartered in Switzerland, but its products can be found all over the world. Many people may be unaware that products they consume on a regular basis are sold by the Swiss giant. Nestlé sells a range of products in the US market including Stouffer's frozen meals and Perrier water. Despite a self-made reference to being the world's food company, the Nestlé name is often hidden in product packaging. In fact, while Nestlé's presence in markets around the globe is huge, its name is not. Instead, the company has chosen an unusual strategy for its international expansion, selling some products the same way around the globe, but developing new products for individual markets as well. The company has found that because food products tend to reflect cultural preferences, the Nestlé product line must acknowledge local preferences and needs in different markets.

Go to Nestlé's US website (**www.nestle.com**) and examine not only the product line, but also how products are presented and promoted. Following the discussion in your text, consider the various elements that make up culture, particularly those that affect food preferences. Identify how Nestlé is responding to cultural preferences in the US market. Next, explore its United Kingdom site (**www.nestle.co.uk**) and its Japanese (**www.nestle.co.jp/japan/index-e.htm**) and Filipino (**www.nestle.com.ph**) sites. How do the other sites differ from the US site? What conclusions can you draw about the local cultures in the United Kingdom, Japan, and the Philippines? In your opinion, is it important for companies expanding into new markets via the Internet to develop individual sites for different cultures? Why or why not?

2 American Internet companies, perhaps because of their relatively rapid success at home, are getting a wake-up call as they expand into Europe, arguably the next big market for e-commerce. Foreign websites are being developed and established on a regular basis. But to the surprise of many of these American companies, the going is not easy. Local competitors have already made a name for themselves, and American companies are finding themselves trying to catch up. Many companies appear to be unsure how they should approach the market across the big pond. Some are taking a cookie-cutter approach and establishing websites that are simply an extension of their American sites, while others seem to be taking a country-by-country approach to the market. The former group seemingly believes that the Internet culture will overcome any differences of national culture, while those companies following the latter strategy appear to believe that a more traditional approach to markets is necessary even in an unconventional business format.

American auction powerhouse eBay.com apparently believes that if you build it, they will come. The company has followed virtually the same approach to attracting business in Europe as it has in the United States—its European site initially even priced products in US dollars. While the company has since revised its strategy to price products in local currencies, it concedes that it may be too late. European competitors such as QXL.com and eurobid.com have followed a different strategy, recognizing cultural and other differences between markets. Go to eBay's American site (**www.ebay.com**) and also its Britiash site (**eBay.co.uk**) and explore the similarities and differences between the sites. Then, examine QXL.com PLC of Britain (**www.qxl.com**) and also eurobid.com. How are the strategies of the European competitors different from that of eBay. In your opinion, is eBay positioned to take market share from its European competitors, or have the European firms already capitalized on first-mover advantages? Do you believe that a cookie-cutter approach will work in e-commerce, or is it necessary, even in electronic business, to follow a more traditional strategy that recognizes differences between markets?

Source: *The Wall Street Journal*, 11/15/99, A25

Disney in France

Until 1992 the Walt Disney Company had experienced nothing but success in the theme park business. Its first park, Disneyland, opened in Anaheim, California, in 1955 and was an instant success. Its theme song, "It's a Small World After All," promoted "an idealized vision of America spiced with reassuring glimpses of exotic cultures all calculated to promote heartwarming feelings about living together as one happy family. There were dark tunnels and bumpy rides to scare the children a little but none of the terrors of the real world . . . The Disney characters that everyone knew from the cartoons and comic books were on hand to shepherd the guests and to direct them to the Mickey Mouse watches."[47]

In the 1970s the triumph was repeated in Florida, and in 1983 Disney proved that the Japanese too have a real affinity for Mickey Mouse with the successful opening of Tokyo Disneyland. Having wooed the Japanese, in 1986 Disney executives turned their attention to Paris, the self-proclaimed capital of European high culture and style. "Why did they pick France?" many asked. When word first got out that Disney wanted to build another international theme park, officials from more than 200 locations all over the world descended on Disney with pleas and cash inducements to work the Disney magic in their hometowns. But Paris was chosen because of demographics and subsidies. About 17 million Europeans live less than a two-hour drive from Paris. Another 310 million can fly there in the same time or less. Also, the French government was so eager to attract Disney to Paris that it offered the company more than $1 billion in various incentives, all in the expectation that the project would create 30,000 French jobs.

From the start cultural gaffes by Disney set the tone for the project.

By late 1986 Disney was deep in negotiations with the French government. To the exasperation of the Disney team, headed by Joe Shapiro, the talks were taking far longer than expected. Jean-Rene Bernard, the chief French negotiator, said he was astonished when Mr. Shapiro, his patience ebbing, ran to the door of the room and in a very un-Gallic gesture, began kicking it repeatedly, shouting, "Get me something to break!"

There was also snipping from Parisian intellectuals who attacked the transplantation of Disney's dream world as an assault on French culture; "a cultural Chernobyl," one prominent intellectual called it. The minister of culture announced he would boycott the opening, proclaiming it to be an unwelcome symbol of American clichés and a consumer society. Unperturbed, Disney pushed ahead with the planned summer 1992 opening of the $5 billion park. Soon after Euro-Disneyland opened, French farmers drove their tractors to the entrance and blocked it. This globally televised act of protest was aimed not at Disney but at the US government, which had been demanding that French agricultural subsidies be cut. Still, it focused world attention on the loveless marriage of Disney and Paris.

Then there were the operational errors. Disney's policy of serving no alcohol in the park, since reversed, caused astonishment in a country where a glass of wine for lunch is a given. Disney thought that Monday would be a light day for visitors and Friday a heavy one and allocated staff accordingly; but the reality was the reverse. Another unpleasant surprise was the hotel breakfast debacle. "We were told that Europeans 'don't take breakfast,' so we downsized the restaurants," recalled one Disney executive. "And guess what? Everybody showed up for

breakfast. We were trying to serve 2,500 breakfasts in a 350-seat restaurant at some of the hotels. The lines were horrendous. Moreover, they didn't want the typical French breakfast of croissants and coffee, which was our assumption. They wanted bacon and eggs." Lunch turned out to be another problem. "Everybody wanted lunch at 12:30. The crowds were huge. Our smiling cast members had to calm down surly patrons and engage in some 'behavior modification' to teach them that they could eat lunch at 11 AM or 2 PM."

There were major staffing problems too. Disney tried to use the same teamwork model with its staff that had worked so well in America and Japan, but it ran into trouble in France. In the first nine weeks of Euro-Disneyland's operation, roughly 1,000 employees, 10 percent of the total, left. One former employee was a 22-year-old medical student from a nearby town who signed up for a weekend job. After two days of "brainwashing," as he called Disney's training, he left following a dispute with his supervisor over the timing of his lunch hour. Another former employee noted, "I don't think that they realized what Europeans were like . . . that we ask questions and don't think all the same way."

One of the biggest problems, however, was that Europeans didn't stay as long at the park as Disney expected. While Disney succeeded in getting close to 9 million visitors a year through the park gates, in line with its plans, most stayed only a day or two. Few stayed the four to five days that Disney had hoped for. Most Europeans regard theme parks as places for day excursions not as destinations for an extended vacation. This was a big shock for Disney; the company had invested billions of dollars in building luxury hotels next to the park—hotels the day-trippers didn't need and that stood half empty most of the time. To make matters worse, the French didn't show up in the expected numbers. In 1994 only 40 percent of the park's visitors were French. One puzzled executive noted that many visitors were Americans living in Europe or, stranger still, Japanese on a European vacation! As a result, by the end of 1994 Euro-Disneyland had cumulative losses of $2 billion.

At this point Euro-Disney changed its strategy. First, the company changed the name to Disneyland Paris in an attempt to strengthen the park's identity. Second, food and fashion offerings were changed. To quote one manager, "We opened with restaurants providing French-style food service, but we found that customers wanted self-service like in the US parks. Similarly, products in the boutiques were initially toned down for the French market, but since then the range has changed to give it a more definite Disney image." Third, the prices for day tickets and hotel rooms were cut by one-third. The result was an attendance of 11.7 million in 1996, up from a low of 8.8 million in 1994.[48]

At the age of 25, Tom West jump-started his international corporate career. He moved from his job with the Ogilvy & Mather Public Relations Group in New York to the Singapore office as a consultant in charge of investor relations. Ogilvy & Mather had decided to expand its investor relations business in Singapore. Tom joined a 26-person staff, which consisted of only one other American. Tom was responsible for helping investment banks market their initial

East Meets West

public offerings (IPOs) to investors.

Living and working abroad was the realization of a dream that germinated when Tom was a schoolboy in Montreal. Because of his father's job, Tom had lived in a number of cities in North America. However, the Montreal experience was a turning point even though Tom was only eight years old. "I discovered that there were other cultures, other foods, other experiences so dif-

ferent from my own," Tom said. His dream was cultivated when Tom enrolled at Washington and Lee University in Lexington, Virginia, to major in French literature and later when he spent a year studying in Paris.

Landing an international position, however, required more than his ability to speak a foreign language and his sheer desire. "You need to lobby extensively for the international opportunity and to find a mentor. Most importantly,

when an opportunity arises you need to make a strong business case to send an expatriate rather than hire a local," advised Tom.

Tom was sent to Singapore because he possessed business skills that the locals did not at the time. His work abroad consisted largely of the same duties he had performed in the United States to raise favorable media awareness of IPOs before they went public. He wrote corporate and financial news releases, brochures, and

speeches for the company officers. He arranged for interviews with company officers and the press. He also handled PR for domestic and multinational companies operating in Singapore.

Tom worked with both domestic and multinational companies. His diverse client base included a manufacturer of local area network products, an oil and gas shipper, a Singaporean taxicab service, and a global telecommunications company.

Surprisingly, Tom's youth was not an obstacle in doing business in a culture that reveres age. Tom revealed that the secret was his New York experience, which was unavailable in Singapore. "My age was not a problem as long as I approached the clients with the attitude of sharing knowledge. They were very eager to obtain my expertise."

Tom found that developing media relations for his clients was far easier in Singapore than in

120

New York. He found that the reporters in Singapore were much more accessible and more receptive to hearing story ideas that involve clients. Tom suggested that the pro-business stance resulted partially from the close ties between the press and the government, which strongly promoted economic growth.

"It was not a hard sell to call up a reporter and go to lunch and talk about your new client. In New York as a rookie PR person I would have about 30 seconds on someone's answering machine to make the pitch before I got cut off," Tom said.

Tom observed the media frequently ran front-page stories supporting the government's efforts to promote healthy lifestyles and socially responsible behavior in addition to economic development. Consequently, a smart PR firm could capitalize on such a trend by developing compatible campaigns. Tom described how one of his clients, a multinational pharmaceutical company, launched a baby formula by sponsoring a question-and-answer forum on nutrition for new mothers. The event was conducted in the midst of an important government effort to promote children's health and thus was widely reported.

Conducting public relations in Singapore presented some challenges. For example, it was not a completely homogenous country. Although predominantly Chinese, there were Malay and Indian minorities. To reach all these segments effectively it was necessary to use a variety of ethnic media, not simply the largest or the English-speaking press.

According to Tom, one could easily make a serious business blunder by causing a client to lose "face by not offering enough respect to a person of authority." Tom quickly learned the value of "face" when he nearly lost an account as the result of an innocent mistake. In writing thank-you letters to two executives with the same surname in the same firm, Tom mixed up their titles. The senior manager was quite distraught and contacted Tom's boss. Even though the error was unintentional, the senior manager was convinced that he had lost face. Tom as well as his superior had to issue separate apologies to smooth over the incident.

"It was also considered disrespectful to challenge a superior in a meeting. Americans must learn to express disagreement very delicately instead of aggressively," Tom advised. "This is difficult for Americans who value conflict believing that it often leads to better ideas."

If Tom were hiring a replacement, he would look for someone with the right skill set who was committed to a foreign experience. "No company will go to campus looking for people who want to travel overseas. They hire people to work in their accounting, sales, and marketing departments. However, to flourish in an overseas assignment, you need to be patient, flexible, and open to understanding cultures other than your own."

four

International Trade
Theory

Chapter

Opening Case   The Gains from
Trade: Ghana and
South Korea

In 1970 living standards in Ghana
and South Korea were roughly comparable. Ghana's 1970 gross national product (GNP) per head was
$250 and South Korea's was $260.
By 1995 the situation had changed
dramatically. South Korea had a
GNP per capita of $9,700, while
Ghana's was only $390, reflecting
vastly different economic growth
rates. Between 1968 and 1995 the
average annual growth rate in
Ghana's GNP was less than 1.4

The international trade policies for Ghana and South Korea offer strikingly contrasting results. What factors could have motivated Ghana's first president, Kwame Nkrumah, to make the decisions he did? How could two countries with similar living standards change so dramatically in 25 years?

Learning Objectives

1 Understand why nations trade with each other.

2 Be aware of the different theories that explain trade flows between nations.

3 Understand why many economists believe that unrestricted (free) trade between nations will raise the economic welfare of all countries that participate in a free trade system.

4 Be familiar with the arguments of those who maintain that government can play a proactive role in promoting national competitive advantage in certain industries.

5 Understand the important implications that international trade theory holds for business practice.

---

percent. In contrast, South Korea achieved a rate of about 9 percent annually between 1968 and 1995.

What explains the difference in the recent economic history of Ghana and South Korea? There is no simple answer, but the attitudes of both countries toward international trade might provide part of the explanation. A study by the World Bank shows that the South Korean government implemented policies that encouraged South Korean

companies to engage in international trade, but the actions of the Ghanaian government discouraged domestic producers from becoming involved in international trade. As a consequence, in 1980 trade accounted for 18 percent of Ghana's GNP, compared to 74 percent of South Korea's.

Ghana in 1957 became the first of Great Britain's West African colonies to become independent. Its first president, Kwame Nkrumah,

influenced the rest of the continent with his theories of pan-African socialism. For Ghana this meant high tariffs on many imports, an import substitution policy aimed at fostering Ghana self-sufficiency in certain manufactured goods, and the adoption of policies that discouraged Ghana's enterprises from exporting. The results were an unmitigated disaster that transformed one of Africa's most prosperous nations into one of the world's poorest.

As an illustration of how Ghana's antitrade policies destroyed the country's economy, consider the government's involvement in the cocoa trade. A combination of favorable climate, good soils, and ready access to world shipping routes has given Ghana an absolute advantage in cocoa production. It is one of the best places in the world to grow cocoa. As a consequence, Ghana was the world's largest producer and exporter of cocoa in 1957. Then the government of the newly independent nation created a state-controlled cocoa marketing board. The board was given the authority to fix prices for cocoa and was designated the sole buyer of all cocoa grown in Ghana. The board held down the prices that it paid farmers for cocoa, while selling the cocoa on the world market at world prices. Thus, it might buy cocoa from farmers at 25 cents a pound and sell it on the world market for 50 cents a pound. In effect, the board was taxing exports by paying farmers considerably less for their cocoa than it was worth on the world market and putting the difference into government coffers. This money was used to fund the government policy of nationalization and industrialization.

Between 1963 and 1979 the price paid by the cocoa marketing board to Ghana's farmers increased by a factor of 6, while the price of consumer goods in Ghana increased by a factor of 22, and the price of cocoa in neighboring countries increased by a factor of 36! In real terms, the Ghanaian farmers were paid less every year for their cocoa by the cocoa marketing board, while the world price increased significantly. Ghana's farmers responded by switching to the production of subsistence food-

stuffs that could be sold within Ghana, and the country's production and exports of cocoa plummeted by more than one-third in seven years. At the same time, the Ghanaian government's attempt to build an industrial base through state-run enterprises was a failure. The resulting drop in Ghana's export earnings plunged the country into recession, led to a decline in its foreign currency reserves, and severely limited its ability to pay for necessary imports.

The inward-oriented trade policy of the Ghanaian government resulted in a shift of that country's resources away from the profitable activity of growing cocoa—where it had an absolute advantage in the world economy—and toward growing subsistence foods and manufacturing, where it had no advantage. This inefficient use of the country's resources severely damaged the Ghanaian economy and held back the country's economic development.

In contrast, consider the trade policy adopted by the South Korean government. The World Bank has characterized the trade policy of South Korea as strongly outward-oriented. The policies of the South Korean government emphasized low import barriers on manufactured goods (but not on agricultural goods) and incentives to encourage South Korean firms to export. Beginning in the late 1950s, the South Korean government progressively reduced import tariffs from an average of 60 percent of the price of an imported good to less than 20 percent in the mid-1980s. On most nonagricultural goods, import tariffs were eliminated. In addition, the number of imported goods subject to quotas was reduced from more

than 90 percent in the late 1950s to zero by the early 1980s. Over the same period South Korea progressively reduced the subsidies given to South Korean exporters from an average of 80 percent of their sales price in the late 1950s to an average of less than 20 percent of their sales price in 1965, and down to zero in 1984. With the exception of the agricultural sector (where a strong farm lobby maintained import controls), South Korea moved progressively toward a free trade stance.

South Korea's outward-looking orientation has been rewarded by a dramatic transformation of its economy. Initially, South Korea's resources shifted from agriculture to the manufacture of labor-intensive goods, especially textiles, clothing, and footwear. An abundant supply of cheap but well-educated labor helped form the basis of South Korea's comparative advantage in labor-intensive manufacturing. More recently, as labor costs have risen, the growth areas in the economy have been in the more capital-intensive manufacturing sectors, especially motor vehicles, semiconductors, consumer electronics, and advanced materials. As a result of these developments, South Korea has gone through some dramatic changes. In the late 1950s, 77 percent of the country's employment was in the agricultural sector; today the figure is less than 20 percent. Over the same period the percentage of its GNP accounted for by manufacturing increased from less than 10 percent to more than 30 percent, while the overall GNP grew at an annual rate of more than 9 percent.[1]

Introduction

The opening case illustrates the gains that come from international trade. For a long time the economic policies of the Ghanaian government discouraged trade with other nations. The result was a shift in Ghana's resources away from productive uses (growing cocoa) and toward unproductive uses (subsistence agriculture). The economic policies of the South Korean government encouraged trade with other nations. The result was a shift in South Korea's resources away from uses where it had no comparative advantage in the world economy (agriculture) and toward more productive uses (labor-intensive manufacturing). As a direct result of their policies toward international trade, Ghana's economy declined while South Korea's grew.

This chapter has two goals that are related to the story of Ghana and South Korea. The first is to review a number of theories that explain why international trade benefits a country. The second goal is to explain the pattern of international trade that we observe in the world economy. We will be primarily concerned with explaining the pattern of exports and imports of products between countries. We will not be concerned with foreign direct investment between countries; that is discussed in Chapter 6.

An Overview of Trade Theory

We open this chapter with a discussion of mercantilism. Propagated in the 16th and 17th centuries, mercantilism advocated that countries should simultaneously encourage exports and discourage imports. Although mercantilism is an old and largely discredited doctrine, its echoes remain in modern political debate and in the trade policies of many countries. Next we will look at Adam Smith's theory of absolute advantage. Proposed in 1776, Smith's theory was the first to explain why unrestricted free trade is beneficial to a country. **Free trade** occurs when a government does not attempt to influence through quotas or duties what its citizens can buy from another country or what they can produce and sell to another country. Smith argued that the invisible hand of the market mechanism, rather than government policy, should determine what a country imports and what it exports. His arguments imply that such a *laissez-faire* stance toward trade is in the best interests of a country. Building on Smith's work are two additional theories that we shall review. One is the theory of comparative advantage, advanced by the 19th century English economist David Ricardo. This theory is the intellectual basis of the modern argument for unrestricted free trade. In the 20th century Ricardo's work was refined by two Swedish economists, Eli Heckscher and Bertil Ohlin, whose theory is known as the Heckscher–Ohlin theory.

free trade Situation in which a government does not attempt to influence through quotas or duties what its citizens can buy from another country or what they can produce and sell to another country.

The Benefits of Trade

The great strength of the theories of Smith, Ricardo, and Heckscher–Ohlin is that they identify the specific benefits of international trade. Common sense suggests that some international trade is beneficial. For example, nobody would suggest that Iceland should grow its own oranges. Iceland can benefit from trade by exchanging some of the products it can produce at a low cost (fish) for some products it cannot produce at all (oranges). Thus, by engaging in international trade, Icelanders are able to add oranges to their diet of fish.

The theories of Smith, Ricardo, and Heckscher–Ohlin go beyond this common-sense notion, however, to show why it is beneficial for a country to engage in international trade *even for products it is able to produce for itself.* This is a difficult concept.

For example, many people in the United States believe that American consumers should buy products produced in the United States by American companies whenever possible to help save American jobs from foreign competition. Such thinking apparently was behind a decision by the International Trade Commission to protect the Louisiana crawfish industry from inexpensive Chinese imports (see the accompanying "Country Focus").

The same kind of nationalistic sentiments can be observed in many other countries. However, the theories of Smith, Ricardo, and Heckscher–Ohlin tell us that a country's economy may gain if its citizens buy from other nations certain products that could be produced at home. The gains arise because international trade allows a country to specialize in the manufacture and export of products that can be produced most efficiently in that country, while importing products that can be produced more efficiently in other countries. So it may make sense for the United States to specialize in the production and export of commercial jet aircraft, since the efficient production of commercial jet aircraft requires resources that are abundant in the United States, such as a highly skilled labor force and cutting-edge technological know-how. On the other hand, it may make sense for the United States to import textiles from India because the efficient production of textiles requires a relatively cheap labor force—and cheap labor is not abundant in the United States.

This economic argument is often difficult for segments of a country's population to accept. With their future threatened by imports, American textile companies and their employees have tried hard to persuade the US government to limit the importation of textiles by demanding quotas and tariffs. Similarly, as the "Country Focus" illustrates, with its future threatened by imports, the Louisiana crawfish industry succeeded in its attempt to persuade the government to limit imports of crawfish from China. Although such import controls may benefit particular groups, such as American textile businesses and their employees or Louisiana crawfish farmers, the theories of Smith, Ricardo, and Heckscher–Ohlin suggest that the economy as a whole is hurt by this kind of action. Limits on imports are often in the interests of domestic producers but not domestic consumers; they are pro-producer and anti-consumer.

The Pattern of International Trade

The theories of Smith, Ricardo, and Heckscher–Ohlin also help to explain the pattern of international trade that we observe in the world economy. Some aspects of the pattern are easy to understand. Climate and natural resources explain why Ghana exports cocoa, Brazil exports coffee, Saudi Arabia exports oil, and China exports crawfish. But much of the observed pattern of international trade is more difficult to explain. For example, why does Japan export automobiles, consumer electronics, and machine tools? Why does Switzerland export chemicals, watches, and jewelry? David Ricardo's theory of comparative advantage offers an explanation in terms of international differences in labor productivity. The more sophisticated Heckscher–Ohlin theory emphasizes the interplay between the proportions in which the factors of production (such as land, labor, and capital) are available in different countries and the proportions in which they are needed for producing particular goods. This explanation rests on the assumption that countries have different endowments of the factors of production. Tests of this theory, however, suggest it is a less powerful explanation of real-world trade patterns than once thought.

One early response to the failure of the Heckscher–Ohlin theory to explain the observed pattern of international trade was the *product life-cycle theory*. Proposed by Raymond Vernon, this theory suggests that early in their life cycle, most new products are produced in and exported from the country in which they were developed.

Once upon a time Louisiana was owned by the French. Napoleon sold the territory to the United States when Thomas Jefferson was president, but many of the French stayed on. Over time, their descendants developed the distinctive Cajun culture that today is celebrated in the United States for its unique cuisine and music. At the heart of that cuisine can be found the venerable crawfish, as Louisianian's call the crayfish. The crawfish is a fresh-water crustacean that is native to the bayous of Louisiana. A central ingredient of crawfish pie, bisque, etouffee, and gumbo, the crawfish is to Cajun Louisiana what wine is to France, a culinary symbol of its culture. It is also a major industry

for native Louisiana crawfish. With a significant price advantage on their side, sales of Chinese imports skyrocketed from 353,000 pounds in 1992 to 5.5 million pounds in 1996. By 1996, Louisiana state officials estimated that 3,000 jobs had been lost in the local industry, mostly minimum-wage crawfish peelers, due to market share gains made by the Chinese.

This was too much for the Louisiana industry. In 1996, Louisiana's Crawfish Promotion and Research Board filed a petition requesting an antidumping action with the International Trade Commission, an arm of the US government. The petition claimed that Chinese crawfish producers were dumping their product, selling at below cost to drive

and benefited from a steadier supply, and good for Louisiana cuisine, because it has become less expensive to cook. The lawyers point out that the action is not in the interests of American consumers because it is nothing more than an attempt by Louisiana producers to reestablish their lucrative monopoly on the production of crawfish, a monopoly that would enable them to extract higher prices from consumers.

However, the International Trade Commission was deaf to such arguments. Using "Alice in Wonderland" reasoning, the commission deemed that China is a "nonmarket economy" since it is not yet a member of the World Trade Organization. The commission then used

Crawfish Wars

that generates $300 million per year in revenues for Louisiana crawfish farmers—or at least it did until the Chinese appeared.

In the early 1990s, Louisiana importers encouraged development of the Chinese industry to meet the growing demand for crawfish. In China, the crawfish industry proved to be attractive for entrepreneurial farmers looking for ways to make profits. Chinese crawfish first started to appear on the Louisiana scene in 1991. Although old-time Cajuns were quick to claim the Chinese crawfish had an inferior taste, consumers didn't seem to notice the difference. More importantly perhaps, they liked the price, which ran between $2 and $3 per pound depending on the season, compared to $5 to $8 per pound

Louisiana producers out of business. The industry requested that a 200 to 300 percent import tax be placed on Chinese crawfish. The State of Louisiana spent $350,000 to support the action.

Lawyers representing the Chinese crawfish industry claimed that lower production costs in China were the reason for the low prices—not dumping. One Louisiana-based importer of Chinese crawfish pointed out that 27 processing plants in China supplied his company. Workers at these plants were given housing and other amenities and in addition paid 15 cents per hour, or $9 for a 60-hour week. Also, claim these lawyers, Chinese crawfish have been good for American consumers, who have saved money

prices in a "market economy," Spain, to establish a benchmark for a "fair market value" for crawfish. Since Spanish crawfish sell for approximately twice the price of Chinese crawfish, and about the same price as Louisiana crawfish, the commission concluded that the Chinese were dumping (selling below costs of production). In August 1997, the commission levied a 110 to 123 percent duty on imports of Chinese crawfish, effectively negating the price advantage enjoyed by Chinese producers. In the interests of protecting American jobs the commission had sided with Louisiana producers and against American consumers, who would now have to pay higher prices for crawfish.[2]

As a new product becomes widely accepted internationally, however, production starts in other countries. As a result, the theory suggests, the product may ultimately be exported back to the country of its original innovation.

In a similar vein, during the 1980s economists such as Paul Krugman of MIT developed what has come to be known as the *new trade theory*. New trade theory stresses that in some cases countries specialize in the production and export of particular products not because of underlying differences in factor endowments, but because in certain industries the world market can support only a limited number of firms. (This is argued to be the case for the commercial aircraft industry.) In such industries, firms that enter the market first build a competitive advantage that is subsequently difficult to challenge. Thus, the observed pattern of trade between nations may in part be due to the ability of firms within a given nation to capture first-mover advantages. The United States predominates in the export of commercial jet aircraft because American firms such as Boeing were first movers in the world market. Boeing built a competitive advantage that has been difficult for firms from countries with equally favorable factor endowments to challenge.

In a work related to the new trade theory, Michael Porter of Harvard Business School has recently developed a theory that attempts to explain why particular nations achieve international success in certain industries. We shall refer to this theory as the theory of national competitive advantage. Like the new trade theorists, in addition to factor endowments, Porter points out the importance of country factors such as domestic demand and domestic rivalry in explaining a nation's dominance in the production and export of particular products.

Trade Theory and Government Policy

Although all these theories agree that international trade is beneficial to a country, they lack agreement in their recommendations for government policy. Mercantilism makes a crude case for government involvement in promoting exports and limiting imports. The theories of Smith, Ricardo, and Heckscher–Ohlin form part of the case for unrestricted free trade. The argument for unrestricted free trade is that both import controls and export incentives (such as subsidies) are self-defeating and result in wasted resources. On the other hand, both the new trade theory and Porter's theory of national competitive advantage can be interpreted as justifying some limited and selective government intervention to support the development of certain export-oriented industries. We will discuss the pros and cons of this argument, known as strategic trade policy, as well as the pros and cons of the argument for unrestricted free trade, in Chapter 5.

Mercantilism

The first theory of international trade emerged in England in the mid-16th century. Referred to as *mercantilism,* its principle assertion was that gold and silver were the mainstays of national wealth and essential to vigorous commerce. At that time, gold and silver were the currency of trade between countries; a country could earn gold and silver by exporting goods. By the same token, importing goods from other countries would result in an outflow of gold and silver to those countries. The main tenet of **mercantilism** was that it was in a country's best interests to maintain a trade surplus, to export more than it imported. By doing so, a country would accumulate gold and silver and, consequently, increase its national wealth and prestige. As the English mercantilist writer Thomas Mun put it in 1630:

> The ordinary means therefore to increase our wealth and treasure is by foreign trade, wherein we must ever observe this rule: to sell more to strangers yearly than we consume of theirs in value.[3]

Consistent with this belief, the mercantilist doctrine advocated government intervention to achieve a surplus in the balance of trade. The mercantilists saw no virtue in a large volume of trade. Rather, they recommended policies to maximize exports and minimize imports. To achieve this, imports were limited by tariffs and quotas, and exports were subsidized.

mercantilism Theory of international trade that believes it is in a country's best interests to export more than it imports.

An inherent inconsistency in the mercantilist doctrine was pointed out by the classical economist David Hume in 1752. According to Hume, if England had a balance-of-trade surplus with France (it exported more than it imported) the resulting inflow of gold and silver would swell the domestic money supply and generate inflation in England. In France, however, the outflow of gold and silver would have the opposite effect. France's money supply would contract, and its prices would fall. This change in relative prices between France and England would encourage the French to buy fewer English goods (because they were becoming more expensive) and the English to buy more French goods (because they were becoming cheaper). The result would be a deterioration in the English balance of trade and an improvement in France's trade balance, until the English surplus was eliminated. Hence, according to Hume, in the long run no country could sustain a surplus in the balance of trade and so accumulate gold and silver as the mercantilists had envisaged.

The flaw with mercantilism was that it viewed trade as a zero-sum game. (A **zero-sum game** is one in which a gain by one country results in a loss by another.) It was left to Adam Smith and David Ricardo to show the shortsightedness of this approach and to demonstrate that trade is a **positive-sum game,** or a situation in which all countries can benefit. We shall discuss the views of Smith next. Before doing so, however, we must note that the mercantilist doctrine is by no means dead.[4] For example, Jarl Hagelstam, a director at the Finnish Ministry of Finance, has observed that in most trade negotiations:

> The approach of individual negotiating countries, both industrialized and developing, has been to press for trade liberalization in areas where their own comparative competitive advantages are the strongest, and to resist liberalization in areas where they are less competitive and fear that imports would replace domestic production.[5]

Hagelstam attributes this strategy to a neo-mercantilist belief held by the politicians of many nations. This belief equates political power with economic power and economic power with a balance-of-trade surplus. Thus, the trade strategy of many nations is designed to simultaneously boost exports and limit imports. For example, many American politicians claim that Japan is a neo-mercantilist nation because its government, while publicly supporting free trade, simultaneously seeks to protect certain segments of its economy from more efficient foreign competition.

Absolute Advantage

In his 1776 landmark book *The Wealth of Nations,* Adam Smith attacked the mercantilist assumption that trade is a zero-sum game. Smith argued that countries differ in their ability to produce goods efficiently. In his time, for example, the English were the world's most efficient manufacturers of textiles because of their superior manufacturing processes. Because of the combination of favorable climate, good soils, and accumulated expertise, the French had the world's most efficient wine industry. The English had an *absolute advantage* in the production of textiles, while the French had an *absolute advantage* in the production of wine. Thus, a country has an **absolute advantage** in the production of a product when it is more efficient than any other country in producing it.

According to Smith, countries should specialize in the production of goods for which they have an absolute advantage and then trade these goods for the goods produced by other countries. In Smith's time this suggested that the English should specialize in the production of textiles while the French should specialize in the production of wine. England could get all the wine it needed by selling its textiles to France and buying wine in exchange. Similarly, France could get all the

Chapter 4 International Trade Theory

In the international arena Japan has long been a strong supporter of free trade agreements. However, the US government has repeatedly suggested that the approach taken by the Japanese is a cynical neo-mercantilist one. The Japanese, US officials say, are happy to sign international agreements that open foreign markets to the products of Japanese companies, but at the same time they protect their home market from foreign competition. As evidence, US officials point to the large trade imbalance between the United States and Japan, which in 1994 ran at over $80 billion (meaning that the United States imported $80 billion more in would have more than doubled and prices in Japan would have fallen substantially.

The study suggested that falling prices would have saved the average Japanese consumer about $890 per year in 1989. At the same time, however, there would have been a fall in Japanese production of more than 20 percent in certain areas including wheat, oilseeds, leaf tobacco, canned fruit and vegetables, and cosmetics. Trade liberalization would also have resulted in the loss of more than 180,000 Japanese jobs. It would seem, therefore, that Japan's government protects these areas from more efficient foreign competition in order to

Other developed countries import between 22 percent and 78 percent of their autos and 16 percent and 60 percent of their auto parts. According to US trade negotiators, the Japanese government limits imports into Japan by requiring stringent safety inspections that are designed to raise the costs to foreigners trying to sell in Japan. For example, the US Commerce Department claims that the addition of front brush guards to a recreational vehicle, a safety feature required only in Japan, necessitates a complete reinspection that costs up to $3,000 per vehicle.

The Japanese government rejects such charges. Officials ar-

Is Japan a Neo-mercantilist Nation?

goods from Japan than it exported to Japan).

The US government recently received support from an unlikely source: three Japanese economists. In a study published in 1994 the three economists cited food products, cosmetics, and chemical production as areas where the Japanese government protected Japanese industry from more efficient foreign competition through a variety of import restrictions, such as quotas (limits) on the amounts of a product that can be imported into Japan. According to the economists, without barriers protecting these areas from foreign competition, imports save jobs, even though the average Japanese consumer has to pay for this action through higher prices. Protection of the food products area in particular may be motivated by the fact that Japanese farmers, who benefit most from this protection, are a powerful political force within Japanese society.

The US government claims that Japan also has taken a neo-mercantilist stance in the importation of automobiles and automobile parts. Japan is a major exporter of autos and auto parts to the United States and Europe, but historically it has imported only 3 percent of its autos and 2 percent of its auto components. gue that US auto companies have not been successful in Japan because they do not make cars suited to the Japanese market. They point out that while 80 percent of the autos sold in the Japanese market have engines smaller than 2,000cc, no US auto company sells cars in Japan in that range. They also point out that imported autos and auto parts are increasing their share of the Japanese market. Between 1990 and 1994, for example, the share of the Japanese market accounted for by imported cars increased from 5.1 percent to 8.1 percent.[6]

textiles it needed by selling wine to England and buying textiles. Smith's basic argument is that you should never produce goods at home that you can buy at a lower cost from other countries. Smith demonstrates that by specializing in the production of goods in which each has an absolute advantage, both countries benefit by engaging in trade.

Consider the effects of trade between Ghana and South Korea. The production of any good (output) requires resources (inputs) such as land, labor, and capital. Assume that Ghana and South Korea both have the same amount of resources and that these resources can be used to produce either rice or cocoa. Assume that 200 units of resources are available in each country. Imagine that in Ghana it

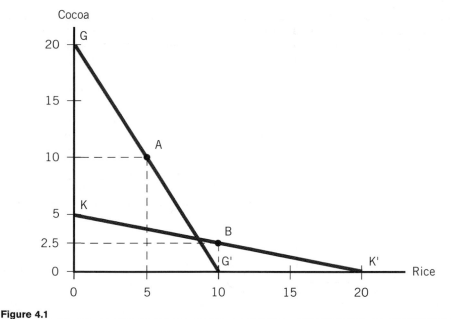

Figure 4.1

The Theory of Absolute Advantage

takes 10 resources to produce one ton of cocoa and 20 resources to produce one ton of rice. Thus, Ghana could produce 20 tons of cocoa and no rice, 10 tons of rice and no cocoa, or some combination of rice and cocoa between these two extremes. The different combinations that Ghana could produce are represented by the line GG′ in Figure 4.1. This is referred to as Ghana's production possibility frontier (PPF). Similarly, imagine that in South Korea it takes 40 resources to produce one ton of cocoa and 10 resources to produce one ton of rice. Thus, South Korea could produce 5 tons of cocoa and no rice, 20 tons of rice and no cocoa, or some combination between these two extremes. The different combinations available to South Korea are represented by the line KK′ in Figure 4.1, which is South Korea's PPF. Clearly, Ghana has an absolute advantage in the production of cocoa. (More resources are needed to produce a ton of cocoa in South Korea than in Ghana.) By the same token, South Korea has an absolute advantage in the production of rice.

Now consider a situation in which neither country trades with any other. Each country devotes half of its resources to the production of rice and half to the production of cocoa. Each country must also consume what it produces. Ghana would be able to produce 10 tons of cocoa and 5 tons of rice (point A in Figure 4.1), while South Korea would be able to produce 10 tons of rice and 2.5 tons of cocoa. Without trade, the combined production of both countries would be 12.5 tons of cocoa (10 tons in Ghana plus 2.5 tons in South Korea) and 15 tons of rice (5 tons in Ghana and 10 tons in South Korea). If each country were to specialize in producing the good for which it had an absolute advantage and then trade with the other for the good it lacks, Ghana could produce 20 tons of cocoa, and South Korea could produce 20 tons of rice. Thus, by specializing, the production of both goods could be increased. Production of cocoa would increase from 12.5 tons to 20 tons, while production of rice would increase from 15 tons to 20 tons. The increase in production that would result from specialization is 7.5 tons of cocoa and 5 tons of rice. These figures are summarized in Table 4.1.

Table 4.1

Absolute Advantage and the Gains from Trade

	Resources Required to Produce 1 Ton of Cocoa and Rice	
	Cocoa	Rice
Ghana	10	20
South Korea	40	10
	Production and Consumption without Trade	
	Cocoa	Rice
Ghana	10.0	5.0
South Korea	2.5	10.0
Total production	12.5	15.0
	Production with Specialization	
	Cocoa	Rice
Ghana	20.0	0.0
South Korea	0.0	20.0
Total production	20.0	20.0
	Consumption after Ghana Trades 6 Tons of Cocoa for 6 Tons of South Korean Rice	
	Cocoa	Rice
Ghana	14.0	6.0
South Korea	6.0	14.0
	Increase in Consumption as a Result of Specialization and Trade	
	Cocoa	Rice
Ghana	4.0	1.0
South Korea	3.5	4.0

By engaging in trade and swapping one ton of cocoa for one ton of rice, producers in both countries could consume more of both cocoa and rice. Imagine that Ghana and South Korea swap cocoa and rice on a one-to-one basis; that is, the price of one ton of cocoa is equal to the price of one ton of rice. If Ghana decided to export 6 tons of cocoa to South Korea and import 6 tons of rice in return, its final consumption after trade would be 14 tons of cocoa and 6 tons of rice. This is four tons more cocoa than it could have consumed before specialization and trade, and one ton more rice. Similarly, South Korea's final consumption after trade would be 6 tons of cocoa and 14 tons of rice. This is 3.5 tons more cocoa than it could have consumed before specialization and trade and 4 tons more rice. Thus, as a result of specialization and trade, output of both cocoa and rice would be increased, and consumers in both nations would be able to consume more. Thus, we can see that trade is a positive-sum game; it produces net gains for all involved.

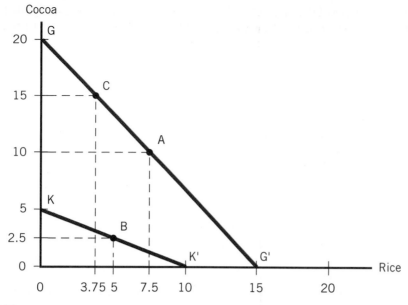

Figure 4.2

Theory of Comparative Advantage

Comparative Advantage

David Ricardo took Adam Smith's theory one step further by exploring what might happen when one country has an absolute advantage in the production of all goods.[7] Smith's theory of absolute advantage suggests that such a country might derive no benefits from international trade. In his 1817 book *Principles of Political Economy,* Ricardo showed that this was not the case. According to Ricardo's theory of **comparative advantage,** it makes sense for a country to specialize in the production of those goods that it produces most efficiently and to buy the goods that it produces less efficiently from other countries, even if this means buying goods from other countries that it could produce more efficiently itself.[8] While this may seem counterintuitive, the logic can be explained with a simple example.

Let us stay with the example of Ghana and South Korea that we used to explain Adam Smith's theory. This time assume that Ghana is more efficient in the production of both cocoa and rice; that is, Ghana has an absolute advantage in the production of both products. In Ghana it takes 10 resources to produce one ton of cocoa and 13⅓ resources to produce one ton of rice. Thus, given its 200 units of resources, Ghana can produce 20 tons of cocoa and no rice, 15 tons of rice and no cocoa, or any combination in between on its PPF (the line GG′ in Figure 4.2). In South Korea it takes 40 resources to produce one ton of cocoa and 20 resources to produce one ton of rice. Thus, South Korea can produce 5 tons of cocoa and no rice, 10 tons of rice and no cocoa, or any combination on its PPF (the line KK′ in Figure 4.2). Again assume that without trade, each country uses half of its resources to produce rice and half to produce cocoa. Thus, without trade, Ghana will produce 10 tons of cocoa and 7.5 tons of rice (point A in Figure 4.2), while South Korea will produce 2.5 tons of cocoa and 5 tons of rice (point B in Figure 4.2).

In light of Ghana's absolute advantage in the production of both goods, why should it trade with South Korea? Although Ghana has an absolute advantage in the production of both cocoa and rice, it has a comparative advantage only in the

comparative advantage Situation in which a country specializes in producing the goods it produces most efficiently and buys the products it produces less efficiently from other countries, even if it could produce the goods more efficiently itself.

production of cocoa: Ghana can produce 4 times as much cocoa as South Korea, but only 1.5 times as much rice. Ghana is *comparatively* more efficient at producing cocoa than it is at producing rice.

Without trade the combined production of cocoa will be 12.5 tons (10 tons in Ghana and 2.5 in South Korea), and the combined production of rice will also be 12.5 tons (7.5 tons in Ghana and 5 tons in South Korea). Without trade each country must consume what it produces. By engaging in trade, the two countries can increase their combined production of rice and cocoa, and consumers in both nations can consume more of both goods.

The Gains from Trade

Imagine that Ghana exploits its comparative advantage in the production of cocoa to increase its output from 10 tons to 15 tons. This uses up 150 units of resources, leaving the remaining 50 units of resources to use in producing 3.75 tons of rice (point C in Figure 4.2). Meanwhile, South Korea specializes in the production of rice, producing 10 tons. The combined output of both cocoa and rice has now increased. Before specialization, the combined output was 12.5 tons of cocoa and 12.5 tons of rice. Now it is 15 tons of cocoa and 13.75 tons of rice (3.75 tons in Ghana and 10 tons in South Korea). The source of the increase in production is summarized in Table 4.2.

Not only is output higher, but also both countries can now benefit from trade. If Ghana and South Korea swap cocoa and rice on a one-to-one basis, with both countries choosing to exchange four tons of their export for four tons of the import, both countries are able to consume more cocoa and rice than they could before specialization and trade (see Table 4.2). Thus, if Ghana exchanges 4 tons of cocoa with South Korea for 4 tons of rice, it is still left with 11 tons of cocoa, which is 1 ton more than it had before specialization. Moreover, the 4 tons of rice it gets from South Korea in exchange for its 4 tons of cocoa, when added to the 3.75 tons it now produces domestically, leaves it with a total of 7.75 tons of rice, which is one-quarter of a ton more than it had before trade. Similarly, after swapping four tons of rice with Ghana, South Korea still ends up with six tons of rice, which is more than it had before specialization. In addition, the 4 tons of cocoa it receives in exchange is 1.5 tons more than it produced before specialization. Thus, consumption of cocoa and rice can increase in both countries as a result of specialization and trade.

The basic message of the theory of comparative advantage is that *potential world production is greater with unrestricted free trade than it is with restricted trade.* Also, Ricardo's theory suggests that consumers in all nations can consume more if there are no restrictions on trade. This occurs even in countries that lack an absolute advantage in the production of any good. To an even greater degree than the theory of absolute advantage, the theory of comparative advantage suggests that trade is a positive-sum game in which all gain. As such, this theory provides a strong rationale for encouraging free trade. So powerful is Ricardo's theory that it remains a major weapon for those who argue for free trade.

Qualifications and Assumptions

The conclusion that free trade is universally beneficial is a rather bold one to draw from such a simple model. Our model has many unrealistic assumptions, including:

1 We have assumed a simple world in which there are only two countries and two goods. In the real world there are many countries and many goods.

2 We have assumed away transportation costs between countries.

Table 4.2

Comparative Advantage and the Gains from Trade

	Resources Required to Produce 1 Ton of Cocoa and Rice	
	Cocoa	Rice
Ghana	10	13.33
South Korea	40	20
	Production and Consumption without Trade	
	Cocoa	Rice
Ghana	10.0	7.5
South Korea	2.5	5.0
Total production	12.5	12.5
	Production with Specialization	
	Cocoa	Rice
Ghana	15.0	3.75
South Korea	0.0	10.0
Total production	15.0	13.75
	Consumption after Ghana Trades 4 Tons of Cocoa for 4 Tons of South Korean Rice	
	Cocoa	Rice
Ghana	11.0	7.75
South Korea	4.0	6.0
	Increase in Consumption as a Result of Specialization and Trade	
	Cocoa	Rice
Ghana	1.0	0.25
South Korea	1.5	1.0

3 We have assumed away differences in the prices of resources in different countries. We have said nothing about exchange rates and instead simply assumed that cocoa and rice could be swapped on a one-to-one basis.

4 We have assumed that while resources can move freely from the production of one good to another within a country, they are not free to move internationally. In reality, some resources are somewhat internationally mobile. This is true of capital and, to a lesser extent, labor.

5 We have assumed constant returns to scale; that is, specialization by Ghana or South Korea has no effect on the amount of resources required to produce one ton of cocoa or rice. In reality, both diminishing and increasing returns to specialization exist. The amount of resources required to produce a good might decrease or increase as a nation specializes in production of that good.

6 We have assumed that each country has a fixed stock of resources and that free trade does not change the efficiency with which a country uses its resources. This static assumption makes no allowances for the dynamic changes in a country's stock of resources and in the efficiency with which the country uses its resources that might result from free trade.

7 We have assumed away the effects of trade on income distribution within a country.

Given these assumptions, can the conclusion that free trade is mutually beneficial be extended to the real world of many countries, many goods, positive transportation costs, volatile exchange rates, internationally mobile resources, nonconstant returns to specialization, and dynamic changes. Although a detailed extension of the theory of comparative advantage is beyond the scope of this book, economists have shown that the basic result derived from our simple model can be generalized to a world composed of many countries producing many different goods.[9] Despite all its shortcomings, research suggests that the basic proposition of the Ricardian model—that countries will export the goods they are most efficient at producing—is supported by the data.[10] However, once all the assumptions are dropped, the case for unrestricted free trade loses some of its strength, according to some economists associated with the "new trade theory."[11] We return to this issue later in this chapter and in the next.

Trade and Economic Growth

Our simple comparative advantage model assumed that trade does not change a country's stock of resources or the efficiency with which it utilizes those resources. This static assumption makes no allowances for the dynamic changes that might result from trade. If we relax this assumption, it becomes apparent that opening an economy to trade is likely to generate dynamic gains.[12] These dynamic gains are of two sorts. First, free trade might increase a country's stock of resources as increased supplies of labor and capital from abroad become available for use within the country. This is occurring now in Eastern Europe, where many Western businesses are investing large amounts of capital in the former Communist countries.

Bill Gates, pictured here speaking at the Kremlin, met with First Deputy Prime Minister Anatoly Chubais in 1997 to talk about the role of information technology in Russia's economy.
© Peter Tunley/CORBIS.

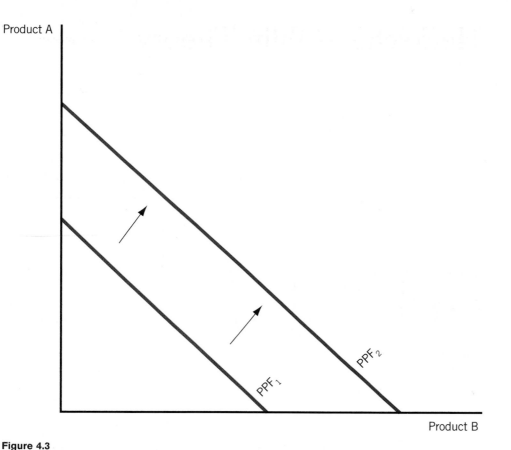

Product A

PPF₁

PPF₂

Product B

Figure 4.3

The Influence of Free Trade on the PPF

Second, free trade might also increase the efficiency with which a country utilizes its resources. Gains in the efficiency of resource utilization could arise from a number of factors. For example, economies of large-scale production might become available as trade expands the size of the total market available to domestic firms. Trade might make better technology from abroad available to domestic firms. In turn, better technology can increase labor productivity or the productivity of land. (The so-called green revolution had this effect on agricultural outputs in developing countries.) Also, opening an economy to foreign competition might stimulate domestic producers to look for ways to increase their efficiency. Again, this phenomenon is arguably occurring in the once-protected markets of Eastern Europe, where many former state monopolies are having to increase the efficiency of their operations to survive in the world market.

Dynamic gains in both the stock of a country's resources and the efficiency with which resources are utilized will cause a country's PPF to shift outward. This is illustrated in Figure 4.3, where the shift from PPF₁ to PPF₂ results from the dynamic gains that arise from free trade. As a consequence of this outward shift, the country in Figure 4.3 can produce more of both goods than it did before introduction of free trade. The theory suggests that opening an economy to free trade not only results in static gains of the type discussed earlier, but also results in dynamic gains that stimulate economic growth. If this is so, the case for free trade becomes stronger, and the World Bank has assembled evidence that suggests a free trade stance does have these kind of beneficial effects on economic growth.[13]

Heckscher–Ohlin Theory

Ricardo's theory stresses that comparative advantage arises from differences in productivity. Thus, whether Ghana is more efficient than South Korea in the production of cocoa depends on how productively it uses its resources. Ricardo argued that differences in labor productivity between nations underlie the notion of comparative advantage. Swedish economists Eli Heckscher (in 1919) and Bertil Ohlin (in 1933) put forward a different explanation of comparative advantage. They argued that comparative advantage arises from differences in national factor endowments.[14] By factor endowments they meant the extent to which a country is endowed with such resources as land, labor, and capital. Nations have different factor endowments, and different factor endowments explain differences in factor costs. The more abundant a factor, the lower its cost. The Heckscher–Ohlin theory predicts that countries will export those goods that make intensive use of those factors that are locally abundant, while importing goods that make intensive use of factors that are locally scarce. Thus, the Heckscher–Ohlin theory attempts to explain the pattern of international trade that we observe in the world economy. Like Ricardo's theory, the Heckscher–Ohlin theory argues that free trade is beneficial. Unlike Ricardo's theory, however, the Heckscher–Ohlin theory argues that the pattern of international trade is determined by differences in factor endowments, rather than differences in productivity.

The Heckscher–Ohlin theory also has commonsense appeal. For example, the United States has long been a substantial exporter of agricultural goods, reflecting in part its large tracts of arable land. In contrast, South Korea has excelled in the export of goods produced in labor-intensive manufacturing industries, such as textiles and footwear. This reflects South Korea's relative abundance of low-cost labor. The United States, which lacks abundant low-cost labor, has been a primary importer of these goods. Note that it is relative, not absolute, endowments that are important; a country may have larger absolute amounts of land and labor than another country, but be relatively abundant in only one of them.

The Leontief Paradox

The Heckscher–Ohlin theory has been one of the most influential in international economics. Most economists prefer the Heckscher–Ohlin theory to Ricardo's theory because it makes fewer simplifying assumptions. It has been subjected to many empirical tests. Beginning with a famous study published in 1953 by Wassily Leontief (winner of the Nobel Prize in economics in 1973), many of these tests have raised questions about the validity of the Heckscher–Ohlin theory.[15] Using the Heckscher–Ohlin theory, Leontief postulated that because the United States was relatively abundant in capital compared to other nations, the United States would be an exporter of capital-intensive goods and an importer of labor-intensive goods. To his surprise, however, he found that US exports were less capital intensive than US imports. Since this result was at variance with the predictions of the theory, it has become known as the Leontief paradox.

No one is quite sure why we observe the Leontief paradox. One possible explanation is that the United States has a special advantage in producing new products or goods made with innovative technologies. Such products may be less capital intensive than products whose technology has had time to mature and become suitable for mass production. Thus, the United States may be exporting goods that heavily use skilled labor and innovative entrepreneurship, while importing heavy manufactures that use large amounts of capital. Some more recent empirical studies tend to confirm this.[16] However, recent tests of the Heckscher–Ohlin theory using data for a large number of countries tend to confirm the existence of the Leontief paradox.[17]

This leaves economists with a difficult dilemma. They prefer Heckscher–Ohlin on theoretical grounds, but it is a relatively poor predictor of real-world international trade patterns. The theory they regard as being too limited, Ricardo's theory of comparative advantage, actually predicts trade patterns with greater accuracy. The best solution to this dilemma may be to return to the Ricardian idea that trade patterns are largely driven by international differences in productivity. Thus, one might argue that the United States exports commercial aircraft and imports automobiles not because its factor endowments are especially suited to aircraft manufacture and not suited to automobile manufacture, but because the United States is more efficient at producing aircraft than automobiles.

The Product Life-Cycle Theory

Raymond Vernon proposed the product life-cycle theory in the mid-1960s.[18] Vernon's theory was based on the observation that for most of the 20th century a very large proportion of the world's new products had been developed by US firms and sold first in the United States (e.g., mass-produced automobiles, televisions, instant cameras, photocopiers, personal computers, and semiconductor chips). Vernon argued that the wealth and size of the market gave US firms a strong incentive to develop new consumer products. In addition, the high cost of labor gave US firms an incentive to develop cost-saving process innovations.

Just because a new product is developed by a US firm and first sold in the US market does not mean the product must be produced in the United States. It could be produced abroad at some low-cost location and then exported back into the United States. However, Vernon argued that most new products were initially produced in America. The pioneering firms might have believed it was better to keep production facilities close to the market and to the firm's center of decision making, given the uncertainty and risks inherent in product introductions. Also, the demand for most new products tends not to be based on price. Consequently, firms can charge relatively high prices for new products, which eliminates the need to look for low-cost production sites in other countries.

Vernon went on to say that early in the life cycle of a typical new product, while demand is starting to grow rapidly in the United States, demand in other advanced countries is limited to high-income groups. The limited initial demand in other advanced countries does not make it worthwhile for firms in those countries to produce the new product, but it does necessitate some exports from the United States to those countries.

Over time, however, demand for the new product starts to grow in other advanced countries (e.g., Great Britain, France, Germany, and Japan). As it does, it becomes worthwhile for foreign producers to begin producing for their home markets. In addition, US firms might set up production facilities in those advanced countries where demand is growing. Consequently, production within other advanced countries begins to limit the potential for exports from the United States.

As the market in the United States and other advanced nations matures, the product becomes more standardized, and price becomes the main competitive weapon. As this occurs, cost considerations start to play a greater role in the competitive process. Producers based in advanced countries where labor costs are lower than in the United States (e.g., Italy and Spain) might now be able to export to the United States.

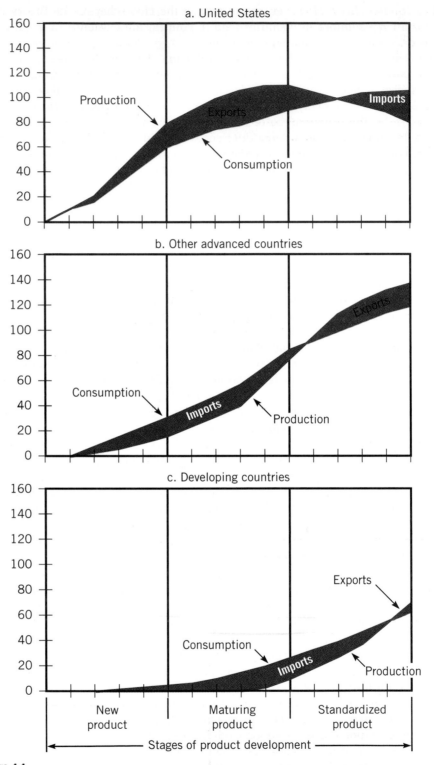

Figure 4.4

The Product Life-Cycle Theory

If cost pressures become intense, the process might not stop there. The cycle by which the United States lost its advantage to other advanced countries might be repeated once more, as developing countries (e.g., Thailand) begin to acquire a production advantage over advanced countries. Thus, the locus of global production initially switches from the United States to other advanced nations, and then from those nations to developing countries.

Over time the United States switches from being an exporter of the product to an importer of the product as production becomes concentrated in lower-cost foreign locations. These dynamics are illustrated in Figure 4.4, which shows the growth of production and consumption in the United States, other advanced countries, and developing countries.

Evaluating the Product Life-Cycle Theory

Historically, the product life-cycle theory provides an accurate explanation of international trade patterns. Consider photocopiers; the product was developed in the early 1960s by Xerox in the United States and sold initially to US users. Xerox exported photocopiers from the United States, primarily to Japan and the advanced countries of Western Europe. As demand began to grow in those countries, Xerox entered into joint ventures to set up production in Japan (Fuji-Xerox) and Great Britain (Rank-Xerox). In addition, once Xerox's patents on the photocopier process expired, other foreign competitors began to enter the market (e.g., Canon in Japan, Olivetti in Italy). As a consequence, exports from the United States declined, and US users began to buy some of their photocopiers from lower-cost foreign sources, particularly from Japan. More recently, Japanese companies have found that their own country is too expensive to manufacture photocopiers, so they have begun to switch production to developing countries such as Singapore and Thailand. As a result, initially the United States and now several other advanced countries (e.g., Japan and Great Britain) have switched from being exporters of photocopiers to being importers. This evolution in the pattern of international trade in photocopiers is consistent with the predictions of the product life-cycle theory. The theory clearly explains the migration of mature industries out of the United States and into low-cost assembly locations.

However, the product life-cycle theory is not without weaknesses. Viewed from an Asian or European perspective, Vernon's argument that most new products are developed and introduced in the United States seems ethnocentric. Although it may be true that from 1945 to 1975 most new products were introduced in the United States, there have always been important exceptions. In recent years these exceptions appear to have become more common. Many new products are now introduced in Japan (e.g., high-definition television or digital audio tapes). More importantly, with the increased globalization and integration of the world economy that we discussed in Chapter 1, a growing number of new products are now introduced simultaneously in the United States, Japan, and the advanced European nations (e.g., laptop computers, compact disks, and electronic cameras). This may be accompanied by globally dispersed production, with particular components of a new product being produced in those locations where the mix of factor costs and skills is most favorable (as predicted by the theory of comparative advantage).

Laptop computers were introduced simultaneously into a number of major national markets by Toshiba. Although various components for Toshiba laptop computers are manufactured in Japan (e.g., display screens, memory chips), other components are manufactured in Singapore and Taiwan, and still others (e.g., hard drives and microprocessors) are manufactured in the United States. All the components are

shipped to Singapore for final assembly, and the completed product is then shipped to the major world markets (the United States, Western Europe, and Japan). The pattern of trade associated with this new product is both different from and more complex than the pattern predicted by Vernon's model. Trying to explain this pattern using the product life-cycle theory would be very difficult. The theory of comparative advantage might better explain why certain components are produced in certain locations and why the final product is assembled in Singapore. In short, although Vernon's theory may be useful for explaining the pattern of international trade during the brief period of American global dominance, its relevance in the modern world is limited.

The New Trade Theory

The new trade theory emerged in the 1970s. A number of economists were questioning the assumption of diminishing returns to specialization used in international trade theory.[19] They argued that in many industries, because of the presence of substantial economies of scale, there are increasing returns to specialization. As output expands with specialization, the ability to realize economies of scale increases and so the unit costs of production should decrease. Economies of scale are primarily derived by spreading fixed costs (such as the costs of developing a new product) over a larger output. Consider the commercial jet aircraft industry. The fixed costs of developing a new commercial jet airliner are astronomical. For example, Boeing spent an estimated $5 billion to develop its 777. The company will have to sell at least 350 of them to recoup these development costs and break even. Thus, due to the high fixed costs of developing a new jet aircraft, the economies of scale are substantial.

The new trade theorists further argue that because of substantial scale economies, world demand will support only a few firms in many industries. This is the case in the commercial jet aircraft industry; estimates suggest that world demand can profitably support at most three major manufacturers. For example, the total world demand for 300-seater commercial jet aircraft similar to Boeing's 777 model will probably be only 1,500 aircraft over the 10 years between 1995 and 2005. If we assume that firms must sell at least 500 aircraft to get an acceptable return on their investment (which is reasonable, given the breakeven point of 300 aircraft), we can see that the world market can profitably support only three firms!

The new trade theorists go on to argue that in those industries where the existence of substantial economies of scale imply that the world market will profitably support only a few firms, countries may export certain products simply because they have a firm that was an early entrant into that industry. Underpinning this argument is the notion of **first-mover advantages,** which are the economic and strategic advantages that accrue to early entrants into an industry.[20] Because they are able to gain economies of scale, the early entrants into an industry may get a lock on the world market that discourages subsequent entry. The ability of first movers to reap economies of scale creates a barrier to entry. In the commercial aircraft industry, for example, the fact that Boeing and Airbus are already in the industry discourages new entry.

This theory suggests that a country may dominate in the export of a good simply because it was lucky enough to have one or more firms among the first to produce that good. This is at variance with the Heckscher–Ohlin theory, which suggests that a country will predominate in the export of a product when it is particularly well endowed with those factors used intensively in its manufacture. Thus, the new

first-mover advantages Economic and strategic advantages that accrue to early entrants into an industry.

trade theorists argue that the United States leads in exports of commercial jet aircraft not because it is better endowed with the factors of production required to manufacture aircraft, but because two of the first movers in the industry, Boeing and McDonnell Douglas, were US firms. However, the new trade theory is not at variance with the theory of comparative advantage. Because economies of scale result in an increase in the efficiency of resource utilization, and hence in productivity, the new trade theory identifies an important source of comparative advantage.

How useful is this theory in explaining trade patterns? It is perhaps too early to say; the theory is so new that little supporting empirical work has been done. Consistent with the theory, however, a study by Harvard business historian Alfred Chandler suggests that the existence of first-mover advantages is an important factor in explaining the dominance of firms in certain industries.[21] Also, the number of firms is very limited in many global industries. This is the case with the commercial aircraft industry, the chemical industry, the heavy construction-equipment industry, the heavy truck industry, the tire industry, the consumer electronics industry, and the jet engine industry, to name but a few examples.

Perhaps the most contentious implication of the new trade theory is the argument that it generates for government intervention and strategic trade policy.[22] New trade theorists stress the role of luck, entrepreneurship, and innovation in giving a firm first-mover advantages. According to this argument, the reason Boeing was the first mover in commercial jet aircraft manufacture—rather than firms such as Great Britain's DeHavilland and Hawker Siddely, or Holland's Fokker, all of which could have been—was that Boeing was both lucky and innovative. One way Boeing was lucky is that DeHavilland shot itself in the foot when its Comet jet airliner, introduced two years earlier than Boeing's first jet airliner, the 707, was found to be full of serious technological flaws. Had DeHavilland not made some serious technological mistakes, Great Britain might now be the world's leading exporter of commercial jet aircraft!

Boeing's innovativeness was demonstrated by its independent development of the technological know-how required to build a commercial jet airliner. Several new trade theorists have pointed out, however, that Boeing's R&D was largely paid for by the US government; that the 707 was a spin-off from a government-funded military program. Herein lies a rationale for government intervention. By the sophisticated and judicious use of subsidies, could a government increase the chances of its domestic firms becoming first movers in emerging industries, as the US government apparently did with Boeing? If this is possible, and the new trade theory suggests it might be, then we have an economic rationale for a proactive trade policy that is at variance with the free trade prescriptions of the trade theories we have reviewed so far. We will consider the policy implications of this issue in Chapter 5.

National Competitive Advantage: Porter's Diamond

In 1990 Michael Porter of Harvard Business School published the results of intensive research to determine why some nations succeed and others fail in international competition.[23] Porter and his team looked at 100 industries in 10 nations. The book that contains the results of this work, *The Competitive Advantage of Nations,* has made an important contribution to thinking about trade. Like the work of the new trade theorists, Porter's work was driven by a belief that the existing theories of international trade told only part of the story. Porter hoped to explain why a nation achieves

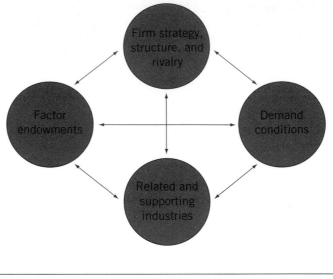

Figure 4.5

Determinants of National Competitive Advantage: Porter's Diamond

international success in a particular industry. Why does Japan do so well in the automobile industry? Why does Switzerland excel in the production and export of precision instruments and pharmaceuticals? Why do Germany and the United States do so well in the chemical industry? These questions cannot be answered easily by the Heckscher–Ohlin theory, and the theory of comparative advantage offers only a partial explanation. The theory of comparative advantage would say that Switzerland excels in the production and export of precision instruments because it uses its resources very efficiently in these industries. Although this may be correct, this does not explain why Switzerland is more productive in this industry than Great Britain, Germany, or Spain. It is this puzzle that Porter tries to solve.

Porter's thesis is that four broad attributes of a nation shape the environment in which local firms compete, and these attributes promote or impede the creation of competitive advantage (see Figure 4.5). These attributes are

- *Factor endowments*–a nation's position in factors of production such as skilled labor or the infrastructure necessary to compete in a given industry.

- *Demand conditions*–the nature of home demand for the industry's product or service.

- *Relating and supporting industries*–the presence or absence in a nation of supplier industries and related industries that are internationally competitive.

- *Firm strategy, structure, and rivalry*–the conditions in the nation governing how companies are created, organized, and managed and the nature of domestic rivalry.

Porter speaks of these four attributes as constituting the *diamond*. He argues that firms are most likely to succeed in industries or industry segments where the diamond is most favorable. He also argues that the diamond is a mutually reinforcing system. The effect of one attribute is contingent on the state of others. For example, Porter argues, favorable demand conditions will not result in competitive advantage unless the state of rivalry is sufficient to cause firms to respond to them.

Porter maintains that two additional variables can influence the national diamond in important ways: chance and government. Chance events, such as major innovations, create discontinuities that can reshape industry structure and provide the opportunity for one nation's firms to supplant another's. Government, by its choice of policies, can detract from or improve national advantage. For example, regulation can alter home demand conditions, antitrust policies can influence the intensity of rivalry within an industry, and government investments in education can change factor endowments.

Factor Endowments

Factor endowments lie at the center of the Heckscher–Ohlin theory. While Porter does not propose anything radically new, he does analyze the characteristics of factors of production in some detail. He recognizes hierarchies among factors, distinguishing between basic factors (e.g., natural resources, climate, location, and demographics) and advanced factors (e.g., communications infrastructure, sophisticated and skilled labor, research facilities, and technological know-how). He argues that advanced factors are the most significant for competitive advantage. Unlike basic

By improving the general skill and knowledge level of the population, and by stimulating advanced research at higher education institutions, government investments in basic and higher education can upgrade a nation's advanced factors. © Photo Disc.

factors (which are naturally endowed), advanced factors are a product of investment by individuals, companies, and governments. Thus, government investments in basic and higher education, by improving the general skill and knowledge level of the population and by stimulating advanced research at higher education institutions, can upgrade a nation's advanced factors.

The relationship between advanced and basic factors is complex. Basic factors can provide an initial advantage that is subsequently reinforced and extended by investment in advanced factors. Disadvantages in basic factors can create pressures to invest in advanced factors. The most obvious example of this phenomenon is Japan, a country that lacks arable land and mineral deposits and yet has built a substantial endowment of advanced factors. Porter notes that Japan's large pool of engineers (reflecting a much higher number of engineering graduates per capita than almost any other nation) has been vital to Japan's success in many manufacturing industries.

Demand Conditions

Porter emphasizes the role home demand plays in providing the impetus for upgrading competitive advantage. Firms are typically most sensitive to the needs of their closest customers. Thus, the characteristics of home demand are important in shaping the attributes of domestically made products and in creating pressures for innovation and quality. Porter argues that a nation's firms gain competitive advantage if their domestic consumers are sophisticated and demanding. Such consumers pressure local firms to meet high standards of product quality and to produce innovative

The cellular telephone equipment industry is one of the great growth stories of the 1990s. The number of cellular subscribers has been expanding rapidly. By the end of 1998 there were over 150 million cellular subscribers worldwide, up from less than 10 million in 1990. Three firms dominate the global market for cellular equipment (e.g., cellular phones, base station equipment, digital switches): Motorola, Nokia, and Ericsson. Of the three, the dramatic rise of Nokia has been the most surprising.

Nokia's roots are in Finland, not a country that jumps to mind when one talks about leading-edge technology companies. In the 1980s Nokia was a rambling Finnish conglomerate with activities that em-

sparsely populated and inhospitably cold nations had good reason to become pioneers; it cost far too much to lay down a traditional wire-line telephone service. Yet those same features make telecommunications all the more valuable; people driving through the Arctic winter and owners of remote northern houses need a telephone to summon help if things go wrong. As a result, Sweden, Norway, and Finland became the first nations in the world to take cellular telecommunications seriously. They found, for example, that while it cost up to $800 per subscriber to bring a traditional wire-line service to remote locations in the far north, the same locations could be linked by wireless cellular for only $500 per per-

These independent and cost-conscious telephone service providers have prevented Nokia from taking anything for granted in its home country. With typical Finnish pragmatism, they have been willing to buy from the lowest-cost supplier, whether that was Nokia, Ericsson, Motorola, or someone else. This situation contrasted sharply with that prevailing in most developed nations until the late 1980s and early 1990s, where domestic telephone monopolies typically purchased equipment from a dominant local supplier or made it themselves. Nokia responded to this competitive pressure by doing everything possible to drive down its manufacturing costs while still staying at the leading edge of cellular technology.

The Rise of Finland's Nokia

braced tire manufacturing, paper production, consumer electronics, and telecommunications equipment. Today it is a focused $10 billion telecommunications equipment manufacturer with a global reach second only to that of Motorola and sales and earnings that are growing more than 30 percent annually.

How has this former conglomerate emerged to take a global leadership position in cellular equipment? Much of the answer lies in the history, geography, and political economy of Finland and its Nordic neighbors.

The story starts in 1981 when the Nordic nations got together to create the world's first international cellular telephone network. The

son. As a consequence, by 1994 12 percent of the people in Scandinavia owned cellular phones, compared with less than 6 percent in the United States, the world's second most developed market.

Nokia, as a longtime telecommunications equipment supplier, was well positioned to take advantage of this development, but there were also other forces at work in Finland that helped Nokia develop its competitive edge. Unlike virtually every other developed nation, Finland has never had a national telephone monopoly. Instead, the country's telephone services have been provided by about 50 or so autonomous local telephone companies, whose elected boards set prices by referendum (which means low prices).

The consequences of these forces are clear. While Motorola remains the number one firm in the cellular equipment, the once obscure Finnish firm Nokia is snapping at its heels. It is Nokia, not Motorola, that is the leader in digital cellular technology, the wave of the future. Nokia has the lead because Scandinavia started switching to digital technology five years before the rest of the world. Spurred on by its cost-conscious Finnish customers, Nokia now has the lowest cost structure of any cellular phone equipment manufacturer in the world, making it more profitable than Motorola. Nokia's operating margins in 1996 were 8.3 percent, compared with 4.1 percent at Motorola.[24]

products. Porter notes that Japan's sophisticated and knowledgeable buyers of cameras helped stimulate the Japanese camera industry to improve product quality and to introduce innovative models. A similar example can be found in the cellular phone equipment industry, where sophisticated and demanding local customers in Scandinavia helped push Nokia of Finland and Ericsson of Sweden to invest in cellular phone technology long before demand for cellular phones took off in other developed nations. As a result, Nokia and Ericsson, along with Motorola, are today dominant players in the global cellular telephone equipment industry. The case of Nokia is reviewed in more depth in the accompanying "Management Focus."

Related and Supporting Industries

The third broad attribute of national advantage in an industry is the presence of suppliers or related industries that are internationally competitive. The benefits of investments in advanced factors of production by related and supporting industries can spill over into an industry, helping it achieve a strong competitive position internationally. Swedish strength in fabricated steel products (e.g., ball bearings and cutting tools) has drawn on strengths in Sweden's specialty steel industry. Technological leadership in the US semiconductor industry until the mid-1980s provided the basis for US success in personal computers and several other technically advanced electronic products. Similarly, Switzerland's success in pharmaceuticals is closely related to its previous international success in the technologically related dye industry.

One consequence of this is that successful industries within a country tend to be grouped into clusters of related industries. This was one of the most pervasive findings of Porter's study. One such cluster is the German textile and apparel sector, which includes high-quality cotton, wool, synthetic fibers, sewing machine needles, and a wide range of textile machinery.

Firm Strategy, Structure, and Rivalry

The fourth broad attribute of national competitive advantage in Porter's model is the strategy, structure, and rivalry of firms within a nation. Porter makes two important points here. His first is that nations are characterized by different "management ideologies," which either help them or do not help them build national competitive advantage. For example, Porter notes the predominance of engineers on the top-management teams of German and Japanese firms. He attributes this to these firms' emphasis on improving manufacturing processes and product design. In contrast, Porter notes a predominance of people with finance backgrounds on the top-management teams of many US firms. He links this to many US firms' lack of attention to improving manufacturing processes and product design, particularly during the 1970s and 1980s. He also argues that the dominance of finance has led to an overemphasis on maximizing short-term financial returns. According to Porter, one consequence of these different management ideologies has been a relative loss of US competitiveness in those engineering-based industries where manufacturing processes and product design issues are important (e.g., the automobile industry).

Porter's second point is that there is a strong association between vigorous domestic rivalry and the creation and persistence of competitive advantage in an industry. Vigorous domestic rivalry induces firms to look for ways to improve efficiency, which makes them better international competitors. Domestic rivalry creates pressures to innovate, to improve quality, to reduce costs, and to invest in upgrading advanced factors. All of this helps to create world-class competitors. As an illustration Porter cites Japan:

> Nowhere is the role of domestic rivalry more evident than in Japan, where it is all-out warfare in which many companies fail to achieve profitability. With goals that stress market share, Japanese companies engage in a continuing struggle to outdo each other. Shares fluctuate markedly. The process is prominently covered in the business press. Elaborate rankings measure which companies are most popular with university graduates. The rate of new product and process development is breathtaking.[25]

A similar point about the stimulating effects of strong domestic competition can be made with regard to the rise of Nokia of Finland to global preeminence in the market for cellular telephone equipment. For details, see the "Management Focus."

Evaluating Porter's Theory

Porter's argument is that the degree to which a nation is likely to achieve international success in a certain industry is a function of the combined impact of factor endowments, domestic demand conditions, related and supporting industries, and domestic rivalry. He argues that for this diamond to boost competitive performance usually requires the presence of all four components (although there are some exceptions). Porter also contends that government can influence each of the four components either positively or negatively. Factor endowments can be affected by subsidies, policies toward capital markets, policies toward education, and the like. Government can shape domestic demand through local product standards or with regulations that mandate or influence buyer needs. Government policy can influence supporting and related industries through regulation and influence firm rivalry through such devices as capital market regulation, tax policy, and antitrust laws.

If Porter is correct, we would expect his model to predict the pattern of international trade that we observe in the real world. Countries should be exporting products from those industries where

Unions and the WTO

At the December 1999 World Trade Organization meeting in Seattle, American unions were protesting competition from countries with low-cost labor. Ironically, at the same time, US economic statistics showed that unemployment in the United States had dropped to its lowest point since World War II. At 4.1 percent nationally, with some parts of the country as low as 3.2 percent, US unemployment was less than half of the unemployment rate in European Union countries. In 1995, US unemployment was at 7 percent. These data indicate that the United States has had a net growth in jobs at the same time trade has been liberalized under the World Trade Organization. What are the concerns of labor in such a scenario?

all four components of the diamond are favorable, while importing in those areas where the components are not favorable. At this point we simply do not know if he is correct. Porter's theory is so new that it has not been subjected to independent empirical testing. Much about the theory rings true, but the same can be said for the new trade theory, the theory of comparative advantage, and the Heckscher–Ohlin theory. In reality it may be that each of these theories explains something about the pattern of international trade. In many respects these theories complement each other.

Implications for Business

Why does all of this matter for business? There are at least three main implications of the material discussed in this chapter for international businesses: location implications, first-mover implications, and policy implications.

Location Implications

One way in which the material discussed in this chapter matters to an international business concerns the link between the theories of international trade and a firm's decision about where to locate its productive activities. Underlying most of the theories we have discussed is the notion that countries have particular advantages in different productive activities. Thus, from a profit perspective, it makes sense for a firm to disperse its various productive activities to those countries where, according to the theory of international trade, they can be performed most efficiently. If design can be performed most efficiently in France, that is where design facilities should be located; if the manufacture of basic components can be performed most efficiently in Singapore, that is where they should be manufactured; and if final assembly can be performed most efficiently in China, that is where final assembly should be performed. The end result is a global web of productive activities, with different activities being performed in varying locations around the globe depending on considerations of comparative advantage, factor endowments, and the like. If the firm does not do this, it may find itself at a competitive disadvantage relative to firms that do.

Consider the production of a laptop computer, a process with four major stages: (1) basic research and development (R&D) of the product design, (2) manufacture of standard electronic components (e.g., memory chips), (3) manufacture of advanced components (e.g., flat-top color display screens and microprocessors), and (4) final assembly. Basic R&D and design requires a pool of highly skilled and educated workers with good backgrounds in microelectronics. The two countries with a comparative advantage in basic microelectronics R&D and design are Japan and the United States, so most producers of laptop computers locate their R&D facilities in one, or both, of these countries. (Apple, IBM, Motorola, Texas Instruments, Toshiba, and Sony all have major R&D facilities in both Japan and the United States.)

The manufacture of standard electronic components is a capital-intensive process requiring semiskilled labor, and cost pressures are intense. The best locations for such activities today are places such as Singapore, Taiwan, Malaysia, and South Korea. These countries have pools of relatively skilled, low-cost labor. Thus, many producers of laptop computers have standard components, such as memory chips, produced at these locations.

The manufacture of advanced components such as microprocessors and display screens is a capital-intensive process requiring skilled labor. Because cost pressures are not so intense at this stage, these components can be manufactured in countries with high labor costs that also have pools of highly skilled labor (primarily Japan and the United States).

Finally, assembly is a relatively labor-intensive process requiring only low-skilled labor, and cost pressures are intense. As a result, final assembly may be carried out in a country such as Mexico, which has an abundance of low-cost, low-skilled labor.

The end result is that when we look at a laptop computer produced by a US manufacturer, we may find that it was designed in California, its standard components were produced in Taiwan and Singapore, its advanced components were produced in Japan and the United States, its final assembly occurred in Mexico, and the finished product was then sold in the United States or elsewhere in the world. By dispersing production activities to different locations around the globe, the US manufacturer is taking advantage of the differences between countries identified by the various theories of international trade.

First-Mover Implications

The new trade theory suggests the importance to firms of building and exploiting first-mover advantages. According to the new trade theory, firms that establish a first-mover advantage with regard to the production of a particular new product may subsequently dominate global trade in that product. This is particularly true in those industries where the global market can profitably support only a limited number of firms, such as the aerospace market, but early commitments also seem to be important in less concentrated industries such as the market for cellular telephone equipment (see the "Management Focus" on Nokia). For the individual firm, it pays to invest substantial financial resources in trying to build a first-mover, or early-mover, advantage, even if that means several years of substantial losses before a new venture becomes profitable. Although the precise details of how to

achieve this are beyond the scope of this book, there is a vast literature on strategies for exploiting first-mover advantages.[26] In recent years Japanese firms, rather than their European or North American competitors, have been prepared to undertake the vast investments and bear the years of losses required to build a first-mover advantage. This has been true in the production of liquid crystal display (LCD) screens for laptop computers. While firms such as Toshiba and NEC invested heavily in this technology during the 1980s, many large European and American firms exited the market. As a result, today Japanese firms dominate global trade in LCD screens, even though the technology was invented in the United States.

Policy Implications

The theories of international trade also matter to international businesses because business firms are major players on the international trade scene. Business firms produce exports, and business firms import the products of other countries. Because of their pivotal role in international trade, firms influence government trade policy. By lobbying government, business firms can help promote free trade or trade restrictions. The message for business contained in the theories of international trade is that promoting free trade is generally in the best interests of the home country, although it may not always be in the best interest of an individual firm. Many firms recognize this and lobby for open markets.

For example, in 1991 when the US government announced its intention to place a tariff on Japanese imports of liquid crystal display (LCD) screens, IBM and Apple Computer protested strongly. Both IBM and Apple pointed out that (1) Japan was the lowest-cost source of LCD screens, (2) they used these screens in their own laptop computers, and (3) the proposed tariff, by increasing the cost of LCD screens, would increase the cost of laptop computers produced by IBM and Apple, making them less competitive in the world market. The tariff, designed to protect US firms, would be self-defeating. In response to these pressures, the US government reversed its posture on this issue.

Unlike IBM and Apple, however, businesses do not always lobby for free trade. In the United States, for example, "voluntary" restrictions on imports on automobiles, machine tools, textiles, and steel are the result of direct pressures by US firms in these industries on the government. The government has responded by getting foreign companies to agree to "voluntary" restrictions on their imports, using the implicit threat of more comprehensive formal trade barriers to get them to adhere to these agreements. As predicted by international trade theory, many of these agreements have been self-defeating. Take the voluntary restriction on machine tool imports agreed to in 1985 as an example.

ANOTHER PERSPECTIVE

US Tariff Rates

Information about international trade is readily available on-line. You can visit the US government's site for business (**http://www.business.gov**) and access an array of information on international trade. You can also review the US government's tariffs at the US Office of Tariff Affairs and Trade Agreements (**http://www.usitc.gov/taffairs.htm**).

Because of limited import competition from more-efficient foreign suppliers, the prices of machine tools in the United States have risen to higher levels than would have prevailed under free trade. Since machine tools are used throughout the manufacturing industry, the result has been an increase in the costs of US manufacturing in general and a corresponding loss in world market competitiveness. Shielded from international competition by import barriers, the US machine tool industry has had no incentive to increase its efficiency. Consequently, it has lost many of its export

markets to more efficient foreign competitors. Thus, the US machine tool industry is now smaller than it was in 1985. For anyone schooled in international trade theory, these events are not surprising.[27]

Finally, Porter's theory of national competitive advantage also contains policy implications. Porter's theory suggests that it is in a firm's best interest to invest in upgrading advanced factors of production; for example, to invest in better training for its employees and to increase its commitment to research and development. It is also in the best interests of business to lobby the government to adopt policies that have a favorable impact on each component of the national "diamond." Thus, according to Porter, businesses should urge government to increase its investment in education, infrastructure, and basic research (because all these enhance advanced factors) and to adopt policies that promote strong competition within domestic markets (because this makes firms stronger international competitors, according to Porter's findings).

Key Terms

Summary

This chapter has reviewed a number of theories that explain why it is beneficial for a country to engage in international trade and has explained the pattern of international trade that we observe in the world economy. We have seen how the theories of Smith, Ricardo, and Heckscher–Ohlin all make strong cases for unrestricted free trade. In contrast, the mercantilist doctrine and, to a lesser extent, the new trade theory can be interpreted to support government intervention to promote exports through subsidies and to limit imports through tariffs and quotas.

In explaining the pattern of international trade, the second objective of this chapter, we have seen that with the exception of mercantilism, which is silent on this issue, the different theories offer largely complementary explanations. Although no one theory may explain the apparent pattern of international trade, taken together, the theory of comparative advantage, the Heckscher–Ohlin theory, the product life-cycle theory, the new trade theory, and Porter's theory of national competitive advantage do suggest which factors are important. Comparative advantage tells us that productivity differences are important; Heckscher–Ohlin tells us that factors endowments matter; the product life-cycle theory tells us that where a new product is introduced is important; the new trade theory tells us that increasing returns to specialization and first-mover advantages matter; and Porter tells us that of these factors may be important insofar as they affect the four components of the national diamond.

The following points have been made in this chapter:

1 Mercantilists argued that it was in a country's best interests to run a balance-of-trade surplus. They viewed trade as a zero-sum game, in which one country's gains cause losses for other countries.

2 The theory of absolute advantage suggests that countries differ in their ability to produce goods efficiently. The theory suggests that a country should specialize in producing goods in areas where it has an absolute advantage and import goods in areas where other countries have absolute advantages.

3 The theory of comparative advantage suggests that it makes sense for a country to specialize in producing those goods that it can produce most efficiently, while buying goods that it can produce relatively less efficiently from other countries—even if that means buying goods from other countries that it could produce more efficiently itself.

4 The theory of comparative advantage suggests that unrestricted free trade brings about increased world production; that is, that trade is a positive-sum game.

5 The theory of comparative advantage also suggests that opening a country to free trade stimulates economic growth, which creates dynamic gains from trade.

6 The Heckscher–Ohlin theory argues that the pattern of international trade is determined by differences in factor endowments. It predicts that countries will export those goods that make intensive use of locally abundant factors and will import goods that make intensive use of factors that are locally scarce.

7 The product life-cycle theory suggests that trade patterns are influenced by where a new product is introduced. In an increasingly integrated global economy, the product life-cycle theory seems to be less predictive than it was between 1945 and 1975.

8 The new trade theory argues that in those industries where substantial economies of scale imply that the world market will profitably support only a few firms, countries may predominate in the export of certain products simply because they had a firm that was a first mover in that industry.

9 Some new trade theorists have promoted the idea of strategic trade policy. The argument is that government, by the sophisticated and judicious use of subsidies, might increase the chances of domestic firms becoming first movers in new industries.

10 Porter's theory of national competitive advantage suggests that the pattern of trade is influenced by four attributes of a nation: (*i*) factor endowments, (*ii*) domestic demand conditions, (*iii*) relating and supporting industries, and (*iv*) firm strategy, structure, and rivalry.

11 Theories of international trade are important to an individual business firm primarily because they can help the firm decide where to locate its various production activities.

12 Firms involved in international trade influence government policy toward trade. By lobbying government bodies, business firms can help promote free trade or trade restrictions.

Critical Thinking and Discussion Questions

1 Mercantilism is a bankrupt theory that has no place in the modern world. Discuss.

2 One "Country Focus" in this chapter reviews the arguments of those who suggest that Japan is a neo-mercantilist nation. Do you agree with this assessment? Can you think of cases in which your country has taken a neo-mercantilist stance to foreign competition?

3 Using the theory of comparative advantage to support your arguments, outline the case for free trade.

4 Using the new trade theory and Porter's theory of national competitive advantage, outline the case for government policies that would build national competitive advantage in a particular industry. What kind of policies would you recommend that the government adopt? Are these policies at variance with the basic free trade philosophy?

5 You are the CEO of a textile firm that designs and manufactures mass-market clothing in the United States. Your manufacturing process is labor-intensive and does not require highly skilled employees. Currently you have design facilities in Paris and New York and manufacturing facilities in North Carolina. Drawing on the theory of international trade, decide whether these are optimal locations for these activities.

6 In general, policies designed to limit competition from low-cost foreign competitors do not help a country to achieve greater economic growth. Discuss this statement.

Internet Exercises

1 The question of national competitiveness often requires delicate handling. Countries are eager to promote their own positions in the global economy, while companies are interested in encouraging countries to adopt policies that facilitate corporate competitiveness. Michael Porter, professor of strategy at Harvard University, has suggested that governments can play a role in a nation's competitiveness, and consequently government actions influence which industries are successful.

Today, however, the global business world is undergoing a revolution, thanks to the Internet. Go to **www.ecommerce.gov/.** Using Porter's diamond of competitive advantage framework, analyze this new business world. Does Porter's framework make sense in the age of the Internet? As a dominant player in an industry, what, if any, changes do you need to make to encourage favorable government actions in an electronically linked world?

2 Understanding cross-border trade—why it occurs and why it follows the patterns it does—is important to our understanding of international business. Several economists, notably Adam Smith and David Ricardo, have theorized that efficiency increases as a result of specialization by countries and free trade. Heckscher and Ohlin explored the role of labor and capital stock in determining trading patterns between nations. More recently, Porter has suggested that industry success depends on factor conditions; demand conditions; the presence, or lack thereof, of related and supporting industries; and firm strategy, structure, and rivalry. While these theories have proved to be powerful tools in increasing our understanding of trade, they were developed to explain "bricks and mortar trade." Today, a new form of cross-border trade is rapidly emerging—electronic trade.

Go to **www.businessweek. com/1999/99_50/b3659074.htm** and explore the ideas presented. Consider each of the trade theories presented in the text and their value in an interconnected world. How well do the existing theories explain international e-commerce? Can policy makers and companies depend on the theories to guide global e-commerce decision making in the same way they utilize the theories for traditional trade issues? Comment on the future of trade in this new environment.

The Rise of the Indian Software Industry

As a relatively poor country India is not normally thought of as a nation that is capable of building a major presence in a high-technology industry, such as computer software. In a little more than a decade, however, the Indian software industry astounded its skeptics and emerged from obscurity into an important force in the global software industry. Between 1991–92 and 1996–97 sales of Indian software companies grew at a compound rate of 53 percent annually. In 1991–92 the industry had sales totaling $388 million. By 1996–97 sales were about $1.8 billion. By 1997 there were more than 760 software companies in India employing 160,000 software engineers, the third-largest concentration of such talent in the world. Much of this growth was powered by exports. In 1985, Indian software exports were worth less than $10 million. Exports hit $1.1 billion in 1996–97 and were projected to reach $4 billion by 2000–01. As a testament to this growth, many foreign software companies are investing heavily in Indian software development operations including Microsoft, IBM, Oracle, and Computer Associates, the four largest US-based software houses.

Most of the growth of the Indian software industry has been based on contract or project-based work for foreign clients. Many Indian companies, for example, maintain applications for their clients, convert code, or migrate software from one platform to another. Increasingly, Indian companies are also involved in important development projects for foreign clients. For example, TCS, India's largest software company, has an alliance with Ernst & Young under which TCS will develop and maintain customized software for Ernst & Young's global clients. TCS also has a development alliance with Microsoft under which the company developed a paperless National Share Depositary system for the Indian stock market based on Microsoft's Windows NT operating system and SQL Server database technology.

The Indian software industry has emerged despite a poor information technology infrastructure. The installed base of personal computers stood at just 1.8 million in 1997 in India, a nation of 1 billion people. With just 1.5 telephone lines per 100 people, India has one of the lowest penetration rates for fixed telephone lines in Asia, if not the world. Internet connections numbered just 45,000 in 1997, compared to 30 million in the United States. But sales of personal computers are starting to take off; more than 500,000 were expected to be sold in 1998. The rapid growth of mobile telephones in India's main cities is compensating to some extent for the lack of fixed telephone lines.

In explaining the success of their industry, India's software entrepreneurs point to a number of factors. Although the general level of education in India is low, India's important middle class is highly educated and its top educational institutions are world class. Also, there has always been an emphasis on engineering in India. Another great plus from an international perceptive is that English is the working language throughout much of middle-class India—a remnant from the days of the British raja. Then there is the wage rate. In America software engineers are increasingly scarce, and the basic salary has been driven up to one of the highest for any occupational group in the country, with entry-level programmers earning $70,000 per year. An entry-level programmer in India, in contrast, starts at about $5,000 per year, which is very low by international standards but high by Indian standards. Salaries for programmers are rising rapidly in India, but so is productivity. In 1992 productivity was about $21,000 per software engineer. By 1996 the figure had risen to $45,000. Many Indian firms now believe they have approached the critical mass required to realize scale economies in software development and to achieve legitimacy in the eyes of important global partners and clients.

Another factor playing to India's hand is that satellite communication has removed distance as an obstacle to doing business for foreign clients. Because software is nothing more than a stream of zeros and one, it can be transported at the speed of light and negligible cost to any point in the world. In a world of instant communications, India's geographical position has given it a time zone advantage. Indian companies have been able to exploit the rapidly expanding international market for outsourced software services including the expanding market for remote maintenance. Indian engineers can fix software bugs, upgrade systems, or process data overnight while their users in Western companies are asleep.

To maintain their competitive position, Indian software companies are now investing heavily in training and leading-edge programming skills. They have also been enthusiastic adopters of international quality standards, and particularly ISO 9000 certification. Indian companies are also starting to make forays into the application and shrink-wrapped software business, primarily with applications aimed at the domestic market. It may only be a matter of time, however, before Indian companies start to compete with companies such as Microsoft, Oracle, PeopleSoft, and SAP in the applications business.[28]

CASE DISCUSSION QUESTIONS

1 To what extent does the theory of comparative advantage explain the rise of the Indian software industry?

2 To what extent does the Heckscher–Ohlin theory explain the rise of the Indian software industry?

3 Use Michael Porter's diamond to analyze the rise of the Indian software industry. Does this analysis help explain the rise of this industry?

4 Which of the above theories— comparative advantage, Heckscher–Ohlin, or Porter's— gives the best explanation of the rise of the Indian software industry? Why?

five

The Political Economy of International Trade

Opening Case	Trade in Hormone-Treated Beef	In the 1970s scientists discovered how to synthesize certain hormones and use them to promote the growth rate of livestock, reduce the fat content of meat, and increase milk production. Bovine somatotropin (BST), a growth hormone produced by beef cattle, was first synthesized by the biotechnolgy firm Genentech. Injections of BST could be used to supplement an animal's own hormone production and increase its growth rate. These hormones soon became

Learning Objectives

1 Discuss the various policy instruments that governments use to restrict imports and promote exports.

2 Understand why some governments intervene in international trade to restrict imports and promote exports.

3 Appreciate the position of those who argue that government intervention in international trade can be self-defeating and typically fails to produce the gains that advocates of intervention claim.

4 Be familiar with the evolution, purpose, current status, and future prospects of the global trading system as embodied in the General Agreement on Tariffs and Trade and the World Trade Organization.

5 Understand the important implications for business practice of government intervention in international trade and of the current global trading system.

---

popular among farmers, who found that they could cut costs and help satisfy consumer demands for leaner meat. Although several of these hormones occurred naturally in animals, consumer groups in several countries soon raised concerns. They argued that the use of hormone supplements was unnatural and that the health consequences of consuming hormone-treated meat were unknown but might include hormonal irregularities and cancer.

In 1989 the European Union (EU) responded to these concerns by banning the use of growth-promoting hormones in the production of livestock and the importation of hormone-treated meat. The ban was controversial because a reasonable consensus existed among scientists that the hormones posed no health risk. Before the ban a number of these hormones had already passed licensing procedures in several EU countries. As part of this process, research had

been assembled that appeared to show that consuming hormone-treated meat had no effects on human health. Although the EU banned hormone-treated meat, many other countries did not, including big meat-producing countries such as Australia, Canada, New Zealand, and the United States. The use of hormones soon became widespread in these countries.

According to trade officials outside the EU, the European ban constituted an unfair restraint on trade. As a result of this ban, exports of meat to the EU fell. For example, US red meat exports to the EU declined from $231 million in 1988 to $98 million in 1994. The complaints of meat exporters were bolstered in 1995 when the Codex Alimentarius Commission, the international food standards body of the UN's Food and Agriculture Organization, and the World Health Organization approved the use of growth hormones. In making this decision, Codex reviewed the scientific literature and found no evidence of a link between the consumption of hormone-treated meat and human health problems, such as cancer.

Fortified by such decisions, the United States in 1995 pressed the EU to drop the ban on the import of hormone-treated beef. The EU refused, citing "consumer concerns about food safety." In response, both Canada and the United States independently filed formal complaints with the World Trade Organization. The United States was joined in its complaint by a number of other countries, including Australia and New Zealand. Created in 1995, the

WTO has powers to enforce fair trading practices between its member states, which included all of the parties to this dispute.

The WTO created a trade panel of three independent experts. After reviewing evidence and hearing from a range of experts, as well as from representatives of both parties, the panel issued a preliminary ruling in May 1997. In a stunning decision, the panel ruled that the EU ban on hormone-treated beef was illegal because it had no scientific justification. The panel also noted that the EU was inconsistent in its application of the ban. The EU takes a very strict view on the use of growth-promoting hormones in the beef sector, where it has a substantial surplus and is not internationally competitive, while it still allows the use of some growth hormones for hog production where the EU has no substantial surplus and does not compete on international markets.

The EU immediately indicated it would appeal the finding to the WTO court of appeals. The WTO court heard the appeal in November 1997 and issued its decision in Feb-

ruary 1998. The appeals body agreed with the findings of the trade panel that the EU had not presented any scientific evidence to justify the hormone ban. This ruling left the EU in a difficult position. Legally, the EU had to lift the ban or face possible trade sanctions. But the ban had wide support among the public in Europe.

After some deliberation, the EU decided to keep the ban. The United States responded by requesting authorization from the WTO to impose trade sanctions on the EU in retaliation. In July 1999 the WTO authorized the United States to impose retaliatory trade sanctions on the EU. On July 29, 1999, the United States imposed punitive 100 percent duties on imports from the EU, including delicacies such as foie gras, truffles, and Roquefort cheese, as well as beef, pork, canned tomatoes, and mustard. The sanctions amounted to about $116.8 million in total and targeted goods from France, Germany, Italy, and Denmark—the countries that were most influential in preserving the 10-year-old beef-hormone ban.[1]

Introduction

Our review of the classical trade theories of Smith, Ricardo, and Heckscher–Ohlin in Chapter 4 showed us that in a world without trade barriers, trade patterns will be determined by the relative productivity of different factors of production in countries. Countries will specialize in the production of products that they can produce most efficiently, while importing products that they can produce less efficiently. Chapter 4 also laid out the intellectual case for free trade. **Free trade** refers to a situation where a government does not attempt to restrict what its citizens can buy from another country or what they can sell to another country. As we saw in Chapter 4, the theories of Smith, Ricardo, and Heckscher–Ohlin predict that the consequences of free trade include both static economic gains (because free trade supports a higher level of domestic consumption and more efficient utilization of resources) and dynamic economic gains (because free trade stimulates economic growth and the creation of wealth).

In this chapter we look at the political reality of international trade. While many nations are nominally committed to free trade, in practice nations tend to intervene in international trade. These political realities are amply illustrated in the opening case. The case describes how the decision by the European Union (EU) to ban hormone-treated beef in Europe has given rise to a contentious trade dispute between

free trade Environment in which a government does not attempt to restrict what its citizens can buy from another country or what they can sell to another country.

the EU and several beef-producing countries such as Canada and the United States. The EU banned the sale of hormone-treated beef for political reasons—it wanted to soothe concerns in Europe about the potential health effects of such meat, even though such concerns have no scientific basis. However, the EU is also a member of the World Trade Organization and has to abide by its rules if it wants to enjoy the benefits of membership. Unfortunately for the EU, the WTO ruled that the EU ban is illegal. This decision placed the EU between a rock and a hard place. On the one hand, the EU is under considerable political pressure from consumer groups within Europe to maintain the ban. On the other, it wants to play by the rules of the WTO—rules that have brought significant benefits to the EU (as we shall discuss later in this chapter). The EU decided to keep the ban in place, pay a penalty for violating WTO rules, and continue to search for scientific evidence to support its position.

In this chapter we explore the political and economic reasons for governmental intervention in international trade. When governments intervene, they often do so by restricting imports of goods and services into their nation while adopting policies that promote exports. Normally their motives are to protect domestic producers and jobs from foreign competition, while at the same time increase the foreign market for the products of domestic producers. However, as the opening case illustrates, "social" issues have intruded into the decision making in recent years. The decision by the EU to ban imports of hormone-treated beef, for example, was only tangentially influenced by a desire to protect the jobs of beef producers in Europe. Rather, it was a political response to social concerns about the health consequences of hormone-treated beef. Social issues are also entering into the trade calculus in other countries. In the United States, for example, there is a movement to ban imports of goods from countries that do not abide by the same labor, health, and environmental regulations as the United States does.

We start this chapter by describing the range of policy instruments that governments use to intervene in international trade. This is followed by a detailed review of the various political and economic motives that governments have for intervention. In the third section of this chapter we consider how the case for free trade stands up in view of the various justifications given for government intervention. Then we look at the emergence of the modern international trading system, which is based on the General Agreement on Tariffs and Trade (GATT) and its successor, the World Trade Organization (WTO). The GATT and WTO are the creations of a series of multinational treaties. The most recent was completed in 1995, involved over 120 countries, and resulted in the creation of the WTO. The purpose of these treaties has been to lower barriers to the free flow of goods and services between nations. Like the GATT before it, the WTO promotes free trade by limiting the ability of national governments to adopt policies that restrict imports. In the final section of this chapter we discuss the implications of this material for business practice.

Instruments of Trade Policy

We review seven main instruments of trade policy in this section: tariffs, subsidies, import quotas, voluntary export restraints, local content requirements, antidumping policies, and administrative policies. Tariffs are the oldest and simplest instrument of trade policy. As we shall see later in this chapter, they are also the instrument that GATT and WTO have been most successful in limiting. A decline in tariff barriers in recent decades has been accompanied by a rise in nontariff barriers such as subsidies, quotas, voluntary export restraints, and antidumping policies.

Tariffs

A **tariff** is a tax levied on imports. The oldest form of trade policy, tariffs fall into two categories. **Specific tariffs** are levied as a fixed charge for each unit of a good imported (for example, $3 per barrel of oil). **Ad valorem tariffs** are levied as a proportion of the value of the imported good. An example of an ad valorem tariff is the 25 percent tariff the US government placed on imported light trucks (pickup trucks, four-wheel-drive vehicles, minivans) in the late 1980s.

A tariff raises the cost of imported products relative to domestic products. Thus, the 25 percent tariff on light trucks imported into the United States increased the price of European and Japanese light truck imports relative to US-produced light trucks. The goal of this tariff was to protect the market share of US auto manufacturers (although a cynic might note that all the tariff did was speed up the plans of European and Japanese automobile companies to build light trucks in the United States). While the principal objective of most tariffs is to protect domestic producers and employees against foreign competition, they also raise revenue for the government. Until introduction of the income tax, for example, the US government raised most of its revenues from tariffs.

The important thing to understand about a tariff is who suffers and who gains. The government gains, because the tariff increases government revenues. Domestic producers gain, because the tariff protects them against foreign competitors by increasing the cost of imported foreign goods. Consumers lose because they must pay more for certain imports. Whether the gains to the government and domestic producers exceed the losses to consumers depends on various factors such as the amount of the tariff, the importance of the imported good to domestic consumers, the number of jobs saved in the protected industry, and so on.

Although detailed consideration of these issues is beyond the scope of this book, two conclusions can be derived from a more advanced analysis.[2] First, tariffs are unambiguously pro-producer and anti-consumer. While they protect producers from foreign competitors, this restriction of supply also raises domestic prices. Thus, as noted in Chapter 4, a study by Japanese economists calculated that restrictions on imports of foodstuffs, cosmetics, and chemicals into Japan in 1989 cost the average Japanese consumer about $890 per year in the form of higher prices.[3] The finding that import tariffs impose significant costs on domestic consumers in the form of higher prices has been the conclusion of almost all studies that have looked at this issue.[4] For another example, see the accompanying "Country Focus," which looks at the cost to US consumers from tariffs.

Tariffs also reduce the overall efficiency of the world economy. A protective tariff encourages domestic firms to produce products at home that, in theory, could be produced more efficiently abroad. The consequence is inefficient utilization of resources. For example, tariffs on the importation of rice into South Korea has meant that the land of South Korean rice farmers has been used in an unproductive manner. It would make more sense for the South Koreans to purchase their rice from lower-cost foreign producers and to use the land in some other way, such as growing foodstuffs that cannot be produced more efficiently elsewhere or for residential and industrial purposes.

Subsidies

subsidy Government payment to a domestic producer.

A **subsidy** is a government payment to a domestic producer. Subsidies take many forms including cash grants, low-interest loans, tax breaks, and government equity participation in domestic firms. By lowering costs, subsidies aid domestic producers in two ways: they help them compete against low-cost foreign imports and they help them gain export markets.

The United States likes to think of itself as a nation that is committed to unrestricted free trade. In negotiations with trading partners, such as China, the European Union, and Japan, US trade representatives can often be heard claiming that the United States economy is an open one with few import tariffs. While it is true that tariffs on the importation of goods into the United States are low when compared to those found in many other industrialized nations, they still exist. A study concluded that during the employees from low-cost foreign competitors. The typical reasoning behind the tariffs was that without such protection, US firms would go out of business and substantial unemployment would result. So the tariffs were presented as having positive effects for the US economy, not to mention the US Treasury, which benefited from the associated revenues.

The study found, however, that while these import tariffs saved about 200,000 jobs in the protected industries that would otherwise have been lost to foreign competition, they also cost American consumers about $32 billion per year in the form of higher prices. Even when the proceeds from the tariff that accrued to the US Treasury were added to the equation, the total cost to the nation still amounted to $10.2 billion per year, or more than $50,000 per job saved.

The two economists who conducted the study argued that these figures understated the true cost to the nation of the tariffs. They maintained that by making imports less competitive with American-made products, tariffs allowed domestic producers to charge more than they might otherwise because they did not have to compete with low-priced imports. By damping competition, even a little, these tariffs removed an incentive for firms in the protected industries to become more efficient, thereby retarding economic progress. Further, the study's authors noted that if the tariffs had not been imposed, some of the $32 billion freed up every year

The Costs of Protectionism in the United States*

1980s tariffs cost US consumers about $32 billion per year.

The study, by Gary Hufbauer and Kim Elliott of the Institute for International Economics, looked at the effect of import tariffs on economic activity in 21 industries with annual sales of $1 billion or more that the United States protected most heavily from foreign competition. The industries included apparel, ceramic tiles, luggage, and sugar. In most of these industries import tariffs had originally been imposed to protect US firms and would have been spent on other goods and services and growth in these areas would have created additional jobs, thereby offsetting the loss of 200,000 jobs in the protected industries.[5]

*S. Nasar, "The High Costs of Protectionism," *New York Times,* November 12, 1993, pp. C1, C2, and C. Hufbauer and K.A. Elliott, *Measuring the Costs of Protectionism in the United States,* Washington, D.C., Institute for International Economics 1993. Reprinted by permission. All rights reserved.

According to official national figures, government subsidies to industry in most industrialized countries amount to between 2 percent and 3.5 percent of the value of industrial output. (These figures exclude subsidies to agriculture and public services.) The average rate of subsidy in the United States was 0.5 percent; in Japan it was 1 percent, and in Europe it ranged from just below 2 percent in Great Britain and West Germany to as much as 6 to 7 percent in Sweden and Ireland.[6] These figures, however, almost certainly underestimate the true value of subsidies because they are based only on cash grants and ignore other kinds of subsidies (e.g., equity participation or low-interest loans). A more detailed study of subsidies within the European Union (EU) was undertaken by the EU Commission. This study found that subsidies to manufacturing enterprises in the early 1990s ranged from a low of 2 percent of total value added in Great Britain to a high of 14.6 percent in Greece. Among the four largest EU countries, Italy was the worst offender; its subsidies are three times those of Great Britain, twice those of Germany, and 1.5 times those of France.[7]

The main gains from subsidies accrue to domestic producers, whose international competitiveness is increased as a result. Advocates of strategic trade policy (which, as you will recall from Chapter 4, is an outgrowth of the new trade theory) favor the use of subsidies to help domestic firms achieve a dominant position in those industries where economies of scale are important and the world market is not large enough to profitably support more than a few firms (e.g., aerospace, semiconductors). According to this argument, subsidies can help a firm achieve first-mover advantages in an emerging industry (just as US government subsidies, in the form of substantial R&D grants, allegedly helped Boeing). If this is achieved, further gains to the domestic economy arise from the employment and tax revenues that a major global company can generate.

But subsidies must be paid for. Governments typically pay for subsidies by taxing individuals. Therefore, whether subsidies generate national benefits that exceed their costs is debatable. In practice many subsidies are not that successful at increasing the international competitiveness of domestic producers. Rather, they tend to protect the inefficient, rather than promote efficiency.

Import Quotas and Voluntary Export Restraints

An **import quota** is a direct restriction on the quantity of some good that may be imported into a country. The restriction is normally enforced by issuing import licenses to a group of individuals or firms. For example, the United States has a quota on cheese imports. The only firms allowed to import cheese are certain trading companies, each of which is allocated the right to import a maximum number of pounds of cheese each year. In some cases the right to sell is given directly to the governments of exporting countries. This is the case for sugar and textile imports in the United States.

A variant on the import quota is the voluntary export restraint. A **voluntary export restraint (VER)** is a quota on trade imposed by the exporting country, typically at the request of the importing country's government. One famous example is the limitation on auto exports to the United States enforced by Japanese automobile producers in 1981. A response to direct pressure from the US government, this VER limited Japanese exports to the United States to no more than 1.68 million vehicles per year. The agreement was revised in 1984 to allow Japanese producers to export 1.85 million vehicles per year. In 1985 the agreement was allowed to lapse, but the Japanese government indicated its intentions at that time to continue to restrict exports to the United States to 1.85 million vehicles per year.[8]

Foreign producers agree to VERs because they fear that if they do not, more damaging punitive tariffs or import quotas might follow. Agreeing to a VER is seen as a way to make the best of a bad situation by appeasing protectionist pressures in a country.

As with tariffs and subsidies, both import quotas and VERs benefit domestic producers by limiting import competition. Quotas do not benefit consumers. An import quota or VER always raises the domestic price of an imported good. When imports are limited to a low percentage of the market by a quota or VER, the price is bid up for that limited foreign supply. In the automobile industry, for example, the VER increased the price for the limited supply of Japanese imports. According to a study by the US Federal Trade Commission, the automobile industry VER cost US consumers about $1 billion per year between 1981 and 1985. That $1 billion per year went to Japanese producers in the form of higher prices.[9]

Local Content Requirements

A **local content requirement** demands that some specific fraction of a good be produced domestically. The requirement can be expressed either in physical terms (e.g., 75 percent of component parts for this product must be produced locally) or in value terms (e.g., 75 percent of the value of this product must be produced locally).

Local content regulations have been widely used by developing countries to try to shift their manufacturing base from the simple assembly of products whose parts are manufactured elsewhere to the local manufacture of component parts. More recently, the issue of local content has been raised by several developed countries. In the United States, for example, pressure is building to insist that 75 percent of the component parts that go into cars built in the United States by Japanese companies such as Toyota and Honda be manufactured in the United States. Both Toyota and Honda have reacted to such pressures by announcing their intention to buy more American-manufactured parts.

For a domestic producer of component parts, local content regulations provide protection in the same way an import quota does: by limiting foreign competition. The aggregate economic effects are also the same; domestic producers benefit, but the import restrictions raise the prices of imported components. Higher prices for imported components are passed on to consumers of the final product in the form of higher final prices. So as with all trade policies, local content regulations tend to benefit producers and not consumers.

Antidumping Policies

In the context of international trade, **dumping** is defined as selling goods in a foreign market at a price below their costs of production or as selling goods in a foreign market at below their "fair" market value. There is a difference between these two definitions, since the "fair" market value of a good is normally judged to be greater than the costs of producing that good because it includes a "fair" profit margin. Firms may unload excess production in foreign markets by dumping and some dumping may be the result of predatory behavior. Producers may use substantial profits from their home markets to subsidize prices in a foreign market with a view to driving indigenous competitors out of that market. Once this has been achieved, the predatory firm can raise prices and earn substantial profits. An alleged example of dumping occurred in 1997, when two South Korean manufacturers of semiconductors, LG Semicon and Hyundai Electronics, were accused of selling dynamic random access memory chips (DRAMs) in the US market at below their costs of production. This action occurred in the middle of a worldwide glut of chip-making capacity. It was alleged that the Korean firms were trying to unload their excess production in the United States.

Antidumping policies are designed to punish foreign firms that engage in dumping. The ultimate objective is to protect domestic producers from "unfair" foreign competition. Although antidumping policies vary somewhat from country to country, the majority are similar to the antidumping policies used in the United States. If a domestic producer believes that a foreign firm is dumping production in the US market, it can file a petition with two government agencies, the Commerce Department and the International Trade Commission. In the Korean DRAM case, the petition was filed by Micron Technology, a US manufacturer of DRAMs. The government agencies then investigate

ANOTHER PERSPECTIVE

What You See Isn't Always What You Get

As you may have learned by visiting the US Office of Tariff Affairs and Trade Agreements site **(http://www.usitc.gov/taffairs.htm),** tariff and quota barriers are readily researched, so they are easy for managers to factor in to their business planning. Non-tariff barriers are often less explicit. In the mid-1980s, just after American trade negotiators pushed Japan to allow imports of American rice into Japan (there were price differentials of 1 to 10 between American and Japanese rice at the time), rumors spread that American rice would cause cancer. These rumors severely impeded imports.

the complaint. If they find it has merit, the Commerce Department may impose an antidumping duty on the offending foreign imports. These duties, which represent a special tariff, can be fairly substantial. For example, after reviewing Micron's complaint, the Commerce Department imposed 9 percent and 4 percent dumping duties on LG Semicon and Hyundai DRAMs, respectively.

Administrative Policies

administrative trade policies Bureaucratic rules that are designed to make it difficult for imports to enter a country.

In addition to the formal instruments of trade policy, governments sometimes use a range of informal or administrative policies to restrict imports and boost exports. **Administrative trade policies** are bureaucratic rules that are designed to make it difficult for imports to enter a country. Some say the Japanese are the masters of this trade barrier. In recent years Japan's formal tariff and nontariff barriers have been among the lowest in the world. However, critics charge that their informal administrative barriers to imports more than compensate for this. One example is that of tulip bulbs; the Netherlands exports tulip bulbs to almost every country in the world except Japan. Japanese customs inspectors insist on checking every tulip bulb by cutting it vertically down the middle, and even Japanese ingenuity cannot put them together again! Another example concerns the US express delivery company Federal Express. Federal Express has had a tough time expanding its global express services into Japan, primarily because Japanese customs inspectors insist on opening a large proportion of express packages to check for pornography—a process that can delay an "express" package for days. Japan is not the only country

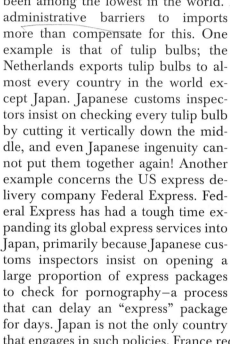

ANOTHER PERSPECTIVE

Local Content Requirements May Stimulate FDI

Local content requirements often lead to business for the domestic sector, but that is not always the case, although it is the intention of the legislation. Sometimes what the local market provides does not meet the needs of the manufacturer, especially in the areas of quality and reliability. In these cases, the foreign suppliers may follow their buyer to the market and piggyback their operations on their buyer's FDI. When Japanese auto manufacturers entered the US market to begin their US operations, a move that was widely understood to be a response to quota threats, local content requirements, and other import restrictions, many of their Japanese suppliers came with them.

that engages in such policies. France required that all imported videotape recorders arrive through a small customs entry point that was both remote and poorly staffed. The resulting delays kept Japanese VCRs out of the French market until a VER agreement was negotiated.[10] As with all instruments of trade policy, administrative instruments benefit producers and hurt consumers, who are denied access to possibly superior foreign products.

The Case for Government Intervention

There are two types of argument for government intervention in international trade—political and economic. Political arguments for intervention are concerned with protecting the interests of certain groups within a nation (normally producers), often at the expense of other groups (normally consumers). Economic arguments for intervention are typically concerned with boosting the overall wealth of a nation (to the benefit of all, both producers and consumers).

Political Arguments for Intervention

Political arguments for government intervention cover a range of issues including protecting jobs, protecting industries deemed important for national security, retaliating to unfair foreign competition, protecting consumers from "dangerous" products, furthering the goals of foreign policy, and protecting the human rights of individuals in exporting countries.

PROTECTING JOBS AND INDUSTRIES   One common political argument for government intervention is that it is necessary for protecting jobs and industries from "unfair" foreign competition. Antidumping policies are frequently justified on such grounds. The voluntary export restraints (VERs) that offered some protection to the US automobile, machine tool, and steel industries during the 1980s were also motivated by such considerations. Similarly, Japan's quotas on rice imports are aimed at protecting jobs in that country's agricultural sector. The same motive underlay the establishment of the Common Agricultural Policy (CAP) by the European Union. The CAP was designed to protect the jobs of Europe's politically powerful farmers by restricting imports and guaranteeing prices. However, the higher prices that resulted from the CAP have cost Europe's consumers dearly. This is true of most attempts to protect jobs and industries through government intervention. As we saw earlier in the chapter the VER in the automobile industry raised the price of Japanese imports, at a cost of $1 billion per year to US consumers.

In addition to hurting consumers, trade controls sometimes hurt the producers they are intended to protect. In Chapter 4, for example, we noted how the VER agreement in the US machine tool industry has been self-defeating. By limiting Japanese and Taiwanese machine tool imports, the VER raised the prices of machine tools purchased by US manufacturers to levels above those prevailing in the world market. This raised the capital costs of the US manufacturing industry in general, thereby decreasing its international competitiveness.

NATIONAL SECURITY   Countries sometimes argue that it is necessary to protect certain industries because they are important for national security. Defense-related industries often get this kind of attention (e.g., aerospace, advanced electronics, semiconductors, and so on). Although not as common as it used to be, this argument is still made occasionally. Those in favor of protecting the US semiconductor industry from foreign competition, for example, argue that semiconductors are now such important components of defense products that it would be dangerous to rely primarily on foreign producers for them. In 1986, this argument helped persuade the federal government to support Sematech, a consortium of 14 US semiconductor companies that accounts for 90 percent of the US industry's revenues. Sematech's mission is to conduct joint research into manufacturing techniques that can be parceled out to members. The government saw the venture as so critical that Sematech was specially protected from antitrust laws. Initially the US government provided Sematech with $100 million per year in subsidies. By the mid-1990s, however, the US semiconductor industry had regained its leading market position, largely through the personal computer boom and demand for microprocessor chips made by Intel. In 1994, the consortium's board voted to end federal funding and since 1996 the consortium has been funded entirely by private money.[11]

RETALIATION   Some argue that governments should use the threat to intervene in trade policy as a bargaining tool to help open foreign markets and force trading partners to play by the rules. Successive US governments have been among those that adopted this "get-tough" approach. The US government has successfully used the threat of punitive trade sanctions to get the Chinese government to enforce its

intellectual property laws. As you will recall from Chapter 2, lax enforcement of these laws had resulted in massive copyright infringements in China that cost US companies such as Microsoft hundreds of millions of dollars per year in lost sales revenues. After the United States threatened to impose 100 percent tariffs on a range of Chinese imports, and after harsh words between officials from the two countries, the Chinese agreed to tighter enforcement of intellectual property regulations.[12]

If it works, such a politically motivated rationale for government intervention may liberalize trade and bring with it resulting economic gains. It is a risky strategy, however, because the country being pressured may not back down and instead may raise its own trade barriers. This is what the Chinese government threatened to do when pressured by the United States, although it ultimately did back down. If a government does not back down, the results could be higher trade barriers all around and an economic loss to all.

PROTECTING CONSUMERS   The opening case describes how the European Union banned the sale and importation of hormone-treated beef. The ban was motivated by concerns for the safety and health of consumers, as opposed to economic considerations. Many governments have long had regulations in place to protect consumers from "unsafe" products. The indirect effect of such regulations often is to limit or ban the importation of such products. In 1998 the Clinton administration permanently banned imports into the United States of 58 types of military-style assault weapons (US-based firms were already prohibited from selling such weapons). The ban was motivated by a desire to increase public safety. It followed on the heels of a rash of random and deadly shootings by individuals using such weapons, including one in the president's home state of Arkansas that left four children and a schoolteacher dead.[13]

The conflict over the importation of hormone-treated beef into the European Union may be a taste of things to come. In addition to the use of hormones to

Biotechnology has made it possible to genetically alter many crops so that they are resistant to common herbicides, produce proteins that are natural insecticides, have dramatically improved yields, or are resistant to inclement weather conditions. Do you think these positive outcomes of genetically altered products overcome the possible negative health effects these products potentially may cause in humans? What about the farmers who would benefit from the higher yields, "natural" protection against pests, or the possibility of growing new crops that they never could before—especially in poorer countries?
© Corbis. All rights reserved.

promote animal growth and meat production, biotechnology has made it possible to genetically alter many crops so that they produce proteins that are natural insecticides, have dramatically improved yields, or are resistant to inclement weather. A new breed of genetically modified tomatoes has an antifreeze gene inserted into its genome and can be grown in colder climates than previously possible. A genetically engineered cotton seed produced by Monsanto has a protein that protects against three common insect pests, the cotton bollworm, tobacco budworm, and pink bollworm. Use of this seed reduces or eliminates the need for traditional pesticide applications for these pests. As enticing as such innovations sound, they have met with intense resistance from consumer groups, particularly in Europe. The fear is that the widespread use of genetically altered seed could have unanticipated and harmful effects on human health and may result in "genetic pollution." (An example of genetic pollution would be when the widespread use of crops that produce "natural pesticides" stimulates the evolution of "super-bugs" that are resistant to those pesticides.) Such concerns have lead Austria and Luxembourg to outlaw the importation, sale, or use of genetically altered organisms. Sentiment against genetically altered organisms also is strong in several other European countries, most notably Germany and Switzerland. It seems increasingly likely, therefore, that the World Trade Organization will be drawn into the conflict between those that want to expand the global market for genetically altered organisms, such as Monsanto, and those that want to limit it, such as Austria and Luxembourg.[14]

FURTHERING FOREIGN POLICY OBJECTIVES   On occasion, governments will use trade policies to support their foreign policy objectives.[15] They may grant preferential trade terms to countries with which they want to build strong relations. Trade policy has also been used several times as an instrument for pressuring or punishing "rogue states" that do not abide by international law or norms. Iraq has labored under extensive trade sanctions since defeated in the 1991 Gulf War. The theory is that such pressure might persuade the "rogue state" to mend its ways or it might hasten a change of government. In the case of Iraq, the sanctions are seen as a way of forcing that country to comply with several UN resolutions. In another example, the United States has maintained long-running trade sanctions against Cuba. The main goal is to impoverish Cuba in the hope that the resulting economic hardship will lead to the downfall of Cuba's Communist government and its replacement with a more democratically inclined (and pro-US) regime. The United States also has long-running trade sanctions in place against Libya and Iran, both of which it accuses of supporting terrorist action against US interests.

Unfortunately, other countries can undermine any unilateral trade sanctions. The US sanctions against Cuba, for example, have not stopped other Western countries from trading with the Communist nation. The US sanctions have done little more than create a vacuum into which other trading nations, such as Canada and Germany, have stepped. In an attempt to put a halt to this, and further tighten the screws on Cuba, in 1996 Congress passed the **Helms-Burton Act.** This act allows Americans to sue foreign firms that use property in Cuba confiscated from them after the 1959 revolution. A similar act, the **D'Amato Act,** aimed at Libya and Iran was also passed that year. The passage of Helms-Burton elicited protest from America's trading partners, including the European Union, Canada, and Mexico, all of which claim the law violates their sovereignty and is illegal under World Trade Organization rules. For example, Canadian companies that have been doing business in Cuba for years see no reason why they should suddenly be sued in US courts when Canada does not restrict trade with Cuba. They are not violating Canadian law and they are not US companies, so why should they be subject to US law? Despite such protests, the law is still on the books in the United States, although the Clinton administration has been less than enthusiastic about

GMOs banned in some countries WTO - drawn in.

Helms-Burton Act
Legislation that allows Americans to sue foreign firms that use property in Cuba confiscated from them after the 1959 revolution.

D'Amato Act Legislation that is similar to the Helms-Burton Act, but aimed at Libya and Iran.

enforcing it—probably because it is unenforceable. The fuss over Helms-Burton illustrates, however, that trade policy is a rather blunt and sometimes counterproductive instrument of foreign policy.

PROTECTING HUMAN RIGHTS   Protecting and promoting human rights in other countries is an important element of foreign policy for many democracies. Governments sometimes use trade policy to try to improve the human rights policies of trading partners. In recent years, the most obvious example of this has been the annual debate in the United States over whether to grant most favored nation (MFN) status to China.

MFN status allows countries to exports goods to the United States under favorable terms. Under MFN rules the average tariff on Chinese goods imported into the United States is 8 percent. If China's MFN status were rescinded, tariffs would probably rise to about 40 percent. Trading partners who are signatories of the World Trade Organization—as most are—automatically receive MFN status. However, China is not yet a member of the WTO, so the decision of whether to grant MFN status to China is a real one. The decision is made more difficult by the perception that China has a poor human rights record. As indications of the country's disregard for human rights, critics of China often point to the 1989 Tiananmen Square massacre, China's contin-

US Trade Representative Charlene Barshefsky and Chinese Minister of Foreign Trade and Economic Cooperation Shi Guangsheng exchange documents after signing an agreement on China's accession into the World Trade Organization on November 15, 1999. The agreement will throw open an immense market of 1.2 billion consumers to unprecedented access by foreign firms.
© AFP/Corbis.

uing subjugation of Tibet (which China occupied in the 1950s), and the squashing of political dissent in China (which has an estimated 1,700 political prisoners).[16] These critics argue the United States should withhold MFN status until China shows measurable improvement in its human rights record. They argue that trade policy should be used as a political weapon to force China to change its internal policies toward human rights.

But some believe that limiting trade because of widespread human right abuses only makes matters worse in those countries. They argue that the best way to change the internal human rights stance of a country is to engage it through international trade. The argument is simple: Growing bilateral trade raises the income levels of both countries, and as a state becomes richer its people begin to demand—and generally receive—better treatment with regard to their human rights. This is a variant of the argument introduced in Chapter 2 that economic progress begets political progress (if political progress is measured by the adoption of a democratic government that respects human rights). This argument has won the day in the United States. In 1997 President Clinton announced he would grant MFN status to China, and in doing so argued that trade and human rights issues should be decoupled. The United States is not alone in taking such a position. In March 1996 France, eager for China to sign a $1.5 billion contract for Airbus Industrie planes, argued within the European Union against a resolution in the United Nations Commission on Human Rights urging improvement of Chinese human rights practices.

Economic Arguments for Intervention

With the development of the new trade theory and strategic trade policy (see Chapter 4), the economic arguments for government intervention have undergone a renaissance. Until the early 1980s, most economists saw little benefit in government intervention and strongly advocated a free trade policy. This position has changed somewhat with the development of strategic trade policy, although as we will see in the next section, there are still strong economic arguments for sticking to a free trade stance.

THE INFANT INDUSTRY ARGUMENT   The infant industry argument is the oldest economic argument for government intervention. It was first proposed by Alexander Hamilton in 1792. According to this argument, many developing countries have a potential comparative advantage in manufacturing, but new manufacturing industries there cannot initially compete with well-established industries in developed countries. To allow manufacturing to get a toehold, governments temporarily support new industries (with tariffs, import quotas, and subsidies) until they have grown strong enough to meet international competition.

This argument has had substantial appeal for the governments of developing nations during the past 40 years. Also, the infant industry argument has been recognized as a legitimate reason for protectionism by the GATT. Nevertheless, many economists remain very critical of this argument. They make two main points. First, protection of manufacturing from foreign competition does no good unless the protection makes the industry efficient. In case after case, however, protection seems to have done little more than foster the development of inefficient industries that have little hope of ever competing in the world market. Brazil, for example, built up the world's 10th-largest auto industry behind tariff barriers and quotas. Once those barriers were removed in the late 1980s, however, foreign imports soared and the Brazilian industry was forced to face up to the fact that after 30 years of protection, it was one of the world's most inefficient.[17]

A second point is that the infant industry argument relies on an assumption that firms are unable to make efficient long-term investments by borrowing money from the domestic or international capital market. Consequently, governments have been required to subsidize long-term investments. Given the development of global capital markets over the past 20 years, this assumption no longer looks as valid as it once did (see Chapter 9 for details). Today, if a developing country really does have a potential comparative advantage in a manufacturing industry, firms in that country should be able to borrow money from the capital markets to finance the required investments. Given financial support, firms based in countries with a potential comparative advantage have an incentive to go through the necessary initial losses in order to make long-run gains. This is what many Taiwanese and South Korean firms did in industries such as textiles, semiconductors, machine tools, steel, and shipping. Thus, given efficient global capital markets, the only industries that would require government protection would be those that are not worthwhile.

STRATEGIC TRADE POLICY   The strategic trade policy argument has been proposed by the new trade theorists.[18] We reviewed the basic argument in Chapter 4 when we considered the new trade theory. The new trade theory argues that in industries where the world market will profitably support only a few firms, countries may predominate in the export of certain products simply because they had firms that were able to capture first-mover advantages. The dominance of Boeing in the commercial aircraft industry is attributed to such factors.

Against this background, there are two components to the strategic trade policy argument. First, it is argued that a government can raise national income if it can ensure that the firms to gain first-mover advantages in such an industry are domestic rather than foreign enterprises. Thus, according to the strategic trade policy argument, a government should use subsidies to support promising firms that are active in emerging industries. Advocates of this argument point out that the substantial R&D grants the US government gave Boeing in the 1950s and 60s probably helped tilt the field of competition in the emerging market for jet passenger planes in Boeing's favor. (Boeing's 707 jet airliner was derived from a military plane.) Similar arguments are now made with regard to Japan's dominance in the production of liquid crystal display screens (used in laptop computers). Although these screens were invented in the United States, the Japanese government, in cooperation with major electronics companies, targeted this industry for research support in the late 1970s and early 80s. The result was that Japanese firms, not US firms, captured the first-mover advantages in this market.

The second component of the strategic trade policy argument is that it might pay government to intervene in an industry if it helps domestic firms overcome the barriers to entry created by foreign firms that have already reaped first-mover advantages. This argument underlies government support of Airbus Industrie, Boeing's major competitor. Airbus is a consortium of four companies from Great Britain, France, Germany, and Spain formed in 1966. When it began production in the mid-1970s it had less than 5 percent of the world commercial aircraft market. By the late 1990s it had increased its share to about 40 percent and was threatening Boeing's dominance. How has Airbus achieved this? According to the US government, the answer is a $13.5 billion subsidy from the governments of Great Britain, France, Germany, and Spain.[19] Without this subsidy, Airbus would have never been able to break into the world market. In another example, the rise to dominance of the Japanese semiconductor industry, despite the first-mover advantages enjoyed by US firms, is attributed to intervention by the Japanese government. In this case the government did not subsidize the costs of domestic manufacturers. Rather, it protected the Japanese home market while pursuing policies that ensured Japanese companies got access to the necessary manufacturing and product know-how.

If these arguments are correct, they clearly suggest a rationale for government intervention in international trade. Specifically, governments should target technologies that may be important in the future and use subsidies to support development work aimed at commercializing those technologies. Government should provide export subsidies until the domestic firms have established first-mover advantages in the world market. Government support may also be justified if it can help domestic firms overcome the first-mover advantages enjoyed by foreign competitors and emerge as viable competitors in the world market (as in the Airbus and semiconductor examples). In this case, a combination of home market protection and export-promoting subsidies may be needed.

The Revised Case for Free Trade

The strategic trade policy arguments of the new trade theorists suggest an economic justification for government intervention in international trade. This justification challenges the rationale for unrestricted free trade found in the work of classic trade theorists such as Adam Smith and David Ricardo. In response to this challenge, a number of economists—including some responsible for the development of the new trade theory, such as Paul Krugman of MIT—have been quick to point out that although strategic trade policy looks nice in theory, in practice it may be unworkable. This response to the strategic trade policy argument constitutes the revised case for free trade.[20]

Retaliation and Trade War

Krugman argues that strategic trade policy aimed at establishing domestic firms in a dominant position in a global industry are beggar-thy-neighbor policies that boost national income at the expense of other countries. A country that attempts to use such policies will probably provoke retaliation. In many cases, the resulting trade war between two or more interventionist governments will leave all countries involved worse off than if a hands-off approach had been adopted. If the US government were to respond to the Airbus subsidy by increasing its own subsidies to Boeing, for example, the result might be that the subsidies would cancel each other out. In the process, both European and US taxpayers would end up supporting an expensive and pointless trade war, and both Europe and the United States would be worse off.

Krugman may be right about the danger of a strategic trade policy leading to a trade war. The problem, however, is how to respond when one's competitors are already being supported by government subsidies; that is, how should Boeing and the United States respond to the subsidization of Airbus? According to Krugman, the answer is not to engage in retaliatory action, but to help establish rules of the game that minimize the use of trade-distorting subsidies. This is what the GATT seeks to do.

Domestic Politics

Governments do not always act in the national interest when they intervene in the economy. Instead they are influenced by politically important interest groups. The European Union's support for the Common Agricultural Policy (CAP), which arose because of the political power of French and German farmers, is an example. The policy benefited inefficient farmers and the politicians who relied on the farm vote, but no one else. Thus, a further reason for not embracing strategic trade policy, according to Krugman, is that such a policy is almost certain to be captured by special interest groups, who will distort it to their own ends. Krugman concludes that with regard to the United States:

> To ask the Commerce Department to ignore special-interest politics while formulating detailed policy for many industries is not realistic; to establish a blanket policy of free trade, with exceptions granted only under extreme pressure, may not be the optimal policy according to the theory but may be the best policy that the country is likely to get.[21]

Development of the Global Trading System

We have seen in this chapter and the previous one that there are strong economic arguments for supporting unrestricted free trade. While many governments have recognized the value of these arguments, they have been unwilling to unilaterally lower their trade barriers for fear that other nations might not follow suit. Consider the problem that two neighboring countries, say France and Italy, face when deciding whether to lower barriers to trade between them. The government of Italy might be in favor of lowering trade barriers, but it might be unwilling to do so for fear that France will not do the same. Instead, the French might take advantage of Italy's low barriers to enter the Italian market, while continuing to shut Italian products out of France through high trade barriers. The French government might believe it faces the same dilemma. The problem is a lack of trust between the governments of France and Italy. Both governments recognize that their nations will benefit from lower trade barriers, but neither government is willing to lower barriers for fear that the other might not follow.[22]

How is such a deadlock to be resolved? One answer is for both countries to negotiate rules that will govern cross-border trade and lower trade barriers. But who is to monitor the governments to make sure they are playing by the trade rules? And

who is to impose sanctions on a government that cheats? Both governments could set up an independent body whose function is to act as a referee. This referee could monitor trade between the countries, make sure that no side cheats, and impose sanctions on a country if it does.

While it might sound unlikely that any government would compromise its national sovereignty by submitting to such an arrangement, since World War II an international trading framework has evolved that has exactly these features. For its first 50 years this framework was known as the General Agreement on Tariffs and Trade. Since 1995 it has been known as the World Trade Organization. Here we look at the evolution and workings of the GATT and the WTO. We begin, however, with a brief discussion of the pre-GATT history of world trade to set the scene.

From Smith to the Great Depression

As we saw in Chapter 4, the intellectual case for free trade goes back to the late 18th century and the work of Adam Smith and David Ricardo. Free trade as a government policy was first officially embraced by Great Britain in 1846, when the British Parliament repealed the Corn Laws. The Corn Laws placed a high tariff on imports of foreign corn. The objectives of the Corn Laws tariff were to raise government revenues and to protect British corn producers. There had been annual motions in Parliament in favor of free trade since the 1820s when David Ricardo was a member of Parliament. However, agricultural protection was withdrawn only when the effects of a harvest failure in Britain were compounded by the imminent threat of famine in Ireland. Faced with considerable hardship and suffering among the populace, Parliament narrowly reversed its long-held position.

During the next 80 years, Great Britain, as one of the world's dominant trading powers, pushed for trade liberalization, but its policy of unilateral free trade was not reciprocated by its major trading partners. The only reason Britain was able to hold on to this policy for so long was that, as the world's largest exporting nation, it had far more to lose from a trade war than did any other country.

By the 1930s, however, the British attempt to stimulate free trade was buried under the economic rubble of the Great Depression. The Depression had roots in the failure of the world economy to mount a sustained economic recovery after the end of World War I in 1918. Things got worse in 1929 with the US stock market collapse and the subsequent run on the US banking system. Economic problems were compounded in 1930 when the US Congress passed the Smoot-Hawley Act. Aimed at avoiding rising unemployment by protecting domestic industries and diverting consumer demand away from foreign products, the Smoot-Hawley Act erected an enormous wall of tariff barriers. Almost every industry was rewarded with its "made-to-order" tariff. An odd aspect of the Smoot-Hawley tariff-raising binge was that the United States was running a balance-of-payment surplus at the time and it was the world's largest creditor nation. The Smoot-Hawley Act had a damaging effect on employment abroad. Other countries reacted to the US action by raising their own tariff. US exports tumbled in response, and the world slid further into the Great Depression.[23]

1947–1979: GATT, Trade Liberalization, and Economic Growth

The economic damage caused by the beggar-thy-neighbor trade policies that the Smoot-Hawley Act ushered in exerted a profound influence on the economic institutions and ideology of the post-World War II world. The United States emerged

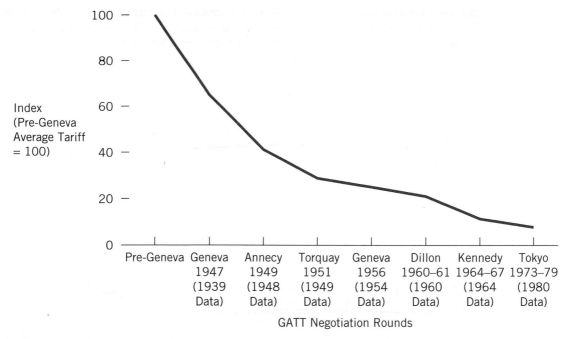

Figure 5.1

Average Reductions in US Tariff Rates, 1947–1979

Indexes are calculated from percentage reductions in average weighted tariff rates given in Finger, 1979 (Table 1, p. 425), *World Development Report* (Oxford University Press, 1987), (Table 8.1, p. 136); and *World Development Report* (Oxford University Press, 1994). Weighted average US tariff rate after Tokyo round was 4.6 percent (World Bank, 1987).

from the war not only militarily victorious but also economically dominant. After the debacle of the Great Depression, opinion in Congress had swung strongly in favor of free trade. Under US leadership, the General Agreement on Tariffs and Trade was established in 1947.

The GATT is a multilateral agreement whose objective was to liberalize trade by eliminating tariffs, subsidies, import quotas, and the like. From its foundation in 1947 until it was superseded by the WTO, the GATT's membership grew from 19 to more than 120 nations. The GATT did not attempt to liberalize trade restrictions in one fell swoop; that would have been impossible. Rather, tariff reduction was spread over eight rounds. The most recent, the Uruguay Round, was launched in 1986 and completed in December 1993. In these rounds mutual tariff reductions were negotiated among all members, who then committed themselves not to raise import tariffs above negotiated rates. GATT regulations were enforced by a mutual monitoring mechanism. If a country believed that one of its trading partners was violating a GATT regulation, it could ask the Geneva-based bureaucracy that administered the GATT to investigate. If GATT investigators found the complaints to be valid, member countries could be asked to pressure the offending party to change its policies. In general, such pressure was sufficient to get an offending country to change its policies. If policies were not changed, the offending country could have been expelled from the GATT.

In its early years the GATT was by most measures very successful. In the United States, for example, the average tariff declined by nearly 92 percent between the Geneva Round of 1947 and the Tokyo Round of 1973–79 (see Figure 5.1). Consistent with the theoretical arguments first advanced by Ricardo and reviewed in Chapter 4, the move toward free trade under the GATT appeared to stimulate economic growth. From 1953 to 1963 world trade grew at an annual rate of 6.1 percent, and world income grew at an annual rate of 4.3 percent. Performance from 1963 to 1973 was even better; world trade grew at 8.9 percent annually, and world income grew at 5.1 percent a year.[24]

1980–1993: Disturbing Trends

During the 1980s and early 1990s the world trading system erected by the GATT began to come under strain as pressures for greater protectionism increased around the world. There were three main reasons for the rise in such pressures during the 1980s. First, Japan's economic success strained the world trading system. Japan was in ruins when the GATT was created. By the early 1980s, however, it had become the world's second-largest economy and its largest exporter. Japan's success in such industries as automobiles and semiconductors might have been enough to strain the world trading system, but things were made worse by the widespread perception in the West that despite low tariff rates and subsidies, Japanese markets were closed to imports and foreign investment because of administrative trade barriers.

Second, the world trading system was further strained by the persistent trade deficit in the world's largest economy, the United States. Although the deficit peaked in 1987 at over $170 billion, by the end of 1992 the annual rate was still running at about $80 billion. From a political perspective, the matter was made worse because in 1992 the United States also ran a $45 billion deficit in its trade with Japan—a country perceived as not playing by the rules. The US deficit caused painful adjustments in industries such as automobiles, machine tools, semiconductors, steel, and textiles, where domestic producers steadily lost market share to foreign competitors. The resulting unemployment gave rise to renewed demands in the US Congress for protection against imports.

A third reason for the trend toward greater protectionism was that many countries found ways to get around GATT regulations. Bilateral voluntary export restraints (VERs) circumvent GATT agreements because neither the importing country nor the exporting country complains to the GATT bureaucracy in Geneva—and without a complaint, the GATT bureaucracy can do nothing. Exporting countries agreed to VERs to avoid more damaging punitive tariffs. One of the best-known examples is the VER between Japan and the United States, under which Japanese producers promised to limit their auto imports into the United States as a way of defusing trade tensions. According to a World Bank study, 13 percent of the imports of industrialized countries in 1981 were subjected to nontariff trade barriers such as VERs. By 1986 this figure had increased to 16 percent. The most rapid rise was in the United States, where the value of imports affected by nontariff barriers (primarily VERs) increased by 23 percent between 1981 and 1986.[25]

The Uruguay Round and the World Trade Organization

Against the background of rising pressures for protectionism, in 1986 the members of the GATT embarked on their eighth round of negotiations to reduce tariffs, the Uruguay Round (so named because they took place in Uruguay). This was the most difficult round of negotiations yet, primarily because it was the most ambitious. GATT rules had applied only to trade in manufactured goods and commodities. In the Uruguay Round member countries sought to extend GATT rules to cover services. They also sought to write rules governing the protection of intellectual property, to reduce agricultural subsidies, and to strengthen the GATT's monitoring and enforcement mechanisms.

The Uruguay Round dragged on for seven years. For a time it looked as if an agreement might not be possible, raising fears that the world might slip into a trade war. The main impediment to an agreement was a long-standing dispute between the United States and the European Union on agricultural subsidies. An agreement had to be reached before December 16, 1993, which was when the "fast-track negotiating authority" granted to President Clinton by Congress would have expired. Had this authority expired, any agreement would have needed the approval of the whole US Congress, rather than just the president, a much more difficult proposition. An 11th-hour compromise on agricultural subsidies, which reduced the level of subsidies significantly but not by as much as the United States had wanted, saved the day, and an agreement was reached December 15, 1993. The agreement was formally signed by member states at a meeting in Marrakech, Morocco, on April 15, 1994. It went into effect July 1, 1995.

The most important components of the Uruguay Round agreement are detailed in Table 5.1. The Uruguay Round contained the following provisions: tariffs on industrial goods were to be reduced by more than one-third; agricultural subsidies were to be substantially reduced; fair trade and market access rules were to be extended to cover a range of services; GATT rules were also to be extended to provide enhanced protection for patents, copyrights, and trademarks (intellectual property); barriers on trade in textiles were to be significantly reduced over 10 years; and a World Trade Organization (WTO) was to be created to implement the GATT agreement.

SERVICES AND INTELLECTUAL PROPERTY   Until the Uruguay Round GATT rules had applied only to industrial goods (i.e., manufactured goods and commodities). In 1997 world trade in services amounted to $1,295 billion, compared to world trade in goods of $5,295 billion.[26] In the long run, extending GATT rules to this important trading arena could significantly increase both the total share of world trade accounted for by services and the overall volume of world trade. Also, the extension of GATT rules to cover intellectual property gives high-technology companies a mechanism to force countries to prohibit the piracy of intellectual property, a problem in some developing nations (see Chapter 2).

THE WORLD TRADE ORGANIZATION   The clarification and strengthening of GATT rules and the creation of the World Trade Organization also hold out the promise of more effective policing and enforcement. This should benefit overall economic growth and development by promoting trade. The WTO acts as an umbrella organization that encompasses the GATT along with two new sister bodies: one for services and the other for intellectual property. The WTO is now responsible for arbitrating trade disputes and monitoring the trade policies of member countries. Previously, member countries involved in disputes could block adoption of arbitration reports, but that changed with the Uruguay Round. Now the WTO will automatically adopt an arbitration panel report on a trade dispute unless there is a consensus to reject it. Countries that have been found by the arbitration panel to violate GATT rules may appeal to a permanent appellate body, but its verdict is binding. If offenders fail to comply with the recommendations of the arbitration panel, trading partners have the right to compensation or, in the last resort, to impose (commensurate) trade sanctions. Every stage of the procedure is subject to strict time limits. Thus, the WTO has something the GATT never had—teeth.[27]

IMPLICATIONS OF THE URUGUAY ROUND   The world is better off with a GATT deal than without it. Without the deal the world might have slipped into increasingly dangerous trade wars, which might have triggered a recession. The current world trading system looks secure, and the world economy is expected to grow faster than it would have without completion of the Uruguay Round. Estimates of the

Table 5.1

Main Features of the Uruguay Round Agreement

Up to 1993	The 1993 Agreement	Main Impact
Industrial Tariffs		
Backbone of previous GATT rounds. Tariffs on industrial goods average 5% in industrialized countries—down from 40% in the late 1940s.	Rich countries will cut tariffs on industrial goods by more than one-third. Tariffs will be scrapped on over 40% of manufactured goods.	Easier access to world markets for exports of industrial goods. Lower prices for consumers.
Agriculture		
High farm subsidies and protected markets in the United States and European Community lead to overproduction and dumping.	Subsidies and other barriers to trade in agricultural products will be cut over six years. Subsidies cut by 20%. All import barriers will be converted to tariffs and cut by 36%.	Better market opportunities for efficient food producers. Lower prices for consumers. Restraint of farm subsidies war.
Services		
GATT rules do not extend to services. Many countries protect service industries from international competition.	Gatt rules on fair trade principles extended to cover many services. Failure to reach agreement on financial services and telecommunications. Special talks will continue.	Increase in trade in services. Further liberalization of trade in services now seems likely.
Intellectual Property		
Standards of protection for patents, copyrights, and trademarks vary widely. Ineffective enforcement of national laws a growing source of trade friction.	Extensive agreements on patents, copyrights, and trademarks. International standards of protection and agreements for effective enforcement established.	Increased protection and reduction of intellectual property piracy will benefit producers of intellectual property (e.g., computer software firms, performing artists). Will increase technology transfer.
Textiles		
Rich countries have restricted imports of textiles and clothing through bilateral quotas under Multi-Fiber Arrangement (MFA).	MFA quotas progressively dismantled over 10 years and tariffs reduced. Normal GATT rules will apply at end of 10 years.	Increased trade in textiles should benefit developing countries. Reduced prices for consumers worldwide.
GATT Rules		
GATT remains the same as when drafted in 1947, even though many more countries have entered the world trading community and trade patterns have shifted.	Many GATT rules revised and updated. They include codes on customs valuation and import licensing, customs unions and free trade areas, and rules dealing with waivers from GATT regulations.	Greater transparency, security, and predictability in trading policies.
World Trade Organization		
GATT originally envisioned as part of an International Trade Organization. ITO never ratified and GATT applied provisionally.	GATT becomes a permanent world trade body covering goods, services, and intellectual property with a common disputes procedure. WTO to implement results of Uruguay Round.	More effective advocacy and policing of the international trading system.

Source: "The GATT Deal: The Longest Round of All," *Financial Times,* December 16, 1993. Reprinted with permission.

overall impact of the GATT agreement, however, are not that dramatic. Three studies undertaken in mid-1993 (before the agreement was finalized) estimated the deal would add between $213 billion and $274 billion in 1992 US dollars to aggregate world income by 2002—or about 0.75 percent to 1 percent of gross global income.[28]. Others argue that these figures underestimated the potential gain because they did not factor in the gains from the liberalization of trade in services, stronger trade rules, and greater business confidence. Considering such factors, it is claimed that due to the GATT agreement global economic output could be as much as 8 percent higher than it would otherwise have been by 2002.[29] The greatest achievement of a successful GATT agreement is what it helps avoid—the risk of a trade war that might reduce global economic growth and raise prices for consumers around the globe.

WTO: Early Experience

One hope expressed by the WTO's creators was that its enforcement mechanisms would make it a more effective guard of global trade rules than the GATT had been. The goal was that the WTO might emerge as an effective advocate and facilitator of future trade deals, particularly in areas such as services. In general, the experience so far has been encouraging.

WTO AS A GLOBAL POLICEMAN   The WTO's policing and enforcement mechanisms are having a positive effect. As of late 1999, more than 150 cases had been brought to the WTO. About 30 were withdrawn following consultations between the countries in dispute; more than 100 are going through consultation, panel adjudication, or appeal; about 20 are in the final stage of implementing a solution; 4 have been settled and the solution implemented; and 7 have been closed without any need for action.[30] The WTO's record compares with a total of 196 cases that were handled by the GATT over almost half a century. The use of the WTO represents an important vote of confidence in the organization's dispute resolution procedures.

The backing of the leading trading powers has been crucial to the organization's early success. Initially, there were fears that the United States might undermine the system by continuing to rely on unilateral measures when it suited or by refusing to accept WTO verdicts. These fears were enhanced in 1995 when the United States refused to bring a dispute with Japan over trade in autos and auto parts to the WTO (that dispute was settled bilaterally). Since then, however, the United States has emerged as the biggest user of the WTO. It has been a party in 78 disputes between 1996 and 1999: 48 as plaintiff, and 30 as defendant. The United States has won about 80 to 85 percent of its cases, about the same percentage as under the GATT.[31] However, the United States lost a major case to Japan when the WTO rejected every element of a US claim that Japan should reorganize its commercial economy so that Kodak could better compete there against its global rival Fuji. Kodak claimed that its access to Japanese markets was unfairly restricted because of the close relationships between Japanese manufacturing companies, banks, and retail outlets. There is little question that these exist, but they are neither unique to Japan nor, the WTO observed, were they created to keep Kodak out of the Japanese markets: They were there long before Kodak came along. Besides, Fuji holds no larger share of the Japanese market than Kodak does of the US market.

Encouraged perhaps by the tougher system, developing countries are also starting to use the settlement procedures more than they did under the GATT. Developing countries had launched over 30 complaints by July 1997, many targeted at developed nations. When Costa Rica complained that US regulations discriminated against its textile exports, the WTO ruled in favor of the Central American nation.

So far the United States has proved willing to accept WTO rulings that go against it. The United States agreed to implement a WTO judgment that called for the country to remove discriminatory antipollution regulations that were applied to gasoline

imports. In a dispute with India over textile imports, the United States rescinded quotas before a WTO panel could start work. And in June 1996, the United States preempted the establishment of a WTO panel by revoking punitive tariffs placed on EU food and drink exports that were imposed in 1988 in retaliation for the EU's ban on hormone-treated beef.

Despite its early success, questions still remain as to how effective the WTO's dispute resolution procedures will ultimately be. The first real test of the procedures will arise when the WTO has to arbitrate a politically sensitive case, particularly one that involves the United States or the European Union where significant and vocal minorities of politicians argue that the WTO infringes on national sovereignty. The WTO rulings on Kodak and hormone-treated beef produced complaints from vocal minorities in the United States and the European Union, respectively.

WTO TELECOMMUNICATIONS AGREEMENT As explained above, the Uruguay Round of GATT negotiations extended global trading rules to cover trade in services. The WTO was given the role of brokering future agreements to open global trade in services. The WTO was also encouraged to extend its reach to encompass regulations governing foreign direct investment, something the GATT had never done. Two of the first industries targeted for reform were global telecommunications and financial services. The WTO came close to reaching an agreement to liberalize global telecommunications services in early 1996, but ultimately failed to close a deal when the United States declined to sanction the draft agreement, arguing that it did not do enough to open national telecommunications markets to foreign investment.

The WTO tried again to reach an agreement in February 1997. Many observers believed the negotiations represented a major test of the credibility of the WTO as a facilitator of future global trade and investment deals. In 1995 the global telecommunications services market was worth just over $600 billion—or 2.5 percent of global GDP—only 20 percent of which was open to competition. Given its importance in the global economy, the telecommunications service industry was clearly a very important target for reform. The goal of the WTO was to get countries to agree to open their telecommunications markets to competition, allowing foreign operators to purchase ownership stakes in domestic telecommunications providers, and to establish a set of common rules for fair competition in the telecommunications sector. The benefits claimed for such agreements where threefold.

First, advocates argued that inward investment and increased competition would stimulate the modernization of telephone networks around the world and lead to higher-quality service. Second, supporters maintained that the increased competition would benefit customers through lower prices. Estimates suggested that a deal would soon reduce the average cost of international telephone calls by 80 percent and save consumers $1,000 billion over three years.[32] Third, the WTO argued that trade in other goods and services depends on flows of information matching buyers to sellers. As telecommunications services improve in quality and decline in price, international trade becomes less costly for traders and increases in volume. Telecommunications reform, therefore, should promote cross-border trade in other goods and services. Although it is difficult to be precise about these matters, Renato Ruggiero, the director-general of the WTO, argued:

> Telecommunications liberalization could mean global income gains of some $1 trillion over the next decade or so. This represents about 4 percent of world GDP at today's prices.[33]

After some last-minute hedging by the United States, a deal was reached February 15, 1997. Under the pact, 68 countries accounting for more than 90 percent of world telecommunications revenues pledged to start opening their markets to foreign competition and to abide by common rules for fair competition in telecommunications. Most of the world's biggest markets, including the United States, European Union, and Japan, were fully liberalized by January 1, 1998, when the pact went into effect. All forms of basic telecommunications service are covered, including voice telephony, data and fax transmissions, and satellite and radio communications. Many telecommunications companies responded positively to the deal, pointing out that it would enhance their ability to offer business customers "one-stop shopping"—a global, seamless service for all their corporate needs and a single bill.[34]

WTO FINANCIAL SERVICES AGREEMENT Fresh from its success in brokering a telecommunications agreement, the WTO embarked in April 1997 on a series of negotiations to liberalize the global financial services industry. Under the negotiating schedule, an agreement had to be reached by December 31, 1997. The financial services industry includes banking, securities businesses, insurance, asset management services, and the like. As with telecommunications, the first attempt at reaching a global deal in 1995 had failed when the United States refused to join a pact. The negotiations stalled because the United States felt developing countries were not prepared to make enough concessions.

The global financial services industry is enormous. The sector executes $1.2 trillion a day in foreign exchange transactions. International financing extended by banks around the world reporting to the Bank for International Settlements is estimated at $6.4 trillion, including $4.6 trillion net international lending. Total world banking assets are put at more than $20 trillion, insurance premiums at $2 trillion, stock market capitalization at over $10 trillion, and market value of listed bonds at around $10 trillion. In addition, almost every international trade deal in goods or services requires credit, capital, foreign exchange, and insurance.[35]

Participants in the negotiations wanted to see more competition in the sector both to allow firms greater opportunities abroad and to encourage greater efficiency. Developing countries need the capital and financial infrastructure for their development. But governments also have to ensure that the system is sound and stable because of the economic shocks that can be caused if exchange rates, interest rates, or other market conditions fluctuate excessively. They also have to avoid economic crisis caused by banks' failures. Therefore, government intervention in the interests of prudential safeguards is an important condition underpinning financial market liberalization.

An agreement was finally reached December 14, 1997.[36] The deal covers more than 95 percent of the world's financial services market. Under the agreement, which took effect in March 1999, 102 countries pledged to open to varying degrees their banking, securities, and insurance sectors to foreign competition. In common with the telecommunications deal, the accord covers not just cross-border trade, but also foreign direct investment. Seventy countries agreed to dramatically lower or eradicate barriers to FDI in their financial services sector. The United States and the European Union are, with minor exceptions, fully open to inward investment by foreign bank, insurance, and securities companies. As part of the deal, many Asian countries made important concessions that allow, for the first time, significant foreign participation in their financial services sectors.

The Future: Unresolved Issues

The WTO has yet to deal with a range of issues. Four of the most important areas for future development are environmentalism, workers' rights, foreign direct investment, and dumping.[37]

High on the list of the WTO's future concerns will be the interaction of environmental and trade policies and how best to promote sustainable development and ecological well-being without resorting to protectionism. The WTO will have to find ways to deal with the increasingly vigorous claims by environmentalists that expanded international trade encourages companies to locate factories in areas of the world where they are freer to pollute and degrade the environment.

In many respects Toyota has been a victim of its own success. Until the 1960s Toyota was an obscure Japanese automobile company. In 1950 Toyota produced a mere 11,700 vehicles. In 1970 it was producing 1.6 million vehicles, and by 1990 the figure had increased to 4.12 million. In the process, Toyota rose to become the third-largest automobile company and the largest automobile exporter in the world. In

world market from its plants in Japan. However, by the early 1980s political pressures and talk of local content regulations in the United States and Europe were forcing an initially reluctant Toyota to rethink its exporting strategy. Toyota had already agreed to "voluntary" export restraints with the United States in 1981. The consequence for Toyota was stagnant export growth between 1981 and

GM in December 1984. The maximum capacity of the Fremont plant was about 250,000 cars per year.

For Toyota, the joint venture provided a chance to find out whether it could build quality cars in the United States using American workers and American suppliers. It also provided Toyota with experience dealing with an American union (the United Auto Work-

*Toyota's Response to Rising Protectionist Pressures in Europe and the United States**

the view of most analysts, Toyota's dramatic rise was due to the company's world-class manufacturing and design skills. These made Toyota not only the most productive automobile company in the world, but also the one that consistently produced the highest-quality and best-designed automobiles.

For most of its history Toyota has exported automobiles to the

1984. Against this background, Toyota began to think about establishing manufacturing operations overseas.

Toyota's first overseas operation was a 50/50 joint venture with General Motors established in February 1983 under the name New United Motor Manufacturing Inc. (NUMMI). NUMMI, based in Fremont, California, began producing Chevrolet Nova cars for

ers) and with a means of circumventing "voluntary"" import restrictions. By the fall of 1986 the NUMMI plant was running at full capacity and the early indications were that the plant was achieving productivity and quality levels close to those achieved at Toyota's major Takaoka plant in Japan.

Encouraged by its success at NUMMI, in December 1985 Toyota announced it would build an

Along with environmental concerns are concerns that free trade encourages firms to shift their production to countries with low labor rates where workers' rights are routinely violated. The United States has repeatedly and unsuccessfully pressed for discussion of common international standards for workers' rights—an idea strongly opposed by poorer nations that fear it is just another excuse for protectionism by the rich.

GATT regulations have yet to be extended to embrace foreign direct investment with the exception of telecom and financial services (investment by a firm based in one country in productive facilities in another country). Given the globalization of production that we are now witnessing in the world economy, barriers to foreign direct investment seem antiquated, and yet they are still widespread (we will discuss these in detail in Chapter 6). Currently many countries limit investment by foreign companies in their economies (e.g., local content requirements, local ownership rules, and even prohibition). Extending GATT to embrace foreign direct investment might require countries to grant establishment rights to foreign companies.

A final issue of concern has been the proliferation of antidumping actions in recent years. WTO rules allow countries to impose antidumping duties on foreign goods that are being sold cheaper than at home, or below their cost of production, when domestic producers can show that they are being harmed. Unfortunately, the

automobile manufacturing plant in Georgetown, Kentucky. The plant, which came on stream in May 1988, officially had the capacity to produce 200,000 Toyota Camrys a year. However, by early 1990 it was producing the equivalent of 220,000 cars per year. This success was followed by an announcement in December 1990 that Toyota would build a second plant in Georgetown with a capacity to produce a further 200,000 vehicles per year. The two plants and NUMMI gave Toyota the capacity to build 660,000 vehicles per year in North America.

In addition to its North American transplant operations, Toyota moved to set up production facilities in Europe in a response to growing protectionist pressures there. Toyota was also anticipating the 1992 lowering of trade barriers among the member states of the European Union (EU). In 1989 the company announced it would build a plant in England with the capacity to manufacture 200,000 cars per year by 1997. The implication was that after 1992, much of the plant's output would be exported to the rest of the EU. This decision prompted the French prime minister to describe Britain as "a Japanese aircraft carrier, sitting off the coast of Europe waiting to attack." Fearing that the EU would limit its expansion, Toyota joined other Japanese automobile companies in agreeing to keep their share of the European auto market to under 11 percent, at least until 2000.

It has not all been smooth sailing for Toyota. A major problem has been building an overseas supplier network that is comparable to Toyota's Japanese network. In a 1990 meeting of Toyota's North American suppliers' association, Toyota executives informed the North American suppliers that the defect ratio for parts produced by 75 North American and European suppliers was 100 times greater than the defect ratio for parts supplied by 147 Japanese suppliers. Toyota executives also pointed out that parts manufactured by North American and European suppliers tended to be significantly more expensive than comparable parts manufactured in Japan.

Because of these problems, Toyota initially imported many parts from Japan for its European and US assembly operations. However, the general increase in imports of automobile components only heightened trade tensions between the United States and Japan. The high volume of such imports was a major sticking point in trade negotiations between the United States and Japan. To diffuse the situation, Toyota worked to increase the local content of cars assembled in North America and Europe. By 1996 70 percent of the value of Toyota cars assembled in Europe and the United States was produced locally, up from less than 40 percent in 1990. To achieve this, Toyota embarked on an aggressive supplier education drive in both Europe and the United States aimed at familiarizing its local suppliers with Japanese production methods.[38]

---

*Charles W. L. Hill and Gareth R. Jones, *Strategic Management: An Integrated Approach, 3rd edition.* Copyright © 1995 by Houghton Mifflin Company. Reprinted with permission.

vague definition of what constitutes "dumping" is being exploited by many countries. In the United States, for example, 26 antidumping cases were launched in 1998, up from 16 cases the previous year. There has also been a rise in cases filed by the European Union. When an industry faces strong foreign competition, the first response of some firms it seems is to cry foul and accuse the foreign producers of dumping. The process then becomes politicized, as representatives of businesses and their employees lobby government officials to "protect domestic jobs from unfair foreign competition." If this trend continues, the WTO will likely try to strengthen the regulations governing the imposition of antidumping duties.

Implications for Business

What are the implications of all this for business practice? Why should the international manager care about the political economy of free trade, about the relative merits of arguments for free trade and protectionism? There are two answers. The first concerns the impact of trade barriers on a firm's strategy. The second concerns the role that business firms can play in promoting free trade and/or trade barriers.

Trade Barriers and Firm Strategy

To understand how trade barriers affect a firm's strategy, consider first the material we covered in Chapter 4. Drawing on the theories of international trade, we discussed how it may make sense for the firm to disperse its various production activities to those countries around the globe where they can be performed most efficiently. Thus, it may make sense for a firm to design and engineer its product in one country, to manufacture components in another, to perform final assembly operations in yet another country, and then export the finished product to the rest of the world.

Trade barriers are a constraint on a firm's ability to disperse its productive activities in such a manner. First, tariff barriers raise the costs of exporting products to a country (or of exporting partly finished products between countries). This may put the firm at a competitive disadvantage vis-à-vis indigenous competitors in that country. In response, the firm may then find it economical to locate production facilities in that country so that it can compete on an even footing. Second, voluntary export restraints (VERs) may limit a firm's ability to serve a country from foreign locations. Again, the response might be to set up production facilities in that country—even though it may result in higher production costs. Such reasoning was one factor behind the rapid expansion of Japanese auto-making capacity in the United States during the 1980s. This followed the establishment of a VER agreement between the United States and Japan that limited US imports of Japanese automobiles. For details, see the accompanying "Management Focus," which describes how Toyota responded to threats of greater protectionism by opening car plants in the United States and Europe.

Third, to conform with local content regulations, a firm may have to locate more production activities in a given market than it would otherwise. Again, from the firm's perspective, the consequence might be to raise costs above the level that could be achieved if each production activity was dispersed to its optimal location. And fourth, even when trade barriers do not exist, the firm may still want to locate some production activities in a given country to reduce the threat of trade barriers being imposed in the future.

All of the above effects are likely to raise the firm's costs above the level that could be achieved in a world without trade barriers. The higher costs that result need not translate into a significant competitive disadvantage, however, if the countries imposing trade barriers do so to the imported products of all foreign firms, irrespective of their national origin. But when trade barriers are targeted at exports from a particular nation, firms based in that nation may be at a competitive disadvantage vis-à-vis the firms of other nations (VERs are in effect targeted trade barriers). To deal with such targeted trade barriers, the firm may move production into the country imposing barriers. Another strategy may be to move production to countries whose exports are not targeted by the trade barrier.

Policy Implications

As noted in Chapter 4, businesses are major players on the international trade scene. Because of their pivotal role in international trade, firms exert a strong influence on government policy toward trade. This influence can encourage protectionism, or it can encourage the government to support the WTO and push for open markets and freer trade among all nations. Also, government policies with regard to international trade can have a direct impact on business.

Consistent with strategic trade policy, examples can be found of government intervention in the form of tariffs, quotas, and subsidies helping firms and industries to establish a competitive advantage in the world economy. In general, however, this chapter suggests that a policy of government intervention has the three following drawbacks. Intervention can be self-defeating because it tends to protect the inefficient rather than help firms become efficient global competitors. Intervention is dangerous because it may invite retaliation and trigger a trade war. Finally, intervention is unlikely to be well executed, given the opportunity for such a policy to be captured by special interest groups. Does this mean that business should simply encourage government to adopt a laissez-faire, free trade policy?

Most economists would probably argue that the best interests of international business are served by a free trade stance, but not a laissez-faire stance. It is probably in the best long-run interests of the business community to encourage the government to aggressively promote greater free trade by, for example, strengthening the WTO. In general, business has much more to gain from government efforts to open protected markets to imports and foreign direct investment than from government efforts to support certain domestic industries in a manner consistent with the recommendations of strategic trade policy.

This conclusion is reinforced by a phenomenon we touched on in Chapter 1—the increasing integration of the world economy and internationalization of production that has occurred over the past two decades. We live in a world where many firms of all national origins increasingly depend for their competitive advantage on globally dispersed production systems. Such systems are the result of free trade. Free trade has brought great advantages to firms that have exploited it and to consumers who benefit from the resulting lower prices. Given the danger of retaliatory action, businesses that lobby their governments to engage in protectionism must realize that by doing so they may be denying themselves the opportunity to build a competitive advantage by constructing a globally dispersed production system. By encouraging their governments to engage in protectionism, their own activities and sales overseas may be jeopardized if other governments retaliate.

→ free trade
stance
not laissez-
faire stance

Key Terms

Summary

The objective of this chapter was to describe how the reality of international trade deviates from the theoretical ideal of unrestricted free trade that we reviewed in Chapter 4. In this chapter we reviewed the various instruments of trade policy, reviewed the political and economic arguments for government intervention in international trade, reexamined the economic case for free trade in light of the strategic trade policy argument, and looked at the evolution of the world trading framework. The main conclusion reached is that, while a policy of free trade may not always be the theoretically optimal policy (given the arguments of the new trade theorists), in practice it is probably the best policy for a government to pursue. The long-run interests of business and consumers may be best served by strengthening international institutions such as the WTO. Given the danger that isolated protectionism might escalate into a trade war, business probably has far more to gain from government efforts to open protected markets to imports and foreign direct investment (through the WTO) than from government efforts to protect domestic industries from foreign competition.

In this chapter the following points have been made:

1 The effect of a tariff is to raise the cost of imported products. Gains accrue to the government (from revenues) and to producers (who are protected from foreign competitors). Consumers lose because they must pay more for imports.

2 By lowering costs, subsidies help domestic producers to compete against low-cost foreign imports and to gain export markets. However, subsidies must be paid for by taxpayers. Also, they tend to be captured by special interests that use them to protect the inefficient.

3 An import quota is a direct restriction imposed by an importing country on the quantity of some good that may be imported. A voluntary export restraint (VER) is a quota on trade imposed from the exporting country's side. Both import quotas and VERs benefit domestic producers by limiting import competition, but they result in higher prices, which hurts consumers.

4 A local content requirement is a demand that some specific fraction of a good be produced domestically. Local content requirements benefit the producers of component parts, but they raise prices of imported components, which hurts consumers.

5 An administrative policy is an informal instrument or bureaucratic rule that can be used to restrict imports and boost exports. Such policies benefit producers but hurt consumers, who are denied access to possibly superior foreign products.

6 There are two types of arguments for government intervention in international trade: political and economic. Political arguments for intervention are concerned with protecting the interests of certain groups, often at the expense of other groups, or with promoting goals with regard to foreign policy, human rights, consumer protection, and the like. Economic arguments for intervention are about boosting the wealth of a nation.

7 The most common political argument for intervention is that it is necessary to protect jobs. However, political intervention often hurts consumers and it can be self-defeating.

8 Countries sometimes argue that it is important to protect certain industries for reasons of national security.

9 Some argue that government should use the threat to intervene in trade policy as a bargaining tool to open foreign markets. This can be a risky policy; if it fails the result can be higher trade barriers.

10 The infant industry argument for government intervention is that governments should temporarily support new industries to let manufacturing get a toehold. In practice, however, governments often end up protecting the inefficient.

11 Strategic trade policy suggests that through subsidies, government can help domestic firms

gain first-mover advantages in global industries where economies of scale are important. Government subsidies may also help domestic firms overcome barriers to entry into such industries.

12 The problems with strategic trade policy are twofold: (*i*) such a policy may invite retaliation, in which case all will lose, and (*ii*) strategic trade policy may be captured by special interest groups, which will distort it to their own ends.

13 The Smoot-Hawley Act, enacted in 1930, erected an enormous wall of tariff barriers. Other countries responded by adopting similar tariffs, and the world slid further into the Great Depression.

14 The GATT was a product of the post-war free trade movement. The GATT was successful in lowering trade barriers on manufactured goods and commodities. The move toward greater free trade under the GATT appeared to stimulate economic growth.

15 The completion of the Uruguay Round of GATT talks and the establishment of the World Trade Organization have strengthened the world trading system by extending GATT rules to services, increasing protection for intellectual property, reducing agricultural subsidies, and enhancing monitoring and enforcement mechanisms.

16 Trade barriers act as a constraint on a firm's ability to disperse its various production activities to optimal locations around the globe. One response to trade barriers is to establish more production activities in the protected country.

17 Business may have more to gain from government efforts to open protected markets to imports and foreign direct investment than from government efforts to protect domestic industries from foreign competition.

Critical Thinking and Discussion Questions

1 Do you think the US government should consider human rights when granting most favored nation status to China? What are the arguments for and against such a position?

2 Whose interests should be the paramount concern of government trade policy—the interests of producers (businesses and their employees) or those of consumers?

3 Given the arguments relating to the new trade theory and strategic trade policy, what kind of trade policy should business be pressuring government to adopt?

4 You are an employee of a US firm that produces personal computers in Thailand and then exports them to the United States and other countries for sale. The personal computers were originally produced in Thailand to take advantage of relatively low labor costs and a skilled workforce. Other possible locations considered at the time were Malaysia and Hong Kong. The US government decides to impose punitive 100 percent ad valorem tariffs on imports of computers from Thailand to punish the country for administrative trade barriers that restrict US exports to Thailand. How should your firm respond? What does this tell you about the use of targeted trade barriers?

Internet Exercises

1 A major topic of debate at the 1999 World Trade Organization (WTO) meeting in Seattle involved global e-commerce. The debate was different from usual WTO discussions in that instead of focusing on breaking down trade barriers between nations, it emphasized stopping trade barriers before they could be put in place. Many countries fear US dominance in international e-commerce. Also, because the language of the Internet is English, many countries and companies believe they could be at a disadvantage. Those interested in preventing interference with the free flow of goods across the Internet point out that the Internet has the potential to level the trading field for small and developing countries, and the technology should be embraced as a trade facilitator. As Rhett Dawson of the Information Technology Industry Council points out, "It's going to happen everyplace, and American hegemony is not going to sustain itself" (*The Wall Street Journal*, November 29, 1999, p. A1).

The United States promoted four key issues at the trade talks. First, it wants a moratorium on Internet tariffs. Second, the United States would like to establish a policy of nondiscrimination for foreign firms trading on the Internet. Third, it would like to ensure that e-commerce flows will not be limited by WTO policies. Finally, the United States supports the notion of technological neutrality (*The Wall Street Journal*, November 29, 1999, p. A1). Go to the WTO's website (**www.wto.org**) and explore the progress that has been made by the WTO with regard to international e-commerce. In your opinion, should there be a separate set of rules for goods and services that are traded electronically, or should all goods, regardless of how they are bought and sold, fall under the same regulations? If a new policy for electronically traded goods and services is established, what does this mean for companies that still do business the old-fashioned way? As the vice president of global and strategic policy at America Online, what should you be doing to protect your company from limitations on the free flow of trade across the Internet?

2 Go to your hotel room, turn on the TV, and start surfing the channels. You have a choice of watching ESPN, MTV, or CNN. Where are you? You might be in China. China appears to be the current destination of choice for American media companies. While this may seem surprising given the tight government control over Chinese airwaves, media giants are finding the market not only to be huge and untapped, but also unusually welcoming. The country boasts some 1.2 billion people who are avidly consuming content via their 305 million TV sets. Still, American companies investing in the market find they have to work closely with government officials. Foreign TV shows can make up only 25 percent of all TV programming, and only 10 foreign films are allowed in theaters in a year.

Media moguls are finding that their entry into the marketplace is greatly facilitated by collaborating with government officials. Some American companies are developing partnerships with Chinese government-owned production companies in an effort to smooth their path to success. The Chinese government seems to be putting out a welcome mat for American investors, anticipating not only the jobs that American investments could bring, but also the increased advertising revenues its state-owned TV and cable companies could collect. Go to **www.accesschina.com** and also to **www.beijing-tv.cn.net/** and **www.asiamedia.ucla.edu/ weekly/11.27.98.** As the head of a foreign media company how would you approach the Chinese marketplace? Some companies have established partnerships with the Chinese government. What are the implications of this type of strategy?

Source: *Businessweek*, March 29, 1999, p. 40.

Shrimps, Turtles, and the WTO

There are seven species of sea turtle in the world; six of them are on the list of endangered species in the United States. A major cause of the decline of sea turtles has been poor fishing practices, particularly by shrimp boats. It is estimated that some 150,000 sea turtles per year are trapped and drown in the nets of shrimp boats. To limit this carnage, in 1989 the US Congress passed a law that required shrimp boats to be equipped with a turtle excluder, a simple grate that fits over the mouth of shrimp trawling nets and prevents sea turtles from becoming trapped. The law also banned the importation of shrimp from countries that fail to mandate the use of turtle excluders by their shrimp fleets.

As with many such laws, the US government dragged its heels on enforcing the import ban. It wasn't until 1996 that the United States placed an embargo on the importation of shrimp from countries that failed to mandate the use of excluders. Even then, it did so only because environmental groups in the United States had sued the government to compel it to enforce its own law. Three countries were targeted by the 1996 ban—India, Pakistan, and Malaysia. The three responded by filing a complaint with the World Trade Organization. They were joined by Thailand, which decided as a matter of principle to pursue the WTO case (Thailand had already satisfied the United States that its turtle protection methods were adequate).

As is normal in such cases, the WTO formed an independent arbitration panel composed of three experts from countries not involved in the dispute. The panel was charged with reviewing the US position to see whether it conflicted with WTO

rules. The United States claimed that WTO rules include provisions for taking restrictive measures if they are related "to the conservation of exhaustible natural resources and if such measures are made effective in conjunction with restrictions on domestic production or consumption." The United States was supported by a number of environmental organizations, including the World Wildlife Fund (WWF). In a brief submitted to the panel, the WWF argued that marine turtles are migratory animals, a global resource that should be subject to stewardship by international society. Even though no multilateral body or resolution had authorized the United States to enact its ban, the WWF claimed that the United States acted in a manner consistent with its obligations and took reasonable measures that reflected the will of the international community.

The four countries that brought the complaint argued that the US ban represented an unfair restraint on trade that was illegal under WTO rules. According to these countries, the United States was violating WTO rules by applying domestic legislation outside its boundaries and by applying it in a discriminatory manner. Influential voices in all these countries accused the United States of hypocrisy. An article in *The Hindu*, an Indian newspaper, stated,

> Compared to what the US as a nation is doing to other global shared resources, the world's climate and atmosphere, what complainant nations like India are doing to the marine turtle is a contemptuously small problem . . . The US leadership has, unfortunately, always put

its national interests before global concerns in its global environmental policies. Its behavior on the climate change issue is one example. Its refusal to sign the bio-diversity treaty is another. Its refusal to pay dues to the United Nations is yet another.[39]

The World Trade Organization panel on April 6, 1998, ruled that the United States was wrong to prohibit shrimp imports from countries that failed to protect sea turtles from entrapment in the nets of shrimp boats. The WTO stated that while environmental considerations were important, the primary aim of international agreements on trade remained the promotion of economic development through unfettered free trade. Further, the WTO stated that even under WTO treaty provisions that allow environmental exceptions, the United States would not be allowed to force other nations to adopt policies to protect an endangered species.

While the WTO has no power to overturn US law, the United States must pay a penalty to the WTO if it decides to keep its law and the import ban, which seems likely. Environmental groups responded with outrage to the WTO's ruling. A Sierra Club spokesman noted, "This is the clearest slap at environmental protection to come out of the WTO to date." Similarly, a spokeswoman for the Washington, D.C.-based Center for Marine Conservation stated, "it is unthinkable that we should not be allowed to mitigate the impacts of our own shrimp markets on endangered sea turtles. This entire life form is threatened with extinction."[40]

CASE DISCUSSION QUESTIONS

1 Do you think the United States is correct to try to use its law and trade policy to force other countries to adopt environmental policies that it perceives to be sound?

2 Does the WTO decision have implications for US national sovereignty? If so what?

3 Do you think it is correct for the WTO to decouple trade policy from environmental policy? Why?

4 Do you think other countries are correct to accuse the United States of hypocrisy on the environmental issue?

5 How should the United States react to the WTO decision in this case?

six

Foreign Direct Investment

Chapter

Opening Case
    Electrolux's Global Investment Strategy

With 1998 sales of over SKr110 billion ($14 billion), Electrolux is the world's largest manufacturer of household appliances (washing machines, dishwashers, refrigerators, vacuum cleaners, etc.). A Swedish company with a small home market, Electrolux has always had to look to other markets for its growth. By 1997 the company was generating more than 85 percent of its sales outside of Sweden. A little over 52 percent of the sales are in Western Europe,

Electrolux's expansion into Asia, Eastern Europe, and Latin America stemmed from the fact that the markets in Western Europe and North America were mature. The company needed to expand globally in order to keep pace with their historic growth rate. © Charles Thatcher/Tony Stone Images.

Learning Objectives

1 Identify the forces underpinning the rising tide of foreign direct investment in the world economy.

2 Understand why firms often prefer direct investment as a strategy for entering a foreign market over alternatives such as exporting and granting foreign entities the right to produce the firm's product under license.

3 Appreciate why firms based in the same industry often undertake foreign direct investment at the same time.

4 Understand why certain locations are favored as the target of foreign direct investment.

5 Appreciate how political ideology influences government policy toward foreign direct investment.

6 Be conversant with the costs and benefits of foreign direct investment for receiving and source countries.

7 Understand the policy instruments governments can use to restrict and to encourage foreign direct investment.

---

with another 27 percent in North America. In recent years, however, the most rapid growth has come from Asia (which accounted for 5.1 percent of 1997 revenues), Eastern Europe (7 percent of revenues), and Latin America (6.4 percent of revenues). As of early 1998 the company employed more than 100,000 people worldwide, had 150 factories and 300 warehouses located in 60 countries, and sold about 55 million products per year in 150 countries.

Electrolux's expansion into Asia, Eastern Europe, and Latin America dates from an early 1990s planning review that concluded demand for household appliances was mature in Western Europe and North America. The company believed future growth in these regions would be limited to replacement demand and the growth in population and would be unlikely to exceed 2 to 3 percent annually. Leif Johansson, the CEO of Electrolux, decided the company

was too dependent on these mature markets. He reasoned the company would have to expand aggressively into the emerging markets of the developing world if it was to maintain its historic growth rate. The company estimated that demand for household appliances in Asia, Eastern Europe, and Latin America could grow at 20 percent annually for at least the next decade and probably beyond. Accordingly, in 1994 he set an ambitious goal for

Electrolux; the company would have to double its sales in these emerging markets from the $1.35 billion it achieved in 1994 to $2.7 billion by 1997 (this target was exceeded). An additional goal was for Electrolux to become one of the top three suppliers of household goods in Southeast Asia by 2000.

In addition to the obvious growth potential, another consideration for Electrolux was that its main global competitors, General Electric and Whirlpool of the United States and Germany's Bosch-Siemans, had recently announced similar plans. Electrolux believed that it better move quickly, lest it be left out in the race to profit from these emerging markets.

Having committed itself to expansion, Electrolux had to decide how to achieve its ambitious goals. A combination of cost considerations and import barriers made direct exporting from its Western European and North American plants uneconomical. Instead, varying approaches were adopted for different regions and countries. Acquisitions of going concerns, green-field developments, joint ventures, and enhanced marketing were all considered. Electrolux stated that it was prepared to spend $200 million per year to increase its presence in these emerging markets.

Electrolux had made its first move into Eastern Europe in 1991 when it acquired Lehel, Hungary's largest manufacturer of household appliances. In the mid-1990s, Electrolux decided to establish wholly owned operating companies in Russia, Poland, and the Czech Republic. Each of these operating subsidiaries would be a green-field development. A different approach was required in Asia. Regulations concerning foreign ownership in India and China, for example, virtually compelled Electrolux to work through joint ventures with local partners. In China, the world's fastest-growing market, the company already had joint ventures in compressors, vacuum cleaners, and water purification equipment in 1994. Between 1994 and 1997 the company spent another $300 million to build five manufacturing plants in the country. In Southeast Asia Electrolux emphasized the marketing of goods imported from China, rather than local production. As for Latin America, here the company expanded through acquisitions, culminating in its 1996 acquisition of Refripar, the largest producer of refrigerator products in Brazil. Electrolux's goal is to turn Refripar, which had 1995 sales of about $600 million, into its Latin American base for the production of household products.

Although Electrolux has been largely successful in its attempt to globalize its production and sales base, the expansion has not been without its problems. In 1997 the company suffered a significant drop in profit due to deteriorating market conditions in Brazil and the Asian Pacific. The profit slump exposed serious weaknesses that had developed in Electrolux's global production system. Although the company had expanded rapidly via acquisitions since the early 1990s, it had not rationalized its production operations. Consequently, there was often considerable duplication of facilities within regions. In early 1998 the company's new CEO, Michael Treschow, announced a restructuring plan that called for the loss of 12,000 jobs and the closing of 25 factories and 50 warehouses worldwide. At the same time, however, Treschow reaffirmed Electrolux's commitment to building a global corporation with significant operations in the world's developing markets.[1]

Introduction

This chapter is concerned with the phenomenon of foreign direct investment (FDI). **Foreign direct investment (FDI)** occurs when a firm invests directly in facilities to produce and/or market a product in a foreign country. Thus, the 1991 purchase of Hungary's Lehel by Electrolux and its 1996 acquisition of Brazil's Refripar are both examples of FDI, as are the company's investments in joint ventures to manufacture products in China, and in new wholly owned production facilities in Russia, Poland, and the Czech Republic (for details, see the opening case). The US Department of Commerce has come up with a more precise definition of FDI. According to the department, FDI occurs whenever a US citizen, organization, or affiliated group takes an interest of 10 percent or more in a foreign business. Once a firm undertakes FDI it becomes a **multinational enterprise** (the meaning of multinational here being "more than one country").

We begin this chapter by looking at the importance of foreign direct investment in the world economy. Next we review the theories that have been used to explain foreign direct investment. The chapter then moves on to look at government policy toward foreign direct investment. As always, the chapter closes with a section on the implications for business.

Foreign Direct Investment in the World Economy

When discussing foreign direct investment, it is important to distinguish between the *flow* of FDI and the *stock* of FDI. The **flow of FDI** refers to the amount of FDI undertaken over a given time period (normally a year). The **stock of FDI** refers to the total accumulated value of foreign-owned assets at a given time. We also talk of **outflows of FDI,** meaning the flow of FDI out of a country, and **inflows of FDI,** meaning the flow of FDI into a country.

The Growth of FDI

During the past 20 years there has been a marked increase in both the *flow* and *stock* of FDI in the world economy. The average yearly *outflow* of FDI increased from about $25 billion in 1975 to a record $644 billion in 1998 (see Figure 6.1).[2] Not only did the flow of FDI accelerate during the 1980s and 1990s, but it also accelerated faster than the growth in world trade. Between 1984 and 1998 the total flow of FDI from all countries increased by over 1,000 percent, while world trade grew by 91 percent, and world output by 27 percent.[3] As a result of the strong FDI flow, by 1997 the global stock of FDI exceeded $3.5 trillion. By 1998 some 60,000 parent companies with more than 500,000 affiliates in foreign markets collectively produced an estimated $11 trillion in global sales, or 25 percent of global output.[4]

There are several reasons FDI is growing more rapidly than world trade and world output. Despite the general decline in trade barriers that we have witnessed over the past 30 years, there is still some fear among businesses of protectionist pressures. Executives see FDI as a way of circumventing future trade barriers. Thus, much of the investment in the United States undertaken by Japanese automobile companies during the 1980s and early 1990s was driven by a desire to reduce exports from Japan, thereby alleviating trade tensions between the two nations.

Second, much of the recent increase in FDI is being driven by the dramatic political and economic changes that have been occurring in many of the world's developing nations. The general shift toward democratic political institutions and free market economics that we discussed in Chapter 2 has encouraged FDI. Across much of Asia, Eastern Europe, and Latin America, increasing economic growth, economic deregulation, privatization programs that are open to foreign investors, and the removal of many restrictions on FDI have all made these countries more attractive to foreign investors. According to the United Nations, between 1991 and 1996 more than 100 countries made 599 changes in legislation governing FDI. Some 95 percent of these changes involved liberalizing a country's foreign investment regulations to make it easier for foreign companies to enter the market. The desire to facilitate FDI has also been reflected in a dramatic increase in the number of bilateral investment treaties designed to protect and promote investment between two countries. As of January 1, 1997, there were 1,330 such treaties in the world involving

flow of foreign direct investment Amount of FDI undertaken during a given period.

stock of foreign direct investment Total accumulated value of foreign-owned assets at a given time.

outflows of foreign direct investment Flow of FDI out of a country.

inflows of foreign direct investment Flow of FDI into a country.

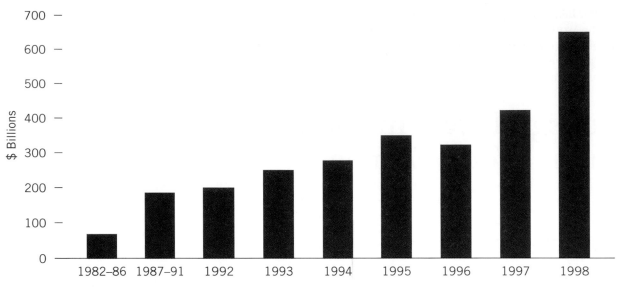

Figure 6.1

FDI Outflows, 1982–1998 ($ billions)*
*Note: 1998 data based on preliminary estimates.
Source: United Nations is the author of the original material. Reprinted with permission.

162 countries, a threefold increase in five years.[5] The pace of liberalization shows no signs of slackening. During 1997, 76 countries made 151 changes in FDI regulations, and 89 percent of the changes created a more favorable environment for FDI.[6] The opening case showed how Electrolux responded to these trends by investing in Eastern Europe and Asia. The acquisition of Lehel of Hungary, for example, was the result of a privatization program that allowed foreign investors to purchase state-owned enterprises.

The globalization of the world economy, a phenomenon that we first discussed in Chapter 1, is also having a positive impact on the volume of FDI. Firms such as Electrolux now see the whole world as their market, and they are undertaking FDI in an attempt to make sure they have a significant presence in every region of the world. For reasons that we shall explore later in this book, many firms now feel that it is important to have production facilities based close to their major customers. This, too, is creating pressures for greater FDI.

The Direction of FDI

Not only has there been rapid growth in the flow of FDI, but there has also been an important shift in the direction of FDI. Historically, most FDI has been directed at the developed nations of the world as firms based in advanced countries invested in each other's markets. The United States has often been the favorite target for FDI inflows. This trend continued in 1997 when $90.7 billion was invested in the country (see Figure 6.2). The country's large and wealthy domestic markets, dynamic and stable economy, favorable political environment, and openness to FDI all attract investment. Investors include firms based in the United Kingdom, Japan, Germany, Holland, and France.

While developed nations still account for the largest share of FDI inflows, there has been a surge of FDI into the world's developing nations (see Figure 6.2). From 1985 to 1990, the annual inflow of FDI into developing nations averaged $27.4 billion, or

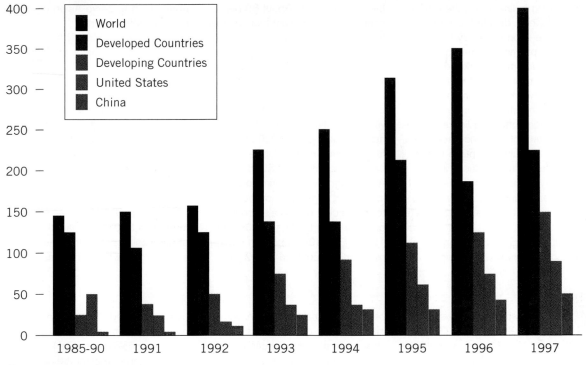

Figure 6.2

FDI Inflows, 1985–1997 ($ billions)

Source: United Nations is the author of the original material. Reprinted with permission.

17.4 percent of the total global flow. By 1998, the inflow into developing nations had risen to $165 billion, or 25.6 percent of the total global flow. However, this was a drop from 1997, when developing nations accounted for 37 percent of total FDI inflows.[7] The 1998 decline reflects the short-term effects of the 1998 Asian economic crisis.

In recent years, most of the inflow into developing nations has been targeted at the emerging economies of South, East, and Southeast Asia, which collectively accounted for $86 billion of the 1997 total. Driving much of the increase has been the growing importance of China as a recipient of FDI (see Figure 6.2). In 1997, China received direct investments valued at $45 billion, making it the second-largest recipient of FDI in the world after the United States. The reasons for the strong flow of investment into China are discussed in the accompanying "Country Focus." Next to China, Singapore was the second-largest investment recipient in the Asian region, with inflows valued at $10 billion.

After South, East, and Southeast Asia, Latin America emerged as the next most important region in the developing world for FDI inflows. In 1997, total inward investments into this region reached a record $56 billion. About $16 billion of this total was invested in Brazil, with another $12 billion targeted at Mexico. Much of this investment was a response to reforms in the region, including privatization, the liberalization of regulations governing FDI, and the growing importance of regional free trade areas such as MERCOSUR and NAFTA (which will be discussed in Chapter 7). At the other end of the scale, Africa received the smallest amount of inward investment, $4.7 billion in 1997. The inability of Africa to attract greater investment is a reflection of the political unrest, armed conflict, and frequent changes in economic policy that have long depressed the region.

Beginning in late 1978, the leadership of China decided to try to move the economy away from a centrally planned system to one that is much more market driven, while still maintaining the rigid political framework of Communist Party control. The strategy had a number of key elements, including a switch to a system of household responsibility in agriculture in place of the old collectivism, increases in the authority of local officials and plant managers in industry, allowing the establishment of small-scale private enterprises in services and light manufacturing, and opening the economy to increased foreign trade

the United States. About 80 percent of that investment has come from other Asian countries, such as Hong Kong (which is now part of China), Singapore, Korea, and Japan, with the balance coming from the United States and Western European nations. Over the past 20 years this inflow has resulted in the establishment of 145,000 foreign-funded enterprises in China with capital investments of $216 billion. According to some estimates, this investment might have provided 20 to 30 percent of China's economic growth during the late 1980s and 1990s. By 1996, firms with foreign ownership accounted for 12 per-

from which to serve Asian or world markets with exports.

What was apparently less obvious, at least to begin with, was how difficult it would be for foreign firms to do business in China. Blinded by the size and potential of China's market, many firms paid scant attention to the complexities of operating a business in this country until after the investment was made. China may have a huge population, but despite two decades of rapid growth it is still a poor country where the average income is little more than $700 per year. The lack of purchasing power translates into a weak market for many Western

Foreign Direct Investment in China

and investment. The result has been a quadrupling of GDP since 1978. Agricultural output doubled in the 1980s, and industry posted major gains, especially in coastal areas near Hong Kong and opposite Taiwan, where foreign investment helped spur output of both domestic and export goods.

Starting from a tiny base, foreign investment surged to an annual average rate of $2.7 billion in the 1985–1990 period and then exploded to reach a record $45.2 billion in 1997, making China the second-biggest recipient of FDI inflows in the world after

cent of industrial production, with manufacturing concentrated in toys, shoes, electrical appliances, and other labor-intensive sectors.

The reasons for the rise in investment are fairly obvious. With a population of 1.2 billion people, China represents one of the largest potential markets in the world. Import tariffs make it difficult to serve this market via exports, so FDI is required to tap into the country's huge potential. Also, a combination of cheap labor and tax incentives, particularly for enterprises that establish themselves in special economic zones, makes China an attractive base

consumer goods from automobiles to household appliances. Another problem is the lack of a well-developed transportation infrastructure or distribution system. PepsiCo discovered this problem at its subsidiary in Chongqing. Perched above the Yangtze River in southwest Sichuan province, Chongqing lies at the heart of China's massive hinterland. The Chongqing municipality, which includes the city and its surrounding regions, contains over 30 million people, but according to Steve Chen, the manager of the Pepsi subsidiary, the lack of well-developed road and distribution

---

gross fixed capital formation The total amount of capital invested in factories, stores, office buildings, and the like.

Another way of looking at the importance of FDI inflows in an economy is to express them as a percentage of gross fixed capital formation. **Gross fixed capital formation** summarizes the total amount of capital invested in factories, stores, office buildings, and the like. Other things being equal, the greater the capital investment in an economy, the more favorable its future growth prospects are likely to be. Viewed this way, FDI can be seen as an important source of capital investment and a determinant of the future growth rate of an economy. Figure 6.3 provides some summary statistics on inward flows of FDI as a percentage of gross fixed capital formation from 1985 to 1996. In general, FDI accounts for between 3 percent and 5 percent of worldwide gross fixed capital formation. In 1996, the latest year for which figures are available, the percentage was 5.6 percent. As Figure 6.3 illustrates, however, when expressed as a percentage of total gross fixed capital formation, FDI is more important to the developing nations of the world. In 1996, for example, 8.7

systems means he can reach only about half of this population with his product.

Other problems include a highly regulated environment that can make it problematic to conduct business transactions and shifting tax and regulatory regimes. For example, in 1997 the Chinese government suddenly scrapped the tax credit scheme that had made it attractive to import capital equipment into China. This immediately made it more expensive to set up operations in the country.

There are also difficulties finding qualified personnel to staff operations. The cultural revolution produced a generation of people who lack the basic educational background that is taken for granted in the West, and because of the country's past, few local people understand the complexities of managing a modern industrial enterprise. There are also problems with local joint venture partners who are inexperienced, opportunistic, or simply operate according to different goals. One US manager explained that when he laid off 200 people to reduce costs, his Chinese joint venture partner hired them all back the next day. When he inquired why they had been hired back, the Chinese partner, which was government owned, explained that as an agency of the government, it had

an "obligation" to reduce unemployment. Increased investment in the coastal regions of China has raised another source of concern. Serious overcapacity now looms in certain sectors, with negative implications for prices and profits.

Reflecting the growing awareness of these problems, Western enterprises slowed the rate of investment into China in late 1997 and early 1998. In July 1997 Chrysler said it would close its sales office in Beijing, citing overcapacity in the automobile market and lower than expected demand for cars. Chrysler also announced that, while it will be maintaining its joint venture in Shanghai to make Jeeps, it will not be looking for new investments in China. Similarly, in August 1997 Chicago-based Ameritech Corp. stated that because of regulatory problems it would drop out of its telecommunications joint venture and pull out of China. About the same time, Caterpillar Inc. stated it would be closing a joint venture in China because there was little demand for the engines produced by the venture. To compound matters further, the financial crisis that swept through Asia in late 1997 and early 1998 seemed likely to drastically curtail the flow of investment money from other Asian countries, a source that historically had been of major importance. Because of these factors, FDI inflows into

China were expected to decline in 1998 to $35 billion, down $10 billion from 1997.

What all this means for long-term inflows of FDI into China, and for the country's long-term growth rate, remains to be seen. Chinese officials have tried a number of tactics to drum up support for FDI. The government has committed itself to invest more than $800 billion in infrastructure projects over the next 10 years, which should improve the nation's poor highway system. By giving preferential tax breaks to companies that invest in special regions, such as that around Chongqing, the government has created incentives for foreign companies to invest in China's vast interior, where markets are currently underserved. They have been pursuing a macroeconomic policy that includes an emphasis on maintaining steady economic growth, low inflation, and a stable currency, all of which are attractive to foreign investors. And to deal with the lack of qualified personnel, in 1997 the government instructed universities to establish 30 business schools to train Chinese in basic skills such as accounting, finance, and human resource management. As a result, although the bloom may be coming off China's boom in FDI inflows, the country likely will continue to be an important magnet for foreign investors well into this century.[8]

percent of all capital investment in developed nations took the form of FDI inflows. These average figures disguise the importance of FDI for certain nations. In 1996, FDI inflows accounted for 17 percent of all gross fixed capital formation in China and 14.2 percent in Mexico. In comparison, FDI inflows accounted for only 7 percent of all capital investment in the United States. It follows that FDI is far more important as a source of investment capital to countries such as China and Mexico, than it is to the United States, even though the United States accounts for a larger absolute amount of FDI inflows.

In many developed nations FDI is far more important as a source of capital than it is in the United States. Examples include the United Kingdom, where FDI inflows accounted for 14.6 percent of all capital investment in 1996, Sweden (14.8 percent in 1996), and Ireland (20.4 percent in 1996). But FDI inflows accounted for less than 0.1 percent of all gross fixed capital formation in the Japanese economy in 1996—a

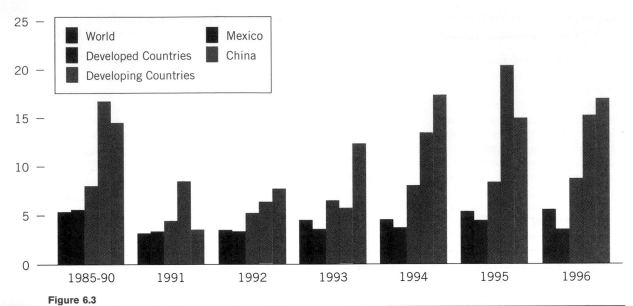

Figure 6.3

Inward FDI Flows as a Percentage of Gross Fixed Capital Formation, 1985–1996
Source: United Nations is the author of the original material. Reprinted with permission.

figure that reflects not only the prolonged economic recession in that country, but also the host of formal regulations and informal barriers that make it difficult for foreign companies to invest in and do business in this nation. To the extent that capital inflows allow a country to achieve higher future growth rates, countries such as Japan may be hurting themselves by adopting restrictive regulations with regard to FDI inflows. We shall return to this issue in the next chapter.

The Source of FDI

For most of the period after World War II, the United States was by far the largest source country for FDI. Even during the late 1970s the United States was still accounting for about 47 percent of all FDI *outflows* from industrialized countries, while the second-place United Kingdom accounted for about 18 percent. US firms so dominated the growth of FDI in the 1960s and 70s that the words American and multinational became almost synonymous. As a result, by 1980, 178 of the world's largest 382 multinationals were US firms, and 40 of them were British.[9] However, during the 1985–90 period the United States slipped to third place behind Japan and the United Kingdom. Since then, as Figure 6.4 illustrates, the United States has once more regained its dominant position, accounting for $114.5 billion of FDI outflows, or 27 percent of the global total, in 1997.

The increase in Japanese FDI outflows during the 1980s and the subsequent stagnation during the 1990s reflect the strong Japanese economy during the 1980s and the prolonged recession that gripped the economy during the 1990s. During the 1980s Japanese firms were making market share gains in industry after industry. This yielded strong growth in profits and cash flows. In addition, the Japanese currency increased in value against many other currencies during this period, including the US dollar. Data from J. P. Morgan & Co. suggest that an index measuring the value of the Japanese yen against 44 other currencies increased from 89.2 in January 1980 to a high of 130.4 in August 1993 (the index was set to 100

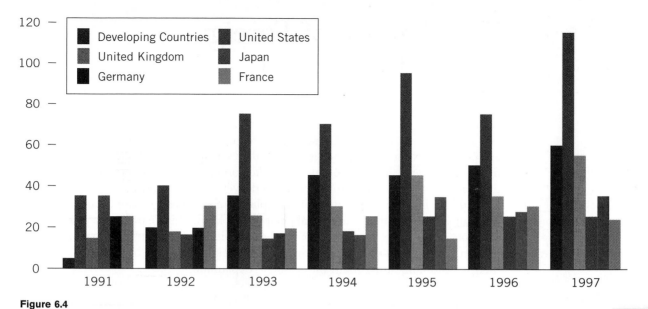

Figure 6.4

FDI Outflows, 1991–1997 ($ billions)
Source: United Nations is the author of the original material. Reprinted with permission.

in 1990).[10] As the yen became more valuable, it became progressively cheaper to acquire assets in countries whose currencies were not as strong, such as the United States. Thus, the combination of strong growth in corporate profits and cash flows and a strong currency made it both easy and relatively inexpensive for Japanese firms to purchase assets—including factories, land, office buildings, and often, whole firms—in countries whose economic performance was less robust and whose currency was weaker. Also, in many countries there was an increased threat that trade barriers might be used to hold back the growing flood of Japanese exports (this was true in the United States). This gave many Japanese firms a strong incentive to invest in production facilities overseas and serve foreign markets from those facilities, as opposed to exporting from Japan. In sum, strong corporate performance, a strong currency, and the threat that foreign countries might erect trade barriers against Japanese exports all helped propel Japanese FDI outflows to record levels from 1985 to 1991. The slowdown in the growth of Japanese FDI outflows since 1991 simply reflected the poor corporate performance in Japan that resulted from the country's economic malaise.

The growth of FDI outflows from the United States was driven by a combination of favorable factors including a strong US economy; strong corporate profits and cash flow, which has given US firms the capital to invest abroad; and a relatively strong currency, particularly since 1995. Similar factors explain the growth of FDI outflows from the United Kingdom during the 1990s.

The other notable trend in the statistics summarized in Figure 6.4 has been the rise of FDI outflows from developing nations. These have increased from an annual average of $10.5 billion in the 1985–1990 time period to a record $61.1 billion in 1997. The biggest investors among developing nations in 1997 were Hong Kong, Singapore, and South Korea. Much of the Hong Kong and Singapore investment was targeted at China and other Southeast Asian nations. While South Korean firms also invested in these regions, they also targeted the United States and Europe.

The Theory of Foreign Direct Investment

In this section we review several theories of foreign direct investment. These theories approach the phenomenon of foreign direct investment from three complementary perspectives. One set of theories seeks to explain why a firm will favor direct investment as a means of entering a foreign market when two other alternatives are possible, exporting and licensing. Another set of theories seeks to explain why firms in the same industry often undertake foreign direct investment at the same time, and why certain locations are favored over others as targets for foreign direct investment. These theories attempt to explain the observed *pattern* of foreign direct investment flows. A third theoretical perspective, known as the **eclectic paradigm,** attempts to combine the two other perspectives into a single holistic explanation of foreign direct investment (the term *eclectic* means picking the best aspects of other theories and combining them into a single explanation).

eclectic paradigm
Theory of foreign direct investment that combines two other perspectives into a single holistic explanation of FDI.

Why Foreign Direct Investment?

Why do firms go to all the trouble of establishing operations abroad through foreign direct investment when two other alternatives are available to them for exploiting the profit opportunities in a foreign market: exporting and licensing? **Exporting** involves producing goods at home and then shipping them to the receiving country for sale. **Licensing** involves granting a foreign entity (the licensee) the right to produce and sell the firm's product in return for a royalty fee on every unit the foreign entity sells. In the opening case, why would a firm such as Electrolux choose to invest directly in a factory in Hungary to build home appliances for sale in that country, when it could have exported home appliances to Hungary from one of its Swedish factories, or it could have allowed a Hungarian firm to build its appliances under license?

exporting Producing goods at home and shipping them to the receiving country for sale.

licensing Granting a foreign entity the right to produce and sell a firm's product in return for a royalty fee on every unit sold.

The question is an important one because foreign direct investment may be both expensive and risky when compared to exporting and licensing. FDI is expensive because a firm must establish production facilities in a foreign country or acquire a foreign enterprise. FDI is risky because of the problems associated with doing business in a different culture where the "rules of the game" may be very different. Relative to indigenous firms, there is a greater probability that a foreign firm undertaking FDI in a country for the first time will make costly mistakes because of ignorance. When a firm exports, it need not bear the costs associated with foreign direct investment, and the risks associated with selling abroad can be reduced by using a native sales agent. Similarly, when a firm allows another enterprise to produce its products under license it need not bear the costs or risks of FDI, since these are born by the licensee. So why do so many firms apparently prefer FDI over either exporting or licensing? The answer can be found in the limitations of exporting and licensing as means for capitalizing on foreign market opportunities.

LIMITATIONS OF EXPORTING The viability of an exporting strategy is often constrained by transportation costs and trade barriers. When transportation costs are added to production costs, it becomes unprofitable to ship some products over a large distance. This is particularly true of products that have a low value-to-weight ratio and that can be produced in almost any location (e.g., cement, soft drinks, and so on). For such products, the attractiveness of exporting decreases relative to either FDI or licensing. For products with a high value-to-weight ratio, however, transport costs are normally a very minor component of total landed cost (e.g., electronic components, personal computers, medical equipment, computer software) and have little impact on the relative attractiveness of exporting, licensing, and FDI.

Transportation costs aside, much foreign direct investment is undertaken as a response to actual or threatened trade barriers such as import tariffs or quotas. By placing tariffs on imported goods, governments can increase the cost of exporting relative to foreign direct investment and licensing. Similarly, by limiting imports through quotas, governments increase the attractiveness of FDI and licensing. For example, the wave of FDI by Japanese auto companies into the United States during the 1980s was partly driven by protectionist threats from Congress and by quotas on the importation of Japanese cars. For Japanese auto companies, these factors decreased the profitability of exporting and increased that of foreign direct investment. Trade barriers do not have to be in place for foreign direct investment to be favored over exporting. Often, the desire to reduce the threat that trade barriers might be imposed is enough to justify foreign direct investment as an alternative to exporting.

LIMITATIONS OF LICENSING   A branch of economic theory known as **internalization theory** seeks to explain why firms often prefer foreign direct investment over licensing as a strategy for entering foreign markets.[11] According to internalization theory, licensing has three major drawbacks as a strategy for exploiting foreign market opportunities. First, *licensing may result in a firm's giving away valuable technological know-how to a potential foreign competitor.* For example, in the 1960s RCA licensed its leading-edge color television technology to a number of Japanese companies, including Matsushita and Sony. At the time RCA saw licensing as a way to earn a good return from its technological know-how in the Japanese market without the costs and risks associated with foreign direct investment. However, Matsushita and Sony quickly assimilated RCA's technology and used it to enter the US market to compete directly against RCA. As a result, RCA is now a minor player in its home market, while Matsushita and Sony have a much bigger market share.

A second problem is that *licensing does not give a firm the tight control over manufacturing, marketing, and strategy in a foreign country that may be required to maximize its profitability.* With licensing, control over manufacturing, marketing, and strategy is granted to a licensee in return for a royalty fee. However, for *both* strategic and operational reasons, a firm may want to retain control over these functions. In terms of *strategy,* a firm might want its foreign subsidiary to price and market very aggressively to keep a foreign competitor in check. Kodak is pursuing this strategy in Japan. The competitive attacks launched by Kodak's Japanese subsidiary are keeping its major global competitor, Fuji, busy defending its competitive position in Japan. Consequently, Fuji has had to pull back from its earlier strategy of attacking Kodak aggressively in the United States. Unlike a wholly owned subsidiary, a licensee would be unlikely to accept such a strategy because the licensee would be allowed to make only a low profit or it might have to take a loss.

The rationale for wanting control over the *operations* of a foreign entity is that the firm might wish to take advantage of differences in factor costs across countries, producing only part of its final product in a given country, while importing other parts from where they can be produced at lower cost. Again, a licensee would be unlikely to accept such an arrangement because it would limit the licensee's autonomy. Thus, when tight control over a foreign entity is desirable, foreign direct investment is preferable to licensing.

A third problem with licensing arises when the firm's competitive advantage is based not so much on its products, as on the management, marketing, and manufacturing capabilities that produce those products. Such capabilities are often not amenable to licensing. While a foreign licensee may be able to physically reproduce the firm's product under license, it often may not be able to do so as efficiently as the firm could itself. As a result, the licensee may not be able to fully exploit the profit potential inherent in a foreign market.

Consider Toyota, a company whose competitive advantage in the global auto industry is acknowledged to come from its superior ability to manage the overall process of designing, engineering, manufacturing, and selling automobiles; that is, from its management and organizational capabilities. Toyota is credited with pioneering the development of a new production process, known as lean production, that enables it to produce higher-quality automobiles at a lower cost than its global rivals.[12] Although Toyota has certain products that could be licensed, its real competitive advantage comes from its management and process capabilities. These kinds of skills are difficult to articulate or codify; they certainly cannot be written down in a simple licensing contract. They are organizationwide and they have been developed over the years. They are not embodied in any one individual, but instead are widely dispersed throughout the company. Toyota's skills are embedded in its organizational culture, and culture cannot be licensed. Thus, if Toyota were to allow a foreign entity to produce its cars under license, chances are the entity could not do so nearly as efficiently as Toyota could. This would limit the ability of the foreign entity to fully develop the market potential of that product. Such reasoning underlies Toyota's preference for direct investment in foreign markets, as opposed to allowing foreign automobile companies to produce its cars under license. The same is true of Wal-Mart, which is profiled in the accompanying "Management Focus." Wal-Mart considered expanding internationally via franchising but decided its culture would be difficult to replicate in franchisees. (Franchising is the market-based mechanism by which firms sell or license the right to use their brand name, subject to the franchisee adhering to certain strict requirements regarding the way it operates its business).

All of this suggests that when one or more of the following conditions holds, FDI is more profitable than licensing: (*i*) when the firm has valuable know-how that cannot be adequately protected by a licensing contract, (*ii*) when the firm needs tight control over a foreign entity to maximize its market share and earnings in that country, and (*iii*) when a firm's skills and know-how are not amenable to licensing.

ADVANTAGES OF FOREIGN DIRECT INVESTMENT A firm will favor foreign direct investment over exporting as an entry strategy when transportation costs or trade barriers make exporting unattractive. The firm also will favor foreign direct investment over licensing (or franchising) when it wishes to maintain control over its technological know-how, or over its operations and business strategy, or when the firm's capabilities are simply not amenable to licensing, as may often be the case.

Founded by Sam Walton in the 1960s, Wal-Mart had grown to become the largest discount retailer in the United States with annual sales of $32.6 billion by the early 1990s. Wal-Mart's spectacular growth from a small Arkansas retailer to a national powerhouse was based on a first-class management team that pursued a number of innovative operations strategies that backed up the company's commitment to deliver a large selection of high-value merchandise at a low cost to consumers.

The firm pioneered the development of a "hub-and-spoke" distribution system, where central

that allow for daily adjustments to orders, inventory, and prices. In addition, the company is famous for a dynamic and egalitarian culture that grants major decision-making authority to store managers, department managers, and individual employees (whom Wal-Mart refers to as "associates"). Wal-Mart is known for treating its employees well but also for demanding commitment and excellent performance from them. This culture is backed up with a generous profit-sharing plan and stock-ownership plan for all employees. By such means, Wal-Mart has developed a culture and control system that creates incentives for as-

vantage was based on the combination of culture and supporting information and logistics systems, and that such a culture and systems would be difficult to transfer to franchisees. In other words, it believed the management know-how behind its culture and systems was not amenable to franchising.

In 1992 Wal-Mart began its foreign adventure by establishing six stores in Mexico. By the end of 1997 it had 402 stores in that country, along with 144 in Canada, 13 in Puerto Rico, 9 in Argentina, 8 in Brazil, 3 in China, and 3 in Indonesia. It had also announced the decision to purchase 21 Wertkauf hypermarket stores

Wal-Mart's International Expansion

distribution warehouses were strategically located to serve clusters of stores. This helped drive down inventory and logistics costs. The firm was also one of the first to utilize computer-based information systems to track in-store sales and transmit this information to suppliers. The information provided by these systems was used to determine pricing and stocking strategy and to better manage inventories. Today Wal-Mart is still a leader in information systems. All Wal-Mart stores, distribution centers, and suppliers are linked via sophisticated information systems and satellite-based communications

sociates and managers to give their best for the company.

Despite its success, by 1991 Wal-Mart was encountering significant problems. With 1,568 stores nationwide, its growth prospects in the United States were looking more limited. Wal-Mart decided to try to expand its operations outside the United States and build a "global brand." The company debated a number of options for expansion, including licensing its brand name to franchisees, but decided that it would be best to expand via wholly owned subsidiaries in foreign countries that permitted such investment. The company concluded that its competitive ad-

in Germany, its first venture in Europe. As part of its entry strategy, once it has established or acquired a store in a foreign country, Wal-Mart transfers some of its US associates to that store for two to three years to help establish the back-office systems and to transfer the Wal-Mart culture to the new associates.

So far the strategy seems to be working. Wal-Mart's international stores contributed over $5 billion in sales to the company's $120 billion revenues in 1997, and they are already posting profits.[13]

The Pattern of Foreign Direct Investment

Firms in the same industry often undertake foreign direct investment at about the same time. There also is a clear tendency for firms to direct their investment activities toward certain locations. The two theories we consider in this section attempt to explain the patterns that we observe in foreign direct investment flows.

FOLLOWING COMPETITORS One theory to explain foreign direct investment patterns is based on the idea that firms follow their domestic competitors overseas. First expounded by F. T. Knickerbocker, this theory has been developed with regard to oligopolistic industries.[14] An **oligopoly** is an industry composed of a limited number of large firms (an industry in which four firms control 80 percent of a domestic

oligopoly Industry composed of a limited number of large firms.

market is considered an oligopoly). A critical competitive feature of such industries is interdependence of the major players: What one firm does can have an immediate impact on the major competitors, forcing a response in kind. Thus, if one firm in an oligopoly cuts prices, this can take market share away from its competitors, forcing them to respond with similar price cuts to retain their market share.

Such imitative behavior can take many forms in an oligopoly. One firm raises prices, the others follow; someone expands capacity, and the rivals imitate lest they be left in a disadvantageous position. Building on this, Knickerbocker argued that the same kind of imitative behavior characterizes foreign direct investment. Consider an oligopoly in the United States in which three firms—A, B, and C—dominate the market. Firm A establishes a subsidiary in France. Firms B and C reflect that if this investment is successful, it may knock out their export business to France and give Firm A a first-mover advantage. Furthermore, Firm A might discover some competitive asset in France that it could repatriate to the United States to torment Firms B and C on their native soil. Given these possibilities, Firms B and C decide to follow Firm A and establish operations in France.

Several studies of US enterprises suggest that firms based in oligopolistic industries tend to imitate each other's FDI.[15] The same phenomenon has been observed with regard to Japanese firms.[16] For example, Toyota and Nissan responded to Honda's investments in the United States and Europe by undertaking their own FDI in the United States and Europe. Similarly, in the opening case we saw how Electrolux's expansion into Eastern Europe and Asia was partly driven by the fact that its global competitors, Whirlpool and GE, were making similar moves.

THE PRODUCT LIFE CYCLE We considered Raymond Vernon's product life-cycle theory in Chapter 4. What we did not dwell on, however, was Vernon's contention that his theory also explains the pattern of FDI over time. Vernon argued that in many cases the establishment of facilities abroad, to produce a product for consumption in that market or for export to other markets, is often undertaken by the same firm or firms that pioneered the product in their home market. Thus, Xerox introduced the photocopier into the US market, and Xerox originally set up production facilities in Japan (Fuji-Xerox) and Great Britain (Rank-Xerox) to serve those markets.

Vernon's view is that firms undertake FDI at particular stages in the life cycle of a product they have pioneered. They invest in other advanced countries when local demand in those countries grows large enough to support local production (as Xerox did). They subsequently shift production to developing countries when product standardization and market saturation give rise to price competition and cost pressures. Investment in developing countries, where labor costs are lower, is seen as the best way to reduce costs.

There is merit to Vernon's theory; firms do invest in a foreign country when demand in that country will support local production, and they do invest in low-cost countries when cost pressures become intense.[17] Vernon's theory fails to explain, however, why it is profitable for a firm to undertake FDI at such times, rather than continuing to export from its home base and rather than licensing a foreign firm to produce its product. Just because demand in a foreign country is large enough to support local production, does not necessarily mean that local production is the most profitable option. It may still be more profitable to produce at home and export to that country (to realize the scale economies that arise from serving the global market from one location). Alternatively, it may be more profitable for the firm to

license a foreign firm to produce its product for sale in that country. The product life-cycle theory ignores these options and, instead, simply argues that once a foreign market is large enough to support local production, FDI will occur. This limits its explanatory power and its usefulness to business in that it fails to identify when it is profitable to invest abroad.

The Eclectic Paradigm

The eclectic paradigm has been championed by the British economist John Dunning.[18] Dunning argues that in addition to the various factors discussed above, location-specific advantages are also of considerable importance in explaining both the rationale for and the direction of foreign direct investment. By **location-specific advantages,** Dunning means the advantages that arise from utilizing resource endowments or assets that are tied to a particular foreign location and that a firm finds valuable to combine with its own unique assets (such as the firm's technological, marketing, or management capabilities). Dunning accepts the argument of the internalization theory that it is difficult for a firm to license its own unique capabilities and know-how. Therefore, he argues that combining location-specific assets or resource endowments *and* the firm's own unique capabilities often requires foreign direct investment. That is, it requires the firm to establish production facilities where those foreign assets or resource endowments are located.

An obvious example of Dunning's arguments are natural resources, such as oil and other minerals, which are by their character specific to certain locations. Dunning suggests that to exploit such foreign resources a firm must undertake FDI. This explains the FDI undertaken by many of the world's oil companies, which have to invest where oil is located in order to combine their technological and managerial capabilities with this valuable location-specific resource. Another obvious example are valuable human resources, such as low-cost, skilled labor. The cost and skill of labor varies from country to country. Because labor is not internationally mobile, according to Dunning it makes sense for a firm to locate production facilities where the cost and skills of local labor are most suited to its production processes. One reason Electrolux is building factories in China is that China has an abundant supply of low-cost but well-educated and skilled labor. Thus, other factors aside, China is a good location for producing household appliances both for the Chinese market and for export elsewhere.

However, Dunning's theory has implications that go beyond basic resources such as minerals and labor. Consider Silicon Valley, which is the world center for the computer and semiconductor industries. Many of the world's major computer and semiconductor companies, such as Apple Computer, Hewlett-Packard, and Intel, are located close to each other in the Silicon Valley region of California. As a result, much of the cutting-edge research and product development in computers and semiconductors occurs here. According to Dunning's arguments, knowledge being generated in Silicon Valley with regard to the design and manufacture of computers and semiconductors is available nowhere else in the world. As it is commercialized, that knowledge diffuses throughout the world, but the leading edge of knowledge generation in the computer and semiconductor industries is in Silicon Valley. In Dunning's language, this means Silicon Valley has a *location-specific advantage* in the generation of knowledge related to the computer and semiconductor industries. In part, this advantage comes from the sheer concentration of intellectual talent in this area, and in part it arises from a network of informal contacts that allows firms to benefit from others' knowledge generation. Economists refer to such knowledge spillovers

location-specific advantages Advantages that arise from using resource endowments or assets that are tied to a particular location and that a firm finds valuable to combine with its own unique assets.

externalities Knowledge spillovers that occur when companies in the same industry locate in the same area.

as **externalities,** and there is a well-established theory suggesting that firms can benefit from such externalities by locating close to their source.[19]

Given this, it may make sense for foreign computer and semiconductor firms to invest in research and (perhaps) production facilities so they can benefit from being where the knowledge is generated, the belief being that externalities will allow firms based there to use valuable new knowledge before those based elsewhere, thereby giving them a competitive advantage in the global marketplace. In support of this argument, we are seeing significant evidence of FDI by European, Japanese, South Korean, and Taiwanese computer and semiconductor firms in the Silicon Valley region.[20] In a similar vein, others have argued that direct investment by foreign firms in the US biotechnology industry has been motivated by desires to gain access to the unique location-specific technological knowledge of US biotechnology firms.[21] Dunning's theory, therefore, seems to be a useful addition to those outlined above; it helps explain like no other how location factors affect the direction of FDI.

ANOTHER PERSPECTIVE

FDI: Not Limited to the Big Players

We tend to think of FDI as an activity that is for large MNEs, yet FDI may be a useful strategy for the smaller company. A small, privately owned company in North Carolina in industrial thermoplastics pelletizing, Gala Industries, Inc., has recently decided to produce in Germany, even though labor costs are higher there. The reasoning? Access to Germany's advanced knowledge about pellet production offsets any increased labor cost.

Part 3 Cross-Border Trade and Investment

Political Ideology and Foreign Direct Investment

Now we are familiar with the theory of FDI, it is time to focus on government policy toward FDI. Government policy has typically been driven by political ideology. Historically, ideology toward FDI has ranged from a radical stance that is hostile to all FDI to the non-interventionist principle of free market economics. In between these two extremes is an approach that might be called pragmatic nationalism.

The Radical View

The radical view traces its roots to Marxist political and economic theory. Radical writers argue that the multinational enterprise (MNE) is an instrument of imperialist domination. They see the MNE as a tool for exploiting host countries to the exclusive benefit of the MNE's capitalist-imperialist home country. They argue that the MNE extracts profits from the host country and takes them to the home country, giving nothing of value to the host country in exchange. They note, for example, that key technology is tightly controlled by the MNE, and that important jobs in the foreign subsidiaries of MNEs go to home country nationals rather than to citizens of the host country. Because of this, according to the radical view, FDI by the MNEs of advanced capitalist nations keeps the less developed countries of the world relatively backward and dependent on advanced capitalist nations for investment, jobs, and technology. Thus, according to the extreme version of this view, no country should ever permit foreign corporations to undertake FDI because they can never be instruments of economic development, only of economic domination. Where MNEs already exist in a country, they should be immediately nationalized.[22]

From 1945 until the 1980s the radical view was very influential in the world economy. Until the collapse of communism between 1989 and 1991, the countries of Eastern Europe were opposed to any FDI. Similarly, Communist countries elsewhere, such as China, Cambodia, and Cuba, were all opposed in principle to FDI (although in practice the Chinese started to allow FDI in mainland China in the 1970s). The radical position was also embraced by many socialist countries, particularly in Africa where one of the first actions of many newly independent states was to nationalize foreign-owned enterprises. The radical position was further embraced by countries whose political ideology was more nationalistic than socialistic. This was true in Iran and India, for example, both of which adopted tough policies restricting FDI and nationalized many foreign-owned enterprises. Iran is an interesting case because its Islamic government, while rejecting Marxist theory, essentially embraced the radical view that FDI by MNEs is an instrument of imperialism.

By the end of the 1980s, however, the radical position was in retreat almost everywhere. There seem to be three reasons for this. First is the collapse of communism in Eastern Europe. Second is the generally abysmal economic performance of those countries that embraced the radical position and the growing belief by many of these countries that, contrary to the radical position, FDI can be an important source of technology and jobs and can stimulate economic growth. And third is the strong economic performance of those developing countries that embraced capitalism rather than radical ideology (e.g., Singapore, Hong Kong, and Taiwan).

radical position

The Free Market View

The free market view traces its roots to classical economics and the international trade theories of Adam Smith and David Ricardo (see Chapter 4). The free market view argues that international production should be distributed among countries according to the theory of comparative advantage. That is, countries should specialize in the production of those goods and services that they can produce most efficiently. Within this framework, the MNE is seen as an instrument for dispersing the production of goods and services to those locations around the globe where they can be produced most efficiently. Viewed this way, FDI by the MNE is a way to increase the overall efficiency of the world economy.

For example, consider a well-publicized decision by IBM in the mid-1980s to move assembly operations for many of its personal computers from the United States to Guadalajara in Mexico. IBM invested about $90 million in an assembly facility with the capacity to produce 100,000 PCs per year, 75 percent of which were exported back to the United States.[23] According to the free market view, moves such as this can be seen as increasing the overall efficiency of resource utilization in the world economy. Mexico, due to its low labor costs, has a comparative advantage in the assembly of PCs. According to the free market view, by moving the production of PCs from the United States to Mexico, IBM frees up US resources for activities in which the United States has a comparative advantage (e.g., the design of computer software, the manufacture of high-value-added components such as microprocessors, or basic R&D). Also, US consumers benefit because the PCs they want now cost less than they would if they were produced domestically. In addition, Mexico gains from the technology, skills, and capital that IBM transfers with its FDI. Contrary to the radical view, the free market view stresses that such resource transfers benefit the host country and stimulate its economic growth. Thus, the free market view argues that FDI is a benefit to both the source country and the host country.

For reasons explored earlier in this book (see Chapter 2), the free market view has been ascendant worldwide in recent years. Consequently, there has been a global move toward the removal of restrictions on inward and outward foreign direct investment. As noted earlier, according to the United Nations, between 1991 and 1996 more than 100 countries made 599 changes in legislation governing FDI. Some 95 percent of these changes involved liberalizing a country's foreign investment regulations to make it easier for foreign companies to enter the markets.[24] However, despite the ascendency of the free market view, in practice no country has adopted the free market view in its pure form (just as no country has adopted the radical view in its pure form). Countries such as Britain and the United States are among the most open to FDI, but the governments of both have demonstrated a tendency to intervene. Britain does so formally by reserving the right to block foreign takeovers of domestic firms if the takeovers are seen as "contrary to national security interests" or if they have the potential for "reducing competition." (In practice this right is rarely exercised.) US controls on FDI are more limited still and largely informal. For political reasons the United States will occasionally restrict US firms from undertaking FDI in certain countries (e.g., Cuba and Iran). In addition, there are some limited restrictions on inward FDI. For example, foreigners are prohibited from purchasing more than 25 percent of any US airline or from acquiring a controlling interest in a US television broadcast network. Also, since 1989 the government has had the right to review foreign investment on the grounds of "national security."

Pragmatic Nationalism

In practice, many countries have adopted neither a radical policy nor a free market policy toward FDI, but instead a policy that can best be described as pragmatic nationalism. The pragmatic nationalist view is that FDI has both benefits and costs. FDI can benefit a host country by bringing capital, skills, technology, and jobs, but those benefits often come at a cost. When products resulting from an investment are produced by a foreign company rather than a domestic company, the profits from that investment go abroad. Many countries are also concerned that a foreign-owned manufacturing plant may import many components from its home country, which has negative implications for the host country's balance-of-payments position.

Recognizing this, countries adopting a pragmatic stance pursue policies designed to maximize the national benefits and minimize the national costs. According to this view, FDI should be allowed only if the benefits outweigh the costs. Japan offers one of the more extreme examples of pragmatic nationalism. Until the 1980s Japan's policy was among the most restrictive in countries adopting a pragmatic nationalist stance. This was due to Japan's perception that direct entry of foreign (especially US) firms with ample managerial resources into the Japanese markets could be detrimental to the development and growth of the country's own industry and technology.[25] This belief led Japan to block the majority of applications by foreign firms to invest in Japan. However, there were always exceptions. Firms that had important technology often received permission to undertake FDI if they insisted that they would neither license their technology to a Japanese firm nor enter into a joint venture with a Japanese enterprise. IBM and Texas Instruments were able to set up wholly owned subsidiaries in Japan by adopting this negotiating position. From the perspective of the Japanese government, the benefits of FDI in such cases—the stimulus that these firms might impart to the Japanese economy—outweighed the perceived costs.

Another aspect of pragmatic nationalism is aggressively courting FDI seen to be in the national interest by, for example, offering subsidies to foreign MNEs in the form of tax breaks or grants. Countries often compete with each other to attract foreign investment, offering large tax breaks and subsidies to enterprises considering investment. In Europe Britain has been the most successful at attracting Japanese investment in the automobile industry, often in the face of major competition from other European nations. In addition to Nissan, Toyota and Honda also now have major assembly plants in Britain. All three now use this country as their base for serving the rest of Europe—with obvious employment and balance-of-payments benefits for Britain.

Shifting Ideology

Recent years have seen a marked decline in the number of countries that adhere to a radical ideology. Although no countries have adopted a *pure* free market policy stance, an increasing number of countries are gravitating toward the free market end of the spectrum and have liberalized their foreign investment regime. This includes many countries that only a few years ago were firmly in the radical camp (e.g., the former Communist countries of Eastern Europe and many of the socialist countries of Africa) and several countries that until recently could best be described as pragmatic nationalists with regard to FDI (e.g., Japan, South Korea, Italy, Spain, and most Latin American countries). One result has been the surge in the volume of FDI worldwide, which as we noted earlier, has been growing twice as fast as the growth in world trade. Another result has been a dramatic increase in the volume of FDI directed at countries that have recently liberalized their FDI regimes, such as China, India, and Vietnam.

Costs and Benefits of FDI to the Nation-State

Many governments can be considered pragmatic nationalists when it comes to FDI. Accordingly, their policy is shaped by a consideration of the costs and benefits of FDI. Here we explore the benefits and costs of FDI, first from the perspective of a host country and then from the perspective of the home country.

Host Country Effects: Benefits

There are three main benefits of inward FDI for a host country: the resource-transfer effect, the employment effect, and the balance-of-payments effect. In the following section we explore the costs of FDI to host countries.

RESOURCE-TRANSFER EFFECTS   Foreign direct investment can make a positive contribution to the host economy by supplying capital, technology, and management resources that would otherwise not be available. If such factors are scarce in a country, the FDI may boost that country's economic growth rate. The accompanying "Country Focus" describes how the Venezuelan government has been encouraging FDI in its petroleum industry in an attempt to benefit from resource-transfer effects.

Many MNEs, by virtue of their size and financial strength, have access to financial resources not available to host country firms. These funds may be available from internal company sources, or, because of their reputation, large MNEs may find it easier to borrow money from capital markets than host country firms would. This consideration was a factor in the Venezuelan government's decision to invite foreign oil companies to enter into joint ventures with PDVSA, the state-owned Venezuelan oil company.

You will recall from Chapter 2 that technology can stimulate a country's economic growth and industrialization.[26] Technology can take two forms, both of which are valuable. It can be incorporated in a production process (e.g., the technology for discovering, extracting, and refining oil) or it can be incorporated in a product

In 1976 Venezuela nationalized its oil industry, effectively closing the sector to foreign investors. The stated goal at the time was to control this important natural resource for the benefit of Venezuela, as opposed to foreign oil companies. The results, however, fell short of expectations. The country's state-owned oil monopoly, Petroleos de Venezuela SA (PDVSA), failed to develop new oil fields to replace the depletion of existing reserves and by the mid-1980s the country's oil output was falling.

Faced with the prospect of declining export revenues from

velop many of Venezuela's oil fields in a timely fashion, it had no alternative but to turn to foreign companies for help. Third, the government believed that PDVSA would be able to use joint ventures with foreign oil companies to learn about modern management techniques in the industry. PDVSA could then use this knowledge to improve the efficiency of its own operations.

Plans call for the investment of $73 billion in the oil industry. The plan, as outlined by Gustavo Roosen, president of PDVSA, is to develop crude oil production potential of 4 million barrels per

coveries of crude oil and has entered into several ventures with other foreign partners to develop these zones. If commercial quantities of oil are discovered, PDVSA will share future production with its partners. Under the terms of most agreements, PDVSA will receive 35 percent of the earnings from any successful exploration venture. Together with foreign investors such as Conoco and Total, PDVSA is investing in state-of-the-art refining facilities that can be used to convert heavy crude oil into a lighter weight, high-value crude oil for export. Finally, PDVSA, Shell,

Foreign Direct Investment in Venezuela's Petroleum Industry

oil, in 1991 Venezuela reversed its policy and began to open its oil industry to foreign investors. The Venezuelan government turned to foreign investors for three reasons. First, it recognized that PDVSA did not have the capital required to undertake the investment alone. Second, it realized that PDVSA lacked the technological resources and skills of many of the world's major oil companies, particularly in the areas of oil exploration, oil field development, and sophisticated refining. The government understood that if PDVSA was to de-

day by 2002 and 7 million barrels per day by 2007 (the country produced about 2.6 million barrels per day in 1991). Of the $73 billion in projected capital spending, PDVSA plans to invest about $45 billion, and foreign oil companies will supply the remaining $28 billion. The first FDI agreement was signed in 1992 with British Petroleum (BP). BP agreed to invest $60 million by 1995 to develop a marginal oil field that it would then be given the rights to for 20 years. Using a BP study, PDVSA identified sectors in Eastern Venezuela with strong prospects for large dis-

Exxon, and Mitsubishi have entered into a $5.6 billion joint venture to produce liquefied natural gas for export.

By 1997 more than 40 development projects were under way in Venezuela involving cooperation between PDVSA and foreign oil companies. Almost all of the world's major oil companies now had some activities in the country, compared to none before to 1991. The country's oil output was also once more expanding, reaching 3.5 million barrels per day in 1997, up from a low of 1.7 million barrels per day in 1985.[27]

(e.g., personal computers). However, many countries lack the research and development resources and skills required to develop their own indigenous product and process technology. This is particularly true of the world's less developed nations. Such countries must rely on advanced industrialized nations for much of the technology required to stimulate economic growth, and FDI can provide it. Thus, as we saw in the "Country Focus" on Venezuela, a lack of relevant technological know-how with regard to the discovery, extraction, and refining of oil was one reason the Venezuelan government invited foreign oil companies into the country.

The foreign management skills provided through FDI may also produce important benefits for the host country. Beneficial spin-off effects arise when local personnel who are trained to occupy managerial, financial, and technical posts in the subsidiary of a foreign MNE subsequently leave the firm and help to establish indigenous firms. Similar benefits may arise if the superior management skills of a foreign MNE stimulate local suppliers, distributors, and competitors to improve their own management skills.

The beneficial effects may be reduced considerably if most management and highly skilled jobs are reserved for home country nationals, depriving citizens of the host country of the benefits of training by the MNE. The percentage of management and skilled jobs that go to citizens of the host country can be a major negotiating point between an MNE wishing to undertake FDI and a potential host government. In recent years most MNEs have responded to host government pressures by agreeing to reserve a large proportion of management and highly skilled jobs for citizens of the host country.

EMPLOYMENT EFFECTS   The beneficial employment effect claimed for FDI is that it brings jobs to a host country that would otherwise not be created there. As we saw in the "Management Focus" on Nissan in the United Kingdom, employment effects are both direct and indirect. Direct effects arise when a foreign MNE directly employs host country citizens. Indirect effects arise when jobs are created in local suppliers as a result of the investment and when jobs are created because of increased spending in the local economy resulting from employees of the MNE. The indirect employment effects are often as large as, if not larger than, the direct effects. In the Nissan case, for example, Nissan's investment in the United Kingdom created 4,250 direct jobs and at least another 4,000 jobs in support industries.

Cynics note that not all of the "new jobs" created by FDI represent net additions in employment. In the case of FDI by Japanese auto companies in the United States, for example, some argue that the jobs created by this investment have been more than offset by the jobs lost in US-owned auto companies, which have lost market share to their Japanese competitors. As a consequence of such substitution effects, the net number of new jobs created by FDI may not be as great as initially claimed by an MNE. The issue of the likely net gain in employment may be a major negotiating point between an MNE wishing to undertake FDI and the host government.

BALANCE-OF-PAYMENTS EFFECTS   The effect of FDI on a country's balance-of-payments accounts is an important policy issue for most host governments. A country's **balance-of-payments accounts** keep track of both its payments to and its receipts from other countries. Governments normally are concerned when their country is running a deficit on the current account of their balance of payments. The **current account** tracks the export and import of goods and services. A current account deficit, or trade deficit as it is often called, arises when a country is importing more goods and services than it is exporting. Governments typically prefer to see a current account surplus rather than a deficit. The only way in which a current account deficit can be supported in the long run is by selling assets to foreigners. (For a detailed explanation of why this is the case, see Krugman and Obstfeld.)[28] For example, the persistent US current account deficit of the 1980s and 1990s was financed by a steady sale of US assets (stocks, bonds, real estate, and whole corporations) to foreigners. Because national governments dislike seeing the assets of their country fall into foreign hands, they prefer a current account surplus. FDI can help a country achieve this goal in two ways.

First, if the FDI is a substitute for imports of goods or services, it improves the current account of the host country's balance of payments. Much of the FDI by Japanese automobile companies in the United States and United Kingdom, for example, substitutes for imports from Japan. Thus, the current account of the US balance of payments has improved somewhat because many Japanese companies are

balance-of-payments account Record of a country's payments to and receipts from other countries.

current account Record of a country's export and import of goods and services.

now supplying the US market from production facilities in the United States, as opposed to facilities in Japan. Insofar as this has reduced the need to finance a current account deficit by asset sales to foreigners, the United States has benefited. A second potential benefit arises when the MNE uses a foreign subsidiary to export goods and services to other countries.

Host Country Effects: Costs

Three main costs of inward FDI concern host countries: the possible adverse effects of FDI on competition within the host nation, adverse effects on the balance of payments, and the perceived loss of national sovereignty and autonomy.

ADVERSE EFFECTS ON COMPETITION   Host governments sometimes worry that the subsidiaries of foreign MNEs operating in their country may have greater economic power than indigenous competitors because they may be part of a larger international organization. As such, the foreign MNE may be able to draw on funds generated elsewhere to subsidize its costs in the host market, which could drive indigenous companies out of business and allow the firm to monopolize the market. Once the market was monopolized, the foreign MNE could raise prices above those that would prevail in competitive markets, with harmful effects on the economic welfare of the host nation. This concern tends to be greater in countries that have few large firms of their own that can compete with the subsidiaries of foreign MNEs (generally less developed countries). It is a relatively minor concern in most advanced industrialized nations.

Another variant of the competition argument is related to the infant industry concern we discussed in Chapter 5. Import controls may be motivated by a desire to let a local industry develop to a stage where it is capable of competing in world markets. The same logic suggests that FDI should be restricted. If a country with a potential comparative advantage in a particular industry allows FDI in that industry, indigenous firms may never have a chance to develop.

The above arguments are often used by inefficient indigenous competitors when lobbying their government to restrict direct investment by foreign MNEs. Although a host government may state publicly in such cases that its restrictions on inward FDI are designed to protect indigenous competitors from the market power of foreign MNEs, they may have been enacted to protect inefficient but politically powerful indigenous competitors from foreign competition.

ADVERSE EFFECTS ON THE BALANCE OF PAYMENTS   The possible adverse effects of FDI on a host country's balance-of-payments position are twofold. First, set against the initial capital inflow that comes with FDI must be the subsequent outflow of income as the foreign subsidiary repatriates earnings to its parent company. Such outflows show up as a debit on the current account of the balance of payments. A second concern arises when a foreign subsidiary imports a substantial number of its inputs from abroad, which also results in a debit on the current account of the host country's balance of payments. One criticism leveled against Japanese-owned auto assembly operations in the United States, for example, was that they imported many component parts from Japan, reducing the favorable impact of this FDI on the current account of the US balance-of-payments position. The Japanese auto companies responded by pledging to purchase 75 percent of their component parts from US-based manufacturers (but not necessarily US-owned manufacturers).

NATIONAL SOVEREIGNTY AND AUTONOMY   Many host governments worry that FDI is accompanied by some loss of economic independence. Key decisions that can affect the host country's economy will be made by a foreign parent that has no real commitment to the host country, and over which the host country's government has no real control. Thirty years ago this concern was expressed by several European countries, who feared that FDI by US MNEs was threatening their national

sovereignty. The same concerns are now surfacing in the United States with regard to European and Japanese FDI. The main fear seems to be that if foreigners own assets in the United States, they can somehow "hold the country to economic ransom." Thirty years ago when officials in the French government were making similar complaints about US investments in France, many US politicians dismissed the charge as silly. Now that the shoe is on the other foot, many US politicians no longer think the notion is silly. However, most economists dismiss such concerns as groundless and irrational. Political scientist Robert Reich spoke of such concerns as the product of outmoded thinking, because they fail to account for the growing interdependence of the world economy.[29] In a world where firms from all advanced nations are increasingly investing in each other's markets, it is not possible for one country to hold another to "economic ransom" without hurting itself.

Home Country Effects: Benefits

Although the cost and benefits of FDI for a host country have received the most attention, there are also costs and benefits to the home (or source) country. Does the US economy benefit or lose from investments by its firms in foreign markets? Does the Swedish economy lose or gain from Electrolux's investment in other nations? Some would argue that FDI is not always in the home country's national interest and should be restricted. Others argue that the benefits far outweigh the costs and that any restrictions would be contrary to national interests. To understand why people take these positions, let us look at the benefits and costs of FDI to the home (source) country.[30]

The benefits of FDI to the home country arise from three sources. First, the current account of the home country's balance-of-payments benefits from the inward flow of foreign earnings. Thus, one benefit to Sweden from Electrolux's investment in other nations are the earnings that are repatriated to Sweden from those countries. FDI can also improve the current account of the home country's balance of payments if the foreign subsidiary creates demands for home country exports of capital equipment, intermediate goods, complementary products, and the like.

Second, benefits to the home country from outward FDI arise from employment effects. As with the balance of payments, positive employment effects arise when the foreign subsidiary creates demand for home country exports of capital equipment, intermediate goods, complementary products, and so on. Thus, Electrolux's investment in foreign manufacturing plants can benefit both the Swedish balance-of-payments position and employment in Sweden, if Electrolux imported some component parts for its foreign plants directly from Sweden.

Third, benefits arise when the home country MNE learns valuable skills from its exposure to foreign markets that can be transferred back to the home country. This amounts to a reverse resource-transfer effect. Through its exposure to a

When a US textile company shuts down its plants and moves production to Mexico, as many have, imports into the United States rise and the trade position deteriorates. One objection raised by US labor leaders to the NAFTA free trade pact between the United States, Mexico, and Canada is that the United States will lose hundreds of thousands of jobs as US firms invest in Mexico to take advantage of cheaper labor and then export back to the US market.
© Corbis. All rights reserved.

foreign market, an MNE can learn about superior management techniques and superior product and process technologies. These resources can then be transferred back to the home country, with a commensurate beneficial effect on the home country's economic growth rate.[31] For example, one reason General Motors and Ford invested in Japanese automobile companies (GM owns part of Isuzu, and Ford owns part of Mazda) was to learn about those Japanese companies' apparently superior management techniques and production processes. If GM and Ford can transfer this know-how back to their US operations, the result may be a net gain for the US economy.

Home Country Effects: Costs

Against these benefits must be set the apparent costs of FDI for the home (source) country. The most important concerns center around the balance-of-payments and employment effects of outward FDI. The home country's trade position (its current account) may deteriorate if the purpose of the foreign investment is to serve the home market from a low-cost production location. For example, when a US textile company shuts its plants in South Carolina and moves production to Central America, imports into the US rise and the trade position deteriorates. The current account of the balance of payments also suffers if the FDI is a substitute for direct exports. Thus, insofar as Toyota's assembly operations in the United States are intended to substitute for direct exports from Japan, the current account position of Japan will deteriorate.

The most serious concerns about employment arise when FDI is seen as a substitute for domestic production. If the labor market in the home country is already very tight, this concern may not be that great. However, if the home country is suffering from unemployment, concern about the "export of jobs" may rise to the fore. For example, one objection frequently raised by US labor leaders to the North American Free Trade Agreement between the United States, Mexico, and Canada (see next chapter) is that the United States will lose hundreds of thousands of jobs as US firms invest in Mexico to take advantage of cheaper labor and then export back to the US market.[32]

International Trade Theory and Offshore Production

When assessing the costs and benefits of FDI to the home country, keep in mind the lessons of international trade theory (see Chapter 4). International trade theory tells us that home country concerns about the negative economic effects of offshore production may be misplaced. The term *offshore production* refers to FDI undertaken to serve the home market. Far from reducing home country employment, such FDI may actually stimulate economic growth (and hence employment) in the home country by freeing up home country resources to concentrate on activities where the home country has a comparative advantage. Also, home country consumers benefit if the price of a product falls as a result of the FDI.

If a company were prohibited from making such investments on the grounds of negative employment effects but its international competitors were able to reap the benefits of low-cost production, the company would undoubtedly lose market share to its international competitors. Under such a scenario, the adverse long-run economic effects for the domestic economy would probably far outweigh the relatively minor balance-of-payments and employment effects associated with offshore production.

Government Policy Instruments and FDI

We have now reviewed the costs and benefits of FDI from the perspective of both home country and host country. Before tackling the important issue of bargaining between the MNE and the host government, we need to discuss the policy instruments that governments use to regulate FDI activity by MNEs. Both home (source) countries and host countries have a range of policy instruments that they can use.

Home Country Policies

By their choice of policies, home countries can both encourage and restrict FDI by local firms. We look at policies designed to encourage outward FDI first. These include foreign risk insurance, capital assistance, tax incentives, and political pressure. Then we will look at policies designed to restrict outward FDI.

ENCOURAGING OUTWARD FDI Many investor nations now have government-backed insurance programs to cover major types of foreign investment risk. The types of risks insurable through these programs include the risks of expropriation (nationalization), war losses, and the inability to transfer profits back home. Such programs are particularly useful in encouraging firms to undertake investments in politically unstable countries.[33] In addition, several advanced countries also have special funds or banks that make government loans to firms wishing to invest in developing countries. As a further incentive to encourage domestic firms to undertake FDI, many countries have eliminated double taxation of foreign income (i.e., taxation of income in both the host country and the home country). Last, and perhaps most significant, a number of investor countries (particularly the United States) have used their political influence to persuade host countries to relax their restrictions on inbound FDI. For example, in response to direct US pressure, Japan relaxed many of its formal restrictions on inward FDI in the early 1980s. Now, in response to further US pressure, Japan is relaxing its informal barriers to inward FDI. One beneficiary of this trend has been Toys R Us, which, after five years of intensive lobbying by the company and US government officials, opened its first retail stores in Japan in December 1991. By the end of 1997 Toys R Us had 51 stores in Japan.

RESTRICTING OUTWARD FDI Virtually all investor countries, including the United States, have exercised some control over outward FDI from time to time. One common policy has been to limit capital outflows out of concern for the country's balance of payments. From the early 1960s until 1979, for example, Britain had exchange-control regulations that limited the amount of capital a firm could take out of the country. Although the main intent was to improve the British balance of payments, an important secondary intent was to make it more difficult for British firms to undertake FDI.

In addition, countries have manipulated tax rules to encourage their firms to invest at home. The objective behind such policies is to create jobs at home rather than in other nations. At one time the British taxed companies' foreign earnings at a higher rate than their domestic earnings, creating an incentive for British companies to invest at home.

Finally, countries sometimes prohibit national firms from investing in certain countries for political reasons. Such restrictions can be formal or informal. For example, formal rules have prohibited US firms from investing in countries such as Cuba,

Libya, and Iran, whose political ideology and actions are judged to be contrary to US interests. Similarly, during the 1980s informal pressure was applied to dissuade US firms from investing in South Africa. In this case, the objective was to put pressure on South Africa to change its apartheid laws, which occurred during the early 1990s. Thus, this policy was successful.

Host Country Policies

Host countries adopt policies designed both to restrict and to encourage inward FDI. As noted earlier in this chapter, political ideology has determined the type and scope of these policies in the past. Now we seem to be moving quickly away from widespread adherence to some version of the radical stance that prohibited much FDI and toward a combination of free market objectives and pragmatic nationalism.

ENCOURAGING INWARD FDI It is increasingly common for governments to offer incentives to foreign firms to invest in their countries. Such incentives take many forms, but the most common are tax concessions, low-interest loans, and grants or subsidies. Incentives are motivated by a desire to gain from the resource-transfer and employment effects of FDI. They are also motivated by a desire to capture FDI away from other potential host countries. Not only do countries compete with each other to attract FDI, but so do regions of countries. In the United States, state governments often compete with each other to attract FDI. It has been estimated that Kentucky offered Toyota a $112 million incentive package to persuade the company to build its US automobile assembly plant in the state. The package included tax breaks, new state spending on infrastructure, and low-interest loans.[34]

RESTRICTING INWARD FDI Host governments use a range of controls to restrict FDI. The two most common are ownership restraints and performance requirements. Ownership restraints can take several forms. In some countries foreign companies are excluded from specific businesses. For example, they are excluded from tobacco and mining in Sweden and from the development of certain natural resources in Brazil, Finland, and Morocco. In other industries, foreign ownership may be permitted, although local investors may be required to own a significant proportion of the equity of the foreign MNE's subsidiary. For example, foreign ownership is restricted to 25 percent or less of an airline in the United States.

The rationale underlying ownership restraints seems to be twofold. First, foreign firms are often excluded from certain sectors on the grounds of national security or competition. Particularly in less developed countries, the feeling seems to be that local firms might not be able to develop unless foreign competition is restricted by a combination of import tariffs and controls on FDI. This is really a variant of the infant industry argument discussed in Chapter 5.

Second, ownership restraints seem to be based on a belief that local owners can help to maximize the resource-transfer and employment benefits of FDI for the host country. Until the early 1980s the Japanese government prohibited most FDI but was prepared to allow joint ventures between Japanese firms and foreign MNEs if the MNE had a particularly valuable technology. The Japanese government clearly felt that such an arrangement would help speed up the subsequent diffusion of the MNE's valuable technology throughout the Japanese economy.

Performance requirements also can take several forms. Performance requirements are controls over the behavior of the local subsidiary. The most common performance requirements are related to local content, exports, technology transfer, and local participation in top management. As with certain ownership restrictions, the logic underlying performance requirements is that such rules help to maximize the benefits and minimize the costs of FDI for the host country. Virtually all countries employ some form of performance requirement when it suits their objectives. However, performance requirements tend to be more common in less developed countries than in advanced industrialized nations. For example, one study found that some 30 percent of the affiliates of US MNEs in less developed countries were subject to performance requirements, while only 6 percent of the affiliates in advanced countries were faced with such requirements.[35]

International Institutions and the Liberalization of FDI

Until recently there had been no consistent involvement by multinational institutions in the governing of FDI. With the formation of the World Trade Organization in 1995, this is now changing rapidly. As noted in Chapter 5, relative to the GATT, the role of the WTO has been expanded to embrace the promotion of international trade in services. By their very nature, many services have to be produced where they are sold, so exporting is not an option (for example, one cannot export McDonald's hamburgers or consumer banking services). Given this, the WTO has become involved in regulations governing FDI. As might be expected for an institution created to promote free trade, the thrust of the WTO's efforts has been to push for the liberalization of regulations governing FDI, particularly in services. Under the auspices of the WTO, in 1997 two extensive multinational agreements were reached to liberalize trade in telecommunications and financial services. Both of these agreements contained detailed clauses that require signatories to liberalize their regulations governing inward FDI, essentially opening their markets to foreign telecommunications and financial services companies.

However, the WTO has had less success at trying to initiate talks aimed at establishing a universal set of rules designed to promote the liberalization of FDI. Led by Malaysia and India, developing nations have so far rejected any attempts by the WTO to start such discussions. In an attempt to make some progress on this issue, in 1995 the **Organization for Economic Cooperation and Development (OECD)** initiated talks between its members. (The OECD is a Paris-based intergovernmental organization of "wealthy" nations whose purpose is to provide its 29 member states with a forum in which governments can compare their experiences, discuss the problems they share, and seek solutions that can be applied within their own national contexts. The members include most European Union countries, the United States, Canada, Japan, and South Korea). The aim of the talks was to draft a **Multilateral Agreement on Investment (MAI)** that would make it illegal for signatory states to discriminate against foreign investors, thus liberalizing rules governing FDI between OECD states. The talks broke down in early 1998, primarily because the United States refused to sign the agreement. According to the United States, the proposed agreement contained too many exceptions that would weaken the pact's powers. For example, the proposed agreement would not have barred discriminatory taxation of foreign-owned companies, and it would have allowed countries to restrict foreign television programs and music in the name of preserving culture. Also campaigning against the MAI were environmental and labor groups, who criticized the proposed agreement on the grounds that it contained no binding environmental or labor agreements. Despite these problems, however, negotiations on a revised MAI treaty likely will restart soon.[36]

Organization for Economic Cooperation and Development (OECD) A Paris-based intergovernmental organization of "wealthy" nations whose purpose is to provide its 29 member states with a forum in which governments can compare their experiences, discuss the problems they share, and seek solutions that can be applied within their own national contexts.

Multilateral Agreement on Investment (MAI) Agreement that would make it illegal for signatory states to discriminate against foreign investors.

Implications for Business

Several implications for business are inherent in the material discussed in this chapter. We deal first with the implications of the theory, and then turn our attention to the implications of government policy.

The Theory of FDI

The implications of the theories of FDI for business practice are straightforward. First, the location-specific advantages argument associated with John Dunning does help explain the *direction* of FDI. However, the location-specific advantages argument does not explain *why* firms prefer FDI to licensing or to exporting. From both an explanatory and a business perspective, perhaps the most useful theories are those that focus on the limitations of exporting and licensing. These theories are useful because they identify how the relative profitability of foreign direct investment, exporting, and licensing vary with circumstances. The theories suggest that exporting is preferable to licensing and foreign direct investment as long as transport costs are minor and trade barriers are trivial. As transport costs and/or trade barriers increase, exporting becomes unprofitable, and the choice is between FDI and licensing. Because FDI is more costly and more risky than licensing, other things being equal, the theories argue that licensing is preferable to FDI. Other things are seldom equal, however. Although licensing may work, it is not attractive when one or more of the following conditions exist: (*a*) the firm has valuable know-how that cannot be adequately protected by a licensing contract, (*b*) the firm needs tight control over a foreign entity to maximize its market share and earnings in that country, and (*c*) a firm's skills and capabilities are not amenable to licensing. Figure 6.5 presents these considerations as a decision tree.

Firms for which licensing is not a good option tend to be clustered in three types of industries:

1 High-technology industries where protecting firm-specific expertise is of paramount importance and licensing is hazardous.

2 Global oligopolies, where competitive interdependence requires that multinational firms maintain tight control over foreign operations so they have the ability to launch coordinated attacks against their global competitors (as Kodak has done with Fuji).

3 Industries where intense cost pressures require that multinational firms maintain tight control over foreign operations (so they can disperse manufacturing to locations around the globe where factor costs are most favorable in order to minimize costs).

Although empirical evidence is limited, the majority seems to support these conjectures.[37]

Firms for which licensing is a good option tend to be in industries whose conditions are opposite to those specified above. Licensing tends to be more common (and more profitable) in fragmented, low-technology industries in which globally dispersed manufacturing is not an option. A good example is the fast food industry.

By using a **franchising** strategy, McDonald's has expanded globally, but can continue to guarantee (relatively) that a Big Mac anywhere in Asia is the same as a Big Mac in the United States.
© Ric Ergenbright/CORBIS.

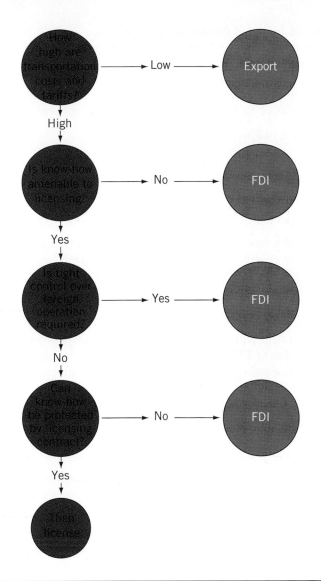

Figure 6.5

A Decision Framework

McDonald's has expanded globally by using a franchising strategy. Franchising is essentially the service industry version of licensing—although it normally involves much longer-term commitments than licensing. With franchising, the firm licenses its brand name to a foreign firm in return for a percentage of the franchisee's profits. The franchising contract specifies the conditions that the franchisee must fulfill if it is to use the franchisor's brand name. Thus, McDonald's allows foreign firms to use its brand name as long as they agree to run their restaurants on exactly the same lines as McDonald's restaurants elsewhere in the world. This strategy makes sense for McDonald's because (*a*) like many services, fast food cannot be exported; (*b*) franchising economizes the costs and risks associated with opening foreign markets; (*c*) unlike technological know-how, brand names are relatively easy to protect using a contract, (*d*) there is no compelling reason for McDonald's to have tight control over franchisees; and (*e*) McDonald's know-how, in terms of how to run a fast food restaurant, is amenable to being specified in a written contract (e.g., the contract specifies the details of how to run a McDonald's restaurant).

Finally, it should be noted that the product life-cycle theory and Knickerbocker's theory of FDI tend to be less useful from a business perspective because they are descriptive rather than analytical. They do a good job of describing the historical evolution of FDI, but they do a relatively poor job of identifying the factors that influence the relative profitability of FDI, licensing, and exporting. The issue of licensing as an alternative to FDI is ignored by both these theories.

Government Policy

A host government's attitude toward FDI should be an important variable in decisions about where to locate foreign production facilities and where to make a foreign direct investment. Other things being equal, investing in countries that have permissive policies toward FDI is clearly preferable to investing in countries that restrict FDI.

However, often the issue is not this straightforward. Despite the move toward a free market stance in recent years, many countries still have a rather pragmatic view toward FDI. In such cases, a firm considering FDI must often negotiate the specific terms of the investment with the country's government. Such negotiations center on two broad issues. If the host government is trying to attract FDI, the central issue is likely to be the kind of incentives the host government is prepared to offer to the MNE and what the firm will commit in exchange. If the host government is uncertain about the benefits of FDI and might choose to restrict access, the central issue is likely to be the concessions the firm must make to be allowed to go forward with a proposed investment.

The outcome of any negotiated agreement depends to a large degree on the relative bargaining power of both parties. Each side's bargaining power depends on three factors:

- The value each side places on what the other has to offer.
- The number of comparable alternatives available to each side.
- Each party's time horizon.

From the perspective of a firm negotiating the terms of an investment with a host government, the firm's bargaining power is high when the host government places a high value on what the firm has to offer, the number of comparable alternatives open to the firm is greater, and the firm has a long time in which to complete the negotiations. The converse also holds. The firm's bargaining power is low when the host government places a low value on what the firm has to offer, the number of comparable alternatives open to the firm is fewer, and the firm has a short time in which to complete the negotiations.[38]

Key Terms

Summary

The objectives of this chapter were to review theories that attempt to explain the pattern of FDI between countries and to examine governmental influence on firms' decisions to invest in foreign countries. The following points have been made:

1 Any theory seeking to explain FDI must explain why firms go to the trouble of acquiring or establishing operations abroad, when exporting and licensing are available to them.

2 High transportation costs and/or tariffs imposed on imports help explain why many firms prefer FDI or licensing over exporting.

3 Firms often prefer FDI to licensing when (*i*) a firm has valuable know-how that cannot be adequately protected by a licensing contract, (*ii*) a firm needs tight control over a foreign entity to maximize its market share and earnings in that country, and (*iii*) a firm's skills and capabilities are not amenable to licensing.

4 Knickerbocker's theory suggests that much FDI is explained by imitative behavior by rival firms in an oligopolistic industry.

5 Vernon's product life-cycle theory suggests that firms undertake FDI at particular stages in the life cycle of products they have pioneered. However, Vernon's theory does not address the issue of whether FDI is more efficient than exporting or licensing for expanding abroad.

6 Dunning has argued that location-specific advantages are of considerable importance in explaining the nature and direction of FDI. According to Dunning, firms undertake FDI to exploit resource endowments or assets that are location-specific.

7 Political ideology is an important determinant of government policy toward FDI. Ideology ranges from a radical stance that is hostile to FDI to a noninterventionist, free market stance. Between the two extremes is an approach best described as pragmatic nationalism.

8 Benefits of FDI to a host country arise from resource-transfer effects, employment effects, and balance-of-payments effects.

9 The costs of FDI to a host country include adverse effects on competition and balance of payments and a perceived loss of national sovereignty.

10 The benefits of FDI to the home (source) country include improvement in the balance of payments as a result of the inward flow of foreign earnings, positive employment effects when the foreign subsidiary creates demand for home country exports, and benefits from a reverse resource-transfer effect. A reverse resource-transfer effect arises when the foreign subsidiary learns valuable skills abroad that can be transferred back to the home country.

11 The costs of FDI to the home country include adverse balance-of-payments effects that arise from the initial capital outflow and from the export substitution effects of FDI. Costs also arise when FDI exports jobs abroad.

12 Home countries can adopt policies designed to both encourage and restrict FDI. Host countries try to attract FDI by offering incentives and try to restrict FDI by dictating ownership restraints and requiring that foreign MNEs meet specific performance requirements.

Critical Thinking and Discussion Questions

1 In recent years Japanese FDI in the United States has grown far more rapidly than US FDI in Japan. Why do you think this is the case? What are the implications of this trend?

2 Compare these explanations of FDI: internalization theory, Vernon's product life-cycle theory, and

Knickerbocker's theory of FDI. Which theory do you think offers the best explanation of the historical pattern of FDI? Why?

3 You are the international manager of a US business that has just developed a revolutionary new personal computer that can perform the same functions as IBM and Apple computers and their clones but costs only half as much to manufacture. Your CEO has asked you to formulate a recommendation for how to expand into the Western European market. Your options are (*i*) to export from the United States, (*ii*) to license a European firm to manufacture and market the computer in Europe, and (*iii*) to set up a wholly owned subsidiary in Europe. Evaluate the pros and cons of each alternative and suggest a course of action to your CEO.

4 Explain how the political ideology of a host government might influence the process of negotiating access between the host government and a foreign MNE.

Internet Exercises

1 Walt Disney Company, the quintessential example of Americana, is expending its reach again. The company's efforts to bring the Magic Kingdom to foreign markets is well known, from its success story in Tokyo to its struggle for acceptance in France. Disney's most recent investment will be in Hong Kong. Government officials in Hong Kong think that Mickey Mouse and his friends will bring the magic needed to pull the economy out of its slump. The government has gone to great lengths to make the investment attractive to Disney.

Hong Kong is providing $2.83 billion in equity financing, low-interest rate loans, and public works spending to assist in the $4 billion project (*The Wall Street Journal,* November 4, 1999, p. A26). The local government expects its payoff to come in the form of jobs. Some 16,000 jobs will be created as the park is built, and another 18,400 jobs are expected to be created once the park is running. Controversy surrounds the Hong Kong deal. Some experts suggest the government has overstepped its bounds and argue that the financing assistance amounts to a payout of about $100,000 for every job that is created once the park is open (*The Wall Street Journal,* November 4, 1999, p. A26). Others believe the price is worthwhile given the expected influx of visitors to the city.

Governments frequently provide assistance, similar to the Disney deal, to foreign companies in an effort to attract foreign investment. Go to **www.business.gov.hk/english/index.htm** and consider the position of the Hong Kong government with regard to foreign investment. In your opinion, should governments sponsor foreign investment? Should governments solicit, via the Internet, new investment? How does a deal like the Disney agreement affect the relationship between a government and local corporations? Does the fact that Disney provides a unique product/service affect your opinion? As the manager of a local company that will provide services to Disney, what does the Hong Kong deal mean to you?

2 China is considered to be one of the hottest markets in the world. Its vast number of consumers are a magnet to firms from around the globe. The country's recent deal to join the World Trade Organization (WTO) is expected to increase the attraction. One area that shows tremendous promise involves Web ventures. Prior to the deal with the WTO, foreign ownership of Internet companies had been restricted, however, with the agreement the ban has been lifted, sparking interest from would-be investors. E-commerce has proved to be an especially propitious segment in the Chinese business environment. Not only is electronic commerce free of the traditional bureaucracy that makes doing business so difficult in the state-dominated market, but Beijing is also actively promoting Internet usage. Currently, over 4 million Chinese are on-line, and within 10 years the Chinese market is expected to have some 85 million users.

Even without the WTO deal and its effect on the ban on foreign ownership of Internet companies, hundreds of Chinese firms have been active in establishing on-line opportunities. With the WTO deal, these companies and others have the potential for investments that should allow the firms to build market share more quickly. Many American companies are linking with Chinese partners to caputre on-line market share in the country, but these companies may find that their task is challenging in the new business environment. Go to **www.meetchina.com** and to **www.chinainfornet.com**. Discuss the options available to American Internet companies interested in expanding into the Chinese market. How can a company develop an on-line presence in the new China? Some experts are concerned that politically motivated restrictions could limit the activities of foreign companies. As the head of global expansion for eBay, would you wait or jump into the market today? How does on-line international expansion strategy differ from traditional bricks-and-mortar investments into new markets?

Source: *Beacon Journal,* November 18, 1999, p. D1.

FDI in Russia

Five years after the launch of economic reforms designed to transform Russia's lumbering state-directed economy into a modern market system, Russia was experiencing unprecedented capital flight. In 1996 some $22.3 billion left the country, most of it illegally. In contrast, a mere $2.2 billion in foreign investment flowed into the country. According to data from the European Bank for Reconstruction and Development, between 1989 and 1996 foreigners invested just $5.3 billion in Russia, compared to foreign investment of about $11.5 billion in much smaller former Communist state, Hungary.

One reason for this is that Russia consistently tops the charts as the riskiest investment destination tracked by the Economist Intelligence Unit. The risks include a complex tax code that is always changing and randomly enforced, often at the expense of foreign companies. Weak and untested property and contract safeguards, endless regulations often enforced by bureaucrats, and a playing field made uneven by trading and tax favors granted by the Russian government to Russian companies are also frequently cited as contributing to the high risks associated with investment in Russia.

Russia's privatization laws have also tended to discriminate against foreign investors. Most privatization schemes in Russia favor incumbent management and/or local companies. For an example, a "shares for loans" scheme in 1995 saw a dozen large companies sold for a fraction of their market value to several large Moscow banks. Foreign investors were not given an opportunity to bid on these assets. Similarly, the privatization of several large-scale companies has seen the majority of stock sold to incumbent managers and employees for a fraction of the price the stock could fetch on the open market.

The failure of the Russian government to capitalize on the sale of state-owned assets is self-defeating given that the country is in desperate need of capital resources to upgrade its crumbling infrastructure, which is suffering from years of neglect and mismanagement under communism. The Russian oil and gas industry is an example. Russia has the largest oil and gas reserves in the world, but it is finding it difficult to get these reserves out of the ground and to the international market. Russian oil output plummeted after the collapse of the Soviet Union, from 569 million tons in 1988 to 305 million tons in 1996. The problems include leaking pipelines, aging oil wells, a lack of new drilling, and conflict between the various states of the former Soviet Union as to who actually owns much of the oil and gas infrastructure. According to estimates by the World Bank, Russia needs to spend between $40 billion and $50 billion per year just to maintain oil and gas production at current levels. Boosting production back to the levels achieved in the 1980s could require investments of $80 billion to $100 billion per year—money that Russia does not have.

In an attempt to reverse this slide, in November 1997 the government of Boris Yeltsin announced that Russia's oil and gas industries would be open to foreign investment. The decree signed by Yeltsin allowed foreign investors to buy 100 percent of Russian oil companies. Within days, Royal Dutch/Shell had teamed up with Gazprom, Russia's giant gas monopoly, to bid for Rosneft, the last big state-owned oil group to be privatized. This was quickly followed by a deal under which British Petroleum announced that it would purchase 10 percent of another Russian company, Sidanco, giving it a stake in a huge oil field near the Chinese border. The benefits that flow to Russia from such investments could be substantial. In a report prepared for the Russian parliament, Western oil companies said foreign development of just six identified oil and gas fields could create more than 550,000 jobs and earn about $450 billion over their operating lives.

However, before they are prepared to make further large-scale investments, many Western companies say they need stronger legal and tax guarantees. Their preferred method of operation would be to sign internationally recognizable production sharing agreements, which leave the ownership of natural resources with the state, but allow foreign developers a defined share of future revenues. Although the Russian government has tried to enact such legislation, the Communist-dominated parliament has resisted any attempt to pass such laws.[39]

CASE DISCUSSION QUESTIONS

1 What are the benefits to the Russian economy from foreign direct investment in general and in the oil industry in particular?

2 What are the risks that foreign companies must bear when making investments in Russia? What is the source of these risks? How substantial are they?

3 Is there any way foreign companies can reduce these risks?

seven

Regional Economic Integration

Opening Case Consolidation in the European Insurance Market

Between 1996 and 1998 a wave of mergers swept through the insurance industry in the European Union. The mergers were the results of a process begun January 1, 1993, when the Single European Act became law among the member states of the European Union. The goal of the Single European Act was to remove barriers to cross-border trade and investment within the confines of the EU, creating a single market instead of a collection of distinct national markets.

The euro—the common currency for the EU member states—will replace all the different currencies across the European Union in January 2002 (more about the euro in the next chapter). For the insurance industry, the coming of the euro helps consumers to compare insurance products offered by companies in different EU states.

Learning Objectives

1 Appreciate all the possible different levels of economic integration between nations.

2 Understand the economic and political arguments for regional economic integration.

3 Understand the economic and political arguments against regional economic integration.

4 Be familiar with the history, current scope, and future prospects of the world's most important regional economic agreements including the European Union, the North American Free Trade Agreement, MERCOSUR, and Asia-Pacific Economic Cooperation.

5 Understand the implications for business that are inherent in regional economic integration agreements.

Under the act, the EU insurance industry was deregulated and liberalized in mid-1994. Before that, there had been wide variations in competitive conditions, regulations, and prices among the national insurance markets. For example, in early 1994 a simple 10-year life insurance policy in Portugal cost three times more than the same policy in France, while automobile insurance for an experienced driver cost twice as much in Ireland as in Italy and four times as much as in Britain. The new rules did

two main things. First, they made genuine cross-border trade possible by allowing insurance companies to sell their products anywhere in the EU on the basis of regulations in their home states, the so-called single license. Second, insurers throughout the EU were allowed to set their own rates for all classes of insurance policy. They no longer needed to submit policy wordings to local officials for approval, thereby dismantling the highly regulated regime behind which much of the industry had

sheltered. Among the expected outcomes of these changes were an increase in competition and downward pressure on prices.

By mid-1997 it looked as if the move toward a single market in the EU was going to be given a further push by the impending adoption of a common currency, the euro, among a majority of the EU's member states. On January 1, 1999, 11 of the EU's 15 member states were scheduled to lock in their currency exchange rates against each other and begin handing over responsibility for monetary policy to the newly created European Central Bank. The second stage will occur January 1, 2002, when the currencies of the participating states will be formally abolished and replaced by a common monetary unit, the euro. The euro will make it much easier for consumers to compare the insurance products offered by companies based in different EU states. This also should increase competition and place a downward pressure on prices.

The initial response to these changes in the competitive environment was muted. However, by mid-1996 insurance companies were realizing that they needed to reposition themselves to compete more effectively in a single market dominated by one currency. This repositioning resulted in a wave of mergers within nations as firms tried to attain the scale economies necessary to compete on a larger European playing field. In 1996 Axa and UAP, two French insurance companies, merged to create the largest European insurance company. As part of the deal, Axa gained control over several subsidiary

companies that UAP had acquired in Germany in 1994, allowing Axa to increase its presence in this important market. Two large British insurance companies, Royal Insurance and Sun Alliance, also joined forces in 1996.

This was followed in 1997 and early 1998 by a number of cross-border mergers, the most notable of which was between Germany's Allianz and AGF, a large French insurance company. The merger between Allianz and AGF was prompted by a takeover bid for AGF launched by the large Italian insurance company Generali. Generali wanted to acquire AGF to expand its presence in France. The bid spurred Allianz into action. Allianz, which dominated the German insurance market, had been feeling threatened by increased competition in its home market arising in part from a merger between Munich-based Hamburg–Mannheimer and Britain's Victoria Insurance and in part from the increased strength of the Axa–UAP combination. Displaying a sensitivity for French sentiments that Generali lacked, Allianz promised that AGF's management would remain French and that Allianz executives would be

in the minority on the board of the merged company. Unwilling to make such concessions, Generali withdrew its counterbid for AGF, but not before it had won significant concessions from Allianz and AGF. In return for Generali withdrawing its bid, the German and French companies agreed to sell several important subsidiaries to the Italian insurer, boosting Generali's premiums by more than half and giving it a sizable presence in both Germany and Italy.

As a result of these developments, by mid-1998 the shape of the EU insurance industry had been substantially altered. Allianz had emerged as the largest pan-European insurer with $64 billion in total premium income. In addition to its leading position in Germany, Allianz had become one of the top five insurers in Belgium, Spain, and France. The Axa–UAP combination had become the second-largest European insurer with significant activities in France and Germany, while Italy's Generali with premium income of $31 billion was now the third-largest pan-European insurance company.[1]

Introduction

regional economic integration Agreement between countries in a geographic region to reduce tariff and nontariff barriers to the free flow of goods, services, and factors of production between each other.

One notable trend in the global economy in recent years has been the accelerated movement toward regional economic integration. By **regional economic integration** we mean agreements among countries in a geographic region to reduce, and ultimately remove, tariff and nontariff barriers to the free flow of goods, services, and factors of production between each other. The last decade has witnessed an unprecedented proliferation of regional arrangements. Between 1948 and 1994, 108 regional trade agreements were notified to the GATT or its successor, the WTO; 38 were in the five years ending in 1994. Since creation of the WTO in 1995, 67 additional regional trade agreements have been reached, some pertaining to trade in services. Out of the total of 175 regional trade agreements notified to the GATT/WTO since 1948, 107 were in force as of mid-1999. Over three-quarters of the operational regional agreements in existence today were established between 1992 and 1999.[2]

Consistent with the predictions of international trade theory, particularly the theory of comparative advantage (see Chapter 4), the belief has been that agreements designed to promote freer trade within regions will produce nontrivial gains from trade for all member countries. As we saw in Chapter 5, the GATT and its successor, the WTO, also seek to reduce trade barriers. However, with close to 130 member states the WTO has a worldwide perspective. By entering into regional agreements, groups of countries aim to reduce trade barriers more rapidly than can be achieved under the WTO.

Nowhere has the movement toward regional economic integration been more successful than in Europe. As noted in the opening case, on January 1, 1993, the European Union effectively became a single market with 340 million consumers. Nor does the EU intend to stop there. The member states of the EU are introducing a single currency, they are moving toward a closer political union, and they are discussing enlargement of the EU from the current 15 countries to ultimately include another 15 Eastern European states. Similar moves toward region integration are being pursued elsewhere in the world. Canada, Mexico, and the United States have implemented the North American Free Trade Agreement (NAFTA). This promises to remove all barriers to the free flow of goods and services between the three countries. Argentina, Brazil, Paraguay, and Uruguay have implemented a 1991 agreement to start reducing barriers to trade between themselves. Known as MERCOSUR, this free trade area is viewed by some as the first step in a move toward creation of a South American Free Trade Area (SAFTA). There is also talk of establishing a hemispherewide Free Trade Agreement of the Americas (FTAA). Along similar lines, 18 Pacific Rim countries, including the NAFTA member states, Japan, and China, have been discussing the creation of a pan-Pacific free trade area under the auspices of the Asia-Pacific Economic Cooperation forum (APEC). There are also active attempts at regional economic integration to be found in Central America, the Andean Region of South America, Southeast Asia, and parts of Africa.

As the opening case on the European insurance industry demonstrates, a move toward greater regional economic integration can deliver important benefits to consumers and present firms with new challenges. In the European insurance industry, the creation of a single EU insurance market is opening protected national markets to increased competition, resulting in lower prices for insurance products. This benefits consumers, who now have more money to spend on other goods and services. The increase in competition and price pressure that has followed the creation of a single market has forced insurance companies to look for cost savings from economies of scale. Companies have also sought to increase their presence in different nations. The mergers occurring in the European insurance industry are seen as a way of achieving both these goals.

The rapid spread of regional trade agreements designed to promote free trade raises the fear among some of a world in which a number of regional trade blocs compete against each other. In this scenario, free trade would exist within each bloc, but each bloc would protect its market from outside competition with high tariffs. The specter of the EU and NAFTA turning into "economic fortresses" that shut out foreign producers through high tariff barriers is particularly worrisome to those who believe in unrestricted free trade. If such a scenario were to materialize, the resulting decline in trade between blocs could more than offset the gains from free trade within blocs.

The main objectives of this chapter are: (1) to explore the economic and political debate surrounding regional economic integration. In doing this we will pay particular attention to the economic and political benefits and costs of integration, (2) to review progress toward regional economic integration around the world, and (3) to map the important implications of regional economic integration for the practice of international business. Before tackling these objectives, however, we first need to examine the levels of integration that are theoretically possible.

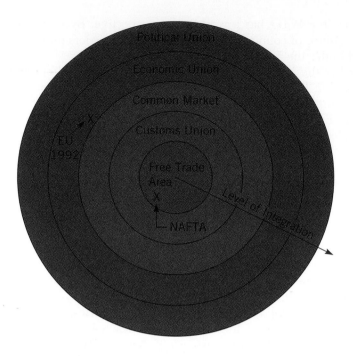

Figure 7.1

Levels of Economic Integration

Levels of Economic Integration

Several levels of economic integration are possible in theory (see Figure 7.1). From least integrated to most integrated, they are a free trade area, a customs union, a common market, an economic union, and, finally, a full political union.

Free Trade Area

In a free trade area all barriers to the trade of goods and services among member countries are removed. In the theoretically ideal free trade area, no discriminatory tariffs, quotas, subsidies, or administrative impediments are allowed to distort trade between member countries. Each country, however, is allowed to determine its own trade policies with regard to nonmembers. Thus, for example, the tariffs placed on the products of nonmember countries may vary among member countries.

 The most enduring free trade area in the world is the European Free Trade Association (EFTA). Established in January 1960, EFTA currently joins four countries—Norway, Iceland, Liechtenstein, and Switzerland—down from seven in 1995 (on January 1, 1996, three EFTA members, Austria, Finland, and Sweden, joined the EU). EFTA was founded by those Western European countries that initially decided not to be part of the European Community (the forerunner of the EU). Its original members included Austria, Britain, Denmark, Finland, and Sweden, all of whom are now members of the EU. EFTA's emphasis has been on free trade in industrial goods. Agriculture was left out of the arrangement, allowing each member to determine its own level of support. Members were also free to determine the level of protection applied to goods coming from outside EFTA. Other free trade areas include the North American Free Trade Agreement (NAFTA).

Customs Union

The customs union is one step further along the road to full economic and political integration. A customs union eliminates trade barriers between member countries and adopts a common external trade policy. Establishment of a common external trade policy requires administrative machinery to oversee trade relations with non-members. Most countries that enter into a customs union desire even greater economic integration down the road. The EU began as a customs union and has moved beyond this stage. Other customs unions include the current version of the Andean Pact (between Bolivia, Colombia, Ecuador, and Peru). The Andean Pact aims to establish free trade between member countries and to impose a common tariff, of 5 to 20 percent, on products imported from outside.[3]

Common Market

Like a customs union, the theoretical common market has no barriers to trade between member countries and a common external trade policy. Unlike in a customs union, a common market allows factors of production to move freely between member countries. Thus, labor and capital are free to move because there are no restrictions on immigration, emigration, or cross-border flows of capital between member countries. Hence, a much closer union is envisaged in a common market than in a customs union. The EU is currently a common market, although its goal is full economic union. The EU is the only successful common market ever established, although several regional groupings have aspired to this goal. Establishing a common market demands a significant degree of harmony and cooperation on fiscal, monetary, and employment policies. Achieving this degree of cooperation has proven very difficult. MERCOSUR, the South America grouping of Brazil, Argentina, Paraguay, and Uruguay, hopes to establish itself as a common market.

Economic Union

An economic union entails even closer economic integration and cooperation than a common market. Like the common market, an economic union involves the free flow of products and factors of production between member countries and the adoption of a common external trade policy. Unlike a common market, a full economic union also requires a common currency, harmonization of the member's tax rates, and a common monetary and fiscal policy. Such a high degree of integration demands a coordinating bureaucracy and the sacrifices of significant sovereignty to that bureaucracy. There are no true economic unions in the world, but the EU is moving in this direction, particularly given the current attempt to create a single EU currency, the euro, by January 1, 2002.

Political Union

The move toward economic union raises the issue of how to make a coordinating bureaucracy accountable to the citizens of member nations. The answer is through political union. The EU is already on the road toward political union. The European Parliament has been directly elected by citizens of the EU countries since the late 1970s. In addition, the Council of Ministers (the controlling, decision-making body of the EU) is composed of government ministers from each EU member. Canada and the United States provide examples of even closer degrees of political union; in each country independent states were combined into a single nation. Ultimately, the EU may move toward a similar federal structure.

The Case for Regional Integration

The case for regional integration is both economic and political. Most attempts to achieve regional economic integration have been contentious and halting. In this section we examine the economic and political cases for integration and two impediments to integration. In the next section we look at the case against integration.

The Economic Case for Integration

The economic case for regional integration is relatively straightforward. We saw in Chapter 4 how economic theories of international trade predict that unrestricted free trade will allow countries to specialize in the production of goods and services that they can make most efficiently. The result is greater world production than would be possible with trade restrictions. We also saw in that chapter how opening a country to free trade stimulates economic growth in the country, which creates dynamic gains from trade. We saw in Chapter 6 how foreign direct investment (FDI) can transfer technological, marketing, and managerial know-how to host nations. Given the central role of knowledge in stimulating economic growth, opening a country to FDI also is likely to stimulate economic growth. In sum, economic theories suggest that free trade and investment is a positive-sum game, in which all participating countries stand to gain.

Given this, the theoretical ideal is an absence of barriers to the free flow of goods, services, and factors of production among nations. However, as we saw in Chapters 5 and 6, a case can be made for government intervention in international trade and FDI. Because many governments have accepted part or all of the case for intervention, unrestricted free trade and FDI have proved to be only an ideal. Although international institutions such as the GATT and WTO have been moving the world toward a free trade regime, success has been less than total. In a world of many nations and many political ideologies, it is very difficult to get all countries to agree to a common set of rules.

Regional economic integration is an attempt to achieve additional gains from the free flow of trade and investment beyond those attainable under international agreements such as GATT and the WTO. It is easier to establish a free trade and investment regime among a limited number of adjacent countries than among the world community as a whole. Problems of coordination and policy harmonization are largely a function of the number of countries that seek agreement. The greater the number of countries involved, the greater the number of perspectives that must be reconciled, and the harder it will be to reach agreement.

The Political Case for Integration

The political case for regional economic integration has also loomed large in most attempts to establish free trade areas, customs unions, and the like. Linking neighboring economies and making them increasingly dependent on each other creates incentives for political cooperation and reduces the potential for violent conflict between the states. In addition, by grouping their economies, the countries can enhance their political weight in the world.

These considerations underlay establishment of the European Community (EC) in 1957 (the EC was the forerunner of the EU). Europe had suffered two devastating wars in the first half of the century, both arising out of the unbridled ambitions of nation-states. Those who have sought a united Europe have always hoped to make another war in Europe unthinkable. Many Europeans also believed that after World War II the European nation-states were no longer large enough to hold their own in world markets and world politics. The need for a united Europe to deal with the United States and the politically alien Soviet Union loomed large in the minds of many of the EC's founders.[4]

Impediments to Integration

Despite the strong economic and political arguments for integration, it has never been easy to achieve or sustain. There are two main reasons for this. First, although economic integration benefits the majority, it has its costs. While a nation as a whole may benefit significantly through a regional free trade agreement, certain groups may lose. Moving to a free trade regime inevitably involves some painful adjustments. For example, as a result of the 1994 establishment of NAFTA some Canadian and US workers in such industries as textiles, which employ low-cost, low-skilled labor, will lose their jobs as firms move production to Mexico. The promise of significant net benefits to the Canadian and US economies is little comfort to those who lose jobs. Such groups were in the forefront of opposition to the NAFTA agreement and will continue to oppose any widening of the agreement.

A second impediment to integration arises from concerns over national sovereignty. For example, Mexico's concerns about maintaining control of its oil interests resulted in an agreement with Canada and the United States to exempt the Mexican oil industry from any liberalization of foreign investment regulations achieved under NAFTA. Concerns about national sovereignty arise because close economic integration demands that countries give up some degree of control over such key issues as monetary policy, fiscal policy (e.g., tax policy), and trade policy. This has been a major stumbling block in the EU. To achieve full economic union, the EU is trying to introduce a common currency to be controlled by a central EU bank. Although most member states have agreed to such a deal, Britain remains an important holdout. A politically important segment of public opinion in that country opposes a common currency on the grounds that it would require relinquishing control of monetary policy to the EU, which many British perceive as a bureaucracy run by foreigners. In 1992 the British won the right to opt out of any single currency agreement and as of 1999, there was little sign that the British government would reverse its decision.

The Case against Regional Integration

Some economists fear that the benefits of regional integration have been oversold, while the costs have often been ignored.[5] They point out that the benefits of regional integration are determined by the extent of trade creation, as opposed to trade diversion. **Trade creation** occurs when high-cost domestic producers are replaced by low-cost producers within the free trade area. It may also occur when higher-cost external producers are replaced by lower-cost external producers within the free trade area (see the accompanying "Country Focus" for an example). **Trade diversion** occurs when

trade creation Occurs when high-cost domestic producers are replaced by low-cost producers within the free trade area.

trade diversion Occurs when lower-cost external suppliers are replaced by higher-cost suppliers within the free trade area.

When the North American Free Trade Agreement went into effect in 1994, many expressed fears that one consequence would be large job losses in the US textile industry as companies moved production from the United States to Mexico. Opponents of NAFTA argued passionately, but unsuccessfully, that the treaty should not be adopted because of the negative impact it would have on employment in the United States, particularly in industries such as textiles.

A glance at the data four years after passage of NAFTA suggests the critics had a point. Between 1994 and mid-1997 about 149,000 US apparel workers lost their jobs, over 15 percent of all employment in the industry. Much of this job loss has occurred because production has moved to Mexico. Between 1994 and 1997 Mexico's apparel

However, the issue becomes more complicated when one takes a closer look at the data. There have been job losses in the US textile industry, but clothing prices in the United States have also fallen since 1994 as textile production shifted from high-cost US producers to lower-cost Mexican producers. This obviously benefits US consumers, who now have more money to spend on other items. The cost of a typical pair of designer jeans, for example, fell from $55 in 1994 to $48 in 1997. Nor is the fall in prices simply a result of the movement of production from the United States to Mexico. The establishment of NAFTA has also resulted in textile production being moved from Asia to Mexico. In 1980, 83 percent of all US textile imports came from Asia. By 1997, Asia accounted for 41 percent of US textile imports as

In addition to lower prices, the shift in textile production to Mexico has also benefited the US economy in other ways. First, it has helped produce a surge in exports from US fabric and yarn makers—many of whom are in the chemical industry (they make artificial yarn). Before passage of NAFTA, US yarn producers, such as Burlington Industries and E.I. du Pont, supplied only small amounts of fabric and yarn to Asian producers. However, as apparel production has moved from Asia to Mexico, exports of fabric and yarn to that country have surged. US producers supply 70 percent of the raw material going to Mexican sewing shops. Between 1994 and 1997 fabric and yarn exports to Mexico, mostly in the form of cut pieces ready for sewing, nearly doubled to around $2.5 billion per year. In addition, US manu-

The Impact of NAFTA on the US Textile Industry

exports to the United States trebled to $3.3 billion. In 1993 the US jeans maker Guess? sourced 95 percent of its product domestically. Now it gets about 60 percent of its clothing from outside the United States, and Mexico is one of the biggest beneficiaries. In 1995 Fruit of the Loom Inc., the largest manufacturer of underwear in the United States, said it would close six of its domestic plants and cut back operations at two others, laying off about 3,200 workers, or 12 percent of its total US workforce. The company announced the closures were part of its drive to move operations to cheaper plants abroad, particularly in Mexico. Before the closures less than 30 percent of its sewing was done outside the United States, but Fruit of the Loom planned to move the majority of that work to Mexico.

companies switched their sources of textiles from Asia to Mexico. An example of this trend is the US clothing retailer The Limited Inc., which in 1997 switched its source for textile products from Sri Lanka to Mexico. According to a spokesman for The Limited, although wages in Mexico are three times the $60 per month that apparel workers make in Sri Lanka, it's cheaper and faster to move goods from Mexico to the United States than from Sri Lanka. Also, under NAFTA there are no tariffs on imports from Mexico, while a 19 percent tariff is levied on textile imports from Sri Lanka. When all these factors are considered, it becomes cheaper to produce textiles in Mexico than Sri Lanka. Thus, as a result of NAFTA, production has been shifted to a lower-cost external source. The Limited plans to pass on its cost savings to consumers in the form of lower prices.

facturers of textile equipment have also seen an increase in sales as apparel factories in Mexico order textile equipment. In 1995 exports of textile equipment to Mexico nearly doubled over the 1994 level to $35.5 million.

In sum, although there have been job losses in the US textile industry, advocates of NAFTA argue that there have been net benefits to the US economy in the form of lower clothing prices and an increase in exports from fabric and yarn producers and from producers of textile machinery. As a result of NAFTA, trade has been created. The gains from trade are being captured by US consumers and by producers in certain sectors. As always, the establishment of a free trade area does create winners and losers, but advocates argue that the gains easily outweigh the losses.[6]

lower-cost external suppliers are replaced by higher-cost suppliers within the free trade area. A regional free trade agreement will benefit the world only if the amount of trade it creates exceeds the amount it diverts.

Suppose the United States and Mexico set up a free trade area, scrapping all trade barriers between them but maintaining tariffs on imports from the rest of the world. If the United States began to import textiles from Mexico, would this change be for the better? If the United States previously produced all its own textiles at a higher cost than Mexico, then the free trade agreement has shifted production to the cheaper source. According to the theory of comparative advantage, trade has been created within the regional grouping, and there would be no decrease in trade with the rest of the world. The change would be for the better. If, however, the United States previously imported textiles from South Korea, which produced them more cheaply than either Mexico or the United States, then trade has been diverted from a low-cost source—a change for the worse.

In theory, WTO rules should ensure that a free trade agreement does not result in trade diversion. These rules allow free trade areas to be formed only if the members set tariffs that are not higher or more restrictive to outsiders than the ones previously in effect. However, as we saw in Chapter 5, a range of nontariff barriers are not covered by the GATT and WTO. As a result, regional trade blocs whose markets are protected from outside competition by high nontariff barriers could emerge. In such cases, the trade diversion effects might outweigh the trade creation effects. The only way to guard against this possibility, according to those concerned about this potential, is to increase the scope of the WTO so that it covers nontariff barriers. There is no sign of this occurring anytime soon, however, so the risk remains that regional economic integration will result in trade diversion.

Regional Economic Integration in Europe

Europe now has two trade blocs: the European Union and the European Free Trade Association. Of the two, the EU is far more significant, not just in terms of membership (the EU has 15 members, and EFTA has 4), but also in terms of economic and political influence in the world economy. Many now see the EU as an emerging economic and political superpower of the same order as the United States and Japan. Accordingly, we will concentrate our attention on the EU.[7]

Evolution of the European Union

The EU is the product of two political factors: (1) the devastation of two world wars on Western Europe and the desire for a lasting peace, and (2) the European nations' desire to hold their own on the world's political and economic stage. In addition, many Europeans were aware of the potential benefits of closer economic integration of the countries.

The original forerunner of the EU, the European Coal and Steel Community, was formed in 1951 by Belgium, France, West Germany, Italy, Luxembourg, and the Netherlands. Its objective was to remove barriers to intragroup shipments of coal, iron, steel, and scrap metal. With the signing of the Treaty of Rome in 1957, the European Community (EC) was established. The name changed again in 1994 when the *European Community* became the *European Union* following the ratification of the Maastricht Treaty (discussed later).

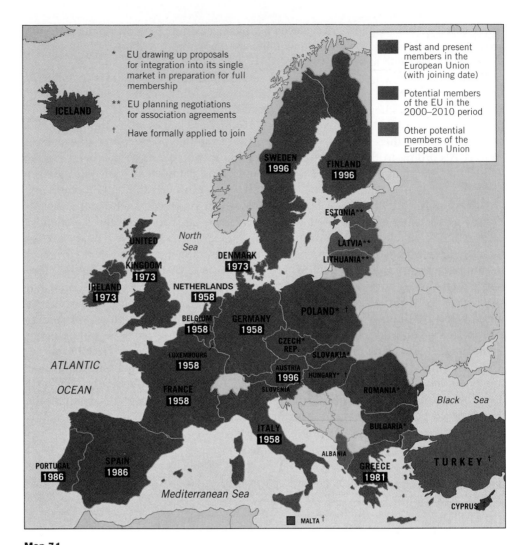

* EU drawing up proposals for integration into its single market in preparation for full membership

** EU planning negotiations for association agreements

† Have formally applied to join

Past and present members in the European Union (with joining date)

Potential members of the EU in the 2000–2010 period

Other potential members of the European Union

ICELAND

SWEDEN 1996

FINLAND 1996

ESTONIA**

LATVIA**

LITHUANIA**

North Sea

UNITED KINGDOM 1973

DENMARK 1973

IRELAND 1973

NETHERLANDS 1958

POLAND* †

BELGIUM 1958

GERMANY 1958

CZECH* REP.

SLOVAKIA*

ATLANTIC OCEAN

LUXEMBOURG 1958

AUSTRIA 1996

HUNGARY* †

SLOVENIA

ROMANIA*

Black Sea

FRANCE 1958

ITALY 1958

BULGARIA*

ALBANIA

TURKEY †

PORTUGAL 1986

SPAIN 1986

GREECE 1981

Mediterranean Sea

CYPRUS †

MALTA †

Map 7.1

The European Union

The Treaty of Rome provided for the creation of a common market. Article 3 of the treaty, called for the elimination of internal trade barriers and the creation of a common external tariff and required member states to abolish obstacles to the free movement of factors of production among the members. To facilitate the free movement of goods, services, and factors of production, the treaty provided for any necessary harmonization of the member-states' laws. The treaty also committed the EC to establish common policies in agriculture and transportation.

The first enlargement of the community occurred in 1973, when Great Britain, Ireland, and Denmark joined. These three were followed in 1981 by Greece, in 1986 by Spain and Portugal, and in 1996 by Austria, Finland, and Sweden (see Map 7.1) bringing the total membership to 15 (East Germany became part of the EC after the reunification of Germany in 1990). With a population of 350 million and a GDP greater than that of the United States, these enlargements made the EU a potential global superpower.

The Single European Act

Two revolutions occurred in Europe in the late 1980s. The first was the collapse of communism in Eastern Europe. The second revolution was much quieter, but its impact on Europe and the world may have been just as profound as the first. It was the 1987 adoption of the Single European Act by the member nations of the EC. This act committed the EC countries to work toward establishment of a single market by December 31, 1992.

THE STIMULUS FOR THE SINGLE EUROPEAN ACT   The Single European Act was born out of frustration among EC member countries that the community was not living up to its promise. By the early 1980s the EC had fallen far short of its objectives to remove barriers to the free flow of trade and investment between member countries and to harmonize the technical and legal standards for doing business. At the end of 1982 the European Commission found itself with 770 cases of intra-EC protectionism to investigate. In addition, some 20 EC directives setting common technical standards for a variety of products ranging from cars to thermometers were deadlocked. Many companies viewed the disharmony of the members' technical, legal, regulatory, and tax standards as the main problem with the EC. The "rules of the game" differed substantially from country to country, which stalled the creation of a true single internal market.

In addition, many member countries were subsidizing national firms, thereby distorting competition. For example, in 1990 the French government decided to pump FFr 6 billion into Groupe Bull, a state-owned computer maker, and Thomson, a defense and electronics group. This brought protests from ICL, a British computer maker, on the grounds that such a subsidy would allow Groupe Bull to capture more of the EC computer market.[8]

In the early 1980s many of the EC's prominent businesspeople campaigned to end the EC's economic divisions. The EC responded by creating the Delors Commission. Under the chairmanship of Jacques Delors, the former French finance minister and president of the EC Commission, the commission produced a discussion paper in 1985. This proposed that all impediments to the formation of a single market be eliminated by December 31, 1992. Two more years passed before the EC persuaded all member countries to accept the proposals contained in the discussion paper. The result was the Single European Act, which was independently ratified by the parliaments of each member country and became EC law in 1987.

THE OBJECTIVES OF THE ACT   The purpose of the Single European Act was to have a single market in place by December 31, 1992. The act proposed the following changes:[9]

1 Remove all frontier controls between EC countries, thereby abolishing delays and reducing the resources required for complying with trade bureaucracy.

2 Apply the principle of "mutual recognition" to product standards. A standard developed in one EC country should be accepted in another, provided it meets basic requirements in such matters as health and safety.

3 Open public procurement to nonnational suppliers. This should reduce costs directly by allowing lower-cost suppliers into national economies and indirectly by forcing national suppliers to compete.

4 Lift barriers to competition in the EC's retail banking and insurance businesses, which should drive down the costs of financial services, including borrowing, throughout the EC.

5 Remove all restrictions on foreign exchange transactions between member countries by the end of 1992.

6 Abolish restrictions on cabotage—the right of foreign truckers to pick up and deliver goods within another member state's borders—by the end of 1992. This could reduce the cost of haulage within the EC by 10 to 15 percent.

All those changes should lower the costs of doing business in the EC, but the single-market program is also expected to have more complicated supply-side effects. For example, the expanded market should give EC firms greater opportunities to exploit economies of scale. In addition, the increase in competitive intensity brought about by removing internal barriers to trade and investment should force EC firms to become more efficient.

To signify the importance of the Single European Act, the European Community also decided to change its name to the European Union once the act took effect.

IMPLICATIONS The implications of the Single European Act are potentially enormous. We discuss the implications for business practice in more detail at the end of the chapter. For now it should be noted that, as long as the EU is successful in establishing a single market, the member countries can expect significant gains from the free flow of trade and investment. These gains may be greater than those predicted by standard trade theory that accrue when regions specialize in producing those goods and services that they make most efficiently. The lower costs of doing business implied by the Single European Act will benefit EU firms, as will the potential economies of scale inherent in serving a single market of 360 million consumers. On the other hand, as a result of the Single European Act many EU firms are facing increased competitive pressure. Countries such as France and Italy have long used administrative trade barriers and subsidies to protect their home markets from foreign competition. Removal of these barriers has increased competition, and some firms may go out of business. Ultimately, however, both consumers and EU firms will benefit. Consumers will benefit from the lower prices implied by a more competitive market. EU firms will benefit if the increased competitive pressure forces them to become more efficient, thereby transforming them into more effective international competitors capable of going head-to-head with US and Asian rivals in the world marketplace.

The shift toward a single market has not been as rapid as many would like. Six years after the Single European Act became EU law, there have been a number of delays in applying the act to certain industries, often because countries have appealed to the Council of Ministers for more time. The insurance industry, for example, was exempt until July 1994 (see the opening case for details). Investment services were not liberalized until January 1996, and there was no compulsion to liberalize basic telephone services until 1998 (and until 2003 in poorer countries such as Greece to protect local telephone companies from being "crushed" by the likes of Britain's BT or America's AT&T).[10] Many European countries have found their dreams of a single market dashed by the realities of deep cultural and language barriers, which still separate many national markets, although not as effectively as formal trade barriers once did. Still, the long-run prognosis remains very strong, and despite all the short-term setbacks the EU will probably have a reasonably well-functioning single market within 10 years.

The Euro

In December 1991 leaders of the EC member states met in Maastricht, the Netherlands, to discuss the next steps for the EC. The results of the Maastricht meeting surprised both Europe and the rest of the world. For months the countries of the EC had been fighting over a common currency. The British in particular had opposed any attempt to establish a common currency. Although many economists believed a common currency was required to cement a closer economic union, deadlock had been predicted. Instead, the 12 members signed a treaty that committed them to adopting a common currency by January 1, 1999, and paved the way for closer political cooperation.

The treaty laid down the main elements of a future European government: a single currency, the euro; a common foreign and defense policy; a common citizenship; and an EU parliament with teeth. It is now just a matter of waiting, some believe, for a "United States of Europe" to emerge. Of more immediate interest are the implications for business of the establishment of a single currency.[11]

The euro currency unit is now used by 11 of the 15 member states of the European Union in what is called the euro zone. Establishment of the euro has rightly been described as an amazing political feat. There are few historic precedents for what the Europeans are doing. Governments do not routinely relinquish control over important economic policy instruments or sacrifice national sovereignty for the greater good. Establishing the euro required the participating national governments not only to give up their own currencies, but also to give up control over monetary policy. By adopting the euro, the EU has created the second-largest currency zone in the world after that of the US dollar. Some believe the euro could someday rival the dollar in importance as the most important currency in the world.

According to the Maastricht Treaty, to join the euro zone member countries had to achieve low inflation rates, low long-term interest rates, a stable exchange rate, public debt limited to no more than 60 percent of a country's GDP, and current budget deficits of no more than 3 percent of GDP. Initially there was considerable skepticism that this would be possible. However, by the spring of 1998 it was clear that of the 12 countries that had signaled their intention to join the euro zone, only Greece would not make the criteria. Three EU countries, Britain, Denmark, and Sweden, are still sitting on the sidelines, although there is speculation that Britain and Sweden may join before 2002. The 11 countries that made the grade and agreed to EMU locked their exchange rates against each other January 1, 1999.

Euro notes and coins will not be issued until January 1, 2002. In the interim, national currencies will continue to circulate in each of the 11 countries. However, in each participating state the national currency will stand for a defined amount of euros. Notes that now look like French francs, or German deutsche marks, or Italian lira are mere denominations of the euro. In each participating nation, banks and businesses will keep two sets of accounts, one in the local currency and one in euros. Many prices are now posted in both euros and the local currency. And increasingly, many business transactions will be conducted in euros.

After January 1, 2002, euro notes and coins will be issued and the national currencies will start to be taken out of circulation. After about six months, only euros will be in circulation, and all prices and routine economic transactions within the euro zone will be in euros. The euro will move from being a virtual currency to a real currency.

BENEFITS OF THE EURO   The Europeans decided to establish a single currency for a number of reasons. First, they believe that businesses and individuals will realize significant savings from having to handle one currency rather than many. These savings come from lower foreign exchange and hedging costs. For example, people going from Germany to France will no longer have to pay a commission to a bank to change deutsche marks into francs. Instead, they will be able to use euros. According to the European Commission, such savings could amount to 0.5 percent of the European Union's GDP, or about $40 billion a year.

Second, and perhaps more importantly, the adoption of a common currency will make it easier to compare prices across Europe. This should increase competition. For example, if Germans find that cars sell for less in France than Germany, they may consider purchasing from a French car dealer rather than their local car dealer. Alternatively, traders may engage in arbitrage to exploit such price differentials, buying cars in France and reselling them in Germany. In the face of such competitive pressures, German car dealers will have to reduce the prices they charge to hold onto business. Because of such pressures, the introduction of a common currency should lead to lower prices across the board. This should translate into substantial gains for European consumers.

Third, faced with lower prices European producers will be forced to look for ways to reduce their production costs in order to maintain their profit margins. To the extent that this occurs, the introduction of a common currency should ultimately produce long-run gains in the economic efficiency of European companies.

Fourth, the introduction of a common currency should boost development of a highly liquid pan-European capital market. Such a capital market should lower the cost of capital and lead to an increase in both the level of investment and the efficiency with which investment funds are allocated. This could be especially helpful to smaller companies that have historically had difficulty borrowing money from domestic banks. For example, the capital market of Portugal is very small and illiquid, which makes it difficult for Portuguese entrepreneurs to borrow money at a reasonable price. However, entrepreneurs and other companies should soon be able to tap a much more liquid pan-European capital market. Now Europe has no continentwide capital market, such as the NASDAQ market in the United States, that funnels investment capital to dynamic young growth companies. Introduction of the euro could facilitate establishment of such a market. The long-term benefits of such a development should not be underestimated.

Finally, the development of a pan-European euro-denominated capital market will increase the range of investment options open to both individuals and institutions. For example, it will now be much easier for individuals and institutions based in, let's say, Holland to invest in Italian or French companies. This will enable European investors to better diversify their risk, which again lowers the cost of capital and should also increase the efficiency with which capital resources are allocated.[12]

COSTS OF THE EURO   The drawback of a single currency is that national authorities would lose control over monetary policy. Thus, the EU's monetary policy must be well-managed. The Maastricht Treaty called for the establishment of an independent European Central Bank (ECB), similar in some respects to the US Federal Reserve, with a clear mandate to manage monetary policy so as to ensure price stability. Like the US Federal Reserve, the ECB, based in Frankfurt, is meant to be independent from political pressure—although critics question this. Among other things, the ECB sets interest rates and determines monetary policy across the euro zone.

The implied loss of national sovereignty to the ECB underlies the decision by Britain, Denmark, and Sweden to stay out of the euro zone for now. Some in these countries are suspicious of the ability of the ECB to remain free from political pressure and to keep inflation under control. In theory, the design of the ECB should ensure that it remains free of political pressure. The ECB is modeled on the German Bundesbank, which has been the most independent and successful central bank in Europe. The language contained in the Maastricht Treaty prohibits the ECB from taking orders from politicians. The executive board of the bank, which consists of a president, vice president, and four other members, carries out policy by issuing instructions to national central banks. Policy is determined by the governing council, which consists of the executive board plus the central bank governors from the 11 euro zone countries. The governing council votes on interest rate changes. Members of the executive board are appointed for eight-year nonrenewable terms, insulating them from political pressures to get reappointed. Nevertheless, the jury is still out on the ECB's independence, and it will take time for the bank to establish its inflation-fighting credentials.

According to critics, another drawback of the euro is that the EU is not an optimal currency area. An optimal currency area exists where similarities in the underlying structure of economic activity make it feasible to adopt a single currency and use a single exchange rate as an instrument of macroeconomic policy. Many of the European economies in the euro zone, however, are very dissimilar. For example, Finland and Portugal are very dissimilar economies. They have different wage rates and tax regimes, different business cycles, and may react very differently to external economic shocks. A change in the euro exchange rate that helps Finland may hurt Portugal. Such differences complicate macroeconomic policy. For example, when euro economies are not growing in unison, a common monetary policy may mean that interest rates are too high for depressed regions and too low for booming regions. It will be interesting to see how the EU copes with the strains caused by such divergent economic performance.

The EU might deal with such divergent effects by engaging in fiscal transfers, taking money from prosperous regions and pumping it into depressed regions. Such a move, however, would open a political can of worms. It is difficult, for example, to imagine the citizens of Germany forgoing their "fair share" of EU funds in order to create jobs for underemployed Portuguese workers.

Reflecting on these issues, several critics believe that the euro puts the economic cart before the political horse. In their view, a single currency should follow, not precede, political union. They argue that the euro will unleash enormous pressures for tax harmonization and fiscal transfers from the center, policies that cannot be pursued without the appropriate political structure. The most apocalyptic vision that flows from these negative views is that the euro will lead to lower economic growth and higher inflation within Europe. To quote one critic:

> Imposing a single exchange rate and an inflexible exchange rate on countries that are characterized by different economic shocks, inflexible wages, low labor mobility, and separate national fiscal systems without significant cross-border fiscal transfers will raise the overall level of cyclical unemployment among EMU members. The shift from national monetary policies dominated by the (German) Bundesbank within the European Monetary System to a European Central Bank governed by majority voting with a politically determined exchange rate policy will almost certainly raise the average future rate of inflation.[13]

Enlargement of the European Union

The other big issue the EU must now grapple with is enlargement. After a bitter dispute between the existing 12 members, in March 1994 they agreed to enlarge the EU to include Austria, Finland, Sweden, and Norway. Most of the opposition came from Britain, which worried that enlargement, and a subsequent reduction in its voting power in the EU's top decision-making body, the Council of Ministers, would limit its ability to block EU developments that it did not like. Britain backed down in the face of strong opposition from other EU members and agreed to enlargement.

Voters in the four countries went to the polls in late 1994. Austria, Finland, and Sweden all voted to join the EU, but Norway voted to stay out. Thus, the EU of 12 became the EU of 15 on January 1, 1996. Next the EU had to deal with membership applications from Hungary, Poland, the Czech Republic, Estonia, Slovenia, Malta, Cyprus, and Turkey.[14] In 1997 the EU responded by formally inviting five former Communist states—Estonia, Poland, the Czech Republic, Slovenia, and Hungary—to join. However, the timetable for this event is uncertain, and any additional expansion is unlikely until a few years after the completion of the euro in 2002. All these countries still have a long way to go before their economies reach the level enjoyed by the current EU members. For example, according to the European Commission, Poland, the country with the largest population among the five, needs to modernize its agricultural sector, speed up its sluggish privatization efforts, and bring its inflation rate down from around 20 percent to about 3 percent.[15]

Fortress Europe?

One concern of the United States and Asian countries is that the EU at some point will impose new barriers on imports from outside the EU. The fear is that the EU might increase external protection as weaker member states attempt to offset their loss of protection against other EU countries by arguing for limitations on outside competition.

In theory, given the free market philosophy that underpins the Single European Act, this should not occur. In October 1988, the European Commission debated external trading policy and published a detailed statement of the EC's trading intentions in the post-1992 era.[16] The commission stressed the EC's interests in vigorous external trade. It noted that exports by EC countries to non-EC countries are equivalent to 20 percent of total world exports, compared to 15 percent for the United States and 9 percent for Japan. These external exports are equivalent to 9 percent of its own GDP, compared to 6.7 percent for the United States and 9.7 percent for Japan. In short, it is not in the EU's interests to adopt a protectionist stance, given the EU's reliance on external trade. The commission has also promised loyalty to GATT and now WTO rules on international trade. As for the types of trade not covered by the WTO, the EU states it will push for reciprocal access. The EU has stated that in certain cases it might replace individual national trade barriers with EU protection against imports, but it also has promised that the overall level of protection would not rise.

Despite such reassurances, there is no guarantee the EU will not adopt a protectionist stance toward external trade, and there are indications that has occurred in two industries, agriculture and automobiles. In agriculture, the EU has continued the Common Agricultural Policy, which limits many food imports. In autos, the EU reached an agreement with the Japanese to limit their market share of the EU auto market. Between 1993 and 1998 those countries that had quotas on Japanese car imports lifted them gradually until the end of 1998, when they were abolished. Meanwhile, Japanese producers committed themselves to voluntarily restraining sales so that by the end of the century they held no more than 17 percent of the European market. After that, all restrictions were to be abolished. These examples of protectionism, however, are not the norm, and in general the EU countries have adopted a relatively liberal trade policy with regard to third parties, such as Japan and the United States. In a published report on the issue, the WTO has stated that the growth of regional trade groups such as the EU has not impeded the growth of freer world trade, as some fear, and may have helped promote it.[17]

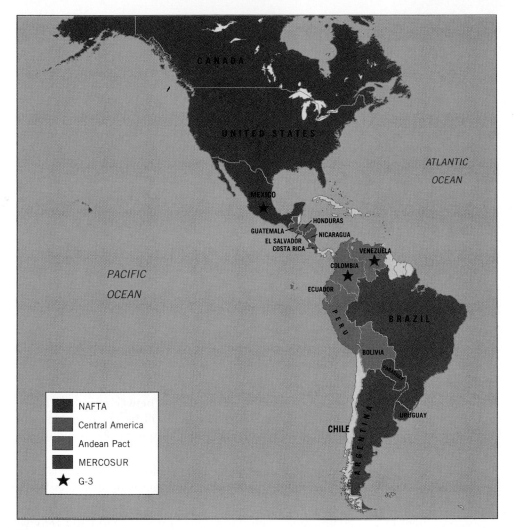

Map 7.2

Economic Integration in the Americas

Regional Economic Integration in the Americas

No other attempt at regional economic integration comes close to the EU in its boldness or its potential implications for the world economy, but regional economic integration is on the rise in the Americas. The most significant attempt is the North American Free Trade Agreement. In addition to NAFTA, several other trade blocs exist in the Americas (see Map 7.2), the most significant being the Andean Group and MERCOSUR. There are also plans to establish a hemisphere wide Free Trade Area of the Americas by 2005.

The North American Free Trade Agreement

In 1988 the governments of the United States and Canada agreed to enter into a free trade agreement (FTA), which took effect January 1, 1989. The goal was to eliminate all tariffs on bilateral trade between Canada and the United States by 1998.

This was followed in 1991 by talks among the United States, Canada, and Mexico aimed at establishing the North American Free Trade Agreement in the three countries. The talks concluded in August 1992 with an agreement in principle to establish NAFTA.

For NAFTA to become a reality, each country had to ratify it. Both Canada and Mexico committed themselves to NAFTA by the fall of 1993, leaving only the US government to signal its support. The Clinton administration had already committed itself to NAFTA, and passage by the US Senate looked likely, but the agreement faced stiff opposition in the US House of Representatives. The vote on NAFTA in the House of Representatives was scheduled for November 17, 1993. Until only hours before the vote the outcome was still in doubt, but a last-minute round of lobbying by President Clinton, which included numerous side deals to buy the support of wavering representatives, led to a surge for NAFTA and the bill passed the House by a comfortable margin.

THE AGREEMENT NAFTA became law January 1, 1994.[18] The contents of the agreement included the following:

- Abolition within 10 years of tariffs on 99 percent of the goods traded between Mexico, Canada, and the United States.
- Removal of most barriers on the cross-border flow of services, allowing financial institutions, for example, unrestricted access to the Mexican market by 2000.
- Protection of intellectual property rights.
- Removal of most restrictions on foreign direct investment between the three member countries, although special treatment (protection) will be given to Mexican energy and railway industries, US airline and radio communications industries, and Canadian culture.
- Application of national environmental standards, provided such standards have a scientific basis. Lowering of standards to lure investment is described as being inappropriate.
- Establishment of two commissions with the power to impose fines and remove trade privileges when environmental standards or legislation involving health and safety, minimum wages, or child labor are ignored.

ARGUMENTS FOR NAFTA Proponents argue that NAFTA should be viewed as an opportunity to create an enlarged and more efficient productive base for the entire region. One likely short-term effect of NAFTA will be that many US and Canadian firms will move some production to Mexico to take advantage of lower labor costs. In 1991 the average hourly labor costs in Mexico were $2.32, compared with $14.31 in the United States and $14.71 in Canada. Movement of production to Mexico is most likely to occur in low-skilled, labor-intensive manufacturing industries where Mexico might have a comparative advantage (e.g., textiles). Many will benefit from such a trend. Mexico benefits because it gets needed investment and employment. The United States and Canada should benefit because the increased incomes of the Mexicans will allow them to import more US and Canadian goods, thereby recycling demand and making up for the jobs lost in industries that moved production to Mexico. US and Canadian consumers will benefit from the lower costs, and hence prices, of products produced in Mexico. In addition, the international competitiveness of US and Canadian firms that move production to Mexico to take advantage of lower labor costs will be enhanced, enabling them to better compete with Asian and European rivals.

Many workers in the United States initially felt that NAFTA would take away their jobs as employers looked for cheaper labor in Mexico. However, in 1996 a study by researchers at the University of California–Los Angeles concluded that the impact on jobs was a net gain of 3,000 for the United States in the first 2 years of the NAFTA regime.
© Joseph Sohm; ChromoSohm Inc./CORBIS.

ARGUMENTS AGAINST NAFTA   Those who opposed NAFTA claimed that ratification would be followed by a mass exodus of jobs from the United States and Canada into Mexico as employers sought to profit from Mexico's lower wages and less strict environmental and labor laws. According to one extreme opponent, Ross Perot, up to 5.9 million US jobs would be lost to Mexico after NAFTA. Most economists, however, dismiss these numbers as being absurd and alarmist. They point out that Mexico would have to run a bilateral trade surplus with the United States of close to $300 billion for job loss on such a scale to occur—and $300 billion is about the size of Mexico's present GDP. In other words, such a scenario is implausible.

More sober estimates of the impact of NAFTA ranged from a net creation of 170,000 jobs in the United States (due to increased Mexican demand for US goods and services) and an increase of $15 billion per year to the US and Mexican GDP, to a net loss of 490,000 US jobs. To put these numbers in perspective, employment in the US economy was predicted to grow by 18 million from 1993 to 2003. As most economists repeatedly stress, NAFTA will have a small impact on both Canada and the United States. It could hardly be any other way, since the Mexican economy is only 5 percent of the size of the US economy. The country that took the economic leap of faith by signing NAFTA was Mexico. Mexican firms are now exposed to highly efficient US and Canadian competitors that have far greater capital resources, access to highly educated and skilled workforces, and much greater technological sophistication. The short-run outcome is bound to be painful economic restructuring and unemployment in Mexico. But if economic theory is any guide, in the long run there should be dynamic gains in the efficiency of Mexican firms as they adjust to a more competitive marketplace. To the extent that this happens, Mexico's long-term rate of economic growth will accelerate, and Mexico might yet become a major market for Canadian and US firms.[19]

Environmentalists have also voiced concerns about NAFTA. They point to the sludge in the Rio Grande and the smog in the air over Mexico City and warn that Mexico could degrade clean air and toxic waste standards across the continent. They claim the lower Rio Grande is the most polluted river in the United States, increasing in chemical waste and sewage along its course from El Paso, Texas, to the Gulf of Mexico.

There is also continued opposition in Mexico from those who fear a loss of national sovereignty. Mexican critics argue that their entire country will be dominated by US firms that will not really contribute to Mexico's economic growth, but instead will use Mexico as a low-cost assembly site, while keeping their high-paying, high-skilled jobs north of the border.

THE EARLY EXPERIENCE   The first year after NAFTA turned out to be a largely positive experience for all three countries. US trade with Canada and Mexico expanded at about twice the rate of trade with non-NAFTA countries in the first nine months of 1994, compared with the same period in 1993. US exports to Mexico grew by 22 percent, while Mexican exports to the United States grew by 23 percent. Anti-NAFTA campaigners had warned of doom for the US auto industry, but exports of autos to Mexico from the United States increased by nearly 500 percent in the first nine months of 1994. The US Commerce Department estimated that the surge in exports to Mexico secured about 130,000 US jobs, while only 13,000 people applied for aid under a program designed to help workers displaced by the movement of jobs to Mexico, suggesting that job losses from NAFTA had been small.[20]

However, the early euphoria over NAFTA was snuffed out in December 1994 when the Mexican economy was shaken by a financial crisis. Through 1993 and 1994 Mexico's trade deficit with the rest of the world had grown sharply, while Mexico's inflation rate had started to accelerate. This put increasing pressure on the Mexican currency, the peso. Traders in the foreign exchange markets, betting that there would be a large decline in the value of the peso against the dollar, began to sell pesos and buy dollars. As a result, in December 1994 the Mexican government was forced to devalue the peso by about 35 percent against the US dollar. This effectively increased the cost of imports from the United States by 35 percent. The devaluation of the peso was followed quickly by a collapse in the value of the Mexican stock market, and the country suddenly and unexpectedly appeared to be in the midst of a major economic crisis. Shortly afterward, the Mexican government introduced an austerity program designed to rebuild confidence in the country's financial institutions and reign in growth and inflation. The program was backed by a $20 billion loan guarantee from the US government.[21]

One result of this turmoil was a sharp decline in Canadian and US exports to Mexico. Many companies also reduced or put on hold their plans for expansion into Mexico. As might be expected, critics of NAFTA seized on Mexico's financial crisis to crow that they had been right all along. But just as the celebrations of NAFTA's success were premature, so were claims of its sudden demise. Early studies of the impact of NAFTA suggest that its impact has been muted.[22] The most comprehensive study to date was undertaken by researchers at the University of California, Los Angeles, and funded by the US government.[23] Their findings are enlightening. First, they conclude that the growth in trade between Mexico and the United States began to change nearly a decade before the implementation of NAFTA when Mexico started to liberalize its own trade regime to conform with GATT standards. The period since NAFTA went into effect has had little impact on trends already in place. The study found that trade growth in those sectors that underwent tariff liberalization in the first two and a half years of NAFTA was only marginally higher than trade growth in sectors not yet liberalized. For example, between 1993 and 1996, US exports to Mexico in sectors liberalized under NAFTA grew by 5.83 percent annually, while exports in sectors not liberalized under NAFTA grew by 5.35 percent. The authors argue that NAFTA has so far had only a marginal impact on the level of trade between the United States and Mexico.

As for NAFTA's impact on jobs in the United States, the study concluded that the effect was positive but very small. The study found that while NAFTA created 31,158 new jobs in the United States, 28,168 jobs were also lost due to imports from Mexico, for a net job gain of about 3,000 in the first two years of the NAFTA regime.

However, as the report's authors point out, trade flows and employment in 1995 and 1996 were significantly affected by the peso devaluation and subsequent economic crisis that gripped Mexico in early 1995. It is probably too early to draw conclusions about the true impact of NAFTA on trade flows and employment; it will probably be at least a decade before any meaningful conclusions can be reached. While the optimistic picture of job creation painted by NAFTA's advocates has not yet come to pass, neither has the apocalyptic vision of widespread job losses in the United States and Canada propagated by NAFTA's opponents.

ENLARGEMENT   One big issue now confronting NAFTA is that of enlargement. A number of other Latin American countries have indicated their desire to eventually join NAFTA. The governments of both Canada and the United States are adopting a wait-and-see attitude with regard to most countries. The Canadian, Mexican, and US governments began talks in May 1995 with Chile regarding that country's possible entry into NAFTA. So far, however, these talks have yielded little progress, primarily because of political opposition in the US Congress.

The Andean Pact

The Andean Pact was formed in 1969 when Bolivia, Chile, Ecuador, Colombia, and Peru signed the Cartagena Agreement. The Andean Pact was largely based on the EC model, but it has been far less successful at achieving its stated goals. The integration begun in 1969 included an internal tariff reduction program, creation of a common external tariff, a transportation policy, a common industrial policy, and special concessions for the smallest members, Bolivia and Ecuador.

By the mid-1980s the Andean Pact had all but collapsed. It had failed to achieve any of its stated objectives. There was no tariff-free trade between member countries, no common external tariff, and no harmonization of economic policies. The attempt to achieve cooperation between member countries seems to have been hindered by political and economic problems. The countries of the Andean Pact have had to deal with low economic growth, hyperinflation, high unemployment, political unrest, and crushing debt burdens. All these problems made it extremely difficult to achieve cooperation. In addition, the dominant political ideology in many of the Andean countries during this period tended toward the radical/socialist end of the political spectrum. Because such an ideology is hostile to the free market economic principle on which the Andean Pact was based, progress toward closer integration could not be expected.

The tide began to turn in the late 1980s when, after years of economic decline, the governments of Latin America began to adopt free market economic policies. In 1990 the heads of the five current members of the Andean Pact—Bolivia, Ecuador, Peru, Colombia, and Venezuela—met in the Galápagos Islands. The resulting Galápagos Declaration re-launched the Andean Pact. The declaration's objectives included establishment of a free trade area by 1992, a customs union by 1994, and a common market by 1995.

Since the Galápagos Declaration, internal tariff levels have been reduced by all five members, and a customs union with a common external tariff was established in mid-1994, six months behind schedule. And for the first time, the controlling political ideology of the Andean countries is at least consistent with the free market principles underlying a common market.

But significant differences between member countries still exist that may make harmonization of policies and close integration difficult. For example, Venezuela's GNP per person is four times that of Bolivia's, and Ecuador's tiny production-line industries can hardly compete with Colombia's and Venezuela's more advanced industries. Such differences are a recipe for disagreement and suggest that many of the adjustments required to achieve a true common market will be painful, even though the net benefits will probably outweigh the costs.[24] To complicate matters even further, in recent years Peru and Ecuador have fought a border war, Venezuela has remained aloof during a banking crisis, and Colombia has suffered from domestic political turmoil and problems related to its drug trade. This has led some to argue that the pact is more "formal than real."[25] However, in 1998 the outlook for the Andean Pact started to change when the group entered into negotiations with MERCOSUR to establish a South American free trade area.

MERCOSUR

MERCOSUR originated in 1988 as a free trade pact between Brazil and Argentina. The modest reductions in tariffs and quotas accompanying this pact reportedly helped bring about an 80 percent increase in trade between the two countries in the late 1980s.[26] Encouraged by this success, the pact was expanded in March 1990 to include Paraguay and Uruguay. The initial aim of the MERCOSUR pact was to establish a full free trade area by the end of 1994 and a common market sometime thereafter. The four countries of MERCOSUR have a combined population of 200 million. With a market of this size, MERCOSUR could have a significant impact on the economic growth rate of the four economies.

In December 1995 MERCOSUR's members agreed to a five-year program under which they hoped to perfect their free trade area and move toward a full customs union. The four member states of MERCOSUR also have now committed themselves to establishment of a wider free trade area, the South American Free Trade Area (SAFTA). The goal is to bring other South American countries into the agreement, including the nations of the Andean Pact, and to have internal free trade for not less than 80 percent of goods produced in the region by 2005.[27]

MERCOSUR seems to be making a positive contribution to the economic growth rates of its member states. Trade between MERCOSUR's four members grew from $4 billion in 1990 to $16.9 billion in 1996. Also, the combined GDP of the four member states grew at an annual average rate of 3.5 percent between 1990 and 1996, a performance that is significantly better than the four attained during the 1980s.[28]

However, MERCOSUR has its critics, including Alexander Yeats, a senior economist at the World Bank, who wrote a stinging critique of MERCOSUR that was leaked to the press in October 1996.[29] According to Yeats, the trade diversion effects of MERCOSUR outweigh its trade creation effects. Yeats points out that the fastest-growing items in intra-MERCOSUR trade were cars, buses, agricultural equipment, and other capital-intensive goods that are produced relatively inefficiently in the four member countries. In other words, MERCOSUR countries, insulated from outside competition by external tariffs that run as high as 70 percent of the value on motor vehicles, are investing in factories that build products that are too expensive to sell to anyone but themselves. The result, according to Yeats, is that MERCOSUR countries might not be able to compete globally once the group's external trade barriers come down. In the meantime, capital is being drawn away from more efficient enterprises. In the near term, countries with more efficient manufacturing enterprises lose because MERCOSUR's external trade barriers keep them out of the market.

The leak of Yeats's report caused a storm at the World Bank, which typically does not release reports that are critical of member states (the MERCOSUR countries are members of the World Bank). It also drew strong protests from Brazil, which was one of the primary targets of Yeats's critique. Still, in admission that at least some of Yeats's arguments have merit, a senior MERCOSUR diplomat let it be known that external trade barriers will gradually be reduced, forcing member countries to compete globally. Already many external MERCOSUR tariffs, which average 14 percent, are lower than they were before the group's creation, and there are plans for a hemispheric free trade area of the Americas to be established by 2005 (which will combine MERCOSUR, NAFTA, and other American countries). If that occurs, MERCOSUR will have no choice but to reduce its external tariffs further.

Central American Common Market and CARICOM

There are two other trade pacts in the Americas, although neither has made much progress. In the early 1960s, Costa Rica, El Salvador, Guatemala, Honduras, and Nicaragua attempted to set up a Central American common market. It collapsed in 1969 when war broke out between Honduras and El Salvador after a riot at a soccer match. Now the five countries are trying to revive their agreement, although no definite progress had been made.

Then there is the customs union that was to have been created in 1991 between the English-speaking Caribbean countries under the auspices of the Caribbean Community. Referred to as CARICOM, it was originally established in 1973. However, it has repeatedly failed to progress toward economic integration. A formal commitment to economic and monetary union was adopted by CARICOM's member states in 1984, but since then little progress has been made. In October 1991 the CARICOM governments failed, for the third consecutive time, to meet a deadline for establishing a common external tariff.

Free Trade Area of the Americas

Flush from the early success with NAFTA and MERCOSUR, in December 1994 at a hemispherewide "Summit of the Americas" a proposal was made to establish the Free Trade Area of the Americas (FTAA). It took over three years for talks to begin, but in April 1998, 34 heads of state traveled to Santiago, Chile, for the second Summit of the Americas where they formally inaugurated talks to establish the FTAA by 2005. The talks will continue for seven years and will address a range of economic, political, and environmental issues related to cross-border trade and investment. Although the United States was an early advocate of the FTAA, at this point US support seems to be mixed at best. Because the United States has by far the largest economy in the region, strong US support is a precondition for establishment of the FTAA.

ANOTHER PERSPECTIVE

What Does This Mean to Me?

Think about how different levels of economic integration can influence business practice. A Belgian dentist can set up a practice in southern Spain and move his family there with no additional governmental licensing or approval. Yet a Mexican dentist cannot set up his practice in Boston without emigrating and becoming relicensed in the United States. The ability of labor to move without barriers will tend to harmonize work conditions, salary levels, and benefits over time.

Canada has the job of chairing the crucial first stage of negotiations and will host the next Summit of the Americas, either in 2001 or 2002. If the FTAA is eventually established, it will have major implications for cross-border trade and investment flows within the hemisphere, but it is clearly a long way off.

Regional Economic Integration Elsewhere

Outside of Western Europe and the Americas, there have been few significant attempts at regional economic integration. Although there are a number of groupings throughout Asia and Africa, few exist in anything other than name. Perhaps the most significant group is the Association of Southeast Asian Nations (ASEAN). In addition, the Asia-Pacific Economic Cooperation (APEC) forum has recently emerged as the kernel of a potential free trade region.

Association of Southeast Asian Nations

Formed in 1967, ASEAN currently includes Brunei, Indonesia, Laos, Malaysia, Myanmar, the Philippines, Singapore, Thailand, and Vietnam. Laos, Myanmar, and Vietnam all joined recently, and their inclusion complicates matters because their economies trail those of the original members. The basic objectives of ASEAN are to foster freer trade between member countries and to achieve some cooperation in their industrial policies. Progress has been very limited, however. For example, although some progress has been made in tariff reduction between ASEAN countries, only 5 percent of intra-ASEAN trade currently consists of goods whose tariffs have been reduced through ASEAN's preferential trade arrangement. Future progress seems limited given that the financial crisis that swept through Southeast Asia in 1997 hit several ASEAN countries particularly hard, most notably Indonesia, Malaysia, and Thailand. Until these countries can get back on their economic feet, it is unlikely that much progress will be made.

Asia Pacific Economic Cooperation

Asia-Pacific Economic Cooperation was founded in 1990 at the suggestion of Australia. APEC currently has 18 member states including such economic powerhouses as the United States, Japan, and China (see Map 7.3). Collectively the 18 member states account for half of the world's gross national product, 40 percent of world trade, and most of the growth in the world economy. The stated aim of APEC is to increase multilateral cooperation in view of the economic rise of the Pacific nations and the growing interdependence within the region. US support for APEC was based on the belief that it might prove a viable strategy for heading off any moves to create Asian groupings from which it would be excluded.

Interest in APEC was heightened considerably in November 1993 when the heads of APEC member states met for the first time for a two-day conference in Seattle. Debate before the meeting focused on the likely future role of APEC. One view was that APEC should commit itself to the ultimate formation of a free trade area. Such a move would transform the Pacific Rim from a geographical expression into the world's largest free trade area. Another view was that APEC would produce no more than hot air and lots of photo opportunities for the leaders involved. As it turned out, the APEC meeting produced little more than some vague commitments from member states to work closely together for greater economic integration and a general lowering of trade barriers. However, member states did not rule out the possibility of closer economic cooperation in the future.[30]

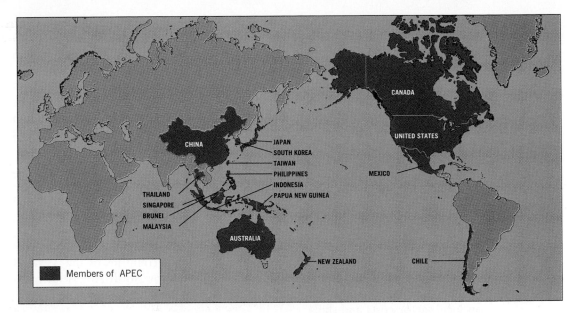

Map 7.3

Asia-Pacific Economic Cooperation

The heads of state met again in November 1994 in Jakarta, Indonesia. This time they agreed to take more concrete steps, and the joint statement at the end of the meeting formally committed APEC's industrialized members to remove their trade and investment barriers by 2010 and for developing economies to do so by 2020. They also called for a detailed blueprint charting out how this might be achieved, which was presented and discussed at the next APEC summit, held in Osaka in November 1995.[31] This was followed by further meetings in 1996 and 1997. At the 1997 meeting member states endorsed proposals designed to remove trade barriers in 15 sectors, ranging from fish to toys. However, the plan is vague and commits APEC to doing no more than holding further talks. Commenting on the vagueness of APEC pronouncements, the influential Brookings Institute, a US-based economic policy institution, noted that APEC "is in grave danger of shrinking into irrelevance as a serious forum." Despite the slow progress, APEC is worth watching, for if it eventually does transform itself into a free trade area, it will probably be the world's largest.[32]

Implications for Business

Currently the most significant developments in regional economic integration are occurring in the EU, NAFTA, and MERCOSUR. Although some of the other Latin American trade blocs may have greater economic significance in the future, as ultimately may APEC, currently the events in the EU, NAFTA, and MERCOSUR have more profound and immediate implications for business practice. Accordingly, in this section we will concentrate on the business implications of the EU, NAFTA, and MERCOSUR. Similar conclusions, however, could be drawn with regard to the creation of a single market anywhere in the world.

Opportunities

The creation of a single market offers significant opportunities because markets that were protected from foreign competition are opened. For example, in Europe before 1992 the large French and Italian markets were among the most protected. These markets are now much more open to foreign competition in the form of both exports and direct investment. Nonetheless, the specter of "Fortress Europe" suggests that to fully exploit such opportunities, it will benefit non-EU firms to set up EU subsidiaries. Many major US firms have long had subsidiaries in Europe. Those that do not would be advised to consider establishing them now, or run the risk of being shut out of the EU by nontariff barriers. In fact, non-EU firms rapidly increased their direct investment in the EU in anticipation of the creation of a single market. From 1985 to 1989, for example, about 37 percent of the FDI inflows into industrialized countries was directed at the EC. By 1991 this figure had risen to 66 percent.[33]

Additional opportunities arise from the inherent lower costs of doing business in a single market—as opposed to 15 national markets in the case of the EU or 3 in the case of NAFTA. Free movement of goods across borders, harmonized product standards, and simplified tax regimes allow firms based in the EU and the NAFTA countries to realize potentially enormous cost economies by centralizing production in those locations where the mix of factor costs and skills is optimal. At the extreme, rather than producing a product in each of the 15 EU countries or the 3 NAFTA countries, a firm may be able to serve the whole EU or North American market from a single location. This location must be chosen carefully, of course, with an eye on local factor costs and skills.

For example, in response to the challenges created by EU after 1992, the Minneapolis-based company 3M consolidated its European manufacturing and distribution facilities to take advantage of economies of scale. Thus, a plant in Great Britain now produces 3M's printing products and a German factory its reflective traffic control materials for all of the EU. In each case, 3M chose a location for centralized production after carefully considering the likely production costs in alternative locations within the EU. The ultimate goal of 3M is to dispense with national distinctions, directing R&D, manufacturing, distribution, and marketing for each product group from an EU headquarters.[34] Similarly, Unilever, one of Europe's largest companies, began rationalizing its production in advance of 1992 to attain scale economies. Unilever concentrated its production of dish-washing powder for the EU in one plant, bath soap in another, and so on.[35]

Even after the removal of barriers to trade and investment, enduring differences in culture and competitive practices often limit companies' ability to realize cost economies by centralizing production in key locations and producing a standardized product for a multicountry market. Consider the case of Atag Holdings NV, a Dutch maker of kitchen appliances that is profiled in the accompanying "Management Focus." Because of enduring differences between nations within the EU's single market, Atag still has to produce various "national brands," which limits the scale economies.

Threats

Just as the emergence of single markets in the EU and the Americas creates opportunities for business, it also presents a number of threats. For one, the business environment within each grouping will become more competitive. The lowering of barriers to trade and investment is likely to lead to increased price competition throughout the EU, NAFTA, and MERCOSUR. For example, before 1992 a Volkswagen Golf cost 55 percent more in Great Britain than in Denmark and 29 percent more in Ireland than in Greece.[36] Such price differentials vanish in a single market. This is a direct threat to any firm doing business in EU, NAFTA, or MERCOSUR countries. To survive in the tougher single-market environment, firms must rationalize their production and reduce their costs or else they will be at a severe disadvantage.

Atag Holdings

Atag Holdings NV is a Dutch company whose main business is kitchen appliances. Atag thought it was well placed to benefit from the single market, but so far it has found it tough going. Atag's plant is just one mile from the German border and near the center of the EU's population. The company thought it could cater to both Southern and Northern Europe by producing two main product lines and selling these standardized "euro-products" to "euro-consumers." The main benefits are the economies of scale derived from mass production of a standardized range of products.

Unfortunately, Atag quickly discovered that the euro-consumer is a myth. Consumer preferences vary much more across nations than Atag had thought. Consider ceramic stove tops; Atag planned to market just 2 varieties throughout the EU but has found it needs 11. Belgians, who cook in huge pots, require extra-large burners. Germans like oval pots and burners to fit. The French need small burners and very low temperatures for simmering sauces and broths. Germans like oven knobs on the top; the French want them on the front. Most Germans and French prefer black and white appliances; the British demand a range of colors including peach, pigeon blue, and mint green. Despite these problems, foreign sales of Atag's kitchenware increased from 4 percent of total revenues in 1985 to 25 percent in 1994. But the company now has a more realistic assessment of the benefits of a single market among a group of countries whose cultures and traditions still differ in deep and often profound ways. Atag now believes that its range of designs and product quality, rather than the magic bullet of a euro-product designed for a euro-consumer, will keep the company competitive. At the same time, Atag has to cope with higher costs than would have been possible with greater product standardization.[37]

A further threat to firms outside these trading blocs arises from the likely long-term improvement in the competitive position of many firms within the blocs. This is particularly relevant in the EU, where many firms are limited in their ability to compete globally with North American and Asian firms by a high cost structure. The creation of a single market and the resulting increased competition in the EU could transform many EU companies into efficient global competitors. The message for non-EU businesses is that they need to prepare for the emergence of more capable European competitors by reducing their own cost structures.

A final threat to firms outside of trading blocs is the threat of being shut out of the single market by the creation of "Trade Fortress." The charge that regional economic integration might lead to a fortress mentality is most often leveled at the EU. As noted earlier in the chapter, although the free trade philosophy underpinning the EU theoretically argues against the creation of any "fortress" in Europe, there are signs that the EU may raise barriers to imports and investment in politically sensitive areas, such as autos. Non-EU firms might be advised, therefore, to set up their own EU operations as quickly as possible. This could also occur in the NAFTA countries, but it seems less likely.

Key Terms

Summary

This chapter pursued three main objectives: to examine the economic and political debate surrounding regional economic integration; to review the progress toward regional economic integration in Europe, the Americas, and elsewhere; and to distinguish the important implications of regional economic integration for the practice of international business. The following points have been made in the chapter.

1 A number of levels of economic integration are possible in theory. In order of increasing integration, they include a free trade area, a customs union, a common market, an economic union, and full political union.

2 In a free trade area, barriers to trade between member countries are removed, but each country determines its own external trade policy. In a customs union, internal barriers to trade are removed and a common external trade policy is adopted. A common market is similar to a customs union except that factors of production also are allowed to move freely between countries. An economic union involves even closer integration, including establishment of a common currency and harmonization of tax rates. A political union is the logical culmination of attempts to achieve closer economic integration.

3 Regional economic integration is an attempt to achieve economic gains from the free flow of trade and investment between neighboring countries.

4 Integration is not easily achieved or sustained. Although integration brings benefits to the majority, it is never without costs for the minority. Concerns over national sovereignty often slow or stop integration attempts.

5 Regional integration will not increase economic welfare if the trade creation effects in the free trade area are outweighed by the trade diversion effects.

6 The Single European Act sought to create a true single market by abolishing administrative barriers to the free flow of trade and investment between EU countries.

7 The Maastricht Treaty aimed to take the EU even further along the road to economic union by establishing a common currency. The economic gains from a common currency, the euro, come from reduced exchange costs, reduced risk associated with currency fluctuations, and increased price competition within the EU.

8 Although no other attempt at regional economic integration comes close to the EU in terms of potential economic and political significance, various other attempts are being made. The most notable include NAFTA in North America, the Andean Pact and MERCOSUR in Latin America, ASEAN in Southeast Asia, and (perhaps) APEC.

9 The creation of single markets in the EU and North America means that many markets that were formerly protected from foreign competition are now more open. This creates major investment and export opportunities for firms within and outside these regions.

10 The free movement of goods across borders, the harmonization of product standards, and the simplification of tax regimes make it possible for firms based in a free trade area to realize potentially enormous cost economies by centralizing production in those locations within the area where the mix of factor costs and skills is optimal.

11 The lowering of barriers to trade and investment between countries within a trade group will probably be followed by increased price competition.

Critical Thinking and Discussion Questions

1 NAFTA is likely to produce net benefits for the US economy. Discuss.

2 What are the economic and political arguments for regional economic integration? Given these arguments, why don't we see more integration in the world economy?

3 What is the likely effect of creation of a single market and a single currency within the EU on competition within the EU? Why?

4 How should a US firm that currently exports only to Western Europe respond to the creation of a single market?

5 How should a firm with self-sufficient production facilities in several EU countries respond to the creation of a single market? What are the constraints on its ability to respond in a manner that minimizes production costs?

Internet Exercises

1 The move toward monetary union within the European Union countries is well under way. The euro was introduced at the central bank level in January 1999, and by 2002 the euro will replace the individual currencies of 11 countries. This unprecedented move is raising numerous issues, chief among them is what does monetary union, and the euro, mean to business? Will the euro change how Europeans shop? The jury is still out on just how consumers will respond to the new currency. Some experts argue that the notion of a euro consumer is simply a myth, while others suggest that the euro, combined with the opportunity for on-line shopping, will lead to more uniform buying behavior among consumers, especially the younger generation. Whatever the effect on consumers, experts do agree that companies must prepare themselves for the change. The Association for the Monetary Union of Europe (AMUE) has established a website to assist companies as they begin positioning themselves to do business in a state of monetary union.

Go to the AMUE website (**www.eubusiness.com/emu/euro-prep.htm**). Click on the page designed to aid companies as they begin their efforts to do business within a state of monetary union. Outline the steps you, as the owner of a small American bearing exporter to France and Germany, would take to prepare for the coming of the euro. How would your strategy change if you were vice president of accounting and finance for a large Australian brewery with deep penetration in the European Union marketplace? Suppose you are in charge of export sales for an on-line music company. Would your task be more difficult, easier, or the same? Explain the challenges faced by these three companies as they prepare for a unified European market.

2 Economic integration among countries is an important part of today's global business environment. For companies, it means larger markets free of trade barriers that restrict the flow of goods and services between countries. For countries, it can produce gains ranging from greater efficiency to improved political relationships.

Four important efforts toward regional economic integration include the North American Free Trade Agreement (NAFTA), the European Union (EU), the Association of Southeast Asia Nations (ASEAN), and MERCOSUR, linking Argentina, Brazil, Paraguay, and Uruguay.

Go to websites for each of these agreements (**www.nafta.net** for NAFTA; **www.europa.eu.int/** for the EU; **www.aseansec.org/** for ASEAN; and **www.mercosurinvestment.com/** for MERCOSUR). Compare the accords using the regional economic integration framework presented in the text. One key benefit of regional economic integration for companies is the absence of trade barriers among participating countries. Companies conducting business on-line may be in a position to circumvent trade barriers regardless of whether countries participate in a regional grouping or not. In your opinion, how will this phenomenon affect the positions of regional economic groupings? Should agreements such as NAFTA become involved in regulating e-commerce?

Martin's Textiles

August 12, 1992, was a really bad day for John Martin. That was the day Canada, Mexico, and the United States announced the planned North American Free Trade Agreement (NAFTA). Under the plan, all tariffs between the three countries would be eliminated within the next 10 to 15 years, with most being cut in 5 years. Most disturbing for John was the plan's provision that all tariffs on trade of textiles among the three countries were to be removed within 10 years. Under the agreement, Mexico and Canada would also be allowed to ship a specific amount of clothing and textiles made from foreign materials to the United States each year, and this quota would rise slightly over the first five years of the agreement. "My God!" thought John. "Now I'm going to have to decide about moving my plants to Mexico."

John is the CEO of a New York-based textile company, Martin's Textiles. The company has been in the Martin family for four generations; it was founded by his great-grandfather in 1910. In 1992 the company employed 1,500 people in three New York plants that produced cotton-based clothes, primarily underwear. All production employees were union members, and the company had a long history of good labor relations. The company had never had a labor dispute, and John, like his father, grandfather, and great-grandfather before him, regarded the workers as part of the "Martin family." John prided himself not only on knowing many of the employees by name, but also on knowing about the family circumstances of many longtime employees.

During the 1970s and 80s, the company had experienced in-creasingly tough competition, both from overseas and at home. The mid-1980s were particularly difficult. The strength of the dollar on the foreign exchange market during that period enabled Asian producers to enter the US market with very low prices. Since then, although the dollar had weakened against many major currencies, the Asian producers had not raised their prices. In a low-skilled, labor-intensive business such as clothing manufacture, costs are driven by wage rates and labor productivity. Not surprisingly, most of John's competitors in the northeastern United States responded to the intense cost competition by moving production south, first to states such as South Carolina and Mississippi, where nonunion labor could be hired for significantly less than in the unionized Northeast, and then to Mexico, where labor costs for textile workers were less than $2 per hour. In contrast, wage rates were $12.50 per hour at John's New York plant and $8 to $10 per hour at nonunion textile plants in the southeastern United States.

The early 90s had been particularly tough at Martin's Textiles. The company had registered a small loss each year, and John knew the company could not go on like this. His major customers, while praising the quality of Martin's products, had warned him that his prices were getting too high and that they might not be able to continue to do business with him. His longtime banker had told him that he must get his labor costs down. John agreed, but he knew of only one surefire way to do that—to move production south to Mexico. He had always been reluctant to do that, but now he seemed to have little choice. He feared that in five years the US market would be flooded with cheap imports from Asian, US, and Mexican companies, all producing in Mexico. It looked like the only way for Martin's Textiles to survive was to close the New York plants and move production to Mexico. All that would be left in the United States would be the sales force.

John's mind spun. How could something that throws good honest people out of work be good for the country? The politicians said it would be good for trade, good for economic growth, good for the three countries. John could not see it that way. What about Mary Morgan, who had worked for Martin's for 30 years. She was 54 years old. How would she and others like her find another job? What about his moral obligation to his workers? What about the loyalty his workers had shown his family over the years? Was this a good way to repay it? How would he break the news to his employees, many of whom had worked for the company 10 to 20 years? And what about the Mexican workers? Could they be as loyal and productive as his present employees? From other US textile companies that had set up production in Mexico he had heard stories of low productivity, poor workmanship, high turnover, and high absenteeism. If this was true, how could he cope with that? John had always felt that the success of Martin's Textiles was partly due to the family atmosphere, which encouraged worker loyalty, productivity, and attention to quality, an atmosphere that had been built up over four generations. How could he replicate that in Mexico with foreign workers who spoke a language he didn't even understand?

CASE DISCUSSION QUESTIONS

1 What are the economic costs and benefits to Martin's Textiles of shifting production to Mexico?

2 What are the social costs and benefits to Martin's Textiles of shifting production to Mexico?

3 Are the economic and social costs and benefits of moving production to Mexico independent of each other?

4 What seems to be the most ethical course of action?

5 What would you have done if you were John Martin?

For Thang Bernard surfing is much more than a sport. It's a lifestyle. "I wear the clothes; do the sport; and listen to surf music." Now Bernard, as he prefers to be called, is striving to make a living from his lifestyle. Bernard, 28, an undergraduate marketing major at California State Polytechnic University, Pomona, has started SPAANK. The company distributes his own line of beachcomber sandals and T-shirts targeted at other surfing aficionados.

Bernard's own love affair with surfing began when he was eight years old in his native Hawaii. It continued when he moved with his family to California at 18. At that

Surf's Up!

time Bernard began working for a major surf clothing retailer. Within a year he was the store manager. However, Bernard quit, what some of his surfer friends might consider a dream job, to pursue a much bigger dream. Bernard wanted to market his own clothing line and he wanted to finish his college education. "I thought I knew everything I needed until I started college," Bernard soon realized.

Four years later, while still managing the surfing store, Bernard designed a pair of surfer sandals, including the name, logo, and colors. According to Bernard, surfers buy the total image not just the

footwear. He showed the design to the store's loyal customers, the buyers, and his friends, all of whom were very supportive.

Bernard started with sandals, a single product line strategy, for a number of reasons. He was financing his business with credit cards and his budget was limited. Sandals did not require the cash outlay of other clothing. Yet sandals are essential for all surfers.

SPAANK sandals were positioned as mid-priced, high quality, and "totally casual." They expressed that their wearers were "casual, confident, and comfortable." The sandals were made from

rubber and plastic. They were available in yellow, blue, green, and red in a variety of sizes, including children's. Bernard's suggested retail price was $12. Competitive sandals sold from $3 for inexpensive, inferior quality to $50 for high-quality leather. Bernard decided to distribute the sandals through small and mid-sized surf shops in Southern California.

The unique brand image Bernard developed revolved around the SPAANK name, the logo, and the slogan. "I liked the sound of SPAANK, which had been the name of a boyhood friend's dog. Bernard reminisced that SPAANK,

whose pedigree was questionable, was the laziest dog in the islands.

The logo was a left ocean wave like the famous Pipeline, which is found on the north shore of Oahu. The colors along the wave moved from orange to gold to yellow, the "hues of Hawaiian sunset," according to Bernard. No other competitor was using a left wave design. Bernard coined the slogan "Casual, Confident, and Comfortable."

Despite being a distinctly Hawaiian sport most of whose participants are American, Bernard quickly became aware of the global aspects of starting his business. When Bernard finalized the

product two years after developing his initial design, he began researching manufacturers in the United States, Mexico, and Taiwan. He ultimately selected a Taiwanese producer because of its low price and minimum order requirements.

To obtain leads on manufacturers, Bernard faxed a rough sketch and product specifications to the Taiwan Chamber of Commerce. The chamber forwarded his request to sandal manufacturers and Bernard was inundated with more than 30 responses. After a month of communicating in English with manufacturers primarily through faxes, Bernard settled on a suitable supplier. He selected a firm that could handle a small order and did not insist on shipping it all at once. He placed an order for 2,000 sandals at $3 each CIF. According to CIF (cost, insurance, freight) terms of sale, the seller quotes a price that includes the cost of the goods, insurance, and all transportation and miscellaneous charges to the named foreign port in the country of final destination.

However, there were several complications to overcome before Bernard could take delivery because the deal was international. He had to hire a freight forwarder to ship the goods. Since he had no previous experience with international freight forwarders, he went to the Yellow Pages of the Los Angeles telephone directory and started making calls. After doing lots of digging, he found a company that specialized in sandals and would handle small shipments.

He needed a letter of credit (L/C), which safeguarded both his and the foreign manufacturer's interests. He contacted the international department of a local bank to help him obtain a letter of credit. The L/C stated that the importer bank would pay the manufacturer for the shipment once it arrived in Los Angeles.

To determine in advance the duty he would pay, Bernard sub-mitted a sample of the sandals to the US Customs Service of the Department of the Treasury for a ruling on the components of the product. Duties vary depending on the component materials. The Customs Office notified Bernard that the country of origin was improperly labeled and "if imported as is, the sandal would not be considered legally marked." Each pair of sandals had "Made In Taiwan" on a tag with other product information, but Customs required that a separate sticker with the country of origin would have to be affixed.

According to the Tariff Act of 1930, "every article of foreign origin imported into the United States shall be marked in a conspicuous place as legibly, indelibly and permanently as the nature of the article will permit, in such a manner as to indicate to the ultimate purchaser in the United States the English name of the country of origin of the article."

The sandals, which wholesale for $6, are being sold on consignment through three midsized surf shops. He has sold over a quarter of his initial inventory despite a limited marketing budget. Bernard initially placed two quarter-page, black-and-white ads in a surfing magazine at a total cost of $1,000. Given his limited resources, he did so more to establish his trademark than build any awareness.

According to Bernard, "The problem is getting the sandals into the stores, not moving them out." Surf retailers often carry and push their exclusive line of clothing. Retailers want their suppliers to support their brands with hefty marketing and cooperative advertising budgets. Promotion can include print advertising as well as paid sponsorships to well-known surfers.

Bernard now spends about one day per week on the sandal line. He services current accounts; makes cold calls to increase his distribution; analyzes the market; and works on his designs.

A year ago Bernard experimented with a second line of T-shirts, embellished with his unique wave logo. He landed a single large account and within a month sold 80 percent of the 500 T-shirts he had placed on consignment. Because of the costs required to produce the shirts, the venture barely broke even. Despite the success of the T-shirts with consumers, the retailer was reluctant to reorder again because of Bernard's inadequate marketing budget. Bernard, however, continues to spend time designing the shirts and trying to land new accounts.

In starting his surfing venture, Bernard occasionally has been tossed off the board. However, this veteran surfer is committed to catching the big wave and riding it for fun and profit.

eight

The Foreign Exchange Market

Opening Case

Foreign Exchange Losses at JAL

One of the world's largest airlines, Japan Airlines (JAL), is also one of the best customers of Boeing, the world's biggest manufacturer of commercial airplanes. Every year JAL spends about $800 million to purchase aircraft from Boeing. Boeing aircraft are priced in US dollars, with prices ranging from about $35 million for a 737 to $160 million for a top-of-the-line 747-400. JAL orders an aircraft two to six years before the plane is actually needed. JAL normally pays Boeing a 10 per-

The **foreign exchange market** enables companies based in countries that use different currencies to trade with each other. However, it can be difficult, and risky, in the interim between when an order is placed and when a final payment is made for an item, as was illustrated by the value change of the Japanese yen against the US dollar for JAL. Why do you suppose companies would not negotiate to purchase a product at an established price according to currency value at the time of the initial deposit?

Learning Objectives

1 Be familiar with the form and function of the foreign exchange market.

2 Understand the difference between spot and forward exchange rates.

3 Understand how currency exchange rates are determined.

4 Appreciate the role of the foreign exchange market in insuring against foreign exchange risk.

5 Be familiar with the merits of different approaches towards exchange rate forecasting.

6 Appreciate why some currencies cannot always be converted into other currencies.

7 Understand how countertrade is used to mitigate problems associated with an inability to convert currencies.

---

cent deposit when ordering an aircraft, and the bulk of the payment is made when the aircraft is delivered.

The long lag between placing an order and making a final payment presents a conundrum for JAL. Most of JAL's revenues are in Japanese yen, not US dollars. JAL must change its yen into dollars to pay Boeing. In the interval between placing an order and making final payment, the value of the Japanese yen against the US dollar may change. This can increase or decrease the

cost of an aircraft when calculated in yen. Consider an order placed in 1985 for a 747 aircraft that was to be delivered in 1990. In 1985 the dollar value of this order was $100 million. The prevailing exchange rate in 1985 was $1 = ¥240 (i.e., one dollar was worth 240 yen), so the price of the 747 in yen was ¥2.4 billion. By 1990 when final payment was due, however, the dollar–yen exchange rate might have changed. For example, the dollar–yen exchange rate might be $1 = ¥300,

and the price of the 747 in yen would have gone from ¥2.4 billion to ¥3.0 billion, an increase of 25 percent. Or the yen might have risen in value against the dollar to $1 = ¥200. If this had occurred, the yen price of the 747 would have fallen 16.7 percent to ¥2.0 billion.

In 1985 JAL has no way of knowing what the value of the yen will be against the dollar by 1990. However, JAL can enter into a contract with foreign exchange traders in 1985 to purchase dollars in 1990

value of yen
against dollar
may change

forward exchange contract *example related to trade*

based on those traders' assessment of what they think the dollar–yen exchange rate will be in 1990. This is called entering into a *forward exchange contract* and it allows JAL to know in 1985 what it will have to pay for the 747 in 1990. For example, if the value of the yen was expected to increase against the dollar between 1985 and 1990, foreign exchange traders might have offered a forward exchange contract that allowed JAL to purchase dollars at a rate of $1 = ¥185 in 1990, instead of the $1 = ¥240 rate that prevailed in 1985. At this forward exchange rate, the 747 would only cost ¥1.85 billion, a 23 percent saving over the yen price implied by the 1985 exchange rate.

JAL was confronted with just this scenario in 1985. At that time JAL entered into a 10-year forward exchange contract with a total value of about $3.6 billion. This contract gave JAL the right to buy US dollars from a consortium of foreign exchange traders at various points during the next ten years for an average exchange rate of $1 = ¥185. To JAL this looked like a great deal given the 1985 exchange rate of $1 = ¥240. However, by September 1994 when the bulk of the contract had been executed, it no longer looked like a good deal. To everyone's surprise, the value of the yen had surged against the dollar. By 1992 the exchange rate stood at $1 = ¥120, and by 1994 it was $1 = ¥99. Un-

fortunately, JAL could not take advantage of this more favorable exchange rate. Instead, JAL was bound by the terms of the contract to purchase dollars at the contract rate of $1 = ¥185, a rate that by 1994 looked outrageously expensive. This misjudgment cost JAL dearly. In 1994 JAL was paying 86 percent more than it needed to for each Boeing aircraft bought with dollars purchased via the forward exchange contract! In October 1994 JAL admitted that in its most recent financial year the loss from this misjudgment amounted to $450 million, or ¥45 billion. Foreign exchange traders speculated that JAL had probably lost a total of ¥155 billion ($1.5 billion) on this contract since 1988.[1]

Introduction

3 objectives

① ② ③

This chapter has three main objectives. The first is to explain how the foreign exchange market works. The second is to examine the forces that determine exchange rates and to discuss the degree to which it is possible to predict future exchange rate movements. The third objective is to map the implications for international business of exchange rate movements and the foreign exchange market. This chapter is the first of two that deal with the international monetary system and its relationship to international business. In the next chapter we will explore the institutional structure of the international monetary system, or the context within which the foreign exchange market functions. As we shall see, changes in the institutional structure of the international monetary system can exert a profound influence on the development of foreign exchange markets.

foreign exchange market Market for converting the currency of one country into that of another country.

exchange rate Rate at which one currency is converted into another.

The **foreign exchange market** is a market for converting the currency of one country into that of another country. An **exchange rate** is simply the rate at which one currency is converted into another. We saw in the opening case how JAL used the foreign exchange market to convert Japanese yen into US dollars. Without the foreign exchange market, international trade and international investment would be impossible on the scale that we see today; companies would have to resort to barter. The foreign exchange market is the lubricant that enables companies based in countries that use different currencies to trade with each other.

foreign exchange risk

We know from earlier chapters that international trade and investment have their risks. As the opening case illustrates, some of these risks exist because future exchange rates cannot be perfectly predicted. The rate at which one currency is converted into another typically changes over time. One function of the foreign exchange market is to provide some insurance against the risks that arise from changes in exchange rates, commonly referred to as foreign exchange risk. Although the foreign exchange market offers some insurance against foreign exchange risk, it cannot provide complete insurance. JAL's loss of $1.5 billion on foreign exchange transactions is an extreme example of what can happen, but it is not unusual for international businesses to suffer losses because of unpredicted changes in exchange rates. Currency fluctuations can make seemingly profitable trade and investment deals unprofitable, and vice versa. The opening case contains an example of this as it relates to trade. For an example that deals with investment, consider the case of Mexico. Between 1976 and 1987, the value of the Mexican peso dropped from 22 per US dollar to 1,500 per US dollar. As a result, a US company with an investment in Mexico that yielded an income of 100 million pesos per year would have seen the dollar value of that income shrink from $4.55 million in 1976 to $66,666 by 1987!

In addition to altering the value of trade deals and foreign investments, currency movements can also open or close export opportunities and alter the attractiveness of imports. In 1984, for example, the US dollar was trading at an all-time high against most other currencies. At that time one dollar could buy one British pound or 250 Japanese yen, compared to 0.55 of a British pound and about 85 yen in early 1995. In the 1984 US presidential campaign, then President Ronald Reagan boasted about how good the strong dollar was for the United States. Many US companies did not see it that way. Companies such as Caterpillar that earned their living by exporting to other countries were being priced out of foreign markets by the strong dollar. In 1980 when the dollar-to-pound exchange rate was $1 = £0.63, a $100,000 Caterpillar earthmover cost a British buyer £63,000. In 1984, with the exchange rate at $1 = £0.99, it cost close to £99,000–a 60 percent increase in four years! At that exchange rate Caterpillar's products were overpriced in comparison to those of its foreign competitors, such as Japan's Komatsu. At the same time, the strong dollar reduced the price of the earthmovers Komatsu imported into the United States, which allowed the Japanese company to take US market share away from Caterpillar.

Thus, while the existence of foreign exchange markets is necessary for large-scale international trade and investment, the movement of exchange rates introduces many risks into international trade and investment. Some of these risks can be insured against by using instruments offered by the foreign exchange market, such as the forward exchange contracts discussed in the opening case; others cannot be.

In this chapter we will examine these issues. We begin by looking at the functions and the form of the foreign exchange market. This includes distinguishing among spot exchange rates and forward exchange rates. Then we will consider the factors that determine exchange rates. We will also look at how foreign trade is conducted when a country's currency cannot be exchanged for other currencies; that is, when its currency is not convertible. The chapter closes with a discussion of these things in terms of their implications for business.

The Functions of the Foreign Exchange Market

The foreign exchange market serves two main functions. The first is to convert the currency of one country into the currency of another. The second is to provide some insurance against **foreign exchange risk,** by which we mean the adverse consequences of unpredictable changes in exchange rates.[2]

Currency Conversion

Each country has a currency in which the prices of goods and services are quoted. In the United States it is the dollar ($); in Great Britain, the pound (£); in Japan, the yen (¥); and so on. In general, within the borders of a particular country one must use the national currency (although as we saw in the previous chapter, within

foreign exchange risk
Adverse consequences of unpredictable changes in exchange rates.

the European Union 11 countries are moving toward full adoption of a single currency, the euro). A US tourist cannot walk into a store in Edinburgh, Scotland, and use US dollars to buy a bottle of Scotch whisky. Dollars are not recognized as legal tender in Scotland; the tourist must use British pounds. Fortunately, the tourist can go to a bank and exchange her dollars for pounds. Then she can buy the whisky.

When a tourist exchanges one currency into another, she is participating in the foreign exchange market. The exchange rate is the rate at which the market converts one currency into another. For example, an exchange rate of $1 = ¥85 specifies that one US dollar has the equivalent value of 85 Japanese yen. The exchange rate allows us to compare the relative prices of goods and services in different countries. Our US tourist may find that she must pay £25 for the bottle of Scotch whisky in Edinburgh, knowing that the same bottle costs $40 in the United States. Is this a good deal? Imagine the current dollar/pound exchange rate is $1 = £0.50. Our tourist takes out her calculator and converts £25 into dollars. (The calculation is 25/0.50.) She discovers that the bottle of Scotch costs the equivalent of $50, and she is surprised that a bottle of Scotch whisky could cost less in the United States than in Scotland. (This is true; alcohol is taxed heavily in Great Britain.)

Tourists are minor participants in the foreign exchange market; companies engaged in international trade and investment are major ones. International businesses have four main uses for foreign exchange markets. First, the payments a company receives for its exports, the income it receives from foreign investments, or the income it receives from licensing agreements with foreign firms may be in foreign currencies. To use those funds in its home country, the company must convert them to its home country's currency. Consider the Scotch distillery that exports its whisky to the United States. The distillery is paid in dollars, but they must be converted into British pounds.

Second, international businesses use foreign exchange markets when they must pay a foreign company for its products or services in its country's currency. For example, our friend Michael runs a company called NST, a large British travel service for school groups. Each year Michael's company arranges vacations for thousands of British schoolchildren and their teachers in France. French hotel proprietors demand payment in euros, so Michael must convert large sums of money from pounds into euros to pay them.

Third, international businesses use foreign exchange markets when they have spare cash that they wish to invest for short terms in money markets. Consider a US company that has $10 million it wants to invest for three months. The best interest rate it can earn on these funds in the United States may be 8 percent. By investing in a Swiss money market account, however, it may be able to earn 12 percent. Thus, the company may change its $10 million into francs and invest it in Switzerland. However, the rate of return it earns on this investment depends not only on the Swiss interest rate, but also on the changes in the value of the Swiss franc against the dollar.

Finally, **currency speculation** is another use of foreign exchange markets. Currency speculation typically involves the short-term movement of funds from one currency to another in the hope of profiting from shifts in exchange rates. Consider again the US company with $10 million to invest for three months. Suppose the company suspects that the US dollar is overvalued against the Swiss franc. That is, the company expects the value of the dollar to depreciate against that of the Swiss franc. Imagine the current dollar/franc exchange rate is $1 = SFr 6. The company exchanges its $10 million into Swiss francs, receiving SFr 60 million. Over the next three months the value of the dollar depreciates until $1 = SFr 5. Now the company exchanges its SFr 60 million back into dollars and finds that it has $12 million. The company has made a $2 million profit on currency speculation in three months on an initial investment of $10 million.

currency speculation Short-term movement of funds from one currency to another in the hopes of profiting from shifts in exchange rates.

One famous currency "speculator" is George Soros, whose Quantum Group of hedge funds controls about $15 billion in assets. The activities of Soros, who has been spectacularly successful, are profiled in the accompanying "Management Focus." In general, however, companies should beware of speculation for it is a very risky business; the company cannot know for sure what will happen to exchange rates. While a speculator may profit handsomely if his speculation about future currency movements is correct, he can also lose vast amounts of money if it is wrong. For example, in 1991 Clifford Hatch, the finance director of the British food and drink company Allied-Lyons, bet large amounts of the company's funds on the speculation that the British pound would rise in value against the US dollar. Over the previous three years Hatch had made over $25 million for Allied-Lyons by placing similar currency bets. His 1991 bet, however, went spectacularly wrong when instead of increasing in value, the British pound plummeted in value against the US dollar. In February 1991 one pound bought $2; by April it bought less than $1.75. The total loss to Allied-Lyons from this speculation was a staggering $269 million, more than the company was to earn from all of its food and drink activities during 1991![3]

Insuring against Foreign Exchange Risk

A second function of the foreign exchange market is to provide insurance to protect against the possible adverse consequences of unpredictable changes in exchange rates (foreign exchange risk). To explain how the market performs this function, we must first distinguish among spot exchange rates and forward exchange rates.

SPOT EXCHANGE RATES   When two parties agree to exchange currency and execute the deal immediately, the transaction is referred to as a spot exchange. Exchange rates governing such "on the spot" trades are referred to as spot exchange rates. The **spot exchange rate** is the rate at which a foreign exchange dealer converts one currency into another currency on a particular day. Thus, when our US tourist in Edinburgh goes to a bank to convert her dollars into pounds, the exchange rate is the spot rate for that day.

Although it is necessary to use a spot rate to execute a transaction immediately, it may not be the most attractive rate. The value of a currency is determined by the interaction between the demand and supply of that currency relative to the demand and supply of other currencies. For example, if lots of people want US dollars and dollars are in short supply, and few people want Swiss francs and Swiss francs are in plentiful supply, the spot exchange rate for converting dollars into Swiss francs will change. The dollar is likely to appreciate against the Swiss franc (or the franc will depreciate against the dollar). Imagine the spot exchange rate is $1 = SFr 5 when the market opens. As the day progresses, dealers demand more dollars and fewer francs. By the end of the day the spot exchange rate might be $1 = SFr 5.3. The dollar has appreciated, and the Swiss franc has depreciated.

spot exchange rate Rate at which a foreign exchange dealer converts one currency into another currency on a particular day.

ANOTHER PERSPECTIVE

Exchange Rates on Vacation

An interesting exchange rate side effect was occurring the summer of 1997 during the currency crisis in Southeast Asia. The currency crisis led to a dramatic political crisis in Indonesia, which caused the overthrow of President Suharto and much unrest in the streets of many major cities. The peaceful beaches of Bali were affected, too, as tourism collapsed. The spot exchange rate moved from 2,500 to 16,000 rupiah to the US dollar, which meant that costs in Bali dropped so much that a suite in the best resort could be had for $40 a night. Imagine the impact on the local economy.

George Soros, a Hungarian-born financier, is the principle partner of the Quantum Group, which controls a series of hedge funds with assets of about $15 billion. A **hedge fund** is an investment fund that not only buys financial assets (such as stocks, bonds, and currencies) but also sells them short. **Short selling** occurs when an investor places a speculative bet that the value of a finan-

broker is significantly less than the income he received from the initial sale of the stock. Imagine that a short seller borrows 100 units of IBM stock and sells it in the market at $150 per share, yielding a total income of $15,000. In one year the short seller has to give the 100 units of IBM stock back to his broker. In the intervening period the value of the IBM stock falls to $50. It now

Along with other hedge funds, Soros' Quantum fund often takes a short position in currencies that he expects to decline in value. For example, if Soros expects the British pound to decline against the US dollar he may borrow 1 billion pounds from a currency trader and immediately sell them for US dollars. Soros will then hope that the value of the pound will decline against the dollar, so

George Soros—The Man Who Can Move Currency Markets

cial asset will decline and profits from that decline. A common variant of short selling occurs when an investor borrows stock from his broker and sells that stock. The short seller has to pay back that stock to his broker. However, he hopes that in the intervening period the value of the stock will decline so that the cost of repurchasing the stock to pay back the

costs the short seller only $5,000 to repurchase the 100 units of IBM stock for his broker. The difference between the initial sales price ($150) and the repurchase price ($50) represents the short seller's profit, which in this case is $100 per unit of stock for a total profit of $10,000. Short selling was developed as a means of reducing risk (of hedging), but it is often used for speculation.

that when he has to repay the 1 billion pounds it will cost him considerably less (in US dollars) than he received from the initial sale.

Since the 1970s Soros has consistently earned huge returns by making such speculative bets. His most spectacular triumph came in September 1992. At that time he believed that the British pound was likely to decline in value against major currencies,

---

Table 8.1 lists spot exchange rate quotes for several currencies on February 8, 2000 at 2:20 PM Eastern US time (quotes can change by the minute). On this day at this time $1 could be exchanged for Australian $1.578, UK £0.6209, and so on. Table 8.1 also tells us what other currencies would purchase. For example, SFr 1 could be exchanged for DMark 1.216, the Germany currency.

FORWARD EXCHANGE RATES The fact that spot exchange rates change daily as determined by the relative demand and supply for different currencies can be problematic for an international business. A US company that imports laptop computers from Japan knows that in 30 days it must pay yen to a Japanese supplier when a shipment arrives. The company will pay the Japanese supplier ¥200,000 for each laptop computer, and the current dollar/yen spot exchange rate is $1 = ¥120. At this rate, each computer costs the importer $1,667 (i.e., 1,667 = 200,000/120). The importer knows she can sell the computers the day they arrive for $2,000 each, which yields a gross profit of $333 on each computer ($2,000 − $1667). However, the importer will not have the funds to pay the Japanese supplier until the computers have been sold. If over the next 30 days the dollar unexpectedly depreciates against the yen, say to $1 = ¥95, the importer will still have to pay the Japanese company ¥200,000 per computer, but in dollar terms that would equal $2,105 per computer, which is more than she can sell the computers for. A depreciation in the value of the dollar against the yen from $1 = ¥120 to $1 = ¥95 would transform a profitable deal into an unprofitable one.

particularly the German deutsche mark. The prevailing exchange rate was £1 = DM2.80. The British government was obliged by a European Union agreement on monetary policy to try to keep the pound above DM2.77. Soros doubted the British could do this, so he shorted the pound, borrowing billions of pounds (using the $12 billion assets of the Quantum Fund as collateral) and immediately selling them for German deutsche marks. His simultaneous sale of pounds and purchase of marks was so large that it helped drive down the value of the pound against the mark. Other currency traders, seeing Soros' market moves and knowing his reputation for making successful currency bets, jumped on the bandwagon and started to sell pounds short and buy deutsche marks. The resulting *bandwagon effect* put enormous pressure on the pound. The British Central Bank, at the request of the British government, spent about 20 billion pounds on September 16 to try to prop up the value of the pound against the deutsche mark (by selling marks and buying pounds), but to no avail. The pound continued to fall and on September 17 the British government gave up and let the pound decline (it actually fell to £1 = DM2.00). As a consequence of this bet, Soros made a $1 billion profit in four weeks!

Like all currency speculators, however, George Soros has had his losses. In February 1994 he bet that the Japanese yen would decline in value against the US dollar and promptly shorted the yen. However, the yen continued to rise, costing his Quantum fund $600 million. Similarly, a series of incorrect bets in 1987 resulted in losses of more than $800 million for Quantum. Despite such defeats, however, Soros' Quantum fund has earned an average annual rate of return of over 40 percent since 1970.

Soros has gained a reputation for being able to move currency markets by his actions. This is the consequence not so much of the money that Soros puts into play, but of the bandwagon effect that results when other speculators follow his lead. This reputation has resulted in Soros being depicted as the archvillain of the 1997 Asian currency crisis. In 1997 the currencies of Thailand, Malaysia, South Korea, and Indonesia all lost between 50 percent and 70 percent of their value against the US dollar. While the reasons for the crisis are complex, a common feature was excessive borrowing by firms based in these countries. Several Asian leaders, however, most notably Mahathir bin Mohamad, the prime minister of Malaysia, blamed the crisis on "criminal speculation" by Soros, who he says had been intent on impoverishing Asian nations. Soros denied that his fund had been involved in shorting Asian currencies.[4]

Table 8.1

Foreign Exchange Quotations

Currency Last Trade	U.S. $ N/A	Aust $ 2:00PM	U.K. £ 2:00PM	Can $ 2:00PM	DMark 2:00PM	FFranc 2:00PM	¥en 2:00PM	SFranc 2:00PM	Euro 1:49PM
U.S. $	1	0.6338	1.61	0.6906	0.5049	0.1505	0.009149	0.6142	0.9872
Aust $	1.578	1	2.541	1.09	0.7966	0.2375	0.01444	0.9691	1.558
U.K. £	0.6209	0.3935	1	0.4288	0.3135	0.09347	0.005681	0.3814	0.613
Can $	1.448	0.9178	2.332	1	0.7311	0.218	0.01325	0.8894	1.429
DMark	1.981	1.255	3.19	1.368	1	0.2981	0.01812	1.216	1.955
FFranc	6.643	4.21	10.7	4.588	3.354	1	0.06078	4.08	6.558
¥en	109.3	69.28	176	75.48	55.19	16.45	1	67.13	107.9
SFranc	1.628	1.032	2.622	1.124	0.822	0.2451	0.0149	1	1.607
Euro	1.013	0.642	1.631	0.6996	0.5114	0.1525	0.009268	0.6222	1

forward exchange
Two parties agree to exchange currency and execute the deal at some specific date in the future.

forward exchange rates Rates for currency exchange quoted for 30, 90, or 180 days into the future.

To avoid the risk of this occurring, the US importer might want to engage in a forward exchange. A **forward exchange** occurs when two parties agree to exchange currency and execute the deal at some specific date in the future. Exchange rates governing such future transactions are referred to as forward exchange rates. For most major currencies, **forward exchange rates** are quoted for 30 days, 90 days, and 180 days into the future. (An example of forward exchange rate quotations appears in Table 8.2.) In some cases, it is possible to get forward exchange rates for several years into the future. The opening case, for example, showed how JAL entered into a contract that predicted forward exchange rates up to 10 years in the future. Let us assume the 30-day forward exchange rate for converting dollars into yen is $1 = ¥110. The laptop computer importer enters into a 30-day forward exchange transaction with a foreign exchange dealer at this rate and is guaranteed that she will have to pay no more than $1,818 for each computer (1,818 = 200,000/110). This guarantees her a profit of $182 per computer ($2,0008 − $1,818), and she insures herself against the possibility that an unanticipated change in the dollar/yen exchange rate will turn a profitable deal into an unprofitable one.

In this example the spot exchange rate ($1 = ¥120) and the 30-day forward rate ($1 = ¥110) differ. Such differences are normal; they reflect the expectations of the foreign exchange market about future currency movements. The fact that $1 bought more yen with a spot exchange than with a 30-day forward exchange indicates that foreign exchange dealers expected the dollar to depreciate against the yen in the next 30 days. When this occurs we say the dollar is selling at a *discount* on the 30-day forward market (i.e., it is worth less than on the spot market). The opposite can also occur. If the 30-day forward exchange rate were $1 = ¥130, for example, $1 would buy more yen with a forward exchange than with a spot exchange. In such a case, we say the dollar is selling at a *premium* on the 30-day forward market. This reflects the foreign exchange dealers' expectations that the dollar will appreciate against the yen over the next 30 days.

The Nature of the Foreign Exchange Market

So far we have dealt with the foreign exchange market only as an abstract concept. It is now time to take a closer look at the nature of this market. The foreign exchange market is not located in any one place. It is a global network of banks, brokers, and foreign exchange dealers connected by electronic communications. When companies wish to convert currencies, they typically go through their banks rather than entering the market directly. In recent years the foreign exchange market has been growing at a rapid pace, reflecting a general growth in the volume of cross-border trade and investment (see Chapter 1). In March 1986, for example, the average total value of global foreign exchange trading was about $200 billion per day. By April 1989 it had soared to over $650 billion per day, by 1995 it was over $1,200 billion per day, and by 1998 it hit $1,500 billion per day.[5] The most important trading centers are London, New York, Tokyo, and Singapore. In April 1998, over $637 billion was traded through London each day, $351 billion through New York, $147 billion through Tokyo, and $139 billion through Singapore.[6] Major secondary trading centers include Zurich, Frankfurt, Paris, Hong Kong, San Francisco, and Sydney.

London's dominance in the foreign exchange market is due to both history and geography. As the capital of the world's first major industrial trading nation, London had become the world's largest center for international banking by the end of

Table 8.2

Spot and Forward Exchange Rates

CURRENCY TRADING

Monday, January 3, 2000

EXCHANGE RATES

The New York foreign exchange mid-range rates below apply to trading among banks in amounts of $1 million and more, as quoted at 4 p.m. Eastern time by Reuters and other sources. Retail transactions provide fewer units of foreign currency per dollar. Rates for the 11 Euro currency countries are derived from the latest dollar-euro rate using the exchange ratios set 1/1/99.

Country	U.S. $ equiv.		Currency per U.S. $	
	Mon	Fri	Mon	Fri
Argentina (Peso)	1.0002	1.0001	.9998	.9999
Australia (Dollar)	.6582	.6560	1.5192	1.5244
Austria Schilling	.07462	.07318	13.402	13.665
Bahrain (Dinar)	2.6525	2.6525	.3770	.3770
Belgium (Franc)	.0255	.0250	39.2885	40.0615
Brazil (Real)	.5495	.5536	1.8200	1.8065
Britain (Pound)	1.6371	1.6153	.6108	.6191
1-month forward	1.6373	1.6156	.6108	.6190
3-months forward	1.6373	1.6154	.6108	.6190
6-months forward	1.6368	1.6148	.6109	.6193
Canada (Dollar)	.6913	.6924	1.4465	1.4442
1-month forward	.6919	.6929	1.4453	1.4432
3-months forward	.6929	.6939	1.4433	1.4411
6-months forward	.6943	.6954	1.4404	1.4381
Chile (Peso) (d)	.001894	.001888	527.85	529.75
China (Renminbi)	.1208	.1208	8.2798	8.2795
Colombia (Peso)	.0005306	.0005333	1884.50	1875.00
Czech. Rep (Koruna)				
Commercial rate	.02814	.02793	35.541	35.805
Denmark (Krone)	.1379	.1353	7.2491	7.3933
Ecuador (Sucre)				
Floating rate	.00004598	.00004866	21750.00	20550.00
Finland (Markka)	.1727	.1694	5.7908	5.9047
France (Franc)	.1565	.1535	6.3887	6.5143
1-month forward	.1569	.1539	6.3736	6.4995
3-months forward	.1576	.1545	6.3460	6.4710
6-months forward	.1586	.1555	6.3054	6.4297
Germany (Mark)	.5250	.5149	1.9049	1.9423
1-month forward	.5262	.5160	1.9004	1.9379
3-months forward	.5285	.5183	1.8921	1.9294
6-months forward	.5319	.5216	1.8800	1.9171
Greece (Drachma)	.003113	.003050	321.26	327.83
Hong Kong (Dollar)	.1286	.1286	7.7763	7.7735
Hungary (Forint)	.004034	.003957	247.90	252.71
India (Rupee)	.02302	.02299	43.435	43.500
Indonesia (Rupiah)	.0001417	.0001431	7055.00	6987.50
Ireland (Punt)	1.3040	1.2789	.7669	.7819
Israel (Shekel)	.2436	.2407	4.1053	4.1548
Italy (Lira)	.0005303	.0005201	1885.83	1922.91

Country	U.S. $ equiv.		Currency per U.S. $	
	Mon	Fri	Mon	Fri
Japan (Yen)	.009843	.009792	101.60	102.12
1-month forward	.009893	.009843	101.08	101.59
3-months forward	.009989	.009937	100.11	100.64
6-months forward	.010141	.010088	98.61	99.13
Jordan (Dinar)	1.4085	1.4085	.7100	.7100
Kuwait (Dinar)	3.2895	3.2862	.3040	.3043
Lebanon (Pound)	.0006634	.0006634	1507.50	1507.50
Malaysia (Ringgit)	.2632	.2632	3.8000	3.8001
Malta (Lira)	2.4643	2.4254	.4058	.4123
Mexico (Peso)				
Floating rate	.1063	.1055	9.4050	9.4750
Netherland (Guilder)	.4659	.4569	2.1463	2.1885
New Zealand (Dollar)	.5255	.5229	1.9029	1.9124
Norway (Krone)	.1266	.1248	7.8969	8.0105
Pakistan (Rupee)	.01927	.01930	51.890	51.815
Peru (new Sol)	.2840	.2850	3.5215	3.5085
Philippines (Peso)	.02503	.02481	39.950	40.300
Poland (Zloty)	.2418	.2418	4.1350	4.1350
Portugal (Escudo)	.005121	.005023	195.26	199.10
Russia (Ruble) (a)	.03643	.03630	27.450	27.550
Saudi Arabia (Riyal)	.2666	.2666	3.7508	3.7510
Singapore (Dollar)	.6038	.6004	1.6562	1.6655
Slovak Rep. (Koruna)	.02427	.02373	41.202	42.132
South Africa (Rand)	.1632	.1625	6.1288	6.1550
South Korea (Won)	.0008869	.0008807	1127.50	1135.50
Spain (Peseta)	.006171	.006052	162.05	165.24
Sweden (Krona)	.1195	.1176	8.3668	8.5030
Switzerland (Franc)	.6391	.6281	1.5647	1.5921
1-month forward	.6416	.6306	1.5585	1.5859
3-months forward	.6459	.6347	1.5483	1.5755
6-months forward	.6527	.6414	1.5321	1.5992
Taiwan (Dollar)	.03188	.03186	31.365	31.385
Thailand (Baht)	.02702	.02655	37.015	37.665
Turkey (Lira)	.00000185	.00000184	539255.00	542400.00
United Arab (Dirham)	.2723	.2723	3.6729	3.6730
Uruguay (New Peso)				
Financial	.08608	.08611	11.618	11.613
Venezuela (Bolivar)	.001540	.001541	649.25	648.75
SDR	1.3761	1.3710	.7267	.7294
Euro	1.0268	1.0068	.9739	.9932

Special Drawing Rights (SDR) are based on exchange rates for the U.S., German, British, French, and Japanese currencies. Source: International Monetary Fund.

a-Russian Central Bank rate. Trading band lowered on 8/17/98. b-Government rate. d-Floating rate; trading band suspended on 9/2/99.

The 3-month and 6-month forward rates for France, Germany, Japan and Switzerland appearing in the Foreign Exchange column were incorrectly calculated for the period beginning with August 13 and ending with October 7. Corrected data is available from Readers' Reference Service (413) 592-3600.

the 19th century, a position it has retained. Today London also has an advantageous location; its central position between Tokyo and Singapore to the east and New York to the west has made it the critical link between the Asian and New York markets. Because of the differences in time zones, London opens as Tokyo and Singapore close for the night and is still open for the first few hours of trading in New York. However, some now argue that the failure of Britain to join the first round of the European Monetary Union might lead to the demise of London as the center of global foreign exchange trading. This is particularly likely to occur if the euro emerges as a major currency unit after 2002, and if Britain stays out of the euro zone (see Chapter 7 for details).

Two features of the foreign exchange market are of particular note. The first is that the market never sleeps. It is a 24-hour-a-day market. Somewhere in the world, a foreign exchange market is open.

The second feature of the market is the integration of the various trading centers. Direct telephone lines and Internet-based computer links between trading centers around the globe have effectively created a single market. The integration of financial centers implies there can be no significant difference in exchange rates quoted in the trading centers. For example, if the dollar/Swiss franc exchange rate quoted in London at 3 PM is $1 = SFr 5.0, the dollar/franc exchange rate quoted in New York at the same time (9 AM New York time) will be identical. If the New York dollar/franc exchange rate were $1 = SFr 5.5, a dealer could make a profit through **arbitrage,** the process of buying a currency low and selling it high. For example, if the prices differed in London and New York as given, a dealer could purchase SFr 550,000 for $100,000 in New York and immediately sell them in London for $110,000, making a quick profit of $10,000. If all dealers tried to cash in on the opportunity, however, the demand for Swiss francs in New York would result in an appreciation of the franc against the dollar, while the increase in the supply of Swiss francs in London would result in their depreciation there. The discrepancy in the New York and London exchange rates would disappear very quickly. Since foreign exchange dealers are continually watching their computer screens for arbitrage opportunities, the few that arise tend to be small, and they disappear in minutes.

Another feature of the foreign exchange market is the important role played by the US dollar. Although a foreign exchange transaction can involve any two currencies, some 87 percent of transactions involve dollars.[7] This is true even when a dealer wants to sell one nondollar currency and buy another. A dealer wishing to sell Czech koruna for Swiss francs, for example, will usually sell the koruna for dollars and then use the dollars to buy Swiss francs. Although this may seem a roundabout way of doing things, it is actually cheaper than trying to find a holder of Swiss francs who wants to buy koruna. The advantage of trading through the dollar is a result of the United States' importance in the world economy. Because the volume of international transactions involving dollars is so great, it is not hard to find dealers who wish to trade dollars for francs or koruna.

Economic Theories of Exchange Rate Determination

At the most basic level, exchange rates are determined by the demand and supply of one currency relative to the demand and supply of another. For example, if the demand for dollars outstrips the supply and if the supply of euros is greater than the demand, the dollar/euro exchange rate will change. The dollar will appreciate against the euro (or, alternatively, the euro will depreciate against the dollar). However, this simple explanation does not tell us what factors underlie the demand for and supply of a currency. Nor does it tell us when the demand for dollars will exceed the

arbitrage Process of buying a currency low and selling it high.

supply (and vice versa) or when the supply of euros will exceed demand for them (and vice versa). Neither does it tell us under what conditions a currency is in demand or under what conditions it is not demanded. In this section we will review economic theory's answers to these questions.

If we understand how exchange rates are determined, we may be able to forecast exchange rate movements. Because future exchange rate movements influence export opportunities, the profitability of international trade and investment deals, and the price competitiveness of foreign imports, this is valuable information for an international business. Unfortunately, there is no simple explanation. The forces that determine exchange rates are complex, and no theoretical consensus exists, even among economists who study the phenomenon every day. Nonetheless, most economic theories of exchange rate movements seem to agree that three factors have an important impact on future exchange rate movements in a country's currency: the country's price inflation, its interest rate, and market psychology.[8]

Prices and Exchange Rates

To understand how prices are related to exchange rate movements, we first need to discuss an economic proposition known as the law of one price. Then we will discuss the theory of purchasing power parity (PPP), which links changes in the exchange rate between two countries' currencies to changes in the countries' price levels.

THE LAW OF ONE PRICE The **law of one price** states that in competitive markets free of transportation costs and barriers to trade (such as tariffs), identical products sold in different countries must sell for the same price when their price is expressed in terms of the same currency.[9] For example, if the exchange rate between the dollar and the Mexican peso is $1 = P5, a jacket that retails for $50 in New York should retail for P250 (50 × 5) in Mexico City. Consider what would happen if the jacket cost P300 in Mexico City ($60 in US currency). At this price, it would pay a company to buy jackets in New York and sell them in Mexico (an example of arbitrage). Initially the company could make a profit of $10 on each jacket by purchasing them for $50 in New York and selling them for P300 in Mexico. (Remember we are assuming away transportation costs and trade barriers.) However, the increased demand for jackets in New York would raise their price in New York, and the increased supply of jackets in Mexico would lower their price there. This would continue until prices were equalized. Thus, prices might equalize when the jacket cost $55 in New York and P275 in Mexico (assuming no change in the exchange rate of $1 = P5).

ANOTHER PERSPECTIVE

Does the Internet Enable Buyers to Invoke the Law of One Price?

The law of one price—identical products sold in different countries must sell for the same price in competitive markets with no trade barriers or transport costs—assumes universal access to price information across borders. The Internet allows people to access pricing information across borders. Limitations might be language, technology, and access to the appropriate currency. There may also be tariff, transportation, and other transaction costs. Can you imagine going to your local Volvo dealer kknowing how much you would have to pay for a Volvo in Stockholm, Sweden? And what if Volvo were trying to build market share in Thailand by operating with lower margins? You might be bargaining with your local dealer based on the price of a Volvo in Bangkok.

PURCHASING POWER PARITY If the law of one price were true for all goods and services, the purchasing power parity (PPP) exchange rate could be found from any individual set of prices. By comparing the prices of identical products in different currencies, it would be possible to determine the "real" or PPP exchange rate that would exist if markets were efficient. (An **efficient market** has no impediments—such as trade barriers—to the free flow of goods and services.)

law of one price Identical products sold in different countries must sell for the same price when their price is expressed in the same currency in competitive markets free of transportation costs and barriers to trade.

efficient market Market that has no impediments to the free flow of goods and services.

A less extreme version of the PPP theory states that given **relatively efficient markets**—that is, markets in which few impediments to international trade and investment exist—the price of a "basket of goods" should be roughly equivalent in each country. To express the PPP theory in symbols, let $P_\$$ be the US dollar price of a basket of particular goods and P_{SF} be the price of the same basket of goods in Swiss francs. The PPP theory predicts that the dollar/SF exchange rate should be equivalent to:

$$\text{\$/SF exchange rate} = P_\$/P_{SF}$$

Thus, if a basket of goods costs \$200 in the United States and SF600 in Switzerland, PPP theory predicts that the dollar/SF exchange rate should be \$200/SF600 or \$0.33 per SF (i.e., \$1 = SF3).

The next step in the PPP theory is to argue that the exchange rate will change if relative prices change. For example, imagine there is no price inflation in the United States, while prices in Switzerland are increasing by 20 percent a year. At the beginning of the year, a basket of goods costs \$200 in the United States and SF600 in Switzerland, so the dollar/SF exchange rate, according to PPP theory, should be \$0.33 = SF1. At the end of the year, the basket of goods still costs \$200 in the United States, but it costs SF720 in Switzerland. PPP theory predicts that the exchange rate should change as a result. By the end of the year, \$0.27 = SF1 (i.e., \$1 = SF3.6). Due to the effects of price inflation, the SF has depreciated against the dollar. One dollar should buy more francs at the end of the year than at the beginning.

MONEY SUPPLY AND PRICE INFLATION   In essence, PPP theory predicts that changes in relative prices will result in a change in exchange rates. Theoretically, a country in which price inflation is running wild should expect to see its currency depreciate against that of countries in which inflation rates are lower. Because the growth rate of a country's money supply and its inflation rate are closely correlated,[10] we can predict the likely inflation rate. Then we can use this to forecast exchange rate movements.

Inflation is a monetary phenomenon. Inflation occurs when the quantity of money in circulation rises faster than the stock of goods and services; that is, when the money supply increases faster than output increases. Imagine what would happen if everyone in the country was suddenly given \$10,000 by the government. Many people would rush out to spend their extra money on things they had always wanted—new cars, new furniture, better clothes, and so on. There would be a surge in demand for goods and services. Car dealers, department stores, and other providers of goods and services would respond to this demand by raising prices. The result would be price inflation.

A government increasing the money supply is analogous to giving people more money. An increase in the money supply makes it easier for banks to borrow from the government and for individuals and companies to borrow from banks. The resulting increase in credit causes increases in demand for goods and services. Unless the output of goods and services is growing at a rate similar to that of the money supply, the result will be inflation. This relationship has been observed time after time in country after country.

Now we have a connection between the growth in a country's money supply, price inflation, and exchange rate movements. When the growth in a country's money supply is faster than the growth in its output, price inflation is fueled. The PPP theory tells us that a country with a high inflation rate will see a depreciation in its currency exchange rate. Consider the case of Bolivia. In the mid-1980s Bolivia experienced hyperinflation—an explosive and seemingly uncontrollable price inflation in which money loses value very rapidly. Table 8.3 presents data on Bolivia's money supply, inflation rate, and its peso's exchange rate with the US dollar during the hy-

Table 8.3

Macroeconomic Data for Bolivia, April 1984–October 1985

Month	Money Supply (billions of pesos)	Price Level Relative to 1982 (average = 1)	Exchange Rate (pesos per dollar)
1984			
April	270	21.1	3,576
May	330	31.1	3,512
June	440	32.3	3,342
July	599	34.0	3,570
August	718	39.1	7,038
September	889	53.7	13,685
October	1,194	85.5	15,205
November	1,495	112.4	18,469
December	3,296	180.9	24,515
1985			
January	4,630	305.3	73,016
February	6,455	863.3	141,101
March	9,089	1,078.6	128,137
April	12,885	1,205.7	167,428
May	21,309	1,635.7	272,375
June	27,778	2,919.1	481,756
July	47,341	4,854.6	885,476
August	74,306	8,081.0	1,182,300
September	103,272	12,647.6	1,087,440
October	132,550	12,411.8	1,120,210

Juan-Antino Morales, "Inflation Stabilization in Bolivia," in *Inflation Stabilization: The Experience of Israel, Argentina, Brazil, Bolivia, and Mexico,* ed. Michael Bruno et al., MIT Press, 1998.

perinflation. The exchange rate is actually the "black market" exchange rate because the Bolivian government prohibited converting the peso to other currencies during the period. The growth in money supply, the rate of price inflation, and the depreciation of the peso against the dollar all moved in step. This is just what PPP theory and monetary economics predict. Between April 1984 and July 1985, Bolivia's money supply increased by 17,433 percent, prices increased by 22,908 percent, and the value of the peso against the dollar fell by 24,662 percent! In October 1985 the Bolivian government instituted a dramatic stabilization plan, which included introduction of a new currency and tight control of the money supply, and by 1987 the country's annual inflation rate was down to 16 percent.[11]

An increase in a country's money supply, which increases the amount of currency available, changes the relative demand and supply conditions in the foreign exchange market. If the US money supply is growing more rapidly than US output, dollars will be relatively more plentiful than the currencies of countries where monetary growth is closer to output growth. As a result of this relative increase in supply of dollars, the dollar will depreciate on the foreign exchange market against the currencies of countries with slower monetary growth.

Government policy determines whether the rate of growth in a country's money supply is greater than the rate of growth in output. Governments generally have significant control over the money supply. A government can increase the money supply simply by telling the country's central bank to print more money. Governments tend to do this to finance public expenditure (building roads, paying government workers, paying for defense, etc.). A government could finance public expenditure by raising taxes, but because nobody likes paying more taxes and politicians do not like to be unpopular, they prefer to print money. Unfortunately, there is no magic money tree. The inevitable result of excessive growth in money supply is price inflation. However, this has not stopped governments around the world from printing money, with predictable results. If an international business is attempting to predict future movements in the value of a country's currency on the foreign exchange market, it should examine that country's policy toward monetary growth. If the government seems committed to controlling the rate of growth in money supply, the country's future inflation rate may be low (even if the current rate is high) and its currency should not depreciate too much on the foreign exchange market. If the government seems to lack the political will to control the rate of growth in the money supply, the future inflation rate may be high, which is likely to cause its currency to depreciate. Historically, many Latin American governments have fallen into this latter category, including Argentina, Bolivia, and Brazil. Recent signs point to many of the newly democratic states of Eastern Europe making the same mistake.

EMPIRICAL TESTS OF PPP THEORY PPP theory predicts that changes in relative prices will result in a change in exchange rates. A country in which price inflation is running wild should expect to see its currency depreciate against that of countries with lower inflation rates. This is intuitively appealing, but is it true in practice? There are several good examples of the connection between a country's price inflation and exchange rate position (such as Bolivia). However, extensive empirical testing of PPP theory has yielded mixed results.[12] While PPP theory seems to yield relatively accurate predictions *in the long run,* it does not appear to be a strong predictor of *short-run* movements in exchange rates covering five years or less. In addition, the theory seems to best predict exchange rate changes for countries with high rates of inflation and underdeveloped capital markets. The theory is less useful for predicting short-term exchange rate movements between the currencies of advanced industrialized nations that have relatively small differentials in inflation rates.

Several factors may explain the failure of PPP theory to predict exchange rates more accurately. PPP theory assumes away transportation costs and barriers to trade and investment. In practice, these factors are significant and they tend to create price differentials between countries. As we saw in Chapters 5 and 6, governments routinely intervene in international trade and investment. Such intervention, by violating the assumption of efficient markets, weakens the link between relative price changes and changes in exchange rates predicted by PPP theory.

Governments also intervene in the foreign exchange market in attempting to influence the value of their currencies. We will look at why and how they do this in Chapter 9. This government intervention further weakens the link between price changes and changes in exchange rates.

Perhaps the most important factor explaining the failure of PPP theory to predict short-term movements in foreign exchange rates, however, is the impact of investor psychology and other factors on currency purchasing decisions and exchange rate movements. We will discuss this issue in more detail later in this chapter.

Interest Rates and Exchange Rates

Economic theory tells us that interest rates reflect expectations about likely future inflation rates. In countries where inflation is expected to be high, interest rates also will be high because investors want compensation for the decline in the value of their money. This relationship was first formalized by economist Irvin Fisher and is referred to as the Fisher Effect. The Fisher Effect states that a country's "nominal" interest rate (i) is the sum of the required "real" rate of interest (r) and the expected rate of inflation over the period for which the funds are to be lent (I). More formally,

$$i = r + I$$

For example, if the real rate of interest in a country is 5 percent and annual inflation is expected to be 10 percent, the nominal interest rate will be 15 percent. As predicted by the Fisher Effect, a strong relationship seems to exist between inflation rates and interest rates.[13]

We can take this one step further and consider how it applies in a world of many countries and unrestricted capital flows. When investors are free to transfer capital between countries, real interest rates will be the same in every country. If differences in real interest rates did emerge between countries, arbitrage would soon equalize them. For example, if the real interest rate in Switzerland was 10 percent and only 6 percent in the United States, it would pay investors to borrow money in the United States and invest it in Switzerland. The resulting increase in the demand for money in the United States would raise the real interest rate there, while the increase in the supply of foreign money in Switzerland would lower the real interest rate there. This would continue until the two sets of real interest rates were equalized. (In practice, differences in real interest rates may persist because of government controls on capital flows; investors are not always free to transfer capital between countries.)

It follows from the Fisher Effect that if the real interest rate is the same worldwide, any difference in interest rates between countries reflects differing expectations about inflation rates. Thus, if the expected rate of inflation in the United States is greater than that in Switzerland, US nominal interest rates will be greater than Swiss nominal interest rates.

Since we know from PPP theory that there is a link (in theory at least) between inflation and exchange rates, and since interest rates reflect expectations about inflation, it follows that there must also be a link between interest rates and exchange rates. This link is known as the International Fisher Effect (IFE). The **International Fisher Effect** states that for any two countries, the spot exchange rate should change in an equal amount but in the opposite direction to the difference in nominal interest rates between two countries. Stated more formally,

$$(S_1 - S_2)/S_2 \times 100 = i_\$ - i_{SF}$$

where $i_\$$ and i_{SF} are the respective nominal interest rates in the United States and Switzerland (for the sake of example), S_1 is the spot exchange rate at the beginning of the period, and S_2 is the spot exchange rate at the end of the period.

International Fisher Effect
For any two countries, the spot exchange rate should change in an equal amount but in the opposite direction to the difference in the nominal interest rates between the two countries.

If the US nominal interest rate is higher than Switzerland's, reflecting greater expected inflation rates, the value of the dollar against the Swiss franc should fall by that interest rate differential in the future. So if the interest rate in the United States is 10 percent, and in Switzerland it is 6 percent, reflecting 4 percent higher expected inflation in the United States, we would expect the value of the dollar to depreciate by 4 percent against the Swiss franc.

Do interest rate differentials help predict future currency movements? The evidence is mixed; as in the case of PPP theory, in the long run there seems to be a relationship between interest rate differentials and subsequent changes in spot exchange rates. However, considerable short-run deviations occur. Like PPP, the International Fisher Effect is not a good predictor of short-term changes in spot exchange rates.[14]

Investor Psychology and Bandwagon Effects

Empirical evidence suggests that neither PPP theory nor the International Fisher Effect are particularly good at explaining *short-term* movements in exchange rates. One reason for this may be the impact of investor psychology on short-term exchange rate movements. Increasing evidence reveals that various psychological factors play an important role in determining market traders' expectations of likely future exchange rates.[15] Expectations have a tendency to become self-filling prophecies. We discussed a good example of this mechanism in the "Management Focus" on George Soros. When George Soros shorted the British pound in September 1992, many foreign exchange traders jumped on the bandwagon, selling British pounds and purchasing German marks (see the "Management Focus" for details). As the bandwagon effect built up, with more and more traders selling British pounds and purchasing deutsche marks in expectation of a decline in the pound, their expectations became a self-fulfilling prophecy with massive selling forcing down the value of the pound against the deutsche mark. The pound declined in value not because of any major shift in macroeconomic fundamentals, but because investors moved in a herd in response to a bet placed by a major speculator, George Soros.

According to a number of recent studies, investor psychology and bandwagon effects play a major role in determining short-run exchange rate movements.[16] However, these effects can be hard to predict. Investor psychology can be influenced by political factors and by microeconomic events, such as the investment decisions of individual firms, many of which are only loosely linked to macroeconomic fundamentals, such as relative inflation rates. Also, bandwagon effects can be both triggered and exacerbated by the idiosyncratic behavior of politicians. Something like this seems to have occurred in Southeast Asia during 1997 when the currencies of Thailand, Malaysia, South Korea, and Indonesia lost between 50 and 70 percent of their value against the US dollar over a few months. For a detailed look at what occurred in South Korea, see the accompanying "Country Focus." The collapse in the value of the Korean currency did not occur because South Korea had a higher inflation rate than the United States. It occurred because of an excessive buildup of dollar-denominated debt among South Korean firms. By mid-1997 these companies were having trouble servicing this debt. Foreign investors, fearing a wave of corporate bankruptcies, took their money out of the country, exchanging won for US dollars. As this began to depress the exchange rate, currency traders jumped on the bandwagon and speculated against the won (selling it short).

Summary

We have seen that relative monetary growth, relative inflation rates, and nominal interest rate differentials are all moderately good predictors of long-run changes in exchange rates. They are poor predictors of short-run changes in exchange rates, however, because of the impact of psychological factors, investor expectations, and bandwagon effects on short-term currency movements. This information is useful for an international business. Insofar as the long-term profitability of foreign investments, export opportunities, and the price competitiveness of foreign imports are all influenced by long-term movements in exchange rates, international businesses would be advised to pay attention to countries' differing monetary growth, inflation, and interest rates. International businesses that engage in foreign exchange transactions on a day-to-day basis could benefit by knowing some predictors of short-term foreign exchange rate movements. Unfortunately, short-term exchange rate movements are difficult to predict.

ANOTHER PERSPECTIVE

Exchange Rates and the Lucky Traveler

You are taking a trip to Japan, and you convert $1,000 to Japanese yen to cover expenses while there. Your bank gives you ¥140,000 for your $1,000. During your two weeks in Japan, the dollar weakens against the yen, to ¥110 to the dollar. Meanwhile, your Japanese friends were so hospitable you have spent only ¥30,000. After you land in Los Angeles, you take ¥110,000 to the bank in the airport to convert to dollars. How much have you spent for your trip? Will you list these expenses on your expense report?

Exchange Rate Forecasting

A company's need to predict future exchange rate variations raises the issue of whether it is worthwhile to invest in exchange rate forecasting services to aid decision making. Two schools of thought address this issue. One school, the efficient market school, argues that forward exchange rates do the best possible job of forecasting future spot exchange rates; therefore, investing in forecasting services would be a waste of money. The other school of thought, the inefficient market school, argues that companies can improve the foreign exchange market's estimate of future exchange rates (as contained in the forward rate) by investing in forecasting services. This school of thought does not believe the forward exchange rates are the best possible predictors of future spot exchange rates.

The Efficient Market School

Forward exchange rates represent market participants' collective predictions of likely spot exchange rates at specified future dates. If forward exchange rates are the best possible predictor of future spot rates, it would make no sense for companies to spend money trying to forecast short-run exchange rate movements. Many economists believe the foreign exchange market is efficient at setting forward rates.[17] An efficient market is one in which prices reflect all available public information. (If forward rates reflect all available information about likely future changes in exchange rates, there is no way a company can beat the market by investing in forecasting services.)

If the foreign exchange market is efficient, forward exchange rates should be unbiased predictors of future spot rates. This does not mean the predictions will be accurate in any specific situation; it means inaccuracies will not be consistently above

Why Did the Korean Won Collapse?

In early 1997 South Korea could look back with pride on a 30-year "economic miracle" that had raised the country from the ranks of the poor and given it the world's 11th-largest economy. By the end of 1997 the Korean currency, the won, had lost a staggering 67 percent of its value against the US dollar, the South Korean economy lay in tatters, and the International Monetary Fund was overseeing a $55 billion rescue package. This sudden turn of events had its roots in investments made by South Korea's large industrial conglomerates, or *chaebol,* during the 1990s, often at the bequest of politicians. In 1993 Kim Young-Sam, a populist politician, became president of South Korea. Mr. Kim took office during a mild recession and promised to boost economic growth by encouraging investment in export-oriented industries. He urged the *chaebol* to invest in new factories. South Korea enjoyed an investment-led economic boom in 1994 and 1995, but at a cost. The *chaebol,* always reliant on heavy borrowing, built up massive debts that were equivalent, on average, to four times their equity.

As the volume of investments ballooned during the 1990s, the *quality* of many of these investments declined significantly. The investments too often were based on projections about future demand conditions that were unrealistic. This resulted in significant excess capacity and falling prices. An example is investments made by Korean *chaebol* in semiconductor factories. Investments in such facilities surged in 1994 and 1995 when a temporary global shortage of dynamic random access memory chips (DRAMs) led to sharp price increases for this product. However, by 1996 supply shortages had disappeared and excess capacity was beginning to make itself felt, just as the South Koreans started to bring new DRAM factories on stream. The results were predictable; prices for DRAMs plunged through the floor and the earnings of South Korean DRAM manufacturers fell by 90 percent, which meant it was extremely difficult for them to make scheduled payments on the debt they had taken on to build the extra capacity. The risk of corporate bankruptcy increased significantly. Nor was this process occurring in just the semiconductor industry. South Korean companies were also investing heavily in a range of other industries, including automobiles and steel.

Much of the borrowing had been in US dollars, as opposed to Korean won. At the time this had seemed like a smart move. The dollar/won exchange rate had been stable at about $1 = W850. Also, interest rates on dollar borrowings were two to three percentage points lower than rates on borrowings in Korean won. Thus, it often made good sense to borrow in dollars. Much of this borrowing was in the form of short-term, dollar-denominated debt that had to be paid back within one year. While the borrowing strategy seemed to make sense, there was a risk. If the won were to depreciate

or below future spot rates, that they will be random. Many empirical tests have addressed the efficient market hypothesis. Although most of the early work confirmed the hypothesis (suggesting companies should not waste their money on forecasting services), more recent studies have challenged it.[18] There is some evidence that forward rates are not unbiased predictors of future spot rates, and that more accurate predictions of future spot rates can be calculated from publicly available information.[19]

The Inefficient Market School

inefficient market
Market in which prices do not reflect all available information.

Citing evidence against the efficient market hypothesis, some economists believe the foreign exchange market is inefficient. An **inefficient market** is one in which prices do not reflect all available information. In an inefficient market, forward exchange rates will not be the best possible predictors of future spot exchange rates.

If this is true, it may be worthwhile for international businesses to invest in forecasting services (as many do). The belief is that professional exchange rate forecasts might provide better predictions of future spot rates than forward exchange rates do. However, the track record of professional forecasting services is not that good. An analysis of the forecasts of 12 major forecasting services from 1978 to 1982 concluded

against the dollar, this would increase the size of the debt burden when measured in the local currency. Currency depreciation would raise borrowing costs, depress corporate earnings, and increase the risk of bankruptcy. This is exactly what happened.

By mid-1997 foreign investors had become alarmed at the rising debt levels of South Korean companies, particularly given the excess capacity and plunging prices in several areas where South Korean companies had made huge investments, including semiconductors, automobiles, and steel. Given increasing speculation that many companies would not be able to service their debt payments, foreign investors began to withdraw their money from the South Korean stock and bond markets. In the process, they sold Korean won and purchased US dollars. The selling of won accelerated in mid-1997 when two of the smaller *chaebol* filed for bankruptcy, citing their inability to meet scheduled debt payments. The increased supply of won and the increased demand for US dollars pushed down the price of won from around W840 = $1 to W900 = $1.

At this point the South Korean central bank stepped into the foreign exchange market to try to keep the exchange rate above W1,000 = $1. It did this by purchasing won with dollars it held in reserve. The idea was to try to push up the price of the won in dollar terms and restore investor confidence in the stability of the exchange rate. This action, however, did not address the underlying debt problem faced by South Korean companies. Against a backdrop of more corporate bankruptcy's in South Korea and the government's stated intentions to take some troubled companies into state ownership, Standard & Poor's, the US credit rating agency, downgraded South Korea's sovereign debt. This caused the South Korean stock market to plunge 5.5 percent and the Korean won to fall to W930 = $1. According to S&P, "the downgrade of . . . ratings reflects the escalating cost to the government of supporting the country's ailing corporate and financial sectors."

The S&P downgrade triggered a sharp sale of the Korean won. In an attempt to protect the won against what was becoming a classic

bandwagon effect, the South Korean central bank raised short-term interest rates to over 12 percent, more than double the inflation rate. The bank also stepped up its intervention in the currency exchange markets, selling dollars and purchasing won in an attempt to keep the dollar/won exchange rate above $1 = W1,000. The main effect of this action, however, was to rapidly deplete South Korea's foreign exchange reserves. These stood at $30 billion November 1, but fell to only $15 billion two weeks later. With its foreign exchange reserves almost exhausted, on November 17 the South Korean central bank gave up its defense of the won. Immediately, the price of won in dollars plunged to about W1,500 = $1, increasing by 60 to 70 percent the amount of won heavily indebted South Korean companies had to pay to meet scheduled payments on their dollar-denominated debt. These losses, due to adverse changes in foreign exchange rates, depressed the profits of many firms. It is estimated that South Korean firms suffered foreign exchange losses of more than $15 billion in 1997.[20]

that the forecasters did not provide better forecasts than the forward exchange rates.[21] Forecasting services also did not predict the 1997 currency crisis that swept through southeast Asia.

Approaches to Forecasting

Assuming the foreign exchange market's estimate of future spot rates can be improved, on what basis should forecasts be prepared? Here again, there are two schools of thought. One adheres to fundamental analysis, while the other uses technical analysis.

FUNDAMENTAL ANALYSIS **Fundamental analysis** draws on economic theory to construct sophisticated econometric models for predicting exchange rate movements. The variables contained in these models typically include those we have discussed, such as relative money supply growth rates, inflation rates, and interest rates. In addition, they may include variables related to balance-of-payments positions.

Running a deficit on the balance-of-payments current account (importing more goods and services than a country is exporting) creates pressures that result in the depreciation of the currency on the foreign exchange market.[22] (For background on

fundamental analysis
Draws on economic theory to construct sophisticated econometric models for predicting exchange rate movements.

the balance of payments, see Chapter 7.) Consider what might happen if the United States were running a persistent current account balance-of-payments deficit. Because the United States would be importing more than it was exporting, people in other countries would be increasing their holdings of US dollars. If these people were willing to hold their dollars, the dollar's exchange rate would not be influenced. However, if these people converted their dollars into other currencies, the supply of dollars in the foreign exchange market would increase (as would demand for the other currencies). This shift in demand and supply conditions would create pressures that could lead to the depreciation of the dollar against other currencies.

This argument hinges on whether people in other countries are willing to hold dollars, and this depends on such factors as US interest rates and inflation rates. Thus, the balance-of-payments position is not a fundamental predictor of future exchange rate movements. For example, from 1981 to 1985, the US dollar appreciated against most major currencies despite a growing balance-of-payments deficit. Relatively high real interest rates in the United States made the dollar very attractive to foreigners, so they did not convert their dollars into other currencies. Given this, we are back to the argument that the fundamental determinants of exchange rates are monetary growth, inflation rates, and interest rates.

TECHNICAL ANALYSIS **Technical analysis** uses price and volume data to determine past trends, which are expected to continue into the future. This approach does not rely on a consideration of economic fundamentals. Technical analysis is based on the premise that analyzable market trends and waves can be used to predict future trends and waves. Because there is no theoretical rationale for this assumption of predictability, many economists compare technical analysis to fortune-telling. Despite this skepticism, technical analysis has gained favor in recent years.[23]

Currency Convertibility

Until this point we have assumed that the currencies of various countries are freely convertible into other currencies. This assumption is invalid. Many countries restrict the ability of residents and nonresidents to convert the local currency into a foreign currency. The result is that international trade and investment are more difficult in those countries. Many international businesses have used countertrade to circumvent problems that arise when a currency is not freely convertible.

Convertibility and Government Policy

Because of government restrictions, a significant number of currencies are not freely convertible into other currencies. A country's currency is said to be **freely convertible** when the government allows both residents and nonresidents to purchase unlimited amounts of a foreign currency with it. A currency is said to be **externally convertible** when only nonresidents may convert it into a foreign currency without any limitations. A currency is **nonconvertible** when neither residents nor nonresidents are allowed to convert it into a foreign currency.

Free convertibility is the exception rather than the rule. Many countries place some restrictions on their residents' ability to convert the domestic currency into a foreign currency (a policy of external convertibility). Restrictions on convertibility for residents range from the relatively minor (such as limiting the amount of foreign currency they may take with them out of the country on trips) to the major (such as restricting domestic businesses' ability to take foreign currency out of the country). External convertibility restrictions can limit domestic companies' ability to invest abroad, but they present few problems for foreign companies wishing to do business in that country.

In many countries, the ability of residents and nonresidents to convert local currency into a foreign currency is restricted by government policy. A government restricts the convertibility of its currency in an attempt to protect the country's foreign exchange reserves and to halt any **capital flight**. ©Photo Disc.

Even if the Japanese government placed tight controls on the ability of its residents to convert the yen into US dollars, all US businesses with deposits in Japanese banks could convert all their yen into dollars and take them out of the country. Thus, a US company with a subsidiary in Japan is assured that it will be able to convert the profits from its Japanese operation into dollars and take them out of the country.

Serious problems arise, however, under a policy of nonconvertibility. This was the practice of the former Soviet Union, and it continued to be the practice in Russia until recently. When strictly applied, nonconvertibility means that although a US company doing business in a country such as Russia may generate ruble profits, it may not convert those rubles into dollars and take them out of the country. This is not desirable for international business.

Governments limit convertibility to preserve their foreign exchange reserves. A country needs an adequate supply of these reserves to service its international debt commitments and to purchase imports. Governments typically impose convertibility restrictions on their currency when they fear that free convertibility will lead to a run on their foreign exchange reserves. This occurs when residents and nonresidents rush to convert their holdings of domestic currency into a foreign currency—generally referred to as capital flight. Capital flight is most likely to occur when the value of the domestic currency is depreciating rapidly because of hyperinflation, or when a country's economic prospects are shaky in other respects. Under such circumstances, both residents and nonresidents tend to feel that their money is more likely to hold its value if it is converted into a foreign currency and invested abroad. Not only will a run on foreign exchange reserves limit the country's ability to service its international debt and pay for imports, but it will also lead to depreciation in the exchange rate as residents and nonresidents unload their holdings of domestic currency on the foreign exchange markets (thereby increasing the market supply of the country's currency). Governments fear that the rise in import prices resulting from currency depreciation will lead to further increases in inflation. This fear provides another rationale for limiting convertibility.

Countertrade

Companies can deal with the nonconvertibility problem by engaging in countertrade. **Countertrade** refers to a range of barterlike agreements by which goods and services can be traded for other goods and services. Countertrade can make sense when a country's currency is nonconvertible. Consider the deal that General Electric struck with the Romanian government in 1984, when that country's currency was nonconvertible. When General Electric won a contract for a $150 million generator project in Romania, it agreed to take payment in the form of Romanian goods that could be sold for $150 million on international markets. The Venezuelan

countertrade
Barterlike agreements by which goods and services can be traded for other goods and services; used in international trade when a country's currency is nonconvertible.

government negotiated a contract with Caterpillar in 1986 under which Venezuela would trade 350,000 tons of iron ore for Caterpillar heavy construction equipment. Caterpillar subsequently traded the iron ore to Romania in exchange for Romanian farm products, which it then sold on international markets for dollars.[24]

How important is countertrade? One estimate is that 20 to 30 percent of world trade in 1985 involved some form of countertrade agreements. Since then, however, more currencies have become freely convertible, and the percentage of world trade that involves some form of countertrade has fallen to between 10 and 20 percent.[25]

Implications for Business

This chapter contains a number of clear implications for business. First, it is critical that international businesses understand the influence of exchange rates on the profitability of trade and investment deals. Adverse changes in exchange rates can make apparently profitable deals unprofitable. The risk introduced into international business transactions by changes in exchange rates is referred to as foreign exchange risk. Means of hedging against foreign exchange risk are available. Forward exchange rates and currency swaps allow companies to insure against this risk.

International businesses must also understand the forces that determine exchange rates. This is particularly true in light of the increasing evidence that forward exchange rates are not unbiased predictors. If a company wants to know how the value of a particular currency is likely to change over the long term on the foreign exchange market, it should take a close look at those economic fundamentals that appear to predict long-term exchange rate movements (i.e., the growth in a country's money supply, its inflation rate, and its nominal interest rates). For example, an international business should be very cautious about trading with or investing in a country with a recent history of rapid growth in its domestic money supply. The upsurge in inflation that is likely to follow such rapid monetary growth could lead to a sharp drop in the value of the country's currency on the foreign exchange market, which could transform a profitable deal into an unprofitable one. This is not to say that an international business should not trade with or invest in such a country. Rather, it means an international business should first take some precautions, such as buying currency forward on the foreign exchange market or structuring the deal around a countertrade arrangement.

Complicating this picture is the issue of currency convertibility. Governments' proclivity to restrict currency convertibility suggests the foreign exchange market does not always provide the lubricant necessary to make international trade and investment possible. Given this, international businesses need to explore alternative mechanisms for facilitating international trade and investment that do not involve currency conversion. Countertrade seems the obvious mechanism.

Key Terms

Summary

This chapter explained how the foreign exchange market works, examined the forces that determine rates, and discussed the implications of these factors for international business. Given that changes in exchange rates can dramatically alter the profitability of foreign trade and investment deals, this is an area of major interest to international business. These points have been made in the chapter:

1 One function of the foreign exchange market is to convert the currency of one country into the currency of another.

2 International businesses participate in the foreign exchange market to facilitate international trade and investment, to invest cash in short-term money market accounts abroad, and to engage in currency speculation.

3 A second function of the foreign exchange market is to provide insurance against foreign exchange risk.

4 The spot exchange rate is the exchange rate at which a dealer converts one currency into another currency on a particular day.

5 Foreign exchange risk can be reduced by using forward exchange rates. A forward exchange rate is an exchange rate governing future transactions.

6 The law of one price is that in competitive markets that are free of transportation costs and barriers to trade, identical products sold in different countries must sell for the same price when their price is expressed in the same currency.

7 Purchasing power parity (PPP) theory states the price of a basket of particular goods should be roughly equivalent in each country. PPP theory predicts that the exchange rate will change if relative prices change.

8 The rate of change in countries' relative prices depends on their relative inflation rates. A country's inflation rate seems to be a function of the growth in its money supply.

9 The PPP theory of exchange rate changes yields relatively accurate predictions of long-term trends in exchange rates, but not of short-term movements. The failure of PPP theory to predict exchange rate changes more accurately may be due to the existence of transportation costs, barriers to trade and investment, and the impact of psychological factors such as bandwagon effects on market movements and short-run exchange rates.

10 Interest rates reflect expectations about inflation. In countries where inflation is expected to be high, interest rates also will be high.

11 The International Fisher Effect states that for any two countries, the spot exchange rate should change in an equal amount but in the opposite direction to the difference in nominal interest rates.

12 The most common approach to exchange rate forecasting is fundamental analysis. This relies on variables such as money supply growth, inflation rates, nominal interest rates, and balance-of-payments positions to predict future changes in exchange rates.

13 In many countries, government policy restricts the ability of residents and nonresidents to convert local currency into a foreign currency. A government restricts the convertibility of its currency to protect the country's foreign exchange reserves and to halt any capital flight.

14 Particularly bothersome for international business is a policy of nonconvertibility, which prohibits residents and nonresidents from exchanging local currency for foreign currency. A policy of nonconvertibility makes it very difficult to engage in international trade and investment in the country.

15 One way of coping with nonconvertibility is to engage in countertrade—to trade goods and services for other goods and services.

Critical Thinking and Discussion Questions

1 The interest rate on South Korean government securities with one-year maturity is 4 percent, and the expected inflation rate for the coming year is 2 percent. The interest rate on US government securities with one-year maturity is 7 percent, and the expected rate of inflation is 5 percent. The current spot exchange rate for Korean won is $1 = W1,200. Forecast the spot exchange rate one year from today. Explain the logic of your answer.

2 Two countries, Britain and the United States, produce just one good: beef. Suppose the price of beef in the United States is $2.80 per pound and in Britain it is £3.70 per pound.

a According to PPP theory, what should the $/£ spot exchange rate be?

b Suppose the price of beef is expected to rise to $3.10 in the United States, and to £4.65 in Britain. What should the one-year forward $/£ exchange rate be?

c Given your answers to parts *a* and *b*, and given that the current interest rate in the United States is 10 percent, what would you expect the current interest rate to be in Britain?

3 You manufacture wine goblets. In mid-June you receive an order for 10,000 goblets from Japan. Payment of ¥400,000 is due in mid-December. You expect the yen to rise from its present rate of $1 = ¥130 to $1 = ¥100 by December. You can borrow yen at 6 percent per annum. What should you do?

Internet Exercises

1 The theory of purchasing power parity (PPP) suggests that in markets where there are few barriers to trade and investment, the price of a basket of goods should be about the same in each country. From this theory, one might surmise that within the European Union, prices on goods ought to be about the same from country to country. However, much to the dismay of British consumers, prices in Britain appear to be generally higher than in the rest of Europe. For example, a British-made Land Rover Discovery costs about $46,000 in Britain, but just $30,500 in the Netherlands. British Prime Minister Tony Blair has even used the phrase "rip off Britain" to describe the disparity in prices.

The EU and the Organization for Economic Cooperation and Development (OECD) have recognized the price differential between Britain and other European countries for years. Studies show that Britons pay anywhere from a 20 to 40 percent premium for many consumer products, even those that are made locally. The problem is so bad that Britain recently instituted a new law known as the Competition Act that will allow heavy fines to be levied against companies that are found guilty of price-fixing. Assume you are guilty of charging higher prices in Britain than in the rest of the EU. What effect will Britain's new law have on your operations? Some retailers have argued that their higher British prices are justified because retailing in the country is costlier than elsewhere. One organization, the Brands Group, which represents British consumer goods manufacturers, has even said that, due to the high costs of wages, retail space, and utilities, it's the retailers that are being ripped off not the consumers. Discuss this proposition.

Source: *The Washington Post*, September 28, 1999, p. A19.

2 Shopping for a new bike? Don't buy it in Britain. A Trek mountain bike costing $499 in the United States retails for nearly twice that in Britain, $818, and that's the sale price! Why the difference? No one knows for sure. Some experts have suggested that Britain's higher prices are the result of market forces, while others point to a culture that resists the notion of competition and lower prices. Still others note that firms may be charging more simply because they can. Whatever the cause, the result is the same. Consumers are becoming outraged, and the problem has become a media magnet.

In the past, price differences such as the one presented above may have been relatively unknown to many people. Today, however, as awareness builds, consumers are demanding that prices be kept in line across similar markets. Armed with a powerful new tool, the Internet, consumers can easily compare prices across markets and voice their displeasure when inequities occur. Go to Lands' End sites (**www.landsend.com** for the United States and **www.landsend .co.uk** for the United Kingdom) or Toys R Us (**www.toysrus.com** for the United States and **www.toysrus .co.uk** for the United Kingdom) and try to identify price differences between markets. As a consumer, do you have the right to demand equal prices? Why? As a company, how should you respond to complaints regarding pricing structures? How can a company defend its higher British prices?

Source: *The Washington Post*, September 28, 1999, p. A19.

The Collapse of the Thai Baht

During the 1980s and 1990s Thailand emerged as one of Asia's most dynamic tiger economies. From 1985 to 1995 Thailand achieved an annual average economic growth rate of 8.4 percent, while keeping its inflation rate at only 5 percent a year (comparable figures for the United States over this period were 1.3 percent economic growth and 3.2 percent inflation). Much of Thailand's economic growth was powered by exports. From 1990 to 1996, for example, the value of exports from Thailand grew by 16 percent per year compounded. The wealth created by export-led growth helped to fuel an investment boom in commercial and residential property, industrial assets, and infrastructure. As demand for property increased, the value of commercial and residential real estate in Bangkok started to soar. This fed a building boom the likes of which had never been seen before in Thailand. Office and apartment buildings were going up all over the city. Heavy borrowing from banks financed much of this construction, and as long as the value of property continued to rise, the banks were happy to lend to property companies.

By early 1997, however, the property boom had produced excess capacity in residential and commercial property. An estimated 365,000 apartment units were unoccupied in Bangkok in late 1996. With another 100,000 units scheduled to be completed in 1997, years of excess demand in the Thai property market had been replaced by excess supply. By one estimate, Bangkok's building boom by 1997 had produced enough excess space to meet its residential and commercial needs for at least five years.

At the same time, Thailand's investments in infrastructure, industrial capacity, and commercial real estate were now sucking in foreign

goods at unprecedented rates. To build infrastructure, factories, and office buildings, Thailand was purchasing capital equipment and materials from America, Europe, and Japan. As a consequence, the current account of the balance of payments shifted strongly into the red during the mid-1990s. Despite strong export growth, imports grew faster. By 1995 Thailand was running a current account deficit equivalent to 8.1 percent of its gross domestic product.

Things started to fall apart February 5, 1997. When Somprasong Land, a Thai property developer, announced it had failed to make a scheduled $3.1 million interest payment on an $80 billion eurobond loan, effectively entering into default. Somprasong Land was the first victim of speculative overbuilding in the Bangkok property market. The Thai stock market had already declined 45 percent from its high in early 1996, primarily on concerns that several property companies might be forced into bankruptcy. Now one had been. The stock market fell another 2.7 percent on the news, but it was only the beginning.

In the aftermath of Somprasong's default it became clear that, along with several other property developers, many of the country's financial institutions, including Finance One, were on the brink of default. Finance One, the country's largest financial institution, had pioneered a practice that had become widespread among Thai institutions—issuing bonds denominated in US dollars and using the proceeds to finance lending to the country's booming property developers. In theory, this practice made sense because Finance One could exploit the interest rate differential between dollar-denominated debt and Thai debt (i.e., Finance One borrowed in US dollars at a low in-

terest rate and lent in Thai Baht at high interest rates). The only problem with this financing strategy was that when the Thai property market began to unravel in 1996 and 1997, the developers could no longer pay back the cash they had borrowed from Finance One. This made it difficult for Finance One to pay back its creditors. As the effects of overbuilding became evident in 1996, Finance One's nonperforming loans doubled, then doubled again in the first quarter of 1997.

In February 1997, trading in the shares of Finance One was suspended while the government tried to arrange for the troubled company to be acquired by a small Thai bank, in a deal sponsored by the Thai central bank. It didn't work, and when trading resumed in Finance One shares in May they fell 70 percent in a single day. By this time bad loans in the Thai property market were swelling daily and had risen to over $30 billion. Finance One was bankrupt, and it was feared that others would follow.

It was at this point that currency traders began a concerted attack on the Thai currency. For the previous 13 years the Thai baht had been pegged to the US dollar at an exchange rate of about $1 = Bt25. This peg, however, had become increasingly difficult to defend. Currency traders, looking at Thailand's growing current account deficit and dollar-denominated debt burden, reasoned that demand for dollars in Thailand would rise while demand for baht would fall. (Businesses and financial institutions would be exchanging baht for dollars to service their debt payments and purchase imports.) There were several attempts to force a devaluation of the baht in late 1996 and early 1997. These speculative attacks typically involved traders selling baht short to profit from a future decline in the value of the baht against the dollar. In this context, short selling involves a currency trader borrowing baht from a financial institution and immediately reselling those baht in the foreign exchange market for dollars. If the value of the baht subsequently falls against the dollar, then when the trader has to buy the baht back to repay the financial institution it will cost fewer dollars than received from the initial sale of baht. For example, a trader might borrow Bt100 from a bank for six months. The trader then exchanges the Bt100 for $4 (at an exchange rate of $1 = Bt25). If the exchange rate subsequently declines to $1 = Bt50 it will cost the trader only $2 to repurchase the Bt100 in six months and pay back the bank, leaving the trader with a 100 percent profit!

In May 1997 short sellers were swarming over the Thai baht. In an attempt to defend the peg, the Thai government used its foreign exchange reserves (which were denominated in US dollars) to purchase Thai baht. It cost the Thai government $5 billion to defend the baht, which reduced its "officially reported" foreign exchange reserves to a two-year low of $33 billion. In addition, the Thai government raised key interest rates from 10 percent to 12.5 percent to make holding baht more attractive, but because this also raised corporate borrowing costs it exacerbated the debt crisis. What the world financial community did not know at this point, was that with the blessing of his superiors, a foreign exchange trader at the Thai central bank had locked up most of Thailand's foreign exchange reserves in forward contracts. The reality was that Thailand had only $1.14 billion in available foreign exchange reserves left to defend the dollar peg. Defending the peg was now impossible.

On July 2, 1997, the Thai government bowed to the inevitable and announced it would allow the baht to float freely against the dollar. The baht immediately lost 18 percent of its value and started a slide that would bring the exchange rate down to $1 = Bt55 by January 1998. As the baht declined, the Thai debt bomb exploded. A 50 percent decline in the value of the baht against the dollar doubled the amount of baht required to serve the dollar-denominated debt commitments taken on by Thai financial institutions and businesses. This created more bankruptcies and further pushed down the battered Thai stock market. The Thailand Set stock market index declined from 787 in January 1997 to a low of 337 in December of that year, and this on top of a 45 percent decline in 1996![26]

CASE DISCUSSION QUESTIONS

1 Identify the main factors that led to the collapse of the Thai baht in 1997.

2 Do you think the sudden collapse of the Thai baht can be explained by the purchasing power parity theorum?

3 What role did speculators play in the fall of the Thai baht? Did they cause its fall?

4 What steps might the Thai government have taken to preempt the financial crisis that swept the nation in 1997?

5 How will the collapse of the Thai baht affect businesses in Thailand, particularly those that purchase inputs from abroad or export finished products?

6 Do you notice any similarities between the collapse of the Thai baht in 1997 and the collapse of the Korean won about the same time (see the "Country Focus" in this chapter)? What are these similarities? Do you think these two events were related? How?

nine

The Global Monetary System

Opening Case   The Tragedy of the Congo (Zaire)

The Democratic Republic of the Congo, formally known as Zaire, gained its independence from Belgium in 1960. The central African nation, rich in natural resources such as copper, seemed to have a promising future. If the country had simply sustained its pre-independence economic growth rate its gross national product would have been $1,400 per head by 1997, making it one of the richest countries in Africa. Instead, by 1997, the

The economic, political, and social collapse of the Democratic Republic of Congo (formerly Zaire) led several prominent critics to claim that IMF policy actually contributed to the economic misery of the country, rather than curing it.
©Liba Taylor/CORBIS

Learning Objectives

1 Understand the role played by the global monetary system in determining exchange rates.

2 Be familiar with the historical development of the modern global monetary system.

3 Appreciate the differences between a fixed and a floating exchange rate system.

4 Understand why the world's fixed exchange rate regime collapsed in the 1970s.

5 Understand the arguments for and against fixed and floating exchange systems.

6 Be familiar with the role played by the International Monetary Fund and World Bank in the global monetary system.

7 Understand the implications of the global monetary system for currency management and business strategy.

country was a wreck. Battered by a brutal civil war that led to the ousting of the country's longtime dictator, Mobutu Sese Seko, the economy had shrunk to its 1958 level with a GNP per capita of less than $100. The annual inflation rate was in excess of 750 percent, an improvement from the 9,800 percent inflation rate recorded in 1994. Consequently, the local currency was almost worthless with all transactions being made by barter or, for

the lucky few, with US dollars. Infant mortality stood at a dismal 106 per 1,000 live births, and life expectancy was 47 years, comparable to that of Europe in the Middle Ages.

What were the underlying causes of the economic, political, and social collapse of Zaire? While the story is a complex one, several influential critics place some of the blame at the feet of two multinational lending institutions, the International Monetary Fund (IMF) and the World Bank.

Both institutions were established in 1944 at the famous Bretton Woods, conference, which paved the way for the post-World War II international monetary system. The IMF was given the task of maintaining order in the international monetary system, while the World Bank was to promote general economic development, particularly among the world's poorer nations. The IMF typically provides loans to countries whose currencies are losing value due to economic

IMF

World Bk.

mismanagement. In return for these loans, the IMF imposes on debtor countries strict financial policies that are designed to rein in inflation and stabilize their economies. The World Bank has historically provided low-interest loans to help countries build basic infrastructure. Both institutions are funded by subscriptions from member states, including significant contributions from all the world's developed nations.

The IMF and the World Bank were major donors to post-independence Zaire. The IMF's involvement with Zaire dates to 1967, when it approved Zaire's first economic stabilization plan, backed by a $27 million line of credit. About the same time the World Bank began to make low-interest-rate infrastructure loans to Mobutu's government. This was followed by a series of further plans and loans between 1976 and 1981. At the urging of the IMF, Zaire's currency was devalued five times during this period to help boost exports and reduce imports, while taxes were raised in an effort to balance Zaire's budget. IMF and other Western officials were also placed in key positions at the Zairian central bank, finance ministry and office of debt management.

Despite all this help, Zaire's economy continued to deteriorate. By 1982, after 15 years of IMF assistance, Zaire had a lower GNP than in 1967 and faced default on its debt. Some critics, including Jeffrey Sachs, the noted development economist from Harvard University, claim this poor performance could in part be attributed to the tight policies imposed by the IMF, which included tax hikes, cuts in government subsidies, and periodic competitive currency devaluations. These policies, critics claim, were ill-suited to such a poor country and created a

vicious cycle of economic decline. The tax hikes drove work into the "underground economy" or created a disincentive to work. Government tax revenues dwindled and the budget deficit expanded, making it difficult for the government to service its debt obligations. The currency devaluations raised import prices and fueled the very phenomenon the IMF was trying to control—inflation. High price and wage inflation soon brought ordinary Zairians into high tax brackets, which drove even more work into the underground economy and further reduced government tax revenues.

When explaining Zaire's malaise, others point to endemic corruption. In 1982, a senior IMF official in Zaire reported that President Mobutu Sese Seko and his cronies were stealing IMF and World Bank loans. Later news reports suggest that the president had accumulated a personal fortune of $4 billion by the mid-1980s, making him one of the richest men in the world at that time.

In 1982 Zaire was suspended from further use of its IMF credit line. However, the position was reversed in 1983 when a new agreement was negotiated that included an additional $356 million in IMF loans. The loans were linked to further devaluation of the Zairian currency, more tax hikes, and cuts in government subsidies. The IMF's decision to turn a blind eye to the corruption problem and extend new loans was influenced by pressure from Western politicians who saw Mobutu's pro-Western regime as a bulwark against the spread of Marxism in Africa. By turning a blind eye to the corruption, the IMF could claim it was abiding by IMF rules, which stated the institution should offer only economic advice and stay out of internal political issues. The

IMF's decision gave credence to Mobutu's government and enabled Zaire to attract more foreign loans. As a consequence, the country's overall foreign debt increased to $5 billion by the mid-1980s, up from $3 billion in 1978.

Unfortunately, the new loans and IMF policies did little to improve Zaire's economic performance, which continued to deteriorate. In 1987 Zaire abandoned its agreement with the IMF because of food riots. The IMF negotiated another agreement for the 1989–91 period, which included a further currency devaluation. This too, however, failed to produce any tangible progress. The Zairian economy continued to implode, while a civil war flared. In 1993 Zaire suspended its debt repayments, effectively going into default. In 1994 the World Bank announced it would shut its operations in the country. About the same time the IMF suspended Zaire's membership in the institution, making the country ineligible for further loans.

After a long civil war, Mobutu Sese Seko was deposed in 1997. The new government inherited $14.6 billion of external debt, including debt arrears exceeding $1 billion. At a formal meeting chaired by the World Bank to discuss rescheduling the country's debt, delegates from the new government claimed the World Bank, IMF, and other institutions acted irresponsibly lending money to Mobutu's regime despite evidence of substantial corruption and Zaire's inability to service such a high level of debt. In an implicit acknowledgment that this may have been the case, the IMF and World Bank began telling debtor countries to stamp out corruption or lose access to IMF and World Bank loans.[1]

IMF policies ill suited to country.

Introduction

Although we discussed the workings of the foreign exchange market in Chapter 8, we did not mention the international monetary system's role in determining exchange rates. Rather, we assumed that currencies were free to float against each other; that is, that a currency's relative value on the foreign exchange market is determined primarily by the impersonal market forces of demand and supply. But contrary to our assumption, many currencies are not free to float against each other. Rather, exchange rates are determined within the context of an international monetary system in which many currencies' ability to float against other currencies is limited by their governments or by intergovernmental arrangements. In 1997 only 51 of the world's viable currencies were freely floating; this number includes the currencies of many of the world's larger industrial nations such as the United States, Canada, Japan, and Britain. A further 50 currencies were pegged to the exchange rates of certain major currencies—particularly the US dollar and the French franc—or to baskets of other currencies, while another 45 currencies were allowed by their governments to float as long as they stayed within a broad range relative to another currency, such as the US dollar.[2]

This chapter explains how the international monetary system works and points out its implications for international business. To understand how the international monetary system works, we must acquire the historical perspective of the system's evolution. Accordingly, we will begin with a discussion of the gold standard and its breakup during the 1930s. Then we will discuss the Bretton Woods conference, which occurred in 1944 and established the basic framework for the post-World War II international monetary system. The Bretton Woods system called for fixed exchange rates against the US dollar. Under this **fixed exchange rate** system the value of most currencies in terms of US dollar was fixed for long periods and allowed to change only under a specific set of circumstances. The Bretton Woods conference also created two major international institutions, both of which are discussed in the opening case, the International Monetary Fund (IMF) and the World Bank. The IMF was given the task of maintaining order in the international monetary system; the World Bank's task was to promote development.

Both of these institutions continue to play a major role in the world economy. In 1997 and 1998, for example, the IMF helped several Asian countries deal with the dramatic decline in the value of their currencies that occurred during the Asian financial crisis that started in 1997. By mid-1999 the IMF had programs in 94 countries. As the opening case on Zaire illustrates, however, there is a growing debate about the role of the IMF and to a lesser extent the World Bank and the appropriateness of their policies for many developing nations. In the case of Zaire, several prominent critics claim that IMF policy contributed to the country's economic misery, rather than curing it. The debate over the role of the IMF has taken on new urgency given the institution's extensive involvement in the economies of Asia and Eastern Europe during the later part of the 1990s. Accordingly, we shall discuss the issue in depth.

The Bretton Woods system of fixed exchange rates collapsed in 1973. Since then the world has operated with a mixed system in which some currencies are allowed to float freely, but many are either managed in some way by government intervention or pegged to another currency. We will explain the reasons for the failure of the Bretton Woods system as well as the nature of the present system. We will also discuss how pegged exchange rate systems work.

fixed exchange rate Value of most currencies in terms of U.S. dollars was fixed for long periods and allowed to change only under a specific set of circumstances.

Nearly three decades after the breakdown of the Bretton Woods system, the debate over what kind of exchange rate regime is best for the world continues. Some economists advocate a system in which major currencies are allowed to float against each other. Others argue for a return to a fixed exchange rate regime similar to the one established at Bretton Woods. This debate is intense and important, and we will examine the arguments of both sides.

Finally, we will discuss the implications of all this material for international business. We will see how the exchange rate policy adopted by a government can have an important impact on the outlook for business operations in a given country. If government exchange rate policies result in currency devaluation, for example, exporters based in that country may benefit as their products become more price competitive in foreign markets. Alternatively, importers will suffer from an increase in the price of their products. We will also look at how the policies adopted by the IMF can affect the economic outlook for a country and, accordingly, the costs and benefits of doing business in that country.

The Gold Standard

The gold standard had its origin in the use of gold coins as a medium of exchange, unit of account, and store of value—a practice that stretches back to ancient times. When international trade was limited in volume, payment for goods purchased from another country was typically made in gold or silver. However, as the volume of international trade expanded in the wake of the Industrial Revolution, a more convenient means of financing international trade was needed. Shipping large quantities of gold and silver around the world to finance international trade seemed impractical. The solution adopted was to arrange for payment in paper currency and for governments to agree to convert the paper currency into gold on demand at a fixed rate.

Nature of the Gold Standard

The practice of pegging currencies to gold and guaranteeing convertibility is known as the **gold standard.** By 1880 most of the world's major trading nations, including Great Britain, Germany, Japan, and the United States, had adopted the gold standard. Given a common gold standard, the value of any currency in units of any other currency (the exchange rate) was easy to determine.

For example, under the gold standard one US dollar was defined as equivalent to 23.22 grains of "fine" (pure) gold. Thus, one could, in theory, demand that the US government convert that dollar into 23.22 grains of gold. Since there are 480 grains in an ounce, one ounce of gold cost $20.67 (480/23.22). The amount of a currency needed to purchase one ounce of gold was referred to as the gold par value. The British pound was defined as containing 113 grains of fine gold. One ounce of gold cost £4.25 (480/113). From the gold par values of pounds and dollars, we can calculate what the exchange rate was for converting pounds into dollars; it was £1 = $4.87 (i.e., $20.67/£4.25).

The Strength of the Gold Standard

The great strength claimed for the gold standard was that it contained a powerful mechanism for simultaneously achieving balance-of-trade equilibrium by all countries.[3] A country is said to be in balance-of-trade equilibrium when the income its residents earn from exports is equal to the money its residents pay to people in other countries for imports (i.e., the current account of its balance of payments is in balance).

Suppose there are only two countries in the world, Japan and the United States. Imagine Japan's trade balance is in surplus because it exports more to the United States than it imports from the United States. Japanese exporters are paid in US dollars, which they exchange for Japanese yen at a Japanese bank. The Japanese bank submits the dollars to the US government and demands payment of gold in return. (This is a simplification of what actually would occur, but it will make our point.)

Under the gold standard, when Japan has a trade surplus there will be a net flow of gold from the United States to Japan. These gold flows automatically reduce the US money supply and swell Japan's money supply. As we saw in Chapter 8, money supply growth and price inflation are connected. An increase in money supply will raise prices in Japan, while a decrease in the US money supply will push US prices downward. The rise in the price of Japanese goods will decrease demand for these goods, while the fall in the price of US goods will increase demand for these goods. Thus, Japan will start to buy more from the United States, and the United States will buy less from Japan, until a balance-of-trade equilibrium is achieved.

This adjustment mechanism seems so simple and attractive that even today, more than half a century after the final collapse of the gold standard, there are people who believe the world should return to a gold standard.

The Period between the Wars, 1918–1939

The gold standard worked reasonably well from the 1870s until the start of World War I in 1914, when it was abandoned. During the war several governments financed part of their massive military expenditures by printing money. This resulted in inflation, and by the war's end in 1918, price levels were higher everywhere. The United States returned to the gold standard in 1919, Great Britain in 1925, and France in 1928.

Great Britain returned to the gold standard by pegging the pound to gold at the prewar gold parity level of £4.25 per ounce, despite substantial inflation between 1914 and 1925. This priced British goods out of foreign markets, which pushed the country into a deep depression. When foreign holders of pounds lost confidence in Great Britain's commitment to maintaining its currency's value, they began converting their holdings of pounds into gold. The British government saw that it could not satisfy the demand for gold without seriously depleting its gold reserves, so it suspended convertibility in 1931.

The United States followed suit and left the gold standard in 1933 but returned to it in 1934, raising the dollar price of gold from $20.67 per ounce to $35 per ounce. Because more dollars were needed to buy an ounce of gold, the implication was that the dollar was worth less. This amounted to a devaluation of the dollar relative to other currencies. Before the devaluation the pound/dollar exchange rate was £1 = $4.87, after the devaluation it was £1 = $8.24. By reducing the price of US exports and increasing the price of imports, the government was trying to create employment in the United States by boosting output. However, a number of other countries adopted a similar tactic, and in the cycle of competitive devaluations that soon emerged, no country could win.

The net result was the shattering of any remaining confidence in the system. With countries devaluing their currencies at will, one could no longer be certain how much gold a currency could buy. Instead of holding onto another country's currency, people often tried to change it into gold immediately, lest the country devalue its currency. This put pressure on the gold reserves of various countries, forcing them to suspend gold convertibility. By the start of World War II in 1939, the gold standard was dead.

In 1944, at the height of World War II, representatives from 44 countries met at Bretton Woods, New Hampshire, to design a new international monetary system. Pictured here is Henry Morgenthau, then Secretary of the Treasury, addressing the opening meeting of the conference where the IMF and the World Bank were established.
©Bettman/CORBIS

The Bretton Woods System

At the height of World War II in 1944, representatives from 44 countries met at Bretton Woods, New Hampshire, to design a new international monetary system. With the collapse of the gold standard and the Great Depression of the 1930s fresh in their minds, these statesmen were determined to build an enduring economic order that would facilitate postwar economic growth. There was a general consensus that fixed exchange rates were desirable. In addition, the conference participants wanted to avoid the senseless competitive devaluations of the 1930s, and they recognized that the gold standard would not assure this. The major problem with the gold standard as previously constituted was that there was no multinational institution that could stop countries from engaging in competitive devaluations.

The agreement reached at Bretton Woods established two multinational institutions—the International Monetary Fund and the World Bank. The task of the IMF would be to maintain order in the international monetary system, and that of the World Bank would be to promote general economic development. The Bretton Woods agreement also called for a system of fixed exchange rates that would be policed by the IMF. Under the agreement, all countries were to fix the value of their currency in terms of gold but were not required to exchange their currencies for gold. Only the dollar remained convertible into gold—at a price of $35 per ounce. The other countries decided what they wanted their exchange rates to be vis-à-vis the dollar and then calculated the gold par value of their currency based on that selected dollar exchange rate. All participating countries agreed to try to maintain the value of their currencies within 1 percent of the par value by buying or selling currencies (or gold) as needed. For example, if foreign exchange dealers were selling more of a country's currency than they demanded, the government of that country would intervene in the foreign exchange markets, buying its currency in an attempt to increase demand and maintain its gold par value.

Another aspect of the Bretton Woods agreement was a commitment not to use devaluation as a weapon of competitive trade policy. However, if a currency became too weak to defend, a devaluation of up to 10 percent would be allowed without any formal approval by the IMF. Larger devaluations required IMF approval.

The Role of the IMF

The IMF Articles of Agreement were heavily influenced by the worldwide financial collapse, competitive devaluations, trade wars, high unemployment, hyperinflation in Germany and elsewhere, and general economic disintegration that occurred between the two world wars. The aim of the Bretton Woods agreement, of which the IMF was the main custodian, was to try to avoid a repetition of that chaos through a combination of discipline and flexibility.

DISCIPLINE A fixed exchange rate regime imposes discipline in two ways. First, the need to maintain a fixed exchange rate puts a brake on competitive devaluations and brings stability to the world trade environment. Second, a fixed exchange rate regime imposes monetary discipline on countries, thereby curtailing price inflation. For example, consider what would happen under a fixed exchange rate regime if Great Britain rapidly increased its money supply by printing pounds. As explained in Chapter 8, the increase in money supply would lead to price inflation. Given fixed exchange rates, inflation would make British goods uncompetitive in world markets, while the prices of imports would become more attractive in Great Britain. The result would be a widening trade deficit in Great Britain, with the country importing more than it exports. To correct this trade imbalance under a fixed exchange rate regime, Great Britain would be required to restrict the rate of growth in its money supply to bring price inflation back under control. Thus, fixed exchange rates are seen as a mechanism for controlling inflation and imposing economic discipline on countries.

FLEXIBILITY Although monetary discipline was a central objective, the Bretton Woods agreement recognized that a rigid policy of fixed exchange rates would be too inflexible. It would probably break down just as the gold standard had. In some cases a country's attempts to reduce its money supply growth and correct a persistent balance-of-payments deficit could force the country into recession and create high unemployment. The architects of the Bretton Woods agreement wanted to avoid high unemployment, so they built some limited flexibility into the system. Two major features of the IMF Articles of Agreement fostered this flexibility: IMF lending facilities and adjustable parities.

The IMF stood ready to lend foreign currencies to members to tide them over during short periods of balance-of-payments deficit, when a rapid tightening of monetary or fiscal policy would hurt domestic employment. A pool of gold and currencies contributed by IMF members funded these lending operations. A persistent balance-of-payments deficit can lead to a depletion of a country's reserves of foreign currency, forcing it to devalue its currency. By providing deficit countries with short-term foreign currency loans, IMF funds would buy countries time in which to bring down their inflation rates and reduce their balance-of-payments deficit. The belief was that such loans would reduce pressures for devaluation and allow for a more orderly and less painful adjustment.

Countries were to be allowed to borrow a limited amount from the IMF without adhering to any specific agreements. However, extensive drawings from IMF funds would require a country to agree to increasingly stringent IMF supervision of its

macroeconomics policies. Heavy borrowers from the IMF must agree to conditions concerning monetary and fiscal policy set down by the IMF, which typically include IMF-mandated targets on domestic money supply growth, exchange rate policy, tax policy, government spending, and so on.

The system of adjustable parities allows for the devaluation of a country's currency by more than 10 percent if the IMF agrees that the country's balance of payments is in "fundamental disequilibrium." The term *fundamental disequilibrium* was not defined in the IMF's Articles of Agreement, but it was intended to apply to countries that have suffered permanent adverse shifts in the demand for their products. Without a devaluation, such a country would experience high unemployment and a persistent trade deficit until the domestic price level had fallen far enough to restore a balance-of-payments equilibrium. The belief was that devaluation could help sidestep a painful adjustment process in such circumstances.

The Role of the World Bank

The official name for the World Bank is the International Bank for Reconstruction and Development (IBRD). When the Bretton Woods participants established the World Bank, the need to reconstruct the war-torn economies of Europe was foremost in their minds. The bank's initial mission was to help finance the building of Europe's economy by providing low-interest loans. As it turned out, the World Bank was overshadowed in this role by the Marshall Plan, under which the United States lent money directly to European nations to help them rebuild. So the bank turned its attention to "development" and began lending money to the less developed nations of the Third World. In the 1950s the bank concentrated its efforts on public-sector projects. Power station projects, road building, and other transportation investments were much in favor. During the 1960s the bank also began to lend heavily in support of agriculture, education, population control, and urban development.

The bank lends money under two schemes. Under the IBRD scheme, money is raised through bond sales in the international capital market. Borrowers pay what the bank calls a market rate of interest—the bank's cost of funds plus a margin for expenses. This "market" rate is lower than commercial banks' market rate. The bank offers low-interest loans to risky customers whose credit rating is often poor.

A second scheme is overseen by the International Development Agency (IDA), an arm of the bank created in 1960. Resources to fund IDA loans are raised through subscriptions from wealthy members such as the United States, Japan, and Germany. IDA loans go only to the poorest countries. (In 1991 those were defined as countries with annual incomes per capita of less than $580.) Borrowers have 50 years to repay at an interest rate of 1 percent a year.

The Collapse of the Fixed Exchange Rate System

The system of fixed exchange rates established at Bretton Woods worked well until the late 1960s, when it began to show signs of strain. The system finally collapsed in 1973, and since then we have had a managed-float system. To understand why the system collapsed, one must appreciate the special role of the US dollar in the system. As the only currency that could be converted into gold and as the currency that served as the reference point for all others, the dollar occupied a central place in the system. Any pressure on the dollar to devalue could wreak havoc with the system, and that is what happened.

Most economists trace the breakup of the fixed exchange rate system to the US macroeconomic policy package of 1965–1968.[4] To finance both the Vietnam conflict and his welfare programs, President Lyndon Johnson backed an increase in US government spending that was not financed by an increase in taxes. It was financed by an increase in the money supply, which led to a rise in price inflation from less than 4 percent in 1966 to close to 9 percent by 1968. At the same time, the rise in government spending had stimulated the economy. With more money in their pockets, people spent more—particularly on imports—and the US trade balance began to deteriorate.

The rise in inflation and the worsening of the US foreign trade position gave rise to speculation in the foreign exchange market that the dollar would be devalued. Things came to a head in spring 1971 when US trade figures were released, which showed that for the first time since 1945, the United States was importing more than it was exporting. This set off massive purchases of deutsche marks in the foreign exchange market by speculators who guessed that the mark would be revalued against the dollar. On a single day, May 4, 1971, the Bundesbank (Germany's central bank) had to buy $1 billion to hold the dollar/deutsche mark exchange rate at its fixed exchange rate given the great demand for marks. On the morning of May 5, the Bundesbank purchased another $1 billion during the first hour of foreign exchange trading! At that point, the Bundesbank allowed its currency to float.

In the weeks following the decision to float the deutsche mark, the foreign exchange market became increasingly convinced that the dollar would have to be devalued. However, devaluation of the dollar was not easy. Under the Bretton Woods provisions, any other country could change its exchange rates against all currencies simply by fixing its dollar rate at a new level. But as the key currency in the system, the dollar could be devalued only if all countries agreed to simultaneously revalue against the dollar. And many countries did not want this, since it would make their products more expensive relative to US products.

To force the issue, in August 1971 President Richard Nixon announced the dollar was no longer convertible into gold. He also announced that a new 10 percent tax on imports would remain in effect until the nation's trading partners agreed to revalue their currencies against the dollar. This brought the trading partners to the bargaining table, and in December 1971 an agreement was reached to devalue the dollar by about 8 percent against foreign currencies. The import tax was then removed.

The problem was not solved, however. The US balance of payments position continued to deteriorate throughout 1972, while the US money supply continued to expand at an inflationary rate. Speculation continued to grow that the dollar was still overvalued and that a second devaluation would be necessary. In anticipation, foreign exchange dealers began converting dollars to deutsche marks and other currencies. After a massive wave of speculation in February, which culminated with European central banks spending $3.6 billion on March 1 to try to prevent their currencies from appreciating against the dollar, the foreign exchange market was closed. When the foreign exchange market reopened on March 19, the currencies of Japan and most European countries were floating against the dollar—although many developing countries continued to peg their currency to the dollar, and many still do. At that time, the switch to a floating system was viewed as a temporary response to unmanageable speculation in the foreign exchange market. But it is now 30 years since the Bretton Woods system of fixed exchange rates collapsed, and the temporary solution looks permanent.

The Bretton Woods system had an Achilles' heel: The system could not work if its key currency, the US dollar, was under speculative attack. The Bretton Woods system could work only as long as the US inflation rate remained low and the United States did not run a balance-of-payments deficit. Once these things occurred, the system became strained to the breaking point.

The Floating Exchange Rate Regime

The floating exchange rate regime that followed the collapse of the fixed exchange rate system was formalized in January 1976 when IMF members met in Jamaica and agreed to the rules for the international monetary system that are in place today. We will discuss the Jamaica agreement before looking at how the floating exchange rate regime has operated.

The Jamaica Agreement

The Jamaica meeting revised the IMF's Articles of Agreement to reflect the new reality of floating exchange rates. The main elements of the Jamaica agreement include the following:

1 Floating rates were declared acceptable. IMF members were permitted to enter the foreign exchange market to even out "unwarranted" speculative fluctuations.

2 Gold was abandoned as a reserve asset. The IMF returned its gold reserves to members at the current market price, placing the proceeds in a trust fund to help poor nations. IMF members were permitted to sell their own gold reserves at the market price.

3 Total annual IMF quotas—the amount member countries contribute to the IMF—were increased to $41 billion. (Since then they have been increased to $195 billion and membership has been expanded to include 182 countries). Non-oil-exporting, less developed countries were given greater access to IMF funds.

   After Jamaica, the IMF continued its role of helping countries cope with macroeconomic and exchange rate problems, albeit within the context of a radically different exchange rate regime.

Exchange Rates since 1973

Since March 1973 exchange rates have become much more volatile and less predictable than they were between 1945 and 1973.[5] This volatility has been partly due to a number of unexpected shocks to the world monetary system, including:

1 The oil crisis in 1971, when the Organization of Petroleum Exporting Countries (OPEC) quadrupled the price of oil. The harmful effect of this on the US inflation rate and trade position resulted in a further decline in the value of the dollar.

2 The loss of confidence in the dollar that followed the rise of US inflation in 1977 and 1978.

3 The oil crisis of 1979, when OPEC doubled the price of oil.

4 The unexpected rise in the dollar between 1980 and 1985, despite a deteriorating balance of payments.

5 The rapid fall of the US dollar against the Japanese yen and German deutsche mark between 1985 and 1987, and against the yen between 1993 and 1995.

6 The partial collapse of the European Monetary System in 1992.

7 The 1997 Asian currency crisis, when the currencies of several countries including South Korea, Indonesia, Malaysia, and Thailand, lost between 50 percent and 80 percent of their value against the US dollar in a few months.

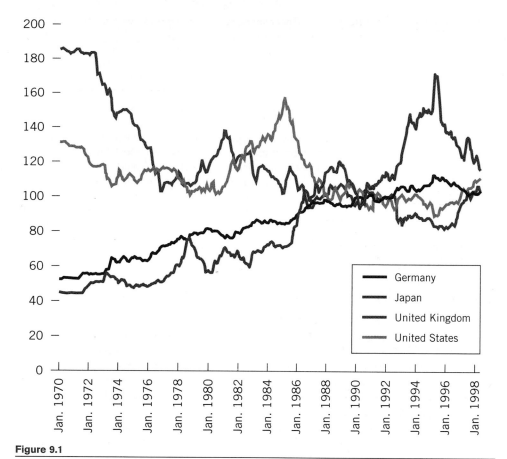

Figure 9.1

Long Term Exchange Rate Trends
Source: JP Morgan. Effective Exchange Rate Index, 1970–1998. (1990 = 100.)

Figure 9.1 summarizes the volatility of four major currencies from 1970 to 1998: the German mark, Japanese yen, British pound, and US dollar. The Morgan Guaranty Index, the basis for Figure 9.1, represents the exchange rate of each of these currencies against a weighted basket of the currencies of 19 industrial countries (the index was set equal to 100 in 1990). All four currencies have been quite volatile. The index value of the Japanese yen, for example, has ranged from a low of 44 in 1970 to a high of 170 in June 1995. Similarly, the US dollar index has been as low as 89.3 in 1995, and as high as 158 in 1985.

The most interesting phenomena in Figure 9.1 are the rapid rise in the value of the dollar between 1980 and 1985 and its subsequent fall between 1985 and 1988 and the similar rise and fall in the value of the Japanese yen between 1990 and 1998. We will briefly discuss the rise and fall of the dollar because this tells us something about how the international monetary system has operated in recent years. The rise and recent fall of the yen are profiled in the accompanying "Country Focus."[6]

The rise in the value of the dollar between 1980 and 1985 is particularly interesting because it occurred when the United States was running a large and growing trade deficit, importing substantially more than it exported. Conventional wisdom would suggest that the increased supply of dollars in the foreign exchange market as a result of the trade deficit should lead to a reduction in the value of the dollar, but it increased in value. Why? A number of favorable factors temporarily overcame the unfavorable effect of a trade deficit. Strong economic growth in the United States

In 1971, before the collapse of the Bretton Woods system of fixed exchange rates, one US dollar purchased 350 Japanese yen. In 1985 the exchange rate was $1 = ¥250; in 1990 it stood at $1 = ¥150; in 1993 it was $1 = ¥125; by March 1995 the exchange rate stood at $1 = ¥85. Much of the decline in the value of the dollar against the yen between 1971 and the 1995 can be explained by differences in relative inflation rates. Between 1983 and 1989, inflation about 30 percent. This overvaluation suggested that differences in US and Japanese inflation rates were not sufficient to explain the rise of the yen.

One explanation for the dramatic rise in the dollar value of the yen between 1993 and 1995 can be found in the behavior of Japanese financial institutions (particularly banks and insurance companies). Japan has long run a large balance-of-trade surplus with the United States. One consequence change rate was relatively stable. However, in the early 1990s Japan entered its worst recession since 1945. The severity of this recession was compounded by a collapse in Japanese stock and property prices, both of which fell by more than 50 percent. This deflation hit Japanese financial institutions hard. Most Japanese financial institutions held many of their assets in the form of Japanese stock and property investments. With stock and property prices plunging,

The Rise and Fall of the Japanese Yen

in Japan averaged 1.1 percent a year, and US price inflation ran at an average annual rate of 3.6 percent. Between 1988 and 1993 inflation in Japan ran at an average annual rate of 2 percent, compared to 4.1 percent in the United States. However, between 1993 and early 1995 the yen appreciated by 50 percent against the dollar. On a purchasing power parity basis, by mid-1995 the yen looked to be overvalued against the dollar by of this surplus is that many Japanese companies have found themselves holding lots of dollars (earned from the sale of products to US consumers). During the 1980s Japanese financial institutions helped recycle these dollars by purchasing them from Japanese companies and reinvesting them in US stocks and bonds.

As long as Japanese financial institutions reinvested dollars in the United States, as opposed to selling them for yen, the dollar/yen ex- Japanese financial institutions saw their balance sheets deteriorate. Their weak balance sheets reduced their appetite for risky investments, so they reduced their purchases of US assets and increased their investments in Japanese government bonds. The financial institutions stopped recycling dollars earned from exports back to the United States. From 1993 onward they changed many of these dollars into yen and reinvested them in

attracted heavy inflows of capital from foreign investors seeking high returns on capital assets. High real interest rates attracted foreign investors seeking high returns on financial assets. At the same time, political turmoil in other parts of the world, along with relatively slow economic growth in the developed countries of Europe, created the view that the United States was a good place to invest. These inflows of capital increased the demand for dollars in the foreign exchange market, which pushed the value of the dollar upward against other currencies.

The fall in the value of the dollar between 1985 and 1988 was caused by a combination of government intervention and market forces. The rise in the dollar, which priced US goods out of foreign markets and made imports relatively cheap, had contributed to a dismal trade picture. In 1985 the United States posted a record high trade deficit of more than $160 billion. This led to demands for protectionism. In September 1985 the finance ministers and central bank governors of the so-called Group of Five major industrial countries (Great Britain, France, Japan, Germany, and the United States) met at the Plaza Hotel in New York and reached what was later referred to as the Plaza Accord. They announced that it would be desirable for most major currencies to appreciate vis-à-vis the US dollar and pledged to intervene

Japan. To make matters worse, many financial institutions started liquidating their holdings of US stocks and bonds to increase the funds available for investment in low-risk Japanese government bonds. Thus, after having doubled their US investments in the two years before 1989, Japanese financial institutions reduced their foreign assets by 20 percent over the next four years.

These developments reduced the demand for dollars and increased the demand for yen; hence the appreciation of the yen against the dollar. As the value of the yen accelerated in 1993, US assets began to look even less attractive (their valuation in yen declined). This increased the reluctance of Japanese institutions to invest in US stocks and bonds. Thus, by 1995 a self-fulfilling bandwagon effect had led to a massive rise in the value of the yen as Japanese investors held back from investing in US assets lest they see the value of those assets reduced by a subsequent appreciation in the value of the yen.

By 1996, this process had reversed itself and the yen started a slide against the dollar that would take it down to $1 = ¥140 by June 1998. As with the rise of the yen, much of the momentum for its subsequent fall can be laid at the feet of Japanese financial institutions. Throughout the 1990s, Japan remained mired in a persistent economic malaise characterized by weak domestic demand. In response, the Japanese government repeatedly cut interest rates in an attempt to stimulate the domestic economy, but to no avail. Japan's economic situation deteriorated even further in 1997 when the collapse of several Asian economies reduced demand for Japanese goods and services. This also threatened to push several Japanese banks with heavy loan exposure to troubled Asian economies into bankruptcy, and the Japanese stock market tumbled to the lowest levels in a decade. The Japanese government responded by further reducing interest rates, and by mid-1998 they stood at a record low 0.5 percent. At the same time, the US economy was entering its seventh year of economic expansion characterized by steady growth and inflation rates that were the lowest since the 1960s. In an attempt to rein in the US economy and keep inflation in check, the US Federal Reserve maintained relatively high interest rates in the United States.

As a consequence of these divergent interest rate policies, by the late 1990s a significant interest rate differential had emerged between the United States and Japan. US Treasury bonds offered a yield of 5.8 percent, while Japanese government bonds provided a yield of 1.4 percent. The US stock market continued its robust performance, while the Japanese stock market continued to flirt with its decadelong lows. Japanese financial institutions reversed their stance of the early 1990s and started plowing money into US bonds and stocks. The reduced demand for yen and increased demand for dollars naturally led to a decline in the value of the yen. As the yen declined against the dollar, the process again began to take on a bandwagon effect, with many Japanese institutions investing in dollar-denominated bonds not only to exploit interest rate differentials but also to profit from the continued decline of the yen against the dollar.[7]

in the foreign exchange markets, selling dollars, to encourage this. The dollar had already begun to weaken in the summer of 1985, and this announcement further accelerated the decline.

The dollar continued to decline until early 1987. The governments of the Group of Five began to worry that the dollar might decline too far. In February 1987 the finance ministers of the Group of Five met in Paris and reached a new agreement known as the Louvre Accord. They agreed that exchange rates had been realigned sufficiently and pledged to support the stability of exchange rates around their current levels by intervening in the foreign exchange markets when necessary to buy and sell currency. Although the dollar continued to decline for a few months after the Louvre Accord, the rate of decline slowed, and by early 1988 the decline had ended. Except for a brief speculative flurry around the time of the Persian Gulf War in 1991, the dollar has been relatively stable since then against most major currencies with the notable exception of the Japanese yen.

In recent history the value of the dollar has been determined by both market forces and government intervention. Under a floating exchange rate regime, market forces have produced a volatile dollar exchange rate. Governments have responded

299

by buying and selling dollars to limit the market's volatility and to correct what they see as overvaluation (in 1985) or potential undervaluation (in 1987) of the dollar. The frequency of government intervenes in the foreign exchange markets explains why the current system is often referred to as a **managed-float system** or a **dirty float system.**

Fixed versus Floating Exchange Rates

The breakdown of the Bretton Woods system has not stopped the debate about the relative merits of fixed versus floating exchange rate regimes. Disappointment with the system of floating rates has led to renewed debate about the merits of a fixed exchange rate system. In this section we review the arguments for fixed and floating exchange rate regimes.[8] We will discuss the case for floating rates before discussing why many commentators are disappointed with the experience under floating exchange rates and yearn for fixed rates.

The Case for Floating Exchange Rates

The case for floating exchange rates has two main elements: monetary policy autonomy and automatic trade balance adjustments.

MONETARY POLICY AUTONOMY   It is argued that under a fixed system, a country's ability to expand or contract its money supply as it sees fit is limited by the need to maintain exchange rate parity. Monetary expansion can lead to inflation, which puts downward pressure on a fixed exchange rate (as predicted by PPP theory; see Chapter 8). Similarly, monetary contraction requires high interest rates (to reduce the demand for money). Higher interest rates lead to an inflow of money from abroad, which puts upward pressure on a fixed exchange rate. Thus, to maintain exchange rate parity under a fixed system, countries were limited in their ability to use monetary policy to expand or contract their economies.

Advocates of a floating exchange rate regime argue that removal of the obligation to maintain exchange rate parity restores monetary control to a government. If a government faced with unemployment wanted to increase its money supply to stimulate domestic demand and reduce unemployment, it could do so unencumbered by the need to maintain its exchange rate. While monetary expansion might lead to inflation, this would lead to a depreciation in the country's currency. If PPP theory is correct, the resulting currency depreciation on the foreign exchange markets should offset the effects of inflation. Although under a floating exchange rate regime, domestic inflation would affect the exchange rate, it should have no impact on the international cost competitiveness of the country's businesses due to exchange rate depreciation. The rise in domestic costs should be offset by the fall in the value of the country's currency on the foreign exchange markets. Similarly, a government could use monetary policy to contract the economy without worrying about the need to maintain parity.

TRADE BALANCE ADJUSTMENTS   Under the Bretton Woods system, if a country developed a deficit in its balance of trade (importing more than it exported) that could not be corrected by domestic policy, the IMF would have to agree to a currency devaluation. Critics of this system argue that the adjustment mechanism works much more smoothly under a floating exchange rate regime. They argue that if a country is running a trade deficit, the imbalance between the supply and demand of that country's currency in the foreign exchange markets (supply exceeding demand) will lead to depreciation in its exchange rate. By making its exports cheaper and its imports more expensive, an exchange rate depreciation should ultimately correct the trade deficit.

The Case for Fixed Exchange Rates

The case for fixed exchange rates rests on arguments about monetary discipline, speculation, uncertainty, and the lack of connection between the trade balance and exchange rates.

MONETARY DISCIPLINE We have already discussed the nature of monetary discipline inherent in a fixed exchange rate system when we covered the Bretton Woods system. The need to maintain a fixed exchange rate parity ensures that governments do not expand their money supplies at inflationary rates. While advocates of floating rates argue that each country should be allowed to choose its own inflation rate (the monetary autonomy argument), advocates of fixed rates argue that governments too often give in to political pressures and expand the monetary supply far too rapidly, causing unacceptably high price inflation. A fixed exchange rate regime will ensure that this does not occur.

SPECULATION Critics of a floating exchange rate regime also argue that speculation can cause fluctuations in exchange rates. They point to the dollar's rapid rise and fall during the 1980s, which they claim had nothing to do with comparative inflation rates and the US trade deficit, but everything to do with speculation. They argue that if foreign exchange dealers see a currency depreciating, they tend to sell the currency in the expectation of future depreciation regardless of the currency's longer-term prospects. As more traders jump on the bandwagon, the expectations of depreciation are realized. Such destabilizing speculation tends to accentuate the fluctuations around the exchange rate's long-run value. It can damage a country's economy by distorting export and import prices. Thus, advocates of a fixed exchange rate regime argue that such a system will limit the destabilizing effects of speculation.

UNCERTAINTY Speculation also adds to the uncertainty surrounding future currency movements that characterizes floating exchange rate regimes. The unpredictability of exchange rate movements in the post-Bretton Woods era has made business planning difficult, and it makes exporting, importing, and foreign investment risky activities. Given a volatile exchange rate, international businesses do not know how to react to the changes—and often they do not react. Why change plans for exporting, importing, or foreign investment after a 6 percent fall in the dollar this month, when the dollar may rise 6 percent next month? This uncertainty, according to the critics, hampers the growth of international trade and investment. They argue that a fixed exchange rate, by eliminating such uncertainty, promotes the growth of international trade and investment. Advocates of a floating system reply that the forward exchange market does a good job of insuring against the risks associated with exchange rate fluctuations (see Chapter 8). Accordingly, the adverse impact of uncertainty on the growth of international trade and investment have been overstated.

TRADE BALANCE ADJUSTMENTS Those in favor of floating exchange rates argue that floating rates help adjust trade imbalances. Critics question the closeness of the link between the exchange rate and the trade balance. They claim trade deficits are determined by the balance between savings and investment in a country, not by the external value of its currency.[9] They also argue that a depreciation in a currency will lead to inflation (due to the resulting increase in import prices). This inflation will wipe out any apparent gains in cost competitiveness that come from currency depreciation. In other words, a depreciating exchange rate will not boost exports and reduce imports, as advocates of floating rates claim; it will simply boost price inflation. Those who favor fixed rates point out that the 40 percent drop in the value of the dollar between 1985 and 1988 did not seem to correct the US trade deficit. In reply, advocates of a floating exchange rate regime argue that between 1985 and 1992, the US trade deficit fell from more than $160 billion to about $70 billion, and they attribute this in part to the decline in the value of the dollar.

Who Is Right?

Which side is right in the vigorous debate between those who favor a fixed exchange rate regime and those who favor a floating exchange rate regime? Economists cannot agree on this issue. From a business perspective, this is unfortunate, because business has a large stake in the resolution of the debate. Would international business be better off under a fixed regime, or are flexible rates better? The evidence is not clear.

We do, however, know that a fixed exchange rate regime modeled along the lines of the Bretton Woods system will not work. Speculation ultimately broke the system; a phenomenon that advocates of fixed rate regimes claim is associated with floating exchange rates! Nevertheless, a different kind of fixed exchange rate system might be more enduring and might foster the stability that would facilitate more rapid growth in international trade and investment. In the next section we look at potential models for such a system and the problems with such systems.

Exchange Rate Regimes in Practice

A number of different exchange rate policies are pursued by governments around the world. These range from a pure "free float" where the exchange rate is determined by market forces to a pegged system that has some aspects of the pre-1973 Bretton Woods system of fixed exchange rates. Figure 9.2 summarizes the different exchange rate policies adopted by member states of the IMF in 1997. While more than half of IMF members allow their currencies to float freely or intervene in only a limited way (the so-called managed float), a significant minority use a more inflexible system under which they peg their currencies to other currencies, such as the US dollar.

Under a pegged exchange rate regime a country will peg the value of its currency to that of a major currency so that, for example, as the US dollar rises in value, its own currency rises too. Pegged exchange rates are popular among many of the world's smaller nations. As with a full fixed exchange rate regime, the great virtue claimed for a pegged exchange rate regime is that it imposes monetary discipline on a country and leads to low inflation. For example, if Mexico pegs the value of the peso to that of the US dollar so that $1 is equal to 8.80 Mexican pesos, then to maintain the value of the peg the Mexican government must make sure the inflation rate in Mexico is similar to that in the United States. If the Mexican inflation rate exceeds the US inflation rate, this will lead to pressure to devalue the Mexican peso (i.e., to alter the peg). To maintain the peg, the Mexican government would be required to cut inflation. For a pegged exchange rate to impose monetary discipline on a country, the country whose currency is chosen for the peg must also pursue sound monetary policy.

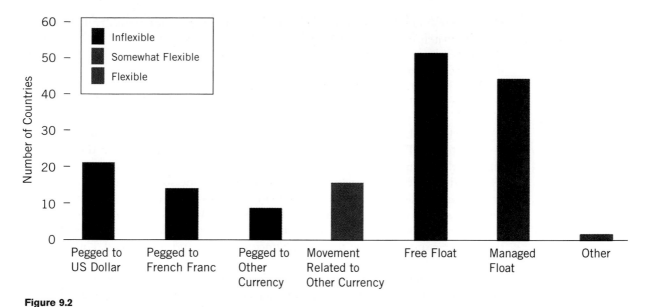

Figure 9.2

How IMF Members Determine Exchange Values
Source: IMF Data.

There is some evidence that adopting a pegged exchange rate regime does moderate inflationary pressures in a country. A recent IMF study concluded that countries with pegged exchange rates regimes had an average annual inflation rate of 8 percent, compared with 14 percent for intermediate regimes, and 16 percent for floating regimes.[10] However, many countries operate with only a "nominal" peg and devalue their currency rather than pursue a tight monetary policy. Also, it can be very difficult for a smaller country to maintain a peg against another currency if capital is flowing out of the country and foreign exchange traders are speculating against the currency. Something like this occurred in 1997 when a combination of adverse capital flows and currency speculation forced several Asian countries, including Thailand and Malaysia, to abandon pegs against the US dollar and let their currencies float freely. Malaysia and Thailand would not have been in this position had they dealt with a number of problems that began to arise in their economies during the 1990s, including the build up of excessive private-sector debt and expanding current account trade deficits.

The experience of Hong Kong during the 1997 Asian currency crisis, however, has added a new dimension to the debate over how to manage a pegged exchange rate. During late 1997 when other Asian currencies were collapsing, Hong Kong maintained the value of its currency against the US dollar at about $1 = HK$7.8 despite several concerted speculative attacks. Hong Kong's **currency board** has been given credit for this success. A country that introduces a currency board commits itself to converting its domestic currency on demand into another currency at a fixed exchange rate. To make this commitment credible, the currency board holds reserves of foreign currency equal at the fixed exchange rate to at least 100 percent of the domestic currency issued. The system used in Hong Kong means that its currency must be fully backed by the US dollar at the specified exchange rate. This is not a true fixed exchange rate regime because the US dollar, and by extension the Hong Kong dollar, floats against other currencies, but it has some features of a fixed exchange rate regime.

Under this arrangement, the currency board can issue additional domestic notes and coins only when there are foreign exchange reserves to back it. This limits the ability of the government to print money and, thereby, create inflationary pressures.

currency board
A governing body that manages the value of a currency by holding foreign currency reserves equal to the amount of domestic currency issued at a fixed exchange rate.

Under a strict currency board system, interest rates adjust automatically. If investors want to switch out of domestic currency into, for example, US dollars, the supply of domestic currency will shrink. This will cause interest rates to rise until it eventually becomes attractive for investors to hold the local currency again. In the case of Hong Kong, the interest rate on three-month deposits climbed as high as 20 percent in late 1997, as investors switched out of Hong Kong dollars and into US dollars. The dollar peg, however, held and interest rates declined again.

Since its establishment in 1983, the Hong Kong currency board has weathered several storms. This success seems to be persuading other countries in the developing world to consider a similar system. Argentina introduced a currency board in 1991, and Bulgaria, Estonia, and Lithuania have all done so in recent years. Despite growing interest in the arrangement, however, critics are quick to point out that currency boards have their drawbacks.[11] If local inflation rates remain higher than the inflation rate in the country to which the currency is pegged, the currencies of countries with currency boards can become uncompetitive and overvalued. Under a currency board system, government lacks the ability to set interest rates. Interest rates in Hong Kong, for example, are effectively set by the US Federal Reserve. Despite these drawbacks, however, Hong Kong's success in avoiding the currency collapse that afflicted its Asian neighbors suggests that other developing countries may adopt a similar system.

Recent Activities and the Future of the IMF

Many observers initially believed that the collapse of the Bretton Woods system in 1973 would diminish the role of the IMF. The IMF's original function was to provide a pool of money from which members could borrow for the short term to adjust their balance-of-payments position and maintain their exchange rate. Under a floating exchange rate regime, the demand for short-term loans was expected to diminish. A trade deficit would presumably lead to a decline in a country's exchange rate, which would help reduce imports and boost exports. No temporary IMF adjustment loan would be needed. After 1973 most industrialized countries let the foreign exchange market determine exchange rates in response to demand and supply. No major industrial country has borrowed funds from the IMF since the mid-1970s, when Great Britain and Italy did. Also, since the early 1970s the rapid development of global capital markets has allowed developed countries such as Great Britain and the United States to finance their deficits by borrowing private money, as opposed to drawing on IMF funds.

Despite these developments, the activities of the IMF have expanded over the past 30 years. By mid-1999 the IMF had 182 members, 94 of which had IMF programs in place, and the institution was implementing its largest rescue packages, committing more than $110 billion in short-term loans to three troubled Asian countries: South Korea, Indonesia, and Thailand. The IMF's activities have expanded as periodic financial crises have hit many economies in the post-Bretton Woods era, particularly among the developing nations of the world. The IMF has repeatedly lent money to nations experiencing financial crises, requesting in return that the governments of these nations enact certain macroeconomic policies. As in the case of Zaire, which was profiled in the opening case, critics of the IMF claim these policies have not always been as beneficial as the IMF might have hoped and in some cases may have made things worse. With the recent extension of IMF loans to several Asian economies, this criticism has reached new levels and a vigorous debate is under way as to the appropriate role of the IMF. In this section we shall discuss the main challenges the IMF has had to deal with over the past 25 years and review the debate over the role of the IMF.

Financial Crises in the Post-Bretton Woods Era

A number of broad types of financial crisis have occurred over the past 25 years, many of which have required IMF involvement. A **currency crisis** occurs when a speculative attack on the exchange value of a currency results in a sharp depreciation in the value of the currency or forces authorities to expend large volumes of international currency reserves and sharply increase interest rates to defend the prevailing exchange rate. A **banking crisis** refers to a situation in which a loss of confidence in the banking system leads to a run on banks, as individuals and companies withdraw their deposits. A **foreign debt crisis** occurs when a country cannot service its foreign debt obligations, whether private sector or government debt. These crises tend to have common underlying macroeconomic causes: high relative price inflation rates, a widening current account deficit, excessive expansion of domestic borrowing, and asset price inflation (such as sharp increases in stock and property prices).[12] At times, elements of currency, banking, and debt crises may be present simultaneously, as in the 1997 Asian crisis.

To assess the frequency of financial crises, the IMF recently looked at the macroeconomic performance of 53 countries from 1975 to 1997 (22 of these countries were developed nations, and 31 were developing countries).[13] The IMF found there were 158 currency crises, including 55 episodes in which a country's currency declined by more than 25 percent. There were also 54 banking crises. The IMF's data, which are summarized in Figure 9.3, suggests that developing nations were more than twice as likely to experience currency and banking crisis as developed nations. It is not surprising, therefore, that most of the IMF's loan activities since the mid-1970s have been targeted toward developing nations.

Four main crises have been of particular significance for the IMF: the Third World debt crisis of the 1980s, the crisis experienced by Russia as that country moved toward a market-based economic system, the 1995 Mexican currency crisis, and the 1997 Asian financial crisis. To varying extent, all were the result of excessive foreign borrowings, a weak or poorly regulated banking system, and high inflation rates. These factors came together to trigger simultaneous debt and currency crises. Checking the resulting crises required IMF involvement. Here we shall look closely at the most recent of these crises, the Mexican currency crisis of 1995, the Russian ruble crisis, and the 1997–1998 Asian financial crisis.

1995 Mexican Currency Crisis

The Mexican peso had been pegged to the dollar since the early 1980s when the International Monetary Fund had made it a condition for lending money to the Mexican government to help bail the country out of a 1982 financial crisis. Under the IMF-brokered arrangement, the peso had been allowed to trade within a tolerance band of plus or minus 3 percent against the dollar. The band was also permitted to "crawl" down daily, allowing for an annual peso depreciation of about 4 percent against the dollar. The IMF believed that the need to maintain the exchange rate within a fairly narrow trading band would force the Mexican government to adopt stringent financial policies to limit the growth in the money supply and contain inflation.

Until the early 1990s it looked as if the IMF policy had worked. However, by 1994 the strains were beginning to show. Since the mid-1980s Mexican producer prices had risen 45 percent more than prices in the United States, and yet there had not been a

currency crisis The situation that occurs when a speculative attack on the exchange value of a currency results in a sharp depreciation in the value of the currency.

banking crisis A situation in which a loss of confidence in the banking system leads to a run on banks.

foreign debt crisis A situation in which a country cannot service its foreign debt obligations.

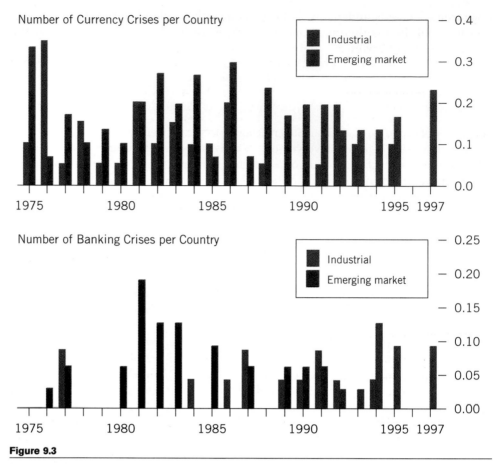

Figure 9.3

Incidence of Currency and Banking Crises, 1975–1997
International Monetary Fund, *World Economic Outlook, 1998* (Washington, D.C.: IMF, May 1998), p. 77.

corresponding adjustment in the exchange rate. By late 1994, Mexico also was running a $17 billion trade deficit, which amounted to 6 percent of the country's gross domestic product and there had been an uncomfortably rapid expansion in the country's public- and private-sector debt. Despite these strains, Mexican government officials had been stating publicly that they would support the peso's dollar peg at around $1 = 3.5 pesos by adopting appropriate monetary policies and by intervening in the currency markets if necessary. Encouraged by such public statements, $64 billion of foreign investment money poured into Mexico between 1990 and 1994 as corporations and mutual fund money managers sought to take advantage of the booming economy.

However, many currency traders concluded that the peso would have to be devalued, and they began to dump pesos on the foreign exchange market. The government tried to hold the line by buying pesos and selling dollars, but it soon found that it lacked the foreign currency reserves required to halt the speculative tide (Mexico's foreign exchange reserves fell from $6 billion at the beginning of 1994 to less than $3.5 billion at the end of the year). In mid-December 1994, the Mexican government abruptly announced a devaluation. Immediately, much of the short-term investment money that had flowed into Mexican stocks and bonds over the previous year reversed its course, as foreign investors bailed out of peso-denominated financial assets. This exacerbated the sale of the peso and contributed to the rapid 40 percent drop in its value.

In the euphoria that followed the January 1, 1994, implementation of the North American Free Trade Agreement no industry looked set to gain more than the auto industry. Because of falling trade barriers and booming demand in Mexico, between January and October 1994 US car exports to Mexico increased 500 percent. For all of 1994 Ford shipped 30,000 vehicles to Mexico, up from 6,000 in 1993. The company planned to ship 50,000 in 1995. General Motors and Chrysler also saw their eral Motors, Nissan, Mercedes-Benz, and Volkswagen.

Over a few days in December 1994, the euphoric bubble of the post-NAFTA boom was rudely burst by the Mexican government's unexpected decision to abandon a system of pegging the value of the peso at 3.5 to the dollar. Instead, the government decided to allow the peso to float freely against the dollar. In the weeks that followed this decision the peso plummeted 40 percent, and by mid-January 1995 it was trading at 5.6 to the dollar. 1995 at the IMF's insistence. The plan tightened credit and raised interest rates.

Demand for autos slumped. For all of 1995 demand was expected to come in between 30 and 50 percent below the levels attained in 1994. Volkswagen, Nissan, Mercedes-Benz, and Ford all temporarily closed their Mexican factories in January in expectation of the drop in demand. In other developments, Fiat of Italy pulled out of plans to build a new auto factory in Mexico, while Nissan an-

The 1995 Mexican Peso Crisis and the Automobile Industry

shipments to Mexico surge in 1994 and were planning for even greater increases in 1995. The number of vehicles sold in Mexico were forecast to rise to 1.2 million by 1999, up from 600,000 in 1994. With this growth in mind, not only had auto companies been exporting more to Mexico, but they had also been investing in Mexican-based production capacity both for serving the Mexican market and for exporting elsewhere. Among the biggest foreign investors were Chrysler, Ford, Gen- As with many other industries, the impact on the auto industry was dramatic and immediate. By February 1995 the price of imported autos had risen by 40 percent. There had also been a substantial rise in the price of most autos assembled in Mexico, such as those coming off Ford's Cuautitlan plant, because many of these operations depended on parts imported from the United States and Canada. Demand for autos was further depressed by the Mexican government's economic austerity plan, introduced in March nounced plans to cut its 1995 production in Mexico from 210,000 to 180,000 vehicles. While the short-term outlook was grim, many auto companies expected to benefit from the fall in the value of the peso in the longer run. The big three US automakers planned to keep their Mexican plants operating at full capacity in the second half of 1995 by boosting exports to the United States.[14]

The IMF stepped in again, this time with the US government and the Bank for International Settlements. Together the three institutions pledged close to $50 billion to help Mexico stabilize the peso and to redeem $47 billion of public- and private-sector debt that was set to mature in 1995. Of this amount, $20 billion came from the US government, with another $18 billion from the IMF (which made Mexico the largest recipient of IMF aid until that point). Without the aid package, Mexico would probably have defaulted on its debt obligations, and the peso would have gone into free fall. As is normal in such cases, the IMF insisted on the imposition of tight monetary policies and further cuts in public spending, both of which helped push the country into a deep recession. However, the recession was relatively short-lived, and by 1997 the country was once more on a growth path, had pared down its debt, and had paid back the $20 billion borrowed from the US government ahead of schedule.[15] (The accompanying "Management Focus" details how this crisis affected the US automobile industry, which before the crisis, was experiencing booming sales in Mexico.)

Russian Ruble Crisis

The IMF's involvement in Russia came about as the result of a persistent decline in the value of the Russian ruble, which was the product of high inflation rates and growing public-sector debt. Between January 1992 and April 1995, the value of the ruble against the US dollar fell from $1 = R125 to $1 = R5,130. This drop occurred while Russia was implementing an economic reform program designed to transform the country's crumbling centrally planned economy into a dynamic market economy. The reform program involved a number of steps, including the removal of price controls on January 1, 1992. Prices surged immediately and inflation was soon running at a *monthly* rate of about 30 percent. For all of 1992 the inflation rate in Russia was 3,000 percent. The annual rate for 1993 was approximately 900 percent.

Several factors contributed to Russia's high inflation. Prices had been held at artificially low levels by state planners during the Communist era. At the same time there was a shortage of many basic goods, so with nothing to spend their money on, many Russians simply hoarded rubles. After the liberalization of price controls, the country was suddenly awash in rubles chasing a still limited supply of goods. The inflationary fires that followed price liberalization were stoked by the Russian government. Unwilling to face the social consequences of the massive unemployment that would follow if many state-owned enterprises quickly were privatized, the government continued to subsidize the operations of many money-losing establishments. The government's budget deficit surged. In the first quarter of 1992 the budget deficit amounted to 1.5 percent of the country's GDP. By the end of 1992 it had risen to 17 percent. Unable or unwilling to finance this deficit by raising taxes, the government found another solution—it printed money, which added fuel to the inflation fire.

With inflation rising, the ruble tumbled. By the end of 1992, the exchange rate was $1 = R480. By the end of 1993 it was $1 = R1,500. As 1994 progressed, it became evident that because of vigorous political opposition, the government would not be able to reduce the budget deficit as quickly as had been thought. By September 1994 the monthly inflation rate was accelerating. October started badly with the ruble sliding more than 10 percent in value against the US dollar in the first 10 days of the month. Then on October 11 the ruble plunged 21.5 percent against the dollar reaching a value of $1 = R3,926 by the time the foreign exchange market closed!

Despite the announcement of a tough budget plan with tight controls on the money supply, the ruble continued to slide and by April 1995 the exchange rate stood at $1 = R5,120. However, by mid-1995 inflation was again on the way down. In June 1995 the monthly inflation rate was at a yearly low of 6.7 percent. The ruble had recovered to stand at $1 = R4,559 by July 6. On that day the Russian government announced it would intervene in the currency market to keep the ruble in a trading range of R4,300 to R4,900 rubles against the dollar. The Russian government thought it was essential to maintain a relatively stable currency. Officials announced that the central bank would be able to draw on $10 billion in foreign exchange reserves to defend the ruble against any speculative selling in Russia's relatively small foreign exchange market.

In the world of international finance, $10 billion is small change and it wasn't long before Russia found that its foreign exchange reserves were being depleted, and the Russian government requested IMF loans. In February 1996 the IMF obliged with its second-largest rescue effort after Mexico, a loan of $10 billion. In return for the loan, Russia agreed to limit the growth in its money supply, reduce public-sector debt, increase government tax revenues, and peg the ruble to the dollar.

Initially the package seemed to have the desired effect. Inflation declined from nearly 50 percent in 1996 to about 15 percent in 1997; the exchange rate stayed within its predetermined band; and the balance-of-payments situation remained broadly favorable. In 1997 the Russian economy grew for the first time since the breakup of the former Soviet Union, if only by a modest half of 1 percent of GDP. However, the public-sector debt situation did not improve. The Russian government continued to spend more than agreed to under IMF targets, while government tax revenues were much lower than projected. Low tax revenues were in part due to falling oil prices (the government collected tax on oil sales), in part due to the difficulties of collecting tax where so much activity was in the "underground economy," and in part due to a complex tax system that was peppered with loopholes. Estimates indicate that in 1997 federal government spending amounted to 18.3 percent of GDP in Russia, while revenues were only 10.8 percent of GDP. The deficit was financed by an expansion in public debt.

The IMF responded by suspending its scheduled payment to Russia in early 1998 pending reform of Russia's complex tax system and a sustained attempt by the Russian government to cut public spending. This put further pressure on the Russian ruble, forcing the Russian central bank to raise interest rates on overnight loans to 150 percent. In June 1998 the US government indicated it would support a new IMF bailout. The IMF was more circumspect, insisting that the Russian government push through a package of corporate tax increases and public spending cuts in order to balance the budget. The Russian government indicated that it would do so, and the IMF released a tranche of $640 million that had been suspended. The IMF followed this with an additional $11.2 billion loan designed to preserve the ruble's stability.

Almost as soon as the funding was announced, however, it began to unravel. The IMF loan required that the Russian government take concrete steps to raise personal tax rates, improve tax collections, and cut government spending. A bill containing the required legislative changes was sent to the Russian parliament, where it was emasculated by antigovernment forces. The IMF responded by withholding $800 million of its first $5.6 billion tranche, undermining the credibility of its own program. The Russian stock market plummeted on the news, closing down 6.5 percent. Selling of rubles accelerated. The central bank began hemorrhaging foreign exchange reserves as it tried to maintain the value of the ruble. Foreign exchange reserves fell by $1.4 billion in the first week of August alone, to $17 billion, while interest rates were surging again.

On the weekend of August 15 and 16, 1998, top Russian officials huddled to develop a response to the most recent crisis. Their options were limited. The patience of the IMF had been exhausted. Foreign currency reserves were being rapidly depleted. Social tensions in the country were running high. Plus, the government faced upcoming redemptions on $18 billion of domestic bonds, with no idea of where the money would come from.

On Monday, August 17, Prime Minister Kiriyenko announced the results of the weekend's conclave. Russia, he said, would restructure the domestic debt market, unilaterally transforming short-term debt into long-term debt. In other words, the government had decided to default on its debt commitments. The government also announced a 90-day moratorium on the repayment of private foreign debt, and stated that it would allow the ruble to decline by 34 percent against the US dollar. Russia had turned its back on the IMF plan.

The effect on Russia was immediate. Overnight, shops marked up the price of goods by 20 percent. As the ruble plummeted, currency exchange points were only prepared to sell dollars at a rate of 9 rubles per dollar, rather than the new official exchange rate of 6.43 rubles to the dollar. As for Russian government debt, that lost 85 percent of its value in a matter of hours, leaving foreign and Russian holders of debt suddenly looking at a huge black hole in their financial assets.[16]

The Asian Crisis

The financial crisis that erupted across Southeast Asia during the fall of 1997 has emerged as the biggest challenge the IMF has had to deal with. Holding the crisis in check required IMF loans to help the shattered economies of Indonesia, Thailand, and South Korea stabilize their currencies. In addition, although they did not request IMF loans, the economies of Japan, Malaysia, Singapore, and the Philippines were also badly hurt by the crisis.

The seeds of this crisis were sown during the previous decade when these countries were experiencing unprecedented economic growth. Although there were and remain important differences between the individual countries, they shared a number of elements. Exports had long been the engine of economic growth in these countries. From 1990 to 1996 the value of exports from Malaysia had grown by 18 percent per year, Thai exports had grown by 16 percent per year, Singapore's by 15 percent per year, Hong Kong's by 14 percent per year, and those of South Korea and Indonesia by 12 percent per year.[17] The nature of these exports had also shifted in recent years from basic materials and products such as textiles to complex and increasingly high-technology products, such as automobiles, semiconductors, and consumer electronics.

THE INVESTMENT BOOM The wealth created by export-led growth fueled an investment boom in commercial and residential property, industrial assets, and infrastructure. The value of commercial and residential real estate in cities such as Hong Kong and Bangkok soared. This fed a building boom the likes of which had never been seen before in Asia. Office and apartment buildings were going up all over the region. Heavy borrowing from banks financed much of this construction, but as long as the value of property continued to rise, the banks were happy to lend. The success of Asian exporters encouraged them to make bolder investments in industrial capacity. This was exemplified most clearly by South Korea's giant diversified conglomerates, or *chaebol,* many of which had ambitions to build a major position in the global automobile and semiconductor industries.

An added factor behind the investment boom in most southeast Asian economies was the government. In many cases the governments had embarked on huge infrastructure projects. In Malaysia, for example, a new government administrative center was being constructed in Putrajaya for M$20 billion (US$8 billion at the pre-July 1997 exchange rate), and the government was funding the development of a massive high-technology communications corridor and the huge Bakun dam, which at a cost of M$13.6 billion was to be the most expensive power generation plant in the country.[18]

Throughout the region, governments also encouraged private businesses to invest in certain sectors of the economy in accordance with "national goals" and "industrialization strategy." In South Korea, long a country where the government played a

The boom in commercial and residential real estate in Asia in the early 1990s was fueled by export-led growth. In Bangkok, the building boom resulted in 365,000 unoccupied apartment units. One 1997 estimate claimed the building boom had produced enough excess space to meet its residential and commercial needs for five years.

proactive role in private-sector investments, President Kim Young-Sam urged the *chaebol* to invest in new factories as a way of boosting economic growth. South Korea had enjoyed an investment-led economic boom in 1994–1995, but at a cost. The *chaebol*, always reliant on heavy borrowings, built up massive debts that were equivalent, on average, to four times their equity.[19]

In Indonesia, President Suharto had supported investments in a network of an estimated 300 businesses that were owned by his family and friends in a system known as "crony capitalism." Many of these businesses were granted lucrative monopolies by the president. For example, in 1995 Suharto announced he had decided to build a national car and the car would be built by a company owned by one of his sons, Hutomo Mandala Putra, in association with Kia Motors of South Korea. To support the venture, a consortium of Indonesian banks was "ordered" by the government to offer almost $700 million in start-up loans to the company.[20]

By the mid-1990s southeast Asia was in the grips of an unprecedented investment boom, much of it financed with borrowed money. Between 1990 and 1995 gross domestic investment grew by 16.3 percent annually in Indonesia, 16 percent in Malaysia, 15.3 percent in Thailand, and 7.2 percent in South Korea. By comparison, investment grew by 4.1 percent annually over the same period in the United States, and 0.8 percent in all high-income economies.[21] And the rate of investment accelerated in 1996. In Malaysia, for example, spending on investment accounted for a remarkable 43 percent of GDP in 1996.[22]

EXCESS CAPACITY   As the volume of investments ballooned during the 1990s, often at the bequest of national governments, the *quality* of many of these investments declined significantly. Often the investments were based on unrealistic projections about future demand. The result was significant excess capacity. Investments by South Korean *chaebol* in semiconductor factories surged in 1994 and 1995 when a temporary global shortage of DRAMs led to sharp price increases for this product. However, supply shortages had disappeared by 1996 and excess capacity was beginning to make itself felt, just as the South Koreans started to bring new DRAM factories on stream. The results were predictable; prices for DRAMs plunged and the earnings of South Korean DRAM manufacturers fell by 90 percent, which meant they had trouble making scheduled payments on the debt they had taken on to build the extra capacity.[23]

In another example, a building boom in Thailand resulted in the emergence of excess capacity in residential and commercial property. By early 1997 an estimated 365,000 apartment units were unoccupied in Bangkok. With another 100,000 units scheduled to be completed in 1997, years of excess demand in the Thai property market had been replaced by excess supply. By one estimate, Bangkok's building boom by 1997 had produced enough excess space to meet its residential and commercial need for five years.[24]

THE DEBT BOMB   By early 1997 what was happening in the South Korean semiconductor industry and the Bangkok property market was being played out elsewhere in the region. Massive investments in industrial assets and property had created excess capacity and plunging prices and left the companies that had made the investments groaning under huge debt burdens they found difficult to service.

To make matters worse, much of the borrowing had been in US dollars, as opposed to local currencies. Originally this had seemed like a smart move. Throughout the region local currencies were pegged to the dollar, and interest rates on dollar borrowings were generally lower than rates on borrowings in domestic currency. Thus, it often made economic sense to borrow in dollars if possible. However, if the governments in the region could not maintain the dollar peg and their currencies started to depreciate against the dollar, this would increase the size of the debt burden that local companies would have to service, when measured in the local currency. Currency depreciation would raise borrowing costs and could result in companies defaulting on their debt obligations.

EXPANDING IMPORTS   A final complicating factor was that by the mid-1990s although exports were still expanding across the region, so were imports. The investments in infrastructure, industrial capacity, and commercial real estate were sucking in foreign goods at unprecedented rates. To build infrastructure, factories, and office buildings, southeast Asian countries were purchasing capital equipment and materials from America, Europe, and Japan. Many southeast Asian states saw the current account of their balance of payments shift strongly into the red during the mid-1990s. By 1995 Indonesia was running a current account deficit that was equivalent to 3.5 percent of its GDP, Malaysia's was 5.9 percent, and Thailand's was 8.1 percent.[25] With deficits like these starting to pile up, it was becoming increasingly difficult for these governments to maintain the peg of their currencies against the US dollar. If that peg could not be held, the local currency value of dollar-dominated debt would increase, raising the specter of large-scale default on debt service payments. The scene was now set for a potentially rapid economic meltdown.

THE CRISIS   The Asian meltdown began in mid-1997 in Thailand when it became clear that several key Thai financial institutions were on the verge of default (see the closing case to Chapter 8 for more details). These institutions had been borrowing dollars from international banks at low interest rates and lending Thai baht at higher interest rates to local property developers. However, due to speculative overbuilding, these developers could not sell their commercial and residential property, forcing them to default on their debt obligations to Thai financial institutions. In turn, the Thai financial institutions seemed increasingly likely to default on their dollar-denominated debt obligations to international banks. Sensing the beginning of the crisis, foreign investors fled the Thai stock market, selling their positions and converting them into US dollars. The increased demand for dollars and increased supply of Thai baht pushed down the dollar/Thai baht exchange rate while the stock market plunged.

Foreign exchange dealers and hedge funds started to speculate against the baht, selling it short. For the previous 13 years the Thai baht had been pegged to the US dollar at an exchange rate of around $1 = Bt25. The Thai government tried to defend the peg, but only succeeded in depleting its foreign exchange reserves. On July 2, 1997, the Thai government abandoned its defense and announced it would allow the baht to float freely against the dollar. The baht started a slide that would bring the exchange rate down to $1 = Bt55 by January 1988. As the baht declined, the Thai debt bomb exploded. The 55 percent decline in the value of the baht against the dollar doubled the amount of baht required to serve the dollar-denominated debt commitments taken on by Thai financial institutions and businesses. This increased the probability of corporate bankruptcies and further pushed down the battered Thai stock market. The Thailand Set stock market index ultimately declined from 787 in January 1997 to a low of 337 in December of that year; this was on top of a 45 percent decline in 1996.

On July 28 the Thai government took the next logical step and called in the International Monetary Fund. With its foreign exchange reserves depleted, Thailand lacked the foreign currency needed to finance its international trade and service debt commitments and desperately needed the capital the IMF could provide. It also needed to restore international confidence in its currency, and it needed the credibility associated with gaining access to IMF funds. Without IMF loans, the baht was likely to increase its free fall against the US dollar, and the whole country might go into default. The IMF agreed to provide the Thai government with $17.2 billion in loans, but the conditions were restrictive.[26] The IMF required the Thai government to increase taxes, cut public spending, privatize several state-owned businesses, and raise interest rates—all designed to cool Thailand's overheated economy. The IMF also required Thailand to close illiquid financial institutions. In December 1997 the government shut 56 financial institutions, laying off 16,000 people in the process and further deepening the recession that now gripped the country.

Following the devaluation of the Thai baht, wave after wave of speculation hit other Asian currencies. In a period of weeks the Malaysian ringgit, Indonesian rupiah and the Singapore dollar were all marked sharply lower. With its foreign exchange reserves down to $28 billion, Malaysia let its currency float on July 14, 1997. Before the devaluation, the ringgit was trading at $1 = 2.525 ringgit. Six months later it had declined to $1 = 4.15 ringgit. Singapore followed on July 17, and the Singapore dollar (S$) quickly dropped in value from $1 = S$1.495 before the devaluation to $1 = S$2.68 a few days later. Next up was Indonesia, whose currency was allowed to float on August 14. This was the beginning of a precipitous decline in the value of Indonesia's currency, which was to fall from $1 = 2,400 rupiah in August 1997 to $1 = 10,000 on January 6, 1998, a loss of 75 percent.

With the exception of Singapore, whose economy is probably the most stable in the region, these devaluations were driven by factors similar to those behind the earlier devaluation of the Thai baht—a combination of excess investment; high borrowings, much of it in dollar-denominated debt; and a deteriorating balance of payments position. Although both Malaysia and Singapore were able to halt the slide in their currencies and stock markets without the help of the IMF, Indonesia was not. Indonesia was struggling with a private-sector dollar-denominated debt of close to $80 billion. With the rupiah sliding precipitously almost every day, the cost of servicing this debt was exploding, pushing more Indonesian companies into technical default.

On October 31, 1997, the IMF announced that in conjunction with the World Bank and the Asian Development Bank it had put together a $37 billion rescue deal for Indonesia. In return, the Indonesian government agreed to close a number of troubled banks, reduce public spending, remove government subsidies on basic foodstuffs and energy, balance the budget, and unravel the widespread crony capitalism. But the government of President Suharto appeared to backtrack several times on commitments made to the IMF. This precipitated further declines in the Indonesian currency and stock markets. Ultimately, Suharto caved in and removed costly government subsidies, only to see the country dissolve into chaos as the populace protested the resulting price increases. This unleashed a chain of events that led to Suharto's removal from power in May 1998.

The final domino to fall was South Korea (for further details, see the "Country Focus" in Chapter 8). During the 1990s South Korean companies had built up huge debt loads as they invested heavily in new industrial capacity. Now they found they had too much industrial capacity and could not generate the income required to service the debt that they had taken on to build the capacity. South Korean banks and companies had also made the mistake of borrowing in dollars, much of it in the form of short-term loans that would come due within a year. Thus, when the South Korean won started to decline in the fall of 1997 in sympathy with the problems elsewhere in Asia, companies saw their debt obligations balloon. Several large companies defaulted on their debt service obligations and filed for bankruptcy. This triggered a decline in the South Korean currency and stock market that was difficult to halt. The South Korean central bank tried to keep the dollar/won exchange rate above $1 = W1,000, but like several countries before it, found that this only depleted its foreign exchange reserves. On November 17 the South Korean central bank gave up the defense of the won, which quickly fell to $1 = W1,500.

With its economy on the verge of collapse, on November 21 the South Korean government requested $20 billion in standby loans from the IMF. As the negotiations progressed, it soon became apparent that South Korea was going to need far more than $20 billion. The country's short-term foreign debt was found to be twice as large as previously thought at close to $100 billion, while its foreign exchange reserves were down to less than $6 billion. On December 3 the IMF and South Korean government reached a deal to lend $55 billion to the country. The agreement with the IMF called for the South Koreans to open their economy and banking system to foreign investors. South Korea also pledged to restrain the *chaebol* by reducing their share of bank financing and requiring them to publish consolidated financial statements and undergo annual independent external audits. The IMF also said South Korea will comply with its commitments to the World Trade Organization to eliminate trade-related subsidies and restrictive import licensing and to streamline its import certification procedures, all of which should open the South Korean economy to greater foreign competition.[27]

Evaluating the IMF's Policy Prescriptions

By early 1998 the IMF was committing more than $110 billion in short-term loans to three Asian countries: South Korea, Indonesia, and Thailand. This was on top of the $20 billion package the IMF gave to Mexico in 1995 and the $10 billion loan to Russia. All these loan packages came with conditions attached. In general, the IMF insists on a combination of tight macroeconomic policies, including cuts in public spending, higher interest rates, and tight monetary policy. It also often pushes for the deregulation of sectors protected from domestic and foreign competition, privatization of state-owned assets, and better financial reporting from the banking sector. In general, these policies are designed to cool down overheated economies by reining in inflation and reducing government spending and debt. This set of policy prescriptions has come in for tough criticisms from many Western observers.[28]

One criticism is that the IMF's "one-size-fits-all" approach to macroeconomic policy is inappropriate for many countries. This point was stressed in the opening case, when we looked at how the IMF's policies toward Zaire may have made things worse rather than better. In the case of the recent Asian crisis, critics argue that the tight macroeconomic policies imposed by the IMF are not well suited to countries that are suffering not from excessive government spending and inflation, but from a private-sector debt crisis with deflationary undertones.[29] In South Korea, for example, the government had been running a budget surplus for years (it was 4 percent of South Korea's GDP in the 1994–1996 period) and inflation was low at about 5 percent. South Korea even had the second-strongest financial position of any country in the Organization for Economic Cooperation and Development. Despite this, say critics, the IMF insisted on the same policies that it applies to countries suffering from high inflation. The IMF is requiring South Korea to maintain an inflation rate of 5 percent. However, given the collapse in the value of its currency and the subsequent rise in the price of imports such as oil, inflationary pressures will inevitably increase. So to hit a 5 percent inflation rate, the South Koreans are being forced to apply an unnecessarily tight monetary policy. Short-term interest rates jumped from 12.5 percent to 21 percent immediately after South Korea signed its initial deal with the IMF. Increasing interest rates make it even more difficult for companies to service their already excessive short-term debt obligations; the cure prescribed by the IMF may actually increase the probability of widespread corporate defaults in South Korea, not reduce them.

The IMF rejects this criticism. According to the IMF, the critical task is to rebuild confidence in the South Korean currency, the won. Once this has been achieved, the won will recover from its extremely oversold levels. This will reduce the size of South Korea's dollar-denominated debt burden when expressed in won, making it easier for companies to service their debt. The IMF also argues that by requiring South Korea to remove restrictions on foreign direct investment, foreign capital will flow into the country to take advantage of cheap assets. This, too, will increase demand for the won, and help improve the exchange rate.

A second criticism of the IMF is that its rescue efforts are exacerbating a problem known to economists as **moral hazard.** Moral hazard arises when people behave recklessly because they know they will be saved if things go wrong. In the case of Asia, critics point out that many Japanese and Western banks were far too willing to lend large amounts of capital to overleveraged Asian companies during the boom years of the 1990s. These critics argue that the banks should now be forced to pay the price for their rash lending policies, even if that means some banks must close.[30] Only by taking such drastic action, the argument goes, will banks not engage in rash lending in the future. By providing support to these countries, the IMF is reducing the probability of debt default and bailing out the banks whose loans gave rise to this situation.

This argument ignores two critical points. First, if Japanese or Western banks with heavy exposure to the troubled Asian economies were forced to write off their loans due to widespread debt default, this would have an impact that would be difficult to contain. The failure of large Japanese banks, for example, could trigger a meltdown in the Japanese financial markets. This would almost inevitably lead to a serious decline in stock markets around the world. That is the very risk the IMF was trying to avoid by stepping in with financial support. Second, it is incorrect to imply that some banks have not had to pay the price for rash lending policies. The IMF has insisted on the closure of banks in South Korea, Thailand, and Indonesia. Also, foreign banks with short-term loans outstanding to South Korean enterprises have rescheduled those loans at interest rates that do not compensate for the extension of the loan maturity.

The final criticism of the IMF is that is has become too powerful for an institution that lacks any real accountability.[31] By the end of 1997, the IMF was engaged in loan programs in 75 developing countries that collectively contain 1.4 billion people. The IMF was determining macroeconomic policies in those countries, yet according to critics such as noted Harvard economist Jeffrey Sachs, with a staff of less than 1,000 the IMF lacks the expertise required to do a good job. Evidence of this, according to Sachs, is that the IMF was singing the praises of the Thai and South

moral hazard A situation in which people behave recklessly because they know they will be saved if things go wrong.

Korean governments only months before both countries lurched into crisis. Then the IMF put together a draconian program for South Korea without having deep knowledge of the country. Sachs's solution to this problem is to reform the IMF so it makes greater use of outside experts and its operations are open to outside scrutiny.

As with many debates about international economics, it is not clear which side has the winning hand. There are cases where one can argue that IMF policies have been counterproductive, such as Zaire, which we discussed in the opening case. But the IMF can point to notable accomplishments, including its success in containing the Asian crisis, which if left unchecked, could have rocked the global international monetary system to its core. Similarly, many observers give the IMF credit for its deft handling of politically difficult situations, such as the Russian ruble crisis, and for successfully promoting a free market philosophy.

Implications for Business

The implications of the material discussed in this chapter for international businesses fall into three main areas: currency management, business strategy, and corporate–government relations.

Currency Management

An obvious implication with regard to currency management is that companies must recognize that the foreign exchange market does not work quite as depicted in Chapter 8. The current system is a mixed system in which a combination of government intervention and speculative activity can drive the foreign exchange market. Companies engaged in significant foreign exchange activities need to be aware of this and to adjust their foreign exchange transactions accordingly. For example, the currency management unit of Caterpillar claims it made millions of dollars in the hours following the announcement of the Plaza Accord by selling dollars and buying currencies that it expected to appreciate on the foreign exchange market following government intervention.

We have seen how under the present system, speculative buying and selling of currencies can create very volatile movements in exchange rates (as exhibited by the rise and fall of the dollar during the 1980s). Contrary to the predictions of the purchasing power parity theory (see Chapter 8), we have seen that exchange rate movements during the 1980s, at least with regard to the dollar, did not seem to be strongly influenced by relative inflation rates. Insofar as volatile exchange rates increase foreign exchange risk, this is not good news for business. On the other hand, as we saw in Chapter 8, the foreign exchange market has developed a number of instruments, such as the forward market and swaps, that can help to insure against foreign exchange risk. Use of these instruments has increased markedly since the breakdown of the Bretton Woods system in 1973.

Business Strategy

The volatility of the present global exchange rate regime presents a conundrum for international businesses. Exchange rate movements are difficult to predict, and yet their movement can have a major impact on the competitive position of a business. Faced with uncertainty about the future value of currencies, firms can utilize the forward exchange market. However, the forward market is far from perfect as a predictor of future exchange rates (see Chapter 8). Also, it is difficult to get adequate insurance coverage for exchange rate changes that might occur several years in the future. The forward market tends to offer coverage for exchange rate changes a few months—not years—ahead. Given this, it makes sense to pursue strategies that will increase the company's strategic flexibility in the face of unpredictable exchange rate movements.

Maintaining strategic flexibility can take the form of dispersing production to different locations around the globe as a hedge against currency fluctuations. Consider the case of Daimler-Benz, Germany's export-oriented automobile and aerospace company. In June 1995 the company stunned the German business community when it announced that it expected to post a $720 million loss in 1995. The cause was Germany's strong currency, which had appreciated by 4 percent against a basket of major currencies since the beginning of 1995 and had risen by over 30 percent against the US dollar since late 1994. By mid-1995 the exchange rate against the dollar stood at $1 = DM1.38. Daimler's management said it could not make money with an exchange rate under $1 = DM1.60. Daimler's senior managers concluded that the appreciation of the mark against the dollar was probably permanent. Their strategy for dealing with this problem was to move substantial production outside of Germany and to increase purchasing of foreign components. This idea will reduce the vulnerability of the company to future exchange rate movements. The Mercedes-Benz division had already begun to implement this move. Even before the 1998 merger with Chrysler, Mercedes planned to produce 10 percent of its cars outside of Germany by 2000, mostly in the United States.[32] Similarly, the Japanese automobile companies have expanded their productive capacity in the United States and Europe. For the Japanese companies, building production capacity overseas is a hedge against appreciation of the yen (as well as against trade barriers).

Another way of building strategic flexibility involves contracting out manufacturing. This allows a company to shift suppliers from country to country in response to shifts in relative costs brought about by exchange rate movements. However, this strategy works only for low-value-added manufacturing (e.g., textiles), in which the individual manufacturers have few if any firm-specific skills that contribute to the value of the product. It is inappropriate in the case of high-value-added manufacturing, in which firm-specific technology and skills add significant value to the product (e.g., the heavy equipment industry) and in which switching costs are correspondingly high. Switching suppliers in high-value-added manufacturing will lead to a reduction in the value that is added, which may offset any cost gains arising from exchange rate fluctuations.

The roles of the IMF and the World Bank in the international monetary system also have implications for business strategy. Increasingly, the IMF has been acting as the macroeconomic policeman of the world economy, insisting that countries coming to it for significant borrowings adopt IMF-mandated macroeconomic policies. These policies typically include anti-inflationary monetary policy and reductions in government spending. In the short run, such policies usually result in a sharp contraction of demand. International businesses selling or producing in such countries need to be aware of this and plan accordingly. In the long run, the kind of policies imposed by the IMF can promote economic growth and an expansion of demand, which create opportunities for international business.

Corporate–Government Relations

As major players in the international trade and investment environment, businesses can influence government policy toward the international monetary system. For example, intense lobbying by US exporters helped convince the US government that intervention in the foreign exchange market was necessary. Similarly, much of the impetus behind the establishment of the exchange rate mechanism of the European monetary system came from European businesspeople, who understood the costs of volatile exchange rates.

Business can and should use its influence to promote an international monetary system that facilitates the growth of international trade and investment. Whether a fixed or floating regime is optimal is a subject for debate. What does seem probable, however, is that exchange rate volatility such as the world experienced during the 1980s and 1990s creates an environment less conducive to international trade and investment than one with more stable exchange rates. Therefore, it would seem to be in the interests of international business to promote an international monetary system that minimizes volatile exchange rate movements, particularly when those movements are unrelated to long-run economic fundamentals.

Key Terms

Summary

This chapter explained the workings of the international monetary systems and pointed out its implications for international business. Specific points include the following:

1 The gold standard is a monetary standard that pegs currencies to gold and guarantees convertibility to gold.

2 It was thought that the gold standard contained an automatic mechanism that contributed to the simultaneous achievement of a balance-of-payments equilibrium by all countries.

3 The gold standard broke down during the 1930s as countries engaged in competitive devaluations.

4 The Bretton Woods system of fixed exchange rates was established in 1944. The US dollar was the central currency of this system; the value of every other currency was pegged to its value. Significant exchange rate devaluations were allowed only with the permission of the IMF.

5 The role of the IMF was to maintain order in the international monetary system (*i*) to avoid a repetition of the competitive devaluations of the 1930s and (*ii*) to control price inflation by imposing monetary discipline on countries.

6 To build flexibility into the system, the IMF stood ready to lend funds to help countries protect their currencies on the foreign exchange market in the face of speculative pressure and to assist countries in correcting a fundamental disequilibrium in their balance-of-payments positions.

7 The fixed exchange rate system collapsed in 1973, primarily due to speculative pressure on the dollar following a rise in US inflation and a growing US balance-of-trade deficit.

8 Since 1973 the world has operated with a floating exchange rate regime, and exchange rates have become more volatile and far less predictable. Volatile exchange rate movements have reopened the debate over the merits of fixed and floating systems.

9 The case for a floating exchange rate regime claims: (*i*) that such a system gives countries autonomy regarding their monetary policy and (*ii*) that floating exchange rates facilitate smooth adjustment of trade imbalances.

10 The case for a fixed exchange rate regime claims: (*i*) that the need to maintain a fixed exchange rate imposes monetary discipline on a country, (*ii*) that floating exchange rate regimes are vulnerable to speculative pressure, (*iii*) that the uncertainty that accompanies floating exchange rates dampens the growth of international trade and investment, and (*iv*) that far from correcting trade imbalances, depreciating a currency on the foreign exchange market tends to cause price inflation.

11 In today's international monetary system, some countries have adopted floating exchange rates and some have pegged their currency to another currency, such as the US dollar.

12 In the post-Bretton Woods era the IMF has continued to play an important role in helping countries navigate their way through financial crises by lending significant capital to embattled governments and by requiring them to adopt certain macroeconomic policies.

13 There is an important debate taking place over the appropriateness of IMF-mandated macroeconomic policies. Critics charge that the IMF often imposes inappropriate conditions on developing nations that are the recipients of its loans.

14 The present managed-float system of exchange rate determination has increased the importance of currency management in international businesses.

15 The volatility of exchange rates under the managed-float system creates both opportunities and threats. One way of responding to this volatility is for companies to build strategic flexibility by dispersing production to different locations around the globe by contracting out manufacturing (in the case of low-value-added manufacturing) and other means.

Critical Thinking and Discussion Questions

1 Why did the gold standard collapse? Is there a case for returning to some type of gold standard? What is it?

2 What opportunities might current IMF lending policies to Third World nations create for international businesses? What threats might they create?

3 Do you think the standard IMF policy prescriptions of tight monetary policy and reduced government spending are always appropriate for developing nations experiencing a currency crisis? How might the IMF change its approach? What would the implications be for international businesses?

4 Debate the relative merits of fixed and floating exchange rate regimes. From the perspective of an international business, what are the most important criteria in a choice between the systems? Which system is the more desirable for an international business?

Internet Exercises

1 The landmark agreement to create a new international monetary system in 1944, commonly referred to as the Bretton Woods agreement, has often been heralded by proponents of fixed exchange rates as the last great monetary agreement. Interested parties frequently debate whether the world would be better off under a fixed exchange agreement. Recently, that debate has taken on a very real perspective as the three major currencies in the world, the dollar, the yen, and the euro have moved toward parity. Those favoring a fixed exchange rate system, and the predictability it provides, are optimistically looking toward a future in which an equivalent unit of exchange would once again exist between markets.

Opposing the fixed exchange regime, are those who note the obvious difficulties with a fixed exchange rate system, including government's loss of a powerful fiscal tool—the ability to devalue a currency. Go to **http://woodrow.mpls.fbr.fed.us/pubs/ar/ar1989.html**. Discuss the benefits of a fixed exchange rate system. From a corporate standpoint, which type of exchange system would be preferable? Why? Does your answer change if you consider the question from the perspective of an exporter versus a large multinational company? Why or why not? In your opinion, could a fixed exchange rate system work in today's global economy? Why or why not?

Source: *Business Week,* December 13, 1999, p. 58.

2 The interconnected nature of today's global monetary system can easily be recognized by examining the effect of Brazil's currency devaluation on Argentina. In 1999, Brazil abruptly devalued its currency, creating havoc for the Argentine economy. Products made in Argentina instantly became more expensive, and the now higher cost of doing business in Argentina relative to its northern neighbor, Brazil, created a critical situation for Argentina as companies shifted production out of the country and into Brazil. After a 35 percent depreciation of the Brazilian real against the Argentine peso, Brazil enjoys an economic recovery while Argentina finds itself in a deep recession.

From a corporate standpoint, Brazil's devaluation of its real provides a strong incentive to reevaluate strategy. Some two dozen companies already have relocated all or part of their manufacturing operations to Brazil to take advantage of a newly cheaper workforce and manufacturing location. Go to www.latinfocus.com and click on Brazil to further explore the current situation. Discuss the role of exchange rates in a company's strategy. As a Dutch exporter to Argentina and Brazil, how does Brazil's currency devaluation affect your operations? How does your response differ if you are vice president of international operations for a Dutch company that manufactures products in Brazil? In Argentina? In the United States?

Source: *Business Week,* January 17, 2000, p. 56.

Caterpillar Inc.

Caterpillar Inc. (Cat) is the world's largest manufacturer of heavy earthmoving equipment. Earthmoving equipment typically represents about 70 percent of the annual dollar sales of construction equipment worldwide. In 1980 Cat held 53.3 percent of the global market for earthmoving equipment. Its closest competitor was Komatsu of Japan, with 60 percent of the Japanese market but only 15.2 percent worldwide.

In 1980 Caterpillar was widely considered one of the premier manufacturing and exporting companies in the United States. The company had enjoyed 50 consecutive years of profits and returns on shareholders equity as high as 27 percent. In 1981, 57 percent of its sales were outside the United States, and roughly two-thirds of these orders were filled by exports. Cat was the third-largest US exporter. Reflecting this underlying strength, in 1981 Cat recorded record pretax profits of $579 million. However, the next three years were disastrous. Caterpillar lost $1 billion and saw its market share slip to as low as 40 percent in 1985, while Komatsu increased its share to 25 percent. Three factors explain this startling turn of events: the higher productivity of Komatsu, the rise in the value of the dollar, and the Third World debt crisis.

Komatsu had been creeping up on Cat for a long time. In the 1960s the company had a minuscule presence outside Japan. By 1974 it had managed to increase its global market share of heavy earthmoving equipment to 9 percent, and by 1980 it was over 15 percent. Part of Komatsu's growth was due to its superior labor productivity; throughout the 1970s it had been able to price its machines 10 to 15 percent below Caterpillar's. However, Komatsu lacked an extensive dealer network outside Japan, and Cat's

worldwide dealer network and superior after-sale service and support functions were seen as justifying a price premium for Cat machines. For these reasons, many industry observers believed Komatsu would not increase its share much beyond its 1980 level.

An unprecedented rise in the value of the dollar against most major world currencies changed the picture. Between 1980 and 1987, the dollar rose an average of 87 percent against the currencies of 10 other industrialized countries. The dollar was driven up by strong economic growth in the United States, which attracted heavy inflows of capital from foreign investors seeking high returns on capital assets. High real interest rates attracted foreign investors seeking high returns on financial assets. At the same time, political turmoil in other parts of the world and relatively slow economic growth in Europe made the United States a good place in which to invest. These inflows of capital increased the demand for dollars in the foreign exchange market, which pushed the value of the dollar upward against other currencies.

The strong dollar substantially increased the dollar price of Cat's machines. At the same time, the dollar price of Komatsu products imported into the United States fell. Due to the shift in the relative values of the dollar and the yen, by 1985 Komatsu priced its machines as much as 40 percent below Caterpillar's prices. Many consumers chose to forgo Caterpillar's superior after-sale service and support and bought Komatsu machines.

The third factor, the Third World debt crisis, became apparent in 1982. During the early 1970s the oil-exporting nations of OPEC quadrupled the price of oil, which resulted in a massive flow of funds into these nations. Commercial banks borrowed

this money from the OPEC members and lent it to the governments of many Third World nations to finance massive construction projects, which led to a global boom in demand for heavy earthmoving equipment. Caterpillar benefited richly from this development. By 1982, however, it became apparent that the commercial banks had lent too much money to risky and unproductive investments, and the governments of several countries (including Mexico, Brazil, and Argentina) threatened to suspend debt payments. The International Monetary Fund stepped in and arranged for new loans to indebted Third World countries, but on the condition that they adopt deflationary macroeconomic policies. For Cat, the party was over; orders for heavy earthmoving equipment dried up almost overnight, and those that were placed went to the lowest bidder—which often was Komatsu.

As a result of these factors, Caterpillar was in deep trouble by late 1982. The company responded quickly and between 1982 and 1985 cut costs by more than 20 percent. This was achieved by a 40 percent reduction in the workforce, the closure of nine plants, and a $1.8 billion investment in flexible manufacturing technologies designed to boost quality and lower cost. At the same time the company launched a campaign of pressing the government to lower the value of the dollar on foreign exchange markets. By 1984 Cat was a leading voice among US exporters in their efforts to get the Reagan administration to intervene in the foreign exchange market.

In early 1985 things began to go Caterpillar's way. Prompted by Cat and other exporters, representatives of the US government met with representatives of Japan, Germany, France, and Great Britain at the Plaza Hotel in New York. In the resulting communiqué—known as the Plaza Accord—the five governments acknowledged that the dollar was overvalued and pledged to take actions that would drive down its price on the foreign exchange market. This called for the central bank of each country to intervene in the foreign exchange market, selling dollars and buying other currencies (including its own). The dollar had already begun to fall in early 1985 in response to a string of record US trade deficits. The Plaza Accord accelerated this trend, and over the next three years the dollar fell back to its 1980 level.

The effect for Caterpillar was almost immediate. Like any major exporter, Caterpillar had its own foreign exchange unit. Suspecting that an adjustment in the dollar would come soon, Cat had increased its holdings of foreign currencies in early 1985, using the strong dollar to purchase them. As the dollar fell, the company was able to convert these currencies back into dollars for a healthy profit. In 1985 Cat had pretax profits of $32 million; without foreign exchange gains of $89 million, it would have lost money. In 1986 foreign exchange gains of $100 million accounted for nearly two-thirds of its pretax profits of $159 million.

More significant for Cat's long-term position, by 1988 the fall in the dollar against the yen and Caterpillar's cost-cutting efforts had helped to eradicate the 40 percent cost advantage that Komatsu had enjoyed over Caterpillar four years earlier. After trying to hold its prices down, Komatsu had to raise its prices that year by 18 percent, while Cat was able to hold its price increase to 3 percent. With the terms of trade no longer handicapping Caterpillar, the company was able to regain some of its lost market share. By 1989 it reportedly held 47 percent of the world market for heavy earthmoving equipment, up from a low of 40 percent three years earlier, while Komatsu's share had slipped to below 20 percent.[33]

CASE DISCUSSION QUESTIONS

1 To what extent is the competitive position of Caterpillar against Komatsu dependent on the dollar/yen exchange rate? Between mid-1996 and early 1998 the dollar appreciated by over 40 percent against the yen. How do you think this would have affected the relatively competitive position of Caterpillar and Komatsu?

2 If you were the CEO of Caterpillar, what actions would you take now to make sure there is no repeat of the early 1980s experience?

3 What potential impact can the actions of the IMF and World Bank have on Caterpillar's business? Is there anything that Cat can do to influence the actions of the IMF and World Bank?

4 As the CEO of Caterpillar, would you prefer a fixed exchange rate regime or a continuation of the current managed-float regime? Why?

Less developed countries benefit from international trade. Their gains, however, do not depend solely on the activities of large, established businesses. These gains can also result from the efforts of the nation's small entrepreneurs, some of whom may be just as comfortable operating in less as well as more developed economies.

For instance, Themba Megagula of Swaziland is one such young and enterprising college student who is studying international business at a California university. Themba, 22, is also operating a part-time import business of Swazi giftware and collectibles. His business grew out of a desire to satisfy the requests of a few close friends and to make a little 1 million people. Its economy is driven by exports, whose value equals over 65 percent of its GDP.

Last summer when Themba returned to visit his family in southern Africa, his friends in the United States asked him to bring back some souvenirs. He returned with an excess of wooden carvings and masks, which he quickly gave to friends or sold on consignment through a local gift store.

Energized by his success and encouraged by his friends, Themba tried to figure out what else he might be able to import from Swaziland. "You are from Swaziland, which has a really unique culture. What do you have there that would be interesting to people here?" questioned his friends.

stores located nearby during the days he was not working at another part-time job or attending classes. He found several that would sell the items on consignment and sell they did except for the elephants.

Themba learned that even with a product such as glass animals one has to be culturally sensitive. His shipment of elephants had their trunks pointing down. "Apparently among some other ethnic groups, the downward trunks are a sign of bad luck. In Africa, at most, it may mean the elephant is thirsty and looking for a drink of water," Themba said.

Themba continues to sell his glass menagerie on consignment. He usually pays $1 to $3 per item excluding shipping costs and tar-

Glass Menagerie

extra cash by capitalizing on his heritage.

Themba is the oldest of five children. His father, a former university administrator, now works as a consultant for the United States Agency for International Development. His mother, an American, is a university professor. Themba started globe-trotting at birth and has already traveled extensively through North America, Europe, and Africa. He was only 18 when he arrived alone in the United States to attend school. He adapted quickly because he is self-reliant and resourceful.

The kingdom of Swaziland is bound on the north, west, and south by South Africa. It is the second smallest country in Africa with

Themba then remembered the glass factory, which was 15 minutes from his home in Africa. He had visited it during a high school field trip. It produced the most exquisite blown glass animal figurines. "If Americans could not go to Africa on safari, he would bring the animals to them. However, these lions, rhinoceros, hippopotami, and elephants would only be three to four inches tall," Themba thought.

With help from his father, Themba ordered a small shipment of a variety of the glass animals. His father helped finance the initial inventory. Through the career center at his university, Themba found a directory of African gift stores in California. Themba called on several

iffs. He tries to set his price to make 60 percent over cost. His next objective is to expand distribution, so he usually carries inventory in the trunk of his car so he can visit prospective retailers whenever he finds some free time.

Because of his drive Themba is able to earn some extra cash while implementing his textbook knowledge. Because of his initiative, a Swazi glass factory, which used to be the site of an old coal mine, now has a small opening to the most developed country in the world.

ten

Global Strategy

Chapter

Opening Case   Global Strategy at General Motors

General Motors is one of the oldest multinational corporations in the world. Founded in 1908, GM established its first international operations in the 1920s. It is now the world's largest industrial corporation and full-line automobile manufacturer with annual revenues of more than $100 billion. The company sells 8 million vehicles per year, 3.2 million of which are produced and marketed outside its North American base. In 1997, GM

With their four new manufacturing plants, and the intention to design and build vehicles that share a common global platform, GM hopes to spread design costs over a greater volume of cars, and also to realize **economies of scale** in the manufacturing of shared components. What are some other problems that may occur with this approach besides the ones mentioned at the end of the opening case?
©PhotoDisc

Part 5 Competing in a Global Marketplace

Learning Objectives

1 Be conversant with the concept of strategy.

2 Understand how firms can profit from expanding their activities globally.

3 Be familiar with the different strategies for competing globally.

4 Understand how cost pressures influence a firm's choice of global strategy.

5 Understand how country differences can influence a firm's choice of global strategy.

6 Understand how firms can use strategic alliances to support their global strategies.

had a 31 percent share of the North American market and an 8.9 percent share of the market in the rest of the world.

Historically, GM's foreign operations have been concentrated in Western Europe. Local brand names such as Opel, Vauxhall, Saab, and Holden helped the company to sell 1.7 million vehicles in 1997 and gain an 11.3 percent market share, second only to that of Ford. Although GM has long had a presence in Latin America and Asia, until recently sales there accounted for only a small fraction of the company's total international business. However, GM's plans call for this to change rapidly. Sensing that Asia, Latin America, and Eastern Europe may be the automobile industry's growth markets, GM has embarked on ambitious plans to invest $2.2 billion in four new manufacturing facilities in Argentina, Poland, China, and Thailand. This expansion goes

hand in hand with a change in GM's philosophy toward management of international operations.

Traditionally, GM saw the developing world as a dumping ground for obsolete technology and outdated models. Just a few years ago, for example, GM's Brazilian factories were churning out US-designed Chevy Chevettes that hadn't been produced in North America for years. GM's Detroit-based executives saw this as a way to squeeze the maximum cash flow from the company's investments in aging technology. GM managers in the developing world, however, took it as an indication that the center did not view developing world operations as significant. This belief was supported by the fact that most operations in the developing world were instructed to carry out manufacturing and marketing plans formulated in the company's Detroit headquarters, rather than creating their own.

In contrast, GM's European operations were traditionally managed on an arm's-length basis. National operations were often allowed to design their own cars and manufacturing facilities and formulate their own marketing strategies. This regional and national autonomy allowed GM's European operations to produce vehicles that were tailored to the needs of local customers. However, it also led to costly duplication of effort in design and manufacturing and to a failure to share valuable technology, skills, and practices among subsidiaries. Thus, while General Motors exerted tight control over its operations in the developing world, its control over operations in Europe was perhaps too lax. The result was a company whose international operations lacked strategic coherence.

GM is trying to change this by switching from its Detroit-centric view of the world to a philosophy that centers of excellence may reside anywhere in the company's global operations. The company is trying to tap these centers of excellence to provide its global operations with the latest technology. The four new manufacturing plants being constructed in the developing world are an embodiment of this new approach. Each is identical, each incorporates state-of-the-art technology, and each has been designed not by Americans, but by a team of Brazilian and German engineers. By building identical plants, GM should be able to mimic Toyota, whose plants are so much alike that a change in a car in Japan can be quickly replicated around the world. The GM plants are modeled after its Eisenach facility in Germany, which is managed by the company's Opel subsidiary. It was at the Eisenach plant that GM figured out how to implement the lean production system pioneered by Toyota. The plant is now the most efficient auto-manufacturing operation in Europe and the best within GM, with a productivity rate at least twice that of most North American assembly operations. When completed, each of these new plants will produce state-of-the-art vehicles for local consumption.

To realize scale economies, GM is also trying to design and build vehicles that share a common global platform. Engineering teams located in Germany, Detroit, South America, and Australia are designing these common vehicle platforms. Local plants will be allowed to customize certain features of these vehicles to match the tastes and preferences of local customers. Adhering to a common global platform will enable the company to spread its costs of designing a car over greater volume and to realize scale economies in the manufacture of shared components—both of which should help GM lower its overall cost structure. The first fruits of this effort include the 1998 Cadillac Seville, which was designed to be sold in more than 40 countries. GM's family of front-wheel-drive minivans was also designed around a common platform that will allow the vehicles to be produced in multiple locations around the globe, as was the 1998 Opel Astra, which is GM's best-selling car in Europe.

Despite making bold moves toward greater global integration, numerous problems can still be seen on GM's horizon. Compared to Ford, Toyota, or the new Mercedes/Chrysler combination, GM still suffers from high costs, low perceived quality, and a profusion of brands. While its aggressive move into emerging markets may be based on the reasonable assumption that demand will grow in these areas, other automobile companies are also expanding their production facilities in the same markets, raising the specter of global excess capacity and price wars. Finally, and perhaps most significantly, some within GM argue that the push toward "global cars" is misconceived. The German-based engineering staff at Opel's Russelsheim design facility, which takes the lead on design of many key global models, has voiced concerns that distinctively European engineering features they deem essential to a cars' local success may be left by the wayside in a drive to devise what they see as blander "global" cars.[1]

Introduction

Our primary concern to this point has been with aspects of the larger environment in which international businesses compete. This environment has included the political, economic, and cultural institutions found in different nations, the international trade and investment framework, and the international monetary system. Now our focus shifts from the environment to the firm itself and, in particular, to the actions that managers can take to compete more effectively as an international business. In this chapter we look at how firms can increase their profitability by expanding their operations in foreign markets. We discuss the different strategies that firms pursue when competing internationally, consider the pros and cons of these strategies, and discuss the various factors that affect a firm's choice of strategy. We also look at why firms often enter into strategic alliances with their global competitors, and we discuss the benefits, costs, and risks of strategic alliances. In subsequent chapters we build on the framework established here to discuss a variety of topics including strategies for entering foreign markets and the various operational, marketing, R&D, and human resource strategies that are pursued by international businesses.

The opening case gives us a preview of some of these issues. General Motors' international expansion is being driven by a belief that emerging markets offer the greatest potential for future growth. GM is not alone in this belief. Not only are many other automobile firms also pursuing a similar expansion strategy, but so are firms based in a range of industries. Although GM has long had operations overseas, until recently these took second place in the company's Detroit-centric view of the world. Now GM is recognizing that if it is to compete successfully in emerging markets, it is no longer enough to transfer outdated technology and designs from Detroit. It must build a globally integrated corporation that draws on centers of excellence whereever they may reside in the world to engineer "global" cars and state-of-the-art production systems. At the same time, for all its economic benefits, the trend toward greater integration of its global operations is raising concerns within GM's European units. They fear they may lose the ability to respond to local market needs. As we shall see in this chapter, GM's struggle with this issue is not unique. Many multinational enterprises are struggling to find the right balance between global integration and local responsiveness.

Strategy and the Firm

The fundamental purpose of any business firm is to make a profit. A firm makes a profit if the price it can charge for its output is greater than its costs of producing that output. To do this, a firm must produce a product that is valued by consumers. Thus, we say that firms engage in value creation. The price consumers are prepared to pay for a product is a measure of the value of the product to consumers.

Firms can increase their profits in two ways: by adding value to a product so consumers are willing to pay more for it and by lowering the costs of value creation (i.e., the costs of production). A firm adds value to a product when it improves the product's quality, provides a service to the consumer, or customizes the product to consumer needs in such a way that consumers will pay more for it; that is, when the firm *differentiates* the

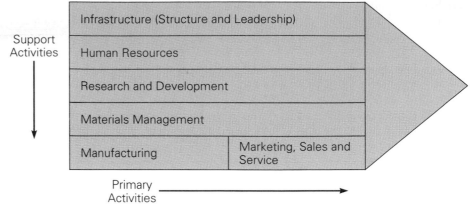

Figure 10.1

The Firm as a Value Chain

product from that offered by competitors. For example, consumers will pay more for a Mercedes-Benz car than a Hyundai because they value the superior quality of the Mercedes. Firms lower the costs of value creation when they find ways to perform value creation activities more efficiently. Thus, there are two basic strategies for improving a firm's profitability—a *differentiation strategy* and a *low-cost strategy.*[2]

The Firm as a Value Chain

It is useful to think of the firm as a value chain composed of a series of distinct value creation activities including production, marketing, materials management, R&D, human resources, information systems, and firm infrastructure. We can categorize these value creation activities as primary activities and support activities (see Figure 10.1).[3]

PRIMARY ACTIVITIES   The primary activities of a firm have to do with creating the product, marketing and delivering the product to buyers, and providing support and after-sale service to the buyers of the product. Here we consider the activities involved in the physical creation of the product as production and those involved in marketing, delivery, and after-sale service as marketing. Efficient production can reduce the costs of creating value (e.g., by realizing scale economies) and can add value by increasing product quality (e.g., by reducing the number of defective products), which facilitates premium pricing. Efficient marketing also can help the firm reduce its costs creating value (e.g., by generating the volume sales necessary to realize scale economies) and can add value by helping the firm customize its product to consumer needs and differentiate its product from competitors' products—both of which facilitate premium pricing.

SUPPORT ACTIVITIES   Support activities provide the inputs that allow the primary activities of production and marketing to occur. The materials management function controls the transmission of physical materials through the value chain—from procurement through production and into distribution. The efficiency with which this is done can significantly reduce the cost of creating value. In addition, an effective materials management function can monitor the quality of inputs into the production process. This results in improved quality of the firm's outputs, which adds value and facilitates premium pricing.

The R&D function develops new product and process technologies. Technological developments can reduce production costs and can result in the creation of more useful and more attractive products that can demand a premium price. Thus, R&D can affect primary production and marketing activities and, through them, value creation.

An effective human resource function ensures that the firm has an optimal mix of people to perform its primary production and marketing activities, that the staffing requirements of the support activities are met, and that employees are trained for their tasks and compensated accordingly. The information systems function makes certain that management has the information it needs to maximize the efficiency of its value chain and to exploit information-based competitive advantages in the marketplace. Firm infrastructure—consisting of such factors as organizational structure, general management, planning, finance, and legal and government affairs—embraces all other activities of the firm and establishes the context for them. An efficient infrastructure helps both to create value and to reduce the costs of creating value.

The Role of Strategy

A firm's **strategy** can be defined as the actions that managers take to attain the goals of the firm. For most firms a primary goal is to be highly profitable. As we have pointed out many times, markets are now extremely competitive due to the liberalization of the world trade and investment environment. To be profitable in such an environment, a firm must pay continual attention to both reducing the costs of value creation and to differentiating its product offering so consumers are willing to pay more for the product than it costs to produce it. Thus, strategy is often concerned with identifying and taking actions that will *lower the costs* of value creation and/or will *differentiate* the firm's product through superior design, quality, service, functionality, and the like.

    To fully understand this, consider the case of Clear Vision, which is profiled in the accompanying "Management Focus." A US-based manufacturer of eyeglasses, Clear Vision found its survival threatened by low-cost foreign competitors. To deal with this threat, Clear Vision adopted a strategy intended to lower its cost structure: It shifted its production from a high-cost location, the United States, to a low-cost location, Hong Kong. Clear Vision later adopted a strategy intended to differentiate its basic product so it could charge a premium price. Reasoning that premium pricing in eyewear depended on superior design, its strategy involved investing capital in French, Italian, and Japanese factories that had reputations for superior design. In sum, Clear Vision's strategies included some actions intended to reduce its costs of creating value and other actions intended to add value to its product through differentiation.

Profiting from Global Expansion

Expanding globally allows firms to increase their profitability in ways not available to purely domestic enterprises.[4] Firms that operate internationally are able to:

1 Earn a greater return from their distinctive skills or core competencies.
2 Realize location economies by dispersing value creation activities to those locations where they can be performed most efficiently.
3 Realize greater experience curve economies, which reduces the cost of value creation.

As we will see, however, a firm's ability to increase its profitability by pursuing these strategies is constrained by the need to customize its product offering, marketing strategy, and business strategy to differing national conditions.

Transferring Core Competencies

The term **core competence** refers to skills within the firm that competitors cannot easily match or imitate.[5] These skills may exist in any of the firm's value creation activities—production, marketing, R&D, human resources, general management, and so

strategy Actions that managers take to attain the firm's goals.

core competence Skills within the firm that competitors cannot easily match or imitate.

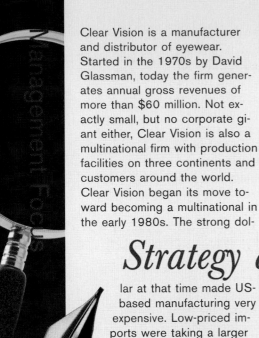

Clear Vision is a manufacturer and distributor of eyewear. Started in the 1970s by David Glassman, today the firm generates annual gross revenues of more than $60 million. Not exactly small, but no corporate giant either, Clear Vision is also a multinational firm with production facilities on three continents and customers around the world. Clear Vision began its move toward becoming a multinational in the early 1980s. The strong dol-

Clear Vision's volume of imports increased, Glassman decided the best way to guarantee quality and delivery was to set up Clear Vision's own manufacturing operation overseas. Accordingly, Clear Vision found a Chinese partner, and together they opened a manufacturing facility in Hong Kong, with Clear Vision as the majority shareholder.

The choice of the Hong Kong location was influenced by its combination of low labor costs, a

this plant are shipped to the Hong Kong factory for final assembly and then distributed to markets in North and South America. The Hong Kong factory now employs 80 people and the China plant between 300 and 400.

At the same time Clear Vision had begun to look for opportunities to invest in foreign eyewear firms with reputations for fashionable design and high quality. Its objective was not to reduce manufacturing costs but to launch a

Strategy at Clear Vision

lar at that time made US-based manufacturing very expensive. Low-priced imports were taking a larger share of the US eyewear market, and Clear Vision realized it could not survive unless it also began to import. Initially the firm bought from independent overseas manufacturers, primarily in Hong Kong. However, the firm became dissatisfied with these suppliers' product quality and delivery. As

skilled workforce, and tax breaks given by the Hong Kong government. By 1986, however, the increasing industrialization of Hong Kong and a growing labor shortage had pushed up wage rates to the extent that it was no longer a "low-cost" location. In response, Glassman and his Chinese partner moved part of their manufacturing to a plant in mainland China to take advantage of the lower wage rates there. The parts for eyewear frames manufactured at

line of high-quality, "designer" eyewear. Clear Vision did not have the design capability in-house to support such a line, but Glassman knew of foreign manufacturers that did. Clear Vision invested in factories in Japan, France, and Italy, taking a minority shareholding in each. These factories now supply eyewear for Clear Vision's Status Eye division, which markets high-priced designer eyewear.[6]

on. Such skills are typically expressed in product offerings that other firms find difficult to match or imitate; thus, the core competencies are the bedrock of a firm's competitive advantage. They enable a firm to reduce the costs of value creation and/or to create value in such a way that premium pricing is possible. For example, Toyota has a core competence in the production of cars. It can produce high-quality, well-designed cars at a lower delivered cost than any other firm in the world. The skills that enable Toyota to do this seem to reside primarily in the firm's production and materials management functions.[7] McDonald's has a core competence in managing fast food operations (it seems to be one of the most skilled firms in the world in this industry); Toys R Us has a core competence in managing high-volume, discount toy stores (it is perhaps the most skilled firm in the world in this business); Procter & Gamble has a core competence in developing and marketing name brand consumer products; Wal-Mart has a core competence in information systems and logistics; and so on.

For such firms, global expansion is a way to further exploit the value creation potential of their skills and product offerings by applying those skills and products in a larger market. The potential for creating value from such a strategy is greatest when the skills and products of the firm are most unique, when the value placed on them by consumers is great, and when there are very few capable competitors with similar skills and/or products in foreign markets. Firms with unique and valuable skills can often realize enormous returns by applying those skills to foreign markets where indigenous competitors lack similar skills and products. As we saw in the opening case, General Motors is trying to create value by leveraging the production skills developed at its Eisenach plant in Germany to plants being built in Argentina, Poland, China, and Thailand. Another example, that of McDonald's, is detailed in the accompanying "Management Focus." McDonald's has profited by leveraging its core competence in running fast food restaurants to foreign markets where indigenous competitors either did not exist or lacked similar skills.

In earlier eras US firms such as Kellogg, Coca-Cola, H. J. Heinz, and Procter & Gamble expanded overseas to exploit their skills in developing and marketing consumer products. These skills and the resulting products—which were developed in the United States during the 1950s and 1960s—yielded enormous returns when applied to European markets, where most indigenous competitors lacked similar marketing skills and products. Their near-monopoly on consumer marketing skills allowed these US firms to dominate many European consumer product markets during the 1960s and 1970s. Similarly, in the 1970s and 1980s many Japanese firms expanded globally to exploit their skills in production, materials management, and new product development—skills that many of their North American and European competitors seemed to lack at the time. Today, retail companies such as Wal-Mart and financial companies such as Citicorp, Merrill Lynch, and American Express are transferring the valuable skills they developed in their core home market to other developed and emerging markets where indigenous competitors lack those skills.

Realizing Location Economies

We know from earlier chapters that countries differ along a range of dimensions, including economic, political, legal, and cultural, and that these differences can either raise or lower the costs of doing business in a country. We also know from the theory of international trade that due to differences in factor costs, certain countries have a comparative advantage in the production of certain products. For example, Japan excels in the production of automobiles and consumer electronics. The United States excels in the production of computer software, pharmaceuticals, biotechnology products, and financial services. Switzerland excels in the production of precision instruments and pharmaceuticals.[8]

What does all this mean for a firm trying to survive in a competitive global market? It means that, *trade barriers and transportation costs* permitting, the firm will benefit by basing each value creation activity where economic, political, and cultural conditions, including relative factor costs, are most conducive to the performance of that activity. Thus, if the best designers for a product live in France, a firm should base its design operations in France. If the most productive labor force for assembly operations is in Mexico, assembly operations should be based in Mexico. If the best marketers are in the United States, the marketing strategy should be formulated in the United States. And so on.

Firms that pursue such a strategy can realize what we refer to as location economies. **Location economies** are the economies that arise from performing a value creation activity in the optimal location for that activity, wherever in the world that might be (transportation costs and trade barriers permitting). Placing a value creation activity in its optimal location can have one or two effects. *It can lower the costs of value creation and help the firm to achieve a low-cost position, and/or it can enable a firm to differentiate its product offering from that of competitors*. Both of these considerations were at work in the case of Clear Vision, which was profiled in an earlier "Management Focus." Clear Vision moved its manufacturing operations out of the United States, first to Hong Kong, and then to mainland China, to take advantage of low labor costs,

location economies
Economies that arise from performing a value creation activity in the optimal location for that activity.

Established in 1955, McDonald's by the early 1980s faced a problem: After three decades of rapid growth, the US fast food market was beginning to show signs of saturation. McDonald's response to the slowdown was to expand abroad rapidly. In 1980, 28 percent of the chain's new restaurant openings were abroad; in 1986 the figure was 40 percent; in 1990 it was close to 60 percent; and in 1997 it was over 70 percent. Since the early 1980s the firm's foreign revenues and profits

McDonald's restaurant for every 25,000 people in the United States. The firm's plans call for this foreign expansion to continue at a rapid rate. In England, France, and Germany combined, the firm opened 500 more restaurants between 1995 and 1997 for a total gain of 37 percent. In 1997 McDonald's stated that it would open 2,000 restaurants per year for the foreseeable future, the majority of them outside the United States. This includes major expansion plans for Latin America, where the

relations were all worked out in advance. In June 1992 a team of 50 employees from the United States, Russia, Germany, and Britain went to Poland to help with the opening of the first four restaurants. A primary objective was to hire and train local personnel. By mid-1994 all these employees except one had returned to their home countries. They were replaced by Polish nationals who had been brought up to the skill level required to run a McDonald's operation.

McDonald's Everywhere

have grown at 22 percent per year. By 1997 the firm had 10,752 restaurants in 108 countries outside the United States. They generated $16.5 billion (53 percent) of the firm's $31 billion in revenues.

McDonald's shows no signs of slowing down. Management notes there is still only one McDonald's restaurant for every 500,000 people in the foreign countries that it currently does business in. This compares to one

company plans to invest $2 billion over the next few years.

One key to the firm's successful foreign expansion is detailed planning. When McDonald's enters a foreign country, it does so only after careful preparation. In what is a fairly typical pattern, before McDonald's opened its first Polish restaurant in 1992 the firm spent 18 months establishing essential contacts and getting to know the local culture. Locations, real estate, construction, supply, personnel, legal, and government

Another key to the firm's international strategy is the export of the management skills that spurred its growth in the United States—not just its fast food products. McDonald's US success was built on a formula of close relations with suppliers, nationwide marketing might, tight control over store-level operating procedures, and a franchising system that encourages entrepreneurial individual franchisees. Although this system has worked flawlessly in the United States, some modifications must

thereby lowering the costs of value creation. At the same time, Clear Vision shifted some of its design operations from the United States to France and Italy. Clear Vision reasoned that skilled Italian and French designers could probably help the firm better differentiate its product. In other words, Clear Vision thinks that the optimal location for performing manufacturing operations is China, whereas the optimal locations for performing design operations are France and Italy. The firm has configured its value chain accordingly. By doing so, Clear Vision hopes to be able to *simultaneously* lower its cost structure and differentiate its product offering. In turn, differentiation should allow Clear Vision to charge a premium price for its product offering.

global web Dispersal of stages of a firm's value chain to those locations around the globe where the value added is maximized or where the costs of value creation are minimized.

CREATING A GLOBAL WEB   One result of this kind of thinking is the creation of a **global web** of value creation activities, with different stages of the value chain being dispersed to those locations around the globe where value added is maximized or where the costs of value creation are minimized. Consider the case of General Motors' Pontiac Le Mans cited in Robert Reich's *The Work of Nations*.[9] Marketed primarily in the United States, the car was designed in Germany; key components were manufactured in Japan, Taiwan, and Singapore; the assembly was performed in South Korea; and the advertising strategy was formulated in Great Britain. The car was designed in Germany because GM believed the designers in its German subsidiary had the skills most suited to the job at hand. (They were the most capable of producing

be made in other countries. One big challenge has been to infuse each store with the same gung-ho culture and standardized operating procedures that have been the hallmark of its success in the United States. To aid in this task, McDonald's has enlisted the help of large partners through joint ventures. The partners play a key role in learning and transplanting the organization's values to local employees.

Foreign partners have also played a key role in helping McDonald's adapt its marketing methods and menu to local conditions. Although US-style fast food remains the staple fare on the menu, local products have been added. In Brazil, for example, McDonald's sells a soft drink made from the guarana, an Amazonian berry. Patrons of McDonald's in Malaysia, Singapore, and Thailand savor shakes flavored with durian, a foul-smelling (to US tastes, at least) fruit considered an aphrodisiac by the locals. In Arab countries, McDonald's restaurants maintain "Halal" menus, which signify compliance with Islamic laws on food preparation, especially beef. In

1995, McDonald's opened the first kosher restaurant in suburban Jerusalem. The restaurant does not serve dairy products. And in India, the big Mac is made with lamb and called the "Maharaja Mac."

McDonald's biggest problem, however, has been to replicate its US supply chain in other countries. US suppliers are fiercely loyal to McDonald's; their fortunes are closely linked to those of McDonald's. McDonald's maintains very rigorous specifications for all the raw ingredients it uses—the key to its consistency and quality control. Outside the United States, however, McDonald's has found suppliers far less willing to make the investments required to meet its specifications. In Great Britain, for example, McDonald's had problems getting local bakeries to produce the hamburger bun. After experiencing quality problems with two local bakeries, McDonald's built its own bakery to supply its stores there. In a more extreme case, when McDonald's decided to open a store in Russia, it found that local suppliers lacked the capability to produce goods

of the quality it demanded. The firm was forced to vertically integrate through the local food industry on a heroic scale, importing potato seeds and bull semen and indirectly managing dairy farms, cattle ranches, and vegetable plots. It also had to construct the world's largest food processing plant, at a cost of $40 million. The restaurant itself cost only $4.5 million.

Now that it has a successful foreign operation, McDonald's is experiencing benefits that go beyond the immediate financial ones. Increasingly the firm is finding that its foreign franchisees are a source for valuable new ideas. The Dutch operation created a prefabricated modular store that can be moved over a weekend, and is now widely used to set up temporary restaurants at outdoor events. The Swedes came up with an enhanced meat freezer that is now used firmwide. And satellite stores, or low overhead mini-McDonald's, which are now appearing in hospitals and sports arenas in the United States, were invented in Singapore.[10]

a design that added value.) Components were manufactured in Japan, Taiwan, and Singapore because favorable factor conditions there—relatively low-cost, skilled labor—suggested that those locations had a comparative advantage in the production of components (which helped reduce the costs of value creation). The car was assembled in South Korea because GM believed that due to its low labor costs, the costs of assembly could be minimized there (also helping to minimize the costs of value creation). Finally, the advertising strategy was formulated in Great Britain because GM believed a particular advertising agency there was the most able to produce an advertising campaign that would help sell the car. (This decision was consistent with GM's desire to maximize the value added.)

In theory, a firm that realizes location economies by dispersing each of its value creation activities to its optimal location should have a competitive advantage vis-à-vis a firm that bases all its value creation activities at one location. It should be able to better differentiate its product offering and lower its cost structure than its single-location competitor. In a world where competitive pressures are increasing, such a strategy may become an imperative for survival (as it seems to have been for Clear Vision).

SOME CAVEATS Introducing transportation costs and trade barriers complicates this picture. Due to favorable factor endowments, New Zealand may have a comparative advantage for automobile assembly operations, but high transportation costs

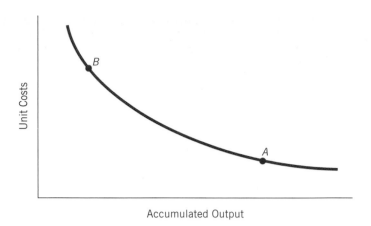

Figure 10.2

The Experience Curve

would make it an uneconomical location. A consideration of transportation costs and trade barriers explains why many US firms are shifting their production from Asia to Mexico. Mexico has three distinct advantages over many Asian countries as a location for value creation activities. First, low labor costs make it a good location for labor-intensive production processes. In recent years wage rates have increased significantly in Japan, Taiwan, and Hong Kong, but they have remained low in Mexico. Second, Mexico's proximity to the large US market reduces transportation costs. This is particularly important in the case of products with high weight-to-value ratios (e.g., automobiles). And third, the North American Free Trade Agreement (see Chapter 8) has removed many trade barriers between Mexico, the United States, and Canada, increasing Mexico's attractiveness as a production site for the North American market. Although value added and the costs of value creation are important, transportation costs and trade barriers also must be considered in location decisions.

Another caveat concerns the importance of assessing political and economic risks when making location decisions. Even if a country looks very attractive as a production location when measured against all the standard criteria, if its government is unstable or totalitarian, the firm might be advised not to base production there. (Political risk is discussed in Chapter 2.) Similarly, if the government appears to be pursuing inappropriate economic policies, that might be another reason for not basing production in that location, even if other factors look favorable.

Realizing Experience Curve Economies

The **experience curve** refers to the systematic reductions in production costs that have been observed to occur over the life of a product.[11] A number of studies have reported that a product's production costs decline by some characteristic about each time accumulated output doubles. The relationship was first observed in the aircraft industry, where each time accumulated output of airframes was doubled, unit costs typically declined to 80 percent of their previous level.[12] Thus, production cost for the fourth airframe would be 80 percent of production cost for the second airframe, the eighth airframe's production costs 80 percent of the fourth's, the sixteenth's 80 percent of the eighth's, and so on. This experience curve relationship between production costs and output is illustrated in Figure 10.2. Two things explain this: learning effects and economies of scale.

LEARNING EFFECTS **Learning effects** refer to cost savings that come from learning by doing. Labor, for example, learns by repetition how to carry out a task, such as assembling airframes, most efficiently. Labor productivity increases over time as individuals learn the most efficient ways to perform particular tasks. Equally important, in new production facilities, management typically learns how to manage the new operation more efficiently over time. Hence, production costs eventually decline due to increasing labor productivity and management efficiency.

Learning effects tend to be more significant when a technologically complex task is repeated because there is more that can be learned about the task. Thus, learning effects will be more significant in an assembly process involving 1,000 complex steps than in one of only 100 simple steps. No matter how complex the task, however, learning effects typically die out after a while. It has been suggested that they are important only during the start-up of a new process and that they cease after two or three years.[13] Any decline in the experience curve after such a point is due to economies of scale.

ECONOMIES OF SCALE The term **economies of scale** refers to reductions in unit cost achieved by producing a large volume of a product. Economies of scale have a number of sources, one of the most important of which seems to be the ability to spread fixed costs over a large volume.[14] Fixed costs are the costs required to set up

Manufacturers of pharmaceuticals use **economies of scale,** or a production of a high volume of product, to overcome the high fixed cost of developing a new drug.
©Corbis. All rights reserved.

a production facility, develop a new product, and the like, and they can be substantial. For example, establishing a new production line to manufacture semiconductor chips costs about $1 billion. According to one estimate, developing a new drug costs about $250 million and takes about 12 years.[15] The only way to recoup such high fixed costs is to sell the product worldwide, which reduces unit costs by spreading them over a larger volume. The more rapidly that cumulative sales volume is built up, the more rapidly fixed costs can be amortized, and the more rapidly unit costs fall.

Another source of scale economies arises from the ability of large firms to employ increasingly specialized equipment or personnel. The theory here goes back over 200 years to Adam Smith, who argued that the division of labor is limited by the extent of the market. As a firm's output expands, it is better able to use specialized equipment and has the output required to justify the hiring of specialized personnel. For example, consider a metal stamping machine that is used in the production of body parts for automobiles. The machine can be purchased in a customized form that is optimized for the production of a particular type of body part, let's say door panels, or a general form that will produce any kind of body part. The general form is less efficient and costs more to purchase than the customized form, but it is more flexible. Because these machines cost millions of dollars each, they have to be used continually to recoup a return on their costs. Fully utilized, a machine can turn out about 200,000 units a year. If an automobile company sells only 100,000 cars per year, it will not be worthwhile to purchase the specialized equipment, and it will have to purchase general machines. This will give it a higher cost structure than a firm that sells 200,000 cars per year, and for which it is economical to purchase a specialized stamping machine. Thus, because a firm with a large output can more fully utilize specialized equipment (and personnel), it should have a lower unit cost than a generalized firm.

STRATEGIC SIGNIFICANCE   The strategic significance of the experience curve is clear. Moving down the experience curve allows a firm to reduce its cost of creating value. The firm that moves down the experience curve most rapidly will have a cost advantage vis-à-vis its competitors. Thus, firm A in Figure 10.2, because it is further down the experience curve, has a clear cost advantage over Firm B.

Many of the underlying sources of experience-based cost economies are plant based. This is true for most learning effects as well as for the economies of scale derived by spreading the fixed costs of building productive capacity over a large output. Thus, the key to progressing downward on the experience curve quickly is to increase the volume produced by a single plant as rapidly as possible. Because global markets are larger than domestic markets, a firm that serves a global market from a single location is likely to build up accumulated volume more quickly than a firm that serves only its home market or that serves multiple markets from multiple production locations. Thus, serving a global market from a single location is consistent with moving down the experience curve and establishing a low-cost position. In addition, to get down the experience curve rapidly, a firm must price and market very aggressively so demand will expand rapidly. It will also need to build sufficient production capacity for serving a global market. The cost advantages of serving the world market from a single location will be all the more significant if that location is the optimal one for performing the value creation activity.

Once a firm has established a low-cost position, it can act as a barrier to new competition. An established firm that is well down the experience curve, such as firm A in Figure 10.2, can price so that it is still making a profit while new entrants, which are further up the curve, such as firm B, are suffering losses.

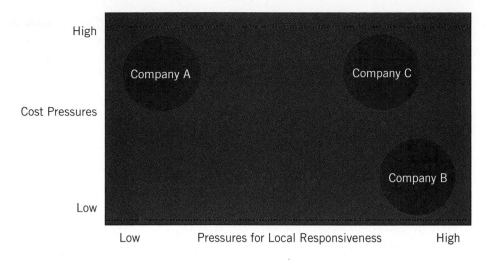

Figure 10.3

Pressures for Cost Reduction and Local Responsiveness

Matsushita has excelled in the pursuit of such a strategy. Along with Sony and Philips, Matsushita was in the race to develop a commercially viable videocassette recorder in the 1970s. Although Matsushita initially lagged behind Philips and Sony, it was able to get its VHS format accepted as the world standard and to reap enormous experience-curve-based cost economies in the process. This cost advantage subsequently constituted a formidable barrier to new competition. Matsushita's strategy was to build global volume as rapidly as possible. To ensure it could accommodate worldwide demand, the firm increased its production capacity 33-fold from 205,000 units in 1977 to 6.8 million units by 1984. By serving the world market from a single location in Japan, Matsushita realized significant learning effects and economies of scale. These allowed Matsushita to drop its prices 50 percent within five years of selling its first VHS-formatted VCR. As a result, Matsushita was the world's major VCR producer by 1983, accounting for approximately 45 percent of world production and enjoying a significant cost advantage over its competitors. The next-largest firm, Hitachi, accounted for only 11.1 percent of world production in 1983.[16]

Pressures for Cost Reductions and Local Responsiveness

Firms that compete in the global marketplace typically face two types of competitive pressure. They face *pressures for cost reductions* and *pressures to be locally responsive* (see Figure 10.3). These competitive pressures place conflicting demands on a firm. Responding to pressures for cost reductions requires that a firm try to minimize its unit costs. Attaining such a goal may necessitate that a firm base its productive activities at the most favorable low-cost location, wherever in the world that might be. It may also necessitate that a firm offer a standardized product to the global marketplace in order to ride down the experience curve as quickly as possible. In contrast, responding to pressures to be locally responsive requires that a firm differentiate its product offering and marketing strategy from country to country in an attempt to accommodate the diverse demands that arise from national differences in consumer tastes and preferences, business practices, distribution channels, competitive conditions, and government policies. Because customizing product offerings to different national requirements can involve significant duplication and a lack of product standardization, the result may be to raise costs.

While some firms, such as firm A in Figure 10.3, face high pressures for cost reductions and low pressures for local responsiveness and others, such as firm B, face low pressures for cost reductions and high pressures for local responsiveness, many firms are in the position of firm C in Figure 10.3. They face high pressures for cost reductions and high pressures for local responsiveness. Dealing with these conflicting and contradictory pressures is a difficult strategic challenge for a firm, primarily because being locally responsive tends to raise costs. In the remainder of this section we shall look at the source of pressures for cost reductions and local responsiveness. In the next section we look at the strategies that firms adopt to deal with these pressures.

Pressures for Cost Reductions

International businesses are increasingly facing pressures for cost reductions. Responding to pressures for cost reduction requires a firm to try to lower the costs of value creation by mass producing a standardized product at the optimal location in the world to try to realize location and experience curve economies. Pressures for cost reductions can be particularly intense in industries producing commodity products where meaningful differentiation on nonprice factors is difficult and price is the main competitive weapon. This tends to be the case for products that serve universal needs. Universal needs exist when the tastes and preferences of consumers in different nations are similar. This is the case for conventional commodity products such as bulk chemicals, petroleum, steel, sugar, and the like. It also tends to be the case for many industrial and consumer products (for example, handheld calculators, semiconductor chips, personal computers, liquid crystal display screens). Pressures for cost re-

Because tires are a commodity product, price is usually the differentiating point among competitors for auto manufacturers' business. In the early 1990s, a decline in the global demand for automobiles created a surplus of tires, which resulted in a worldwide price war. Considering what your text has said about price wars among competitors for the attention of automobile manufacturers' why do you think tire manufacturers try to distinguish themselves with consumers on the basis of such things as safety features, rather than price? ©Corbis. All rights reserved.

ductions are also intense in industries where major competitors are based in low-cost locations, where there is persistent excess capacity, and where consumers are powerful and face low switching costs. Many commentators have also argued that the liberalization of the world trade and investment environment in recent decades, by facilitating greater international competition, has generally increased cost pressures.[17]

Pressures for cost reductions have been intense in the global tire industry. Tires are essentially a commodity product where meaningful differentiation is difficult and price is the main competitive weapon. The major buyers of tires, automobile firms, are powerful and face low switching costs, so they have been playing tire firms off against each other in an attempt to get lower prices. And the decline in global demand for automobiles in the early 1990s created serious excess capacity in the tire industry, with as much as 25 percent of world capacity standing idle. The result was a worldwide price war with almost all tire firms suffering heavy losses in the early 1990s. In response to the resulting cost pressures, most tire firms are now trying to rationalize their operations consistent with the attainment of a low-cost position. This includes moving production facilities to low-cost facilities and offering globally standardized products to try to realize experience curve economies.[18]

Pressures for Local Responsiveness

Pressures for local responsiveness arise from a number of sources including (*i*) differences in consumer tastes and preferences, (*ii*) differences in infrastructure and traditional practices, (*iii*) differences in distribution channels, and (*iv*) host government demands.

DIFFERENCES IN CONSUMER TASTES AND PREFERENCES   Strong pressures for local responsiveness emerge when consumer tastes and preferences differ significantly between countries—as they may for historic or cultural reasons. In such cases, product and/or marketing messages have to be customized to appeal to the tastes and preferences of local consumers. This typically creates pressures for the delegation of production and marketing functions to national subsidiaries.

In the automobile industry, for example, North American consumers like pickup trucks. This is particularly true in the South and West where many families have a pickup truck as a second or third car. But in Europe pickup trucks are seen purely as utility vehicles and are purchased primarily by firms rather than individuals. As a consequence, there is a need to tailor the marketing message to consider the different demand in North America and Europe.

Harvard Business School Professor Theodore Levitt has argued that consumer demands for local customization are on the decline worldwide.[19] According to Levitt, modern communications and transport technologies have created the conditions for a convergence of the preferences of consumers from different nations. The result is the emergence of enormous global markets for standardized consumer products. Levitt cites worldwide acceptance of McDonald's hamburgers, Coca-Cola, Levi Strauss jeans, and Sony television sets, all of which are sold as standardized products, as evidence of the increasing homogeneity of the global marketplace.

Levitt's argument, however, has been characterized as extreme by many commentators. For example, Christopher Bartlett and Sumantra Ghoshal have observed that consumers reacted to an overdose of standardized global products in the consumer electronics industry by showing a renewed preference for products that are differentiated to local conditions.[20] They noted that Amstrad, a British computer and electronics firm, got its start by recognizing and responding to local consumer needs. Amstrad captured a major share of the British audio player market by moving away from the standardized inexpensive music systems marketed by global firms such as Sony and Matsushita. Amstrad's product was encased in teak rather than metal cabinets with a control panel designed to appeal to British consumers' preferences. In response, Matsushita reversed its bias toward standardized global design and placed more emphasis on local customization.

DIFFERENCES IN INFRASTRUCTURE AND TRADITIONAL PRACTICES Pressures for local responsiveness emerge when there are differences in infrastructure and/or traditional practices between countries. Customizing the product may necessitate delegating manufacturing and production functions to foreign subsidiaries. For example, in North America consumer electrical systems are based on 110 volts, while in some European countries 240-volt systems are standard. Thus, domestic electrical appliances have to be customized to this difference in infrastructure. Traditional practices also often vary across nations. For example, in Britain people drive on the left side of the road, creating a demand for right-hand drive cars, but in neighboring France, people drive on the right side of the road, creating a demand for left-hand drive cars.

DIFFERENCES IN DISTRIBUTION CHANNELS A firm's marketing strategies may have to be responsive to differences in distribution channels between countries. This may necessitate the delegation of marketing functions to national subsidiaries. In laundry detergents, for example, five retail chains control 65 percent of the market in Germany, but no chain controls more than 2 percent of the market in neighboring Italy. Thus, retail chains have considerable buying power in Germany, but relatively little in Italy. Dealing with these differences requires varying marketing approaches on the part of detergent companies. Similarly, in the pharmaceutical industry the British and Japanese distribution systems are radically different from the US system. British and Japanese doctors will not accept or respond favorably to an American-style high-pressure sales force. Thus, pharmaceutical firms have to adopt different marketing practices in Britain and Japan compared to the United States (soft sell versus hard sell).

HOST GOVERNMENT DEMANDS Economic and political demands imposed by host country governments may necessitate a degree of local responsiveness. For example, the politics of health care around the world require that pharmaceutical firms manufacture in multiple locations. Pharmaceutical companies are subject to local clinical testing, registration procedures, and pricing restrictions, all of which require that the manufacturing and marketing of a drug meet local requirements. Because governments and government agencies control a significant proportion of the health care budget in most countries, they are in a powerful position to demand a high level of local responsiveness.

Threats of protectionism, economic nationalism, and local content rules (which require that a certain percentage of a product be manufactured locally), all dictate that international businesses manufacture locally. Consider Bombardier, the Canadian-based manufacturer of railcars, aircraft, jet boats, and snowmobiles. Bombardier has 12 railcar factories across Europe. Critics of the firm argue that the resulting duplication of manufacturing facilities leads to high costs and helps explain why Bombardier makes lower profit margins on its railcar operations than on its other business lines. Managers at Bombardier argue that in Europe, informal rules regarding local content favor companies that use local workers. To sell railcars in Germany, you must manufacture in Germany. The same goes for Belgium, Austria, and France. To address its cost structure in Europe, Bombardier has centralized its engineering and purchasing functions, but it has no plans to centralize manufacturing.[21]

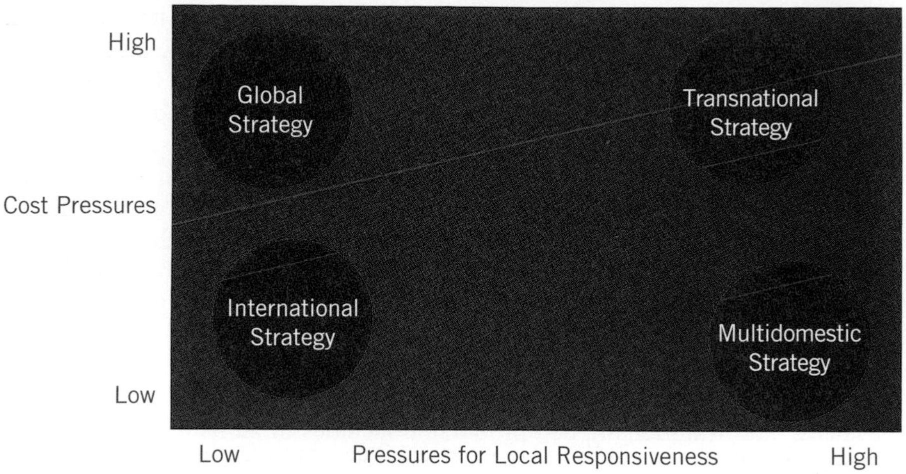

High

Cost Pressures

Low

Low   Pressures for Local Responsiveness   High

Figure 10.4

Four Basic Strategies

IMPLICATIONS   Pressures for local responsiveness imply that it may not be possible for a firm to realize the full benefits from experience curve and location economies. For example, it may not be possible to serve the global marketplace from a single low-cost location, producing a globally standardized product, and marketing it worldwide to achieve experience curve cost economies. The need to customize the product offering to local conditions may work against such a strategy. Automobile firms, for example, have found that Japanese, American, and European consumers demand different kinds of cars and this necessitates producing products that are customized for local markets. Firms such as Honda, Ford, and Toyota are pursuing a strategy of establishing top-to-bottom design and production facilities in each of these regions to better serve local demands. While such customization brings benefits, it also limits a firm's ability to realize significant experience curve cost economies and location economies.

In addition, pressures for local responsiveness imply that it may not be possible to transfer the skills and products associated with a firm's core competencies wholesale from one nation to another. Concessions often have to be made to local conditions. Despite being depicted as "poster boy" for the proliferation of standardized global products, even McDonald's has customized its product offering (i.e., its menu) to account for national differences in tastes and preferences (see the "Management Focus" for details).

Strategic Choice

Firms use four basic strategies to enter and compete in the international environment: an international strategy, a multidomestic strategy, a global strategy, and a transnational strategy.[22] Each strategy has its advantages and disadvantages. The appropriateness of each strategy varies with the extent of pressures for cost reductions and local responsiveness. Figure 10.4 illustrates when each of these strategies is most appropriate. In this section we describe each strategy, identify when it is appropriate, and discuss the pros and cons of each.

International Strategy

Firms that pursue an international strategy try to create value by transferring valuable skills and products to foreign markets where indigenous competitors lack those skills and products. Most international firms have created value by transferring differentiated product offerings developed at home to new markets overseas. They tend to centralize product development functions at home (e.g., R&D). However, they also tend to establish manufacturing and marketing functions in each major country in which they do business. While they may undertake some local customization of product offering and marketing strategy, this tends to be limited. Ultimately, the head office retains tight control over marketing and product strategy in most international firms.

International firms include the likes of Toys R Us, McDonald's, IBM, Kellogg, Procter & Gamble, Wal-Mart, and Microsoft. Microsoft develops the core architecture underlying its products at its Redmond campus in Washington state and also writes the bulk of the computer code there. However, the company allows national subsidiaries to develop their own marketing and distribution strategies and to customize aspects of the product to account for such basic local differences as language and alphabet. Procter & Gamble, which is profiled in the accompanying "Management Focus," has traditionally had production facilities in all its major markets outside the United States, including Britain, Germany, and Japan. These facilities manufactured differentiated products that had been developed by the US parent firm and were often marketed using the message developed in the United States. Historically, P&G's local responsiveness has been limited.

An international strategy makes sense if a firm has a valuable core competence that indigenous competitors in foreign markets lack, and if the firm faces relatively weak pressures for local responsiveness and cost reductions (as is the case for Microsoft). In such circumstances, an international strategy can be very profitable. However, when pressures for local responsiveness are high, firms pursuing this strategy lose to firms that place a greater emphasis on customizing the product offering and market strategy to local conditions. Due to the duplication of manufacturing facilities, firms that pursue an international strategy tend to suffer from high operating costs. This makes the strategy inappropriate in manufacturing industries where cost pressures are high.

Multidomestic Strategy

Firms pursuing a multidomestic strategy orient themselves toward achieving maximum local responsiveness. The distinguishing feature of multidomestic firms is that they extensively customize both their product offering and their marketing strategy to match national conditions. They also tend to establish a complete set of value creation activities—including production, marketing, and R&D—in each major national market in which they do business. As a consequence, they are generally unable to realize value from experience curve effects and location economies. Accordingly, many multidomestic firms have a high-cost structure. They also tend to do a poor job of leveraging core competencies within the firm. General Motors, which we profiled in the opening case, is a good example of a company that has historically functioned as a multidomestic corporation, particularly with regard to its extensive European operations, which are largely self-contained entities.

A multidomestic strategy makes most sense when there are high pressures for local responsiveness and low pressures for cost reductions. The high-cost structure associated with the duplication of production facilities makes this strategy inappropriate in industries where cost pressures are intense (which is the case in the automobile industry, a fact that explains GM's attempts to change its strategic orientation). Another weakness associated with this strategy is that many multidomestic firms have developed into decentralized federations in which each national subsidiary functions in a largely autonomous manner. They often lack the ability to transfer the skills and products derived from core competencies to their national

Procter & Gamble (P&G), the large US consumer products company, has a well-earned reputation as one of the world's best marketers. With over 80 major brands P&G generates more than $20 billion in revenues worldwide. P&G is a dominant global force in laundry detergents, cleaning products, and personal care products. The company expanded abroad in the post-World War II years by pursuing an international strategy—transferring brands and marketing policies developed in the United States to Western Europe—initially with considerable success. Over the next 30 years this policy resulted in development of a classic international firm in which new product development and marketing strategies were pioneered in the United States and then transferred to other countries.

product with a marketing blitz and was quickly rewarded with 30 percent of the market. Only belatedly did P&G realize it had to modify its diapers to accommodate the tastes of Japanese consumers. Now P&G has increased its share of the Japanese market to 30 percent. And in an example of global learning, P&G's trim-fit diapers, developed for the Japanese market, have become a best-seller in the United States.

P&G's experience with disposable diapers in Japan prompted the company to rethink its new product development and marketing philosophy. The company has admitted that its US-centered way of doing business will no longer work. Since the late 1980s P&G has been attempting to delegate more responsibility for new product development and

cent of the market for shampoos in Poland, but in early 1992 sales suddenly plummeted. Then came the rumors: Wash & Go caused dandruff and hair loss—allegations P&G strenuously denied. Next came the jokes. One doing the rounds in Poland was: "I washed my car with Wash & Go and the tires went bald." And when President Lech Walesa proposed that he also become prime minister, critics derided the idea as a "two-in-one solution, just like Wash & Go."

Where did P&G go wrong? The most common theory is that it promoted Wash & Go too hard in a country that has little enthusiasm for brash, American-style advertising. A poll by Pentor, a private market research company in Warsaw, found that almost three times more Poles disliked P&G's commercials

Procter & Gamble's International Strategy

Only minimal adaptation of marketing policies to accommodate country differences was pursued.

The first signs that this strategy was flawed emerged in the 1970s when P&G suffered major setbacks in Japan. By 1985, after 13 years in Japan, P&G was still losing $40 million a year there. After introducing disposable diapers into Japan and commanding an 80 percent share of the market, by the early 1980s P&G had seen its share slip to a miserable 8 percent. Three major Japanese consumer products firms dominated the market. P&G's problem was that its diapers, developed in America, were too bulky for the tastes of Japanese consumers. The Japanese consumer products firm Kao developed a line of trim-fit diapers that appealed more to the tastes of Japanese consumers. Kao supported the introduction of its

marketing strategy to its major subsidiary firms in Japan and Europe. The result has been a company that is more responsive to local differences in consumer tastes and preferences and more willing to admit that good new products can be developed outside the United States.

Despite the apparent changes at P&G, the company's venture into the Polish shampoo market illustrated it still had some way to go in changing long-established practices. In the summer of 1991 P&G entered the Polish market with its Vidal Sasson Wash & Go, an all-in-one shampoo and conditioner that was a best-seller in America and Europe. The product launch was supported by an American-style marketing blitz on a scale never before seen in Poland. At first the campaign seemed to be working as P&G captured more than 30 per-

than liked them. Pentor also argued that the high-profile marketing campaign backfired because years of Communist Party propaganda had led Polish consumers to suspect that advertising is simply a way to shift goods that nobody wants. Some also believe that Wash & Go, which was developed for US consumers who shampoo daily, was too sophisticated for Polish consumers who are less obsessed with personal hygiene. Underlying all of these criticisms seems to be the idea that P&G was once again stumbling because it had transferred a product and marketing strategy from the United States to another country without modification to accommodate the tastes and preferences of local consumers.[23]

343

subsidiaries. This was exemplified by the failure of Philips NV to establish its V2000 VCR format as the dominant design in the VCR industry during the late 1970s. Philips' US subsidiary refused to adopt the V2000 format; instead, it bought VHS-format VCRs produced by Matsushita and put its own label on them!

Global Strategy

Firms that pursue a global strategy focus on increasing profitability by reaping the cost reductions that come from experience curve effects and location economies. That is, they are pursuing a low-cost strategy. The production, marketing, and R&D activities of firms pursuing a global strategy are concentrated in a few favorable locations. Global firms tend not to customize their product offering and marketing strategy to local conditions because customization raises costs (it involves shorter production runs and the duplication of functions). Instead, global firms prefer to market a standardized product worldwide so they can reap the maximum benefits from the economies of scale that underlie the experience curve. They also tend to use their cost advantage to support aggressive pricing in world markets.

This strategy makes most sense where there are strong pressures for cost reductions and where demands for local responsiveness are minimal. Increasingly, these conditions prevail in many industrial goods industries. In the semiconductor industry, for example, enormous demands have emerged for standardized global products. Accordingly, firms such as Intel, Texas Instruments, and Motorola all pursue a global strategy. However, as we noted earlier, these conditions are not found in many consumer goods markets, where demands for local responsiveness remain high (e.g., audio players, automobiles, processed food products). The strategy is inappropriate when demands for local responsiveness are high.

Transnational Strategy

global learning Flow of skills and product offerings from home firm to foreign subsidiary and from foreign subsidiary to home firm and from foreign subsidiary to foreign subsidiary.

transnational strategy Business strategy that seeks experience-based cost economies and location economies, transfers distinctive competencies within the firm, and pays attention to pressures for local responsiveness.

Christopher Bartlett and Sumantra Ghoshal have argued that in today's environment, competitive conditions are so intense that to survive in the global market firms "must exploit experience-based cost economies and location economies, they must transfer core competencies within the firm, and they must do all of this while paying attention to pressures for local responsiveness."[24] They note that in the modern multinational enterprise, core competencies do not just reside in the home country. They can develop in any of the firm's operations. Thus, they maintain that the flow of skills and product offerings should not be all one way, from home firm to foreign subsidiary, as in the case of firms pursuing an international strategy. Rather, the flow should also be from foreign subsidiary to home country and from foreign subsidiary to foreign subsidiary—a process they refer to as **global learning** (for examples of such knowledge flows, see the opening case on General Motors and the "Management Focus" on McDonald's).[25] Bartlett and Ghoshal refer to the strategy pursued by firms that are trying to achieve all of these objective simultaneously as a **transnational strategy.**

A transnational strategy makes sense when a firm faces high pressures for cost reductions and high pressures for local responsiveness. Firms that pursue a transnational strategy are trying to simultaneously achieve low-cost and differentiation advantages. As attractive as this sounds, the strategy is not easy to pursue. Earlier we noted that pressures for local responsiveness and cost reductions place conflicting demands on a firm. Being locally responsive raises costs, which makes cost reductions difficult to achieve. How then, can a firm effectively pursue a transnational strategy?

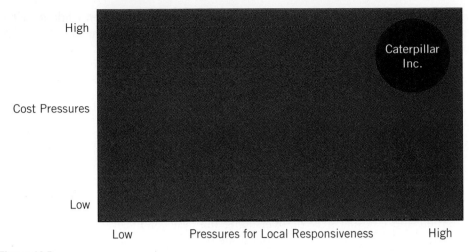

High

Cost Pressures

Low

Low   Pressures for Local Responsiveness   High

Figure 10.5

Cost Pressures and Pressures for Local Responsiveness Facing Caterpillar

Some clues can be derived from the case of Caterpillar Inc. In the late 1970s the need to compete with low-cost competitors such as Komatsu and Hitachi of Japan forced Caterpillar to look for greater cost economies. At the same time, variations in construction practices and government regulations meant that Caterpillar had to remain responsive to local demands. Therefore, as illustrated in Figure 10.5, Caterpillar was confronted with significant pressures for cost reductions and for local responsiveness.

To deal with cost pressures Caterpillar redesigned its products to use many identical components and invested in a few large-scale component manufacturing facilities, sited at favorable locations, to fill global demand and realize scale economics. At the same time the firm augmented the centralized manufacturing of components with assembly plants in each of its major global markets. At these plants, Caterpillar tailored the finished product to local needs. By pursuing this strategy, Caterpillar realized many of the benefits of global manufacturing while responding to pressures for local responsiveness by differentiating its product among national markets.[26] Caterpillar started to pursue this strategy in 1979, and by 1997 had doubled output per employee, significantly reducing its overall cost structure. Meanwhile, Komatsu and Hitachi, which are still wedded to a Japan-centric global strategy, have seen their cost advantages evaporate and have been steadily loosing market share to Caterpillar. (General Motors is trying to pursue a similar strategy with its development of common global platforms for some of its vehicles; see the opening case for details.)

Unilever is another example of a once classic multidomestic firm shifting toward a transnational strategy. A rise in low-cost competition forced Unilever to look for ways of rationalizing its detergents business. During the 1980s Unilever had 17 largely self-contained detergents operations in Europe alone. The duplication, in terms of assets and marketing, was enormous. Because Unilever was so fragmented, it could take as long as four years for the firm to introduce a new product across Europe. Now Unilever is trying to weld its European operation into a single entity, with detergents being manufactured in a handful of cost-efficient plants and standard packaging and advertising being used across Europe. According to firm estimates, the result could be an annual cost saving of more than $200 million. At the same time, however, due to national differences in distribution channels and brand awareness,

Unilever recognizes that it must still remain locally responsive, even while it tries to realize economies from consolidating production and marketing at the optimal locations.[27]

Notwithstanding examples such as Caterpillar, General Motors, and Unilever, Bartlett and Ghoshal admit that building an organization that can support a transnational strategy is complex and difficult. Simultaneously trying to achieve cost efficiencies, global learning, and local responsiveness places contradictory demands on an organization. We will later show how a firm can deal with the dilemmas posed by such difficult organizational issues. For now, it is important to note that the organizational problems associated with pursuing conflicting objectives constitute a major impediment to the pursuit of a transnational strategy. Firms that attempt a transnational strategy can become bogged down in an organizational morass that only leads to inefficiencies.

Bartlett and Ghoshal may be overstating the case for the transnational strategy when they present it as the only viable strategy. While no one doubts that the firm that can adopt a transnational strategy will have a competitive advantage in some industries, global, multidomestic, and international strategies remain viable in other industries. In the semiconductor industry, for example, pressures for local customization are minimal and competition is purely a cost game, in which case a global strategy, not a transnational strategy, is optimal. This is true in many industrial goods markets where the product serves universal needs. But the argument can be made that to compete in certain consumer goods markets, such as the automobile and consumer electronics industry, a firm has to try to adopt a transnational strategy.

Summary

Figure 10.6 summarizes the advantages and disadvantages of each of the four strategies discussed above. While a transnational strategy appears to offer the most advantages, implementing such a strategy raises difficult organizational issues. The appropriateness of each strategy depends on the relative strength of pressures for cost reductions and pressures for local responsiveness.

Strategic Alliances

The term **strategic alliances** refers to cooperative agreements between potential or actual competitors. In this section, we are concerned with strategic alliances between firms from different countries. Strategic alliances run the range from formal joint ventures, in which two or more firms have equity stakes (e.g., Fuji–Xerox), to short-term contractual agreements in which two companies agree to cooperate on a particular task (such as developing a new product). Collaboration between competitors is fashionable; the 1980s and 1990s saw an explosion in the number of strategic alliances.

The Advantages of Strategic Alliances

Firms ally themselves with actual or potential competitors for various strategic purposes.[28] First, as noted earlier in the chapter, strategic alliances may facilitate entry into a foreign market. For example, Motorola initially found it very difficult to gain access to the Japanese cellular telephone market. In the mid-1980s the firm complained loudly about formal and informal Japanese trade barriers. The turning point for Motorola came in 1987 when it allied itself with Toshiba to build microprocessors. As part of the deal, Toshiba provided Motorola with marketing help—including some of its best managers. This helped Motorola in the political game of securing government ap-

Strategy	Advantages	Disadvantages
Global	Exploit experience curve effects Exploit location economies	Lack of local responsiveness
International	Transfer distinctive competencies to foreign markets	Lack of local responsiveness Inability to realize location economies Failure to exploit experience curve effects
Multidomestic	Customize product offerings and marketing in accordance with local responsiveness	Inability to realize location economies Failure to exploit experience curve effects Failure to transfer distinctive competencies to foreign markets
Transnational	Exploit experience curve effects Exploit location economies Customize product offerings and marketing in accordance with local responsiveness Reap benefits of global learning	Difficult to implement due to organizational problems

Figure 10.6

The Advantages and Disadvantages of the Four Strategies

Strategic Alliances: Whose Flight Is This, Anyway?

During boarding for a recent flight between Zurich and Boston, a group of late and perplexed passengers rushed to the announced gate for their flight only to find a Swissair plane and crew. There was a moment of panic because these passengers from Vermont thought they were at the wrong gate in Zurich. They had booked with the American carrier Delta. That morning they had a lesson in strategic alliances. Delta and Swissair have formed a strategic alliance to share aircraft and run flights that have both Swissair and Delta flight numbers. The American passengers weren't lost after all; they were participating in the implementation of a global strategy.

proval to enter the Japanese market and getting radio frequencies assigned for its mobile communications systems. Motorola no longer complains about Japan's trade barriers. Although privately the company admits they still exist, with Toshiba's help Motorola has become skilled at getting around them.[29]

Strategic alliances also allow firms to share the fixed costs (and associated risks) of developing new products or processes. Motorola's alliance with Toshiba was partly motivated by a desire to share the high fixed costs of setting up an operation to manufacture microprocessors. The microprocessor business is so capital intensive—Motorola and Toshiba each contributed close to $1 billion to set up their facility—that few firms can afford the costs and risks by themselves. Similarly, the alliance between Boeing and a number of Japanese companies to build the 767 was motivated by Boeing's desire to share the estimated $2 billion investment required to develop the aircraft.

Third, an alliance is a way to bring together complementary skills and assets that neither company could easily develop on its own. An example is the alliance between France's Thomson and Japan's JVC to manufacture videocassette recorders. JVC and Thomson are trading core competencies; Thomson needs product technology and manufacturing skills, while JVC needs to learn how to succeed in the fragmented European market. Both sides believe there is an equitable chance for gain. Similarly, in 1990 AT&T struck a deal with NEC Corporation of Japan to trade technological skills. AT&T gave NEC some of its computer-aided design technology, and NEC gave AT&T access to the technology underlying its advanced-logic computer chips. Such trading of core competencies seems to underlie many of the most successful strategic alliances.

Fourth, it can make sense to form an alliance that will help the firm establish technological standards for the industry that will benefit the firm. For example, in 1992 Philips NV allied with its global competitor Matsushita to manufacture and market the digital compact cassette (DCC) system Philips had developed. Philips hoped this linking with Matsushita would help it establish the DCC system as a new technological standard in the recording and consumer electronics industries. Sony had developed a competing "mini compact disc" technology that it wanted to establish as the new technical standard. Because the two technologies did very similar things, there was room for only one new standard. Philips saw its alliance with Matsushita as a tactic for winning the race.[30]

The Disadvantages of Strategic Alliances

Strategic alliances have been criticized for giving competitors a low-cost route to new technology and markets. Robert Reich and Eric Mankin have argued that strategic alliances between US and Japanese firms are part of an implicit Japanese strategy to keep higher-paying, higher-value-added jobs in Japan while gaining the project engineering and production process skills that underlie the competitive success of many US companies.[31] They argue that Japanese successes in the machine tool and semiconductor industries were largely built on US technology acquired through strategic alliances. And they argue that, increasingly, US managers are aiding the Japanese in achieving their goals by entering alliances that channel new inventions to Japan and provide a US sales and distribution network for the resulting products. Although such deals may generate short-term profits, Reich and Mankin argue, the long-run result is to "hollow out" US firms, leaving them with no competitive advantage in the global marketplace.

Alliances do have risks. Unless a firm is careful, it can give away more than it receives. But there are so many examples of apparently successful alliances between firms—including alliances between US and Japanese firms—that Reich Mankin's position seems more than a little extreme. It is difficult to see how the Motorola–Toshiba alliance or the Fuji–Xerox alliance fit their thesis. In these cases, both partners seem to have gained from the alliance. Why do some alliances benefit both firms while others benefit one firm and hurt the other? The next section answers this question.

Making Alliances Work

The failure rate for international strategic alliances seems to be quite high. One study of 49 international strategic alliances found that two-thirds run into serious managerial and financial troubles within two years of their formation, and that although many of these problems are solved, 33 percent are ultimately rated as failures by the parties involved.[32] The accompanying "Management Focus" provides a close look at one strategic alliance that failed. Below we argue that the success of an alliance seems to be a function of three main factors: partner selection, alliance structure, and the manner in which the alliance is managed.

technological

In June 1984 General Motors and the Daewoo Group of South Korea signed an agreement that called for each to invest $100 million in a South Korean-based 50/50 joint venture, Daewoo Motor Company, that would manufacture a subcompact car, the Pontiac Le Mans, based on GM's popular German-designed Opel Kadett (Opel is a wholly owned German subsidiary of GM). Much of the day-to-day management of the alliance was to be placed in the hands of Daewoo executives, with managerial and technical advice being provided by a limited number of GM executives. At the time, many hailed the alliance as a smart move for both companies. GM doubted that a small car could be built profitably in the

production line. South Korea had lurched toward democracy, and workers throughout the country demanded better wages. Daewoo Motor was hit by a series of bitter strikes that repeatedly halted Le Mans production. To calm the labor troubles Daewoo Motor more than doubled wages. Suddenly it was cheaper to build Opels in Germany than in South Korea (German wages were still higher, but German productivity was also much higher, which translated into lower labor costs).

Equally problematic was the poor quality of the cars rolling off the Daewoo production line. Electrical systems often crashed on the Le Mans, and the braking system tended to fail after just a few thousand miles. The Le Mans soon

cars in Eastern Europe. GM executives immediately tried to kill the deal, telling Mr. Kim that Europe was the territory of GM's German subsidiary, Opel. Daewoo ultimately agreed to limit the sale to 3,000 cars and never sell again in Eastern Europe. To make matters worse, when Daewoo developed a new sedan car and asked GM to sell it in the United States, GM said no. Also, Daewoo management believed the poor sales of the Le Mans in the United States were not due to quality problems, but to GM's poor marketing efforts.

Things came to a head in 1991 when Daewoo asked GM to agree to expand the joint venture's manufacturing facilities. The plan called for each partner to put in another

Anatomy of a Failed Alliance

United States because of high labor costs, and it saw enormous advantages in this marriage of German technology and Korean labor. At the time, Roger Smith, GM's chairman, told South Korean reporters that GM's North American operation would probably import 80,000 to 100,000 cars a year from Daewoo Motor. The Daewoo Group would get access to the superior engineering skills of GM and an entrée into the world's largest car market—the United States.

Eight years of financial losses later the joint venture collapsed in a blizzard of mutual recriminations between Daewoo and General Motors. From the perspective of GM, things started to go seriously wrong in 1987, just as the first Le Mans was rolling off Daewoo's

gained a reputation for poor quality, and US sales plummeted to 37,000 vehicles in 1991, down 86 percent from their 1988 high. Hurt by the car's reputation as a lemon, Daewoo's share of the rapidly growing South Korean car market also slumped from a high of 21.4 percent in 1987 to 12.3 percent in 1991.

If General Motors was disappointed in Daewoo, that was nothing compared to Daewoo's frustration with GM. Daewoo Group Chairman Kim Woo-Choong complained publicly that GM executives were arrogant and treated him shabbily. Mr. Kim was angry that GM tried to prohibit him from expanding the market for Daewoo's cars. In late 1988, Mr. Kim negotiated a deal to sell 7,000 Daewoo Motor's

$100 million, and for Daewoo Motor to double its output. GM management refused on the grounds that increasing output would not help Daewoo Motor unless the venture could first improve its product quality. The matter festered until late 1991 when GM management delivered a blunt proposal to Daewoo—either GM would buy out Daewoo's stake, or Daewoo would buy out GM's stake in the joint venture. Much to GM's surprise, Daewoo agreed to buy out GM's stake. The divorce was completed in November 1992 with an agreement by Daewoo to pay GM $170 million over three years for its 50 percent stake in Daewoo Motor Company.[33]

Partner Selection

One key to making a strategic alliance work is to select the right ally. A good ally, or partner, has three principal characteristics. First, a good partner helps the firm achieve its strategic goals—whether they are market access, sharing the costs and risks of new product development, or gaining access to critical core competencies. The partner must have capabilities that the firm lacks and that it values. Second, a good partner shares the firm's vision for the purpose of the alliance. If two firms approach an alliance with radically different agendas, the chances are great that the relationship will not be harmonious, will not flourish, and will end in divorce.

Third, a good partner is unlikely to try to exploit the alliance for its own ends; that is, to expropriate the firm's technological know-how while giving away little in return. In this respect, firms with good reputations to maintain probably make the best allies. For example, IBM is involved in so many strategic alliances that it would not pay the company to trample over individual alliance partners. Such action would tarnish IBM's hard-won reputation of being a good ally and would make it more difficult to attract alliance partners in the future. Because IBM attaches great importance to its alliances, it is unlikely to engage in the kind of opportunistic behavior that Reich and Mankin highlight. Similarly, their reputations make it less likely (but by no means impossible) that such Japanese firms as Sony, Toshiba, and Fuji, which have histories of alliances with non-Japanese firms, would exploit an alliance partner.

To select a partner with these three characteristics, a firm needs to study potential alliance candidates. To increase the probability of selecting a good partner, the firm should:

1 Collect as much pertinent, publicly available information on potential allies as possible.

2 Collect data from informed third parties. These include firms that have had alliances with the potential partners, investment bankers who have had dealings with them, and some of their former employees.

3 Get to know the potential partner as well as possible before committing to an alliance. This should include face-to-face meetings between senior managers (and perhaps middle-level managers) to ensure that the chemistry is right.

Alliance Structure

Having selected a partner, the alliance should be structured so that the firm's risks of giving too much away to the partner are reduced to an acceptable level. Figure 10.7 depicts the four safeguards against opportunism by alliance partners that we discuss here. (Opportunism includes the "theft" of technology and/or markets that Reich and Mankin describe.) First, alliances can be designed to make it difficult (if not impossible) to transfer technology not meant to be transferred. The design, development, manufacture, and service of a product manufactured by an alliance can be structured so as to "wall off" sensitive technologies to prevent their leakage to the other participant. In the alliance between General Electric and Snecma to build commercial aircraft engines, for example, GE reduced the risk of "excess transfer" by walling off certain sections of the production process. The modularization effectively cut off the transfer of what GE regarded as key competitive technology, while permitting Snecma access to final assembly. Similarly, in the alliance between Boeing and the Japanese to build the 767, Boeing walled off research, design, and marketing functions considered central to its competitive position, while allowing the Japanese to share in production technology. Boeing also walled off new technologies not required for 767 production.[34]

Second, contractual safeguards can be written into an alliance agreement to guard against the risk of opportunism by a partner. For example, TRW, Inc., has three strategic alliances with large Japanese auto component suppliers to produce seat belts,

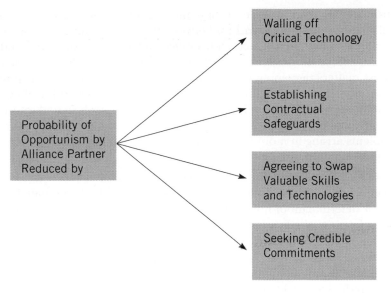

Figure 10.7

Structuring Alliances to Reduce Opportunism

engine valves, and steering gears for sale to Japanese-owned auto assembly plants in the United States. TRW has clauses in each of its alliance contracts that bar the Japanese firms from competing with TRW to supply US-owned auto companies with component parts. By doing this, TRW protects itself against the possibility that the Japanese companies are entering into the alliances merely to gain access to the North American market.

Third, both parties to an alliance can agree in advance to swap skills and technologies that the other covets, thereby ensuring a chance for equitable gain. Cross-licensing agreements are one way to achieve this goal. For example, in the alliance between Motorola and Toshiba, Motorola has licensed some of its microprocessor technology to Toshiba, and in return Toshiba has licensed some of its memory chip technology to Motorola.

Fourth, the risk of opportunism by an alliance partner can be reduced if the firm extracts a significant credible commitment from its partner in advance. The long-term alliance between Xerox and Fuji to build photocopiers for the Asian market illustrates this. Rather than enter into an informal agreement or some kind of licensing arrangement (which Fuji initially wanted), Xerox insisted that Fuji invest in a 50/50 joint venture to serve Japan and East Asia. This venture constituted such a significant investment in people, equipment, and facilities that Fuji was committed from the outset to making the alliance work in order to earn a return on its investment. By agreeing to the joint venture, Fuji essentially made a credible commitment to the alliance. Given this, Xerox felt secure in transferring its photocopier technology to Fuji.[35]

Managing the Alliance

Once a partner has been selected and an appropriate structure has been agreed on, the task facing the firm is to maximize its benefits from the alliance. As in all international business deals, an important factor is sensitivity to cultural differences (see Chapter 3). Many differences in management style are attributable to cultural differences, and managers need to make allowances for these in dealing with their partner. Beyond this, maximizing the benefits from an alliance seems to involve building trust between partners and learning from partners.[36]

BUILDING TRUST   Part of the trick of managing an alliance successfully seems to be to build interpersonal relationships between the firms' managers. This is one lesson that can be drawn from a successful strategic alliance between Ford and Mazda. Ford and Mazda set up a framework of meetings within which their managers not only discuss matters pertaining to the alliance, but also get to know each other better. The belief is that the resulting friendships help build trust and facilitate harmonious relations between the two firms. Personal relationships foster an informal management network between the two firms. This network can then be used to help solve problems arising in more formal contexts (such as in joint committee meetings between personnel from the two firms).

LEARNING FROM PARTNERS   After a five-year study of 15 strategic alliances between major multinationals, Gary Hamel, Yves Doz, and C. K. Prahalad concluded that a major determinant of how much a company gains from an alliance is its ability to learn from its alliance partner.[37] They focused on a number of alliances between Japanese companies and Western (European or American) partners. In every case in which a Japanese company emerged from an alliance stronger than its Western partner, the Japanese company had made a greater effort to learn. Few Western companies studied seemed to want to learn from their Japanese partners. They tended to regard the alliance purely as a cost-sharing or risk-sharing device, rather than as an opportunity to learn how a potential competitor does business.

Consider the 10-year alliance between General Motors and Toyota to build the Chevrolet Nova. This alliance, constituted in 1985, was structured as a formal joint venture, called New United Motor Manufacturing, Inc., and each party had a 50 percent equity stake. The venture owned an auto plant in Fremont, California. According to one Japanese manager, Toyota quickly achieved most of its objectives from the alliance: "We learned about US supply and transportation. And we got the confidence to manage US workers."[38] All that knowledge was then transferred to Georgetown, Kentucky, where Toyota opened its own plant in 1988. But all that GM got from the alliance was a new product, the Chevrolet Nova. Some GM managers complained that the knowledge they gained from Toyota has never been put to good use inside GM. They believe they should have been kept together as a team to educate GM's engineers and workers about the Japanese system. Instead, they were dispersed to various GM subsidiaries.

To maximize the learning benefits of an alliance, a firm must try to learn from its partner and then apply the knowledge within its own organization. It has been suggested that all operating employees should be briefed on the partner's strengths and weaknesses and should understand how acquiring particular skills will bolster their firm's competitive position. Hamel, Doz, and Prahalad note that this is standard practice among Japanese companies. For example, they made this observation:

> We accompanied a Japanese development engineer on a tour through a partner's factory. This engineer dutifully took notes on plant layout, the number of production stages, the rate at which the line was running, and the number of employees. He recorded all this despite the fact that he had no manufacturing responsibility in his own company, and that the alliance did not encompass joint manufacturing. Such dedication greatly enhances learning.[39]

For such learning to be of value, it must be diffused throughout the organization. To achieve this, the managers involved in the alliance should be explicitly used to educate their colleagues in the firm about the skills of the alliance partner.

Key Terms

Summary

In this chapter we reviewed the ways in which firms can profit from global expansion, we reviewed the strategies that firms can adopt to compete globally, and we looked at the issue of strategic alliances. The following points have been made in this chapter:

1. For some firms international expansion represents a way to earn greater returns by transferring the skills and product offerings derived from their core competencies to markets where indigenous competitors lack those skills.

2. Due to national differences, it pays a firm to base each value creation activity where factor conditions are most conducive to the performance of that activity. We refer to this strategy as focusing on the attainment of location economies.

3. By building sales volume more rapidly, international expansion can help a firm move down the experience curve.

4. The best strategy for a firm to pursue may depend on a consideration of the pressures for cost reductions and the pressures for local responsiveness.

5. Pressures for cost reductions are greatest in industries producing commodity products where price is the main competitive weapon.

6. Pressures for local responsiveness arise from differences in consumer tastes and preferences, national infrastructure and traditional practices, distribution channels, and host government demands.

7. Firms pursuing an international strategy transfer the skills and products derived from distinctive competencies to foreign markets, while undertaking limited local customization.

8. Firms pursuing a multidomestic strategy customize their product offering, marketing strategy, and business strategy to national conditions.

9. Firms pursuing a global strategy focus on reaping the cost reductions that come from experience curve effects and location economies.

10. Many industries are now so competitive that firms must adopt a transnational strategy. This involves a simultaneous focus on reducing costs, transferring skills and products, and being locally re-sponsive. Implementing such a strategy, however, is not easy.

11. Strategic alliances are cooperative agreements between actual or potential competitors.

12. The advantages of alliances are that they facilitate entry into foreign markets, enable partners to share the fixed costs and risks associated with new products and processes, facilitate the transfer of complementary skills between companies, and help firms establish technical standards.

13. The disadvantages of a strategic alliance are that the firm risks giving away technological know-how and market access to its alliance partner in return for very little.

14. The disadvantages associated with alliances can be reduced if the firm selects partners carefully, paying close attention to the issue of reputation, and structures the alliance so as to avoid unintended transfers of know-how.

15. Two keys to making alliances work seem to be (i) building trust and informal communications networks between partners and (ii) taking proactive steps to learn from alliance partners.

Critical Thinking and Discussion Questions

1. In a world of zero transportation costs, no trade barriers, and non-trivial differences between nations with regard to factor conditions, firms must expand internationally if they are to survive. Discuss.

2. Plot the position of the following firms on Figure 10.3—Procter & Gamble, IBM, Coca-Cola, Dow Chemicals, US Steel, McDonald's. Justify your answer.

3. Are the following global industries or multidomestic industries: bulk chemicals, pharmaceuticals, branded food products, moviemaking, television manufacture, personal computers, airline travel?

4 Discuss how the need for control over foreign operations varies with the strategy and core competencies of a firm. What are the implications of this for the choice of entry mode?

5 What do you see as the main organizational problems likely to be associated with implementation of a transnational strategy?

Internet Exercises

1 Christopher Bartlett and Sumantra Ghoshal, two international strategy experts, have suggested that firms that follow a transnational strategy, and respond to both cost pressures and pressures for local responsiveness, are more likely to find success in today's highly competitive global marketplace than firms that do not. However, the traditional rules of the game may be a little different in cyberspace. Yahoo! Japan enjoys a commanding position in Japan's burgeoning Internet market, and it got there not by responding to local market differences but by closely imitating its American parent. The Yahoo! Japan Internet site is virtually identical to the American Yahoo! site, except that category headlines are in Japanese rather than English. Instead of approaching the market slowly and with patience, both traditional practices when entering the Japanese marketplace, management at Yahoo! Japan determined that speed was of the essence and committed to establishing the site within two months.

Today, despite its dominance, Yahoo! Japan is changing its site to better meet the needs of its users and also to fend off local competitors such as NTT. Overall, however, the company has retained its American roots and continues to maintain a leading position in the market. Go to Yahoo! (**www.yahoo.com**). Click on the Japanese site and compare it to its American counterpart as well as some of its other foreign sites. Then consider Bartlett and Ghoshal's theory. Does the theory make sense in international e-commerce? Discuss how the Internet is changing the traditional rules of international strategy. What impact will these changes have on companies that rely primarily on traditional business channels?

Source: *The Wall Street Journal,* July 28, 1999, p. B1.

2 You might think that Sony and banking have nothing in common, but you would be wrong. Sony, the Japanese electronics powerhouse, is going into banking. In an effort to diversify its revenue base, the company plans to expand into financial services to reduce its dependency on its traditional electronics products. The company plans to start an Internet bank within the next two years that will allow customers to obtain loans and pay bills on-line. Sony, while perhaps new to banking, is not a stranger to the Internet. The company has been involved in on-line music distribution and has also invested in an Internet broker.

Sony maintains that its emphasis will still be on electronics manufacturing, but concedes that it will be difficult to make a profit in that area in the new millennium. The company believes that its entrée into the banking world is linked to its core business, noting that on-line services such as banking could incorporate the use of smart cards. Using the strategy framework provided in the text, analyze Sony's (**www.Sony.com**) latest moves. How will Sony's forays into cyberspace affect its internal operations? Is Sony in a position to deal with the fast-paced world of e-commerce?

Source: *The Wall Street Journal,* December 13, 1999, p. B12.

Established in the 1940s in Sweden by Ingvar Kamprad, IKEA has grown rapidly in recent years to become one of the world's largest retailers of home furnishings. In its initial push to expand globally, IKEA largely ignored the retailing rule that international success involves tailoring product lines closely to national tastes and preferences. Instead, IKEA stuck with the vision, articulated by founder Kamprad, that the company should sell a basic product range that is "typically Swedish" wherever it ventures in the world. The company also remained primarily production oriented; that is, the Swedish management and design group decided what it was going to sell and then presented it to the worldwide public—often with little research as to what the public actually wanted. The company also emphasized its Swedish roots in its international advertising, even insisting on a "Swedish" blue-and-gold color scheme for its stores.

Despite breaking some key rules of international retailing, the formula of selling Swedish-designed products in the same manner everywhere seemed to work. Between 1974 and 1997, IKEA expanded from a company with 10 stores, only one of which was outside Scandinavia, and annual revenues of $210 million to a group with 138 stores in 28 countries and sales of close to $6 billion. In 1997 only 11 percent of its sales were generated in Sweden. Of the balance, 29.6 percent of sales came from Germany, 42.5 percent from the rest of Western Europe, and 14.4 percent from North America. IKEA is now beginning to expand in Asia, with the opening of stores in mainland China.

The foundation of IKEA's success has been to offer consumers good value for their money. IKEA's approach starts with a global network of suppliers, which now numbers 2,400 firms in 65 countries. An IKEA supplier gains long-term contracts, technical advice, and leased equipment from the company. In return, IKEA demands an exclusive contract and low prices. IKEA's designers work closely with suppliers to build savings into the products by designing products that can be produced at a low cost. IKEA displays its enormous range of more than 10,000 products in cheap out-of-town stores. It sells most of its furniture as kits for customers to take home and assemble themselves. The firm reaps huge economies of scale from the size of each store and the big production runs made possible by selling the same products all over the world. This strategy allows IKEA to match its rivals on quality, while undercutting them by up to 30 percent on price and still maintaining a healthy after-tax return on sales of about 7 percent.

This strategy worked well until 1985 when IKEA decided to enter the North American market. Between 1985 and 1996 IKEA opened 26 stores in North America, but unlike the company's experience across Europe, the stores did not quickly become profitable. By 1990 it was clear that IKEA's North American operations were in trouble. Part of the problem was an adverse movement in exchange rates. In 1985 the exchange rate was $1 = 8.6 Swedish kronar; by 1990 it was $1 = SKr5.8. At this exchange rate many products imported from Sweden did not look inexpensive to American consumers.

But there was more to IKEA's problems than adverse exchange rates. IKEA's unapologetically Swedish products, which had sold so well across Europe, jarred with American tastes and sometimes physiques. Swedish beds were narrow and measured in centimeters. IKEA did not sell the matching bedroom suites that Americans liked. Its kitchen cupboards were too narrow for large dinner plates. Its glasses were too small for a nation that adds ice to everything. The drawers in IKEA's bedroom chests were too shallow for American consumers, who tend to store sweaters in them. And the company made the mistake of selling European-sized curtains that did not fit American windows. As one senior IKEA manager joked later, "Americans just wouldn't lower their ceilings to fit our curtains."

By 1991, the company's top management realized it would have to customize its product offering to North American tastes to succeed. The company redesigned its product range. The drawers in bedroom chests were designed to be two inches deeper—and sales immediately increased by 30 to 40 percent. IKEA now sells American-style king- and queen-size beds, measured in inches, and it sells them as part of complete bedroom suites. It redesigned its range of kitchen furniture and kitchenware to better appeal to American tastes. The company also boosted the amount of products being sourced locally from 15 percent in 1990 to 45 percent in 1997, a move that makes the company far less vulnerable to adverse movements in exchange rates. By 1997 about one-third of IKEA's total product offerings were designed exclusively for the US market.

This break with IKEA's traditional strategy seems to be paying off. Between 1990 and 1994 IKEA's North American sales tripled to $480 million, and they nearly doubled again to about $900 million in 1997. The company claims it has been making a profit in North America since early 1993, although it does not release precise figures and does admit that its profit rate is lower in America than in Europe. Still, the company keeps expanding in America, including the 1998 opening of a $50 million IKEA superstore near Chicago, Illinois.[40]

CASE DISCUSSION QUESTIONS

1 What strategy was IKEA pursuing as it expanded throughout Europe during the 1970s and early 1980s—a multidomestic strategy, a global strategy, or an international strategy?

2 Why do you think this strategy did not work as well in North America as it did in Europe?

3 As of 1998 what strategy was IKEA pursuing? Does this strategy make sense? Can you see any drawbacks with this strategy?

eleven

Entering Foreign Markets

Opening Case   Merrill Lynch in Japan

Merrill Lynch is an investment banking titan. The US-based financial services institution is the world's largest underwriter of debt and equity and the third-largest mergers and acquisitions advisor behind Morgan Stanley and Goldman Sachs. Merrill Lynch's investment banking operations have long had a global reach. The company has a dominant presence not only in New York, but also in London and Tokyo. However, until recently Merrill Lynch's

Merrill Lynch's initial decision to enter Japan's private client market for investments was too early. By 1997, the regulatory climate in Japan and the bankruptcy of Yamaichi Securities made it possible for them to re-enter the market successfully, and much sooner than other foreign financial services firms. What do you suppose were some of the disadvantages to Merrill Lynch in their decision to buy Yamaichi Securities for both their Japanese and U.S. operations?
Stone/Mike Blank

Learning Objectives

1 Explore the three basic decisions that a firm contemplating foreign expansion must make: which markets to enter, when to enter those markets, and on what scale?

2 Review the different modes that firms use to enter a foreign market.

3 Understand the advantages and disadvantages of each entry mode.

4 Appreciate the relationship between strategy and a firm's choice of entry mode.

5 Appreciate some pitfalls of exporting.

6 Be familiar with the steps a firm can take to improve its export performance.

7 Understand the mechanics of export and import financing.

---

international presence was limited to investment banking. Its private client business, which offers banking, financial advice, and stockbrokerage services to individuals, has historically been concentrated in the United States. This is changing rapidly. In 1995 Merrill Lynch purchased Smith New Court, the largest stockbrokerage in Britain. This was followed in 1997 by the acquisition of Mercury Asset Management, the United Kingdom's leading manager

of mutual funds. Then in 1998 Merrill Lynch acquired Midland Walwyn, Canada's last major independent stockbrokerage. The company's boldest moves, however, have probably been in Japan.

Merrill Lynch first started to establish a private client business in Japan in the 1980s, but it met with limited success. It was the first foreign firm to enter Japan's private client investment market. The company found it extremely difficult to

attract employee talent and customers away from Japan's big four stockbrokerages, which had monopolized the Japanese market. Also, restrictive regulations made it almost impossible for Merrill Lynch to offer its Japanese private clients the range of services it offered clients in the United States. For example, foreign exchange regulations meant it was very difficult for Merrill Lynch to sell non-Japanese stocks, bonds, and mutual funds to Japanese investors. In 1993 the company admitted defeat, closed its six retail branches in Kobe and Kyoto, and withdrew from the private client market in Japan.

Over the next few years, however, things started to change. In the mid-1990s Japan began to deregulate its financial services industry. This led to the removal of many of the restrictions that had made it so difficult for Merrill Lynch to do business in Japan. For example, the relaxation of foreign exchange controls meant that by 1998, it was possible for Japanese citizens to purchase foreign stocks, bonds, and mutual funds. Meanwhile, Japan's big four stockbrokerages continued to struggle with serious financial problems that resulted from the 1991 crash of Japan's stock market. In November 1997, in what was a shock to many Japanese, one of these firms, Yamaichi Securities, declared that it was bankrupt due to $2.2 billion in accumulated "hidden losses" and would shut its doors. Recognizing the country's financial system was strained and in need of fresh capital, know-how, and the stimulus of greater competition, the Japanese government signaled that it would adopt a more relaxed attitude toward foreign entry into its financial services industry. This attitude underlay Japan's wholehearted endorsement of a 1997 deal brokered by the World Trade Organization to

liberalize global financial services. The WTO deal made it much easier for foreign firms to sell financial service products to Japanese investors.

By 1997 Merrill Lynch decided the climate in Japan had changed significantly. The big attraction of the market was still the same—the financial assets owned by Japanese households are huge, amounting to a staggering ¥1,220 trillion in late 1997, only 3 percent of which were then invested in mutual funds (most are invested in low-yielding bank accounts and government bonds). However, attitudes were changing and it looked as if it would be much easier to do business in Japan. Accordingly, in mid-1997 Merrill Lynch started to investigate reentering the Japanese private client market. Initially, the company considered a joint venture with Sanwa Bank to sell Merrill Lynch's mutual fund products to Japanese consumers through Sanwa's 400 retail branches. The proposed alliance had the advantage of allowing Merrill Lynch to leverage Sanwa's existing distribution system, rather than having to build its own distribution system. However, such a strategy would not have given Merrill Lynch the presence that it felt it needed to build a solid financial services business in Japan. Company executives reasoned that it was important to make a major commitment to the Japanese market in order to establish Merrill Lynch's brand name as a premier

provider of investment products and financial advice to individuals. This would enable the company to entrench itself as a major player before other foreign institutions entered the market—and before Japan's own stockbrokerages rose to the challenge. At the same time, given their prior experience in Japan, Merrill Lynch's executives were hesitant to go down this road because of the huge costs and risks involved.

The problem of how best to enter the Japanese market was solved by the bankruptcy of Yamaichi Securities. Suddenly Yamaichi's nationwide network of offices and 7,000 employees were up for grabs. In late December 1997, Merrill Lynch announced it would hire some 2,000 of Yamaichi's employees and acquire up to 50 of Yamaichi's branch offices. The deal, which was enthusiastically endorsed by the Japanese government, significantly lowered Merrill Lynch's costs of establishing a retail network in Japan. The goal for the new subsidiary was to have $20 billion under management by 2000. The company got off to a quick start. In February 1998, Merrill Lynch launched its first mutual fund in Japan and saw the value of its assets swell to $1 billion by April. The company now has a significant head start over other foreign financial service institutions contemplating building a private client network in Japan.[1]

Introduction

This chapter is concerned with three closely related topics: (1) The decision of which foreign markets to enter, when to enter them, and on what scale; (2) the choice of entry mode; and (3) the mechanics of exporting. Any firm contemplating foreign expansion must first struggle with the issue of which foreign markets to enter and the timing and scale of entry. The choice of which markets to enter should be driven by an assessment of relative long-term growth and profit potential. For example, in the opening case we saw how Merrill Lynch's entry into the Japanese private client financial services market was driven by a desire to participate in a market that is potentially huge. Japanese households have ¥1,220 trillion in financial assets, only a tiny fraction of which are invested in stocks. If Merrill Lynch can tap into even a small percentage of this savings pool, Japan will quickly become its second-biggest market after the United States. Thus, it makes sense for Merrill Lynch to focus on Japan rather than a country with a much smaller savings pool such as, for example, India.

As for the timing and scale of entry, the opening case illustrates the issues involved. Merrill Lynch first entered Japan's private client market on a small scale in the mid-1980s, only to exit in 1993 after admitting it was making no progress. The reasons for this lack of progress included an adverse regulatory environment that made it difficult for Merrill Lynch to expand and an inability to recruit talented people away from Japan's domestic financial institutions. The company was too early. By 1997, however, the regulatory climate in Japan had changed significantly. This coupled with the bankruptcy of Yamaichi Securities and the resulting increase in the supply of talented financial services people made it feasible for Merrill Lynch to reenter the market on a much larger scale. The timing now seemed right. A significant feature of Merrill Lynch's reengagement in Japan's private client market is that the company is still an early mover among foreign financial services. It is also an early mover relative to Japanese financial service firms. This preemptive move, combined with the substantial scale of Merrill Lynch's commitment, bodes well for the firm's objective of establishing itself as a dominant player in Japan's potentially huge private client market.

The choice of mode for entering a foreign market is another major issue for international businesses. The various modes for serving foreign markets include exporting, licensing or franchising to host country firms, joint venturing with a host country firm, and setting up a wholly owned subsidiary in a host country to serve its market. Each option has advantages and disadvantages. The magnitude of the advantages and disadvantages associated with each entry mode are determined by a number of factors, including transport costs, trade barriers, political risks, economic risks, and firm strategy. The optimal entry mode varies, depending on these factors. Thus, whereas some firms may best serve a given market by exporting, other firms may better serve the market by setting up a wholly owned subsidiary or by using some other entry mode. In the opening case, we saw how Merrill Lynch at one point was reportedly considering a joint venture with Sanwa Bank to serve the Japanese private client market, although it ultimately chose to establish a wholly owned subsidiary.

Although we review a variety of entry modes in this chapter, we shall discuss exporting in more depth than we discuss the other entry modes. Most firms start as exporters and only later switch to other entry modes. Although large multinational enterprises have long been conversant with the steps that must be taken to export successfully, smaller enterprises can find the process intimidating. The firm wishing to export must identify foreign market opportunities, avoid a host of problems that are often associated with doing business in a foreign market, familiarize itself with the mechanics of export and import financing, learn where it can get financing and export credit insurance, and learn how it should deal with foreign exchange risk. The whole process is made all the more problematic when currencies are not freely convertible.

Basic Entry Decisions

In this section, we look at three basic decisions that a firm contemplating foreign expansion must make: Which markets to enter, when to enter those markets, and on what scale?

Which Foreign Markets?

There are more than 160 nation-states in the world. They do not all hold the same profit potential for a firm contemplating foreign expansion. Ultimately, the choice between foreign markets must be made on an assessment of their long-run profit potential. This is a function of a large number of factors, many of which we have already considered in earlier chapters. In Chapter 2 we looked at the economic and political factors that influence the potential attractiveness of a foreign market. The attractiveness of a country as a potential market for an international business depends on balancing the benefits, costs, and risks associated with doing business in that country.

Also in Chapter 2, we noted that the long-run economic benefits of doing business in a country are a function of factors such as the size of a market (in terms of demographics), the present wealth (purchasing power) of consumers in that market, and the likely future wealth of consumers. While some markets are very large, when measured by numbers of consumers (e.g., China and India), low living standards may imply limited purchasing power and a relatively small market when measured in economic terms. We also argued that the costs and risks associated with doing business in a foreign country are typically lower in economically advanced and politically stable democratic nations, whereas they are greater in less developed and politically unstable nations.

However, this calculus is complicated by the fact that the potential *long-run* benefits bear little relationship to a nation's current stage of economic development or political stability. Rather, long-run benefits are dependent on likely future economic growth rates. Economic growth appears to be a function of a free market system and a country's capacity for growth (which may be greater in less developed nations). Other things being equal, the benefit, cost, risk trade-off is likely to be most favorable in the case of politically stable developed and developing nations that have free market systems, and where there is not a dramatic upsurge in either inflation rates or private-sector debt. It is likely to be least favorable in politically unstable developing nations that operate with a mixed or command economy or in developing nations where speculative financial bubbles have led to excess borrowing (see Chapter 2 for further details).

By applying the type of reasoning processes alluded to above, and discussed in more detail in Chapter 2, a firm can come up with a ranking of countries in terms of their attractiveness and long-run profit potential. Preference is then given to entering markets that rank highly. In the case of Merrill Lynch, for example, its recent international ventures in the private client business have been focused on the United Kingdom, Canada, and Japan (see the opening case). All three of these countries have a large pool of private savings and exhibit relatively low political and economic risks—so they are attractive to Merrill Lynch. By offering its financial services products, such as mutual funds and investment advice, Merrill Lynch should be able to capture a large enough proportion of the private savings pool in each country to justify its investment in setting up business there. Of the three countries, Japan is probably the most risky given the fragile state of its financial system, which is still suffering from a serious bad debt problem. However, the large size of the Japanese market, and the fact that its government seems to be embarking upon significant reform, explains why Merrill Lynch has been attracted to this nation.

One fact that has not been discussed, is the value that an international business can create in a foreign market. This depends on the suitability of its product offering to that market and the nature of indigenous competition.[2] If the international business can offer a product that has not been widely available in that market and that product satisfies an unmet need, the value of that product to consumers is likely to be much greater than if the international business simply offers the same type of product that indigenous competitors and other foreign entrants are already offering. Greater value translates into an ability to charge higher prices and/or to build unit sales volume more rapidly. On this count Japan is clearly very attractive to Merrill Lynch. Japanese households invest only 3 percent of their savings in individual stocks and mutual funds (much of the balance being in low-yielding bank accounts for government bonds). In comparison, more than 40 percent of US households invest in individual stocks and mutual funds. Japan's own indigenous financial institutions have been very slow to offer stock-based mutual funds to retail investors, and other foreign firms have yet to establish a significant presence in the market. It follows that Merrill Lynch can create potentially enormous value by offering Japanese consumers a range of products that they have previously not been offered and that satisfy unmet needs for greater returns from their savings.

Timing of Entry

Once attractive markets have been identified, it is important to consider the **timing of entry.** We say that entry is early when an international business enters a foreign market before other foreign firms and late when it enters after other international businesses have already established themselves. Several advantages frequently associated with entering a market early are commonly known as **first mover advantages.**[3] One first-mover advantage is the ability to preempt rivals and capture demand by establishing a strong brand name. A second advantage is the ability to build sales volume in that country and ride down the experience curve ahead of rivals. This gives the early entrant a cost advantage over later entrants. This cost advantage may enable the early entrant to cut prices below the (higher) cost structure of later entrants, thereby driving them out of the market. A third advantage is the ability to create switching costs that tie customers into their products or services. Such switching costs make it difficult for later entrants to win business.

Merrill Lynch's experience in Japan illustrates these concepts. By entering the private client market in Japan early, Merrill Lynch hopes to establish a brand name that later entrants will find difficult to match. Also, by entering early with a valuable product offering, the company hopes to build its sales volume rapidly. This will enable it to spread the fixed costs associated with setting up operations in Japan over a large volume, thereby realizing scale economies. These fixed costs include the costs of establishing a network of appropriately equipped branches in Japan. In addition, as Merrill Lynch trains its Japanese employees, their productivity should rise due to learning economies, which again translates into lower costs. Thus, Merrill Lynch should be able to ride down the experience curve, and this will give it a lower cost structure than later entrants. Finally, the firm's business philosophy is to establish close relationships between its financial advisors (i.e., stockbrokers) and private clients. The financial advisors are taught to get to know the needs of their clients and help manage their finances more effectively. Once established, people rarely change these relationships. In other words, due to switching costs they are unlikely to shift their business to later entrants. This effect is likely to be particularly strong in a country such as Japan, where long-term relationships have traditionally been very important in business and social settings. For all these reasons, Merrill Lynch may be able to capture first-mover advantages that will enable it to enjoy a strong competitive position in Japan for years to come.

There can also be disadvantages associated with entering a foreign market before other international businesses (these are often referred to as **first-mover disadvantages**).[4] These disadvantages may give rise to **pioneering costs,** or

timing of entry Entry is early when an international business enters a foreign market before other foreign firms and late when it enters after other international firms are already established.

first-mover advantages Advantages frequently associated with entering a market early.

first-mover disadvantages Disadvantages associated with entering a foreign market before other international businesses.

pioneering costs Costs that an early entrant has to bear that a later entrant can avoid.

costs that an early entrant has to bear that a later entrant can avoid. Pioneering costs arise when the business system in a foreign country is so different from that in a firm's home market that the enterprise has to devote considerable effort, time, and expense to learning the rules of the game. Pioneering costs include the costs of business failure if the firm, due to its ignorance of the foreign environment, makes some major mistakes. There is a certain liability associated with being a foreigner, and this liability is greater for foreign firms that enter a national market early.[5] Recent research seems to confirm that the probability of survival increases if an international business enters a national market *after* several other foreign firms have already done so.[6] The late entrant, it would appear, benefits by observing and learning from the mistakes made by early entrants.

Pioneering costs also include the costs of promoting and establishing a product offering, including the costs of educating customers. These costs can be significant when local consumers are not familiar with the product being promoted. Merrill Lynch will have to bear such pioneering costs in Japan. Most Japanese are not familiar with the type of investment products and services that Merrill Lynch sells, so it will have to invest significant resources in customer education. In contrast, later entrants may get a "free ride" on an early entrant's investments in learning and customer education by watching how the early entrant proceeded in the market, by avoiding costly mistakes made by the early entrant, and by exploiting the market potential created by the early entrant's investments in customer education. For example, KFC introduced the Chinese to American-style fast food, but McDonald's, a later entrant, has capitalized on the market in China.

An early entrant may be at a severe disadvantage, relative to a later entrant, if regulations change in a way that diminishes the value of an early entrant's investments. This is a serious risk in many developing nations where the rules that govern business practices are still evolving. In such circumstances, early entrants can find themselves at a disadvantage if a change in regulations invalidates prior assumptions about the best business model for operating in that country. For an illustration of the potential difficulties and hazards here, consider the experience of the Amway Corporation in China, which is described in the accompanying "Management Focus."

Scale of Entry and Strategic Commitments

The final issue that an international business needs to consider when contemplating market entry is the scale of entry. Entering a market on a large scale involves the commitment of significant resources. Not all firms have the resources necessary to enter on a large scale, and even some large firms prefer to enter foreign markets on a small scale and then build their presence slowly as they become more familiar with the market. The original entry by Merrill Lynch into the private client market in Japan was on a small scale, involving only a handful of branches. In contrast, Merrill's reentry into the Japanese market in 1997 was on a significant scale, as was Amway's entry into China.

The consequences of entering on a significant scale are associated with the value of the resulting strategic commitments.[7] A **strategic commitment** has a long-term impact and is difficult to reverse. Deciding to enter a foreign market on a significant scale is a major strategic commitment. Strategic commitments, such as large-scale market entry, can influence the nature of competition in a market. For example, by entering Japan's private client business on a significant scale, Merrill Lynch signaled its commitment to the market. This will have several effects. On the positive side, it will make it easier for Merrill Lynch to attract clients. The scale of entry gives potential clients reason to believe that Merrill Lynch will remain in the market for the long run. The

Amway is a US-based direct sales company that sells a variety of household and personal products using a grassroots marketing approach. The company signs up individual consumers as "distributors" who then earn a commission on sales of Amway products. Almost anyone can become an Amway distributor by purchasing for a few hundred dollars a "starter kit" that contains an assortment of Amway products and promotional literature and by attending a few meetings for training about the Amway system, products, and sales techniques. The distributors are taught to engage in door-to-door selling and are encouraged to sell to friends, relatives, and acquaintances. In 1997 the company

ety that emphasizes social relations and interpersonal networks.

Amway was determined to be one of the first direct marketers to establish a significant presence in China. Accordingly, it entered the country on a significant scale, quickly surpassing Avon and Mary Kay to become the largest direct marketer in China. By early 1998 Amway seemed to be doing well. The company had signed up 80,000 distributors in 37 cities across mainland China. It had opened a major factory in Guangzhou and had plans to invest $30 million in a second factory in Shanghai. Sales reached $178 million in 1997, an 80 percent increase from the previous year. Then, unexpectedly, on April

of China's governing Communist party, complained that the meetings encouraged "excessive hugging" and references to "God."

Facing the loss of their Chinese investments, the US companies called in US Trade Representative Charlene Barshefsky. After intense pressure, the Chinese government agreed to a partial reversal of the ban. Under the new regulations, issued in July 1998, the ban on direct selling stays, but Amway, Avon, and Mary Kay will be allowed to sell their products through retail outlets. In addition, they can use their sales representatives for service and delivery but not for direct selling. The new regulations also state that only companies with an investment of more

Amway Goes Astray in China

racked up $7 billion in sales using this approach, more than half outside the United States.

Amway entered the Chinese market in 1995, closely behind rival direct marketers Avon and Mary Kay. Several features attracted Amway to China. With a population of 1.2 billion people, the country offered a potentially huge consumer market. Given Amway's emphasis on direct selling, the lack of well-developed retail distribution systems in China seemed to play right into the company's hands. An Amway representative could offer a far broader range of products than could be found at most Chinese retail outlets, and often at a lower price. Plus, the strategy of selling to friends, relatives, and acquaintances made great sense in a soci-

22, 1998, the Chinese government announced a ban on direct selling!

According to the Chinese government, direct selling practices such as those employed by Amway spawned "weird cults, triads, superstitious groups, and hooliganism." The success of Amway and its American kin had encouraged thousands of local imitators, including a number of fraudulent enterprises and fly-by-night operators that sold everything from fake gold to potency pills. The government also objected to the motivational meetings used by Amway and others to reward top sellers and recruit new ones. The official Chinese media compared such gatherings—at which people sang and chanted company slogans—to religious cults. The *People's Daily*, the mouthpiece

than $10 million may establish direct sales agents.

Amway restarted its business in China the day after the regulatory change was announced. However, the three-month shutdown had cost the company millions of dollars in lost sales. More significantly, the ban on direct selling made it impossible for Amway to follow its normal business model in China. Given this, the company might not be able to grow as quickly as planned. An unforeseen change in the regulations governing a critical element of business practice in China has now significantly diminished the value of the company's investment in the country and negated much of its early-mover advantage.[8]

scale of entry may also make other foreign institutions think twice about entering Japan's market because now they would have to compete not only against Japan's indigenous institutions but also against an aggressive and successful US institution. On the negative side, the move may wake up Japan's financial institutions and elicit a vigorous competitive response from them. Also, by committing itself heavily to Japan, Merrill Lynch may have fewer resources available to support expansion in other desirable markets. The commitment to Japan limits the company's strategic flexibility.

As suggested by this example, significant strategic commitments are neither unambiguously good nor bad. Rather, they tend to change the competitive playing field and unleash a number of changes, some of which may be desirable and some of which will not be. It is therefore important for a firm to think through the implications of large-scale entry into a market and act accordingly. Of particular relevance is trying to identify how actual and potential competitors might react to large-scale entry into a market. Also, there is a connection between large-scale entry and first-mover advantages. The large-scale entrant is more likely than the small-scale entrant to be able to capture the first-mover advantages associated with demand preemption, scale economies, and switching costs.

The value of the commitments that flow from large-scale entry into a foreign market must be balanced against the resulting risks and lack of flexibility associated with significant commitments. But strategic inflexibility also has value. A famous example from military history illustrates the value of inflexibility. When Hernán Cortés landed in Mexico, he ordered his men to burn all but one of his ships. Cortés reasoned that by eliminating their only method of retreat, his men had no choice but to fight hard to win against the Aztecs—and ultimately they did.[9]

Balanced against the value and risks of the commitments associated with large-scale entry are the benefits of small-scale entry. Small-scale entry allows a firm to learn about a foreign market while limiting the firm's exposure. Small-scale entry is a way to gather more information about a market before deciding whether to enter on a significant scale and how best to enter. By giving the firm time to collect information, small-scale entry reduces the risks associated with large-scale entry. But the lack of commitment associated with small-scale entry may make it more difficult for the small-scale entrant to build market share and to capture first-mover or early-mover advantages. The risk-averse firm that enters a foreign market on a small scale may limit its potential losses, but it may also limit the chance to capture first-mover advantages.

Summary

There are no "right" decisions here, just decisions that are associated with different levels of risk and reward. Entering a large developing nation such as China or India before most other international businesses in the industry and entering on a large scale will be associated with high levels of risk. The liability of being foreign is increased by the absence of prior foreign entrants whose experience can be a useful guide. But the potential long-term rewards associated with such a strategy are great. The early large-scale entrant into a major developing nation may be able to capture significant first-mover advantages that will bolster its long-term position. In contrast, entering developed nations such as Australia or Canada after other international businesses in the industry and entering on a small scale in order to learn more about those markets will be associated with much lower levels of risk. However, the potential long-term rewards are also likely to be lower because the firm is forgoing the opportunity to capture first-mover advantages and because the lack of commitment to the market signaled by small-scale entry may limit its future growth potential.

Entry Modes

Once a firm has decided to enter a foreign market, the question arises as to the best mode of entry. Firms have six modes to use when entering foreign markets: exporting, turnkey projects, licensing, franchising, establishing joint ventures with a host country firm, and setting up a wholly owned subsidiary in the host country. Each entry mode has advantages and disadvantages. Managers need to consider these carefully when deciding which to use.[10]

Exporting

Many manufacturing firms begin their global expansion as exporters and later switch to another mode for serving a foreign market. We take a close look at the mechanics and processing of exporting later in the next chapter. Here we focus on the advantages and disadvantages of exporting as an entry mode.

ADVANTAGES Exporting has two distinct advantages. First, it avoids the often substantial costs of establishing manufacturing operations in the host country. Second, exporting may help a firm achieve experience curve and location economies (see Chapter 10). By manufacturing the product in a centralized location and exporting it to other national markets, the firm may be able to realize substantial scale economies from its global sales volume. This is how Sony came to dominate the global TV market, how Matsushita came to dominate the VCR market, and how many Japanese auto firms made inroads into the US auto market.

DISADVANTAGES Exporting has a number of drawbacks. First, exporting from the firm's home base may not be appropriate if there are lower-cost locations for manufacturing the product abroad (i.e., if the firm can realize location economies by moving production elsewhere). Thus, particularly for firms pursuing global or transnational strategies, it may be preferable to manufacture in a location where the mix of factor conditions is most favorable for value creation and to export to the rest of the world from that location. This is not so much an argument against exporting as an argument against exporting from the firm's home country. Many US electronics firms have moved some of their manufacturing to the Far East because of the availability of low-cost, highly skilled labor there. They then export from that location to the rest of the world, including the United States.

A second drawback to exporting is that high transport costs can make exporting uneconomical, particularly for bulk products. One way of getting around this is to manufacture bulk products regionally. This strategy enables the firm to realize some economies from large-scale production and at the same time to limit its transport costs. For example, many multinational chemical firms manufacture their products regionally, serving several countries from one facility.

Another drawback to exporting is that tariffs can make it uneconomical, and the threat of tariff barriers by the host country government can make it risky. An implicit threat of the US Congress to impose tariffs on imported Japanese autos led to many Japanese firms decisions to set up manufacturing plants in the United States. As a consequence, by 1990 almost 50 percent of all Japanese cars sold in the United States were manufactured locally—up from 0 percent in 1985.

A fourth drawback to exporting arises when a firm delegates its marketing in each country where it does business to a local agent. (This is common for firms that are just beginning to export.) Foreign agents often carry the products of competing firms and have divided loyalties. In such cases, the foreign agent may not do as good a job as the firm would if it managed its marketing itself. Firms can get around this problem by setting up wholly owned subsidiaries in the country to handle local marketing. By doing this, the firm can exercise tight control over marketing in the country while reaping the cost advantages of manufacturing the product in a single location.

Turnkey Projects

Firms that specialize in the design, construction, and start-up of turnkey plants are common in some industries. In a **turnkey project,** the contractor agrees to handle every detail of the project for a foreign client, including the training of operating personnel. At completion of the contract, the foreign client is handed the "key" to a plant that is ready for full operation—hence the term *turnkey*. This is actually a

(handwritten margin notes:)
(1) lower cost locations for manufacturing abroad
(2) high transport costs
(3) tariffs
(4) mktg delegated to local agent.

turnkey project Project in which contractor handles every detail of the project for a foreign client, including the training of operating personnel, and then hands the foreign client the key to a plant that is ready for operation.

means of exporting process technology to other countries. Turnkey projects are most common in the chemical, pharmaceutical, petroleum refining, and metal refining industries, all of which use complex, expensive production technologies.

ADVANTAGES   The know-how required to assemble and run a technologically complex process, such as refining petroleum or steel, is a valuable asset. Turnkey projects are a way of earning great economic returns from that asset. The strategy is particularly useful in cases where FDI is limited by government regulations. For example, the governments of many oil-rich countries have set out to build their own petroleum refining industries and, as a step toward that goal, have restricted FDI in their oil and refining sectors. Because many of these countries lacked petroleum refining technology, however, they had to gain it by entering into turnkey projects with foreign firms that had the technology. Such deals are often attractive to the selling firm because without them, they would have no way to earn a return on their valuable know-how in that country.

A turnkey strategy can also be less risky than more conventional FDI. In a country with unstable political and economic environments, a longer-term investment might expose the firm to unacceptable political and/or economic risks (e.g., the risk of nationalization or of economic collapse).

DISADVANTAGES   Three main drawbacks are associated with a turnkey strategy. First, the firm that enters into a turnkey deal will have no long-term interest in the foreign country. This can be a disadvantage if that country subsequently proves to be a major market for the output of the process that has been exported. One way around this is to take a minority equity interest in the operation set up by the turnkey project.

Second, the firm that enters into a turnkey project with a foreign enterprise may inadvertently create a competitor. For example, many of the Western firms that sold oil refining technology to firms in Saudi Arabia, Kuwait, and other Gulf states now find themselves competing with these firms in the world oil market. Third, and related to the second point, if the firm's process technology is a source of competitive advantage, then selling this technology through a turnkey project is also selling competitive advantage to potential and/or actual competitors.

Licensing

A **licensing agreement** is an arrangement whereby a licensor grants the rights to intangible property to another entity (the licensee) for a specified period, and in return, the licensor receives a royalty fee from the licensee.[11] Intangible property includes patents, inventions, formulas, processes, designs, copyrights, and trademarks. For example, as described in the accompanying "Management Focus," in order to enter the Japanese market Xerox, the inventor of the photocopier, established a joint venture with Fuji Photo that is known as Fuji-Xerox. Xerox then licensed its xerographic know-how to Fuji-Xerox. In return, Fuji-Xerox paid Xerox a royalty fee equal to 5 percent of the net sales revenue that Fuji-Xerox earned from the sales of photocopiers based on Xerox's patented

Smirnoff: A License to Fail

Smirnoff used licensing to develop overseas. This was a tremendously successful strategy in Anglo countries where Smirnoff managers from the United States had some understanding of local market practices. However, in Japan Smirnoff ran into a problem: Its Japanese licensee was a major producer of alcoholic beverages that used the license to lock up the market while it developed its own white spirits brands. The US company could only sit by and watch because the Japanese managers always met their minimal contractual obligations for the Smirnoff brand.

know-how. In the Fuji-Xerox case, the license was originally granted for 10 years, and it has been renegotiated and extended several times since. The licensing agreement between Xerox and Fuji-Xerox also limited Fuji-Xerox's direct sales to the Asian Pacific region (although Fuji-Xerox does supply Xerox with photocopiers that are sold in North America under the Xerox label).[12]

ADVANTAGES In the typical international licensing deal, the licensee puts up most of the capital necessary to get the overseas operation going. Thus, a primary advantage of licensing is that the firm does not have to bear the development costs and risks associated with opening a foreign market. Licensing is a very attractive option for firms lacking the capital to develop operations overseas. In addition, licensing can be attractive when a firm is unwilling to commit substantial financial resources to an unfamiliar or politically volatile foreign market. Licensing is also often used when a firm wishes to participate in a foreign market but is prohibited from doing so by barriers to investment. This was one of the original reasons for the formation of the Fuji-Xerox joint venture (see the "Management Focus" for details). Xerox wanted to participate in the Japanese market but was prohibited from setting up a wholly owned subsidiary by the Japanese government. So Xerox set up the joint venture with Fuji and then licensed its know-how to the joint venture. Finally, licensing is frequently used when a firm possesses some intangible property that might have business applications, but when it does not want to develop those applications itself. For example, Bell Laboratories at AT&T invented the transistor circuit in the 1950s, but AT&T decided it did not want to produce transistors, so it licensed the technology to a number of other companies, such as Texas Instruments. Similarly, Coca-Cola has licensed its famous trademark to clothing manufacturers, which have incorporated the design into their clothing.

DISADVANTAGES Licensing has three serious drawbacks. First, it does not give a firm the tight control over manufacturing, marketing, and strategy that is required for realizing experience curve and location economies (as global and transnational firms must do; see Chapter 10). Licensing typically involves each licensee setting up its own production operations. This limits the firm's ability to realize experience curve and location economies by producing its product in a centralized location. Thus, when these economies are important, licensing may not be the best way to expand overseas.

Second, competing in a global market may require a firm to coordinate strategic moves across countries by using profits earned in one country to support competitive attacks in another (again, see Chapter 10). Licensing severely limits a firm's ability to do this. A licensee is unlikely to allow a multinational firm to use its profits (beyond those due in the form of royalty payments) to support a different licensee operating in another country.

A third problem with licensing is one that we first encountered in Chapter 6 when we reviewed the economic theory of FDI. This is the risk associated with licensing technological know-how to foreign companies. Technological know-how constitutes the basis of many multinational firms' competitive advantage. Most firms wish to maintain control over how their know-how is used, and a firm can quickly lose control over its technology by licensing it. Many firms have made the mistake of thinking they could maintain control over their know-how within the framework of a licensing agreement. RCA Corporation, for example, once licensed its color TV technology to a number of Japanese firms including Matsushita and Sony. The Japanese firms quickly assimilated the technology, improved it, and used it to enter the US market. Now the Japanese firms have a bigger share of the US market than the RCA brand. Similar concerns surfaced over the 1989 decision by Congress to allow

Fuji-Xerox

Fuji-Xerox is one of the most enduring and reportedly successful alliances between two companies from different countries. Established in 1962, Fuji-Xerox is structured as a 50/50 joint venture between the Xerox Group, the US maker of photocopiers, and Fuji Photo Film, Japan's largest manufacturer of film products. With sales of close to $10 billion, Fuji-Xerox provides Xerox with over 20 percent of its worldwide revenues.

A prime motivation for the establishment of the joint venture was that in the early 1960s the Japanese government did not allow foreign companies to set up wholly owned subsidiaries in Japan. The joint venture was conceived as a marketing organization to sell xerographic products that would be manufactured by Fuji Photo under license from Xerox. However, when the Japanese government refused to approve the establishment of a joint venture intended solely as a sales company, the joint venture agreement was revised to give Fuji-Xerox manufacturing rights.

Management of the venture was placed in the hands of Japanese managers who were given considerable autonomy to develop their own operations and strategy, subject to oversight by a board of directors that contained representatives from both Xerox and Fuji Photo.

Initially, Fuji-Xerox followed the lead of Xerox in manufacturing and selling the large, high-volume copiers developed by Xerox in the United States. These machines were sold at a premium price to the high end of the market. However, Fuji-Xerox noticed that new competitors, such as Canon and Ricoh, were making significant inroads in the Japanese market by building small, low-volume copiers and focusing on the mid- and low-priced segments of the market. This led to Fuji-Xerox's development of its first "homegrown" copier, the FX2200, which at the time was billed as the world's smallest copier. Introduced in 1973, the FX2200 hit the market just in time to allow Fuji-Xerox to hold its own against a blizzard of new competition in Japan that fol-

lowed the expiration of many of Xerox's key patents.

About the same time, Fuji-Xerox also embarked on a total quality control (TQC) program to speed up the development of new products, reduce waste, improve quality, and lower manufacturing costs. The first fruit of this program was the FX3500. Introduced in 1977, the FX3500 by 1979 had broken the Japanese record for the number of copiers sold in one year. Partly because of the success of the FX3500, in 1980 the company won Japan's prestigious Deming Prize. The success of the FX3500 was all the more notable because at the same time Xerox was canceling a series of programs to develop low- to mid-level copiers and reaffirming its commitment to serving the high end of the market. Because of these cancellations, Tony Kobayashi, the CEO of Fuji-Xerox, was initially told to stop work on the FX3500. He refused, arguing that the FX3500 was crucial for the survival of Fuji-Xerox in the Japanese market. Given the arm's-length relationship between

Japanese firms to produce the advanced FSX fighter plane under license from McDonnell Douglas. Critics fear the Japanese will use the FSX technology to support the development of a commercial airline industry that will compete with Boeing in the global marketplace.

There are ways of reducing these risks. One way is by entering into a cross-licensing agreement with a foreign firm. Under a **cross-licensing agreement**, a firm might license some valuable intangible property to a foreign partner, but in addition to a royalty payment, the firm might also request that the foreign partner license some of its valuable know-how to the firm. Such agreements are designed to reduce the risks associated with licensing technological know-how because the licensee realizes that if it violates the spirit of a licensing contract (by using the knowledge obtained to compete directly with the licensor), the licensor can do the same to it. Cross-licensing agreements enable firms to hold each other hostage, which reduces the probability that they will behave opportunistically toward each other.[13] Such cross-licensing agreements are increasingly common in high-technology industries. For example, the US biotechnology firm Amgen has licensed one of its key drugs, Nuprogene, to Kirin, the Japanese pharmaceutical company. The license gives

cross-licensing agreement Arrangement whereby a company grants the rights to intangible property to another firm for a specified time period in exchange for royalties and a license from the foreign partners for some of its technological know-how.

Xerox and Fuji-Xerox, Kobayashi was able to prevail.

By the early 1980s Fuji-Xerox was number two in the Japanese copier market with between 20 and 22 percent of the market, just behind market leader Canon. In contrast, Xerox was running into all sorts of problems in the United States. As Xerox's patents had expired, a number of companies, including Canon, Ricoh, Kodak, and IBM, began to take market share from Xerox. Canon and Ricoh were particularly successful by focusing on that segment of the market that Xerox had ignored—the low end. As a result, Xerox's market share in the Americas fell from 35 percent in 1975 to 25 percent in 1980, and its profitability slumped.

In an attempt to recapture share, Xerox began to sell Fuji-Xerox's FX3500 copier in the United States. Not only did the FX3500 help Xerox to halt the rapid decline in its share of the US market, but it also opened Xerox's eyes to the benefits of Fuji-Xerox's TQC program. Xerox found that the reject rate for Fuji-Xerox parts was only a fraction of the reject rate for American-produced parts. Visits to Fuji-Xerox revealed another important

truth: Quality in manufacturing does not increase real costs; it reduces costs by reducing defective products and service costs.

These developments forced Xerox to rethink the way it did business. From being the main provider of products, technology, and management know-how to Fuji-Xerox, Xerox in the 1980s became the willing pupil of Fuji-Xerox. In 1983 Xerox introduced its leadership through quality program, which was based upon Fuji-Xerox's TQC program. As part of this, Xerox launched a quality training effort with its suppliers and was rewarded when the number of defective parts from suppliers fell from 25,000 per million in 1983 to 300 per million by 1992.

In 1985 and 1986 Xerox began to focus on new product development. One goal was to design products that, while customized to market conditions in different countries, contained a large number of globally standardized parts. Another goal was to reduce the time it took to design new products and bring them to market. To achieve these goals Xerox set up joint product development teams with Fuji-Xerox. Each team managed the design, component

sources, manufacturing, distribution, and follow-up customer service on a worldwide basis. The use of design teams cut as much as one year from the overall product development cycle and saved millions of dollars.

One consequence of the new approach to product development was the 5100 copier. This was the first product designed jointly by Xerox and Fuji-Xerox for the worldwide market. The 5100 is manufactured in US plants. It was launched in Japan in November 1990 and the US the following February. The 5100's global design reportedly reduced the overall time to market and saved the company more than $10 million in development costs.

As a result of the skills and products acquired from Fuji-Xerox, Xerox's position improved markedly during the 1980s. Because of its improved quality, lower costs, shorter product development time, and more appealing product range, Xerox was able to gain market share back from its competitors and to boost its profits and revenues. Xerox's share of the US copier market increased from a low of 10 percent in 1985 to 18 percent in 1991.[14]

Kirin the right to sell Nuprogene in Japan. In return, Amgen receives a royalty payment and the right to sell some of Kirin's products in the United States.

Another way of reducing the risk associated with licensing is to follow the Fuji-Xerox model and link an agreement to license know-how with the formation of a joint venture in which the licensor and licensee take an important equity stake. Such an approach aligns the interests of licensor and licensee because both have a stake in ensuring that the venture is successful. Thus, the risk that Fuji Photo might appropriate Xerox's technological know-how, and then compete directly against Xerox in the global photocopier market, was substantially reduced by the establishment of a joint venture in which both Xerox and Fuji Photo had an important stake.

Franchising

Franchising is similar to licensing, although franchising tends to involve longer-term commitments than licensing. **Franchising** is basically a specialized form of licensing in which the franchiser not only sells intangible property to the franchisee (normally a trademark), but also insists that the franchisee agree to abide by strict rules

franchising Specialized form of licensing in which the franchisor sells intangible property to the franchisee and insists that the franchisee agree to follow strict rules in operating the business.

as to how it does business. The franchiser will also often assist the franchisee to run the business on an ongoing basis. As with licensing, the franchiser typically receives a royalty payment, which amounts to some percentage of the franchisee's revenues. While licensing is pursued primarily by manufacturing firms, franchising is employed primarily by service firms.[15] McDonald's has grown by using a franchising strategy. McDonald's strict rules as to how franchisees should operate a restaurant extend to control over the menu, cooking methods, staffing policies, and the design and location of a restaurant. McDonald's also organizes the supply chain for its franchisees and provides management training and financial assistance.[16]

ADVANTAGES   The advantages of franchising as an entry mode are very similar to those of licensing. The firm is relieved of many of the costs and risks of opening a foreign market on its own. Instead, the franchisee typically assumes those costs and risks. This creates a good incentive for the franchisee to build a profitable operation as quickly as possible. Thus, using a franchising strategy, a service firm can build a global presence quickly and at a relatively low cost and risk, as McDonald's has.

DISADVANTAGES   The disadvantages are less pronounced than in licensing. Because franchising is often used by service companies, there is no reason to consider the need for coordination of manufacturing to achieve experience curve and location economies. But franchising may inhibit the firm's ability to take profits out of one country to support competitive attacks in another.

A more significant disadvantage of franchising is quality control. The foundation of franchising arrangements is that the firm's brand name conveys a message to consumers about the quality of the firm's product. Thus, a business traveler checking in at a Hilton International hotel in Hong Kong can reasonably expect the same quality

A business traveler may have certain expectations about a hotel, and others in that hotel chain, based on the impression he or she gained from visits to other locations. Is this always valid? Have you ever made reservations with a chain hotel in one city based on your favorable experiences with that chain in another city, only to find one inferior to the other you had visited? This is often a concern of business travelers who are rewarded with "points" or other perks for staying with the same hotel in different locations.
Stone/Mike Blank

of room, food, and service that she would receive in New York. The Hilton name is supposed to guarantee consistent product quality. But foreign franchisees may not be as concerned about quality as they are supposed to be, and the result of poor quality can extend beyond lost sales in a particular foreign market to a decline in the firm's worldwide reputation. If the business traveler has a bad experience at the Hilton in Hong Kong, she may never go to another Hilton hotel and may urge her colleagues to do likewise. The geographical distance of the firm from its foreign franchisees can make poor quality difficult for the franchiser to detect. In addition, the sheer numbers of franchisees—in the case of McDonald's, tens of thousands—can make quality control difficult. Due to these factors, quality problems may persist.

One way around this disadvantage is to set up a subsidiary in each country or region in which the firm expands. The subsidiary might be wholly owned by the company or a joint venture with a foreign company. The subsidiary assumes the rights and obligations to establish franchises throughout the country or region. McDonald's, for example, establishes a master franchisee in many countries. Typically, this master franchisee is a joint venture between McDonald's and a local firm. The combination of proximity and the smaller number of franchises to oversee reduces the quality control challenge. In addition, because the subsidiary (or master franchisee) is at least partly owned by the firm, the firm can place its own managers in the subsidiary to help ensure that it is doing a good job monitoring the franchises in that country or region. This organizational arrangement has proven very satisfactory, and in addition to McDonald's, it has been used by Kentucky Fried Chicken, Hilton International, and others to expand their international operations.

Joint Ventures

A **joint venture** entails the establishment of a firm that is jointly owned by two or more otherwise independent firms. Fuji-Xerox, for example, was set up as a joint venture between Xerox and Fuji Photo (see the "Management Focus"). Establishing a joint venture with a foreign firm has long been a popular mode for entering a new market. The most typical joint venture is a 50/50 venture, in which there are two parties, each of which holds a 50 percent ownership stake (as is the case with the Fuji-Xerox joint venture) and contributes a team of managers to share operating control. Some firms, however, have sought joint ventures in which they have a majority share and thus tighter control.[17]

joint venture Establishment of a firm that is jointly owned by two or more otherwise independent firms.

ADVANTAGES   Joint ventures have a number of advantages. First, a firm can benefit from a local partner's knowledge of the host country's competitive conditions, culture, language, political systems, and business systems. Thus, for many US firms, joint ventures have involved the US company providing technological know-how and products and the local partner providing the marketing expertise and the local knowledge necessary for competing in that country. This was the case with the Fuji-Xerox joint venture. Second, when the development costs and/or risks of opening a foreign market are high, a firm might gain by sharing these costs and/or risks with a local partner. Third, in many countries, political considerations make joint ventures the only feasible entry mode. Again, this was a consideration in the establishment of the Fuji-Xerox venture. Research suggests that joint ventures with local partners face a low risk of being subject to nationalization or other forms of government interference.[18] Local equity partners, who may have some influence on host government policy, have a vested interest in speaking out against nationalization or government interference.

DISADVANTAGES   Despite these advantages, there are two major disadvantages with joint ventures. First, just as with licensing, a firm that enters into a joint venture risks giving control of its technology to its partner. The joint venture between

Boeing and a consortium of Japanese firms to build the 767 airliner raised fears that Boeing was unwittingly giving away its commercial airline technology to the Japanese. However, joint venture agreements can be constructed to minimize this risk. One option is to hold majority ownership in the venture. This allows the dominant partner to exercise greater control over its technology, but it can be difficult to find a foreign partner that is willing to settle for minority ownership.

A second disadvantage is that a joint venture does not give a firm the tight control over subsidiaries that it might need to realize experience curve or location economies. Nor does it give a firm the tight control over a foreign subsidiary that it might need for engaging in coordinated global attacks against its rivals. Consider the entry of Texas Instruments (TI) into the Japanese semiconductor market. When TI established semiconductor facilities in Japan, it did so for the dual purpose of checking Japanese manufacturers' market share and limiting their cash available for invading TI's global market. TI was engaging in global strategic coordination. To implement this strategy, TI's subsidiary in Japan had to be prepared to take instructions from corporate headquarters regarding competitive strategy. The strategy also required the Japanese subsidiary to run at a loss if necessary. Few if any potential joint venture partners would have been willing to accept such conditions because it would have necessitated a willingness to accept a negative return on their investment. Thus, to implement this strategy, TI set up a wholly owned subsidiary in Japan.

A third disadvantage with joint ventures is that the shared ownership arrangement can lead to conflicts and battles for control between the investing firms if their goals and objectives change, or if they take different views as to what the venture's strategy should be. This has apparently not been a problem with the Fuji-Xerox joint venture. According to Tony Kobayashi, the CEO of Fuji-Xerox, a primary reason for this is that both Xerox and Fuji Photo adopted a very arm's-length relationship with Fuji-Xerox, giving the venture's managers considerable freedom to determine their own strategy.[19] However, much research indicates that conflicts of interest over strategy and goals often arise in joint ventures, that these conflicts tend to be greater when the venture is between firms of different nationalities, and that they often end in the dissolution of the venture.[20] Such conflicts tend to be triggered by shifts in the relative bargaining power of venture partners.

For example, it has been argued that in the case of ventures between a foreign firm and a local firm, as the foreign partner's knowledge about local market conditions increases over time, it comes to depend less on the expertise of the local partner. This increases the bargaining power of the foreign partner and ultimately leads to conflicts over control of the venture's strategy and goals.[21]

Wholly Owned Subsidiaries

wholly owned subsidiary
Company in which the parent firm owns 100 percent of the stock.

In a **wholly owned subsidiary,** the firm owns 100 percent of the stock. Establishing a wholly owned subsidiary in a foreign market can be done two ways. The firm can either set up a new operation in that country or it can acquire an established firm and use that firm to promote its products in the country's market.

ADVANTAGES   There are three clear advantages of wholly owned subsidiaries. First, when a firm's competitive advantage is based on technological competence, a wholly owned subsidiary will often be the preferred entry mode because it reduces the risk of losing control over that competence. Many high-tech firms prefer this entry mode for overseas expansion (e.g., firms in the semiconductor, electronics, and pharmaceutical industries). Second, a wholly owned subsidiary gives a firm the kind of tight control over operations that is necessary for engaging in global strategic coordination (i.e., using profits from one country to support competitive attacks in another). Third, a wholly owned subsidiary may be required if a firm is trying to realize location and experience curve economies (as firms pursuing global and transnational strategies try to do). As we saw in Chapter 10, when cost pressures are intense, it may benefit a firm to configure its value chain to maximize the value added at each stage. Thus, a national subsidiary may specialize in manufacturing only part of the product line or certain components of the end product, exchanging parts and products with other subsidiaries in the firm's global system. Establishing such a global production system requires a high degree of control over the operations of each affiliate. The various operations must be prepared to accept centrally determined decisions as to how they will produce, how much they will produce, and how their output will be priced for transfer to the next operation. Because licensees or joint venture partners are unlikely to accept such a subservient role, establishment of wholly owned subsidiaries may be necessary.

DISADVANTAGES   On the other hand, establishing a wholly owned subsidiary is generally the most costly method of serving a foreign market. Firms doing this must bear the full costs and risks of setting up overseas operations. The risks associated with learning to do business in a new culture are less if the firm acquires an established host country enterprise. However, acquisitions raise additional problems, including those associated with trying to marry divergent corporate cultures. These problems may more than offset any benefits derived by acquiring an established operation.[22]

Selecting an Entry Mode

As the preceding discussion demonstrated, there are advantages and disadvantages associated with all the entry modes; they are summarized in Table 11.1. Trade-offs are inevitable when selecting an entry mode. For example, when considering entry into an unfamiliar country with a track record for nationalizing foreign-owned enterprises, a firm might favor a joint venture with a local enterprise. Its rationale might be that the local partner will help it establish operations in an unfamiliar environment and will speak out against nationalization should the possibility arise. However, if the firm's core competence is based on proprietary technology, entering a joint venture might risk losing control of that technology to the joint venture partner, in which case the strategy may seem unattractive. Despite the existence of such trade-offs, it is possible to generalize about the optimal choice of entry mode. That is what we do in this section.[23]

Core Competencies and Entry Mode

We saw in Chapter 10 that firms often expand internationally to earn greater returns from their core competencies—transferring the skills and products derived from their core competencies to foreign markets where indigenous competitors lack those skills. We say that such firms are pursuing an international strategy. The optimal entry mode for these firms depends on the nature of their core competencies. A distinction can be drawn between firms whose core competency is in technological know-how and those whose core competency is in management know-how.

Table 11.1

Advantages and Disadvantages of Entry Modes

Entry Mode	Advantages	Disadvantages
Exporting	Ability to realize location and experience curve economies	High transport costs Trade barriers Problems with local marketing agents
Turnkey contracts	Ability to earn returns from process technology skills in countries where FDI is restricted	Creating efficient competitors Lack of long-term market presence
Licensing	Low development costs and risks	Lack of control over technology Inability to realize location and experience curve economies Inability to engage in global strategic coordination
Franchising	Low development costs and risks	Lack of control over quality Inability to engage in global strategic coordination
Joint ventures	Access to local partner's knowledge Sharing developing costs and risks Politically acceptable	Lack of control over technology Inability to engage in global strategic coordination Inability to realize location and experience economies
Wholly owned subsidiaries	Protection of technology Ability to engage in global strategic coordination Ability to realize location and experience economies	High costs and risks

TECHNOLOGICAL KNOW-HOW   If a firm's competitive advantage (its core competence) is based on control over proprietary technological know-how, licensing and joint venture arrangements should be avoided if possible to minimize the risk of losing control over that technology. Thus, if a high-tech firm sets up operations in a foreign country to profit from a core competency in technological know-how, it will probably do so through a wholly owned subsidiary.

This rule should not be viewed as hard and fast, however. One exception is when a licensing or joint venture arrangement can be structured so as to reduce the risks of a firm's technological know-how being expropriated by licensees or joint venture partners. Another exception exists when a firm perceives its technological advantage to be only transitory—when it expects rapid imitation of its core technology by competitors. Then the firm might want to license its technology as rapidly as possible to foreign firms to gain global acceptance for its technology before the imitation occurs.[24] Such a strategy has some advantages. By licensing its technology to competitors, the firm may deter them from developing their own, possibly superior, technology. Further, by licensing its technology, the firm may be able to establish its technology as the dominant design in the industry (as Matsushita did with its VHS format for VCRs). This may ensure a steady stream of royalty payments. However, the attractions of licensing are probably outweighed by the risks of losing control over technology, and thus licensing should be avoided.

MANAGEMENT KNOW-HOW The competitive advantage of many service firms is based on management know-how (e.g., McDonald's). For such firms, the risk of losing control over their management skills to franchisees or joint venture partners is not that great. These firms' valuable asset is their brand name, and brand names are generally protected by international laws pertaining to trademarks. Many of the issues arising in the case of technological know-how are of less concern here. As a result, many service firms favor a combination of franchising and subsidiaries to control the franchises within countries or regions. The subsidiaries may be wholly owned or joint ventures, but most service firms have found that joint ventures with local partners work best for the controlling subsidiaries. A joint venture is often politically more acceptable and brings a degree of local knowledge to the subsidiary.

Pressures for Cost Reductions and Entry Mode

The greater the pressures for cost reductions are, the more likely a firm will want to pursue some combination of exporting and wholly owned subsidiaries. By manufacturing in those locations where factor conditions are optimal and then exporting to the rest of the world, a firm may be able to realize substantial location and experience curve economies. The firm might then want to export the finished product to marketing subsidiaries based in various countries. These subsidiaries will typically be wholly owned and have the responsibility for overseeing distribution in their countries. Setting up wholly owned marketing subsidiaries is preferable to joint venture arrangements and to using foreign marketing agents because it gives the firm the tight control over marketing that might be required for coordinating a globally dispersed value chain. It also gives the firm the ability to use the profits generated in one market to improve its competitive position in another market. Firms pursuing global or transnational strategies tend to prefer establishing wholly owned subsidiaries.

The Promise and Pitfalls of Exporting

The great promise of exporting is the huge revenue and profit opportunities to be found in foreign markets. Studies have shown that while many large firms tend to be *proactive* about seeking opportunities for profitable exporting, systematically scanning foreign markets to find opportunities for leveraging their technology, products, and marketing skills, many medium-sized and small firms are very *reactive*.[25] Typically, such reactive firms do not even consider exporting until their domestic market is saturated and the emergence of excess productive capacity at home forces them to look for growth opportunities in foreign markets. Also, many small and medium-sized firms tend to wait for the world to come to them, rather than going out into the world to seek opportunities. Even when the world does come to them, they may not respond.

An example is MMO Music Group, which makes sing-along tapes for karaoke machines. Foreign sales accounted for about 15 percent of MMO's revenues of $8 million in the mid-1990s, but the firm's CEO admits that this figure would probably have been much higher had he paid attention to building international sales during the 1980s and early 1990s. Unanswered faxes and phone messages from Asia and Europe piled up while he was trying to manage the burgeoning domestic side of the business. By the time MMO turned its attention to foreign markets, other competitors had stepped in and MMO found it tough going to build export volume.[26]

MMO's experience is common, and it suggests a need for firms to become more proactive about seeking out export opportunities. One reason more firms are not proactive, however, is that they are unfamiliar with foreign market opportunities; they simply do not know how big the opportunities are, or where they might be. Simple ignorance of the potential opportunities is a huge barrier to exporting.[27] Many would-be exporters are often intimidated by the complexities and mechanics of exporting to countries where business practices, language, culture, legal systems, and currency are all different from their home market. This combination of unfamiliarity and intimidation helps explain why less than 2 percent of US firms are exporters, according to the Small Business Administration.[28]

To make matters worse, many neophyte exporters have run into significant problems when first trying to do business abroad and this has soured them on future exporting ventures. Common pitfalls include poor market analysis, a poor understanding of competitive conditions in the foreign market, a failure to customize the product offering to the needs of foreign customers, a lack of an effective distribution program, and a poorly executed promotional campaign in the foreign market.[29] Neophyte exporters also tend to underestimate the time and expertise needed to cultivate business in foreign countries.[30] Few realize the amount of management resources that have to be dedicated to this activity. Many foreign customers require face-to-face negotiations on their home turf. An exporter may have to spend months learning about a country's trade regulations, business practices, and more before a deal can be closed.

Exporters also often face voluminous paperwork, complex formalities, and many potential delays and errors. According to a United Nations report on trade and development, a typical international trade transaction may involve 30 parties, 60 original documents, and 360 document copies, all of which have to be checked, transmitted, reentered into various information systems, processed, and filed. The United Nations has calculated that the time involved in preparing documentation, along with the costs of common errors in paperwork, often amounts to 10 percent of the final value of goods exported.[31]

Improving Export Performance

Inexperienced exporters can gain information about foreign market opportunities and avoid some common pitfalls that tend to discourage and frustrate neophyte exporters. In this section we look at information sources that exporters can use to increase their knowledge of foreign market opportunities, we consider the pros and cons of utilizing export management companies (EMCs) to assist in the export process, and we review various exporting strategies that can be adopted to increase the probability of successful exporting. We begin with a look at how several nations try to assist domestic firms in the export process.

Government Information Sources

Most national governments maintain departments that can help firms establish exporting opportunities. In the United States, the most comprehensive source of information is the US Department of Commerce and its district offices all over the country. Within that department are two organizations dedicated to providing businesses with intelligence and assistance for attacking foreign markets: the International Trade Administration and the United States and Foreign Commercial Service Agency. Similar agencies can be found in many other countries.

These agencies provide the potential exporter with a "best prospects" list, which gives the names and addresses of potential distributors in foreign markets along with businesses they are in, the products they handle, and their contact person. In addition, the Department of Commerce has assembled a "comparison shopping service" for 14 countries that are major markets for US exports. For a small fee, a firm can receive a customized market research survey on a product of its choice. This survey provides information on marketability, the competition, comparative prices, distribution channels, and names of potential sales representatives. Each study is conducted on-site by an officer of the US Department of Commerce.

The Department of Commerce also organizes trade events that help potential exporters make foreign contacts and explore export opportunities. The department organizes exhibitions at international trade fairs, which are held regularly in major cities worldwide. The department also has a matchmaker program, in which department representatives accompany groups of US businesspeople abroad to meet with qualified agents, distributors, and customers.

In addition to the Department of Commerce, nearly every state and many large cities maintain active trade commissions whose purpose is to promote exports. Most of these provide business counseling services, information-gathering service, technical assistance, and financing service. Unfortunately, some have fallen victim to budget cuts or to turf battles for political and financial support with other export agencies.

A number of private organizations are also beginning to gear up to provide more assistance to would-be exporters. Commercial banks and major accounting firms are more willing to assist small firms in starting export operations than they were a decade ago. In addition, large multinationals that have been successful in the global arena are typically willing to discuss opportunities overseas with the owners or managers of small firms.[32]

Utilizing Export Management Companies

One way for first-time exporters to identify the opportunities associated with exporting and to avoid many of the associated pitfalls is to hire an **export management company** (EMC). EMCs are export specialists who act as the export marketing department or international department for their client firms. EMCs normally accept two types of export assignments. In one they start exporting operations for a firm, with the understanding that the firm will take over operations after they are established. In another, start-up services are performed with the understanding that the EMC will have continuing responsibility for selling the firm's products. Many EMCs specialize in serving firms in particular industries and in particular areas of the world. Thus, one EMC may specialize in selling agricultural products in the Asian market, while another may focus on exporting electronics products to Eastern Europe. One drawback of overrelying on EMCs is that the company fails to develop its own exporting capabilities in-house.

In theory, the advantage of EMCs is that they are experienced specialists who can help the neophyte exporter identify opportunities and avoid common pitfalls. A good EMC will have a network of contacts in potential markets, will have multilingual employees, will have a good knowledge of different business mores, and will be conversant with the ins and outs of the exporting process and with local business regulations. However, studies have revealed a large variation in the quality of EMC.[33] While some perform their functions very well, others appear to add little value to the exporting company. Therefore, it is important for an exporter to review a number of EMCs and check references from an EMC's past clients before deciding.

export management company Export specialist that acts as the export marketing department or international department for client firms.

Chapter 11 Entering Foreign Markets

Established in 1903 and based in Evansville, Indiana, Red Spot Paint & Vanish is in many ways typical of the companies that can be found in the small towns of America's heartland. The closely held company, whose CEO, Charles Storms, is the great-grandson of the founder, has 500 employees and annual sales of close to $90 million. The company's main product is paint for plastic components used in the automobile industry. Red Spot products are seen on automobile bumpers, wheel covers, grilles, headlamps, instrument

award in the early 1960s. To further its international business, in the late 1980s Red Spot hired a Central Michigan University professor, Bryan Williams. Williams, who was hired because of his language skills (he speaks German, Japanese, and some Chinese), was the first employee at Red Spot whose exclusive focus was international marketing and sales. The first problem Williams faced was the lack of staff skilled in the business of exporting. He found that it was difficult to build an international business without in-house expert-

A second problem that Williams encountered was the clash between the quarter-to-quarter mentality that frequently pervades management practice in the United States and the long-term perspective that is often necessary to build a successful international business. Williams has found that building long-term personal relationships with potential foreign customers is often the key to getting business. When foreign customers visit Evansville, Williams often invites them home for dinner. His young children even started

Red Spot Paint & Varnish

panels, door inserts, radio buttons, and other components. Unlike many other companies of a similar size and location, however, Red Spot has a thriving international business. International sales (which include exports and local production by licensees) now account for between 15 percent and 25 percent of revenue and Red Spot does business in about 15 countries.

Red Spot has long had international sales and won an export

ise in the basic mechanics of exporting. According to Williams, Red Spot needed people who understood the nuts and bolts of exporting—letters of credit, payment terms, bills of lading, and so on. As might be expected for a business based in the heartland of America, there was not a ready supply of such individuals in the vicinity. It took Williams several years to solve this problem. Now Red Spot has a full-time staff of two who have been trained in the principles of exporting and international operations.

calling one visitor from Hong Kong "uncle." Even with such efforts, however, the business may not come quickly. Meeting with potential foreign customers yields no direct business 90 percent of the time, although Williams points out it often yields benefits in terms of competitive information and relationship building. He has found that perseverance pays. For example, Williams and Storms called on a major German automobile parts manufacturer for seven years before finally landing some business from the company.[34]

Exporting Strategy

In addition to using EMCs, a firm can reduce the risks associated with exporting if it is careful about its choice of exporting strategy. A few guidelines can help firms improve their odds of success. For example, one successful exporter, Red Spot Paint & Varnish, emphasizes the importance of cultivating personal relationships when trying to build an export business (see the accompanying "Management Focus"). The probability of exporting successfully can be increased dramatically by taking a handful of simple strategic steps. First, particularly for the neophyte exporter, it helps to hire an EMC, or at least an experienced export consultant, to help with the identification of opportunities and navigate through the paperwork and regulations involved in exporting. Second, it often makes sense to initially focus on one or a handful of markets. Learn about what is required to succeed in those markets before moving on to other markets. The firm that enters many markets at once runs the risk of spreading its limited management resources too thinly. The result may be a failure to become established in any market. Third, it may be best to enter a foreign market on a fairly small scale to reduce the costs of any subsequent failure. Entering on a small scale gives the firm the time and opportunity to learn about the foreign country before making significant capital commitments. Fourth, the exporter needs to recognize the time and managerial commitment involved in building export sales and should hire additional personnel to oversee this activity, lest the existing management be stretched too thin. Fifth, in many countries it is important to devote a lot of attention to building strong and enduring relationships with local distributors and/or customers (see the "Management focus" on Red Spot Paint for an example). Sixth, it is important to hire local personnel to help the firm establish itself in a foreign market. Local people are likely to have a much greater sense of how to do business in a given country than a manager from an exporting firm that has previously never set foot in that country.

Finally, the exporter should keep the option of local production in mind. Once exports build up to a sufficient volume to justify cost-efficient local production, the exporting firm should consider establishing production facilities in the foreign market. Such localization fosters good relations with the foreign country and can lead to greater market acceptance. Exporting is often not an end in itself, but merely a step on the road toward the establishment of foreign production.

Export and Import Financing

Mechanisms for financing exports and imports have evolved over the centuries in response to a problem that can be particularly acute in international trade: the lack of trust that exists when one must put faith in a stranger. In this section we examine the financial devices that have evolved to cope with this problem in the context of international trade: the letter of credit, the draft (or bill of exchange), and the bill of lading. Then we will trace the 14 steps of a typical export–import transaction.

Lack of Trust

Firms engaged in international trade face the problem of having to trust someone they may have never seen, who lives in a different country, who speaks a different language, who abides by (or does not abide by) a different legal system, and who could be very difficult to track down if he or she defaults on an obligation. Consider, for example, a US firm exporting to a distributor in France. The US businessman might be concerned that if he ships the products to France before he receives payment for them from the French businesswoman, she might take delivery of the products and not pay him. Conversely, the French importer might worry that if she pays for the products before they are shipped, the US firm might keep the money and never ship the products—or might ship defective products. Neither party to the exchange completely trusts the other. This lack of trust is exacerbated by the distance between the two parties—in space, language, and culture—and by the problems of using an underdeveloped international legal system to enforce contractual obligations.

Due to the (quite reasonable) lack of trust between the two parties, each has its own preferences as to how it would like the transaction to be configured. To make sure he is paid, the manager of the US firm would prefer the French distributor to pay for the products before he ships them (see Figure 11.1). Alternatively, to ensure she receives the products, the French distributor would prefer not to pay for them until they arrive (see Figure 11.2). Thus, each party has a different set of preferences. Unless there is some way of establishing trust between the parties, the transaction might never take place.

The problem is solved by using a third party trusted by both—normally a reputable bank—to act as an intermediary. What happens can be summarized as follows (see Figure 11.3). First, the French importer obtains the bank's promise to pay on

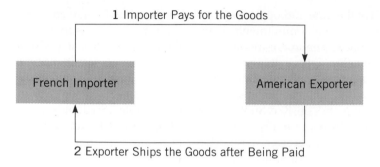

Figure 11.1

Preference of the US Exporter

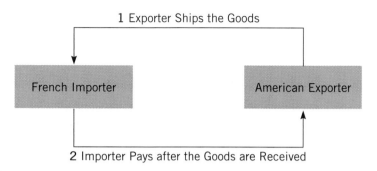

Figure 11.2

Preference of the French Importer

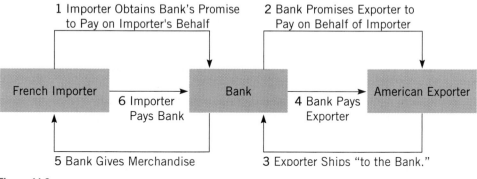

Figure 11.3

The Use of a Third Party

her behalf, knowing the US exporter will trust the bank. This promise is known as a letter of credit. Having seen the letter of credit, the US exporter ships the products to France. Title to the products is given, in due course, to the bank in the form of a document called a bill of lading. In return, the US exporter tells the bank to pay for the products, which the bank does. The document for requesting this payment is referred to as a draft. The bank, having paid for the products, now passes the title on to the French importer, whom the bank trusts. At that time or later, depending on their agreement, the importer reimburses the bank. In the remainder of this section, we will examine how this system works in more detail.

Letter of Credit

A letter of credit, abbreviated as L/C, stands at the center of international commercial transactions. Issued by a bank at the request of an importer, the letter of credit states that the bank will pay a specified sum of money to a beneficiary, normally the exporter, on presentation of particular, specified documents.

Consider again the example of the US exporter and the French importer. The French importer applies to her local bank, let us say the Bank of Paris, for the issuance of a letter of credit. The Bank of Paris then undertakes a credit check of the importer. If the Bank of Paris is satisfied with her creditworthiness, it will issue a letter of credit. However, the Bank of Paris might require a cash deposit or some other form of collateral from her first. In addition, the Bank of Paris will charge the importer a fee for this service. Typically this amounts to between 0.5 percent and 2 percent of the value of the letter of credit, depending on the importer's creditworthiness and the size of the transaction. (As a rule, the larger the transaction, the lower the percentage.)

Let us assume the Bank of Paris is satisfied with the French importer's creditworthiness and agrees to issue a letter of credit. The letter states that the Bank of Paris will pay the US exporter for the merchandise as long as it is shipped in accordance with certain, specified instructions and conditions. At this point, the letter of credit becomes a financial contract between the Bank of Paris and the US exporter. The Bank of Paris then sends the letter of credit to the US exporter's bank, let us say the Bank of New York. The Bank of New York tells the exporter that it has received a letter of credit and that he can ship the merchandise. After the exporter has shipped the merchandise, he draws a draft against the Bank of Paris in accordance with the terms of the letter of credit, attaches the required documents, and presents the draft to his own bank, the Bank of New York, for payment. The Bank of New York then forwards the letter of credit and associated documents to the Bank of Paris. If all the terms and conditions contained in the letter of credit have been complied with, the Bank of Paris will honor the draft and will send payment to the Bank of New York. When the Bank of New York receives the funds, it will pay the US exporter.

As for the Bank of Paris, once it has transferred the funds to the Bank of New York, it will collect payment from the French importer. The Bank of Paris may allow the importer some time to resell the merchandise before requiring payment. This is not unusual, particularly when the importer is a distributor and not the final consumer of the merchandise because it helps the importer's cash flow position. Of course, the Bank of Paris will treat such an extension of the payment period as a loan to the importer and will charge an appropriate rate of interest.

The advantage of this system is that both the French importer and the US exporter are likely to trust reputable banks, even if they do not trust each other. Once the US exporter has seen a letter of credit, he knows he is guaranteed payment and will ship the merchandise. An exporter may find that having a letter of credit will facilitate obtaining pre-export financing. For example, having seen the letter of credit, the Bank of New York might be willing to lend the exporter funds to process and prepare the merchandise for shipping to France. This loan may not have to be repaid until the exporter has received his payment for the merchandise. As for the French importer, the great advantage of the letter of credit is that she does not have to pay out funds for the merchandise until the documents have arrived and unless all conditions stated in the letter of credit have been satisfied. The drawback for the importer is the fee she must pay the Bank of Paris for the letter of credit. In addition, because the letter of credit is a financial liability against her, it may reduce her ability to borrow funds for other purposes.

Draft

A draft, sometimes referred to as a bill of exchange, is the instrument normally used in international commerce for payment. A draft is simply an order written by an exporter instructing an importer, or an importer's agent, to pay a specified amount of money at a specified time. In the example of the US exporter and the French importer, the exporter writes a draft that instructs the Bank of Paris, the French importer's agent, to pay for the merchandise shipped to France. The person or business initiating the draft is known as the maker (in this case, the US exporter). The party to whom the draft is presented is known as the drawee (in this case, the Bank of Paris).

International practice is to use drafts to settle trade transactions. This differs from domestic practice in which a seller usually ships merchandise on an open account, followed by a commercial invoice that specifies the amount due and the terms of payment. In domestic transactions, the buyer can often obtain possession of the merchandise without signing a formal document acknowledging his or her obligation to pay. In contrast, due to the lack of trust in international transactions, payment or a formal promise to pay is required before the buyer can obtain the merchandise.

Drafts fall into two categories, sight drafts and time drafts. A sight draft is payable on presentation to the drawee. A time draft allows for a delay in payment—normally 30, 60, 90, or 120 days. It is presented to the drawee, who signifies acceptance of it by writing or stamping a notice of acceptance on its face. Once accepted, the time draft becomes a promise to pay by the accepting party. When a time draft is drawn on and accepted by a bank, it is called a banker's acceptance. When it is drawn on and accepted by a business firm, it is called a trade acceptance.

Time drafts are negotiable instruments; that is, once the draft is stamped with an acceptance, the maker can sell the draft to an investor at a discount from its face value. Imagine the agreement between the US exporter and the French importer calls for the exporter to present the Bank of Paris (through the Bank of New York) with a time draft requiring payment 120 days after presentation. The Bank of Paris stamps the time draft with an acceptance. Imagine further that the draft is for $100,000.

The exporter can either hold onto the accepted time draft and receive $100,000 in 120 days or he can sell it to an investor, let's say the Bank of New York, for a discount from the face value. If the prevailing discount rate is 7 percent, the exporter could receive $96,500 by selling it immediately (7 percent per annum discount rate for 120 days for $100,000 equals $3,500, and $100,000 − $3,500 = $96,500). The Bank of New York would then collect the full $100,000 from the Bank of Paris in 120 days. The exporter might sell the accepted time draft immediately if he needed the funds to finance merchandise in transit and/or to cover cash flow shortfalls.

Bill of Lading

The third key document for financing international trade is the bill of lading. The bill of lading is issued to the exporter by the common carrier transporting the merchandise. It serves three purposes: it is a receipt, a contract, and a document of title. As a receipt, the bill of lading indicates that the carrier has received the merchandise described on the face of the document. As a contract, it specifies that the carrier is obligated to provide a transportation service in return for a certain charge. As a document of title, it can be used to obtain payment or a written promise of payment before the merchandise is released to the importer. The bill of lading can also function as collateral against which funds may be advanced to the exporter by its local bank before or during shipment and before final payment by the importer.

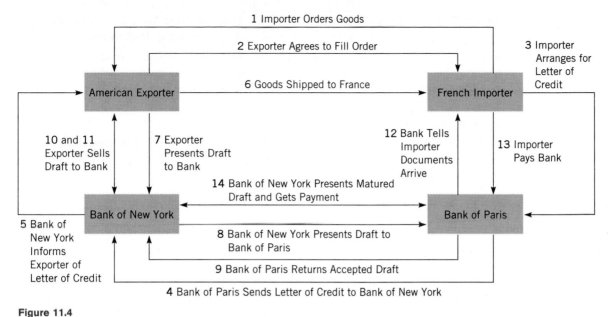

Figure 11.4

A Typical International Trade Transaction

A Typical International Trade Transaction

Now that we have reviewed all the elements of an international trade transaction, let us see how the whole process works in a typical case, sticking with the example of the US exporter and the French importer. The typical transaction involves 14 steps (see Figure 11.4).

Step 1: The French importer places an order with the US exporter and asks the American if he would be willing to ship under a letter of credit.

Step 2: The US exporter agrees to ship under a letter of credit and specifies relevant information such as prices and delivery terms.

Step 3: The French importer applies to the Bank of Paris for a letter of credit to be issued in favor of the US exporter for the merchandise the importer wishes to buy.

Step 4: The Bank of Paris issues a letter of credit in the French importer's favor and sends it to the US exporter's bank, the Bank of New York.

Step 5: The Bank of New York advises the US exporter of the opening of a letter of credit in his favor.

Step 6: The US exporter ships the goods to the French importer on a common carrier. An official of the carrier gives the exporter a bill of lading.

Step 7: The US exporter presents a 90-day time draft drawn on the Bank of Paris in accordance with its letter of credit and the bill of lading to the Bank of New York. The US exporter endorses the bill of lading so title to the goods is transferred to the Bank of New York.

Step 8: The Bank of New York sends the draft and bill of lading to the Bank of Paris. The Bank of Paris accepts the draft, taking possession of the documents and promising to pay the now-accepted draft in 90 days.

Step 9: The Bank of Paris returns the accepted draft to the Bank of New York.

Step 10: The Bank of New York tells the US exporter that it has received the accepted bank draft, which is payable in 90 days.

Step 11: The exporter sells the draft to the Bank of New York at a discount from its face value and receives the discounted cash value of the draft in return.

Step 12: The Bank of Paris notifies the French importer of the arrival of the documents. She agrees to pay the Bank of Paris in 90 days. The Bank of Paris releases the documents so the importer can take possession of the shipment.

Step 13: In 90 days the Bank of Paris receives the importer's payment, so it has funds to pay the maturing draft.

Step 14: In 90 days the holder of the matured acceptance (in this case, the Bank of New York) presents it to the Bank of Paris for payment. The Bank of Paris pays.

Key Terms

Summary

In this chapter we discussed the basic entry decision. We reviewed different entry modes and examined the steps that firms must take to undertake exporting. The following points have been made in this chapter:

1. Basic entry decisions include identifying which markets to enter, when to enter those markets, and on what scale.

2. The most attractive foreign markets tend to be found in politically stable developed and developing nations that have free market systems and where there is not a dramatic upsurge in either inflation rates or private-sector debt.

3. There are several advantages associated with entering a national market early, before other international businesses have established themselves. These advantages must be balanced against the pioneering costs that early entrants often have to bear, including the greater risk of business failure.

4. Large-scale entry into a national market constitutes a major strategic commitment that is likely to change the nature of competition in that market and limit the entrant's future strategic flexibility. The firm needs to consider the implications of such commitments before embarking on a large-scale entry. Although making major strategic commitments can yield many benefits, there are also risks associated with such a strategy.

5. There are six modes of entering a foreign market: exporting, turnkey projects, licensing, franchising, establishing a joint venture, and setting up a wholly owned subsidiary.

6. Exporting has the advantages of facilitating the realization of experience curve economies and avoiding the costs of setting up manufacturing operations in another country. Disadvantages include high transport costs and trade barriers and problems with local marketing agents. The latter can be overcome if the firm sets up a wholly owned marketing subsidiary in the host country.

7. Turnkey projects allow firms to export their process know-how to countries where FDI might be prohibited, thereby enabling the firm to earn a greater return from this asset. The disadvantage is that the firm may inadvertently create efficient global competitors.

8. The main advantage of licensing is that the licensee bears the costs and risks of opening a foreign market. Disadvantages include the risk of losing technological know-how to the licensee and a lack of tight control over licensees.

9. The main advantage of franchising is that the franchisee bears the costs and risks of opening a foreign market. Disadvantages center on problems of quality control of distant franchisees.

10. Joint ventures have the advantages of sharing the costs and risks of opening a foreign market and of gaining local knowledge and political influence. Disadvantages include the risk of losing control over technology and a lack of tight control.

11. The advantages of wholly owned subsidiaries include tight control over operations and tight control over technological know-how. The main disadvantage is that the firm must bear all the costs and risks of opening a foreign market.

12. The optimal choice of entry mode depends on the strategy of the firm.

13. When technological know-how constitutes a firm's core competence, wholly owned subsidiaries are preferred because they best control technology.

14. When management know-how constitutes a firm's core competence, foreign franchises controlled by joint ventures seem to be optimal. This gives the firm the cost and risk benefits associated with franchising, while enabling it to monitor and control franchisee quality effectively.

15. When the firm is pursuing a global or transnational strategy, the need for tight control over operations in order to realize location and experience curve economies suggests wholly owned subsidiaries are the best entry mode.

16. One big impediment to exporting is ignorance of foreign market opportunities. Neophyte exporters often become discouraged or frustrated with the exporting process

because they encounter many problems, delays, and pitfalls. The way to overcome ignorance is to gather information. Government agencies and export management companies can also help an exporter identify export opportunities.

17 Many of the pitfalls associated with exporting can be avoided if a company hires an experienced export management company or export consultant and if it adopts the appropriate export strategy.

18 Firms engaged in international trade must do business with people they cannot trust, people who may be very difficult to track down if they default on an obligation. Due to the lack of trust, each party to an international transaction has a different set of preferences regarding the configuration of the transaction.

19 The problems arising from lack of trust between exporters and importers can be solved by using a third party that is trusted by both—normally a reputable bank.

20 A letter of credit is issued by a bank at the request of an importer. It states that the bank promises to pay a beneficiary, normally the exporter, on presentation of documents specified in the letter.

21 A draft is the instrument normally used in international commerce for payment. It is an order written by an exporter instructing an importer, or an importer's agent, to pay a specified amount of money at a certain time. Drafts are either sight drafts or time drafts. Time drafts are negotiable instruments.

22 A bill of lading is issued to the exporter by the common carrier transporting the merchandise. It serves as a receipt, a contract, and a document of title.

Critical Thinking and Discussion Questions

1 Review Merrill Lynch's 1997 reentry into the Japanese private client market (see the opening case for details). Pay close attention to the timing and scale of entry and the nature of the strategic commitments Merrill Lynch is making in Japan. What are the potential benefits associated with this strategy? What are the costs and risks? Do you think the trade-off between benefits and risks and costs, makes sense? Why?

2 Licensing proprietary technology to foreign competitors is the best way to give up a firm's competitive advantage. Discuss.

3 What kinds of companies stand to gain the most from entering into strategic alliances with potential competitors? Why?

4 Discuss how the need for control over foreign operations varies with firms' strategies and core competencies. What are the implications for the choice of entry mode?

5 A small Canadian firm that has developed valuable medical products using its unique biotechnology know-how is trying to decide how best to serve the European Community market. Its choices are:

a Manufacture the products at home and let foreign sales agents handle marketing.

b Manufacture the products at home and set up a wholly owned subsidiary in Europe to handle marketing.

c Enter into a strategic alliance with a large European pharmaceutical firm. The product would be manufactured in Europe by the 50/50 joint venture and marketed by the European firm.

The cost of investment in manufacturing facilities will be a major one for the Canadian firm, but it is not outside its reach. If these are the firm's only options, which one would you advise it to choose? Why?

6 You are the assistant to the CEO of a small textile firm that manufactures high-quality, premium-priced, stylish clothing. The CEO has decided to see what the opportunities are for exporting and has asked you for advice as to the steps the company should take. What advice would you give to the CEO?

Internet Exercises

1 The term *managed care* sends shivers down the spines of many Americans, but the idea is catching on in the rest of the world. It has become a major new export for the United States. Latin America now boasts more health maintenance organizations (HMOs) than the United States, and in the Philippines, the industry is growing at 20 percent annually. Most countries, citing managed care's negative image in the United States, have avoided using the term *managed care*, choosing alternative names such as "evidence-based medicine" instead, and American companies expanding into foreign markets have found it necessary to change parts of their strategies as well.

Cigna Corporation and Aetna Inc., two of America's largest

providers of managed care, have poured hundreds of millions of dollars into developing their foreign markets over the past few years. Aetna formed a joint venture with Brazil's largest health insurers, Sul America, to develop the Brazilian market and has also used joint ventures to expand into other parts of Latin America, such as Chile, Argentina, and Colombia. Similarly, America's UnitedHealthcare has formed a number of joint ventures with a New York-based global general and life insurer, American International Group, to gain a presence in foreign markets. UnitedHealthcare has taken a more cautious approach to expansion and is concentrating on consulting in Europe as it gets to know foreign markets. Notes Mark Moody, vice president for international operations at UnitedHealthcare, "You cant just say 'take this and plug it in,' we're not exporting widgets." Go to UnitedHealthcare's global site (www. uhcglobal.com) and explore its international operations. Note that America's biggest HMOs have chosen to follow a joint venture-based strategy for their international expansion. Discuss the differences and similarities of international expansion for service providers versus consumer products companies. What challenges do the HMO providers face as they grow their international divisions? How can joint ventures facilitate their entry into new markets?

Source: *The Wall Street Journal*, December 20, 1999, p. B1.

2 General Motors Corporation (GM), the US auto maker, currently has about 4 percent of the Asian market (including Australia). The company wants to have 10 percent by 2004. Sound impossible? Not if GM has its way. The American auto giant sees alliances with Asian partners as the means to achieve its ambitious goal. GM has already partnered with Isuzu Motors and Suzuki Motors and is in talks with Fuji Heavy Industries, the maker of Subaru cars; Honda Motor Company; and Daewoo Motors. In addition, GM has factories in Thailand, Indonesia, and India. Experts argue though, that despite the boost it should get as a result of its alliances, GM still has its work cut out for it. The company needs to develop more cars tailored to the local marketplace and establish an extensive distribution network. Furthermore, GM has yet to convince local customers that it can compete with rivals.

If GM's talks with prospective partners prove to be successful, the company's Asian operations will involve a web of strategic alliances with local automakers. Go to GM's site (**www.generalmotors. com**) and explore its international operations. Discuss the pros and cons of GM's Asian strategy. In relying so heavily on alliances, can GM maintain strategic control over its density in the Asian market? In your opinion, would GM be better off entering the market more slowly, using fewer alliances and more wholly owned subsidiaries? Why or why not?

Source: *Business Week*, December 20, 1999, p. 64.

Downey's is an Irish tavern in Philadelphia created over 20 years ago by Jack Downey. Over the years, the fortunes of the restaurant have wavered, but the strength of some favorite menu items has helped it survive economic downturns. In particular, the lobster bisque soup has met with increasing popularity, but Downey's efforts to market it have been sporadic. Never did Downey imagine that his lobster bisque would someday be the cause of an international trade dispute.

Unbeknown to Downey, the Japanese have a penchant for lobster. When the Philadelphia office of the Japanese External Trade Organization (Jetro) asked Downey to serve his lobster bisque at a small trade show in 1991, he began to think about mass production of his soups. The Japanese loved the lobster bisque. They gave Downey the impression that the soup would sell very well in Japan. At that time, Downey did not have a formal product line but that seemed to be only a minor obstacle.

After the trade show, Michael Fisher, executive vice president for the newly formed Downey Foods Inc., was sent on an all-expenses-paid 10-day marketing trip to Japan by Jetro. (Jetro sponsors approximately 60 Americans for similar trips each year.) Although interest expressed by the food brokers and buyers he met seemed to be more polite than enthusiastic, he did get an initial order for 1,000 cases of the lobster bisque. The only condition placed by the buyer was to have the salt content reduced to comply with local Japanese tastes. Both Jetro and Fisher considered this initial order the beginning of a rich export relationship with Japan.

Fisher contracted with a food processor in Virginia, adapted the recipe for the new salt content, and shipped the soup to Japan. Visions of expanded sales in Japan were quickly dashed as the cases of soup were detained at customs. Samples were sent to a government laboratory and eventually denied entry for containing polysorbate, an emulsifying and antifoaming agent used by food processors. Though it is considered harmless in the United States, polysorbate is not on Jetro's list of 347 approved food additives.

Fisher and Downey did not give up. They reformulated the soup to improve the taste and comply with Jetro's additive regulations. They had the soup tested and certified by a Japanese-approved lab, the Oregon Department of Agriculture's Export Service Center, to meet all Japanese standards. Then, in the fall of 1993, they sent another 1,000 cases to Japan.

The soup was denied entry again. Japanese officials said the expiration date on the Oregon tests had passed, so they retested the cans. Traces of polysorbate were found. A sample from that shipment was sent back to Oregon, and it passed. Two identical cans of soup were sent back to Japan and tested. They failed. In Oregon a sample of the same shipment was tested again and no traces of polysorbate were found.

Japanese officials refused to allow the soup into Japan. By this time, Downey's had been paid $20,000 that it could not afford to give back. "It stunned the customer," says Fisher. "But it stunned me a lot more. I was counting on dozens of reorders."

Fisher filed appeals with the US Embassy in Tokyo to no avail. "It became a bureaucratic/political issue,"

says Fisher. "There was a face-saving problem. The Japanese had rejected the soup twice. There was no way they could reverse the decision."

The final irony came when a New York-based Japanese trader sent a few cases of Downey's regular (no reduced salt content) lobster bisque to Japan. This shipment sailed through customs without a problem.

Where was Jetro when Downey's soups were stalled in customs? Fisher thought he had everything covered. He followed the advice of Jetro, adjusted the soups to meet Japanese palates, and had them tested to meet Japanese food standards. Apparently, Jetro failed to inform Fisher of the apparent need for a local partner to sell and distribute in Japan. Most food companies have trouble getting into Japan, whether large or small. Agricultural products are one of the most difficult things to get into the Japanese market.

Jetro's agricultural specialist, Tatsuya Kajishima, contradicts this claim that Japan is hostile to food imports by stating the following statistic—30 percent of Japan's food imports come from the United States. Further, Japan is the fourth-largest importer of US soups, purchasing $6.5 million worth of soup in 1993. Most of these sales came from Campbell Soup Company.

Although this venture was not profitable for Downey Foods Inc., the company redirected its research and development efforts to build its domestic product line. Through its local broker, Santucci Associates, Downey Foods attracted the attention of Liberty Richter Inc., a national distributor of gourmet and imported food items.[35]

CASE DISCUSSION QUESTIONS

1 Did Downey Foods' export opportunity occur as a result of proactive action by Downey or was its strategy reactive?

2 Why did Downey experience frustrations when trying to export to Japan? What actions might Downey take to improve its prospects of succeeding in the Japanese market?

3 You have been hired by Downey Foods to develop an exporting strategy for the firm. What steps do you think Downey should take to increase the volume of its exports?

twelve

Global Marketing and Product Development

Opening Case

Proctor & Gamble
in Japan: From
Marketing Failure
to Success

Procter & Gamble, the large US
consumer products company, has a
well-earned reputation as one of
the world's best marketers. With its
80-plus major brands, P&G generates more than $37 billion in annual
revenues worldwide. Along with
Unilever, P&G is a dominant global
force in laundry detergents, cleaning products, and personal care
products. P&G expanded abroad in
the post-World War II years by exporting its brands and marketing

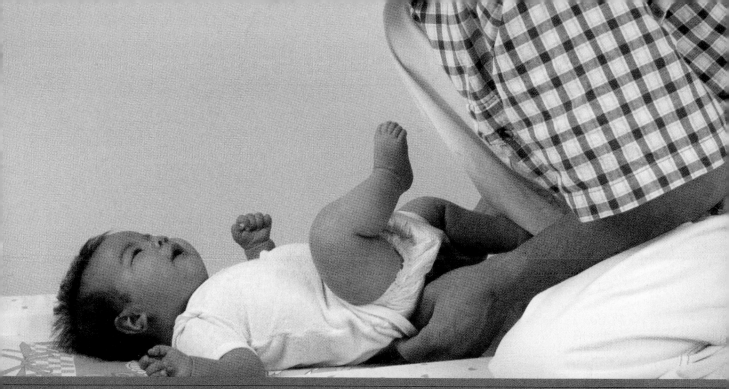

P&G realized that to effectively market diapers in Japan, they had to reduce the bulk of the diaper because Japanese consumers liked a more trim-fitting diaper. Research and development into consumer needs, along with the right marketing message, can lead to a successful launch of a product abroad. Do you think it is possible to launch a product abroad without sufficient research and development? Can you think of a product created domestically that has transferred to another country without any changes?

© Jennie Woodcock; Reflections Photolibrary/CORBIS.

Learning Objectives

1 Understand why and how it may make sense to vary the attributes of a product among countries.

2 Appreciate why and how a firm's distribution strategy might vary among countries.

3 Understand why and how advertising and promotional strategies might vary among countries.

4 Understand why and how a firm's pricing strategy might vary among countries.

5 Understand how the globalization of the world economy is affecting the new product development process within international businesses.

policies to Western Europe, initially with considerable success. Over the next 30 years this policy of developing new products and marketing strategies in the United States and then transferring them to other countries became entrenched. Adaptation of marketing policies to accommodate country differences was minimal.

The first signs that this policy was no longer effective emerged in the 1970s, when P&G suffered a number of major setbacks in Japan. By 1985, after 13 years in Japan, P&G was still losing $40 million a year there. It had introduced disposable diapers in Japan and at one time had commanded 80 percent of the market, but by the early 1980s it held a miserable 8 percent. Three large Japanese consumer products companies were dominating the market. P&G's problem was that Japanese consumers did not like its bulky diapers, developed in the United States.

Kao, a Japanese company, had developed a line of trim-fit diapers that appealed more to Japanese tastes. Kao introduced its product with a marketing blitz and was quickly rewarded with 30 percent of the market. P&G realized it would have to modify its diapers if it were to compete in Japan. So it did, and the company now has a 30 percent share of the Japanese market, plus P&G's trim-fit diapers have become a best-seller in the United States.

P&G had a similar experience in marketing education in the Japanese laundry detergent market. In the early 1980s P&G introduced its Cheer laundry detergent in Japan. Developed in the United States, Cheer was promoted in Japan with the US marketing message—Cheer works in all temperatures and produces lots of rich suds. However, many Japanese consumers wash their clothes in cold water, which made the claim of working in all temperatures irrelevant. Also, many Japanese add fabric softeners to their water, which reduces detergents' sudsing action, so Cheer did not suds as advertised. After a disastrous launch, P&G knew it had to adapt its marketing message. Cheer is now promoted as a product that works effectively in cold water with fabric softeners added, and it is one of P&G's best-selling products in Japan.

P&G's experience with disposable diapers and laundry detergents in Japan forced the company to rethink its product development and marketing philosophy. The company now admits that its US-centered way of doing business no longer works. Since the late 1980s P&G has been delegating more responsibility for new product development and marketing to its major subsidiaries in Japan and Europe. The company is more responsive to local differences in consumer tastes and preferences and more willing to admit that good new products can be developed outside the United States.

Evidence that this new approach is working can be found in the company's activities in Japan. Until 1995 P&G did not sell dish soap in Japan. By 1998 it had Japan's best-selling brand, Joy, which now has a 20 percent share of Japan's $400 million market for dish soap. In the process it made major inroads against the products of two domestic firms, Kao and Lion Corp., each of which marketed multiple brands and controlled nearly 40 percent of the market before P&G's entry. P&G's success with Joy was because of its ability to develop a product formula that was targeted at the unmet needs of Japanese consumers, design a packaging format that appealed to retailers, and develop a compelling advertising campaign.

In researching the market in the early 1990s, P&G discovered an odd habit; Japanese homemakers, one after another, squirted out excessive amounts of detergent onto dirty dishes—a sign of dissatisfaction with existing products. P&G found that this behavior was the result of the changing eating habits of Japanese consumers. The Japanese are consuming more fried food, and existing dish soaps did not effectively remove grease. Armed with this knowledge, P&G researchers in Japan went to work to create a highly concentrated soap formula based on a new technology developed by the company's scientists in Europe that was highly effective in removing grease. The

company also set about designing novel packaging for the product. The packaging of existing products had a clear weakness—their long-necked bottles wasted space on supermarket shelves. P&G's dish soap containers were compact cylinders that took less space in stores, warehouses, and delivery trucks. This improved the efficiency of distribution and allowed supermarkets to use their shelf space more effectively, which made them receptive to stocking Joy. P&G also devoted considerable attention to the development of an advertising campaign for Joy. P&G's ad agency, Dentsu Inc., created commercials in which a famous comedian dropped in on homemakers, unannounced, with a camera crew to test Joy on the household's dirty dishes. The camera zoomed in on a patch of oil in a pan full of water. After a drop of Joy, the oil dramatically disappeared.

With the product, packaging, and advertising strategy carefully worked out, P&G launched Joy throughout Japan in March of 1996. Almost immediately the product gained a 10 percent market share. Within three months the product's share had increased to 15 percent, and by year-end it was close to 18 percent. Because of strong demand, P&G was also able to raise prices, as were the retailers that stocked the product, all of which translated into fatter margins for the retailers and helped consolidate Joy's position in the market.[1]

Introduction

This chapter focuses on how marketing and R&D can reduce the costs of value creation and add value by better serving customer needs. In Chapter 10 we spoke of the tension existing in most international businesses between the needs to reduce costs and at the same time to respond to local conditions, which tends to raise costs. This tension is a theme in this chapter too. A global marketing strategy, which views the world's consumers as similar in their tastes and preferences, is consistent with the mass production of a standardized output. By mass producing a standardized output, the firm can realize substantial unit cost reductions from experience curve and other scale economies. But ignoring country differences in consumer tastes and preferences can lead to failure. Thus, an international business's marketing function needs to determine when product standardization is appropriate and when it is not. Similarly, the firm's R&D function needs to be able to develop globally standardized products when appropriate as well as products customized to local requirements.

Marketing and R&D have a close relationship. A critical aspect of the marketing function is identifying gaps in the market so new products can be developed to fill those gaps. Developing new products requires R&D; thus, the linkage between marketing and R&D. New products should be developed with market needs in mind, and only marketing can define those needs for R&D personnel. Also, only marketing can tell R&D whether to produce globally standardized or locally customized products. Research has long maintained that a major factor of success for new products is the closeness of the relationship between marketing and R&D. The closer the linkage, the greater the success rate.[2]

The opening case illustrates some of the issues that we will be discussing in this chapter. Many of P&G's problems in Japan were due to a failure to tailor its marketing strategy to the specific demands of the Japanese market. P&G learned from its experience with disposable diapers and laundry detergent that a marketing approach that works in one context might not necessarily work in another. The company's subsequent success with Joy drives home the point that in many consumer product markets, it is important to customize the product offering, packaging, and advertising message to the specific needs of consumers in that country. Joy was developed by Procter & Gamble's R&D staff in Kobe, Japan, specifically to meet the evolving needs of Japanese consumers. This illustrates the benefits of locating R&D activities close to the market for the product when that market demands a customized product offering.

But it would be wrong to generalize too much from this case. For other firms in other industries, it may make sense to pursue a global strategy, producing a standardized product for global consumption and using the same basic market message to sell that product worldwide. Some product markets are truly global. The market for semiconductor chips, for example, is a global market where consumers demand the same standardized product worldwide—in such cases a global marketing strategy, supported by a global R&D strategy, might make sense.

In this chapter we examine the roles of marketing and R&D in international businesses. We begin by reviewing the debate on the globalization of markets. Then we discuss the issue of market segmentation. Next, we look at four elements that constitute a firm's marketing mix: product attributes, distribution strategy, communication strategy, and pricing strategy. The **marketing mix** is the set of choices the firm offers to its targeted market(s). Many firms vary their marketing mix from country to country depending on differences in national culture, economic development, product standards, distribution channels, and so on. The chapter closes with a look at new product development in an international business and at the implications of this for the organization of the firm's R&D function.

marketing mix
The set of choices the firm offers to its targeted market(s).

The Globalization of Markets?

In a now-famous *Harvard Business Review* article, Theodore Levitt wrote lyrically about the globalization of world markets.[3] Levitt's arguments have become a lightning rod in the debate about globalization. According to Levitt:

A powerful force drives the world toward a converging commonalty, and that force is technology. It has proletarianized communication, transport, and travel. The result is a new commercial reality—the emergence of global markets for standardized consumer products on a previously unimagined scale of magnitude.

Levitt mentions Hollywood movies as "confirmation" of the disappearance of national tastes due to the globalization of markets. Do you think this is so? How do movies differ from something like MTV in feeding this "standardization," as Levitt calls it? © Corbis. All rights reserved.

Gone are accustomed differences in national or regional preferences . . . The globalization of markets is at hand. With that, the multinational commercial world nears its end, and so does the multinational corporation. The multinational corporation operates in a number of countries and adjusts its products and practices to each—at high relative costs. The global corporation operates with resolute consistency—at low relative cost—as if the entire world were a single entity; it sells the same thing in the same way everywhere.

Commercially, nothing confirms this as much as the success of McDonald's from the Champs Elysees to the Ginza, of Coca-Cola in Bahrain and Pepsi-Cola in Moscow, and of rock music, Greek salad, Hollywood movies, Revlon cosmetics, Sony television, and Levi's jeans everywhere.

Ancient differences in national tastes or modes of doing business disappear. The commonalty of preference leads inescapably to the standardization of products, manufacturing, and the institutions of trade and commerce.

This is eloquent and evocative writing, but is Levitt correct? The rise of global media such as MTV (see the accompanying "Management Focus") and CNN, and the ability of such media to help shape a global culture, seem to lend weight to Levitt's argument. If Levitt is correct, his argument has major implications for the marketing strategies pursued by international business. However, the current consensus among academics seems to be that Levitt overstates his case.[4] Although Levitt may have a point when it comes to many basic industrial products—such as steel, bulk chemicals, and semiconductor chips—globalization seems to be the exception rather than the rule in many consumer goods markets and many industrial markets. Even a firm such as McDonald's, which Levitt holds up as the archetypal example

In a world where there are still major differences in the tastes, preferences, and purchasing habits of consumers in different countries, no one group is more homogenous in its tastes and preferences than those in their teens and early 20s. Whether they live in Los Angeles or London, Tokyo or Prague, Rio de Janeiro or Sydney, young adults the world over wear baggy jeans and Doc Martens, listen to the music of Fiona Apple, drink Coke or Pepsi, and eat at McDonald's. Increasingly, they also watch MTV, the music channel owned by Viacom.

MTV has been singled out by many observers as a major cause of the global homogenization of teen culture and also as a major beneficiary. Both charges are probably true. Introduced in the United States in the late 1970s, MTV is now the most widely distributed cable network in the world. MTV currently broadcasts in 85 countries and has a global audience among 12- to 34-year-olds. By mid-1998 the channel reached an impressive 80 million households in the United States and Canada, but most of the recent growth has occurred outside of North America. MTV Europe, which was established in 1987, is now received by more than 80 million households across the continent. In Asia, over 50 million households receive MTV Asia, and the number is growing exponentially. And in Central and South America, where MTV launched its service in 1994, 30 million households received the channel by mid-1998.

MTV is keenly aware of the concerns and interest of those in their teens and early 20s, and its global program strategy reflects this. As in the United States, its international services broadcast news and socially conscious programming that are of interest to the target audience the world over, such as features on global warming, the destruction of the rain forests, and AIDS. The guts of MTV, however, is its music programming. Initially, MTV's music programming was dominated by US and British artists, and MTV broadcast Anglo-American music to the rest of the world. It was thanks to MTV that grunge rock became a global phenomenon, and teens from Italy to Japan came to know Seattle not as the home of Boeing or Microsoft, but as the birthplace of grunge. Increasingly, however, MTV is championing little-known artists from other parts of the world, and it has shown that it has the power to make them international stars. MTV Europe helped discover the Swedish pop group Ace of Base in 1992. Its global programming of the group's single and video, "All That She Wants," gave the group a top 10 hit in Britain, Germany, Italy, and the United States. Thanks to MTV Asia, one of the best-selling albums of 1993 in India was by Cheb Khaled singing in his native Algerian. In Japan, the Swedish "gothic rock" guitarist Yngwie Malmsteen became a huge star, in part due to promotion by MTV Japan. And for heavily anticipated new albums by big international stars, MTV stages what it calls "planetary premieres," airing a new video in 24 hours in all the countries it covers.

This worldwide marketing reach has made MTV a premier conduit for many companies hoping to profit from the globalization of teen culture. MTV's roster of 200 major advertisers includes Levi Strauss, Procter & Gamble, Johnson & Johnson, Apple Computer, and Pepsi-Cola. According to Donald Holdsworth, head of sales and marketing for Pepsi-Cola International, "MTV not only has broad global coverage, it's also targeted exactly at that segment we want to reach: teenagers." MTV President Tom Freston argues that marketing to those in their teens and early 20s through global communications media such as MTV is becoming increasingly important for many global consumer products companies. He sees music as the most global of communications medium: "You could argue that this is a business even more global than movies, because music is more pervasive than any other form of culture." Because of this pervasiveness, MTV is a natural communications conduit for advertisers trying to build a global brand. Today it is still difficult to sell the same products to 35-year-olds in different countries. They prefer traditional food and fashion. In part that's because they never bonded with international brands as teenagers. But MTV's Freston believes that because of media such MTV members of the younger generation are becoming more homogenized in their tastes and preferences.

However, while the international success of MTV is a testament to the global convergence of tastes and preferences among those in their teens and early 20s in different countries, it is easy to overstate the importance of such globalization. Although there is no doubt that music is, as MTV President Freston notes, the most pervasive and global form of culture, important differences still exist between the tastes and preferences of teens in different nations. MTV may have helped to turn Yngwie Malmsteen into a big star in Japan, but this Swedish master of "gothic rock" didn't break any records in the US market. Even in one of the most global of industries—the music industry—and even among the most homogenous group in the world—teenagers—product standardization has its limits and national differences in tastes and preferences are still important.[5]

MTV Rocks the World

of a consumer products firm that sells a standardized product worldwide, modifies its menu from country to country in light of local consumer preferences.[6] And as we saw in the opening case, although Procter & Gamble may sell dish soap, disposable diapers, and laundry detergent worldwide, and although it may use the same brand names worldwide (e.g., Pampers for diapers), it still customizes the final product offering and marketing strategy to the conditions that pertain in individual national markets.

But Levitt is probably correct to assert that modern transportation and communications technologies, such as MTV, are facilitating a convergence of the tastes and preferences of consumers in the more advanced countries of the world. The popularity of sushi in Los Angeles, hamburgers in Tokyo, and grunge rock almost everywhere support this. In the long run, such technological forces may lead to the evolution of a global culture. At present, however, the persistence of cultural and economic differences between nations acts as a major brake on any trend toward global consumer tastes and preferences. In addition, trade barriers and differences in product and technical standards also constrain a firm's ability to sell a standardized product to a global market. We discuss the sources of these differences in subsequent sections when we look at how products must be altered from country to country. Levitt's globally standardized markets seem a long way off in many industries.

Market Segmentation

Market segmentation refers to the process of identifying distinct groups of consumers whose purchasing behavior differs from other groups in important ways. Markets can be segmented in numerous ways: by geography, demography (sex, age, income, race, education level, etc.), social-cultural factors (social class, values, religion, lifestyle choices), and psychological factors (personality). Because different segments exhibit different patterns of purchasing behavior, firms often adjust their marketing mix from segment to segment. Thus, the precise design of a product, the pricing strategy, the distribution channels used, and the choice of communication strategy may all be varied. The goal is to optimize the fit between the purchasing behavior of consumers in a given segment and the marketing mix, thereby maximizing sales to that segment. Automobile companies, for example, use a different marketing mix to sell cars to different socioeconomic segments. Thus, Toyota uses its Lexus division to sell high-priced luxury cars to high-income consumers, while selling its entry-level models, such as the Toyota Corolla, to lower-income consumers. Similarly, personal computer manufacturers will offer different computer models, embodying different combinations of product attributes and price points, precisely to appeal to consumers from different market segments (e.g., business users and home users).

When managers in an international business consider market segmentation in foreign countries, they need to be aware of two main issues—the extent to which there are differences between countries in the structure of market segments, and the existence of segments that transcend national borders. The structure of market segments may differ significantly from country to country. Thus, a company should not assume there is a one-to-one mapping between market segments in its home country and market segments in a foreign country. An important market segment in a foreign country may have no parallel in the firm's home country, and vice versa. The firm may have to develop a unique marketing mix to appeal to the unique purchasing behavior of a unique segment in a given country. For example, a research project published in 1998 identified a segment of consumers in China in the 45-to-55 age range that have few parallels in other countries.[7] This group came of age during China's violent and repressive Cultural Revolution in the late 1960s and early 1970s. The values of this group have been shaped by their experiences during the Cultural Revolution. They tend to be highly sensitive to price and respond negatively to new products and most forms of marketing. The existence of this group implies that firms doing business in China may need to customize their marketing mix to address the unique values and purchasing behavior of the group.

In contrast, the existence of market segments that transcend national borders enhances the ability of an international business to view the global marketplace as a single entity and pursue a global strategy, selling a standardized product worldwide and using the same basic marketing mix to help position and sell that product in a variety of national markets. For a segment to transcend national borders, consumers in that segment must have some compelling similarities along important dimensions—such as age, values, lifestyle choices—and those similarities must translate into very similar purchasing behavior. Although such segments exist in certain industrial markets, they are rare in consumer markets. However, one emerging global segment beginning to attract the attention of international marketers of consumer goods is the so-called global teen segment. As noted in the "Management Focus" on MTV, the global media are paving the way for a global teen segment. Evidence that such a segment exists comes from a study of the cultural attitudes and purchasing behavior of more than 6,500 teenagers in 26 countries.[8] The findings suggest that teens around the world are increasingly living parallel lives, including the sharing of many common values. It follows that they are likely to purchase the same kind of consumer goods and for the same reasons. Even here though, marketing specialists argue that some customization to account for differences among countries is required.

Product Attributes

A product can be viewed as a bundle of attributes.[9] For example, the attributes that make up a car include power, design, quality, performance, fuel consumption, and comfort; the attributes of a hamburger include taste, texture, and size; a hotel's attributes include atmosphere, quality, comfort, and service. Products sell well when their attributes match consumer needs (and when their prices are appropriate). BMW cars sell well to people who have high needs for luxury, quality, and performance because BMW builds those attributes into its cars. If consumer needs were the same the world over, a firm could sell the same product worldwide. However, consumer needs vary from country to country depending on culture and the level of economic development. A firm's ability to sell the same product worldwide is further constrained by countries' differing product standards. In this section we review each of these issues and discuss how they influence product attributes.

Cultural Differences

We discussed countries' cultural differences in Chapter 3. Countries differ along a range of dimensions, including social structure, language, religion, and education. These differences have important implications for marketing strategy. For example, "hamburgers" do not sell well in Islamic countries, where the consumption of ham is forbidden by Islamic law. The most important aspect of cultural differences is the impact of tradition. Tradition is particularly important in foodstuffs and beverages. For example, the Findus frozen food division of Nestlé, the Swiss food giant, markets fish cakes and fish fingers in Great Britain, but beef bourguignon and coq au vin in France, and vitèllo con funghi and braviola in Italy. Similarly, in addition to its normal range of products, Coca-Cola in Japan markets Georgia, a cold coffee in a can, and Aquarius, a tonic drink, products that appeal to traditional Japanese tastes.

For historical and idiosyncratic reasons, a range of other cultural differences exist between countries. For example, scent preferences differ from one country to another. S. C. Johnson Wax, a manufacturer of waxes and polishes, encountered resistance to its lemon-scented Pledge furniture polish among older consumers in Japan. Market research revealed the polish smelled similar to latrine disinfectant used widely in Japan in the 1940s. Sales rose sharply after the scent was adjusted.[10] In another example, Cheetos, the bright orange and cheesy-tasting snack from PepsiCo's Frito-Lay unit, do not have a cheese taste in China. Chinese consumers generally do not like the taste of cheese because it has never been part of traditional cuisine and because many Chinese are lactose-intolerant.[11]

There is some evidence of the trends Levitt talked about. Tastes and preferences are becoming more cosmopolitan. Coffee is gaining ground against tea in Japan and Great Britain, while American-style frozen dinners have become popular in Europe (with some fine-tuning to local tastes). Taking advantage of these trends, Nestlé can market its instant coffee, spaghetti bolognese, and Lean Cuisine frozen dinners in essentially the same manner in both North America and Western Europe. However, there is no market for Lean Cuisine dinners in most of the rest of the world, and there may never be. A calorie-conscious Asian is difficult to find. Although some cultural convergence has occurred, particularly among the advanced industrial nations of North America and Western Europe, Levitt's global culture is still a long way off.

Economic Differences

Just as important as differences in culture are differences in the level of economic development. We discussed the extent of country differences in economic development in Chapter 2. Consumer behavior is influenced by the level of economic development of a country. Firms based in highly developed countries such as the United States tend to build extra performance attributes into their products. These extra attributes are not usually demanded by consumers in less developed nations, where the preference is for more basic products. Thus, cars sold in less developed nations typically lack many of the features found in the West, such as air-conditioning, power steering, power windows, radios, and cassette players. For most consumer durables, product reliability may be more important in less developed nations, where such a purchase may account for a major proportion of a consumer's income, than it is in advanced nations.

Contrary to Levitt's suggestions, consumers in the most developed countries are often not willing to sacrifice their preferred attributes for lower prices. Consumers in the most advanced countries often shun globally standardized products that have been developed with the lowest common denominator in mind. They are willing to pay more for products that have additional features and attributes customized to their tastes and preferences. For example, demand for top-of-the-line four-wheel-drive sport utility vehicles is largely restricted to the United States. This is due to a combination of factors, including the high income level of US consumers, the country's vast distances, the relatively low cost of gasoline, and the culturally grounded "outdoor" theme of American life.

Product and Technical Standards

Levitt's vision of global markets may still be a long way off due to national differences in product and technological standards.

Differing product standards mandated by governments can rule out mass production and marketing of a standardized product. For example, Caterpillar, the US construction equipment firm, manufactures backhoe-loaders for all of Europe in Great Britain. These tractor-type machines have a bucket in front and a digger at the back. Several special parts must be built into backhoe-loaders that will be sold in Germany: a separate brake attached to the rear axle, a special locking mechanism on the backhoe operating valve, specially positioned valves in the steering system, and a lock on the bucket for traveling. These extras account for 5 percent of the total cost of the product in Germany.[12] The European Union (EU) is trying to harmonize such divergent product standards among its members. If the EU is successful, the need to customize products will be reduced, at least within the boundaries of the EU.

Differences in technical standards also constrain the globalization of markets. Some of these differences result from idiosyncratic decisions made at particular points in history, rather than from government actions. Their long-term effects are nonetheless profound. For example, video equipment manufactured for sale in the United States will not play videotapes recorded on equipment manufactured for sale in Great Britain, Germany, and France (and vice versa). Different technical standards for television signal frequency emerged in the 1950s that require television and video equipment to be customized to countries' prevailing standards. RCA stumbled in the 1970s when it failed to account for this in its marketing of TVs in Asia. Although several Asian countries had adopted the US standard, Singapore, Hong Kong, and Malaysia had adopted the British standard. The result: People who bought RCA TVs in those countries could receive a picture but no sound![13]

Distribution Strategy

A critical element of a firm's marketing mix is its distribution strategy, the means it chooses for delivering the product to the consumer. The way the product is delivered is determined by the firm's entry strategy, which we discussed in Chapter 11. In this section we examine a typical distribution system, discuss how its structure varies between countries, and look at how appropriate distribution strategies vary from country to country.

A Typical Distribution System

Figure 12.1 illustrates a typical distribution system consisting of a channel that includes a wholesale distributor and a retailer. If the firm manufactures its product in the particular country, it can sell directly to the consumer, to the retailer, or to the wholesaler. The same options are available to a firm that manufactures outside the country, or this firm may decide to sell to an import agent, who then deals with the wholesale distributor, the retailer, or the consumer. The factors that determine the firm's choice of channel are considered later in this section.

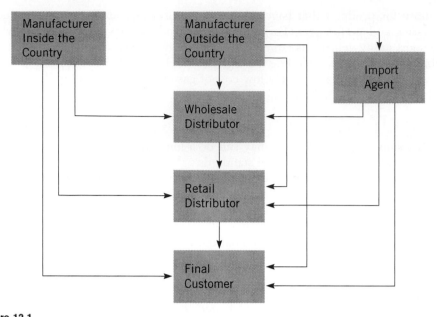

Figure 12.1

A Typical Distribution System

Differences between Countries

The three main differences between countries' distribution systems are retail concentration, channel length, and channel exclusivity.

RETAIL CONCENTRATION   In some countries the retail system is very concentrated, but in others it is fragmented. In a concentrated system, a few retailers supply most of the market. A fragmented system has many retailers, no one of which has a major share of the market. In Germany, for example, four retail chains control 65 percent of the market for food products. In neighboring Italy, retail distribution is fragmented, with no chain controlling more than 2 percent of the market.

Many of the differences in concentration are rooted in history and tradition. In the United States the importance of the automobile and the relative youth of many urban areas has resulted in a retail system centered around large stores or shopping malls to which people can drive. This has facilitated the concentration of the system. Japan's much greater population density, together with the large number of urban centers that grew up before the advent of the automobile, has resulted in a more fragmented retail system of many small stores that serve local neighborhoods and to which people frequently walk. In addition, the Japanese legal system protects small retailers. By law, small retailers can block the establishment of a large retail outlet by petitioning their local government.

Three factors contribute to a tendency for greater retail concentration in developed countries: increased car ownership, number of households with refrigerators and freezers, and number of two-income households. These factors have changed shopping habits and facilitated the growth of large retail establishments sited away from traditional shopping areas.

CHANNEL LENGTH   Channel length refers to the number of intermediaries between the producer (or manufacturer) and the consumer. If the producer sells directly to the consumer, the channel is very short. If the producer sells through an import agent, a wholesaler, and a retailer, a long channel exists. The choice of a short or long channel is primarily a strategic decision for the producing firm. However, some countries have longer distribution channels than others. Channel length is determined largely by the degree to which the retail system is fragmented. Fragmented retail systems tend to promote the growth of wholesalers to serve retailers, which lengthens channels.

The reason for this is simple economics: The more fragmented the retail system, the more expensive it is for a firm to make contact with each individual retailer. Imagine, for example, a firm that sells toothpaste in a country that has 50,000 small retailers. To sell directly to the retailers, the firm would have to build a huge sales force. This would be very expensive, particularly because each sales call would yield a very small order. Imagine, however, that there are 50 wholesalers in the country that supply retailers not only with toothpaste but also with all other personal care and household products. Because these wholesalers carry a range of products, they get bigger orders with each sales call. Thus, it becomes worthwhile for them to deal directly with the retailers. Accordingly, it makes economic sense for the firm to sell to the wholesalers and the wholesalers to deal with the retailers.

As a result of such factors, countries with fragmented retail systems also tend to have long channels of distribution. The classic example is Japan, where there are often two or three layers of wholesalers between the manufacturer and retail outlets. In contrast, in countries such as Great Britain, Germany, and the United States where the retail system is more concentrated, channels

Invisible Distribution Barriers

In Tokyo, inventory to local cigarette shops is supplied daily. So small are these shops that they carry merely a day's inventory, much of which is displayed on their shelves. To change the array of products offered to the consumer, the shop owner would need to accept products from a new wholesaler. This would mean, in Omoto-san's situation, telling a wholesaler with whom she has a strong and personal relationship—she's been having tea with Higashi-san after his delivery for the last 15 years—that she will carry less of his product. Why, she wonders, should she do this? True, the margins may be nicer from the newcomer to the market, which happens to be an American cigarette, yet she doesn't even know the distributor and her loyalty is with Higashi-san.

are much shorter. When the retail sector is very concentrated, it makes sense for the firm to deal directly with retailers because a relatively small sales force is required to deal with a concentrated retail sector, and the orders generated from each sales call can be large. Such circumstances tend to prevail in the United States, where large food companies sell directly to supermarkets rather than going through wholesale distributors.

CHANNEL EXCLUSIVITY An exclusive distribution channel is difficult for outsiders to access. For example, it is often difficult for a new firm to get access to shelf space in US supermarkets. Retailers tend to prefer to carry the products of long-established manufacturers of foodstuffs with national reputations, rather than gamble on the products of unknown firms. How exclusive a distribution system is varies between countries. Japan's system is very exclusive. In Japan, relationships between manufacturers, wholesalers, and retailers often go back decades. Many of these relationships are based on the understanding that distributors will not carry the products of competing firms. In return, the distributors are guaranteed an attractive markup by the manufacturer. As many US and European manufacturers have learned, the close ties that result from this arrangement can make access to the Japanese market very difficult. But as the opening case illustrates, it is possible to break into the Japanese market with a new consumer product, as Procter & Gamble did with its Joy brand of dish soap. P&G was able to overcome a tradition of exclusivity for two reasons. First, after a decade of lackluster economic performance, Japan is changing. In their search for profits, retailers are more willing to violate the old norms of exclusivity. Second, P&G has been in Japan long enough and has a broad enough portfolio of consumer products to give it leverage with distributors, enabling it to push new products out through the distribution channel.

Choosing a Distribution Strategy

A choice of distribution strategy determines which channel the firm will use to reach potential consumers. Should the firm try to sell directly to the consumer or should it go through retailers? Should it go through a wholesaler? Should it use an import agent? The optimal strategy is determined by the relative costs and benefits of each alternative. The relative costs and benefits of each alternative vary from country to country depending on the three factors we have just discussed: retail concentration, channel length, and channel exclusivity.

Because each intermediary in a channel adds its own markup to the products, there is generally a critical link among channel length, the final selling price, and the firm's profit margin. The longer a channel, the greater is the aggregate markup, and the higher the price that consumers are charged for the final product. To ensure that prices do not get too high due to markups by multiple intermediaries, a firm might have to operate with lower profit margins. Thus, if price is an important competitive weapon and if the firm does not want to see its profit margins squeezed, other things being equal, the firm would prefer to use a shorter channel.

However, the benefits of using a longer channel often outweigh these drawbacks. A longer channel economizes on selling costs when the retail sector is very fragmented. Thus, it makes sense for an international business to use longer channels in countries where the retail sector is fragmented and shorter channels in countries where the retail sector is concentrated.

Another benefit of using a longer channel is market access—the ability to enter an exclusive channel. Import agents may have long-term relationships with wholesalers, retailers, and/or important consumers and thus be better able to win orders and get access to a distribution system than the firm will on its own. Similarly, wholesalers may have long-standing relationships with retailers and be better able to persuade them to carry the firm's product than the firm itself would.

Import agents are not limited to independent trading houses; any firm with a strong local reputation could serve just as well. To break down channel exclusivity and gain greater access to the Japanese market, in 1991 and 1992 Apple Computer signed distribution agreements with five large Japanese firms including business equipment giant Brother Industries, stationery leader Kokuyo, Mitsubishi, Sharp, and Minolta. These firms used their long-established distribution relationships with consumers, retailers, and wholesalers to push Apple Macintosh computers through the Japanese distribution system. As a result, Apple's share of the Japanese market increased from less than 1 percent in 1988 to 6 percent in 1991 and 13 percent by 1994.[14]

If such an arrangement is not possible, the firm might want to consider other, less traditional alternatives to gaining market access. Frustrated by channel exclusivity in Japan, some foreign manufacturers of consumer goods have attempted to sell directly to Japanese consumers using direct mail and catalogs. REI, a retailer of outdoor clothing and equipment based in the northwestern United States, had trouble persuading Japanese wholesalers and retailers to carry its products. Instead, it began a direct mail campaign in Japan that is proving very successful.

Communication Strategy

Another critical element in the marketing mix is communicating the attributes of the product to prospective customers. Available communications channels include direct selling, sales promotion, direct marketing, and advertising. A firm's communication strategy is partly defined by its choice of channel. Some firms rely primarily on direct selling, others on point-of-sale promotions or direct marketing, others on mass advertising; still others use several channels simultaneously to communicate their message to prospective customers. In this section we will look first at the barriers to international communication. Then we will survey the various factors that determine which communication strategy is most appropriate in a particular country. After that we discuss global advertising.

Barriers to International Communication

International communication occurs whenever a firm uses a marketing message to sell its products in another country. The effectiveness of a firm's international communication can be jeopardized by three potentially critical variables: cultural barriers, source effects, and noise levels.

CULTURAL BARRIERS   Cultural barriers can make it difficult to communicate messages across cultures. We discussed some sources and consequences of cultural differences between nations in Chapter 3 and in the previous section of this chapter. Because of cultural differences, a message that means one thing in one country may mean something quite different in another. For example, when Procter & Gamble promoted its Camay soap in Japan in 1983 it ran into unexpected trouble. In a TV commercial, a Japanese man walked into the bathroom while his wife was bathing. The woman began telling her husband all about her new beauty soap, but the husband, stroking her shoulder, hinted that suds were not on his mind. This ad had been very popular in Europe, but it flopped in Japan because it is considered very bad manners there for a man to intrude on his wife.[15] Benetton, the Italian clothing manufacturer and retailer, also has run into cultural problems with its advertising. The company launched a worldwide advertising campaign in 1989 with the theme "United Colors of Benetton" that had won awards in France. One ad featured a black woman breast-feeding a white baby, and another one showed a black man and a white man handcuffed together. Benetton was surprised when the ads were attacked by US civil rights groups for promoting white racial domination. Benetton withdrew its ads and fired its French advertising agency.

The best way for a firm to overcome cultural barriers is to develop cross-cultural literacy (see Chapter 3). In addition, it should employ some local input in developing its marketing message, such as using a local advertising agency. If the firm uses direct selling rather than advertising to communicate its message, it would be advised to develop a local sales force whenever possible. Cultural differences limit a firm's ability to use the same marketing message the world over. What works well in one country may be offensive in another.

SOURCE EFFECTS   Source effects occur when the receiver of the message (the potential consumer in this case) evaluates the message based on the status or image of the sender. Source effects can be damaging for an international business when potential consumers in a target country have a bias against foreign firms. For example, a wave of Japan bashing swept the United States in 1992. Worried that US consumers might view its advertisements negatively, Honda created advertisements that emphasized the US-content of its cars to show how American the company had become. Many international businesses try to counter negative source effects by deemphasizing their foreign origins. When British Petroleum acquired Mobil Oil's extensive network of US gas stations, it changed its name to BP, diverting attention away from the fact that one of the biggest operators of gas stations in the United States is a British firm.

Source effects can also be positive. French wine, Italian clothes, and German luxury cars benefit from nearly universal positive source effects. Far from downplaying national origins, in such cases it may pay a firm to emphasize its foreign origins. In Japan, for example, there is strong demand for high-quality foreign goods, particularly those from Europe. It has become chic to carry a Gucci handbag, sport a Rolex watch, drink expensive French wine, and drive a BMW.

NOISE LEVELS   Noise reduces the probability of effective communication. In this context, noise refers to the amount of other messages competing for a potential consumer's attention, and this too varies across countries. In highly developed countries such as the United States, noise from firms competing for the attention of target consumers is extremely high. Fewer firms vie for the attention of prospective customers in developing countries, and the noise level is lower.

Push versus Pull Strategies

The main decision with regard to communication strategy is the choice between a push strategy and a pull strategy. A push strategy emphasizes personal selling rather than mass media advertising in the promotional mix. Although very effective as a promotional tool, personal selling requires intensive use of a sales force and is relatively costly. A pull strategy depends more on mass media advertising to communicate the marketing message.

Although some firms employ only a pull strategy and others only a push strategy, still other firms combine direct selling with mass advertising to maximize communication effectiveness. Factors that determine the relative attractiveness of push and pull strategies include product type relative to consumer sophistication, channel length, and media availability.

PRODUCT TYPE AND CONSUMER SOPHISTICATION   A pull strategy is generally favored by firms in consumer goods industries that are trying to sell to a large segment of the market. For such firms, mass communication has cost advantages, and direct selling is rarely used. In contrast, a push strategy is favored by firms that sell industrial products or other complex products. A great strength of direct selling is that it allows the firm to educate potential consumers about the features of the product. This may not be necessary in advanced nations where a complex product has been in use for some time, where the product's attributes are well understood, and where consumers are sophisticated. However, customer education may be very important when consumers have less sophistication toward the product, which can be the case in developing nations, or in more advanced nations when a complex product is being introduced.

CHANNEL LENGTH   The longer the distribution channel, the more intermediaries there are that must be persuaded to carry the product. This can lead to inertia in the channel, which can make entry very difficult. Using direct selling to push a product through many layers of a distribution channel can be very expensive. In such circumstances, a firm may try to pull its product through the channels by using mass advertising to create consumer demand—the theory being that once demand is created, intermediaries will feel obliged to carry the product.

While US distribution channels are relatively short, in other countries they can be quite long. As discussed earlier, products often pass through two, three, or even four wholesalers before they reach the final retail outlet in Japan. This can make it difficult for foreign firms to break into the Japanese market. Not only must the foreigner persuade a Japanese retailer to carry the product, but also every intermediary in the chain must be persuaded to carry the product. Mass advertising may be one way to break down channel resistance.

MEDIA AVAILABILITY   A pull strategy relies on access to advertising media. A large number of media are available in the United States, including print media (newspapers and magazines) and electronic media (television and radio). Also, the rise of cable television in the United States has facilitated extremely focused advertising targeted at particular segments of the market (e.g., MTV for teens and young adults, Lifetime for women, ESPN for sports enthusiasts). With a few exceptions such as Canada and Japan, this level of media sophistication is not found outside the United States. Even many advanced nations have far fewer electronic media available for advertising. In many developing nations the situation is even more restrictive; mass media of all types are typically more limited. A firm's ability to use a pull strategy is limited in some countries by media availability. In such circumstances, a push strategy is more attractive.

Media availability is limited by law in some cases. Few countries allow advertisements for tobacco and alcohol products on television and radio, though they are usually permitted in print media. When the leading Japanese whiskey distiller, Suntory, entered the US market, it had to do so without television, its preferred medium. The firm spends about $50 million annually on television advertising in Japan.

THE PUSH–PULL MIX   The optimal mix between push and pull strategies depends on product type and consumer sophistication, channel length, and media sophistication. Push strategies tend to be emphasized:

- For industrial products and/or complex new products.
- When distribution channels are short.
- When few print or electronic media are available.

Pull strategies tend to be emphasized:

- For consumer goods.
- When distribution channels are long.
- When sufficient print and electronic media are available to carry the marketing message.

Global Advertising

In recent years, largely inspired by the work of visionaries such as Theodore Levitt, there has been much discussion about the pros and cons of standardizing advertising worldwide. One of the most successful standardized campaigns has been Philip Morris's promotion of Marlboro cigarettes. The campaign was instituted in the 1950s, when the brand was repositioned, to assure smokers that the flavor would be unchanged by the addition of a filter. The campaign theme of "Come to where the flavor is. Come to Marlboro country" was a worldwide success. Marlboro built on this when it introduced "the Marlboro man," a rugged cowboy smoking his Marlboro while riding his horse through the great outdoors. This ad proved successful in almost every major market around the world, and it helped propel Marlboro to the top of the world market share table.

FOR STANDARDIZED ADVERTISING   The support for global advertising is three-fold. First, it has significant economic advantages. Standardized advertising lowers the costs of value creation by spreading the fixed costs of developing the advertisements over many countries. For example, in the early 1980s Levi Strauss paid an advertising agency $550,000 to produce a series of TV commercials. By reusing this series in many countries, rather than developing a series for each country, the company enjoyed significant cost savings. Over a 20-year period Coca-Cola's advertising agency, McCann-Erickson, claims to have saved Coca-Cola $90 million by using certain elements of its campaign globally.

Second, there is the concern that creative talent is scarce and hence that one large effort to develop a campaign will produce better results than 40 or 50 smaller efforts.

A third justification for a standardized approach is that many brand names are global. With the substantial amount of international travel today and the considerable overlap in media across national borders, many international firms want to project a single brand image to avoid confusion caused by local campaigns that conflict with each other. This is particularly important in regions such as Western Europe, where travel across borders is almost as common as travel across state lines in the United States.

AGAINST STANDARDIZED ADVERTISING   There are two main arguments against globally standardized advertising. First, as we have seen repeatedly in this chapter and in Chapter 3, cultural differences between nations are such that a message that works in one nation can fail miserably in another. For an example, see the case of Polaroid, which is reviewed in the accompanying "Management Focus." Because of cultural diversity, it is extremely difficult to develop a single advertising theme that is effective worldwide. Messages directed at the culture of a given country may be more effective than global messages.

Second, country differences in advertising regulations may block the implementation of standardized advertising. For example, Kellogg could not use a television commercial it produced in Great Britain to promote its cornflakes in many other European countries. A reference to the iron and vitamin content of its cornflakes was not permissible in the Netherlands, where claims relating to health and medical benefits are outlawed. A child wearing a Kellogg T-shirt had to be edited out of the commercial before it could be used in France because French law forbids the use of children in product endorsements. Plus, the key line, "Kellogg's makes their cornflakes the best they have ever been," was disallowed in Germany because of a prohibition against competitive claims.[16] American Express ran afoul of regulatory authorities in Germany when it launched a promotional scheme that had proved very successful in other countries. The scheme advertised the offer of bonus points every time an American Express cardholder used his or her card. According to the advertisements, these bonus points could be used toward air travel with three airlines and hotel accommodations. American Express soon found itself charged with breaking Germany's competition law, which prevents an offer of free gifts in connection with the sale of goods, and the firm had to withdraw the advertisements at considerable cost.[17]

Polaroid introduced its SX-70 instant camera in Europe in the mid-1970s with the same marketing strategy, TV commercials, and print ads it had used in North America. Polaroid's headquarters believed the camera served a universal need—the pleasure of instant photography—and that the communication strategy should be the same the world over. The television commercials featured testimonials of personalities well known in the United States. Few of these personalities were known in Europe, however, and paign in no way helped its performance.

The lesson was remembered a decade later when Polaroid's European management launched a pan-European program to reposition Polaroid's instant photography from the "party camera" platform to a serious, "utilitarian" platform. This time headquarters did not assume it had the answers. Instead, it looked for inspiration in the various advertising practices of its European subsidiaries, and it found it in the strategy of one of its smallest those in Japan and Australia, liked the strategy so much that they adopted it.

What made this campaign different from the SX-70 campaign a decade earlier was the decentralized decision making. Instead of headquarters imposing on Europe an advertising campaign developed in the United States, the European subsidiaries developed their own campaign. Equally important, even after the pan-European program was adopted, European managers had the freedom to adapt the campaign to lo-

Global Advertising at Polaroid

managers of Polaroid's European operations pointed this out to headquarters. Unperturbed by these concerns, headquarters management set strict guidelines to discourage deviation from the global plan. The European personnel were proved correct. The testimonials by "unknown" personalities left consumers cold. The commercials failed to raise awareness of Polaroid's instant camera. Even though the camera later became successful in Europe, local management believes the misguided introductory cam-

subsidiaries in Switzerland. With considerable success, the Swiss subsidiary had promoted the functional uses of instant photography as a means of communicating with family and friends. A task force was set up to test this concept in other markets. The tests showed that the Swiss strategy was transferable and that it produced the desired impact. Thus was born Europe's "Learn to Speak Polaroid" campaign, one of the firm's most successful advertising efforts. Non-European subsidiaries, including

cal tastes and needs. For example, where tests showed that the "Learn to Speak Polaroid" tag did not convey the intended meaning in the local language, the subsidiary was free to change it. By adopting this approach, Polaroid reaped some benefits of standardized advertisements, while it customized its message to local conditions when that proved necessary.[18]

DEALING WITH COUNTRY DIFFERENCES Some firms have been experimenting with capturing some of the benefits of global standardization while recognizing differences in countries' cultural and legal environments. A firm may select some features for all of its advertising campaigns and localize other features. By doing so, it may save on some costs and build international brand recognition and yet customize its advertisements to different cultures.

This is what Polaroid did with the "Learn to Speak Polaroid" campaign (see the "Management Focus" for details). Pepsi-Cola used a similar approach in a 1980s advertising campaign. The company wanted to use modern music to connect its products with local markets. Pepsi hired US singer Tina Turner and rock stars from six countries to team up in singing and performing the Pepsi-Cola theme song in a big rock concert. The commercials are customized for each market by showing Turner with the rock stars from that country. Except for the footage of the local stars, all the commercials are identical. The campaign was extended to 30 countries, which relieved the local subsidiaries or bottlers of having to develop their own campaigns.[19]

Pricing Strategy

Pricing strategy is an important component of the overall international marketing mix. In this section we look at three aspects of international pricing strategy. First, we examine the case for pursuing price discrimination, charging different prices for the same product in different countries. Second, we look at what might be called strategic pricing. Third, we review some regulatory factors, such as government-mandated price controls and antidumping regulations, that limit a firm's ability to charge the prices it would prefer in a country.

Price Discrimination

In an international context, price discrimination exists whenever consumers in different countries are charged different prices for the same product. Price discrimination involves charging whatever the market will bear; in a competitive market, prices may have to be lower than in a market where the firm has a monopoly. Price discrimination can help a company maximize its profits. It makes economic sense to charge different prices in different countries.

Two conditions are necessary for profitable price discrimination. First, the firm must be able to keep its national markets separate. If it cannot, individuals or businesses may undercut its attempt at price discrimination through arbitrage. Arbitrage occurs when an individual or business capitalizes on a price differential by purchasing the product in the country where prices are lower and reselling it in the country where prices are higher. For example, many automobile firms have long practiced price discrimination in Europe. At one point a Ford Escort cost $2,000 more in Germany than it did in Belgium. This policy broke down when car dealers bought Escorts in Belgium and drove them to Germany, where they sold them at a profit for slightly less than Ford was selling Escorts in Germany. To protect the market share of its German auto dealers, Ford had to bring its German prices into line with those being charged in Belgium. In other words, Ford could not keep these markets separate.

However, Ford still practices price discrimination between Great Britain and Belgium. A Ford car can cost up to $3,000 more in Great Britain than in Belgium. Arbitrage has not been able to equalize the price, because right-hand-drive cars are sold in Great Britain and left-hand-drive cars in the rest of Europe. Because there is no market for left-hand-drive cars in Great Britain, Ford has been able to keep the markets separate.

The second necessary condition for profitable price discrimination is different price elasticities of demand. The price elasticity of demand is a measure of the responsiveness of demand for a product to changes in price. Demand is said to be elastic when a small change in price produces a large change in demand; it is said to be inelastic when a large change in price produces only a small change in demand. Figure 12.2 illustrates elastic and inelastic demand curves. Generally, a firm can charge a higher price in a country where demand is inelastic.

THE DETERMINANTS OF DEMAND ELASTICITY   The elasticity of demand for a product in a given country is determined by a number of factors; the two most important are income level and competitive conditions. Price elasticity tends to be greater (more elastic) in countries with low income levels. Consumers with limited incomes tend to be very price conscious; they have less to spend, so they look much more closely at price. Thus, price elasticities for products such as television sets are greater in countries such as India, where a television set is still a luxury item, than in the United States, where it is considered a necessity.

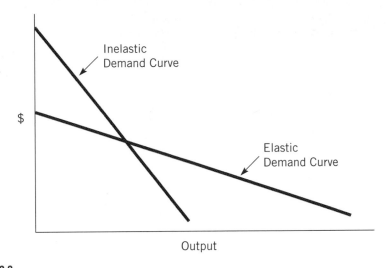

$

Inelastic
Demand Curve

Elastic
Demand Curve

Output

Figure 12.2

Elastic and Inelastic Demand Curves

Generally, the more competitors there are, the greater consumers' bargaining power will be and the more likely consumers will be to buy from the firm that charges the lowest price. Thus, a large number of competitors causes high elasticity of demand. In such circumstances, if a firm raises its prices above those of its competitors, consumers will switch to the competitors' products. The opposite is true when a firm faces few competitors. When competitors are limited, consumers' bargaining power is weaker and price is less important as a competitive weapon. Thus, a firm may charge a higher price for its product in a country where competition is limited than in a country where competition is intense.

PROFIT MAXIMIZING UNDER PRICE DISCRIMINATION   For those readers with some grasp of economic logic, we can offer a more formal presentation of the above argument. (Readers unfamiliar with basic economic terminology may want to skip this subsection.) Figure 12.3 shows the situation facing a firm that sells the same product in only two countries, Japan and the United States. The Japanese market is very competitive, so the firm faces an elastic demand curve (D_J) and marginal revenue curve (MR_J). The US market is not competitive, so there the firm faces an inelastic demand curve (D_U) and marginal revenue curve (MR_U). Also shown in the figure are the firm's total demand curve (D_{J+U}), total marginal revenue curve (MR_{J+U}), and marginal cost curve (MC). The total demand curve is simply the summation of the demand facing the firm in Japan and the United States, as is the total marginal revenue curve.

To maximize profits, the firm must produce at the output where MR = MC. In Figure 12.3 this implies an output of 55 units. If the firm does not practice price discrimination, it will charge a price of $43.58 to sell an output of 55 units. Thus, without price discrimination the firm's total revenues are

$$\$43.58 \times 55 = \$2,396.90$$

Now look what happens when the firm decides to engage in price discrimination. It will still produce 55 units, since that is where MR = MC. However, the firm must now allocate this output between the two countries to take advantage of the difference in demand elasticity. Proper allocation of output between Japan and the United States can be determined graphically by drawing a line through their respective

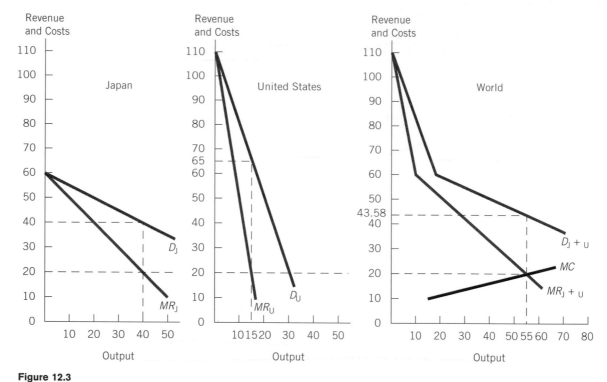

Figure 12.3

Price Discrimination

graphs at $20 to indicate that $20 is the marginal cost in each country (see Figure 12.3). To maximize profits in each country, prices are now set at that level where the marginal revenue for that country equals marginal costs. In Japan this is a price of $40, and the firm sells 40 units. In the United States the optimal price is $65, and it sells 15 units. Thus, reflecting the different competitive conditions, the price charged in the United States is over 50 percent more than the price charged in Japan. Look at what happens to total revenues. With price discrimination, the firm earns revenues of

$$\$40 \times 40 \text{ units} = \$1,600$$

in Japan and

$$\$65 \times 15 \text{ units} = \$975$$

in the United States. By engaging in price discrimination, the firm can earn total revenues of

$$\$1,600 + \$975 = \$2,575,$$

which is $178.10 more than the $2,396.90 it earned before. Price discrimination pays!

Strategic Pricing

The concept of strategic pricing has three aspects, which we will refer to as predatory pricing, multipoint pricing, and experience curve pricing. Both predatory pricing and experience curve pricing can result in problems with antidumping regulations. After we review predatory and experience curve pricing, we will look at antidumping rules and other regulatory policies.

PREDATORY PRICING Predatory pricing is the use of price as a competitive weapon to drive weaker competitors out of a national market. Once the competitors have left the market, the firm can raise prices and enjoy high profits. For such a pricing strategy to work, the firm must normally have a profitable position in another national market, which it can use to subsidize aggressive pricing in the market it is trying to monopolize. Many Japanese firms have been accused of pursuing this strategy. The argument runs like this: Because the Japanese market is protected from foreign competition by high informal trade barriers, Japanese firms can charge high prices and earn high profits at home. They then use these profits to subsidize aggressive pricing overseas, which drives competitors out of those markets. Once this has occurred, it is claimed, the Japanese firms raise prices. For example, Matsushita has been accused of using this strategy to enter the US TV market. As one of the major TV producers in Japan, Matsushita earned high profits at home. It then used these profits to subsidize the losses it made in the United States during its early years there, when it priced low to increase its market penetration. Ultimately, Matsushita became the world's largest manufacturer of TVs.[20]

MULTIPOINT PRICING STRATEGY Multipoint pricing strategy becomes an issue where two or more international businesses compete against each other in two or more distinct (national) markets. For example, multipoint pricing is an issue for Kodak and Fuji Photo because both companies compete against each other in different national markets for film products around the world. The concept of **multipoint pricing** refers to the fact a firm's pricing strategy in one market may have an impact on its rival's pricing strategy in another market. Aggressive pricing in one market may elicit a competitive response from a rival in another market that is important to the firm. In the case of Kodak and Fuji, for example, in January 1997 Fuji launched an aggressive competitive attack against Kodak in the American company's home market, cutting prices on multiple-roll packs of 35mm film by as much as 50 percent.[21] This price cutting resulted in a 28 percent increase in shipments of Fuji color film during the first six months of 1997, while Kodak's shipments dropped by 11 percent. This attack created a dilemma for Kodak because the company did not want to start price discounting in its largest and most profitable market. Kodak's response was to aggressively cut prices in Fuji's largest market, Japan. This strategic response recognized the interdependence between Kodak and Fuji, and the fact that they compete against each other in many different nations. Fuji responded to Kodak's counterattack by pulling back from its aggressive stance in the US market.

> **multipoint pricing** A firm's pricing strategy in one market may have an impact on its rival's pricing strategy in another market.

The Kodak versus Fuji story illustrates an important aspect of multipoint pricing—aggressive pricing in one market may elicit a response from rivals in another market. A firm needs to consider how its global rivals will respond to any changes in its pricing strategy before embarking on them. A second aspect of multipoint pricing arises when two or more global companies focus on particular national markets and launch vigorous price wars in those markets in an attempt to gain market dominance. In the Brazil market for disposable diapers, for example, two US companies, Kimberly-Clark Corp. and Procter & Gamble, started a price war as each of these companies struggled to establish dominance in the market.[22] The cost of disposable diapers fell from $1 per diaper in 1997 to 33 cents per diaper in 1997, while several other competitors, including indigenous Brazilian firms, were driven out of the market. Kimberly-Clark and Procter & Gamble can afford this behavior, even though it dramatically reduces their profits in Brazil, because they have profitable operations elsewhere in the world that can subsidize losses incurred in Brazil.

Pricing decisions around the world need to be centrally monitored. It is tempting to delegate full responsibility for pricing decisions to the managers of various national subsidiaries, thereby reaping the benefits of decentralization. However, because pricing strategy in one part of the world can elicit a competitive response in another part, central management needs to at least monitor and approve pricing decisions in a given national market, and local managers need to recognize that their actions can affect competitive conditions in other countries.

EXPERIENCE CURVE PRICING   We first encountered the experience curve in Chapter 10. As a firm builds its accumulated production volume over time, unit costs fall due to experience effects. Learning effects and economies of scale underlie the experience curve. Price comes into the picture because aggressive pricing (along with aggressive promotion and advertising) is a way to build accumulated sales volume rapidly and thus move down the experience curve. Firms further down the experience curve have a cost advantage vis-à-vis firms further up the curve.

Many firms pursuing an experience curve pricing strategy on an international scale price low worldwide in attempting to build global sales volume as rapidly as possible, even if this means taking large losses initially. Such a firm believes that several years in the future, when it has moved down the experience curve, it will be making substantial profits and have a cost advantage over its less-aggressive competitors.

Regulatory Influences on Prices

Firms' abilities to engage in either price discrimination or strategic pricing may be limited by national or international regulations. Most important, a firm's freedom to set its own prices is constrained by antidumping regulations and competition policy.

ANTIDUMPING REGULATIONS   Both predatory pricing and experience curve pricing can run afoul of antidumping regulations. Technically speaking, dumping occurs whenever a firm sells a product for a price that is less than the cost of producing it. Most regulations, however, define dumping more vaguely. For example, a country is allowed to bring antidumping actions against an importer under Article 6 of GATT as long as two criteria are met: sales at "less than fair value" and "material injury to a domestic industry." The problem with this terminology is that it does not indicate what is a fair value. The ambiguity has led some to argue that selling abroad at prices below those in the country of origin, as opposed to below cost, is dumping.

Such logic led the Bush administration to place a 25 percent duty on imports of Japanese light trucks in 1988. The Japanese manufacturers protested that they were not selling below cost. Admitting that their prices were lower in the United States than in Japan, they argued that this simply reflected the intensely competitive nature of the US market (i.e., different price elasticities). In a similar example, the European Commission found Japanese exporters of dot-matrix printers to be in violation of dumping regulations. To correct what it saw as dumping, the EU placed a 47 percent import duty on imports of dot-matrix printers from Japan. According to EU rules, this import duty must be passed on to European consumers as a price increase.[23]

Antidumping rules set a floor under export prices and limit firms' ability to pursue strategic pricing. The rather vague terminology used in most antidumping actions suggests that a firm's ability to engage in price discrimination also may be challenged under antidumping legislation.

COMPETITION POLICY   Most industrialized nations have regulations designed to promote competition and to restrict monopolies. These regulations can be used to limit the prices a firm can charge in a given country. For example, during the 1960s and 1970s the Swiss pharmaceutical manufacturer Hoffmann-LaRoche had a monopoly on the supply of Valium and Librium tranquilizers. In 1973 the company was investigated by the British Monopolies and Mergers Commission, which is responsible for promoting fair competition in Great Britain. The commission found that Hoffmann-LaRoche was overcharging for its tranquilizers and ordered the company to reduce its prices 35 to 40 percent. Hoffmann-LaRoche maintained unsuccessfully that it was merely engaging in price discrimination. Similar actions were later brought against Hoffmann-LaRoche by the German cartel office and by the Dutch and Danish governments.[24]

Configuring the Marketing Mix

A firm might want to vary aspects of its marketing mix from country to country to take into account local differences in culture, economic conditions, competitive conditions, product and technical standards, distribution systems, government regulations, and the like. Such differences may require some variation in product attributes, distribution strategy, communications strategy, and pricing strategy. As a result of the cumulative effect of these factors, rarely can a firm adopt the same marketing mix worldwide.

For example, financial services is often thought of as an industry where global standardization of the marketing mix is the norm. However, while a financial services company such as American Express may sell the same basic charge card service worldwide, utilize the same basic fee structure for that product, and adopt the same basic global advertising message ("never leave home without it"), differences in national regulations still mean it has to vary aspects of its communication strategy from country to country (as pointed out earlier, the promotional strategy it had developed in the United States was illegal in Germany). Similarly, while McDonald's is often thought of as the quintessential example of a firm that sells the same basic standardized product worldwide, in reality it varies one important aspects of its marketing mix—its menu—from country to country. McDonald's also varies its distribution strategy from country to country. In Canada and the United States most McDonald's are located in areas that are easily accessible by car, but in more densely populated and less automobile-reliant societies of the world, such as Japan and Great Britain, location decisions are driven by the accessibility of a restaurant to pedestrian traffic. Because countries typically still do differ along one or more of the dimensions discussed above, some customization of the marketing mix is normal.

However, there are often significant opportunities for standardization in one or more elements of the marketing mix. Firms may find that it is possible and desirable to standardize their global advertising message and/or core product attributes to realize substantial cost economies. At the same time, they may find it desirable to customize their distribution and pricing strategy on a country-by-country basis to take advantage of local differences. The "customization versus standardization" debate is not an all or nothing issue; it frequently makes sense to standardize some aspects of the marketing mix and customize others, depending on conditions prevailing in various national markets. The accompanying "Management Focus" looks at Castrol, which sells a standardized product worldwide—lubricating oil—and yet varies other aspects of its marketing mix from country to country, depending on economic conditions, competitive conditions, and distribution systems. Decisions about what to customize and what to standardize should be driven by a detailed examination of the costs and benefits of doing so for each element in the marketing mix.

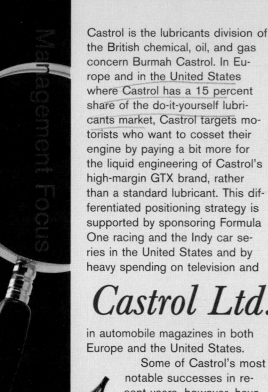

Castrol is the lubricants division of the British chemical, oil, and gas concern Burmah Castrol. In Europe and in the United States where Castrol has a 15 percent share of the do-it-yourself lubricants market, Castrol targets motorists who want to cosset their engine by paying a bit more for the liquid engineering of Castrol's high-margin GTX brand, rather than a standard lubricant. This differentiated positioning strategy is supported by sponsoring Formula One racing and the Indy car series in the United States and by heavy spending on television and

Castrol Ltd.

in automobile magazines in both Europe and the United States.

Some of Castrol's most notable successes in recent years, however, have been in the developing nations of Asia where Castrol reaps only one-sixth of its sales, but more than one-quarter of its operating profits. In Vietnam automobiles are still relatively rare, so Castrol has targeted the vast army of motorcycle owners. Castrol's strategy is to target people who want to take care of their new motorcycles. The long-term goal is to

build brand loyalty, so when automobile ownership becomes common in Vietnam, as Castrol believes it will, former motorcycle owners will stick with Castrol when they trade up to cars. This strategy has already worked in Thailand. Castrol has held the leading share of the motorcycle market in Thailand since the early 1980s, and it now holds the leading share in that country's rapidly growing automobile market.

Unlike its practice in more developed countries, Castrol's communications strategy in Vietnam does not focus on television and glossy print media (there is relatively little of either in Vietnam). Rather, Castrol focuses on building consumer awareness through extensive use of billboards, car stickers, and some 4,000 signboards at Vietnam's ubiquitous roadside garages and motorcycle cleaning shops. Castrol also developed a unique slogan that has a rhythmic quality in Vietnamese *"Dau nhot tot nhat"* ("best quality lubricants") and sticks in consumers' minds. Castrol's researchers say the slogan is recognized by a remarkable 99 percent of people in Ho Chi Minh City.

As elsewhere, Castrol has adopted a premium pricing strategy in Vietnam, which is consistent with the company's attempt to build a global brand image of high quality. Castrol oil costs about $1.5 per liter in Vietnam, about three times as much as cheaper oil imported from countries such as Taiwan and Thailand. Despite the high price of its product, Castrol claims it is gaining share in Vietnam as its branding strategy wins converts.

Castrol has had to tailor its distribution strategy to Vietnam's unique conditions. In most countries where it operates, Castrol divides the country into regions and has a single distributor in each region. In Vietnam, however, Castrol will often have two distinct distributors in a region—one to deal with state-owned customers, of which there are still many in this still nominally Communist country, and one to deal with private customers. Castrol acknowledges that the system is costly but says it is the only way to operate in a country where there is still some tension between state and private entities.[25]

New Product Development

Firms that successfully develop and market new products can earn enormous returns. Examples include Du Pont, which has produced a steady stream of successful innovations such as cellophane, nylon, Freon, and Teflon (nonstick pans); Sony, whose successes include the Walkman and the compact disk; Merck, the drug company that during the 1980s produced seven major new drugs; 3M, which has applied its core competency in tapes and adhesives to developing a range of new products; Intel, which has consistently managed to lead in the development of innovative new microprocessors to run personal computers; and Cisco Systems, which developed the routers that sit at the hubs of Internet connections, directing the flow of digital traffic.

In today's world, competition is as much about technological innovation as anything else. The pace of technological change has accelerated since the Industrial Revolution in the 18th century, and it continues to do so today. The result has been a dramatic shortening of product life cycles. Technological innovation is both creative and destructive.[26] An innovation can make established products obsolete overnight, but it can also make a host of new products possible. Witness recent changes in the electronics industry. For 40 years before the early 1950s, vacuum valves were a major component in radios and then in record players and early computers. The advent of transistors destroyed the market for vacuum valves, but at the same time it created new opportunities connected with transistors. Transistors took up far less space than vacuum valves, creating a trend toward miniaturization that continues today. The transistor held its position as the major component in the electronics industry for just a decade. In the 1970s microprocessors were developed, and the market for transistors declined rapidly. At the same time, however, the microprocessor created yet another set of new product opportunities—handheld calculators (which destroyed the market for slide rules), compact disk players (which destroyed the market for analog record players), personal computers (which destroyed the market for typewriters), to name a few.

This process of creative destruction unleashed by technological change makes it critical that a firm stay on the leading edge of technology, lest it lose out to a competitor's innovations. As we explain in the next subsection, this not only creates a need for the firm to invest in R&D, but it also requires the firm to establish R&D activities at those locations around the globe where expertise is concentrated. But leading-edge technology on its own is not enough to guarantee a firm's survival. The firm must also apply that technology to developing products that satisfy consumer needs, and it must design the product so it can be manufactured cost effectively. To do that, the firm needs to build links between R&D, marketing, and manufacturing. This is difficult enough for the domestic firm, but it is even more problematic for the international business competing in an industry where consumer tastes and preferences differ from country to country. We now examine the issues of locating R&D activities and building links between R&D, marketing, and manufacturing.

The Location of R&D

Ideas for new products are stimulated largely by the interactions of scientific research, demand conditions, and competitive conditions. Other things being equal, the rate of new product development seems to be greater in countries where:

- More money is spent on basic and applied research and development.
- Underlying demand is strong.
- Consumers are affluent.
- Competition is intense.[27]

Basic and applied research and development discovers new technologies and then commercializes them. Strong demand and affluent consumers create a potential market for new products. Intense competition between firms stimulates innovation as the firms try to beat their competitors and reap potentially enormous first-mover advantages that result from successful innovation.

For most of the post–World War II period, the country that ranked highest on these criteria was the United States. The United States devoted a greater proportion of its gross domestic product to R&D than any other country did. Its scientific establishment was the largest and most active in the world. US consumers were the most affluent in the world, the market was large, and competition among US firms was brisk. Because of these factors, the United States was the lead market—the market where most new products were developed and introduced. Accordingly, it was the best location for R&D activities—it was where the action was.

Over the past 20 years things have been changing fast. The US monopoly on new product development has weakened considerably. Although US firms are still at the leading edge of many new technologies, Japanese and European firms are also strong players, with companies such as Sony, Sharp, Ericsson, Nokia, and Philips NV driving product innovation in their respective industries. Both Japan and Germany are now devoting a greater proportion of their GDP to nondefense R&D than is the United States.[28] In addition, both Japan and the European Union are large, affluent markets, and the wealth gap between them and the United States is closing.

While it is no longer appropriate to consider the United States the lead market, it is questionable if any country is. To succeed today, it is often necessary to simultaneously introduce new products in all major industrialized markets. Because leading-edge research is now carried out in many locations around the world, the argument for centralizing R&D activity in the United States is now much weaker than it was two decades ago. (It used to be argued that centralized R&D eliminated duplication.) Much leading-edge research is now occurring in Japan and Europe. Such dispersion allows a firm to stay close to the center of leading-edge activity to gather scientific and competitive information and to draw on local scientific resources.[29] This may result in some duplication of R&D activities, but the cost disadvantages of duplication are outweighed by the advantages of dispersion.

For example, to expose themselves to the research and product development work now being done in Japan, many US firms have set up satellite R&D centers in Japan. Kodak's $65 million R&D center in Japan employs approximately 200 people. The company hired about 100 professional Japanese researchers and directed the lab to concentrate on electronic imaging technology. Other US firms that have established R&D facilities in Japan are Corning, Texas Instruments, IBM, Digital Equipment, Procter & Gamble, Upjohn, Pfizer, Du Pont, and Monsanto.[30] The National Science Foundation (NSF) has documented a sharp increase in the proportion of total R&D spending by US firms that is now made abroad. According to NSF data, between 1985 and 1993 the amount of funds committed to foreign R&D soared nine-fold, while R&D spending in the United States remained essentially flat.[31] For example, Motorola now has 14 dedicated R&D facilities in seven countries, and Bristol-Myers Squibb has 12 facilities in six countries. To internationalize their own research and gain access to US research talent, many European and Japanese firms have begun to invest in US-based research facilities, according to the NSF.

Integrating R&D, Marketing, and Production

Although a firm that is successful at developing new products may earn enormous returns, new product development has a high failure rate. One study of product development in 16 companies in the chemical, drug, petroleum, and electronics industries suggested that only about 20 percent of R&D projects ultimately result in commercially successful products or processes.[32] Another case study of product development in three companies (one in chemicals and two in drugs) reported that about 60 percent of R&D projects reached technical completion, 30 percent were commercialized, and only 12 percent earned an economic profit that exceeded the company's cost of capital.[33] Similarly, a study by the consulting division of Booz, Allen & Hamilton found that more than one-third of 13,000 consumer and industrial products introduced between 1976 and 1981 failed to meet company-specific financial and strategic performance criteria.[34] A more recent study found that 45 percent of new products introduced into the marketplace did not meet their profitability goals.[35] This evidence suggests that many R&D projects do not result in a commercial product, and that between 33 percent and 60 percent of all new products that do reach the marketplace fail to generate an adequate economic return.

The reasons for such high failure rates are various and include development of a technology for which demand is limited, failure to adequately commercialize promising technology, and inability to manufacture a new product in a cost-effective manner. Firms can avoid such mistakes by insisting on tight cross-functional coordination and integration between three core functions involved in the development of new products: R&D, marketing, and production.[36] Tight cross-functional integration between R&D, production, and marketing can help a company to ensure that

1 Product development projects are driven by customer needs.
2 New products are designed for ease of manufacture.
3 Development costs are kept in check.
4 Time to market is minimized.

Close integration between R&D and marketing is required to ensure that product development projects are driven by the needs of customers. A company's customers can be a primary sources of new product ideas. Identification of customer needs, particularly unmet needs, can spur successful product innovation. As the point of contact with customers, a company's marketing function can provide valuable information about customer needs. Integration of R&D and marketing are crucial if a new product is to be properly commercialized. Without integration of R&D and marketing, a company runs the risk of developing products for which there is little or no demand.

Integration between R&D and production can help a company to ensure that products are designed with manufacturing requirements in mind, which can lower manufacturing costs and increase product quality. Integrating R&D and production can also help lower development costs and speed products to market. If a new product is not designed with manufacturing capabilities in mind, it may prove too difficult to build, given existing manufacturing technology. Then the product will have to be redesigned, and both overall development costs and the time it takes to bring the product to market may increase significantly. For example, making design changes during product planning could increase overall development costs by 50 percent and add 25 percent to the time it takes to bring the product to market.[37] Many quantum product innovations require new processes to manufacture them, which makes it all the more important to achieve close integration between R&D and production.[38]

Cross-Functional Teams

One way to achieve cross-functional integration is to establish cross-functional product development teams composed of representatives from R&D, marketing, and production. Because these functions may be located in different countries, the team will sometimes have a multinational membership. The team's objective should be to take a product development project from the initial concept development through to market introduction. A number of attributes seem to be important for a product development team to function effectively and meet its development milestones.[39]

First, the team should be led by a "heavyweight" project manager who has high status within the organization and has the power and authority required to get the financial and human resources the team needs to succeed. This leader should be dedicated primarily, if not entirely, to the project. The leader should be someone who believes in the project (a champion) and is skilled at integrating the perspectives of different functions and at helping personnel from different functions and countries work together for a common goal. The leader should also be able to act as an advocate of the team to senior management.

Cross-functional teams are one of the best ways to achieve cross-functional development on new products. Your text mentions a few problems with these types of teams (like lack of camaraderie), especially when members are located across the globe. What are some other potential problems with having team members located in different countries?
© PhotoDisc.

Second, the team should be composed of at least one member from each key function. The team members should have an ability to contribute functional expertise, a high standing within their function, a willingness to share responsibility for team results, and an ability to put functional and national advocacy aside. It is generally preferable if core team members are 100 percent dedicated to the project for its duration so their focus is on the project, not on the ongoing work of their function.

Third, if possible the team members should be physically located to create a sense of camaraderie and to facilitate communication. This presents problems if the team members are drawn from facilities in different nations. One solution is to transfer key individuals to one location for the duration of a product development project. Fourth, the team should have a clear plan and clear goals, particularly with regard to critical development milestones and development budgets. The team should have incentives to attain those goals, for example, pay bonuses when major development milestones are hit. Fifth, each team needs to develop its own processes for communication and conflict resolution. For example, one product development team at Quantum Corporation, a California-based manufacturer of disk drives for personal computers, instituted a rule that all major decisions would be made and conflicts resolved at meetings that were held every Monday afternoon. This simple rule helped the team to meet its development goals. In this case, it was also common for team members to fly in from Japan, where the product was to be manufactured, to the US development center for the Monday morning meetings.[40]

Implications for International Business

The need to integrate R&D and marketing to adequately commercialize new technologies poses special problems in the international business because commercialization may require different versions of a new product to be produced for different countries. We saw an example of this in the opening case, which described how Procter & Gamble's R&D center in Kobe, Japan, developed a dish soap formula specifically for the Japanese market. To do this, the firm must build close links between its R&D centers and its various country operations. A similar argument applies to the need to integrate R&D and production, particularly in those international businesses that have dispersed various production activities to different locations around the globe.

Integrating R&D, marketing, and production in an international business may require R&D centers in North America, Asia, and Europe that are closely linked by formal and informal integrating mechanisms with marketing operations in each country in their regions, and with the various manufacturing facilities. In addition, the international business may have to establish cross-functional teams whose members are dispersed around the globe. This complex endeavor requires the company to utilize a range of formal and informal integrating mechanisms to knit its far-flung operations together so they can produce new products in an effective and timely manner.

While there is no one best model for allocating product development responsibilities to various centers, one solution adopted by many international businesses involves establishing a global network of R&D centers. Within this model, fundamental research is undertaken at **basic research centers** located around the globe. These centers for fundamental research are normally located in regions or cities where valuable scientific knowledge is being created, and where there is a pool of skilled research talent (e.g., Silicon Valley in the United States, Cambridge in England, Kobe in Japan). These centers are the innovation engines of the firm; they develop the basic technologies that ultimately become new products.

basic research centers Centers for fundamental research located in regions or cities where valuable scientific knowledge is being created, and where there is a pool of skilled research talent.

These technologies are then picked up by R&D units attached to global product divisions and are used to generate new products to serve the global marketplace. This level emphasizes commercialization of the technology and design for manufacturing. If there is a need to further customize the product so that it appeals to the tastes and preferences of consumers in individual countries, any such redesign work will be done by an R&D group based in a subsidiary in that country or at a regional center that customizes products for several different countries in the region.

Consider the case of Hewlett-Packard (HP).[41] HP has four basic research centers. They are located in Palo Alto, California; Bristol, England; Haifa, Israel; and Tokyo, Japan. These labs are the seedbed for technologies that ultimately become new products and businesses. They are the company's innovation engines. The Palo Alto center, for example, pioneered HP's thermal ink-jet technology. The products are developed by R&D centers associated with HP's global product divisions. Thus, the Consumer Products Group, which has its worldwide headquarters in San Diego, California, designs, develops, and manufactures a range of imaging products using HP-pioneered thermal ink-jet technology. The process does not stop here, however; certain subsidiaries might then take the lead in customizing the product so that it best matches the needs of important national markets. HP's subsidiary in Singapore, for example, is responsible for the design and production of thermal ink-jet printers for Japan and other Asian markets. This subsidiary takes products originally developed in San Diego and redesigns them for the Asian market. In addition, the Singapore subsidiary has taken the lead from San Diego in the design and development of certain portable thermal ink-jet printers. HP has delegated this responsibility to Singapore because it has built important competencies in the design and production of thermal ink-jets products, so it has become one of the best places in the world to undertake this activity.

Microsoft offers a similar example. The company has basic research sites in Redmond, Washington (its headquarters), Cambridge, England, and Silicon Valley, California. Staff at these sites work on the fundamental problems that underlie the design of future products. For example, a group at Redmond is working on natural language recognition software, while another works on artificial intelligence. These research centers don't produce new products as such, rather they produce the technology that is used to enhance existing products or help produce new products. The products themselves are made by dedicated product groups (e.g., desktop operating systems, applications). Customization of the products to match the needs of local markets is then sometimes carried out at local subsidiaries. Thus, the Chinese subsidiary in Singapore will do some basic customization of programs such as Microsoft Office, adding Chinese characters and customizing the interface.

Key Terms

Summary

This chapter discussed the marketing and R&D functions in international business. A persistent theme of the chapter is the tension that exists between the need to reduce costs and the need to be responsive to local conditions, which raises costs. The following points have been made:

1 Theodore Levitt has argued that, due to the advent of modern communications and transport technologies, consumer tastes and preferences are becoming global, which is creating global markets for standardized consumer products. However, this position is regarded as extreme by many commentators, who argue that substantial differences still exist between countries.

2 Market segmentation refers to identifying distinct groups of consumers whose purchasing behavior differs from other groups in important ways. Managers in an international business need to be cognizant of two main issues relating to segmentation—the extent to which there are differences between countries in the structure of market segments, and the existence of segments that transcend national borders.

3 A product can be viewed as a bundle of attributes. Product attributes need to be varied from country to country to satisfy different consumer tastes and preferences.

4 National variations in consumer tastes and preferences are due to differences in culture and economic development. In addition, differences in product and technical standards may require the firm to customize product attributes from country to country.

5 A distribution strategy decision is an attempt to define the optimal channel for delivering a product to the consumer.

6 Significant country differences exist in distribution systems. In some countries the retail system is concentrated; in others it is fragmented. In some countries channel length is short; in others it is long. Access to some countries' distribution channels is difficult to achieve.

7 A critical element in the marketing mix is communication strategy, which defines the process the firm will use in communicating the attributes of its product to prospective customers.

8 Barriers to international communication include cultural differences, source effects, and noise levels.

9 A communication strategy is either a push strategy or a pull strategy. A push strategy emphasizes personal selling, and a pull strategy emphasizes mass media advertising. Whether a push strategy or a pull strategy is optimal depends on the type of product, consumer sophistication, channel length, and media availability.

10 A globally standardized advertising campaign, which uses the same marketing message all over the world, has economic advantages, but it fails to account for differences in culture and governmental advertising regulations.

11 Price discrimination exists when consumers in different countries are charged different prices for the same product. Price discrimination can help a firm maximize its profits. For price discrimination to be effective, the national markets must be separate and their price elasticities of demand must differ.

12 Predatory pricing is the use of profit gained in one market to support aggressive pricing in another market for the purpose of driving competitors out of that market.

13 Multipoint pricing refers to the fact a firm's pricing strategy in one market may affect a rivals' pricing strategy in another market. In particular, aggressive pricing in one market may elicit a competitive response from a rival in another market.

14 Experience curve pricing is the use of aggressive pricing to build accumulated volume as rapidly as possible to move the firm down the experience curve quickly.

15 New product development is a high-risk, potentially high-return activity. To build a competency in new product development, an international business must do two things: (i) disperse R&D activities to those countries where new products are being pioneered and (ii) integrate R&D with marketing and manufacturing.

16 Achieving tight integration among R&D, marketing, and manufacturing requires the use of cross-functional teams.

Internet Exercises

1 Maybelline products can be found in nearly any discount store across America. The products can also be found in China, where the products' American roots are used in promotional strategies. But Maybelline products are not made by an American company; they are made by the French cosmetics giant L'Oreal. L'Oreal has enjoyed unprecedented growth in recent years, expanding its reach in markets from China to Mexico. It could be said that the company is transforming the highly competitive global cosmetics industry. The secret to L'Oreal success comes not from standardizing its brands across markets, but from adapting brands to each market to make them culturally palatable.

L'Oreal's strategy is a direct contradiction of other international success stories such as Coca-Cola's, where the emphasis has been on pushing the same brand around the world. The strategy has been so successful that competitors such as Japan's Shiseido Company are beginning to follow it as well, a threat that could make it more difficult for L'Oreal to succeed. Another major challenge facing the cosmetics powerhouse is the threat of new competition from

the Internet. Go to L'Oreal's website (**www.loreal.com**) and also to www.businessweek.com and search under L'Oreal. How should L'Oreal respond to the Internet? In your opinion, should the company develop its own Internet retail outlet? As the owner of an Internet cosmetics start-up company, how would you approach international product and brand development? Would you follow a strategy similar to that of L'Oreal and offer a range of culture-specific products, or would you attempt to create a global brand that sells across a range of cultures? What are the advantages and disadvantages of each strategy? How, if at all, is selling cosmetics electronically different from selling cosmetics through traditional retail outlets?

Source: *Business Week*, June 28, 1999, pp. 70–75.

2 Beiersdorf is not a commonly recognized name. But you might be familiar with Nivea skin cream. Beiersdorf, a German company, has been making Nivea since 1912, but it has made no effort to draw attention to that fact. Instead, the company has tried to make the global product local. Rolf Kunisch, CEO of Beiersdorf, notes, "Polish

people love Nivea . . . and think that it is the oldest Polish brand." The company sells its Nivea brand all over the world and holds some 15 percent of the world market in skin-care products making it the top-selling brand in the world.

Consider the difference between Beiersdorf's strategy and that of French cosmetics giant L'Oreal (see previous exercise). L'Oreal has very successfully transformed itself from a local company into a global powerhouse, not by pushing a single brand, but by focusing on cultural differences in the marketplace and developing products designed to meet consumer preferences. How has Beiersdorf managed to succeed with a single brand? One challenge L'Oreal expects to face in the near future is electronic sales in cosmetics. Go to Beiersdorf's website (**www.beiersdorf.de/** –the English version is at a button off to the right) and also to L'Oreal's (**www.loreal.com**). Which company do you feel is in a better position to meet the threat posed by the Internet? Why?

Source: *Business Week Online*, June 28, 1999.

Critical Thinking and Discussion Questions

1 Imagine you are the marketing manager for a US manufacturer of disposable diapers. Your firm is considering entering the Brazilian market. Your CEO believes the advertising message that has been effective in the United States will suffice in Brazil. Outline some possible objections to this. Your CEO also believes that the pricing decisions in Brazil can be delegated to local managers. Why might she be wrong?

2 Within 20 years, we will have seen the emergence of enormous global markets for standardized consumer products. Do you agree with this statement? Justify your answer.

3 You are the marketing manager of a food products company that is considering entering the South Korean market. The retail system in South Korea tends to be very fragmented, and retailers and

wholesalers tend to have long-term ties with South Korean food companies, which makes access to distribution channels difficult. What distribution strategy would you advise the company to pursue? Why?

4 Price discrimination is indistinguishable from dumping. Discuss the accuracy of this statement.

5 You work for a company that designs and manufactures per-

424

sonal computers. Your company's R&D center is located in North Dakota. The computers are manufactured under contract in Taiwan. Marketing strategy is currently delegated to the heads of three regional groups: a North American group (based in Chicago), a European group (based in Paris), and an Asian group (based in Singapore). Each regional group develops the marketing approach within its region. In order of importance, the largest markets for your products are North America, Germany, Britain, China, and Australia. Your company is experiencing problems in its product development and commercialization process. Products are late to market, the manufacturing quality is poor and costs are higher than projected, and market acceptance of new products is less then hoped for. What might be the source of these problems? How would you fix them?

Nike—The Ugly American?

Nike has always cultivated its rebel image—James Dean in sneakers. Nike was founded in 1972 by Phil Knight, a former university track star, and Bill Bowerman, who had been his coach. Since then the Beaverton, Oregon, company has grown from a niche supplier of running shoes for hard-core athletes into a global colossus in the athletic footwear and apparel business with sales of $10 billion, 40 percent of which are generated outside the United States. Three factors seem to underpin the company's success—the quality and innovation of its products, its sponsorship of key athletes with star appeal such as Michael Jordan and Tiger Woods, and its global advertising that has established a strong brand image for the company.

The image of Nike as the cool iconoclastic rebel shines through strongly in its advertising. Tough and gritty, Nike ads urge consumers to damn the consequences and Just Do It! while wearing Nike gear, of course. In America, the rebel has done extraordinarily well. Nike dominates the market, selling $20 in footwear and apparel per year for every man, woman, and child in the country. The company has been so successful that it is difficult to see how it can continue to grow in the now mature US market. This is not a pleasant thought for an aggressive, ambitious risk-taker like CEO Phil Knight. Knight has set a goal of increasing revenues by 15 percent annually and has focused the company's attention on international markets where the opportunities for growth seem much greater. In contrast to the saturated US market, annual per capita Nike sales in Japan are $4, in Germany they are $3, and in China just over 2 cents. Knight wants to see foreign sales exceed 50 percent of total sales.

There is only one problem with this vision. Basketball is still a fringe sport outside the United States; jogging is a distinctly American passion; and as for baseball and football, don't ask! If Nike is going to grow its international business, it is going to have to focus on the dominant global sport, soccer. But in many countries soccer is imbued with nationalistic passions and pride, and Nike is American, and Americans aren't very good at soccer (at least American men aren't; the women's team are world champions). Also, soccer already has its dominant footwear and apparel suppliers, Adidas and Umbro, which have tied up most of the world's top teams and stars in sponsorship deals.

However, Knight and his team don't shy from a competitive challenge. Underdog once more, Nike embarked on an aggressive advertising campaign to build awareness for its brand in the world of soccer. In the spring of 1996, Nike announced its intentions to the world with a series of ads in soccer magazines around the world. "Europe, Asia, and Latin America," the ad screamed, "Barricade your stadiums. Hide your trophies. Invest in some deodorant. As Asia and Latin America have been crushed, so shall Europe . . . the world has been warned." The world, as it turned out, was not amused. The reaction was more along the lines of "who do these Americans think they are, and what's in the gibe about deodorant?" Nike, however, had only just begun.

Next came the TV commercial portraying Satan and his demons playing soccer against a team of Nike endorsers. The ad, which set a company record for costs, ran worldwide. Knight declared the ad his favorite Nike commercial ever, and it certainly went down well in America. In contrast, several European broadcasters deemed it too scary and offensive to show in prime time when kids were watching. The ad also drew a spate of angry letters from viewers. But this is all grist for the mill of the American rebel, so Nike plunged ahead with an ad for British TV that featured a French soccer star and perennial "bad boy" proudly detailing how his spitting at a fan and calling his coach a bag of s___ had won him a Nike contract. This ad provoked a scathing editorial against Nike in the newsletter of soccer's governing federation, FIFA. Sepp Blatter, now president of FIFA, condemned an "advertising trend that glorifies violence or bad taste . . . technically clever and futuristic as it may be, such style does nothing to promote values, especially among impressionable youngsters."

What really set anti-American tongues wagging among soccer's ruling establishment, however, was Nike's coup in Brazil. The Brazilian soccer team is legendary, having won a record five World Cups. It is also a vibrant symbol of Brazil's samba culture and a huge source of national pride. Imagine the shock when the loud American waltzed into town with bundles of money and purchased the rights to sponsor Brazil's national team for the next 10 years, pushing aside the existing sponsor, Umbro. The deal, which cost $200 million, commits Brazil to appearances in Nike-produced exhibition matches and community events, in addition to the requirement that team members wear Nike shoes and uniforms sporting the Nike "swoosh" logo. To the soccer establishment, it looked as if the Visigoths had just stormed the high temple of soccer.

While Nike may have alienated soccer's establishment, it is not clear that the same is true of Nike's target market—the youth of the world. The establishment may have hated Nike's Satan soccer ad, but Nike managers tell about a focus audience of teens being mesmerized when French soccer star Cantona, flips up his collar, says *"au revoir,"* and kicks the winning goal through the devil. As they left the room, the youngsters all flipped their collars and said *"au revoir."* The kids, apparently, got it![42]

CASE DISCUSSION QUESTION

1 Is Nike wrong to try to leverage its American rebel image to build brand awareness in the global market for soccer footwear and apparel? What are the potential drawbacks of such an approach?

2 Is Nike's promotional strategy for soccer an example of the ugly American abroad, or is it clever marketing by one of the world's shrewdest promoters?

3 How might Nike alter its marketing approach in order to woo soccer players over to the Nike brand, without generating the kind of negative reaction that it has apparently generated among the soccer establishment?

thirteen

Global Operations Management

Opening Case Li & Fung

Established in 1906, Hong Kong-based Li & Fung is now one of the largest multinational trading companies in the developing world, with annual sales of about $2 billion. The company, which is run by the grandson of the founder, Victor Fung, does not see itself as a traditional trading enterprise. Rather, it sees itself as an expert in supply chain management for its 350 or so customers. These customers are a diverse group and include clothing re-

Li & Fung manages a complex network of suppliers for a diverse group of customers, including The Limited, Gymboree, and Warner Brothers, with a customer-focused division for each of these customers. Overall costs are minimized because Li & Fung is able to break up the value chain and disperse activities to different manufacturers in different countries.
William Taufic/The Stock Market.

Learning Objectives

1 Become familiar with the important influence that operations management can have on the competitive position of an international business.

2 Understand how country differences, manufacturing technology, and product features all affect the choice of where to locate production operations.

3 Appreciate the factors that influence a firm's decision of whether

to source component parts from within the company or purchase them from a foreign supplier.

4 Understand what is required to efficiently coordinate a globally dispersed manufacturing system.

---

tailers and consumer electronics companies. Li & Fung takes orders from customers and then sifts through its network of 7,000 independent suppliers located in 26 countries to find the right manufacturing enterprises to produce the product at the most attractive combination of cost and quality. Attaining this goal frequently requires Li & Fung to break up the value chain and disperse productive activities to manufacturers located in different

countries depending on an assessment of factors such as labor costs, trade barriers, transportation costs, and so on. Li & Fung then coordinates the process, managing the logistics and arranging for the shipment of the finished product to the customer.

Typical of its customers is The Limited, Inc., a large US-based chain of retail clothing stores. The Limited outsources much of its manufacturing and logistics functions to

Li & Fung. The process starts when The Limited comes to Li & Fung with designer sketches of clothes for the next fashion season. Li & Fung takes the basic product concepts and researches the market to find the right kind of yarn, dye, buttons, and so on, and then assembles these into prototypes The Limited can inspect. Once The Limited has settled on a prototype, it will give Li & Fung an order, say for 100,000 garments, and ask for delivery within five weeks.

The short time between an order and requested delivery is necessitated by the rapid rate of product obsolescence in the fashion clothing industry (personal computer manufacturers also live with very compressed product life cycles).

With order in hand, Li & Fung distributes the various aspects of the overall manufacturing process to different producers depending on their capabilities and costs. For example, Li & Fung might decide to purchase yarn from a Korean company but have it woven and dyed in Taiwan. Li & Fung will arrange for the yarn to be picked up from Korea and shipped to Taiwan. The Japanese might have the best zippers and buttons, but they manufacture them mostly in China. So Li & Fung will go to YKK, a big Japanese zipper manufacturer, and order the right zippers from its Chinese plants. Then Li & Fung might decide

that because of constraints imposed by export quotas and labor costs, the best place to make the final garments is in Thailand. So everything will be shipped to Thailand. In addition, because The Limited needs quick delivery, Li & Fung might divide the order across five factories in Thailand. Five weeks after the order has been received, the garments will arrive on the shelves of The Limited, all looking like they came from one factory, with colors perfectly matched. The result is a product labeled "Made in Thailand," but it is a global product.

To better serve the needs of its customers, Li & Fung is divided into numerous small, customer-focused divisions. A theme store division serves a handful of customers such as Warner Brothers and Rainforest Café. There is a division for The Limited and another for Gymboree, a US-based children's clothing store.

Walk into one of these divisions, such as the Gymboree division, and you will see that every one of the 40 or so people in the division is focused on meeting Gymboree's needs. On every desk is a computer with a direct software link to Gymboree. The staff is organized into specialized teams in areas such as design, technical support, merchandising, raw material purchasing, quality assurance, and shipping. These teams also have direct electronic links to dedicated staff in Li & Fung's branch offices in various countries where Gymboree buys in volume, such as China, Indonesia, and the Philippines. Thus, Li & Fung uses information systems to manage, coordinate, and control the globally dispersed design, production, and shipping processes to ensure that the time between receipt of an order and delivery is minimized, as is overall cost.[1]

Introduction

In the opening case Li & Fung deals with a number of issues that many other firms competing in today's global economy also deal with. To serve the needs of its customers, Li & Fung has to decide how best to distribute manufacturing activities between operations based in various countries so as to minimize costs, produce products that have an acceptable level of quality, and do so in a timely manner. Li & Fung scans its global network of 7,500 suppliers in 26 countries to make these decisions, weighing factors such as labor costs, trade barriers, transportation costs, and product quality, and only then deciding what should be produced where and in what quantities. Li & Fung often unbundles the value chain associated with producing a product, dispersing various parts of the chain to different locations depending on an assessment of the value that can be created by performing an activity in a particular location. Li & Fung must then coordinate and control the globally dispersed value chain so that it minimizes the time between receipt of an order and delivery of the finished product.

In this chapter we look at the problems that Li & Fung and many other enterprises are facing and at the various solutions. We will answer three central questions:

- Where in the world should productive activities be located?
- How much production should be performed in-house and how much should be outsourced to foreign suppliers?
- What is the best way to coordinate a globally dispersed supply chain?

We shall examine each of the three questions posed above in turn. We begin, however, by reviewing how the information covered in this chapter fits into the "big picture" of global strategy that we introduced in Chapter 10.

Strategy, Manufacturing, and Materials Management

In Chapter 10 we introduced the concept of the value chain and discussed value creation activities, including production, marketing, materials management, R&D, human resources, and information systems. In this chapter we focus on two of these activities—production and materials management—and attempt to clarify how they might be performed internationally to lower the costs of value creation and add value by better serving customer needs.

In Chapter 10 we defined **production** as the activities involved in creating a product. We used the term *production* to denote both service and manufacturing activities because one can produce a service or a physical product. In this chapter we focus more on manufacturing than on service activities, so we will use the term *manufacturing* rather than production. **Materials management** is the activity that controls the transmission of physical materials through the value chain, from procurement through production and into distribution. Materials management includes **logistics,** which refers to the procurement and physical transmission of material through the supply chain, from suppliers to customers. Manufacturing and materials management are closely linked because a firm's ability to perform its manufacturing function efficiently depends on a continuous supply of high-quality material inputs, for which materials management is responsible.

The manufacturing and materials management functions of an international firm have a number of important strategic objectives.[2] Two important objectives that are shared by both manufacturing and materials management are to *lower costs* and to *simultaneously increase product quality* by eliminating defective products from both the supply chain and the manufacturing process.[3]

These two objectives are not independent of each other. As illustrated in Figure 13.1, the firm that improves its quality control will also reduce its costs of value creation. Improved quality reduces costs in three ways:

- Productivity increases because time is not wasted manufacturing poor-quality products that cannot be sold. This leads to a direct reduction in unit costs.
- Rework and scrap costs decline.
- Warranty and rework costs decrease.

The effect is to lower the costs of value creation by reducing both manufacturing and service costs.

The main management technique that companies are using to boost their product quality is **total quality management** (TQM). TQM is a management philosophy that takes as its central focus the need to improve the quality of a company's products and services. The TQM concept was first developed by a number of American consultants, including the late W. Edward Deming, Joseph Juran, and A. V. Feigenbaum.[4] Deming identified a number of steps that should be part of any TQM program. He argued that management should embrace the philosophy that mistakes, defects, and poor-quality materials are not acceptable and should be eliminated. He suggested that the quality of supervision should be improved by allowing more time for supervisors to work with employees and by providing them with the tools they need to do the job. Deming recommended that management should create an environment in which employees will not fear reporting problems or recommending improvements. He believed that work standards should be defined not only as numbers or quotas, but also should include some notion of

production The activities involved in creating a product.

materials management The activity that controls the transmission of physical materials through the value chain, from procurement through production and into distribution.

logistics The procurement and physical transmission of material through the supply chain, from suppliers to customers.

total quality management Management philosophy that takes as its central focus the need to improve the quality of a company's products and services.

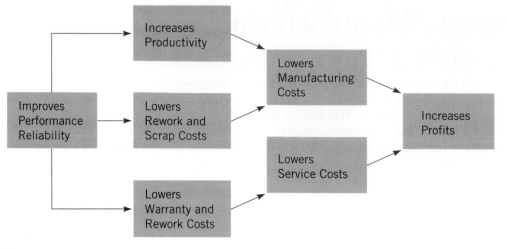

Figure 13.1

The Relationship Between Quality and Costs
Reprinted from "What Does Product Quality Really Mean?" by David A. Garvin, *Sloan Management Review* 26, Fall 1984, p. 37, by permission of publisher. Copyright 1984 by Sloan Management Review Association. All rights reserved.

quality to promote the production of defect-free output. He argued that management has the responsibility to train employees in new skills to keep pace with changes in the workplace. In addition, he believed that achieving better quality requires the commitment of everyone in the company.

The growth of international standards has also focused attention on the importance of product quality. In Europe, for example, the European Union requires that the quality of a firm's manufacturing processes and products be certified under a quality standard known as **ISO 9000** before the firm is allowed access to the European Union marketplace. Although the ISO 9000 certification has proved to be somewhat bureaucratic and costly for many firms, it does focus management attention on the need to improve the quality of products and processes.[5]

In addition to lowering costs and improving quality, two other objectives have particular importance in international businesses. First, manufacturing and materials management must be able to accommodate demands for local responsiveness. As we saw in Chapter 10, demands for local responsiveness arise from national differences in consumer tastes and preferences, infrastructure, distribution channels, and government demands. Demands for local responsiveness create pressures to decentralize manufacturing activities to the major national or regional markets in which the firm does business.

Second, manufacturing and materials management must be able to respond quickly to shifts in customer demand. In recent years time-based competition has grown more important.[6] When consumer demand is prone to large and unpredictable shifts, the firm that can adapt most quickly to these shifts will gain an advantage. Both manufacturing and materials management play critical roles here. The opening case showed that one of Li & Fung's core competencies is its ability to respond to customer needs in a timely manner by ensuring that products arrive just when they are needed, not too late or too soon (which would mean the customer would have to bear the costs of storing the inventory until it was needed).

ISO 9000 Certification that requires certain quality standards must be met.

Where to Manufacture

An essential decision facing an international firm is *where to locate its manufacturing activities* to achieve the twin goals of minimizing costs and improving product quality. For the firm that considers international production to be a feasible option, a number of factors must be considered. These factors can be grouped under three broad headings: country factors, technological factors, and product factors.[7]

Country Factors

Political economy, culture, and relative factor costs differ from country to country. In Chapter 4 we saw that because of differences in factor costs, some countries have a comparative advantage for producing certain products. In Chapters 2 and 3 we saw how differences in political economy and national culture influence the benefits, costs, and risks of doing business in a country. Other things being equal, a firm should locate its various manufacturing activities where the economic, political, and cultural conditions, including relative factor costs, are more conducive to the performance of those activities. In Chapter 10 we referred to the benefits derived from such a strategy as location economies. We argued that one result of the strategy is the creation of a global web of value creation activities.

Of course, other things are not equal. Other country factors that impinge on location decisions include formal and informal trade barriers (see Chapter 5) and rules and regulations regarding foreign direct investment (see Chapter 6). Thus, although relative factor costs may make a country look attractive as a location for performing a manufacturing activity, regulations prohibiting foreign direct investment may eliminate this option. Similarly, a consideration of factor costs might suggest that a firm should source production of a certain component part from a particular country, but trade barriers could make this uneconomical.

Another country factor is expected future movements in the currency's exchange rate (see Chapter 8). Adverse changes in exchange rates can quickly alter a country's attractiveness as a manufacturing base. Currency appreciation can transform a low-cost location into a high-cost location. Many Japanese corporations grappled with this problem during the 1990s. The relatively low value of the yen on foreign exchange markets between 1950 and 1980 strengthened Japan's position as a low-cost location for manufacturing. Between 1980 and the mid-1990s, however, the yen's steady appreciation against the dollar increased the dollar cost of products exported from Japan, making Japan less attractive as a manufacturing location. In response, many Japanese firms moved their manufacturing offshore to lower-cost locations in East Asia.

Technological Factors

The type of technology a firm uses in its manufacturing can be pivotal in location decisions. Because of technological constraints, in some cases it is feasible to perform certain manufacturing activities in only one location and serve the world market from there. In other cases, the technology may make it possible to perform an activity in multiple locations. Three characteristics of a manufacturing technology are of interest here: the level of its fixed costs, its minimum efficient scale, and its flexibility.

FIXED COSTS   As we noted in Chapter 10, sometimes the fixed costs of setting up a manufacturing plant are so high that a firm must serve the world market from a single location or from a very few locations. For example, it can cost more than $1 billion to set up a plant to manufacture semiconductor chips. Given this, serving the world market from a single plant sited at the optimal location makes sense.

A relatively low level of fixed costs can make it economical to perform a particular activity in several locations at once, allowing the firm to better accommodate demands for local responsiveness. Manufacturing in multiple locations may also help the firm avoid becoming too dependent on one location, which can be risky in a world of floating exchange rates.

MINIMUM EFFICIENT SCALE The concept of economies of scale tells us that as plant output expands, unit costs decrease. The reasons for this relationship include the greater utilization of capital equipment and the productivity gains that come with greater specialization of employees within the plant.[8] However, beyond a certain level of output, few additional scale economies are available. Thus, the "unit cost curve" declines with output until a certain output level is reached, at which point further increases in output realize little reduction in unit costs. The level of output at which most plant-level scale economies are exhausted is referred to as the minimum efficient scale of output. This is the scale of output a plant must operate at to realize all major plant-level scale economies. (See Figure 13.2.)

The larger the minimum efficient scale of a plant, the greater the argument for centralizing production in a single location or a limited number of locations. When the minimum efficient scale of production is relatively low, it may be economical to manufacture a product at several locations. As in the case of low fixed costs, this allows the firm to better meet demands for local responsiveness or to hedge against currency risk by manufacturing the same product in several locations.

FLEXIBLE MANUFACTURING (LEAN PRODUCTION) Central to the concept of economies of scale is the idea that the best way to achieve high efficiency, and hence low unit costs, is through the mass production of a standardized output. The trade-off is one of unit costs and product variety. Producing greater product variety from a factory implies shorter production runs, which implies an inability to realize economies of scale. Increasing product variety makes it difficult for a company to increase its manufacturing efficiency and thus reduce its unit costs. According to this logic, the way to increase efficiency and drive down unit costs is to limit product variety and produce a standardized product in large volumes.

This view of manufacturing efficiency has been challenged by the recent rise of flexible manufacturing technologies. The term **flexible manufacturing technology**—or *lean production* as it is often called—covers a range of manufacturing technologies designed to reduce setup times for complex equipment, increase the utilization of individual machines through better scheduling, and improve quality control at all stages of manufacturing.[9] Flexible manufacturing technologies allow a company to produce a wide variety of end products at a unit cost that at one time could be achieved only through the mass production of a standardized output. The term **mass customization** has been coined to describe this ability.[10] Mass customization implies that a firm may be able to customize its product range to suit the needs of different customer groups without a cost penalty. Research suggests that the adoption of flexible manufacturing technologies may increase efficiency and lower unit costs relative to what can be achieved by the mass production of a standardized output.[11]

Flexible manufacturing technologies vary in their sophistication and complexity. One of the most famous examples of a flexible manufacturing technology, Toyota's production system, is relatively unsophisticated, but it has been credited with making Toyota the most efficient auto company in the global industry. Toyota's flexible manufacturing system was developed by one of the company's engineers, Ohno Taiichi. After working for Toyota for five years and visiting Ford's US plants, Ohno became convinced that the mass production philosophy for making cars was flawed. He detected numerous problems. First, long production runs

flexible manufacturing technology Manufacturing technologies designed to reduce setup times for complex equipment, increase the utilization of individual machines through better scheduling, and improve quality control at all stages of manufacturing.

mass customization Production of a wide variety of end products at a unit cost that at one time could be achieved only through the mass production of a standardized output.

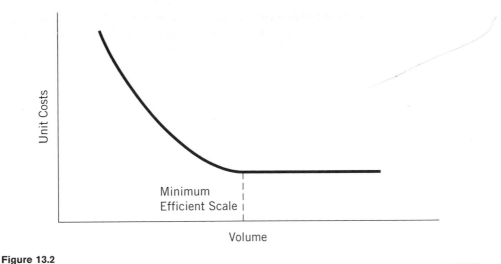

Figure 13.2

A Typical Unit Cost Curve

created massive inventories that had to be stored in large warehouses. This was expensive, both because of the cost of warehousing and because inventories tied up capital in unproductive uses. Second, if the initial machine settings were wrong, long production runs resulted in a large number of defects (i.e., waste). Third, the mass production system was unable to accommodate consumer preferences for product diversity.

In response, Ohno looked for ways to make shorter production runs economical. He developed a number of techniques designed to reduce setup times for production equipment (a major source of fixed costs). By using a system of levers and pulleys he was able to reduce the time required to change dies on stamping equipment from a full day in 1950 to 3 minutes by 1971. This made small production runs economical, which allowed Toyota to respond better to consumer demands for product diversity. Small production runs also eliminated the need to hold large inventories, thereby reducing warehousing costs. Plus, small product runs and the lack of inventory meant that defective parts were produced only in small numbers and entered the assembly process immediately. This reduced waste and helped in tracing defects back to their source and fixing the problem. In sum, Ohno's innovations enabled Toyota to produce a more diverse product range at a lower unit cost than was possible with conventional mass production.[12]

Flexible machine cells are another common flexible manufacturing technology. A flexible machine cell is a grouping of various types of machinery, a common materials handler, and a centralized cell controller (computer). Each cell normally contains four to six machines capable of performing a variety of operations. The typical cell is dedicated to the production of a family of parts or products. The settings on machines are computer controlled. This allows each cell to switch quickly between the production of different parts or products.

Improved capacity utilization and reductions in work-in-progress inventory and waste are major efficiency benefits of flexible machine cells. Improved capacity utilization arises from the reduction in setup times and from the computer-controlled coordination of production flow between machines, which eliminates bottlenecks. The tight coordination between machines also reduces work in progress (e.g., stockpiles of partly finished products). Reductions in waste arise from the ability of computer-controlled machinery to identify how to transform inputs into outputs while

flexible machine cells A grouping of various types of machinery, a common materials handler, and a centralized cell controller (computer).

producing a minimum of unusable waste material. While a freestanding machine might be in use 50 percent of the time, these factors enable the same machines, when grouped into a cell, to be used more than 80 percent of the time and produce the same end product with half the waste. This increases efficiency and results in lower costs.

The efficiency benefits of installing flexible manufacturing technology can be dramatic. For example, after introducing a flexible manufacturing system, General Electric's locomotive operations reduced the time it took to produce locomotive motor frames from 16 days to 16 hours. Similarly, after it introduced a flexible manufacturing system, Fireplace Manufacturers, Inc., one of the country's largest fireplace businesses, reduced scrap from the manufacturing process by 60 percent, increased inventory turnover threefold, and increased labor productivity by more than 30 percent.[13]

As these examples make clear, the adoption of flexible manufacturing technologies can improve a company's efficiency. Not only do flexible manufacturing technologies allow companies to lower costs, but they also enable companies to customize products to the unique demands of small consumer groups—and to do so at a cost that at one time could be achieved only by mass producing a standardized output. Thus, they help a company increase its customer responsiveness. Most important for an international business, flexible manufacturing technologies can help the firm customize products for different national markets. The importance of this advantage cannot be overstated. When flexible manufacturing technologies are available, a firm can manufacture products customized to various national markets at a single factory sited at the optimal location. And it can do this without absorbing a significant cost penalty. Thus, the idea that manufacturing facilities must be established in each major national market in which the firm does business to provide products that satisfy the specific consumer tastes and preferences (part of the rationale for a multidomestic strategy) is becoming outdated (see Chapter 10).

SUMMARY A number of technological factors support the economic arguments for concentrating manufacturing facilities in a few choice locations or even in a single location. Most important, other things being equal, when fixed costs are substantial, the minimum efficient scale of production is high, and/or flexible manufacturing technologies are available, the arguments for concentrating production at a few choice locations are strong. This is true even when substantial differences in consumer tastes and preferences exist between national markets because flexible manufacturing technologies allow the firm to customize products to national differences at a single facility.

Alternatively, when fixed costs are low, the minimum efficient scale of production is low, and flexible manufacturing technologies are not available, the arguments for concentrating production at one or a few locations are not as compelling. In such cases, it may make more sense to manufacture in each major market in which the firm is active if this helps the firm better respond to local demands. However, this holds only if the increased local responsiveness more than offsets the cost disadvantages of not concentrating manufacturing. With the advent of flexible manufacturing technologies, such a strategy is becoming less attractive. In sum, technological factors are making it feasible, and necessary, for firms to concentrate their manufacturing facilities at optimal locations. Trade barriers and transportation costs are probably the major brakes on this trend.

Product Factors

Two product features affect location decisions. The first is the product's *value-to-weight* ratio because of its influence on transportation costs. Many electronic components and pharmaceuticals have high value-to-weight ratios; they are expensive and they do not weigh very much. Thus, even if they are shipped halfway around the world, their transportation costs account for a very small percentage of total costs. Given this, other things being equal, there is great pressure to manufacture these products in the optimal location and to serve the world market from there. The opposite holds for products with low value-to-weight ratios. Refined sugar, certain bulk chemicals, paints, and petroleum products all have low value-to-weight ratios; they are relatively inexpensive products that weigh a lot. Accordingly,

Products such as circuit boards have high value-to-weight ratios, meaning they are expensive in their worth, but do not weigh very much. This, in turn, means their transportation costs are a very small percentage of total costs and thus, the products can be easily shipped across the world.

when they are shipped long distances, transportation costs account for a large percentage of total costs. Thus, other things being equal, there is great pressure to manufacture these products in multiple locations close to major markets to reduce transportation costs.

The other product feature that can influence location decisions is whether the product serves **universal needs,** needs that are the same all over the world. Examples include many industrial products (e.g., industrial electronics, steel, bulk chemicals) and modern consumer products (e.g., handheld calculators and personal computers). Because there are few national differences in consumer taste and preference for such products, the need for local responsiveness is reduced. This increases the attractiveness of concentrating manufacturing at an optimal location.

universal needs
Needs that are the same all over the world.

Locating Manufacturing Facilities

There are two basic strategies for locating manufacturing facilities: concentrating them in the optimal location and serving the world market from there, and decentralizing them in various regional or national locations that are close to major markets. The appropriate strategic choice is determined by the various country, technological, and product factors we have discussed in this section. They are summarized in Table 13.1. Concentration of manufacturing makes most sense when:

- Differences between countries in factor costs, political economy, and culture have a substantial impact on the costs of manufacturing in various countries.
- Trade barriers are low.
- Important exchange rates are expected to remain relatively stable.
- The production technology has high fixed costs and a high minimum efficient scale, or a flexible manufacturing technology exists.
- The product's value-to-weight ratio is high.
- The product serves universal needs.

Alternatively, decentralization of manufacturing is appropriate when:

- Differences between countries in factor costs, political economy, and culture do not have a substantial impact on the costs of manufacturing in various countries.

Table 13.1

Location Strategy and Manufacturing

	Favored Manufactured Strategy	
	Concentrated	**Decentralized**
Country factors		
Differences in political economy	Substantial	Few
Differences in culture	Substantial	Few
Differences in factor costs	Substantial	Few
Trade barriers	Few	Many
Technological factors		
Fixed costs	High	Low
Minimum efficient scale	High	Low
Flexible manufacturing technology	Available	Not available
Product factors		
Value-to-weight ratio	High	Low
Serves universal needs	Yes	No

- Trade barriers are high.
- Volatility in important exchange rates is expected.
- The production technology has low fixed costs and low minimum efficient scale, and flexible manufacturing technology is not available.
- The product's value-to-weight ratio is low.
- The product does not serve universal needs (that is, significant differences in consumer tastes and preferences exist between nations).

Location decisions are seldom clear cut. It is not unusual for differences in factor costs, technological factors, and product factors to point toward concentrated manufacturing while a combination of trade barriers and volatile exchange rates points toward decentralized manufacturing. This is the case in the world automobile industry. Although the availability of flexible manufacturing and cars' relatively high value-to-weight ratios suggest concentrated manufacturing, the combination of formal and informal trade barriers and the uncertainties of the world's current floating exchange rate regime (see Chapter 9) have inhibited firms' ability to pursue this strategy.

For these reasons, Honda is establishing "top-to-bottom" manufacturing operations in its three major markets: Japan, North America, and Western Europe. Honda can treat Western Europe as a single market because the European Community has removed trade barriers and stabilized exchange rates in the member countries.

Another auto firm that treats Western Europe as a single market is Ford. Figure 13.3 shows how Ford of Europe dispersed the various manufacturing activities for its Fiesta to different locations in Western Europe. (This figure shows only

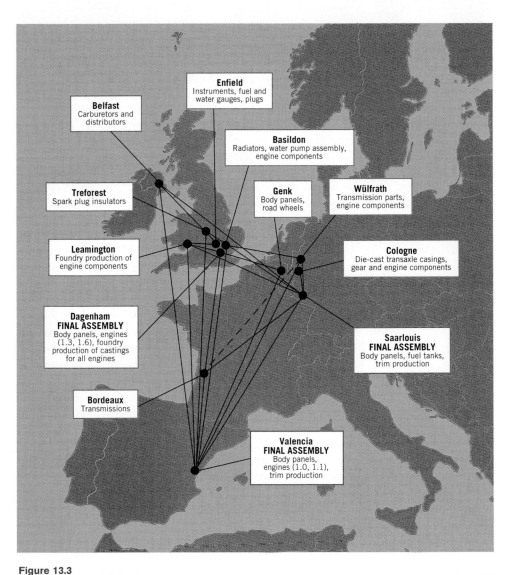

Figure 13.3

The Ford Fiesta Production Network in Europe

the geographical pattern of the network within Ford; independent component suppliers are not shown.) Some components are single sourced to take advantage of economies of scale. For example, all carburetors are supplied by the Belfast plant; all transmissions are built at Bordeaux; Basildon supplies radiator assemblies; Treforest makes spark plugs. Final assembly operations are performed at three locations: Dagenham in Great Britain, Saarlouis in Germany, and Valencia in Spain. Ford reasons that it can better customize the product to local needs by doing this. In addition, it can make up for production shortfalls at one location by shipping cars from one of the other locations. The result is a complex network of cross-border flows of finished vehicles and components. Presumably, Ford locates the various activities in particular locations because it believes these are the most favorable locations for performing those activities.

The Strategic Role of Foreign Factories

Whatever the rationale behind the initial establishment of a foreign manufacturing facility, the strategic role of foreign factories can evolve.[14] Initially, many foreign factories are established where labor costs are low. Their strategic role is to produce labor-intensive products at as low a cost as possible. For example, beginning in the 1970s, many US firms in the computer and telecommunications equipment businesses established factories across southeast Asia to manufacture electronic components, such as circuit boards and semiconductors, at the lowest possible cost. They located their factories in countries such as Malaysia, Thailand, and Singapore precisely because these countries offered an attractive combination of low labor costs, adequate infrastructure, and a favorable tax and trade regime. Initially, the components produced by these factories were designed elsewhere and the final product would be assembled elsewhere. Over time, however, the strategic role of some of these factories has expanded so they have become important centers for the design and final assembly of products for the global marketplace. Hewlett-Packard's operation in Singapore was established as a low-cost location for the production of circuit boards but the facility has now become the center for the design and final assembly of portable ink-jet printers for the global marketplace (see the accompanying "Management Focus").

Such upward migration in the strategic role of foreign factories arises because many foreign factories upgrade their capabilities.[15] This improvement comes from two sources. First, pressure from the center to improve a factory's cost structure and/or customize a product to the demands of consumers in a particular nation can set in motion a chain of events that ultimately leads to the development of additional capabilities at that factory. For example, to meet centrally mandated directions to drive down costs, engineers at HP's Singapore factory argued that they needed to redesign products so they could be manufactured at a lower cost. This led to the establishment of a design center in Singapore. As this design center proved its worth, management at HP realized the importance of co-locating design and manufacturing operations. They increasingly transferred more design responsibilities to the Singapore factory. In addition, the Singapore factory ultimately became the center for the design of products that were tailored to the needs of the Asian market. This too made good strategic sense because the products were being designed by engineers who were close to the Asian market and so probably had a good understanding of the needs of that market, as opposed to engineers located in the United States.

A second source of improvement in the capabilities of a foreign factory can be an increasing abundance of advanced factors of production. Many nations that were considered economic backwaters a generation ago experienced rapid economic development during the 1980s and 1990s and improved their communications and transporta-

In the late 1960s Hewlett-Packard was looking around Asia for a low-cost location to produce electronic components that were manufactured using labor-intensive processes. The company looked at several Asian locations and eventually selected Singapore, opening its first factory there in 1970. Although Singapore did not have the lowest labor costs in the region, costs were low relative to North America. Also, Singapore had several important benefits that could not be found at many other locations in Asia. The education level of the local workforce was high. English was widely spoken. The government of Singapore seemed stable and committed to economic development. The city-state had

dle entire products, as opposed to just components, HP's management transferred other products to Singapore over the next few years including keyboards, solid-state displays, and integrated circuits. All these products, however, were still designed, developed, and initially produced in the United States.

A shift in the status of the plant occurred in the early 1980s when HP embarked on a worldwide campaign to boost product quality and reduce costs. HP transferred the production of its HP41C hand-held calculator to Singapore. The managers at the Singapore plant were given the goal of substantially reducing manufacturing costs. They argued that this could

pressed with the progress made at the factory, that in 1983 HP transferred production of the entire calculator line to Singapore. This was followed by the partial transfer of ink-jet printer production to Singapore in 1984 and keyboard production in 1986. In all cases, the facility redesigned the products and often succeeded in reducing unit manufacturing costs by more than 30 percent. The initial development and design of all these products, however, still occurred in the United States.

In the late 1980s and early 1990s the Singapore plant took on added responsibilities, particularly in the ink-jet printer business. In 1990 the factory was given the job of redesigning an HP ink-jet

Hewlett-Packard in Singapore

one of the better-developed infrastructures in the region, including good communications and transportation networks and a rapidly developing industrial and commercial base. HP also extracted favorable terms from the Singapore government with regard to taxes, tariffs, and subsidies.

The plant initially manufactured nothing more than basic components. The combination of low labor costs and a favorable tax regime made the plant profitable early. In 1973 HP transferred the manufacture of one of its basic handheld calculators from the United States to Singapore. The objective was to reduce manufacturing costs, which the Singapore factory was quickly able to do. Increasingly confident in the capability of the Singapore factory to han-

be achieved only if they were allowed to redesign the product so it could be manufactured at a lower overall cost. HP's central management agreed, and 20 engineers from the Singapore facility were transferred to the United States for one year to learn how to design application-specific integrated circuits. They then brought this expertise back to Singapore and set about redesigning the HP41C.

The results were a huge success. By redesigning the product, the Singapore engineers reduced manufacturing costs for the HP41C by 50 percent. Using this newly acquired capability for product design, the Singapore facility then set about redesigning other products they produced. HP's corporate management was so im-

printer for the Japanese market. Although the initial product redesign was a market failure, the managers at Singapore pushed to be allowed to try again, and in 1991 they were given the job of redesigning HP's DeskJet 505 printer for the Japanese market. This time the redesigned product was a success, garnering significant sales in Japan. Emboldened by this success, the plant has continued to take on additional design responsibilities. It is now viewed as a "lead plant" within HP's global network, with primary responsibility not just for manufacturing, but also for the development and design of a family of small ink-jet printers targeted at the Asian market.[16]

tion infrastructure and the education level of their population. While these countries once lacked the advanced infrastructure required to support sophisticated design, development, and manufacturing operations, this is often no longer the case. This has made it much easier for factories based in these nations to take on a greater strategic role.

Because of such developments many international businesses are moving away from a system in which their foreign factories were viewed as nothing more than low-cost manufacturing facilities and toward one where foreign factories are viewed as globally dispersed centers of excellence. In this new model, different foreign factories take the lead role for the design and manufacture of products to serve important national or regional markets or even the global market. The development of such dispersed centers of excellence is consistent with the transnational strategy introduced in Chapter 10. A major aspect of a transnational strategy is a belief in global learning—the idea that valuable knowledge may be found in a firm's foreign subsidiaries.

Rather than viewing foreign factories simply as sweatshops where unskilled labor churns out low-cost goods, managers of international businesses need to view them as potential centers of excellence and to encourage and foster attempts by local managers to upgrade their factories' capabilities and, thereby, enhance their strategic standing within the corporation.

Make-or-Buy Decisions

International businesses frequently face **sourcing decisions,** decisions about whether they should make or buy the component parts that go into their final product. Should the firm vertically integrate into the manufacture of its own component parts, or should it outsource them—buy them from independent suppliers? Make-or-buy decisions are important factors of many firms' manufacturing strategies. The typical car contains more than 10,000 components, so automobile firms constantly face make-or-buy decisions. Ford of Europe, for example, produces only about 45 percent of the value of the Fiesta in its own plants. The remaining 55 percent, mainly accounted for by component parts, comes from independent suppliers. In the athletic shoe industry the make-or-buy issue has been taken to an extreme. Companies such as Nike and Reebok have no involvement in manufacturing; all production has been outsourced, primarily to manufacturers based in low-wage countries.

Make-or-buy decisions pose plenty of problems for purely domestic businesses but even more problems for international businesses. These decisions in the international arena are complicated by the volatility of countries' political economies, exchange rate movements, changes in relative factor costs, and the like. In this section we examine the arguments for making components and for buying them, and we consider the trade-offs involved in these decisions. Then we discuss strategic alliances as an alternative to manufacturing component parts within the company.

The Advantages of Make

The arguments that support making component parts in-house—vertical integration— are fourfold. Vertical integration is associated with lower costs, facilitates investments in highly specialized assets, protects proprietary product technology, and facilitates the scheduling of adjacent processes.

LOWER COSTS It may pay a firm to manufacture a product or component part in-house, as opposed to outsourcing it to an independent manufacturer, if the firm is more efficient at that production activity than any other enterprise. Boeing, for example, recently reviewed its make-or-buy decisions with regard to commercial jet aircraft (for details see the accompanying "Management Focus"). It decided that although it would outsource the production of some component parts to other

The Boeing Company is the world's largest manufacturer of commercial jet aircraft with a 55 to 60 percent share of the global market. Despite its large market share, in recent years Boeing has found it tough going competitively. The company's problems are twofold. First, Boeing faces a very aggressive competitor in Europe's Airbus Industrie. The dogfight between Boeing and Airbus for market share has enabled major airlines to play the two companies against each other to bargain down the prices for commercial jet aircraft. Second, several of the world's major airlines went through some very rough years during the 1990s. Many lack the financial resources required to

make a profit is if it also drives down its cost structure. With this in mind, in the early 1990s Boeing undertook a companywide review of its make-or-buy decisions. The objective was to try to identify activities that could be outsourced to subcontractors, both in the United States and abroad to drive down production costs.

When making these decisions, Boeing applied a number of criteria. First, Boeing looked at the *basic economics* of the outsourcing decision. The central issue was whether an activity could be performed more cost-effectively by an outside manufacturer or by Boeing. Second, Boeing considered the *strategic risk* associated with outsourc-

plier in a given country to help secure orders for commercial jet aircraft from that country. This practice is known as *offsetting,* and it is common in many industries. For example, Boeing decided to outsource the production of certain components to China. This decision was influenced by the fact that current forecasts suggest the Chinese will purchase over $100 billion worth of commercial jets over the next 20 years. Boeing's hope is that pushing some subcontracting work China's way will help it gain a larger share of this market than its global competitor, Airbus.

One of the first decisions to come out of this process was a decision to outsource the produc-

Make-or-Buy Decisions at Boeing

purchase new aircraft, so they are holding onto their used aircraft longer. Thus, while the typical service life of a Boeing 737 was once believed to be about 15 years, many airlines are now making the aircraft last as long as 25 years. This translates into lower orders for new aircraft. Confronted with this new reality, Boeing has concluded that the only way it can persuade cash-starved airlines to replace their used planes with new aircraft is if it prices very aggressively.

Thus, Boeing has had to face up to the fact that its ability to raise prices for commercial jet aircraft, which was once quite strong, has been limited. Falling prices might even be the norm. The only way that Boeing can continue to

ing an activity. Boeing decided it would not outsource any activity that it deemed to be part of its long-term competitive advantage. For example, the company decided not to outsource the production of wings because it believed that doing so might give away valuable technology to potential competitors. Third, Boeing looked at the *operational risk* associated with outsourcing an activity. The basic objective was to make sure Boeing did not become too dependent on a single outside supplier for critical components. Boeing's philosophy is to hedge operational risk by purchasing from two or more suppliers. Finally, Boeing considered whether it made sense to outsource certain activities to a sup-

tion of insulation blankets for 737 and 757 aircraft to suppliers in Mexico. Insulation blankets are wrapped around the fuselage of an aircraft to keep the interior warm at high altitudes. Boeing has traditionally made these blankets in-house, but it found that it could save $50 million per year by outsourcing production to a Mexican supplier. In total, Boeing reckons that outsourcing cut its cost structure by $500 million per year between 1994 and 1997. By the time the outsourcing is complete, the amount of an aircraft that Boeing builds will have been reduced from 52 percent to 48 percent.[17]

enterprises, it would keep the production of aircraft wings in-house. Its rationale was that Boeing has a core competence in the production of wings, and it is more efficient at this activity than any other enterprise. Therefore, it makes little sense for Boeing to outsource this activity.

FACILITATING SPECIALIZED INVESTMENTS   Imagine Ford of Europe has developed a high-performance, high-quality, and uniquely designed carburetor. The carburetor's increased fuel efficiency will help sell Ford cars. Ford must decide whether to make the carburetor in-house or to contract out the manufacturing to an independent supplier. Manufacturing these uniquely designed carburetors requires investments in equipment that can be used only for this purpose; it cannot be used to make carburetors for any other auto firm. In such cases, we say that this constitutes an investment in **specialized assets.**

specialized assets
Asset designed to perform a specific task, whose value is significantly reduced in its next-best use.

Consider this scenario from the perspective of an independent supplier who has been asked by Ford to make this investment. The supplier might reason that once it has made the investment it will become dependent on Ford for business because Ford is the only possible customer for the output of this equipment. The supplier perceives this as putting Ford in a strong bargaining position and worries that once the specialized investment has been made, Ford might cut prices for the carburetors. Given this risk, the supplier declines to make the investment in specialized equipment.

Now take the position of Ford. Ford might reason that if it contracts out production of the carburetors to an independent supplier, it might become too dependent on that supplier for a vital input. Because specialized equipment is required to produce the carburetors, Ford cannot easily switch its orders to other suppliers who lack that equipment. (It would face high switching costs.) Ford perceives this as increasing the bargaining power of the supplier and worries that the supplier might use its bargaining strength to demand higher prices.

Thus, the mutual dependency that outsourcing would create makes Ford nervous and scares away potential suppliers. The problem is lack of trust. Neither party completely trusts the other to play fair. Consequently, Ford might reason that the only safe way to get the new carburetors is to manufacture them itself. It may be unable to persuade any independent supplier to manufacture them. Thus, Ford decides to make rather than buy.

When substantial investments in specialized assets are required to manufacture a component, the firm generally will prefer to make the component internally rather than contract it out to a supplier. A growing amount of empirical evidence supports this.[18]

PROPRIETARY PRODUCT TECHNOLOGY PROTECTION Proprietary product technology is unique to a firm. If it enables the firm to produce a product containing superior features, proprietary technology can give the firm competitive advantage. Obviously the firm would not want this technology to fall into the hands of competitors. If the firm contracts out the manufacture of components containing proprietary technology, it runs the risk that those suppliers will expropriate the technology for their own use or that they will sell it to the firm's competitors. Thus, to maintain control over its technology, the firm might make such component parts in-house. The "Management Focus" looks at how Boeing decided not to outsource the manufacture of wings and cockpits, primarily because it believed that doing so would give away key technology to potential competitors.

IMPROVED SCHEDULING The weakest argument for vertical integration is that production cost savings result from it because it makes planning, coordination, and scheduling of adjacent processes easier.[19] This is particularly important in firms with just-in-time inventory systems (which we discuss later in the chapter). In the 1920s Ford profited from tight coordination and scheduling made possible by backward vertical integration into steel foundries, iron ore shipping, and mining. Deliveries at Ford's foundries on the Great Lakes were coordinated so well that ore was turned into engine blocks within 24 hours. This substantially reduced Ford's production costs by eliminating the need to hold excessive ore inventories.

For international businesses that source worldwide, scheduling problems can be exacerbated by the time and distance between the firm and its suppliers. This is true whether the firms use their own subunits as suppliers or independent suppliers. Ownership is not the issue here. As discussed in the closing case, Timberland may be able to achieve tight scheduling with its globally dispersed parts suppliers without vertical integration. Thus, although this argument for vertical integration is often made, it is not compelling.

The Advantages of Buy

Buying component parts from independent suppliers can give the firm greater flexibility, help drive down the firm's cost structure, and help the firm capture orders from international customers.

STRATEGIC FLEXIBILITY The great advantage of buying component parts from independent suppliers is that the firm can maintain its flexibility, switching orders between suppliers as circumstances dictate. This is particularly important in the international context, where changes in exchange rates and trade barriers can alter the attractiveness of supply sources. One year Hong Kong might be the lowest-cost source for a particular component, and the next year Mexico may be.

Sourcing component parts from independent suppliers can also be advantageous when the optimal location for manufacturing a product is beset by political risks. Under such circumstances, foreign direct investment to establish a component manufacturing operation in that country would expose the firm to political risks. The firm can avoid many of these risks by buying from an independent supplier in that country, maintaining the flexibility to switch sourcing to another country if a war, revolution, or other political change alters that country's attractiveness as a supply source.

However, maintaining strategic flexibility has its downside. If a supplier perceives the firm will change suppliers in response to changes in exchange rates, trade barriers, or general political circumstances, that supplier might not be willing to make specialized investments in plant and equipment that would ultimately benefit the firm.

LOWER COSTS Although vertical integration is often undertaken to lower costs, it may end up raising costs. One potential source of higher costs arises because vertical integration into the manufacture of component parts increases an organization's scope, and the resulting increase in organizational complexity can raise a firm's cost structure. There are three reasons for this.

First, the greater the number of subunits in an organization, the harder it is to coordinate and control those units. Coordinating and controlling subunits requires top management to effectively process large amounts of information. The greater the number of subunits, the more information top management must process and the harder it is for them to do this well. Theoretically, when the firm becomes involved in too many activities, headquarters management will be unable to effectively control all of them, and the resulting inefficiencies will more than offset any advantages derived from vertical integration.[20] This problem can be particularly serious in an international business, where the difficulty of controlling subunits is exacerbated by distance and differences in time, language, and culture.

Second, the firm that vertically integrates into component part manufacture may find that because its internal suppliers have a captive customer in the firm, they will lack an incentive to reduce costs. The fact that they do not have to compete for orders with other suppliers may result in high operating costs. The managers of the supply operation may be tempted to pass on any cost increases to other parts of the firm in the form of higher transfer prices, rather than looking for ways to reduce those costs.

Third, vertically integrated firms have to determine appropriate prices for goods transferred to subunits within the firm. This is a challenge in any firm, but it is even more complex in international businesses. Different tax regimes, exchange rate movements, and headquarters' ignorance about local conditions all increase the complexity of transfer pricing decisions. This complexity enhances internal suppliers' ability to manipulate transfer prices to their advantage, passing cost increases downstream rather than looking for ways to reduce costs.

The firm that buys its components from independent suppliers can avoid all these problems and the associated costs. The firm that sources from independent suppliers has fewer subunits to control. The incentive problems that occur with internal suppliers do not arise when independent suppliers are used. Independent suppliers know they must continue to be efficient if they are to win business from the firm. Also, because independent suppliers' prices are set by market forces, the transfer pricing problem does not exist. In sum, the bureaucratic inefficiencies and resulting costs that can arise when firms vertically integrate backward and manufacture their own components are avoided by buying component parts from independent suppliers.

OFFSETS Another reason for outsourcing some manufacturing to independent suppliers based in other countries is that it may help the firm capture more orders from that country. As noted in the "Management Focus" on Boeing, the practice of offsets is common in the commercial aerospace industry. For example, before Air India places a large order with Boeing, the Indian government might ask Boeing to push some subcontracting work to Indian manufacturers. This kind of quid pro quo is not unusual in international business, and it affects far more than just the aerospace industry. Representatives of the US government have repeatedly urged Japanese automobile companies to purchase more component parts from US suppliers to partially offset the large volume of automobile exports from Japan to the United States.

Trade-offs

Make-or-buy decisions involve trade-offs. The benefits of manufacturing components in-house seem to be greatest when highly specialized assets are involved, when vertical integration is necessary for protecting proprietary technology, or when the firm is simply more efficient than external suppliers at performing a particular activity.

When these conditions are not present, the risk of strategic inflexibility and organizational problems suggest it may be better to contract out component part manufacturing to independent suppliers. Because issues of strategic flexibility and organizational control loom even larger for international businesses than for purely domestic ones, an international business should be particularly wary of vertical integration into component part manufacture. In addition, some outsourcing in the form of offsets may help a firm gain larger orders in the future.

Strategic Alliances with Suppliers

Several international businesses have tried to reap some of the benefits of vertical integration without the associated organizational problems by entering strategic alliances with essential suppliers. For example, we have seen an alliance between Kodak and Canon, under which Canon builds photocopiers for sale by Kodak, and an alliance between Apple and Sony, under which Sony builds laptop computers for Apple. Through these alliances, Kodak and Apple have committed themselves to long-term relationships with these suppliers, which encourages the suppliers to undertake specialized investments. A lack of trust can inhibit suppliers from making specialized investments to supply a firm with inputs. Strategic alliances are a way to build trust between the firm and its suppliers. Trust is built when a firm makes a credible commitment to continue purchasing from a supplier on reasonable terms. For example, the firm may invest money in a supplier—perhaps by taking a minority shareholding—to signal its intention to build a productive, mutually beneficial long-term relationship.

This kind of arrangement between the firm and its parts suppliers was pioneered in Japan by large auto companies such as Toyota. Many of the Japanese automakers have cooperative relationships with their suppliers that go back for decades. In these relationships the auto companies and their suppliers collaborate on ways to increase value added by, for example, implementing just-in-time inventory systems or cooperating in the design of component parts to improve quality and reduce assembly costs. These relationships have been formalized when the auto firms acquired minority shareholdings in many of their essential suppliers to symbolize their desire for long-term cooperative relationships. At the same time, the relationship between the firm and each essential supplier remains market mediated and terminable if the supplier fails to perform up to standard. By pursuing such a strategy, the Japanese automakers have been able to capture many of the benefits of vertical integration, particularly those arising from investments in specialized assets, without suffering the organizational problems that come with formal vertical integration. The parts suppliers also benefit from these relationships because they grow with the firm they supply and share in its success. Because of these strategies, Toyota manufactures only 27 percent of its component parts in-house, compared to 48 percent at Ford and 67 percent at GM. Of these three firms, Toyota appears to spend the least on component parts, suggesting it has captured many of the benefits that induced Ford and GM to vertically integrate while avoiding organizational inefficiencies.[21]

In general, the trends toward just-in-time systems (JIT), computer-aided design (CAD), and computer-aided manufacturing (CAM) seem to have increased pressures for firms to establish long-term relationships with their suppliers. JIT, CAD, and CAM systems all rely on close links between firms and their suppliers supported by substantial specialized investment in equipment and information systems hardware. To get a supplier to agree to adopt such systems, a firm must make a credible commitment to an enduring relationship with the supplier. In other words, it must build trust with the supplier. It can do this within the framework of a strategic alliance.

Alliances are not all good. Like formal vertical integration, a firm that enters long-term alliances may limit its strategic flexibility by the commitments it makes to its alliance partners. Also, a firm that allies itself with another firm risks giving away key technological know-how to a potential competitor.

Coordinating a Global Manufacturing System

We have been discussing aspects of manufacturing strategy, but now we turn our attention to materials management. Materials management, which encompasses *logistics*, embraces the activities necessary to get materials to a manufacturing facility, through the manufacturing process, and out through a distribution system to the end user.[22] The twin objectives of materials management are to achieve this at the lowest possible cost and in a way that best serves customer needs, thereby lowering the costs of value creation and helping the firm establish a competitive advantage through superior customer service.

The potential for reducing costs through more efficient materials management is enormous. For the typical manufacturing enterprise, material costs account for between 50 and 70 percent of revenues, depending on the industry. Even a small reduction in these costs can have a substantial impact on firm profitability. According to one estimate, for a firm with revenues of $1 million, a return on investment rate of 5 percent, and materials costs that are 50 percent of sales revenues, a $15,000 increase in profits could be achieved either by increasing sales revenues 30 percent or by reducing materials costs by 3 percent.[23] In a saturated market it would be much easier to reduce materials costs by 3 percent than to increase sales revenues by 30 percent.

Materials management is a major undertaking in a firm with a globally dispersed manufacturing system and global markets. Consider Bose Corporation, which is presented in the accompanying "Management Focus." Bose purchases component parts from suppliers scattered over North America, Europe, and the Far East. It assembles its high-fidelity speakers in Massachusetts and ships them to customers the world over. Bose's materials management function must coordinate the flow of component parts so they arrive at the assembly plant just in time to enter the production system. Then it must oversee the timely distribution of finished speakers to customers around the globe. These tasks are complicated by the vast distances involved and by the fact that component parts and finished products are shipped across national borders, where they must pass customs. Plus, as explained in the "Management Focus," Bose must be able to interrupt the normal supply chain to accelerate the delivery of essential components to respond to sudden upsurges in demand for Bose's products.

The Power of Just-in-Time

Pioneered by Japanese firms during the 1950s and 60s, just-in-time inventory systems now play a major role in most manufacturing firms. The basic philosophy behind just-in-time (JIT) systems is to economize on inventory holding costs by having materials arrive at a manufacturing plant just in time to enter the production process, and not before. The major cost saving comes from speeding up inventory turnover; this reduces inventory holding costs, such as warehousing and storage costs.

In addition to the cost benefits, JIT systems can also help firms improve product quality. Under a JIT system, parts enter the manufacturing process immediately; they are not warehoused. This allows defective inputs to be spotted right away. The problem can then be traced to the supply source and fixed before more defective parts are produced. Under a more traditional system, the practice of warehousing parts for months before they are used allows many defective parts to be produced by a supplier before a problem is recognized.

The drawback of a JIT system is that it leaves a firm without a buffer stock of inventory. Although buffer stocks are expensive to store, they can help tide a firm over shortages caused by disruptions (such as a labor dispute in an essential supplier). Buffer stocks can also help a firm respond quickly to increases in demand. However, there are ways around these limitations. To reduce the risks associated with depending on one supplier for an important input, some firms source these inputs from several suppliers. The experience of Bose Corporation shows that it is possible to respond

Bose Corporation manufactures some of the world's best high-fidelity speakers. The Massachusetts corporation annually generates about $300 million in revenues. Its worldwide esteem is evidenced by the fact that Bose speakers are best-sellers in Japan, the world leader in consumer electronics. Bose's core competence is its electronic engineering skills, but the company attributes much of its business success to tightly coordinated materials management.

Bose purchases most of its electronic and nonelectronic components from independent suppliers scattered around North America, the Far East, and Europe. Roughly 50 percent of its pur-

respond rapidly to increased demand for component parts.

Responsibility for coordinating the supply chain to meet both objectives—minimizing transportation and inventory holding costs and yet responding quickly to customer demands—falls on Bose's materials management function. This function achieves coordination through a sophisticated logistics operation. Most of Bose's imports from the Far East come via ships to the West Coast and then across North America to its Massachusetts plant via train. Most of the company's exports also move by ocean freight, but Bose does not hesitate to use airfreight when goods are needed in a hurry. To

also allows Bose to run simulations that allow its logistics managers to examine a variety of factors, such as the effect of duties on the cost of goods sold.

Procter provides several other services to Bose, such as selecting overseas agents who can help move goods out of the Far East. Procter's well-established network of overseas contacts is especially useful when shipments must be expedited through foreign customs. Procter also is electronically linked into the US customs system, which allows it to clear freight electronically as much as five days before a ship arrives at a US port or hours before an international airfreight shipment arrives. This can get

Materials Management at Bose

chases are from foreign suppliers, the majority of them in the Far East. Bose attempts to coordinate this globally dispersed supply chain so that material holding and transportation costs are minimized. This requires component parts to arrive at Bose's Massachusetts assembly plant just in time to enter the production process. But because Bose must remain responsive to customer demands, it sometimes must respond quickly to increases in customer demand for certain speakers. If it does not, it can lose a big order to competitors. Since Bose does not want to hold extensive inventories at its Massachusetts plant, this need for responsiveness requires Bose's globally dispersed supply chain to

control this supply chain, Bose has a long-standing relationship with W. N. Procter, a Boston-based freight forwarder and customs broker. Procter handles customs clearance and shipping from suppliers to Bose. Procter provides Bose with up-to-the-minute electronic data interchange (EDI) capabilities, which gives it the ability to track parts as they move through its global supply chain. Whenever a shipment leaves a supplier, it is entered in this "ProcterLink" system. Bose can then fine-tune its production scheduling so supplies enter the production process just in time. ProcterLink is more than a simple tracking system, however. The EDI system

goods to Bose's manufacturing plant several days sooner.

Just how well this system can work was demonstrated when a Japanese customer doubled its order for Bose speakers. Bose needed to gear up its manufacturing immediately, but many of the essential components were far from Massachusetts. Using ProcterLink, Bose located the needed parts in its supply chain, pulled them out of the normal delivery chain, and airfreighted them to the manufacturing line to satisfy the accelerated schedule. Bose was able to fill the doubled order for its Japanese customer.[24]

quickly to increases in consumer demand while maintaining a JIT system—even if it involves shipping component parts by air rather than overland or by ship (see the "Management Focus").

The Role of Information Technology

As we saw in the "Management Focus" on Bose Corporation, information systems play a crucial role in modern materials management. By tracking component parts as they make their way across the globe toward an assembly plant, information systems enable a firm to optimize its production scheduling according to when components are expected to arrive. By locating component parts in the supply chain precisely, good information systems allow the firm to accelerate production when needed by pulling key components out of the regular supply chain and having them flown to the manufacturing plant.

Firms are increasingly using electronic data interchange and the Internet to coordinate the flow of materials into manufacturing, through manufacturing, and out to customers. EDI systems require Internet-based computer links between a firm, its suppliers, and its shippers. Sometimes customers also are integrated into the system. These electronic linkages are then used to place orders with suppliers, to register parts leaving a supplier, to track them as they travel toward a manufacturing plant, and to register their arrival. Suppliers typically use an EDI link to send invoices to the purchasing firm. An EDI system allows suppliers, shippers, and the purchasing firm to communicate with each other in "real time" (with no time delay), which vastly increases the flexibility and responsiveness of the supply system. EDI also eliminates much of the paperwork between suppliers, shippers, and the purchasing firm. Furthermore, good EDI systems can help a firm decentralize materials management decisions to the plant level by giving corporate-level managers the information they need for coordinating and controlling decentralized materials management groups.

Key Terms

Summary

This chapter explained how efficient manufacturing and materials management functions can improve an international business's competitive position by lowering the costs of value creation and by performing these activities so customer service is enhanced and the value added is maximized. We looked closely at three issues central to international manufacturing and materials management: where to manufacture, what to make and what to buy, and how to coordinate a globally dispersed manufacturing and supply system. The following points were made in the chapter:

1 The choice of an optimal manufacturing location must consider country factors, technological factors, and product factors.

2 Country factors include the influence of factor costs, political economy, and national culture on manufacturing costs.

3 Technological factors include the fixed costs of setting up manufacturing facilities, the minimum efficient scale of production, and the availability of flexible manufacturing technologies.

4 Product factors include the value-to-weight ratio of the product and whether the product serves universal needs.

5 Location strategies either concentrate or decentralize manufacturing. The choice should be made in light of country, technological, and product factors. All location decisions involve trade-offs.

6 Foreign factories can improve their capabilities over time, and this can be of immense strategic benefit to the firm. Managers need to view foreign factories as potential centers of excellence and to encourage and foster attempts by local managers to upgrade the capabilities of their factories.

7 An essential issue in many international businesses is determining which component parts should be manufactured in-house and which should be outsourced to independent suppliers.

8 Making components in-house may facilitate investments in specialized assets and help the firm protect its proprietary technology. It may improve scheduling between adjacent stages in the value chain, also. In-house production also makes sense if the firm is an efficient low-cost producer of a technology.

9 Buying components from independent suppliers facilitates strategic flexibility and helps the firm avoid the organizational problems associated with extensive vertical integration. Outsourcing might also be employed as part of an "offset" policy, which is designed to win more orders for the firm from a country by pushing some subcontracting work to that country.

10 Several firms have tried to attain the benefits of vertical integration and avoid its associated organizational problems by entering long-term strategic alliances with essential suppliers.

11 Although alliances with suppliers can give a firm the benefits of vertical integration without dispensing entirely with the benefits of a market relationship, alliances have drawbacks. The firm that enters a strategic alliance may find its strategic flexibility limited by commitments to alliance partners.

12 Materials management encompasses all the activities that move materials to a manufacturing facility, through the manufacturing process, and out through a distribution system to the end user. The materials management function is complicated in an international business by distance, time, exchange rates, custom barriers, and other things.

13 Just-in-time systems generate major cost savings from reduced warehousing and inventory holding costs. In addition, JIT systems help the firm spot defective parts and remove them from the manufacturing process quickly, thereby improving product quality.

14 Information technology, particularly electronic data interchange, plays a major role in materials management. EDI facilitates the tracking of inputs, allows the firm to optimize its production schedule, allows the firm and its suppliers to communicate in real time, and eliminates the flow of paperwork between a firm and its suppliers.

Critical Thinking and Discussion Questions

1. An electronics firm is considering how best to supply the world market for microprocessors used in consumer and industrial electronic products. A manufacturing plant costs approximately $500 million to construct and requires a highly skilled workforce. The total value of the world market for this product over the next 10 years is estimated to be between $10 billion and $15 billion. The tariffs prevailing in this industry are currently low. What kind of manufacturing strategy do you think the firm should adopt—concentrated or decentralized? What kind of location(s) should the firm favor for its plant(s)?

2. A chemical firm is considering how best to supply the world market for sulfuric acid. A manufacturing plant costs approximately $20 million to construct and requires a moderately skilled workforce. The total value of the world market for this product over the next 10 years is estimated to be between $20 billion and $30 billion. The tariffs prevailing in this industry are moderate. Should the firm favor concentrated manufacturing or decentralized manufacturing? What kind of location(s) should the firm seek for its plant(s)?

3. A firm must decide whether to make a component part in-house or to contract it out to an independent supplier. Manufacturing the part requires a nonrecoverable investment in specialized assets. The most efficient suppliers are located in countries with currencies that many foreign exchange analysts expect to appreciate substantially over the next decade. What are the pros and cons of (a) manufacturing the component in-house and (b) outsourcing manufacture to an independent supplier? Which option would you recommend? Why?

4. Explain how an efficient materials management function can help an international business compete more effectively in the global marketplace.

Internet Exercises

1. Aaeon Technology, a Taiwanese specialty computer maker, is incorporating a $500,000 software system into its business. The system will allow Aaeon Technology to manage procurement, inventory, sales, and finances over the Internet. The company claims it must make the change if it is to stay competitive, that it needs "to have e-commerce." Aaeon Technology is not alone in its strategic move. All over the world, companies are putting software systems in place that will enable them to conduct a large portion of their operations on-line. The business-to-business segment is Asia's fastest-growing area of e-commerce. It is projected that software sales in the region will be more than $1.3 billion by 2003.

The switch to on-line operations is not easy. Particularly in Asia, face-to-face dealings are important, and relationships are often cultivated over many years. In addition, for an electronic supply chain to work effectively, companies must be willing to put sensitive information on the Internet. Consider the pros and cons of incorporating a software system such as Aaeon Technology's. By shifting all or part of the supply chain management process to the Internet, does a company decrease the physical, cultural, economic, and/or political distance that is often a complicating factor in international materials management? Aaeon Technology claims that competition is forcing it to go on-line. Is this force present in other industries as well?

Source: *Business Week*, October 25, 1999, p. 62.

2. "It is clear that network computing will play a fundamental role in meeting and exploiting the global economy. Only those organizations that opt to leverage Internet technologies encompassing intranets and extranets as well as electronic commerce have the chance to enter the next century (21st) with a significant competitive advantage," argues the British trade organization Interforum. In fact, Internet technology has so revolutionized the business world that it is now possible for smaller companies to compete in an international marketplace with large multinational corporations, making the process of globalization occur at an even faster pace.

While the ongoing transformation of business-to-business relationships may not attract the attention that consumer websites do, its impact on the business world and on firm operations should not be minimized. Go to the British Department of Trade and Industry website (**www.enterprisenetwork.co.uk**). Explore the various components relating to the Internet. As the CEO of a small bicycle company, what are the advantages of incorporating the Internet into company operations? As the vice president of a large, multinational fiber optics firm, what are the advantages of incorporating the Internet into the operations of your company? Does firm size matter in the decision to adopt an electronic supply-chain management system? Why or why not?

Source: *The Sunday Times*, November 21, 1999, sec. 3, p. 13.

Timberland, a New Hampshire-based manufacturer of rugged, high-quality shoes, is one of the world's fastest-growing companies. From small beginnings in the late 1970s, Timberland grew into a global business with sales of $797 million in 1997. The company's global expansion began in 1979 when an Italian distributor walked into the then-small US outfitter and expressed an interest in shoe #100-81, a hand-sewn moccasin with a lug sole. The Italian felt the shoe would sell well in Italy—the land of high-style Gucci shoes. He was right; Timberland quickly became a phenomenon in Italy where Timberland shoes often sold for a 60 percent premium over prices in the United States. Other countries followed, and by the mid-1990s Timberland was generating 50 percent of its sales from 50 foreign countries, including Italy, Germany, France, Britain, and Japan.

Ignored during this rapid growth, however, was any attempt to build a tightly managed and coordinated global manufacturing and logistics system. By the early 1990s Timberland was confronted with an extremely complex global manufacturing and logistics network. To take advantage of lower wage costs outside the United States, the company had established manufacturing facilities in the Dominican Republic and Puerto Rico (by 1997, 27 percent of its shoes were made at these locations). Timberland had also found it cost-efficient to source footwear and apparel from independent suppliers based in dozens of other low-wage countries in Asia, Europe, and Latin America. At the same time, Timberland's distribution network had grown to serve consumers in more than 50 countries. To complicate things further, the average shipment of footwear to retailers was for less than 12 pairs of each type of shoe, which made for an enormous volume of individual shipments to track.

By the early 1990s Timberland's logistics systems was breaking down under the strains imposed by rapid volume growth, a globally dispersed supply and distribution chain, and a large volume of individual shipments. The company simply lacked the information systems required to coordinate and control its dispersed production and distribution network. No common information systems linked suppliers, Timberland, and retailers. Nor was there any attempt to consolidate shipments from different regions of the world to realize shipping economies. Products were shipped from six countries in Southeast Asia to the United States and Europe, as opposed to being consolidated at one location and then shipped.

In the mid-1990s Timberland decided to reorganize its global logistics system, by first streamlining its logistics information pipeline and then its cargo pipeline. The information challenge was to come up with a system that would enable Timberland to track a product from the factory to its final destination. But the various links in the supply chain—which included manufacturers, warehouses, shippers, and retailers—did not share common data links and as a consequence were not sharing any information. As Timberland's director of distribution explains it: "At every link in the chain, you can make a decision about cargo that would make it flow better, but only if you have the information about the product and the ability to communicate with that location in real time to direct the product." For example, when a product leaves the factory, Timberland can in theory direct a freight forwarder to send the product by air or by ocean carrier, depending on the urgency of the shipment. When a shipment lands in, say, Los Angeles, it can be shipped to a distribution center or shipped directly to a customer, again depending on need. These kinds of choices, however, can be made only if Timberland has the requisite information systems. Until 1994 the company lacked such systems.

The company developed the required information systems in conjunction with ACS, a freight forwarder, and The Rockport Group, a software house. To simplify its system at the level of physical distribution and to make implementation of its information systems easier, Timberland switched to consolidated regional warehousing. Timberland had separate warehouses in a dozen Asian countries, several in the United States, and three in Europe. Under the new system sources in Asia feed into one warehouse. The company also has single continental distribution centers in North America and Europe. By centralizing its warehousing at three locations, the company can better track where a product is located so that it can be routed quickly and flexibly to where it is needed. The result is a dramatic improvement in Timberland's ability to deliver products to customers exactly when they need them, as opposed to delivering products too late or too soon. Also, by consolidating warehousing, Timberland now has the ability to consolidate shipments from a region into one transoceanic shipment, which should enable the company to negotiate much better shipping rates.[25]

CASE DISCUSSION QUESTIONS

1 What were the causes of Timberland's logistical problems in the 1990s? What do you think were

453

the competitive and financial consequences of these problems?

2 What was the key to solving Timberland's logistical problems? Why? What are the consequences of this solution likely to be for Timberland's competitive position and financial performance?

3 Timberland makes almost no products in the United States. Instead, it chose to manufacture some products in the Dominican Republic and Puerto Rico, while outsourcing the remaining products from third-party manufacturers. Explain the probable thinking behind this strategy. Why does the company not outsource all its production? Why does the company make shoes in the Dominican Republic and Puerto Rico, but not the United States?

fourteen

Global Human Resource Management

Opening Case   Global Human Resource Management at Coca-Cola

The Coca-Cola Company is one of the most successful multinational enterprises. With operations in close to 200 countries and nearly 80 percent of its operating income derived from businesses outside the United States, Coca-Cola is perceived as the quintessential global corporation. Coca-Cola, however, likes to think of itself as a "multi-local" company that just happens to be headquartered in Atlanta and that presents the Coca-Cola brand with a

Coca-Cola tries to staff its local operations with local personnel, such as this Russian woman working in a local bottling plant. "Local people are better equipped to do business at their home locations."
Stone/Steven Weinberg.

Learning Objectives

1 Discuss the pros and cons of different approaches to staffing policy in international businesses.

2 Understand why managers may fail to thrive in foreign postings.

3 Understand what can be done to increase an executive's chance of succeeding in a foreign posting.

4 Appreciate the role that training, management development, and compensation practices can play in managing human resources within an international business.

"local face" in every country where it does business. The philosophy is best summarized by the phrase "think globally, act locally," which captures the essence of Coca-Cola's cross-border management mentality. A dominant theme at Coca-Cola is to grant businesses the freedom to conduct operations in a manner that is appropriate to the market in which they are competing. At the same time, the company tries to establish a common

mind-set among all its employees.

Coca-Cola manages its global operations through 25 operating divisions that are organized under six regional groups: North America, the European Union, the Pacific, the Northeast Europe/Middle East, Africa, and Latin America. Corporate human resources management (HRM) is charged with providing the glue that binds these various divisions and groups into the Coca-Cola family. The corporate HRM

function achieves this in two main ways: first, by propagating a common human resources philosophy within the company, and second, by developing a group of internationally minded mid-level executives for future senior management responsibility.

The corporate HRM group sees its mission as one of developing and providing the underlying philosophy around which local businesses can develop their own human resource practices. For example, rather than have a standard salary *policy* for all its national operations, Coca-Cola has a common salary *philosophy,* which is for its total compensation package to be competitive with the best companies in the local market. Twice a year the corporate HRM group also conducts a two-week HRM orientation session for the human resource staff from each of its 25 operating divisions. These sessions give an overview of the company's HRM philosophy and talk about how local businesses can translate that philosophy into human resource policies in their own area. Coca-Cola has found that information sharing is one of the great benefits of bringing HRM professionals together. For example, tools that have been developed in Brazil to deal with a specific HRM problem might also be useful in Australia. The sessions provide a medium through which HRM professionals can communicate and learn from each other, which facilitates the rapid transfer of innovative and valuable HRM tools from region to region.

As much as possible Coca-Cola tries to staff its local operations with local personnel. To quote one senior executive: "We strive to have a limited number of international people in the field because generally local people are better equipped to do business at their home locations." However, there is still a need for expatriates in the system for two main reasons. One is to fill a need for a specific set of skills that might not exist at a particular location. For example, when Coca-Cola started operations in Eastern Europe it had to bring in an expatriate from Chicago, who was of Polish decent, to be finance manager. The second reason for using expatriates is to improve the employee's own skill base. Coca-Cola believes that because it is a global company, before anyone takes on serious senior management responsibility that person should have international exposure.

The corporate HRM group has about 500 high-level managers that are involved in what it calls its global service program. Coca-Cola char-

acterizes these managers as people who have knowledge of their particular field, plus knowledge of the company, and who can do two things in an international location—add value by the expertise they bring to each assignment and enhance their contribution to the company by having international experience. Of the 500 participants in the program, about 200 move each year. To ease the costs of transfer for these employees, Coca-Cola gives those in its global service program a US-based compensation package. They are paid according to US benchmarks, as opposed to the benchmark prevailing in the country in which they are currently located. Thus, an Indian manager in this program who is currently working in Britain will be paid according to US salary benchmarks—and not those prevailing in either India or Britain. One goal of this program is to build a cadre of internationally minded high-level managers from which the future senior managers of Coca-Cola will be drawn.[1]

Introduction

human resource management Activities an organization carries out to utilize its human resource effectively.

Continuing our survey of operations functions within an international business, in this final chapter we examine international human resource management (HRM). **Human resource management** refers to the activities an organization carries out to utilize its human resource effectively.[2] These activities include determining the firm's human resource strategy, staffing, performance evaluation, management development, compensation, and labor relations. As the opening case on Coca-Cola makes clear, none of these activities is performed in a vacuum; all are related to the strategy of the firm because HRM has an important strategic component.[3] Most importantly, through its influence on the character, development, quality, and productivity of the firm's human resources, the HRM function can help the firm achieve its primary strategic goals of reducing the costs of value creation and adding value by better serving customer needs.

The strategic role of HRM is complex in a domestic firm, but it is more complex in an international business, where staffing, management development, performance evaluation, and compensation activities are complicated by profound differences in labor markets, culture, legal systems, economic systems, and the like (see Chapters 2 and 3). For example,

- Compensation practices may have to vary from country to country depending on prevailing management customs.

- Labor laws may prohibit union organization in one country and mandate it in another.
- Equal employment legislation may be strongly pursued in one country and not in another.

If it is to build a cadre of international managers, the HRM function must deal with a host of issues related to expatriate managers. (An **expatriate manager** is a citizen of one country who is working abroad in one of the firm's subsidiaries.)

The opening case shows how Coca-Cola deals with some of these issues. Coca-Cola copes with differences between countries by articulating a common HRM *philosophy,* but by letting each national operation translate this philosophy into HRM *policies* that are best suited to a particular operating environment. Coca-Cola also tries to build a cadre of internationally minded executives through its global service program, which involves the HRM function identifying and managing the career development of a key group of executives from which future senior management will be selected. Finally, and perhaps most importantly, Coca-Cola sees the HRM function as a vital link in the implementation of its strategic goal of thinking globally and acting locally.

In this chapter we will look closely at the role of HRM in an international business. We focus on four major tasks of the HRM function—staffing policy, management training and development, performance appraisal, and compensation policy. Throughout these sections we will point out the strategic implications of each of these tasks. The chapter closes with a look at international labor relations and the relationship between the firm's management of labor relations and its overall strategy.

Staffing Policy

Staffing policy is concerned with the selection of employees for particular jobs. At one level this involves selecting individuals who have the skills required to do particular jobs. At another level, staffing policy can be a tool for developing and promoting corporate culture.[4] By corporate culture we mean the organization's norms and value systems. A strong corporate culture can help a firm pursue its strategy. General Electric, for example, is not just concerned with hiring people who have the skills required for performing particular jobs; it wants to hire individuals whose behavioral styles, beliefs, and value systems are consistent with those of GE. This is true whether an American is being hired, an Italian, a German, or an Australian and whether the hiring is for a US operation or a foreign operation. The belief is that if employees are predisposed toward the organization's norms and value systems by their personality type, the firm will be able to attain higher performance.

Types of Staffing Policy

Research has identified three types of staffing policies in international businesses: the ethnocentric approach, the polycentric approach, and the geocentric approach.[5] We will review each policy and link it to the strategy pursued by the firm. The most attractive staffing policy is probably the geocentric approach, although there are several impediments to adopting it.

THE ETHNOCENTRIC APPROACH   An **ethnocentric staffing** policy is one in which all key management positions are filled by parent country nationals. This practice was very widespread at one time. Firms such as Procter & Gamble, Philips NV, and Matsushita originally followed it. In the Dutch firm Philips, for example, all important positions in most foreign subsidiaries were at one time held by Dutch nationals who were

expatriate manager A citizen of one country who is working abroad in one of the firm's subsidiaries.

staffing policy Policy concerned with the selection of employees for particular jobs.

ethnocentric staffing All key management positions are filled by parent country nationals.

referred to by their non-Dutch colleagues as the "Dutch Mafia." In many Japanese and South Korean firms today, such as Toyota, Matsushita, and Samsung, key positions in international operations are still often held by home country nationals. According to the Japanese Overseas Enterprise Association, in 1996 only 29 percent of foreign subsidiaries of Japanese companies had presidents that were not Japanese. In contrast, 66 percent of the Japanese subsidiaries of foreign companies had Japanese presidents.[6]

Firms pursue an ethnocentric staffing policy for three reasons. First, the firm may believe the host country lacks qualified individuals to fill senior management positions. This argument is heard most often when the firm has operations in less developed countries. Second, the firm may see an ethnocentric staffing policy as the best way to maintain a unified corporate culture. Many Japanese firms, for example, prefer their foreign operations to be headed by expatriate Japanese managers because these managers will have been socialized into the firm's culture while employed in Japan.[7] Similarly, until recently Procter & Gamble preferred to staff important management positions in its foreign subsidiaries with US nationals who had been socialized into P&G's corporate culture by years of employment in its US operations. Such reasoning predominates when a firm places a high value on its corporate culture.

Third, if the firm is trying to create value by transferring core competencies to a foreign operation, as firms pursuing an international strategy are, it may believe that the best way to do this is to transfer parent country nationals who have knowledge of that competency to the foreign operation. Imagine what might occur if a firm tried to transfer a core competency in marketing to a foreign subsidiary without supporting the transfer with a corresponding transfer of home country marketing management personnel. The transfer would probably fail to produce the anticipated benefits, because the knowledge underlying a core competency cannot easily be articulated and written down. Such knowledge often has a significant tacit dimension; it is acquired through experience. Just like the great tennis player who cannot instruct others how to become great tennis players simply by writing a handbook, the firm that has a core competency in marketing—or anything else—cannot just write a handbook that tells a foreign subsidiary how to build the firm's core competency anew in a foreign setting. It must also transfer management personnel to the foreign operation to show foreign managers how to become good marketers, for example. The need to transfer managers overseas arises because the knowledge that underlies the firm's core competency resides in the heads of its domestic managers. They have acquired this knowledge through years of experience, not by reading a handbook. Thus, if a firm is to transfer a core competency to a foreign subsidiary, it must also transfer the appropriate managers.

Despite this rationale for pursuing an ethnocentric staffing policy, the policy is now on the wane in most international businesses. There are two reasons for this. First, an ethnocentric staffing policy limits advancement opportunities for host country nationals. This can lead to resentment, lower productivity, and increased turnover among that group. Resentment can be greater still if, as often occurs, expatriate managers are paid significantly more than host country nationals.

Second, an ethnocentric policy can lead to "cultural myopia," the firm's failure to understand host country cultural differences that require different approaches to marketing and management. The adaptation of expatriate managers can take a long time, during which they may make major mistakes. For example, expatriate managers may fail to appreciate how product attributes, distribution strategy, communication strategy, and pricing strategy should be adapted to host country conditions. The result may be costly blunders. In one highly publicized case in the United States, Mitsubishi Motors was sued by the federal Equal Employment Opportunity Commission for allegedly tolerating extensive and systematic sexual harassment in a plant in Illinois. The plant's top managers, all Japanese expatriates, denied the allegations. The Japanese managers failed to realize that behavior that would be viewed as acceptable in Japan was not acceptable in the United States.[8]

THE POLYCENTRIC APPROACH   A **polycentric staffing** policy requires host country nationals to be recruited to manage subsidiaries, while parent country nationals occupy key positions at corporate headquarters. In many respects a polycentric approach is a response to the shortcomings of an ethnocentric approach. One advantage of a polycentric approach is that the firm is less likely to suffer from cultural myopia. Host country managers are unlikely to make the mistakes arising from cultural misunderstandings to which expatriate managers are vulnerable. A second advantage is that a polycentric approach may be less expensive. Expatriate managers can be very expensive to maintain. Using host country nationals can reduce the costs of value creation.

However, a polycentric approach also has its drawbacks. Host country nationals have limited opportunities to gain experience outside their own country and thus cannot progress beyond senior positions in their own subsidiary. As in the case of an ethnocentric policy, this may cause resentment. Perhaps the major drawback with a polycentric approach, however, is the gap that can form between host country managers and parent country managers. Language barriers, national loyalties, and a range of cultural differences may isolate the corporate headquarters staff from the foreign subsidiaries. The lack of management transfers from home to host countries, and vice versa, can exacerbate this isolation and lead to a lack of integration between corporate headquarters and foreign subsidiaries. The result can be a federation of largely independent national units with only nominal links to the corporate headquarters. Within such a federation, the coordination required to transfer core competencies or to pursue experience curve and location economies may be difficult to achieve. Thus, although a polycentric approach may be effective for firms pursuing a multidomestic strategy, it is inappropriate for other strategies.

The federation that may result from a polycentric approach also can be a force for inertia within the firm. For example, after decades of pursing a polycentric staffing policy, food and detergents giant Unilever found that shifting from a multidomestic strategic posture to a transnational posture was very difficult. Unilever's foreign subsidiaries had evolved into quasi-autonomous operations, each with its own strong national identity. These "little kingdoms" objected strenuously to corporate headquarters' attempts to limit their autonomy and to rationalize global manufacturing.[9]

THE GEOCENTRIC APPROACH   A **geocentric staffing** policy seeks the best people for key jobs throughout the organization, regardless of nationality. There are a number of advantages to this policy. First, it enables the firm to make the best use of its human resources. Second, and perhaps more important, a geocentric policy enables the firm to build a cadre of international executives who feel at home working in a number of cultures. Creation of such a cadre may be a critical first step toward building a strong unifying corporate culture and an informal management network, both of which are required for global and transnational strategies.[10] Firms pursuing a geocentric staffing policy may be better able to create value from the pursuit of experience curve and location economies and from the multidirectional transfer of core competencies than firms pursuing other staffing policies. In addition, the multinational composition of the management team that results from geocentric staffing tends to reduce cultural myopia and to enhance local responsiveness. Thus, other things being equal, a geocentric staffing policy seems the most attractive.

However, a number of problems limit the firm's ability to pursue a geocentric policy. Many countries want foreign subsidiaries to employ their citizens, so they use immigration laws to require the employment of host country nationals if they are available in adequate numbers and have the necessary skills. Most countries (including the United States) require firms to provide extensive documentation if they wish to hire a foreign national instead of a local national. This documentation can be time consuming, expensive, and at times futile. A further problem is that a geocentric staffing policy can be very expensive. There are increased training costs, relocation costs involved in transferring managers from country to country, and the need for a compensation structure with a standardized international base pay level that may be higher than national levels in many countries. In addition, the higher pay enjoyed by managers placed on an international fast track may be a source of resentment within a firm.

SUMMARY   The advantages and disadvantages of the three approaches to staffing policy are summarized in Table 14.1. An ethnocentric approach is compatible with an international strategy, a polycentric approach is compatible with a multidomestic strategy, and a geocentric approach is compatible with both global and transnational strategies. (See Chapter 10 for details of the strategies.)

Finally, it should be noted that while the staffing policy typology described here is well known and widely used among both practitioners and scholars of international businesses, recently some critics have claimed that the typology is too simplistic and that it may obscure the internal differentiation of management practices within international businesses. The critics claim that within some international businesses, staffing policies vary significantly from national subsidiary to national subsidiary so that while some are managed on an ethnocentric basis, others are managed in a polycentric or geocentric manner.[11] Other critics note that the staffing policy adopted by a firm is primarily driven by its geographic scope, as opposed

Table 14.1

Comparison of Staffing Approaches

Staffing Approach	Strategic Appropriateness	Advantages	Disadvantages
Ethnocentric	International	Overcomes lack of qualified managers in host nation Unified culture Helps transfer core competencies	Produces resentment in host country Can lead to cultural myopia
Polycentric	Multidomestic	Alleviates cultural myopia Inexpensive to implement	Limits career mobility Isolates headquarters from foreign subsidiaries
Geocentric	Global and transnational	Uses human resources efficiently Helps build strong culture and informal management network	National immigration policies may limit implementation Expensive

to its strategic orientation, with firms that have a very broad geographic scope being the most likely to have a geocentric mind-set.[12] Thus, Coca-Cola, which is involved in about 200 countries, is by this argument more likely to have a geocentric mind-set than a firm that is involved in only 3 countries.

The Expatriate Problem

Two of the three staffing policies we have discussed—the ethnocentric and the geocentric—rely on extensive use of expatriate managers. With an ethnocentric policy, the expatriates are all home country nationals who are transferred abroad. With a geocentric approach, the expatriates need not be home country nationals; the firm does not base transfer decisions on nationality. A prominent issue in the international staffing literature is **expatriate failure**—the premature return of an expatriate manager to his or her home country.[13] Here we briefly review the evidence on expatriate failure before discussing a number of ways in which the expatriate failure rate can be minimized.

expatriate failure The premature return of an expatriate manager to his or her home country.

EXPATRIATE FAILURE RATES   Expatriate failure represents a failure of the firm's selection policies to identify individuals who will not thrive abroad. The costs of expatriate failure are high. One estimate is that the average cost per failure to the parent firm can be as high as three times the expatriate's annual domestic salary plus the cost of relocation (which is affected by currency exchange rates and location of assignment).[14] Research suggests that between 16 and 40 percent of all American employees sent abroad to developed nations return from their assignments early, and almost 70 percent of employees sent to developing nations return home early.[15] Although detailed data are not available for other nationalities, one suspects that high expatriate failure is a universal problem. Estimates of the costs of each failure run between $250,000 and $1 million.[16] In addition, approximately 30 to 50 percent of American expatriates, whose average compensation package runs to $250,000 a year, stay at their international assignments but are considered ineffective or marginally effective by their firms.[17] In a seminal study, R. L. Tung surveyed a number of US, European, and Japanese multinationals.[18] Her results, summarized in Table 14.2,

Table 14.2

Expatriate Failure Rates

Recall Rate Percent	Percent of Companies
US multinationals	
20–40%	7%
10–20	69
<10	24
European multinationals	
11–15%	3%
6–10	38
<5	59
Japanese multinationals	
11–19%	14%
6–10	10
<5	76

Source: Data from R. L. Tung, "Selection and Training Procedures of U.S., European, and Japanese Multinationals," *California Management Review* 25 (1982), pp. 57–71.

suggested that 76 percent of US multinationals experienced expatriate failure rates of 10 percent or more, and 7 percent of US multinationals experienced a failure rate of more than 20 percent. Tung's work also suggests that US-based multinationals experience a much higher expatriate failure rate than either European or Japanese multinationals.

Tung asked her sample of multinational managers to indicate reasons for expatriate failure. For US multinationals, the reasons, in order of importance, were

1 Inability of spouse to adjust.
2 Manager's inability to adjust.
3 Other family problems.
4 Manager's personal or emotional maturity.
5 Inability to cope with larger overseas responsibility.

Managers of European firms gave only one reason consistently to explain expatriate failure: the inability of the manager's spouse to adjust to a new environment. For the Japanese firms, the reasons for failure, in order of importance, were

1 Inability to cope with larger overseas responsibility.
2 Difficulties with new environment.
3 Personal or emotional problems.
4 Lack of technical competence.
5 Inability of spouse to adjust.

Perhaps the most striking difference between these lists is that "inability of spouse to adjust" was the top reason for expatriate failure among US and European multinationals but only the number-five reason among Japanese multinationals. Tung comments that this difference is not surprising, given the role and status to which Japanese society traditionally relegates the wife and the fact that most of the Japanese expatriate managers in the study were men.

Since Tung's study a number of other studies have confirmed that the inability of a spouse to adjust, the inability of the manager to adjust, or other family problems remain major reasons for continuing high levels of expatriate failure. One study by International Orientation Resources, an HRM consulting firm, found that 60 percent of expatriate failures occur due to these three reasons.[19] The inability of expatriate managers to adjust to foreign postings seems to be caused by a lack of cultural skills on the part of the manager being transferred. According to one HRM management consulting firm, this is because the expatriate selection process at many firms is flawed:

> Expatriate assignments rarely fail because the person cannot accommodate to the technical demands of the job. Typically, the expatriate selections are made by line managers based on technical competence. They fail because of family and personal issues and lack of cultural skills that haven't been part of the selection process.[20]

The failure of spouses to adjust to a foreign posting seems to be related to a number of factors. Often spouses find themselves in a foreign country without the familiar network of family and friends. Language differences make it difficult for them to make new friends. While this may not be too great a problem for the manager, who can make friends at work, it can be difficult for the spouse who might feel trapped at home. The problem is often exacerbated by immigration regulations prohibiting the spouse from taking employment. With the recent rise of two-career families in many developed nations, this has become much more important. Recent research suggests that a main reason managers now turn down international assignments is

Shell International is a global petroleum company with joint headquarters in both London and The Hague in the Netherlands. The company employs over 100,000 people, about 5,500 of whom are at any one time living and working as expatriates. The expatriates at Shell are a very diverse group, made up of over 70 nationalities and located in more than 100 countries. Shell has long recognized that as a global corporation, the international mobility of its workforce is essential to its success. By the early 1990s, however, Shell was finding it harder to recruit key personnel for foreign postings. To discover why, in 1993 the company interviewed more than 200 expatriate employees and their spouses to determine their biggest concerns. The data were used to construct a survey that was sent to 17,000 current and former expatriate employees, expatriate spouses, and employees who had declined international assignments.

The survey registered a phenomenal 70 percent response rate, indicating that many employees thought this was an important issue. According to the survey, five issues had the greatest impact on the willingness of an employee to accept an international assignment. In order of importance, these were (1) separation from children during their secondary education (the children of British and Dutch expatriates were often sent to boarding schools in their home countries while their parents worked abroad), (2) harm done to a spouse's career and employment, (3) a failure to recognize and involve a spouse in the relocation decision, (4) a failure to provide adequate information and assistance regarding relocation, and (5) health issues. The underlying message here: The family is the basic unit of expatriation, not the individual, and Shell needed to do more to recognize this.

Beginning in 1994, Shell implemented a number of programs designed to deal with some of these problems. To help with the education of children, Shell built elementary schools for Shell employees where there was a heavy concentration of expatriates. As for secondary school education, it worked with local schools, often providing grants, to help them upgrade their educational offerings. It also offered an education supplement to help expatriates send their children to private schools in the host country (before 1994, it would pay for a child's boarding school education only in its home country).

Helping spouses with their careers is a more vexing problem. According to the survey data, half of the spouses accompanying Shell staff on assignment were employed until the transfer. When expatriated, only 12 percent were able to secure employment, while a further 33 percent wished to be employed. Shell set up a Spouse Employment Center to help address the problem. The center provides career counseling and assistance in locating employment opportunities both during and immediately after an international assignment. The company also agreed to reimburse up to 80 percent of the costs of vocational training, further education, or reaccreditation, up to $4,400 per assignment.

Shell also set up a global information and advice network known as "The Outpost" to provide support for families contemplating a foreign posting. The Outpost has its headquarters in The Hague and now runs 40 information centers in more than 30 countries. Staffed by spouses and fully supported by Shell, this network had by 1998 helped more than 1,000 couples prepare for placement overseas. The center recommends schools, medical facilities, and housing and provides up-to-date information on employment, study, self-employment, and volunteer work.[21]

Managing Expatriates at Shell International Petroleum

concern over the impact such an assignment might have on their spouses' careers.[22] The accompanying "Management Focus" examines how one large multinational company, Shell International Petroleum, has tried to come to grips with this issue.

EXPATRIATE SELECTION   One way of reducing expatriate failure rates is through improved selection procedures to screen out inappropriate candidates in advance. In a review of the research, Mendenhall and Oddou stated that a major problem in many firms is that HRM managers tend to equate domestic performance with

If you were transferred abroad and didn't like the local cuisine, this might mean that you lacked attributes of Mendenhall and Oddou's **self-orientation** dimension.
© PhotoDisc

overseas performance potential, selecting candidates for foreign postings accordingly.[23] Domestic performance and overseas performance potential are not the same thing. An executive who performs well in a domestic setting may not be able to adapt to managing in a different cultural setting. From their review of the research, Mendenhall and Oddou identified four dimensions that seem to predict success in a foreign posting: self-orientation, others-orientation, perceptual ability, and cultural toughness.

1 *Self-orientation.* The attributes of this dimension strengthen the expatriate's self-esteem, self-confidence, and mental well-being. Expatriates with high self-esteem, self-confidence, and mental well-being were more likely to succeed in foreign postings. Mendenhall and Oddou concluded that such individuals were able to adapt their interests in food, sport, and music; had interests outside of work that could be pursued (e.g., hobbies); and were technically competent.

2 *Others-orientation.* The attributes of this dimension enhance the expatriate's ability to interact effectively with host country nationals. The more effectively the expatriate interacts with host country nationals, the more likely he or she is to succeed. Two factors seem to be particularly important here: relationship development and willingness to communicate. Relationship development refers to the ability to develop long-lasting friendships with host country nationals. Willingness to communicate refers to the expatriate's willingness to use the host country language. Although language fluency helps, an expatriate need not be fluent to show willingness to communicate. Making the effort to use the language is what is important. Such gestures tend to be rewarded with greater cooperation by host country nationals.

3 *Perceptual ability.* This is the ability to understand why people of other countries behave in the way they do; that is, the ability to empathize with them. This dimension seems critical for managing host country nationals. Expatriate managers who lack this ability tend to treat foreign nationals as if they were home country nationals. As a result, they may experience significant management problems and considerable frustration. As one expatriate executive from Hewlett-Packard observed, "It took me six months to accept the fact that my staff meetings would start 30 minutes late, and that it would bother no one but me." According to Mendenhall and Oddou, well-adjusted expatriates tend to be nonjudgmental and nonevaluative in interpreting the behavior of host country nationals and willing to be flexible in their management style, adjusting it as cultural conditions warrant.

4 *Cultural toughness.* This dimension refers to the fact that how well an expatriate adjusts to a particular posting tends to be related to the country of assignment. Some countries are much tougher postings than others because their cultures are more unfamiliar and uncomfortable. For example, many Americans regard Great Britain as a relatively easy foreign posting, and for good reason—US and British cultures have much in common. On the other hand, many Americans find postings in non-

Western cultures, such as India, Southeast Asia, and the Middle East, to be much tougher.[24] The reasons are many, including poor health care and housing standards, inhospitable climate, a lack of Western entertainment, and language difficulties. It is also important to stress that many cultures are extremely male dominated and thus may be particularly difficult postings for female Western managers.

Mendenhall and Oddou note that standard psychological tests can be used to assess the first three of these dimensions, and a comparison of cultures can give managers a feeling for the fourth dimension. Their point is that in addition to domestic performance, these four dimensions should be given weight when selecting a manager for foreign posting. However, practice does not conform to Mendenhall and Oddou's recommendations. Tung's research, for example, showed that only 5 percent of the firms in her sample used formal procedures and psychological tests to assess the personality traits and relational abilities of potential expatriates.[25] Similarly, recent work by International Orientation Resources suggests that when selecting employees for foreign assignments, only 10 percent of the 50 Fortune 500 firms they surveyed tested for important psychological traits such as cultural sensitivity, interpersonal skills, adaptability, and flexibility. Instead, 90 percent of the time employees were selected on the basis of their technical expertise, not their cross-cultural fluency.[26]

One factor that Mendenhall and Oddou do not address is the problem of expatriate failure due to a spouse's inability to adjust. According to a number of other researchers, a review of the family situation should be part of the expatriate selection process (see the "Management Focus" on Shell for an example).[27] A survey by Windam International, another international HRM

Women in International Assignments

Women managers have had notable success in international management postings, especially in cultures that are perceived to be male-dominated, largely because they are perceived first as foreign and treated by locals within the "foreign" category and only secondly as women. Just look at US Trade Representative Charlene Barshefsky, US Secretary of State Madeleine Albright, and Carly Fiorina, now of Hewlett-Packard. Women also have salience in their new environment—they are noticeable—which can be a business advantage. We must gather data from women who have had international postings and not rely on the opinions of Western male managers who may not fully appreciate the challenges or understand the foreign cultures from a women's perspective.

management consulting firm, found that spouses were included in preselection interviews for foreign postings only 21 percent of the time, and that only half of them ever receive any cross-cultural training. Again, it should be emphasized that the rise of dual-career families has added an additional and difficult dimension to this long-standing problem.[28] Increasingly, spouses wonder why they should have to sacrifice their own career to further that of their partner.[29]

Training and Management Development

Selection is just the first step in matching a manager with a job. The next step is training the manager to do the job. For example, an intensive training program might be used to give expatriate managers the skills required for success in a foreign posting. Management development is a much broader concept. It is intended to develop the manager's skills over his or her career with the firm. Thus, as part of a management development program, over a number of years a manager might be sent on several foreign postings to build her cross-cultural sensitivity and experience. At the same time, along with a group of other managers in the firm, she might attend management education programs at regular intervals.

Historically, most international businesses have been more concerned with training than with management development. They tended to focus their training efforts on preparing home country nationals for foreign postings. Recently, however, the shift toward greater global competition and the rise of transnational firms have brought about changes. It is increasingly common for firms to provide general management development programs in addition to training for particular posts. In many international businesses, the explicit purpose of these management development programs is strategic. The belief is that management development can be used to help the firm achieve its strategic goals.

With this distinction between training and management development in mind, in this section we examine the types of training managers receive for foreign postings. Then we discuss the connection between management development and strategy in the international business.

Training for Expatriate Managers

Earlier in the chapter we saw that the two most common reasons for expatriate failure were the inability of a manager's spouse to adjust to a foreign environment and the manager's own inability to adjust to a foreign environment. Training can help both the manager and his or her spouse. Cultural training, language training, and practical training all seem to reduce expatriate failure. We discuss each of these kinds of training here.[30] Despite the usefulness of training, evidence suggests that many managers receive no training before they are sent on foreign postings. One study found that only about 30 percent of managers sent on one- to five-year expatriate assignments received training before their departure.[31]

CULTURAL TRAINING   Cultural training seeks to foster an appreciation for the host country's culture. The belief is that understanding a host country's culture will help the manager empathize with the culture, which will enhance effectiveness in dealing with host country nationals. It has been suggested that expatriates should receive training in the host country's culture, history, politics, economy, religion, and social and business practices.[32] If possible, it is also advisable to arrange for a trip to the host country before the formal transfer; this seems to ease culture shock. Given the problems related to spouse adaptation, it is important that the spouse, and perhaps the whole family, be included in cultural training programs.

LANGUAGE TRAINING   English is the language of world business; it is quite possible to conduct business all over the world using only English. For example, in ABB, a Swiss electrical equipment giant, the company's top 13 managers hold frequent meetings in different countries. Because they share no common first language, they speak only English, a foreign tongue to all but one.[33] Despite the prevalence of English, however, an exclusive reliance on English diminishes an expatriate manager's ability to interact with host country nationals. As noted earlier in the chapter, a willingness to communicate in the language of the host country, even if the expatriate is far from fluent, can help build rapport with local employees and improve the manager's effectiveness. Despite this, J. C. Baker's study of 74 executives of US multinationals found that only 23 believed knowledge of foreign languages was necessary for conducting business abroad.[34] Those firms that did offer foreign language training for expatriates believed it improved their employees' effectiveness and enabled them to relate more easily to a foreign culture, which fostered a better image of the firm in the host country.

PRACTICAL TRAINING Practical training is aimed at helping the expatriate manager and family ease themselves into day-to-day life in the host country. The sooner a routine is established, the better are the prospects that the family will adapt successfully. One of the most critical needs is for a support network of friends for the expatriate. Where an expatriate community exists, firms often devote considerable effort to ensuring the new expatriate family is quickly integrated into that group. The expatriate community can be a useful source of support and information and can be invaluable in helping the family adapt to a foreign culture.

Repatriation of Expatriates

A largely overlooked but critical issue in the training and development of expatriate managers is to prepare them for reentry into their home country organization.[35] Repatriation should be seen as the final link in an integrated, circular process that connects good selection and cross-cultural training of expatriate managers with completion of their term abroad and reintegration into their national organization. However, instead of employees coming home to share their knowledge and encourage other high-performing managers to take the same international career track, expatriates too often face a different scenario.[36]

Often when they return home after a stint abroad—during which they have typically been autonomous, well-compensated, and celebrated as a big fish in a little pond—they face an organization that doesn't know what they have done for the past few years, doesn't know how to use their new knowledge, and doesn't particularly care. In the worst cases reentering employees have to scrounge for jobs, or firms will create standby positions that don't use the expatriate's skills and capabilities and fail to make the most of the business investment the firm has made in that individual.

Research illustrates the extent of this problem. According to one study of repatriated employees, 60 percent to 70 percent didn't know what their position would be when they returned home. Also, 60 percent said their organizations were vague about repatriation, about their new roles, and about their future career progression within the company, while 77 percent of those surveyed actually took jobs at a lower level in their home organization than in their international assignments.[37] It is a small wonder then that 15 percent of returning expatriates leave their firm within a year of arriving home, while 40 percent leave within three years.[38]

The key to solving this problem is good human resource planning. Just as the HRM function needs to develop good selection and training programs for its expatriates, it also needs to develop good programs for reintegrating expatriates back into work life within their home country organization once their foreign assignment is over and for utilizing the knowledge they acquired while abroad. For an example of the kind of program that might be used, read the accompanying "Management Focus," which looks at the repatriation program developed at Monsanto.

Management Development and Strategy

Management development programs are designed to increase the overall skill levels of managers through a mix of ongoing management education and rotation of managers through a number of jobs to give them varied experiences. Management development programs attempt to improve the overall productivity and quality of the firm's management resources.

Increasingly, international businesses are using management development as a strategic tool. Management development programs help build a unifying corporate culture by socializing new managers into the norms and value systems of the firm. In-house company training programs and intense interaction during off-site training can foster esprit de corps—shared experiences, informal networks, perhaps a company language

Monsanto is a global agricultural, chemical, and pharmaceutical company with revenues in excess of $10 billion and 30,000 employees. At any one time the company will have 100 mid- and high-level managers who are on extended postings abroad. Two-thirds of these are Americans who are being posted overseas, while the remainder are foreign nationals being employed in the United States. At Monsanto the process of managing expatriates and their repatriation begins with a rigorous selection process and intensive cross-cultural training, both abroad to do the job and what their contributions to Monsanto will be when they return. As part of this process, sponsoring managers are expected to be explicit about the kind of job opportunities the expatriate will have on returns.

Once they do arrive back in their home country, expatriate managers meet with cross-cultural trainers during debriefing sessions. They are also given the opportunity to showcase their experience to their peers, subordinates, and superiors in special information exchange sessions.

ties. About three months after they return home, expatriates meet for three hours at work with several colleagues of their choice. The debriefing session is a conversation aided by a trained facilitator who has an outline to help the expatriate cover the important aspects of the repatriation. The debriefing allows the employee to share important experiences and to enlighten managers, colleagues, and friends about his or her expertise so that others within the organization can use some of the global knowledge.

Monsanto's Repatriation Program

for the managers and for their families. As at many other global companies, the idea is to build an internationally minded cadre of highly capable managers who will lead the organization in the future.

One strong feature of this program is that employees and their sending and receiving managers, or sponsors, develop an agreement about their understanding of this assignment and how it will fit into the firm's business objectives. The focus is on why they are sending assignees

However, Monsanto's repatriation program focuses on more than just business—it also attends to the family's reentry. Monsanto has found that difficulties with repatriation often have more to do with personal and family-related issues, than with work-related issues. But the personal matters obviously affect an employee's job performance, so it is important for the company to pay attention to such issues.

This is why Monsanto offers returning employees an opportunity to work through personal difficul-

According to one participant, "It sounds silly, but it's such a hectic time in the family's life you don't have time to sit down and take stock of what's happening. You're going through the move, transitioning to a new job, a new house, the children may be going to a new school. This is a kind of oasis; a time to talk and put your feelings on the table." Apparently it works; since the program was introduced in 1992 the attrition rate among returning expatriates has dropped sharply.[39]

---

or jargon—as well as develop technical competencies. These training events often include songs, picnics, and sporting events that promote feelings of togetherness. These rites of integration may include "initiation rites" wherein personal culture is stripped, company uniforms are donned (e.g., T-shirts bearing the company logo), and humiliation is inflicted (e.g., a pie in the face). The aim of these activities is to strengthen a manager's identification with the company.[40]

Bringing managers together in one location for extended periods and rotating them through different jobs in several countries helps the firm build an informal management network. Consider the Swedish telecommunications company L. M. Ericsson. Interunit cooperation is extremely important at Ericsson, particularly for transferring know-how and core competencies from the parent to foreign subsidiaries, from foreign subsidiaries to the parent, and between foreign subsidiaries. To facilitate cooperation, Ericsson transfers large numbers of people back and forth between headquarters and subsidiaries. Ericsson sends a team of 50 to 100 engineers and managers from one unit to another for a year or two. This establishes a network of interpersonal contacts. This policy is effective for both solidifying a common culture in the company and coordinating the company's globally dispersed operations.[41]

Performance Appraisal

A particularly thorny issue in many international businesses is how best to evaluate expatriate managers' performances.[42] In this section we look at this issue and consider some guidelines for appraising expatriate performance.

Performance Appraisal Problems

The intrusion of unintentional bias makes it difficult to evaluate the performance of expatriate managers objectively. In most cases, two groups evaluate the performance of expatriate managers, host nation managers and home office managers, and both are subject to bias. The host nation managers may be biased by their own cultural frame of reference and set of expectations. For example, Oddou and Mendenhall report the case of a US manager who introduced participative decision making while working in an Indian subsidiary.[43] The manager subsequently received a negative evaluation from host country managers. Because of the strong social stratification that exists in India, managers are seen as experts who should not have to ask subordinates for details. The local employees apparently viewed the US manager's attempt at participatory management as an indication that he was incompetent and did not know his job. This negatively affected his host country managers' evaluation of his performance.

Home country managers' appraisals may be biased by distance and by their own lack of experience working abroad. Because of distance, home office management is often not aware of what is going on in a foreign operation, so managers tend to rely on "hard" data in evaluating an expatriate's performance—data such as the subunit's productivity, profitability, or market share. But such criteria may reflect factors outside the expatriate manager's control (e.g., adverse changes in exchange rates, economic downturns). Also, hard data do not take into account many less visible "soft" variables that are also important, such as an expatriate's ability to develop cross-cultural awareness and to work productively with local managers.

Many expatriate managers appear to believe that headquarters management evaluates them unfairly and does not fully appreciate the value of their skills and experience. This could be one reason many expatriates believe a foreign posting does not benefit their careers. In one study of personnel managers in US multinationals, 56 percent of the managers surveyed stated that a foreign assignment is either detrimental or immaterial to one's career.[44]

Guidelines for Performance Appraisal

Several things can reduce bias in performance appraisal.[45] First, most expatriates appear to believe more weight should be given to an on-site manager's appraisal than to an off-site manager's appraisal. Due to proximity, an on-site manager is more likely to be able to evaluate the soft variables that are important aspects of an expatriate's performance. The evaluation may be especially valid when the on-site manager is of the same nationality as the expatriate, since cultural bias should be alleviated.

In practice, however, home office managers often write performance evaluations after receiving input from on-site managers. When this is the case, most experts recommend that a former expatriate who served in the same location should be involved in the appraisal to help reduce bias. When the policy is for foreign on-site managers to write performance evaluations, home office managers should probably be consulted before an on-site manager completes a formal termination evaluation. This gives the home office manager the opportunity to balance what could be a very hostile evaluation based on a cultural misunderstanding.

Compensation

Two issues are raised in every discussion of compensation practices in an international business. One is how compensation should be adjusted to reflect national differences in economic circumstances and compensation practices. The other issue is how expatriate managers should be paid.

National Differences in Compensation

Substantial differences exist in the compensation of executives at the same level in various countries. For example, in 1996 the average CEO of a large *public* company in the United States made $2.3 million in salary and bonuses, and this went up to $5.8 million when stock options were included in the calculations. In 1997 the figure soared to $7.8 million. In comparison, the average pay of foreign executives is much lower. The CEO of a large public Japanese firm, such as Sony or Matsushita, makes $1.2 million to $1.5 million per year. In Europe, when it was announced that Pierre Suard, then the CEO of French-based telecommunications equipment supplier Alcatel Alsthom, made $2.5 million, it sparked a scandal and much hand-ringing about the excesses of executive pay. According to Towers Perrin, an international human relations consulting firm, the average CEO of a firm in the United States, big or small, public or private, made $927,896 in salary and bonuses (excluding stock options) in 1996. By contrast, the average total pay was $600,052 for a French CEO, $512,651 for a German, $483,815 for a British, and $558,457 for a Japanese. These figures almost certainly underestimate the true differential, since many US executives earn considerable money from stock options and grants; the practice of granting options is still relatively rare in other nations.[46]

These differences in compensation practices raise a perplexing question for an international business: Should the firm pay executives in different countries according to the prevailing standards in each country, or should it equalize pay on a global basis? The problem does not really arise in firms pursuing ethnocentric or polycentric staffing policies. In ethnocentric firms the issue can be reduced to that of how much home country expatriates should be paid (which we will consider later). As for polycentric firms, the lack of managers' mobility among national operations implies that pay can and should be kept country-specific. There would seem to be no point in paying executives in Great Britain the same as US executives if they never work side by side.

This problem is very real in firms with geocentric staffing policies, which is consistent with a transnational strategy. One aspect of this policy, from the HRM perspective, is the need for a cadre of international managers. This cadre may comprise managers of many different nationalities. Should all members of such a cadre be paid the same salary and the same incentive pay? For a US-based firm this would mean raising the compensation of foreign nationals to US levels, which, given the high pay rates prevailing in the United States, could be very expensive. If the firm does not equalize pay, it could cause resentment among foreign nationals who are members of the international cadre and work side by side with US nationals. In general, if a firm is serious about building an international cadre, it may have to pay its international executives the same basic salary irrespective of their country of origin or assignment. The accompanying "Management Focus" contains several examples of how some international businesses have tried to deal with this problem.

Expatriate Pay

The most common approach to expatriate pay is the balance sheet approach. This approach equalizes purchasing power across countries so employees can enjoy the same living standard in their foreign posting that they enjoyed at home. In addition,

A survey of human resource professionals undertaken by Organizational Resources Consulting—an international HRM consulting firm, found that of the 45 large US multinational companies it surveyed all 45 viewed differing pay levels and perks as their biggest problem when trying to develop an international workforce. In contrast, only 60 percent of these companies stated that cultural differences and repatriation processes were a serious problem. The root of the problem is cost; expatriate pay packages that are based on American salaries and needs are increasingly seen as too expensive. In an

from high-pay countries, such as Germany, to lower-pay countries, such as Britain, HP offers temporary bridging payments to ease the adjustment.

The Minnesota Mining and Manufacturing Co. (3M) has a different type of program for longer-term expatriates. The company developed the program because it drastically altered its international organization. In Europe, for example, 3M used to organize its operations on a country-by-country basis. Now, however, 3M has established Europeanwide divisions. As a result many 3M executives who might have spent their entire career in one country are now being asked to move—perhaps permanently—to another country.

higher housing costs through a special payment scheme, the way many traditional expatriate pay policies did. Any housing subsidy that resulted could last for the rest of an executive's career following a transfer—and this would be very expensive.

The large oil company Phillips Petroleum has adopted yet another policy. At Phillips the policy used to be that when a third-country national, such as a British citizen, was transferred abroad (for example, from Britain to Kuwait), he would be paid in US dollars and his salary would be raised to a level equivalent to that of someone in the United States

Executive Pay Policies for Global Managers

attempt to deal with this issue, many international businesses are trying to develop special pay schemes for their internationally mobile managers.

At Hewlett-Packard about 600 people a year are transferred across national borders. Although most of these transferees are on short-term (one to two years) assignments, up to 25 percent are on indefinite assignments. HP ties the pay of short-term transferees to pay scales in their home country, but longer-term HP transferees are quickly switched to the pay scale of their host country and paid according to prevailing local standards. For employees moving

The 3M program compares net salaries in both the old and new country by subtracting the major costs, such as taxes and housing, from gross pay. The transferred executive then gets the highest pay packet. Thus, when 3M transfers a German executive to France, the German remains on her home country pay scale. But a British employee transferred to Germany—where salaries are higher—can expect to be switched to the German pay scale. However, although the policy does consider local housing costs, it doesn't compensate for

doing a similar job. This, however, was a very expensive policy given the generally high level of pay prevailing in the United States. Thus, now Phillips has a third-country nationals program. Under this program, the transferred employee is given generous housing allowances and educational assistance for his children. However, his salary is now pegged to the level prevailing in his home country, and not that in the United States or the country to which the employee is being transferred.[47]

the approach provides financial incentives to offset qualitative differences between assignment locations.[48] Figure 14.1 shows a typical balance sheet. Note that home country outlays for the employee are designated as income taxes, housing expenses, expenditures for goods and services (food, clothing, entertainment, etc.), and reserves (savings, pension contributions, etc.) The balance sheet approach attempts to provide expatriates with the same standard of living in their host countries as they enjoy at home plus a financial inducement (i.e., premium or incentive) for accepting an overseas assignment.

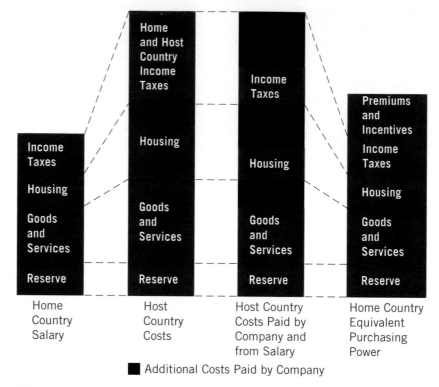

Income Taxes	Home and Host Country Income Taxes	Income Taxes	Premiums and Incentives
Housing	Housing		Income Taxes
		Housing	Housing
Goods and Services	Goods and Services	Goods and Services	Goods and Services
Reserve	Reserve	Reserve	Reserve
Home Country Salary	Host Country Costs	Host Country Costs Paid by Company and from Salary	Home Country Equivalent Purchasing Power

■ Additional Costs Paid by Company

Figure 14.1

A Typical Balance Sheet

C. Reynolds, "Compensation of Overseas Personnel," in *Handbook of Human Resource Administration, 2nd ed.,* J.J. Famularo, ed., McGraw-Hill, 1986, p. 51. Reproduced with permission of The McGraw-Hill Companies, Inc.

The components of the typical expatriate compensation package are a base salary, a foreign service premium, allowances of various types, tax differentials, and benefits. We shall briefly review each of these components.[49] An expatriate's total compensation package may amount to three times what he or she would cost the firm in a home country posting. Because of the high cost of expatriates, many firms have reduced their use of them in recent years. However, their ability to do so is often limited by their desire to build a cadre of international managers. Thus, a firm's ability to reduce its use of expatriates may be limited, particularly if it is pursuing an ethnocentric or geocentric staffing policy.

BASE SALARY An expatriate's base salary is normally in the same range as the base salary for a similar position in the home country. The base salary is normally paid in either the home country currency or in the local currency.

FOREIGN SERVICE PREMIUM A foreign service premium is extra pay the expatriate receives for working outside his or her country of origin. It is offered as an inducement to accept foreign postings. It compensates the expatriate for having to live in an unfamiliar country isolated from family and friends, having to deal with a new culture and language, and having to adapt to new work habits and practices. Many firms pay foreign service premiums as a percentage of base salary ranging from 10 to 30 percent after tax with 16 percent being the average premium.[50]

ALLOWANCES Four types of allowances are often included in an expatriate's compensation package: hardship allowances, housing allowances, cost-of-living allowances, and education allowances. A hardship allowance is paid when the expatriate is being

Expatriates receive an education allowance for their children so that they may receive the same standard of schooling as they would in their home country.
© PhotoDisc.

sent to a difficult location. A difficult location is usually defined as one where such basic amenities as health care, schools, and retail stores are grossly deficient by the standards of the expatriate's home country. A housing allowance is normally given to ensure that the expatriate can afford the same quality of housing in the foreign country as at home. In locations where housing is very expensive (e.g., London, Tokyo), this allowance can be substantial—as much as 10 to 30 percent of the expatriate's total compensation package. A cost-of-living allowance ensures that the expatriate will enjoy the same standard of living in the foreign posting as at home. An education allowance ensures that an expatriate's children receive adequate schooling (by home country standards). Host country public schools are sometimes not suitable for an expatriate's children, in which case they must attend a private school.

TAXATION Unless a host country has a reciprocal tax treaty with the expatriate's home country, the expatriate may have to pay income tax to both the home and host country. When a reciprocal tax treaty is not in force, the firm typically pays the expatriate's income tax in the host country. In addition, firms normally make up the difference when a higher income tax rate in a host country reduces an expatriate's take-home pay.

BENEFITS Many firms also ensure that their expatriates receive the same level of medical and pension benefits abroad that they received at home. This can be very costly for the firm because many benefits that are tax deductible for the firm in the home country (e.g., medical and pension benefits) may not be deductible out of the country.

International Labor Relations

The HRM function of an international business is typically responsible for international labor relations. From a strategic perspective, the key issue in international labor relations is the degree to which organized labor can limit the choices of an international business. A firm's ability to integrate and consolidate its global operations to realize experience curve and location economies can be limited by organized labor. Labor unions can constrain a firm's ability to pursue a transnational or global strategy. Prahalad and Doz give the example of General Motors, which bought peace with labor unions by agreeing not to integrate and consolidate their operations in the most efficient manner.[51] In the early 1980s General Motors made substantial investments in Germany—matching its new investments in Austria and Spain—at the demand of the German metal workers' unions.

One task of the HRM function is to foster harmony and minimize conflict between the firm and organized labor. With this in mind, this section is divided into three parts. First, we review the concerns of organized labor about multinational enterprises. Second, we look at how organized labor has tried to deal with these concerns. And third, we look at how international businesses manage their labor relations to minimize labor disputes.

The Concerns of Organized Labor

Labor unions generally try to get better pay, greater job security, and better working conditions for their members through collective bargaining with management. The unions' bargaining power is derived largely from their ability to threaten to disrupt production, either by a strike or some other form of work protest (e.g., refusing to work overtime). This threat is credible, however, only if management has no alternative but to employ union labor.

A principal concern of domestic unions about multinational firms is that the multinational can counter their bargaining power with the power to move production to another country. Ford, for example, very clearly threatened British unions with a plan to move manufacturing to Continental Europe unless British workers abandoned work rules that limited productivity, showed restraint in negotiating for wage increases, and curtailed strikes and other work disruptions.[52]

Another concern of organized labor is that an international business will keep highly skilled tasks in its home country and farm out only low-skilled tasks to foreign plants. Such a practice makes it relatively easy for an international business to switch production from one location to another as economic conditions warrant. Consequently, the bargaining power of organized labor is once more reduced.

A final union concern arises when an international business attempts to import employment practices and contractual agreements from its home country. When these practices are alien to those traditional in the host country, organized labor fears the change will reduce its influence and power. This concern has surfaced in response to Japanese multinationals that have been trying to export their style of labor relations to other countries. For example, much to the annoyance of the United Auto Workers (UAW), most Japanese auto plants in the United States are not unionized. As a result, union influence in the auto industry is on the decline.

The Strategy of Organized Labor

Organized labor has responded to the increased bargaining power of multinational corporations by taking three actions: (1) trying to establish international labor organizations, (2) lobbying for national legislation to restrict multinationals, and (3) trying to achieve international regulations on multinationals through such organizations as the United Nations. These efforts have not been very successful.

In the 1960s organized labor began to establish a number of International Trade Secretariats (ITSs) to provide worldwide links for national unions. The long-term goal was to be able to bargain transnationally with multinational firms. Organized labor believed that by coordinating union action across countries through an ITS, it could effectively counter the power of a multinational corporation by threatening to disrupt production on an international scale. For example, Ford's threat to move production from Great Britain to other European locations would not have been credible if the unions in various European countries had united to oppose it.

In practice, however, the ITSs have had virtually no real success. Although national unions may want to cooperate, they also compete with each other to attract investment from international businesses, and hence jobs for their members. For example, in attempting to gain new jobs for their members, national unions in the auto industry often court auto firms that are seeking locations for new plants. One reason Nissan chose to build its European production facilities in Great Britain rather than Spain was that the British unions agreed to greater concessions than the Spanish unions did. As a result of such competition between national unions, cooperation is difficult to establish.

A further impediment to cooperation has been the variation in union structure. Trade unions developed independently in each country. As a result, the structure and ideology of unions tends to vary significantly from country to country, as does the nature of collective bargaining. For example, in Great Britain, France, and Italy many unions are controlled by left-wing socialists, who view collective bargaining through the lens of "class conflict." In contrast, most union leaders in Germany, the Netherlands, Scandinavia, and Switzerland are far more moderate politically. Such divergent ideologies are reflected in radically different views about the role of a union in society and the stance unions should take toward multinationals, making cooperation difficult.

Organized labor has also met with only limited success in its efforts to get national and international bodies to regulate multinationals. Such international organizations as the International Labor Organization (ILO) and the Organization for Economic Cooperation and Development (OECD) have adopted codes of conduct for multinational firms to follow in labor relations. However, these guidelines are not as far-reaching as many unions would like. They also do not provide any enforcement mechanisms. Not surprisingly, many researchers report that such guidelines are of only limited effectiveness.[53]

Approaches to Labor Relations

International businesses differ markedly in their approaches to international labor relations. The main difference is the degree to which labor relations activities are centralized or decentralized. Historically, most international businesses have decentralized international labor relations activities to their foreign subsidiaries because labor laws, union power, and the nature of collective bargaining varied so much from country to country. It made sense to decentralize the labor relations function to local managers because central management could not effectively handle the complexity of simultaneously managing labor relations in a number of different environments.

Although this logic still holds, there is now a trend toward greater centralized control over international labor relations in international businesses. This trend reflects international firms' attempts to rationalize their global operations. The general rise in competitive pressure in industry after industry has made it more important for firms to control their costs. Because labor costs account for such a large percentage of total costs, many firms are now using the threat to move production to another country in their negotiations with unions to change work rules and limit wage increases (as Ford did in Europe). Because such a move would involve major new investments and plant closures, this bargaining tactic requires the input of headquarters management. Thus, the level of centralized input into labor relations is increasing.

In addition, there is growing realization that the way work is organized within a plant can be a major source of competitive advantage. Much of the competitive advantage of Japanese automakers, for example, has been attributed to the use of self-managing teams, job rotation, cross-training, and the like in their Japanese plants.[54] To re-create their domestic performance in foreign plants, the Japanese firms have tried to replicate their work practices there. This often brings them into direct conflict with traditional work practices in those countries, as sanctioned by the local labor unions, so the Japanese firms have often made their foreign investments contingent on the local union accepting a radical change in work practices. To achieve this, the headquarters of many Japanese firms bargains directly with local unions to get union agreement to changes in work rules before committing to an investment. For example, before Nissan decided to invest in northern England, it got a commitment from British unions to agree to a change in traditional work practices. Pursuing such a strategy requires centralized control over the labor relations function.

Key Terms

Summary

This chapter has focused on human resource management in international businesses. HRM activities include human resource strategy, staffing, performance evaluation, management development, compensation, and labor relations. None of these activities is performed in a vacuum; all must be appropriate to the firm's strategy. The following points were made in the chapter:

1 Firm success requires HRM policies to be congruent with the firm's strategy.

2 Staffing policy is concerned with selecting employees who have the skills required to perform particular jobs. Staffing policy can be a tool for developing and promoting a corporate culture.

3 An ethnocentric approach to staffing policy fills all key management positions in an international business with parent country nationals. The policy is congruent with an international strategy. A drawback is that ethnocentric staffing can result in cultural myopia.

4 A polycentric staffing policy uses host country nationals to manage foreign subsidiaries and parent country nationals for the key positions at corporate headquarters. This approach can minimize the dangers of cultural myopia, but it can create a gap between home and host country operations. The policy is best suited to a multidomestic strategy.

5 A geocentric staffing policy seeks the best people for key jobs throughout the organization, regardless of their nationality. This approach is consistent with building a strong unifying culture and informal management network and is well suited to both global and transnational strategies. Immigration policies of national governments may limit a firm's ability to pursue this policy.

6 A prominent issue in the international staffing literature is expatriate failure, defined as the premature return of an expatriate manager to his or her home country. The costs of expatriate failure can be substantial.

7 Expatriate failure can be reduced by selection procedures that screen out inappropriate candidates. The most successful expatriates seem to be those who have high self-esteem and self-confidence, get along well with others, are willing to attempt to communicate in a foreign language, and can empathize with people of other cultures.

8 Training can lower the probability of expatriate failure. It should include cultural training, language training, and practical training, and it should be provided to both the expatriate manager and the spouse.

9 Management development programs attempt to increase the overall skill levels of managers through a mix of ongoing management education and rotation of managers through different jobs within the firm to give them varied experiences. Management development is often used as a strategic tool to build a strong unifying culture and informal management network, both of which support transnational and global strategies.

10 It can be difficult to evaluate the performance of expatriate managers objectively because of unintentional bias. A number of steps can be taken to reduce this bias.

11 Country differences in compensation practices raise a difficult question for an international business: Should the firm pay executives in different countries according to the standards in each country or equalize pay on a global basis?

12 The most common approach to expatriate pay is the balance sheet approach. This approach aims to equalize purchasing power so employees can enjoy the same living standard in their foreign posting that they had at home.

13 A key issue in international labor relations is the degree to which organized labor is able to limit the choices available to an international business. A firm's ability to pursue a transnational or global strategy can be significantly constrained by the actions of labor unions.

14 A principal concern of organized labor is that the multinational can counter union bargaining power with threats to move production to another country.

15 Organized labor has tried to counter the bargaining power of multinationals by forming international labor organizations. In general, these efforts have not been successful.

Internet Exercises

1 What's hot in Europe today? People with dot.com experience. As the Internet and e-commerce begin to take off in Europe, there is a shortage of people who can run Internet companies. Both European and American companies are desperately recruiting talent, often luring managers away from their current employers with enticing offers that include signing bonuses and equity stakes. Some headhunters have begun to take a global approach to filling the shortage. One such example is e9ᶜ Ventures Ltd., a British executive search firm. The company has turned to Silicon Valley as a source of talent, for both Americans and Europeans who had relocated to the United States.

As it has done in so many other ways, the Internet is challenging the traditional process of hiring and recruiting, taking it from a primarily localized process to a much broader, internationally oriented one. Job candidates can now post their resumes at on-line sites (e.g., **www.monster.com** and **www.hotjobs.com**) for the world to see. As a prospective employee, how can you improve your chances for success in the job search process? As the manager of an executive search firm, what do you need to do differently in today's market than you did three or five years ago?

Source: The Wall Street Journal, December 21, 1999, p. B1.

2 Finding a job in a foreign country used to be an arduous process for some people. Today, as many executive search firms approach their task on a global basis, the process may be getting easier. Headhunters in Europe are scanning the globe in a desperate search for managers with dot.com experience to fill the tremendous number of openings in Europe. However, while the process of getting the job may be simplified, the challenges awaiting expatriates in their new locations are probably much the same.

Many people relocating to foreign countries go through culture shock. Some individuals have such a difficult time adjusting to their new environment that they quit and go home. Others stay, but frequently find the adjustment to be difficult. Today's expatriates may find their reaction to their new environment, and their adjustment process, is facilitated by the Internet. Expatriate groups offering support and mentoring have sprung up on the Web, making it easier for individuals taking foreign assignments to not only prepare themselves for their new lives, but also to share their experiences with others. Go to **http://dir.yahoo.com/society_and_culture/cultures_and_groups/expatriates/**. Explore the site. How would you prepare yourself for a foreign assignment? How could a site assist you in your preparation process? How could the site help you make the adjustment once you move to the new country?

Critical Thinking and Discussion Questions

1 What are the main advantages and disadvantages of the ethnocentric, polycentric, and geocentric approaches to staffing policy? When is each approach appropriate?

2 Research suggests that many expatriate employees encounter problems that limit both their effectiveness in a foreign posting and their contribution to the company when they return home. What are the main causes and consequences of these problems, and how might a firm reduce the occurrence of such problems?

3 What is the link between an international business's strategy and its human resource management policies, particularly with regard to the use of expatriate employees and their pay scale?

4 In what ways can organized labor constrain the strategic choices of an international business? How can an international business limit these constraints?

Colgate-Palmolive, the $6 billion a year personal products giant, earns nearly two-thirds of its revenues outside the United States. For years Colgate succeeded, as many US multinationals have, by developing products at home and then "throwing them over the wall" to foreign subsidiaries. Each major foreign subsidiary was responsible for local manufacturing and marketing. Senior management positions in these subsidiaries were typically held by Americans, and most of the company's US-based managers were US citizens.

In the early 1980s Colgate realized that if it was going to succeed in the rapidly changing international business environment, it would have to develop a transnational orientation. Its competitors, such as Procter & Gamble, Unilever, and Kao, were trying to become transnational companies, and Colgate needed to follow suit. One important aspect of becoming a transnational company is developing an international cadre of executive managers who are as at home working in one culture as in another and who have the ability to rise above their ethnocentric perspectives.

As a first step toward building such a cadre, Colgate began recruiting college graduates in 1987 and putting them through an intensive international training program. The typical recruit holds an MBA from a US university, speaks at least one foreign language, has lived outside the United States, and has strong computer skills and business experience. Over one-quarter of the participants are foreign nationals.

The trainees spend 24 months in a US program. During three-month stints, they learn global business development secrets of, for example, Colgate toothpaste, compiling a guide for introducing a new product or revamping an existing one in various national markets. Participants also receive additional language instruction and take international business trips. When they have completed the program, the participants become associate product managers in the United States or abroad. Unlike most US companies, Colgate does not send foreign-born trainees to their native countries for their initial jobs. Instead, it is more likely that a French national will remain in the United States, a US national will be sent to Germany, and a British national will go to Spain. The foreigners receive the same generous expatriate compensation packages the Americans do, even if they are assigned to their home country. This extra pay can create resentment among locally hired managers of foreign subsidiaries, so Colgate is urging its foreign subsidiaries to send their brightest young managers to the training program.

Colgate also has taken a number of other steps to develop its international cadre of managers. In Europe, for example, the company is trying to develop "Euromanagers," managers who have experience working in several European countries. This is a departure from the established practice of having managers spend most (if not all) of their working careers in their home country. Also, Colgate now makes efforts to ensure that project teams contain managers from several countries.[55]

CASE DISCUSSION QUESTIONS

1 What is the relationship between HRM and strategy at Colgate-Palmolive?

2 How might Colgate-Palmolive's international training program improve the company's economic performance?

3 What potential problem do you see with Colgate-Palmolive's international training program?

Unlike most college students, Mauricio Acevedo, 23, looks forward to the end of summer—not the beginning. The fall is when Mauricio's business of exporting mostly used motorcycles to Chile picks up significantly.

Mauricio, who attends college in southern California, has been shipping three to four cycles a month to Chile for the past year. Living in the United States, where the seasons are the opposite of Chile's, is an advantage in this

Selling Cycles

business. As summer ends in the United States, motorcycle owners are more likely to sell their machines because inclement weather reduces their riding opportunities. Meanwhile, in Chile demand picks up as the winter rains end and the numerous cobblestone roads dry off.

Mauricio is a partner in J and M Trading Company, a part-time venture run jointly with his father, a corporate controller, and his uncle. Mauricio's father, who emigrated

to the United States in the early 70s, hates motorcycles, but his younger brother, who still lives in Chile, has been racing them since his teens. Mauricio, like his uncle, is a motorcycle enthusiast. "It is an advantage to be able to keep this in the family, particularly in South America where business is built on relationships and it is especially important to find partners whom you can trust," Mauricio said,

How does the partnership work? Mauricio locates the cycles

in a variety of ways, including motorcycle shops, publications like the *Cycle Trader,* and the Internet. For used cycles, the Web is his most important source. Mauricio spends 10 to 12 hours a week scouring on-line specialized publications devoted to reselling cycles, bulletin boards, and Internet classified sites, searching for just the right cycle. "The Web makes it so much easier because you can customize your search to particular models, years, prices, and loca-

tions. Plus you can see a clear picture of the merchandise," Mauricio explained. Many of the Chilean customers, especially the guys at the track, are looking for larger bikes like the Suziki GRX 750, which are difficult to find used. It is possible to buy such bikes new from a motorcycle shop at a discount and without sale tax as long as the cycle is shipped out of the country and does not touch an American street. Retailers require a bill of lading as proof.

Both Mauricio and his father check out the used merchandise. If it meets their requirements—low miles, low price, and good condition—Mauricio rides it home. Mauricio's father deals with the freight forwarders and sometimes finances the deal. Mauricio's uncle finds the buyers, often through his contacts at the tract or by placing classified ads in a Chilean newspaper. Frequently the buyers provide the cash up front and the money is wired to the United States.

Chile, with a population of 14,161,216, is a lucrative market for motorcycles. Traffic on the often narrow streets is very congested, making it quicker to get around on two wheels instead of four. The Chilean economy has been improving steadily. There were no motorcycle dealerships in Chile when Mauricio started exporting the cycles.

The cycles sell for twice their cost and shipping expenses. "For example, we recently purchased a larger cruiser for $9,000. Shipping and duties increased our costs to approximately $14,000, but we were able to sell it for nearly $30,000," Mauricio said.

Mauricio relies on a freight forwarder to handle his shipping and complete the documentation. Selecting the right freight forwarder is very important. Mauricio is aware of friends and family whose businesses have suffered because of their freight forwarders. Some of the perfume his uncle was importing in another deal was stolen from the shipping containers. A friend's shipment of machinery was delivered two weeks later than promised. When it did finally arrive it could not be released because the invoice was missing. A freight forwarder can also be quite useful in a tough situation. For example, in order to expedite a recent shipment, the freight forwarder loaded the cycles on a near-empty banana boat, which was returning to Chile much earlier than the regularly scheduled carrier. J and M Trading selected its freight forwarder based on the company's ad in the Yellow Pages, which featured a Chilean flag. Mauricio's father believed that he could deal better with people who were from his own country.

Mauricio's fascination with trading started in his teens as he listened to family members and friends discuss deals around the dining room table. "My father has always shipped stuff." Before the cycles, he and his father exported used luxury cars for nearly two years. Mauricio enjoyed not only tracking down the automobiles but also the added perk of driving a Porsche or Mercedes while it awaited shipping.

For the future, on his frequent trips to Chile he is investigating exporting other items such as surfing and snowboard equipment. Both sports are spreading in popularity in Chile, which has 6,435 km of coastline and some of the highest mountains in the world.

For the time being, Mauricio is content to limit his business ventures to Chile. It is a country whose language he speaks fluently and whose culture he understands from his family and his frequent visits. There is a lot of pentup demand in a country like Chile that established manufacturers have not yet discovered. "If you are observant and stick to things you know and love it can be rewarding to try to satisfy those needs."

Glossary

absolute advantage A country has an absolute advantage in the production of a product when it is more efficient than any other country at producing it.

ad valorem tariff A tariff levied as a proportion of the value of an imported good.

administrative trade policies Administrative policies, typically adopted by government bureaucracies, that can be used to restrict imports or boost exports.

Andean Pact A 1969 agreement between Bolivia, Chile, Ecuador, Colombia, and Peru to establish a customs union.

antidumping policies Policies designed to punish foreign firms that engage in dumping and thus protect domestic producers from unfair foreign competition.

antidumping regulations Regulations designed to restrict the sale of goods for less than their fair market price.

arbitrage The purchase of securities in one market for immediate resale in another to profit from a price discrepancy.

ASEAN (Association of South East Asian Nations) Formed in 1967, an attempt to establish a free trade area between Brunei, Indonesia, Malaysia, the Philippines, Singapore, and Thailand.

balance-of-payments accounts National accounts that track both payments to and receipts from foreigners.

banking crisis A loss of confidence in the banking system that leads to a run on banks, as individuals and companies withdraw their deposits.

barriers to entry Factors that make it difficult or costly for firms to enter an industry or market.

barter The direct exchange of goods or services between two parties without a cash transaction.

basic research centers Centers for fundamental research located in regions where valuable scientific knowledge is being created; they develop the basic technologies that become new products.

bill of exchange An order written by an exporter instructing an importer, or an importer's agent, to pay a specified amount of money at a specified time.

bill of lading (or draft) A document issued to an exporter by a common carrier transporting merchandise. It serves as a receipt, a contract, and a document of title.

Bretton Woods A 1944 conference in which representatives of 40 countries met to design a new international monetary system.

bureaucratic controls Achieving control through establishment of a system of rules and procedures.

capital account In the balance of payments, records transactions involving the purchase or sale of assets.

capital controls Restrictions on cross-border capital flows that segment different stock markets; limit amount of a firm's stock a foreigner can own; and limit a citizen's ability to invest outside the country.

CARICOM An association of English-speaking Caribbean states that are attempting to establish a customs union.

caste system A system of social stratification in which social position is determined by the family into which a person is born, and change in that position is usually not possible during an individual's lifetime.

centralized depository The practice of centralizing corporate cash balances in a single depository.

channel length The number of intermediaries that a product has to go through before it reaches the final consumer.

civil law system A system of law based on a very detailed set of written laws and codes.

class consciousness A tendency for individuals to perceive themselves in terms of their class background.

class system A system of social stratification in which social status is determined by the family into which a person is born and by subsequent socioeconomic achievements. Mobility between classes is possible.

collectivism A political system that emphasizes collective goals as opposed to individual goals.

COMECON Now-defunct economic association of Eastern European Communist states headed by the former Soviet Union.

command economy An economic system where the allocation of resources, including determination of what goods and services should be produced, and in what quantity, is planned by the government.

common law system A system of law based on tradition, precedent, and custom. When law courts interpret common law, they do so with regard to these characteristics.

common market A group of countries committed to (1) removing all barriers to the free flow of goods, services, and factors of production between each other and (2) the pursuit of a common external trade policy.

communist totalitarianism A version of collectivism advocating that socialism can be achieved only through a totalitarian dictatorship.

communists Those who believe socialism can be achieved only through revolution and totalitarian dictatorship.

comparative advantage The theory that countries should specialize in the production of goods and services they can produce most efficiently. A country is said to have a comparative advantage in the production of such goods and services.

competition policy Regulations designed to promote competition and restrict monopoly practices.

constant returns to specialization The units of resources required to produce a good are assumed to remain constant no matter where one is on a country's production possibility frontier.

controlling interest A firm has a controlling interest in another business entity when it owns more than 50 percent of that entity's voting stock.

copyright Exclusive legal rights of authors, composers, playwrights, artists, and publishers to publish and dispose of their work as they see fit.

core competence Firm skills that competitors cannot easily match or imitate.

counterpurchase A reciprocal buying agreement.

countertrade The trade of goods and services for other goods and services.

cross-cultural literacy Understanding how the culture of a country affects the way business is practiced.

cross-licensing agreement An arrangement in which a company licenses valuable intangible property to a foreign partner and receives a license for the partner's valuable knowledge; reduces risk of licensing.

cultural controls Achieving control by persuading subordinates to identify with the norms and value systems of the organization (self-control).

culture The complex whole that includes knowledge, belief, art, morals, law, custom, and other capabilities acquired by a person as a member of society.

currency board Means of controlling a country's currency.

currency crisis Occurs when a speculative attack on the exchange value of a currency results in a sharp depreciation in the value of the currency or forces authorities to expend large volumes of international currency reserves and sharply increase interest rates to defend the prevailing exchange rate.

currency speculation Involves short-term movement of funds from one currency to another in hopes of profiting from shifts in exchange rates.

currency swap Simultaneous purchase and sale of a given amount of foreign exchange for two different value dates.

currency translation Converting the financial statements of foreign subsidiaries into the currency of the home country.

current account In the balance of payments, records transactions involving the export or import of goods and services.

current account deficit The current account of the balance of payments is in deficit when a country imports more goods and services than it exports.

current account surplus The current account of the balance of payments is in surplus when a country exports more goods and services than it imports.

current cost accounting Method that adjusts all items in a financial statement to factor out the effects of inflation.

current rate method Using the exchange rate at the balance sheet date to translate the financial statements of a foreign subsidiary into the home currency.

customs union A group of countries committed to (1) removing all barriers to the free flow of goods and services between each other and (2) the pursuit of a common external trade policy.

D'Amato Act Act passed in 1996, similar to the Helms-Burton Act, aimed at Libya and Iran.

democracy Political system in which government is by the people, exercised either directly or through elected representatives.

deregulation Removal of government restrictions concerning the conduct of a business.

diminishing returns to specialization Applied to international trade theory, the more of a good that a country produces, the greater the units of resources required to produce each additional item.

dirty-float system A system under which a country's currency is nominally allowed to float freely against other currencies, but in which the government will intervene, buying and selling currency, if it believes that the currency has deviated too far from its fair value.

draft See **bill of lading.**

drawee The party to whom a bill of lading is presented.

dumping Selling goods in a foreign market for less than their cost of production or below their "fair" market value.

eclectic paradigm Argument that combining location-specific assets or resource endowments and the firm's own unique assets often requires FDI; it requires the firm to establish production facilities where those foreign assets or resource endowments are located.

e-commerce Conducting business on-line through the Internet.

economic exposure The extent to which a firm's future international earning power is affected by changes in exchange rates.

economic risk The likelihood that events, including economic mismanagement, will cause drastic changes in a country's business environment that adversely affect the profit and other goals of a particular business enterprise.

economic union A group of countries committed to (1) removing all barriers to the free flow of goods, services, and factors of production between each other, (2) the adoption of a common currency, (3) the harmonization of tax rates, and (4) the pursuit of a common external trade policy.

economies of scale Cost advantages associated with large-scale production.

ecu A basket of EU currencies that serves as the unit of account for the EMS.

efficient market A market where prices reflect all available information.

ending rate The spot exchange rate when budget and performance are being compared.

ethical systems Cultural beliefs about what is proper behavior and conduct.

ethnocentric behavior Behavior that is based on the belief in the superiority of one's own ethnic group or culture; often shows disregard or contempt for the culture of other countries.

ethnocentric staffing A staffing approach within the MNE in which all key management positions are filled by parent country nationals.

eurobonds A bond placed in countries other than the one in whose currency the bond is denominated.

eurocurrency Any currency banked outside its country of origin.

eurodollar Dollar banked outside the United States.

European Free Trade Association (EFTA) A free trade association including Norway, Iceland, and Switzerland.

European Monetary System (EMS) EU system designed to create a zone of monetary stability in Europe, control inflation, and coordinate exchange rate policies of EU countries.

European Union (EU) An economic group of 15 European nations: Austria, Belgium, Denmark, Finland, France, Germany, Great Britain, Greece, the Netherlands, Ireland, Italy, Luxembourg, Portugal, Spain, and Sweden. Established as a customs union, it is now moving toward economic union. (Formerly the European Community.)

exchange rate The rate at which one currency is converted into another.

exchange rate mechanism (ERM) Mechanism for aligning the exchange rates of EU currencies against each other.

exclusive channels A distribution channel that outsiders find difficult to access.

expatriate failure The premature return of an expatriate manager to the home country.

expatriate manager A national of one country appointed to a management position in another country.

experience curve Systematic production cost reductions that occur over the life of a product.

experience curve pricing Aggressive pricing designed to increase volume and help the firm realize experience curve economies.

export management company Export specialists who act as an export marketing department for client firms.

Export-Import Bank (Eximbank) Agency of the US government whose mission is to provide aid in financing and facilitate exports and imports.

exporting Sale of products produced in one country to residents of another country.

externalities Knowledge spillovers.

externally convertible currency Nonresidents can convert their holdings of domestic currency into foreign currency, but the ability of residents to convert the currency is limited in some way.

factor endowments A country's endowment with resources such as land, labor, and capital.

factors of production Inputs into the productive process of a firm, including labor, management, land, capital, and technological know-how.

financial structure Mix of debt and equity used to finance a business.

first-mover advantages Advantages accruing to the first to enter a market.

first-mover disadvantages Disadvantages associated with entering a foreign market before other international businesses.

Fisher Effect Nominal interest rates (i) in each country equal the required real rate of interest (r) and the expected rate of inflation over the period of time for which the funds are to be lent (I). That is, $i = r + I$.

fixed exchange rates A system under which the exchange rate for converting one currency into another is fixed.

fixed-rate bond Offers a fixed set of cash payoffs each year until maturity, when the investor also receives the face value of the bond in cash.

flexible machine cells Flexible manufacturing technology in which a grouping of various machine types, a common materials handler, and a centralized cell controller produce a family of products.

flexible manufacturing technologies Manufacturing technologies designed to improve job scheduling, reduce setup time, and improve quality control.

floating exchange rates A system under which the exchange rate for converting one currency into another is continuously adjusted depending on the laws of supply and demand.

flow of foreign direct investment The amount of foreign direct investment undertaken over a given time period (normally one year).

folkways Routine conventions of everyday life.

foreign bonds Bonds sold outside the borrower's country and denominated in the currency of the country in which they are issued.

Foreign Corrupt Practices Act US law regulating behavior regarding the conduct of international business in the taking of bribes and other unethical actions.

foreign debt crisis Situation in which a country cannot service its foreign debt obligations, whether private-sector or government debt.

foreign direct investment (FDI) Direct investment in business operations in a foreign country.

foreign exchange exposure The risk that future changes in a country's exchange rate will hurt the firm.

foreign exchange market A market for converting the currency of one country into that of another country.

foreign exchange risk The risk that changes in exchange rates will hurt the profitability of a business deal.

foreign portfolio investment (FPI) Investments by individuals, firms, or public bodies (e.g., national and local governments) in foreign financial instruments (e.g., government bonds, foreign stocks).

forward exchange When two parties agree to exchange currency and execute a deal at some specific date in the future.

forward exchange rate The exchange rates governing forward exchange transactions.

franchising A specialized form of licensing in which the franchiser sells intangible property to the franchisee and insists on rules to conduct the business.

free trade The absence of barriers to the free flow of goods and services between countries.

free trade area A group of countries committed to removing all barriers to the free flow of goods and services between each other, but pursuing independent external trade policies.

freely convertible currency A country's currency is freely convertible when the government of that country allows both residents and nonresidents to purchase unlimited amounts of foreign currency with the domestic currency.

fronting loans A loan between a parent company and a foreign subsidiary that is channeled through a financial intermediary.

fundamental analysis Draws on economic theory to construct sophisticated econometric models for predicting exchange rate movements.

gains from trade The economic gains to a country from engaging in international trade.

General Agreement on Tariffs and Trade (GATT) International treaty that committed signatories to lowering barriers to the free flow of goods across national borders and led to the WTO.

geocentric staffing A staffing policy where the best people are sought for key jobs throughout an MNE, regardless of nationality.

global learning The flow of skills and product offerings from foreign subsidiary to home country and from foreign subsidiary to foreign subsidiary.

global matrix structure Horizontal differentiation proceeds along two dimensions: product divisions and areas.

global strategy Strategy focusing on increasing profitability by reaping cost reductions from experience curve and location economies.

global web When different stages of value chain are dispersed to those locations around the globe where value added is maximized or where costs of value creation are minimized.

globalization Trend away from distinct national economic units and toward one huge global market.

globalization of markets Moving away from an economic system in which national markets are distinct entities, isolated by trade barriers and barriers of distance, time, and culture, and toward a system in which national markets are merging into one global market.

globalization of production Trend by individual firms to disperse parts of their productive processes to different locations around the globe to take advantage of differences in cost and quality of factors of production.

gold par value The amount of currency needed to purchase one ounce of gold.

gold standard The practice of pegging currencies to gold and guaranteeing convertibility.

gross domestic product (GDP) The market value of a country's output attributable to factors of production located in the country's territory.

gross fixed capital formation Summarizes the total amount of capital invested in factories, stores, office buildings, and the like.

gross national product (GNP) The market value of all the final goods and services produced by a national economy.

group An association of two or more individuals who have a shared sense of identity and who interact with each other in structured ways on the basis of a common set of expectations about each other's behavior.

Heckscher-Ohlin theory Countries will export those goods that make intensive use of locally abundant factors of production and import goods that make intensive use of locally scarce factors of production.

hedge fund Investment fund that not only buys financial assets (stocks, bonds, currencies) but also sells them short.

Helms-Burton Act Act passed in 1996 that allowed Americans to sue foreign firms that use Cuban property confiscated from them after the 1959 revolution.

home country The source country for foreign direct investment.

horizontal differentiation The division of the firm into subunits.

horizontal foreign direct investment Foreign direct investment in the same industry abroad as a firm operates in at home.

host country Recipient country of inward investment by a foreign firm.

Human Development Index An attempt by the United Nations to assess the impact of a number of factors on the quality of human life in a country.

human resource management Activities an organization conducts to use its human resources effectively.

import quota A direct restriction on the quantity of a good that can be imported into a country.

individualism An emphasis on the importance of guaranteeing individual freedom and self-expression.

individualism versus collectivism Theory focusing on the relationship between the individual and his or her fellows. In individualistic societies, the ties between individuals are loose and individual achievement is highly valued. In societies where collectivism is emphasized, ties between individuals are tight, people are born into collectives, such as extended families, and everyone is supposed to look after the interests of his or her collective.

inefficient market One in which prices do not reflect all available information.

infant industry argument New industries in developing countries must be temporarily protected from international competition to help them reach a position where they can compete on world markets with the firms of developed nations.

inflows of FDI Flow of foreign direct investment into a country.

initial rate The spot exchange rate when a budget is adopted.

innovation Development of new products, processes, organizations, management practices, and strategies.

integrating mechanisms Mechanisms for achieving coordination between subunits within an organization.

intellectual property Products of the mind, ideas (e.g., books, music, computer software, designs, technological know-how). Intellectual property can be protected by patents, copyrights, and trademarks.

internal forward rate A company-generated forecast of future spot rates.

internalization theory Marketing imperfection approach to foreign direct investment.

International Accounting Standards Committee (IASC) Organization of representatives of 106 professional accounting organizations from 79 countries that is attempting to harmonize accounting standards across countries.

international business Any firm that engages in international trade or investment.

international division Division responsible for a firm's international activities.

International Fisher Effect For any two countries, the spot exchange rate should change in an equal amount but in the opposite direction to the difference in nominal interest rates between countries.

International Monetary Fund (IMF) International institution set up to maintain order in the international monetary system.

international strategy Trying to create value by transferring core competencies to foreign markets where indigenous competitors lack those competencies.

international trade Occurs when a firm exports goods or services to consumers in another country.

ISO 9000 Certification process that requires certain quality standards that must be met.

joint venture A cooperative undertaking between two or more firms.

just-in-time (JIT) Logistics systems designed to deliver parts to a production process as they are needed, not before.

lag strategy Delaying the collection of foreign currency receivables if that currency is expected to appreciate, and delaying payables if that currency is expected to depreciate.

late-mover advantage Benefits enjoyed by a company that is late to enter a new market, such as consumer familiarity with the product or knowledge gained about a market.

late-mover disadvantage Handicap experienced by being a late entrant in a market.

law of one price In competitive markets free of transportation costs and barriers to trade, identical products sold in different countries must sell for the same price when their price is expressed in the same currency.

lead market Market where products are first introduced.

lean production systems Flexible manufacturing technologies pioneered at Toyota and now used in much of the automobile industry.

learning effects Cost savings from learning by doing.

legal risk The likelihood that a trading partner will opportunistically break a contract or expropriate intellectual property rights.

legal system System of rules that regulate behavior and the processes by which the laws of a country are enforced and through which redress of grievances is obtained.

Leontief paradox The empirical finding that, in contrast to the predictions of the Heckscher-Ohlin theory, US exports are less capital intensive than US imports.

letter of credit Issued by a bank, indicating that the bank will make payments under specific circumstances.

licensing Occurs when a firm (the licensor) licenses the right to produce its product, use its production processes, or use its brand name or trademark to another firm (the licensee). In return for giving the licensee these rights, the licensor collects a royalty fee on every unit the licensee sells.

licensing agreement Arrangement in which a licensor grants the rights to intangible property to the licensee for a specified period and receives a royalty fee in return.

local content requirement A requirement that some specific fraction of a good be produced domestically.

location economies Cost advantages from performing a value creation activity at the optimal location for that activity.

location-specific advantages Advantages that arise from using resource endowments or assets that are tied to a particular foreign location and that a firm finds valuable to combine with its own unique assets (such as the firm's technological, marketing, or management know-how).

logistics The procurement and physical transmission of material through the supply chain, from suppliers to customers.

Maastricht Treaty Treaty agreed to in 1991, but not ratified until January 1, 1994, that committed the 12 member states of the European Community to a closer economic and political union.

maker Person or business initiating a bill of lading (draft).

managed-float system System under which some currencies are allowed to float freely, but the majority are either managed by government intervention or pegged to another currency.

management networks A network of informal contact between individual managers.

market economy An economic system in which the interaction of supply and demand determines the quantity in which goods and services are produced.

market imperfections Imperfections in the operation of the market mechanism.

market makers Financial service companies that connect investors and borrowers, either directly or indirectly.

market power Ability of a firm to exercise control over industry prices or output.

market segmentation Identifying groups of consumers whose purchasing behavior differs from others in important ways.

marketing mix Choices about product attributes, distribution strategy, communication strategy, and pricing strategy that a firm offers its targeted markets.

masculinity versus femininity Theory of the relationship between gender and work roles. In masculine cultures, sex roles are sharply differentiated and traditional "masculine values" such as achievement and the effective exercise of power determine cultural ideals. In feminine cultures, sex roles are less sharply distinguished, and little differentiation is made between men and women in the same job.

mass customization The production of a variety of end products at a unit cost that could once be

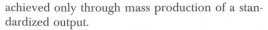

achieved only through mass production of a standardized output.

materials management The activity that controls the transmission of physical materials through the value chain, from procurement through production and into distribution.

mercantilism An economic philosophy advocating that countries should simultaneously encourage exports and discourage imports.

MERCOSUR Pact between Argentina, Brazil, Paraguay, and Uruguay to establish a free trade area.

minimum efficient scale The level of output at which most plant-level scale economies are exhausted.

MITI Japan's Ministry of International Trade and Industry.

mixed economy Certain sectors of the economy are left to private ownership and free market mechanisms, while other sectors have significant government ownership and government planning.

money management Managing a firm's global cash resources efficiently.

Moore's Law The power of microprocessor technology doubles and its costs of production fall in half every 18 months.

moral hazard Arises when people behave recklessly because they know they will be saved if things go wrong.

mores Norms seen as central to the functioning of a society and to its social life.

multidomestic strategy Emphasizing the need to be responsive to the unique conditions prevailing in different national markets.

Multilateral Agreement on Investment (MAI) An agreement that would make it illegal for signatory states to discriminate against foreign investors; would have liberalized rules governing FDI between OECD states.

multinational enterprise (MNE) A firm that owns business operations in more than one country.

multipoint competition Arises when two or more enterprises encounter each other in different regional markets, national markets, or industries.

multipoint pricing Occurs when a pricing strategy in one market may have an impact on a rival's pricing strategy in another market.

new trade theory The observed pattern of trade in the world economy may be due in part to the ability of firms in a given market to capture first-mover advantages.

nonconvertible currency A currency is not convertible when both residents and nonresidents are prohibited from converting their holdings of that currency into another currency.

norms Social rules and guidelines that prescribe appropriate behavior in particular situations.

North American Free Trade Agreement (NAFTA) Free trade area between Canada, Mexico, and the United States.

oligopoly An industry composed of a limited number of large firms.

Organization for Economic Cooperation and Development (OECD) A Paris-based intergovernmental organization of "wealthy" nations whose purpose is to provide its 29 member states with a forum in which governments can compare their experiences, discuss the problems they share, and seek solutions that can then be applied within their own national contexts.

outflows of FDI Flow of foreign direct investment out of a country.

output controls Achieving control by setting goals for subordinates, expressing these goals in terms of objective criteria, and then judging performance by a subordinate's ability to meet these goals.

Paris Convention for the Protection of Industrial Property International agreement to protect intellectual property; signed by 96 countries.

patent Grants the inventor of a new product or process exclusive rights to the manufacture, use, or sale of that invention.

performance ambiguity Occurs when the causes of good or bad performance are not clearly identifiable.

personal controls Achieving control by personal contact with subordinates.

pioneering costs Costs an early entrant bears that later entrants avoid, such as the time and effort in learning the rules, failure due to ignorance, and the liability of being a foreigner.

political economy The political, economic, and legal systems of a country.

political risk The likelihood that political forces will cause drastic changes in a country's business environment that will adversely affect the profit and other goals of a particular business enterprise.

political system System of government in a nation.

polycentric staffing A staffing policy in an MNE in which host country nationals are recruited to manage subsidiaries in their own country, while parent country nationals occupy key positions at corporate headquarters.

positive-sum game A situation in which all countries can benefit even if some benefit more than others.

power distance Theory of how a society deals with the fact that people are unequal in physical and intellectual capabilities. High power distance cultures are found in countries that let inequalities grow over time into inequalities of power and wealth. Low power distance cultures are found in societies that try to play down such inequalities as much as possible.

predatory pricing Reducing prices below fair market value as a competitive weapon to drive weaker competitors out of the market ("fair" being cost plus some reasonable profit margin).

price discrimination The practice of charging different prices for the same product in different markets.

price elasticity of demand A measure of how responsive demand for a product is to changes in price.

privatization The sale of state-owned enterprises to private investors.

product life-cycle theory The optimal location in the world to produce a product changes as the market for the product matures.

production Activities involved in creating a product.

projected rate The spot exchange rate forecast for the end of the budget period.

property rights Bundle of legal rights over the use to which a resource is put and over the use made of any income that may be derived from that resource.

pull strategy A marketing strategy emphasizing mass media advertising as opposed to personal selling.

purchasing power parity (PPP) An adjustment in gross domestic product per capita to reflect differences in the cost of living.

push strategy A marketing strategy emphasizing personal selling rather than mass media advertising.

regional economic integration Agreements among countries in a geographic region to reduce and ultimately remove tariff and nontariff barriers to the free flow of goods, services, and factors of production between each other.

relatively efficient market One in which few impediments to international trade and investment exist.

religion A system of shared beliefs and rituals concerned with the realm of the sacred.

representative democracy A political system in which citizens periodically elect individuals to represent them in government.

right-wing totalitarianism A political system in which political power is monopolized by a party, group, or individual that generally permits individual economic freedom but restricts individual political freedom, including free speech, often on the grounds that it would lead to the rise of communism.

royalties Remuneration paid to the owners of technology, patents, or trade names for the use of same.

short selling Occurs when an investor places a speculative bet that the value of a financial asset will decline, and profits from that decline.

sight draft A draft payable on presentation to the drawee.

Single European Act A 1997 act, adopted by members of the European Community, that committed member countries to establishing an economic union.

Smoot-Hawley Act Enacted in 1930 by the US Congress, this tariff erected a wall of barriers against imports into the United States.

social democrats Those committed to achieving socialism by democratic means.

social mobility The extent to which individuals can move out of the social strata into which they are born.

social strata Hierarchical social categories often based on family background, occupation, and income.

social structure The basic social organization of a society.

socialism A political philosophy advocating substantial public involvement, through government ownership, in the means of production and distribution.

society Group of people who share a common set of values and norms.

sogo shosha Japanese trading companies; a key part of the *keiretsu*, the large Japanese industrial groups.

sourcing decisions Whether a firm should make or buy component parts.

specialized asset An asset designed to perform a specific task, whose value is significantly reduced in its next-best use.

specific tariff Tariff levied as a fixed charge for each unit of good imported.

spot exchange rate The exchange rate at which a foreign exchange dealer will convert one currency into another that particular day.

staffing policy Strategy concerned with selecting employees for particular jobs.

state-directed economy An economy in which the state plays a proactive role in influencing the direction and magnitude of private sector investments.

stock of foreign direct investment The total accumulated value of foreign-owned assets at a given time.

strategic alliances Cooperative agreements between two or more firms.

strategic commitment A decision that has a long-term impact and is difficult to reverse, such as entering a foreign market on a large scale.

strategic trade policy Government policy aimed at improving the competitive position of a domestic industry and/or domestic firm in the world market.

strategy Actions managers take to attain the firm's goals.

Structural Impediments Initiative A 1990 agreement between the United States and Japan aimed at trying to decrease nontariff barriers restricting imports into Japan.

subsidy Government financial assistance to a domestic producer.

swaps The simultaneous purchase and sale of a given amount of foreign exchange for two different value dates.

systematic risk Movements in a stock portfolio's value that are attributable to macroeconomic forces affecting all firms in an economy, rather than factors specific to an individual firm (unsystematic risk).

tariff A tax levied on imports.

tax credit Allows a firm to reduce the taxes paid to the home government by the amount of taxes paid to the foreign government.

tax haven A country with exceptionally low, or even no, income taxes.

tax treaty Agreement between two countries specifying what items of income will be taxed by the authorities of the country where the income is earned.

technical analysis Uses price and volume data to determine past trends, which are expected to continue into the future.

temporal method Translating assets valued in a foreign currency into the home currency using the exchange rate that existed when the assets were originally purchased.

theocratic totalitarianism A political system in which political power is monopolized by a party, group, or individual that governs according to religious principles.

time draft A promise to pay by the accepting party at some future date.

time-based competition Competing on the basis of speed in responding to customer demands and developing new products.

timing of entry Entry is early when a firm enters a foreign market before other foreign firms and late when a firm enters after other international businesses have established themselves.

total quality management Management philosophy that takes as its central focus the need to improve the quality of a company's products and services.

totalitarianism Form of government in which one person or political party exercises absolute control over all spheres of human life and opposing political parties are prohibited.

trade creation Trade created due to regional economic integration; occurs when high-cost domestic producers are replaced by low-cost foreign producers in a free trade area.

trade deficit See **current account deficit.**

trade diversion Trade diverted due to regional economic integration; occurs when low-cost foreign suppliers outside a free trade area are replaced by higher-cost foreign suppliers in a free trade area.

trade surplus See **current account surplus.**

trademark Designs and names, often officially registered, by which merchants or manufacturers designate and differentiate their products.

transaction costs The costs of exchange.

transaction exposure The extent to which income from individual transactions is affected by fluctuations in foreign exchange values.

transfer fee A bank charge for moving cash from one location to another.

transfer price The price at which goods and services are transferred between subsidiary companies of a corporation.

translation exposure The extent to which the reported consolidated results and balance sheets of a corporation are affected by fluctuations in foreign exchange values.

transnational corporation A firm that tries to simultaneously realize gains from experience curve economies, location economies, and global learning, while remaining locally responsive.

transnational strategy Plan to exploit experience-based cost and location economies, transfer core competencies with the firm, and pay attention to local responsiveness.

Treaty of Rome The 1957 treaty that established the European Community.

tribal totalitarianism A political system in which a party, group, or individual that represents the interests of a particular tribe (ethnic group) monopolizes political power.

turnkey project A project in which a firm agrees to set up an operating plant for a foreign client and hand over the "key" when the plant is fully operational.

unbundling Relying on more than one financial technique to transfer funds across borders.

uncertainty avoidance Extent to which cultures socialize members to accept ambiguous situations and to tolerate uncertainty.

universal needs Needs that are the same all over the world, such as steel, bulk chemicals, and industrial electronics.

value creation Performing activities that increase the value of goods or services to consumers.

values Abstract ideas about what a society believes to be good, right, and desirable.

vehicle currency A currency that plays a central role in the foreign exchange market (e.g., the US dollar and Japanese yen).

vertical differentiation The centralization and decentralization of decision-making responsibilities.

vertical foreign direct investment Foreign direct investment in an industry abroad that provides input into a firm's domestic operations, or foreign direct investment into an industry abroad that sells the outputs of a firm's domestic operations.

vertical integration Extension of a firm's activities into adjacent stages of productions (i.e., those providing the firm's inputs or those that purchase the firm's outputs).

voluntary export restraint (VER) A quota on trade imposed from the exporting country's side, instead of the importer's; usually imposed at the request of the importing country's government.

wholly owned subsidiary A subsidiary in which the firm owns 100 percent of the stock.

World Bank International institution set up to promote general economic development in the world's poorer nations.

World Trade Organization (WTO) The organization that succeeded the General Agreement on Tariffs and Trade (GATT) as a result of the successful completion of the Uruguay Round of GATT negotiations.

worldwide area structure Business organizational structure under which the world is divided into areas.

worldwide product division structure Business organizational structure based on product divisions that have worldwide responsibility.

zero-sum game A situation in which an economic gain by one country results in an economic loss by another.

Notes

Chapter 1

1 A. Kupfer, "The Big Switch," *Fortune,* October 13, 1997, pp. 105–16; S. Schiesel, "AT&T and British Telecom Merge Overseas Operations," *New York Times,* July 27, 1998, p. A1; F. Cairncross, *The Death of Distance* (Boston: Harvard Business School Press, 1997); and S. Baker, K. Capell, and J. Ewing, "Running Scared," *Business Week,* December 6, 1999, pp. 62–63.

2 A. Stewart, "Easier Access to World Markets," *Financial Times,* December 3, 1997, p. 8.

3 The product is the Anir Ergonomic Mouse.

4 T. Levitt, "The Globalization of Markets," *Harvard Business Review,* May–June 1983, pp. 92–102.

5 M. Dickerson, L. Romney, "Small Business: New Trends and Help for Growing Companies," *Los Angeles Times,* November 17, 1999, p. 10.

6 See F. T. Knickerbocker, *Oligopolistic Reaction and Multinational Enterprise* (Boston: Harvard Business School Press, 1973), and R. E. Caves, "Japanese Investment in the US: Lessons for the Economic Analysis of Foreign Investment," *The World Economy* 16 (1993), pp. 279–300.

7 I. Metthee, "Playing a Large Part," *Seattle Post-Intelligencer,* April 9, 1994, p. 13.

8 C. S. Tranger, "Enter the Mini-Multinational," *Northeast International Business,* March 1989, pp. 13–14.

9 R. B. Reich, *The Work of Nations* (New York: A. A. Knopf, 1991).

10 J. Bhagwati, *Protectionism* (Cambridge, MA: MIT Press, 1989).

11 F. Williams, "Trade Round Like This May Never Be Seen Again," *Financial Times,* April 15, 1994, p. 8.

12 United Nations, *World Investment Report, 1997* (New York and Geneva: United Nations, 1997).

13 United Nations, *World Investment Report, 1998* (New York and Geneva: United Nations, 1998).

14 *World Trade Organization Annual Report,* November 1999.

15 United Nations press release, TAD/1880, "Global Foreign Direct Investment Boomed in 1998," June 22, 1999.

16 *World Trade Organization Annual Report, 1998* (Geneva: WTO, 1998). United Nations, *World Investment Report, 1998* (New York and Geneva: United Nations, 1998).

17 United Nations press release TAD/1880, and *World Investment Report, 1998.*

18 World Trade Organization, "Beyond Borders: Managing a World of Free Trade and Deep Interdependence," press release 55, September 10, 1996.

19 Moore's Law is named after Intel founder Gorden Moore.

20 Data compiled from various sources and listed at http://cyberatlas.internet.com.

21 Data on number of host computer can be found at http://www.nw.com/zone/WWW.

22 V. Houlder, "Fear and Enterprise As the Net Closes In," *Financial Times,* May 20, 1998, p. 18.

23 Data estimates from http://cyberatlas.internet.com.

24 M. Dickerson, "All Those Inflated Expectations Aside, Many Firms Are Finding the Internet Invaluable in Pursuing International Trade," *Los Angeles Times,* October 14, 1998, p. 10. The company's website is http://www.cardiacscience.com.

25 S. G. Steinberg, "Seek and Ye Shall Find (Maybe)," *Wired,* May 1996; L. Himelstein, H. Green, and R. Siklos, "Yahoo! The Company, the Strategy, the Stock," *Business Week,* September 7, 1998, p. 66; S. Moran, "For Yahoo, GeoCities May Only Be the Start," *Internet World,* March 15, 1999; and *Yahoo! 1998 Annual Report* and 1999 press release archives.

26 "Delivering the Goods," *The Economist,* November 15, 1997, pp. 85–86.

27 P. Dicken, *Global Shift* (New York: Guilford Press, 1992).

28 Interviews with Hewlett-Packard personnel by the author.

29 "War of the Worlds," *The Economist: A Survey of the Global Economy,* October 1, 1994, pp. 3–4.

30 One of the classics being J. J. Servan-Schreiber, *The American Challenge* (New York: Atheneum, 1968).

31 Data from the United Nations, *World Investment Report 1998.*

32 L. Nakarmi, "A Flying Leap toward the 21st Century," *Business Week,* March 20, 1995, pp. 78–80; J. Burton, "Samsung Drives on towards Globalization," *Financial Times,* October 25, 1994, p. 21; G. de Jonquieres and J. Burton, "Big Gamble on a European Thrust," *Financial Times,* October 2, 1995, p. 13; and United Nations, *World Investment Report 1998.*

33 R. A. Mosbacher, "Opening Up Export Doors for Smaller Firms," *Seattle Times,* July 24, 1991, p. A7.

34 "Small Companies Learn How to Sell to the Japanese," *Seattle Times,* March 19, 1992.

35 W. J. Holstein, "Why Johann Can Export but Johnny Can't," *Business Week,* November 4, 1991, pp. 64–65.

36 P. Engardio and L. Curry, "The Fifth Tiger Is on China's Coast," *Business Week,* April 6, 1992, pp. 42–43.

37 See for example, Ravi Batra. *The Myth of Free Trade* (New York: Touchstone Books, 1993); William Greider, *One World, Ready or Not: The Manic Logic of Global Capitalism* (New York: Simon and Schuster, 1997); and D. Rodrik, *Has Globalization Gone too Far?* (Washington, DC: Institution for International Economics, 1997).

38 James Goldsmith, "The Winners and the Losers," in *The Case Against the Global Economy,* ed. J. Mander and E. Goldsmith (San Franciso: The Sierra Book Club, 1996).

39 D. L. Bartlett and J. B. Steele, "America: Who Stole the Dream," *Philadelphia Inquirer,* September 9, 1996.

40 For example, see Paul Krugman, *Pop Internationalism* (Cambridge, MA: MIT Press, 1996).

41 Peter Gottschalk and Timothy M. Smeeding, "Cross-National Comparisons of Earnings and Income Inequality," *Journal of Economic Literature* 35 (June 1997), pp. 633–87, and Susan M. Collins,

Exports, Imports, and the American Worker (Washington, DC: Brookings Institution, 1998).

42 Organization for Economic Cooperation and Development, "Income Distribution in OECD Countries," *OECD Policy Studies,* no. 18 (October 1995).

43 See Krugman, *Pop Internationalism;* D. Belman and T. M. Lee, "International Trade and the Performance of U.S. Labor Markets," in *U.S. Trade Policy and Global Growth,* ed. R. A. Blecker (New York: Economic Policy Institute, 1996).

44 See Robert Lerman, "Is Earnings Inequality Really Increasing? Economic Restructuring and the Job Market," Brief No. 1, Urban Institute, Washington, DC, March 1997.

45 E. Goldsmith, "Global Trade and the Environment," in *The Case Against the Global Economy,* ed. J. Mander and E. Goldsmith (San Francisco: The Sierra Book Club, 1996).

46 Batra, *The Myth of Free Trade.* See also J. Brecher and T. Costello, *Global Village or Global Pillage* (Cambridge, MA: South End Press, 1998).

47 P. Choate, *Jobs at Risk: Vulnerable U.S. Industries and Jobs under NAFTA* (Washington, DC: Manufacturing Policy Project, 1993).

48 Krugman, *Pop Internationalism.*

49 R. Kuttner, "Managed Trade and Economic Sovereignty," in *U.S. Trade Policy and Global Growth,* ed. R. A. Blecker (New York: Economic Policy Institute, 1996).

50 Ralph Nader and Lori Wallach, "GATT, NAFTA, and the Subversion of the Democratic Process," in *U.S. Trade Policy and Global Growth,* ed. R. A. Blecker (New York: Economic Policy Institute, 1996), pp. 93–94.

51 "Perestrokia in Soapland," *The Economist,* June 10, 1989, pp. 69–71, and Bartlett and Ghoshal, *Managing across Borders: The Transnational Solution* (Boston: Harvard Business School Press, 1989).

52 C. J. Loomis, "Citicorp: John Reed's Second Act," *Fortune,* April 29, 1996, pp. 89–98; K. Klee, "Brand Builders," *Institutional Investor,* March 1997, pp. 89–101; M. Siconolfi, "Big Umbrella," *The Wall Street Journal,* April 7, 1998, pp. A1, A6; and L. N. Spiro and G. Silverman, "Will Citigroup's Parade Get Rained On?" *Business Week,* September 28, 1998, pp. 111–14.

1 "Let the Party Begin," *The Economist,* April 26, 1997, pp. 57–58, and "A Very Big Deal, A Survey of Business in Latin America," *The Economist* December 6, 1997, pp. S9–S12.

2 M. Kreinin, "Brazil: the Land of Telecom Opportunity: US Firms Profit from Privatization," *USA Today,* December 1, 1997, p. B12.

3 As we shall see, there is not a strict one-to-one correspondence between political systems and economic systems. A. O. Hirschman, "The On-and-Off Again Connection between Political and Economic Progress," *American Economic Review* 84, no. 2 (1994), pp. 343–48.

4 For a discussion of the roots of collectivism and individualism, see H. W. Spiegel, *The Growth of Economic Thought* (Durham, NC: Duke University Press, 1991). An easily assessable discussion of collectivism and individualism can be found in M. Friedman and R. Friedman, *Free to Choose* (London: Penguin Books, 1980).

5 For a classic summary of the tenets of Marxism details, see A. Giddens, *Capitalism and Modern Social Theory* (Cambridge: Cambridge University Press, 1971).

6 For details see "A Survey of China," *The Economist,* March 18, 1995.

7 J. S. Mill, *On Liberty* (London: Longman's, 1865), p. 6.

8 A. Smith, *The Wealth of Nations, Vol. 1* (London: Penguin Books) p. 325.

9 R. Wesson, *Modern Government–Democracy and Authoritarism,* 2nd ed. (Englewood Cliffs, NJ: Prentice Hall, 1990).

10 For a detailed but accessible elaboration of this argument, see Friedman and Friedman, *Free to Choose.* Also see P. M. Romer, "The Origins of Endogenous Growth," *Journal of Economic Perspectives* 8, no. 1 (1994), pp. 2–32.

11 M. Borrus, L. A. Tyson, and J. Zysman, "Creating Advantage: How Government Policies Created Trade in the Semiconductor Industry," in *Strategic Trade Policy and the New International Economics,* ed. P. Krugman, (Cambridge, MA: MIT Press, 1986).

12 See Lester Thurow, *Head to Head* (New York: Warner Books, 1993).

13 D. North, *Institutions, Institutional Change, and Economic Performance* (Cambridge: Cambridge University Press, 1991).

14 P. Klebnikov, "Russia's Robber Barons." *Forbes,* November 21, 1994, pp. 74–84; C. Mellow, "Russia: Making Cash from Chaos," *Fortune,* April 17, 1995, pp. 145–51; and "Mr. Tatum Checks Out," *The Economist,* November 9, 1996, p. 78.

15 "Godfather of the Kremlin?" *Fortune,"* December 30, 1996, pp. 90–96.

16 "Mr Tatum Checks Out."

17 K. van Wolferen, *The Enigma of Japanese Power* (New York: Vintage Books, 1990), pp. 100–05.

18 P. Bardhan, "Corruption and Development: A Review of the Issues," *Journal of Economic Literature,* September 1997, pp. 1320–46.

19 K. M. Murphy, A. Shleifer, and R. Vishny, "Why Is Rent Seeking so Costly to Growth," *American Economic Review* 83, no. 2 (1993), pp. 409–14.

20 Keiran Cooke, "Honeypot of as Much as $4 Billion down the Drain," *Financial Times,* February 26, 1994, p. 4.

21 Douglass North has argued that the correct specification of intellectual property rights is one of the factors that lowers the costs of doing business and, thereby, stimulates economic growth and development. See North, *Institutions, Institutional Change, and Economic Performance.*

22 Business Software Alliance, *Global Software Piracy Report: Facts and Figures, 1994–1999.* Available from http://www.bsa.org.

23 J. Greenberger and C. S. Smith, "CD Piracy Flourishes in China and the West Supplies Equipment," *The Wall Street Journal,* April 27, 1997, pp. A1, A4.

24 "Trade Tripwires," *The Economist,* August 27, 1994, p. 61.

25 Business Software Alliance, "Software Piracy in China," press release, November 18, 1996.

26 S. Bilello, "US Wages War on China's Pirates," *Newsday,* February 7, 1995, p. A41; C. S. Smith, "Microsoft May Get Help in China from its Uncle Sam," *The Wall Street Journal,* November 21, 1994, p. B4; "Making War on China's Pirates,"

The Economist, February 11, 1995, pp. 33–34; interviews with Microsoft officials; M. O'Neill, "Microsoft Chairman Says China Has Key Future Role," *South China Morning Post,* December 12, 1997, p. 1; "Intellectual Property: Bazar Software," *The Economist,* March 8, 1997, pp. 77–78; and X. Wang, "Microsoft Wins Landmark Piracy Case," *South China Morning Post,* March 8, 1999, p. 1.

27 "A Survey of the Legal Profession," *The Economist,* July 18, 1992, pp. 1–18.

28 The World Bank, *World Development Report, 1999/2000: Entering the 21st Century* (Oxford: Oxford University Press, 1999).

29 G. M. Grossman and E. Helpman, "Endogenous Innovation in the Theory of Growth," *Journal of Economic Perspectives* 8, no. 1 (1994), pp. 23–44, and Romer, "The Origins of Endogenous Growth."

30 F. A. Hayek, *The Fatal Conceit: Errors of Socialism* (Chicago: University of Chicago Press, 1989).

31 James Gwartney, Robert Lawson, and Walter Block, *Economic Freedom of the World: 1975–1995* (London: Institute of Economic Affairs, 1996).

32 North, *Institutions, Institutional Change, and Economic Performance.* See also Murphy, Shleifer, and Vishny, "Why Is Rent Seeking so Costly to Growth?"

33 Hirschman, "The On-and-Off Again Connection between Political and Economic Progress," and A. Przeworski and F. Limongi, "Political Regimes and Economic Growth," *Journal of Economic Perspectives* 7, no. 3 (1993), pp. 51–59.

34 As an example see "Why Voting Is Good for You," *The Economist,* August 27, 1994, pp. 15–17.

35 Ibid.

36 For details of this argument, see M. Olson, "Dictatorship, Democracy, and Development," *American Political Science Review,* September 1993.

37 See Jarad Diamond, *Guns, Germs, and Steel* (New York: W. W. Norton, 1997). Also J. Sachs, "Nature, Nurture and the Limits of Growth," *The Economist,* June 14, 1997, pp. 19–22.

38 Sachs, "Nature, Nurture, and the Limits of Growth," p. 19.

39 "What Can the Rest of the World Learn from the Classrooms of Asia?" *The Economist,* September 21, 1996, p. 24.

40 J. Fagerberg, "Technology and International Differences in Growth Rates," *Journal of Economic Literature,* September 1994, pp. 1147–75.

41 Freedom House, "Freedom in the World: The Annual Survey of Political Rights and Civil Liberties, 1998–1999," http://freedomhouse.org/survey99.

42 "1997 Freedom Around the World," *Freedom Review,* January–February 1997, pp. 5–29.

43 L. Conners, "Freedom to Connect," *Wired,* August 1997, pp. 105–06.

44 F. Fukuyama, "The End of History," *The National Interest* 16 (Summer 1989), p. 18.

45 S. P. Huntington, *The Clash of Civilizations and the Remaking of World Order* (New York: Simon & Schuster, 1996).

46 Ibid., p. 116.

47 S. Fisher, R. Sahay, and C. A. Vegh, "Stabilization and the Growth in Transition Economies: the Early Experience," *Journal of Economic Perspectives* 10 (Spring 1996), pp. 45–66.

48 B. T. Johnson, K. R. Holmes, and M. Kirpatrick, *1999 Index of Economic Freedom* (New York: Heritage Foundation, 1999).

49 S. Moshavi and P. Endarido, "India Shakes off Its Shackles," *Business Week,* January 30, 1995, pp. 48–49; "A Survey of India: The Tiger Steps Out," *The Economist,* January 21, 1995; J. F. Burns, "India Now Winning US Investment," *New York Times,* February 3, 1995, pp. C1, C5; "Tarnished Silver," *The Economist,* September 6, 1997, pp. 64–65; and P. Moore, "Three Steps Forward," *Euromoney,* September 1997, pp. 190–95.

50 N. Weinberg, "First the Pain, Then the Gain," *Forbes,* May 5, 1997, pp. 134–37.

51 J. C. Brada, "Privatization Is Transition—Is It?" *Journal of Economic Perspectives,* (Spring 1996), pp. 67–86.

52 M. S. Borish and M. Noel, "Private Sector Development in the Visegrad Countries," *World Bank,* March 1997.

53 Ibid.

54 Fischer, Sahay, and Vegh, "Stabilization and Growth in Transition Economies."

55 M. Bleaney, "Economic Liberalization in Eastern Europe: Problems and Prospects," *The World Economy* 17, no. 4, (1994), pp. 497–507.

56 M. Wolf and C. Freeland, "The Long Day's Journey to Market," *Financial Times,* March 7, 1995, p. 15.

57 "Lessons of Transition," *The Economist,* June 29, 1996, p. 81.

58 For a discussion of first-mover advantages, see M. Liberman and D. Montgomery, "First-Mover Advantages," *Strategic Management Journal* 9 (Summer Special Issue 1988), pp. 41–58.

59 "Of Liberty and Prosperity," *The Economist,* January 13, 1996, pp. 21–23.

60 S. H. Robock, "Political Risk: Identification and Assessment," *Columbia Journal of World Business,* July/August 1971, pp. 6–20.

61 Steven L. Myers, "Report Says Business Interests Overshadow Rights," *New York Times,* December 5, 1996, p. A8.

62 Jo-Ann Mort, "Sweated Shopping," *The Guardian,* September 8, 1997, p. 11.

63 Bardhan Pranab, "Corruption and Development," *Journal of Economic Literature* 36 (September 1997), pp. 1320–46.

64 A. Shleifer and R. W. Vishny, "Corruption," *Quarterly Journal of Economics* 108 (1993), pp. 599–617.

65 P. Mauro, "Corruption and Growth." *Quarterly Journal of Economics* 110 (1995), pp. 681–712.

66 J. Perlez, "GE Finds Tough Going in Hungary," *New York Times,* July 25, 1994, pp. C1, C3; C. R. Whitney, "East Europe's Hard Path to New Day," *New York Times,* September 30, 1994, pp. A1, A4; and T. Agassi, "Hungary for Capitalism," *Jerusalem Post,* June 18, 1997, p. 8.

Chapter 3

1 S. Sugawara, "Odd Man In," *Washington Post,* October 10, 1996, p. C1; M. A. Lev, "Ford Exec Retools Mazda," *Chicago Tribune,* March 31, 1997, p. 1; M. Nakamoto, "New Driver Takes the Wheel," *Financial Times,* April 22, 1996, p. 18; I. Morton, "The Height of Mazda's Empire," *The Times,* June 7, 1997; and Y. Kageyama, "West Meets East," *Chicago Tribune,* November 24, 1996, p. 3.

2 See R. Dore, *Taking Japan Seriously* (Stanford, CA: Stanford University Press, 1987).

3 E. B. Tylor, *Primitive Culture* (London: Murray, 1871).

4 Geert Hofstede, *Culture's Consequences: International Differences in Work Related Values* (Beverly Hills, CA: Sage, 1984), p. 21.

5 J. Z. Namenwirth and R. B. Weber, *Dynamics of Culture* (Boston: Allen & Unwin, 1987), p. 8.

6 R. Mead, *International Management: Cross Cultural Dimensions* (Oxford: Blackwell Business, 1994), p. 7.

7 "Iraq: Down but Not Out," *The Economist,* April 8, 1995, pp. 21–23.

8 S. P. Huntington, *The Clash of Civilizations* (New York: Simon & Schuster, 1996).

9 M. Thompson, R. Ellis, and A. Wildavsky, *Cultural Theory* (Boulder, CO: Westview Press, 1990).

10 M. Douglas, "Cultural Bias," in the *Active Voice* (London: Routledge, 1982), pp. 183–254.

11 M. L. Dertouzos, R. K. Lester, and R. M. Solow, *Made in America* (Cambridge, MA: MIT Press, 1989).

12 C. Nakane, *Japanese Society* (Berkeley, CA: University of California Press, 1970).

13 Ibid.

14 For details see, M. Aoki, *Information, Incentives, and Bargaining in the Japanese Economy* (Cambridge: Cambridge University Press, 1988), and Dertouzos, Lester, and Solow, *Made in America.*

15 For an excellent historical treatment of the evolution of the English class system, see E. P. Thompson, *The Making of the English Working Class* (London: Vintage Books, 1966). See also R. Miliband, *The State in Capitalist Society* (New York: Basic Books, 1969), especially chap. 2. For more recent studies of class in British societies, see Stephen Brook, *Class: Knowing Your Place in Modern Britain* (London: Victor Gollancz, 1997); A. Adonis and S. Pollard, *A Class Act: The Myth of Britain's Classless Society* (London: MacMillan 1997); and J. Gerteis and M. Savage, "The Salience of Class in Britain and American: A Comparative Analysis," *British Journal of Sociology,* June 1998.

16 Adonis and Pollard, *A Class Act: The Myth of Britain's Classless Society.*

17 N. Goodman, *An Introduction to Sociology* (New York: Harper Collins, 1991).

18 M. Weber, *The Protestant Ethic and the Spirit of Capitalism* (New York: Scribner's Sons, 1958, original 1904–1905). For an excellent review of Weber's work see A. Giddens, *Capitalism and Modern Social Theory* (Cambridge: Cambridge University Press, 1971).

19 Ibid, p. 35.

20 See S. M. Abbasi, K. W. Hollman, and J. H. Murrey, "Islamic Economics: Foundations and Practices," *International Journal of Social Economics* 16, no. 5 (1990), pp. 5–17, and R. H. Dekmejian, *Islam in Revolution: Fundamentalism in the Arab World* (Syracuse, NY: Syracuse University Press, 1995).

21 T. W. Lippman, *Understanding Islam* (New York: Meridian Books, 1995).

22 Dekmejian, *Islam in Revolution.*

23 M. K. Nydell, *Understanding Arabs* (Yarmouth, ME: Intercultural Press, 1987).

24 Lippman, *Understanding Islam.*

25 The material in this section is based largely on Abbasi, Hollman, and Murrey, "Islamic Economics: Foundations and Practices."

26 "The Cracks in the Kingdom," *The Economist,* March 18, 1995, pp. 21–25; B. Deans, "Saudi-US Ties Show New Strains," *Atlanta Constitution,* August 18, 1996, p. 16A; and J. Keen, "Winds Shifting in Saudi Arabia," *USA Today,* June 26, 1996, p. 3A.

27 "Islam's Interest," *The Economist,* January 18, 1992, pp. 33–34.

28 For details of Weber's work and views see Giddens, *Capitalism and Modern Social Theory.*

29 See for example the views expressed in "A Survey of India: The Tiger Steps Out," *The Economist,* January 21, 1995.

30 See Dore, *Taking Japan Seriously;* C. W. L. Hill, "Transaction Cost Economizing as a Source of Comparative Advantage: The Case of Japan," *Organization Science* 6 (1995).

31 See Aoki, *Information, Incentives, and Bargaining in the Japanese Economy,* and J. P. Womack, D. T. Jones, and D. Roos, *The Machine that Changed the World* (New York: Rawson Associates, 1990).

32 This hypothesis dates back to two anthropologists, Edward Sapir and Benjamin Lee Whorf. See E. Sapir, "The Status of Linguistics as a Science," *Language* 5 (1929), pp. 207–14, and B. L. Whorf, *Language, Thought, and Reality* (Cambridge, MA: MIT Press, 1956).

33 D. A. Ricks, *Big Business Blunders: Mistakes in Multinational Marketing* (Homewood, IL: Dow Jones Irwin, 1983).

34 N. Goodman, *An Introduction to Sociology* (New York: Harper Collins, 1991).

35 M. E. Porter, *The Competitive Advantage of Nations* (New York: Free Press, 1990).

36 Ibid., pp. 395–97.

37 G. Hofstede, "The Cultural Relativity of Organizational Practices and Theories," *Journal of International Business Studies,* Fall 1983, pp. 75–89.

38 For more a detailed critique see Mead, *International Management: Cross-Cultural Dimensions,* pp. 73–75.

39 For example, see W. J. Bigoness and G. L. Blakely, "A Cross-National Study of Managerial Values," *Journal of International Business Studies,* December 1996, p. 739; D. H. Ralston, D. H. Holt, R. H. Terpstra, Y. Kai-Cheng, "The Impact of National Culture and Economic Ideology on Managerial Work Values," *Journal of International Business Studies* 28, no. 1 (1997), pp. 177–208; and P. B. Smith, M. F. Peterson, Z. Ming Wang, "The Manager as a Mediator of Alternative Meanings," *Journal of International Business Studies* 27, no. 1 (1996), pp. 115–37.

40 Mead, *International Management: Cross-Cultural Dimensions,* chap. 17.

41 "Free, Young, and Japanese," *The Economist,* December 21, 1991.

42 Namenwirth and Weber, *Dynamics of Culture.*

43 G. Hofstede, "National Cultures in Four Dimensions," *International Studies of Management and Organization* 13, no. 1, pp. 46–74.

44 See "The Long March from Harmony," *The Economist,* July 9, 1994, pp. 6–10, and L. Swanson, "Meeting Global Business Challenges the Japanese Way, *CMA Magazine,* February 1997, pp. 23–25.

45 R. J. Barnet and J. Cavanagh, *Global Dreams: Imperial Corporations and the New World Order.* (New York: Touchstone, 1994).

46 See Aoki, *Information, Incentives, and Bargaining in the Japanese Economy;* Dertouzos, Lester, and Solow, *Made in America;* and Porter, *The Competitive Advantage of Nations,* pp. 395–97.

47 Barnet and Cavanagh, *Global Dreams,* p. 33.

48 P. Gumble and R. Turner, "Mouse Trap: Fans Like Euro Disney But Its Parent's Goofs Weigh

the Park Down," *The Wall Street Journal,* March 10, 1994, p. A1; Barnet and Cavanagh, *Global Dreams,* pp. 33–34; J. Huey, "Eisner Explains Everything," *Fortune,* April 17, 1995, pp. 45–68;

R. Anthony, "Euro-Disney: The First 100 Days," Harvard Business School case #9-693-013; and Charles Masters, "French Fall for the Charms of Disney," *Sunday Telegraph,* April 13, 1997, p. 21.

Chapter 4

1 "Poor Man's Burden: A Survey of the Third World," *The Economist,* September 23, 1989; World Bank, *World Development Report, 1997* (Oxford: Oxford University Press, 1997), Tables 1 and 2; and J. Wha-Lee, "International Trade, Distortions, and Long-Run Economic Growth," *International Monetary Fund Staff Papers* 40, no. 2, p. 299. June 1993.

2 Donna St. George, "Crawfish Wars: Cajun Country vs China," *New York Times,* May 7, 1997, pp. B1, B10; P. Passell, "Protecting America's Shores from Those Chinese Crawfish," *New York Times,* August 28, 1997, p. D2; and N. Dunne, "Shellfish Imports Stick in the Cajun Craw," *Financial Times,* August 21, 1997, p. 16.

3 H. W. Spiegel, *The Growth of Economic Thought* (Durham, NC: Duke University Press, 1991).

4 G. de Jonquieres, "Mercantilists Are Treading on Thin Ice," *Financial Times,* July 3, 1994, p. 16.

5 Jarl Hagelstam, "Mercantilism Still Influences Practical Trade Policy at the End of the Twentieth Century," *Journal of World Trade,* 1991, pp. 95–105.

6 Y. Sazanami, S. Urata, and H. Kawai, *Measuring the Costs of Protection in Japan* (Washington, DC: Institute for International Economics, 1994); M. Nakamoto, "All Action and No Talk," *Financial Times,* March 17, 1995, p. 5; and N. Dunne, "US Threatens WTO Complaint against Japan," *Financial Times,* March 29, 1995, p. 6.

7 S. Hollander, *The Economics of David Ricardo* (Buffalo, NY: University of Toronto Press, 1979).

8 D. Ricardo, *The Principles of Political Economy and Taxation* (Homewood, IL: Richard D. Irwin, 1967, first published in 1817).

9 For example, R. Dornbusch, S. Fischer, and P. Samuelson, "Comparative Advantage: Trade and Payments in a Ricardian Model with a Continuum of Goods," *American Economic Review* 67 (December 1977), pp. 823–39.

10 B. Balassa, "An Empirical Demonstration of Classic Comparative Cost Theory," *Review of Economics and Statistics,* 1963, pp. 231–38.

11 See P. R. Krugman, "Is Free Trade Passé?" *Journal of Economic Perspectives* 1 (Fall 1987), pp. 131–44.

12 P. Samuelson, "The Gains from International Trade Once Again," *Economic Journal* 72 (1962), pp. 820–29.

13 For a summary see "The Gains from Trade," *The Economist,* September 23, 1989, pp. 25–26.

14 B. Ohlin, *Interregional and International Trade* (Cambridge, MA: Harvard University Press, 1933). For a summary see R. W. Jones and J. P. Neary, "The Positive Theory of International Trade," in *Handbook of International Economics,* eds. R. W. Jones and P. B. Kenen (Amsterdam: North Holland, 1984).

15 W. Leontief, "Domestic Production and Foreign Trade: The American Capital Position Re-Examined," *Proceedings of the American Philosophical Society* 97 (1953), pp. 331–49.

16 R. M. Stern and K. Maskus, "Determinants of the Structure of U.S. Foreign Trade," *Journal of International Economics* 11 (1981), pp. 207–44.

17 See H. P. Bowen, E. E. Leamer, and L. Sveikayskas, "Multicountry, Multifactor Tests of the Factor Abundance Theory," *American Economic Review* 77 (1987), pp. 791–809.

18 R. Vernon, "International Investments and International Trade in the Product Life Cycle," *Quarterly Journal of Economics,* May 1966, pp. 190–207, and R. Vernon and L. T. Wells, *The Economic Environment of International Business,* 4th ed. (Englewood Cliffs, NJ: Prentice Hall, 1986).

19 For a good summary of this literature, see E. Helpman and P. Krugman, *Market Structure and Foreign Trade: Increasing Returns, Imperfect Competition, and the International Economy* (Boston: MIT Press, 1985). Also see P. Krugman, "Does the New Trade Theory Require a New Trade Policy?" *World Economy* 15, no. 4 (1992), pp. 423–41.

20 M. B. Lieberman and D. B. Montgomery, "First-Mover Advantages," *Strategic Management Journal* 9, special issue (Summer 1988), pp. 41–58.

21 A. D. Chandler, *Scale and Scope* (New York: Free Press, 1990).

22 Krugman, "Does the New Trade Theory Require a New Trade Policy?"

23 M. E. Porter, *The Competitive Advantage of Nations* (New York: Free Press, 1990). For a good review of this book, see R. M. Grant, "Porter's Competitive Advantage of Nations: An Assessment," *Strategic Management Journal* 12 (1991), pp. 535–48.

24 "Lessons from the Frozen North," *The Economist,* October 8, 1994, pp. 76–77; G. Edmondson, "Grabbing Markets from the Giants," *Business Week, Special Issue: 21st Century Capitalism,* 1995, p. 156; and company news releases.

25 Porter, *Competitive Advantage of Nations,* p. 121.

26 Lieberman and Montgomery, "First-Mover Advantages."

27 C. A. Hamilton, "Building Better Machine Tools," *Journal of Commerce,* October 30, 1991, p. 8, and "Manufacturing Trouble," *The Economist,* October 12, 1991, p. 71.

28 P. Taylor, "Poised for Global Growth," *Financial Times,* December 3, 1997, pp. 1, 8; P. Taylor, "An Industry on the Up and Up," *Financial Times,* December 3, 1997, p. 3; and Krishna Guha, "Strategic Alliances with Global Partners," *Financial Times,* December 3, 1997, p. 6.

Chapter 5

1 C. Southey, "Hormones Fuel a Meaty EU Row," *Financial Times,* September 7, 1995, p. 2; E. L. Andrews, "In Victory for U.S., European Ban on Treated Beef Is Ruled Illegal," *New York Times,* May 9, 1997, p. A1; F. Williams and G. de Jonquieres, "WTO's Beef Rulings Give Europe Food for Thought," *Financial Times,* February 13, 1998, p. 5; *EC Measures Concerning Meat and Meat Products* (Geneva: World Trade Organization, August 18, 1997); and F. Williams, "US Wins Approval for Beef Sanctions," *Financial Times,* July 27, 1999, p. 8.

2 For a detailed welfare analysis of the effect of a tariff, see P. R. Krugman and M. Obstfeld, *International Economics: Theory and Policy* (New York: Harper Collins, 1994), chap. 9.

3 Y. Sazanami, S. Urata, and H. Kawai, *Measuring the Costs of Protection in Japan* (Washington, DC: Institute for International Economics, 1994).

4 See J. Bhagwati, *Protectionism* (Cambridge, MA: MIT Press, 1988), and "Costs of Protection," *Journal of Commerce,* September 25, 1991, p. 8A.

5 G. Hufbauer and K. A. Elliott, *Measuring the Costs of Protectionism in the United States* (Washington, DC: Institute for International Economics, 1993), and S. Nasar, "The High Costs of Protectionism," *New York Times,* November 12, 1993, pp. C1, C2.

6 "From the Sublime to the Subsidy," *The Economist,* February 24, 1990, p. 71.

7 "Aid Addicts," *The Economist,* August 8, 1992, p. 61, and "State Aid: The Addicts in Europe," *The Economist,* November 22, 1997, p. 75.

8 R. W. Crandall, *Regulating the Automobile* (Washington, DC: Brookings Institute, 1986).

9 Quoted in Krugman and Obstfeld, *International Economics.*

10 Bhagwati, *Protectionism,* and "Japan to Curb VCR Exports," *New York Times,* November 21, 1983, p. D5.

11 Alan Goldstein, "Sematech Members Facing Dues Increase; 30% Jump to Make up for Loss of Federal Funding," *Dallas Morning News,* July 27, 1996, p. 2F.

12 N. Dunne and R. Waters, "US Waves a Big Stick at Chinese Pirates," *Financial Times,* January 6, 1995, p. 4.

13 John Broder, "Clinton to Impose Ban on 58 Types of Imported Guns," *New York Times,* April 6, 1998, sec. A; p. 1.

14 Bill Lambrecht, "Monsanto Softens Its Stance on Labeling in Europe," *St. Louis Post-Dispatch,* March 15, 1998, p. E1.

15 Peter. S. Jordan, "Country Sanctions and the International Business Community," *American Society of International Law Proceedings of the Annual Meeting* 20, no. 9 (1997), pp. 333–42.

16 "Waiting for China; Human Rights and International Trade," *Commonwealth,* March 11, 1994, and "China: The Cost of Putting Business First," *Human Rights Watch,"* July 1996.

17 "Brazil's Auto Industry Struggles to Boost Global Competitiveness," *Journal of Commerce,* October 10, 1991, p. 6A.

18 For review see J. A. Brander, "Rationales for Strategic Trade and Industrial Policy," in *Strategic Trade Policy and the New International Economics,* ed. P. R. Krugman (Cambridge, MA: MIT Press, 1986); P. R. Krugman, "Is Free Trade Passé?" *Journal of Economic Perspectives* 1 (1987), pp. 131–44; and P. R. Krugman, "Does the New Trade Theory Require a New Trade Policy?" *World Economy* 15, no. 4 (1992), pp. 423–41.

19 "Airbus and Boeing: The Jumbo War," *The Economist,* June 15, 1991, pp. 65–66.

20 For details see Krugman, "Is Free Trade Passé?" and Brander, "Rationales for Strategic Trade and Industrial Policy."

21 Krugman, "Is Free Trade Passé?"

22 This dilemma is a variant of the famous Prisoner's Dilemma, which has become a classic metaphor for the difficulty of achieving cooperation between self-interested and mutually suspicious entities. For a good general introduction, see A. Dixit and B. Nalebuff, *Thinking Strategically: The Competitive Edge in Business, Politics, and Everyday Life* (New York: W. W. Norton & Co., 1991).

23 The Smoot-Hawley Act did not cause the Great Depression. However the beggar-thy-neighbor trade policies that it ushered in certainly made things worse. See Bhagwati, *Protectionism.*

24 Bhagwati, *Protectionism.*

25 World Bank, *World Development Report* (New York: Oxford University Press, 1987).

26 World Trade Organization, "World Trade Growth Accelerated in 1997," WTO press release, March 19, 1998.

27 Frances Williams, "WTO—New Name Heralds New Powers," *Financial Times,* December 16, 1993, p. 5, and Frances Williams, "GATT Successor to Be Given Real Clout," *Financial Times,* April 4, 1994, p. 6.

28 The studies are *Trade Liberalization: The Global Economic Implications* (Paris and Washington: OECD and the World Bank, 1993), *Assessing the Effects of the Uruguay Round* (Paris: OECD, 1993), and *Background Paper: The Uruguay Round* (Geneva: GATT, 1993).

29 Martin Wolf, "Doing Good Despite Themselves," *Financial Times,* December 16, 1993, p. 15.

30 World Trade Organization, http://www.wto.org/wto/faqs/faq.htm.

31 L. Abruzzese, "In Defense of the WTO," *Journal of Commerce,* October 21, 1997, p. 8A.

32 Alan Cane, "Getting Through: Why Telecommunications Talks Matter," *Financial Times,* February 14, 1997.

33 "Ruggiero Congratulates Governments on Landmark Telecommunications Agreement," World Trade Organization press release, February 17, 1997.

34 Francis Williams, "Telecoms: World Pact Set to Slash Costs of Calls," *Financial Times,* February 17, 1997.

35 "Financial Services," WTO Press Brief, September 1996.

36 G. de Jonquieres, "Happy End to a Cliff Hanger," *Financial Times,* December 15, 1997, p. 15.

37 "A Disquieting New Agenda for Trade," *The Economist,* July 16, 1994, pp. 55–56, and Francis Williams, "Trade Round Like This May Never Be Seen Again," *Financial Times,* December 16, 1993, p. 7.

38 C. W. L. Hill, "The Toyota Corporation in 1994," in C. W. L. Hill and G. R. Jones, *Strategic Management: An Integrated Approach* (Boston: Houghton Mifflin, 1995).

39 A. Aggarwal and S. Narain, "Politics of Conservation," *The Hindu,* October 26, 1997, p. 26.

40 J. H. Cushman, "Trade Group Strikes a Blow at U.S. Environmental Law," *New York Times,* April 7, 1998, p. D1; "WTO Ruling in Turtle Protection Dispute," *Bangkok Post,* March 18, 1998; and J. Maggs, "WTO Shrimp Ruling Heightens Environment vs Trade Debate," *Journal of Commerce,* April 7, 1998, p. 3A.

Chapter 6

1 C. Brown-Humes, "Electrolux Plugs into Households All over Asia," *Financial Times,* April 27, 1995, p. 15; C. Brown-Humes, "Electrolux Buys Control of Brazilian Group," *Financial Times,* January 11, 1996, p. 30; G. McIvor, "Electrolux Comes under the Scalpel," *Financial Times,* October 29, 1997, p. 27; and Electrolux's website www.electrolux.com.

2 "Global Foreign Direct Investment Boomed in 1998," United Nations press release TAD/1880, June 22, 1999.

3 World Trade Organization, *Annual Report, 1998* (Geneva: WTO, 1998), and United Nations, *World Investment Report, 1998* (New York and Geneva: United Nations, 1998).

4 "Global Foreign Direct Investment Boomed in 1998," and United Nations, *World Investment Report, 1998.*

5 United Nations, *World Investment Report, 1998.*

6 Ibid.

7 United Nations. *World Investment Report,* 1998, and "Global Foreign Direct Investment Boomed in 1998."

8 Interviews by the author while in China, March 1998; Liz Sly, "China Losing Its Golden Glow," *Chicago Tribune,* September 15, 1997, p. 1; Matthew Miller, "Search for Fresh Capital Widens," *South China Morning Post,* April 9, 1998, p. 1; and Steve Mufson, "China Says Asian Crisis Will Have an Impact," *Washington Post,* March 8, 1998, p. A27.

9 M. Kidron and R. Segal, *The New State of the World Atlas* (New York: Simon & Schuster, 1987).

10 The data can be found on J. P. Morgan's website: www.jpmorgan.com.

11 For example, see S. H. Hymer, *The International Operations of National Firms: A Study of Direct Foreign Investment* (Cambridge, MA: MIT Press, 1976); A. M. Rugman, *Inside the Multinationals: The Economics of Internal Markets* (New York: Columbia University Press, 1981); D. J. Teece, "Multinational Enterprise, Internal Governance, and Industrial Organization," *American Economic Review* 75 (May 1983), pp. 233–38; C. W. L. Hill and W. C. Kim, "Searching for a Dynamic Theory of the Multinational Enterprise: A Transaction Cost Model," *Strategic Management Journal* (special issue) 9 (1988), pp. 93–104.

12 J. P. Womack, D. T. Jones, and D. Roos, *The Machine that Changed the World* (New York: Rawson Associates, 1990).

13 Source material from Wal-Mart annual reports, 1996 and 1997, and news releases and other information posted on the company's website: www.wal-mart.com.

14 F. T. Knickerbocker, *Oligopolistic Reaction and Multinational Enterprise* (Boston: Harvard Business School Press, 1973).

15 R. E. Caves, *Multinational Enterprise and Economic Analysis* (Cambridge: Cambridge University Press, 1982).

16 See R. E. Caves, "Japanese Investment in the U.S.: Lessons for the Economic Analysis of Foreign Investment," *The World Economy* 16 (1993), pp. 279–300; B. Kogut and S. J. Chang, "Technological Capabilities and Japanese Direct Investment in the United States," *Review of Economics and Statistics* 73 (1991), pp. 401–43; J. Anand and B. Kogut, "Technological Capabilities of Countries, Firm Rivalry, and Foreign Direct Investment," *Journal of International Business Studies,* Third Quarter 1997, pp. 445–65.

17 For the use of Vernon's theory to explain Japanese direct investment in the United States and Europe, see S. Thomsen, "Japanese Direct Investment in the European Community," *The World Economy* 16 (1993), pp. 301–15.

18 J. H. Dunning, *Explaining International Production* (London: Unwin Hyman, 1988).

19 P. Krugman, "Increasing Returns and Economic Geography," *Journal of Political Economy* 99, no. 3 (1991), pp. 483–99.

20 J. H. Dunning and R. Narula, *Transpacific Foreign Direct Investment and the Investment Development Path*, South Carolina Essays in International Business, No. 10 (May 1995), CIBER: University of South Carolina.

21 W. Shan and J. Song, "Foreign Direct Investment and the Sourcing of Technological Advantage: Evidence from the Biotechnology Industry," *Journal of International Business Studies,* Second Quarter 1997, pp. 267–84.

22 For elaboration see S. Hood and S. Young, *The Economics of the Multinational Enterprise* (London: Longman, 1979), and P. M. Sweezy and H. Magdoff, *The Dynamics of US Capitalism* (New York: Monthly Review Press, 1972).

23 S. Weiss, "The Long Path to the IBM-Mexico Agreement: An Analysis of Micro-computer Investment Decisions," Working paper #3, New York University School of Business, 1989.

24 United Nations, *World Investment Report, 1997* (New York and Geneva: United Nations, 1997).

25 M. Itoh and K. Kiyono, "Foreign Trade and Direct Investment," in *Industrial Policy of Japan,* ed. R. Komiya, M. Okuno, and K. Suzumura (Tokyo: Academic Press, 1988).

26 P. M. Romer, "The Origins of Endogenous Growth," *Journal of Economic Perspectives* 8, no. 1 (1994), pp. 3–22.

27 J. Mann, "A Little Help from Their Friends," *Financial Times,* November 10, 1993, p. 28; "Venezuela: A Survey," *The Economist,* October 14, 1994; and E. Luce "Oil: Foreign Investment: Finding a Balanced Approach, *Financial Times,* October 21, 1997, p. 6.

28 P. R. Krugman and M. Obstfeld, *International Economics: Theory and Policy* (New York: Harper Collins, 1994), chap. 9. Also see P. Krugman, *The Age of Diminished Expectations* (Cambridge, MA: MIT Press, 1990).

29 Robert B. Reich, *The Work of Nations: Preparing Ourselves for the 21st Century* (New York: Alfred A. Knopf, 1991).

30 For a review see John H. Dunning, "Reevaluating the Benefits of Foreign Direct Investment," *Transnational Corporations* 3, no. 1 (February 1994), pp. 23–51.

31 This idea has been articulated, although not quite in this form, by C. A. Bartlett and S. Ghoshal, *Managing across Borders: The Transnational Solution* (Boston: Harvard Business School Press, 1989).

32 P. Magnusson, "The Mexico Pact: Worth the Price?" *Business Week,* May 27, 1991, pp. 32–35.

33 C. Johnston, "Political Risk Insurance," in *Assessing Corporate Political Risk,* ed. D. M. Raddock (Totowa, NJ: Rowan & Littlefield, 1986).

34 Martin Tolchin and Susan Tolchin, *Buying into America: How Foreign Money Is Changing the Face of Our Nation* (New York: Times Books, 1988).

35 J. Behrman and R. E. Grosse, *International Business and Government: Issues and Institutions* (Columbia: University of South Carolina Press, 1990).

36 G. de Jonquieres and S. Kuper, "Push to Keep Alive Effort to Draft Global Investment Rules," *Financial Times,* April 29, 1998, p. 5.

37 See Caves, *Multinational Enterprise and Economic Analysis.*

38 For a good general introduction to negotiation strategy, see M. H. Bazerman, *Negotiating Rationally* (New York: Free Press, 1995); A. Dixit and B. Nalebuff, *Thinking Strategically: The Competitive Edge in Business, Politics, and Everyday Life* (New York: W. W. Norton, 1991); and H. Raiffa, *The Art and Science of Negotiation* (Cambridge, MA: Harvard University Press, 1982).

39 C. S. Nicandros, "The Russian Investment Dilemma," *Harvard Business Review,* May–June 1994, p. 40; T. Carrington, "World Bank President Says Economists Were Too Optimistic on Soviet Bloc" *The Wall Street Journal,* October 14, 1994, p. 13; R. Holman, "Russia to Lift Oil Restrictions," *The Wall Street Journal,* December 6, 1994, p. 24A; R. Corzine, "The Beginning of Russia's Oil Rush," *Financial Times,* November 19, 1997, p. 18; and M. Kaminski, "Russia: Foreign Direct Investment," *Financial Times,* April 9, 1997, p. 6.

Chapter 7

1 R. Lapper, "Hard Work to Be Free and Single," *Financial Times,* July 1, 1994, p. 19; "A Singular Market," *The Economist,* October 22, 1994, pp. 10–16; "Insurance: Can the Empire Strike Back?" *The Economist,* April 25, 1998, p. 76; and C. Adams, A. Jack, and A. Fisher, "Allianz Bid Mirrors its Global Ambitions," *Financial Times,* November 11, 1997, p. 20.

2 See http://www.wto.org/wto/develop/regional. htm. Also from a speech given by R. Ruggiero, director-general of the World Trade Organization, to the third conference of the Transatlantic Business Dialogue in Rome, November 7, 1997, "Regional Initiatives, Global Impact: Cooperation and the Multinational System."

3 The Andean Pact has been through a number of changes since its inception. The latest version was established in 1991. See "Free-Trade Free for All," *The Economist,* January 4, 1991, p. 63.

4 D. Swann, *The Economics of the Common Market,* 6th ed. (London: Penguin Books, 1990).

5 See J. Bhagwati, "Regionalism and Multilateralism: An Overview," Columbia University discussion paper 603, Department of Economics, Columbia University, New York; Augusto de la Torre and Margaret Kelly, "Regional Trade Arrangements," occasional paper 93 (Washington, DC: International Monetary Fund, March 1992); and J. Bhagwati, "Fast Track to Nowhere," *The Economist,* October 18, 1997, pp. 21–24.

6 C. Palmeri and J. Aguayo, "Good-bye Guangdong, Hello Jalisco," *Forbes,* February 10, 1997, pp. 76–77; "NAFTA Open Market Bolsters Mexican Textile Industry," *Journal of Commerce,* December 6, 1996, p. 4A; B. J. Feder, "Fruit of the Loom to Close Six U.S. Plants," *New York Times,* October 31, 1995, p. 6; and P. Green, "US

Textile Machinery Sector Battles Deficit as Exports Inch Up," *Journal of Commerce,* March 23, 1995, p. 8B.

7 The material in this section is based on N. Colchester and D. Buchan, *Europower: The Essential Guide to Europe's Economic Transformation in 1992* (London: The Economist Books, 1990); and Swann, *The Economics of the Common Market.*

8 "The Aid Plague: Business in Europe, A Survey," *The Economist,* June 8, 1991, pp. 12–18.

9 "One Europe, One Economy," *The Economist,* November 30, 1991, pp. 53–54, and "Market Failure: A Survey of Business in Europe," *The Economist,* June 8, 1991, pp. 6–10.

10 "A Singular Market."

11 See C. Wyploze, "EMU: Why and How It Might Happen," *Journal of Economic Perspectives* 11 (1997), pp. 3–22, and M. Feldstein, "The Political Economy of the European Economic and Monetary Union," *Journal of Economic Perspectives* 11 (1997), pp. 23–42.

12 "One Europe, One Economy," and Feldstein, "The Political Economy of the European Economic and Monetary Union."

13 Feldstein, "The Political Economy of the European Economic and Monetary Union," p. 41.

14 "From the Arctic to the Mediterranean," *The Economist,* March 5, 1994, pp. 52, 57; Lionel Barber, "More Does Not Mean Merrier," *Financial Times,* March 14, 1994, p. 13; and L. Barber, "Hopes of Wider Union Turn to Fear of No Union," *Financial Times,* December 9, 1994, p. 2.

15 J. Perles, "Europe Invites 5 Ex-Communist Nations to Join," *New York Times,* July 17, 1997, p. A6.

16 "What Are They Building? Survey of Europe's Internal Market," *The Economist,* July 8, 1989, pp. 5–7; and Colchester and Buchan, *Europower.*

17 World Trade Organization, *Regionalism and the World Trading System* (Geneva: World Trade Organization, 1995).

18 "What Is NAFTA?" *The Economist,* November 17, 1993, p. 6, and Susan Garland, "Sweet Victory," *Business Week,* November 29, 1993, pp. 30–31.

19 "NAFTA: The Showdown," *The Economist,* November 13, 1993 pp. 23–36.

20 "Happy Ever NAFTA?" *The Economist,* December 10, 1994, pp. 23–24, and Douglas Harbrecht, "What Has NAFTA Wrought? Plenty of Trade?" *Business Week,* November 21, 1994, pp. 48–49.

21 P. B. Carroll and C. Torres, "Mexico Unveils Program of Harsh Fiscal Medicine," *The Wall Street Journal,* March 3, 1995, pp. A1, A6.

22 N. C. Lustog, "NAFTA: Setting the Record Straight," *The World Economy,* 1997, pp. 605–14.

23 Raúl Hinojosa Ojeda, Curt Dowds, Robert McCleery, Sherman Robinson, David Runsten, Craig Wolff, Goetz Wolff, "NAFTA–How Has It Done? North American Integration Three Years after NAFTA," *North American Integration and Development Center at UCLA,* December 1996.

24 "NAFTA Is Not Alone," *The Economist,* June 18, 1994, pp. 47–48; P. Sweeney, "First Latin American Customs Union Looms over Venezuela," *Journal of Commerce,* September 26, 1991, p. 5A; and "The Business of the American Hemisphere," *The Economist,* August 24, 1991, pp. 37–38.

25 The comment was made by the Colombian ambassador. See K. G. Hall, "Andean Pact Nations to Work Together at Talks," *Journal of Commerce,* April 8, 1998, p. 2A.

26 Business of the American Hemisphere."

27 "NAFTA Is Not Alone."

28 "Murky Mercosur," *The Economist,* July 26, 1997, pp. 66–67.

29 See Michael Philips, "South American Trade Pact Under Fire," *The Wall Street Journal,* October 23, 1996, p. A2; Alexander J. Yeats, *Does MERCOSUR's Trade Performance Justify Concerns about the Global Welfare-Reducing Effects of Free Trade Arrangements? Yes!* (Washington, DC: World Bank, 1996); and D. M. Leipziger et al; "MERCOSUR: Integration and Industrial Policy," *The World Economy,* 1997, pp. 585–604.

30 "Aimless in Seattle," *The Economist,* November 13, 1993, pp. 35–36.

31 Guy de Jonquieres, "Different Aims, Common Cause," *Financial Times,* November 18, 1995, p. 14.

32 G de Jonquieres, "APEC Grapples with Market Turmoil," *Financial Times,* November 21, 1997, p. 6, and G. Baker, "Clinton Team Wins Most of the APEC Tricks," *Financial Times,* November 27, 1997, p. 5.

33 "World Economic Survey," *The Economist,* September 19, 1992, p. 17.

34 P. Davis, "A European Campaign: Local Companies Rush for a Share of EC Market while

Barriers Are Down," *Minneapolis-St. Paul City Business,* January 8, 1990, p. 1.

35 "The Business of Europe," *The Economist,* December 7, 1991, pp. 63–64.

36 E. G. Friberg, "1992: Moves Europeans Are Making," *Harvard Business Review,* May–June 1989, pp. 85–89.

37 T. Horwitz, "Europe's Borders Fade," *The Wall Street Journal,* May 18, 1993, pp. A1, A12; "A Singular Market"; "Something Dodgy in Europe's Single Market," *The Economist,* May 21, 1994, pp. 69–70.

Chapter 8

1 W. Dawkins, "JAO to Disclose Huge Currency Hedge Loss," *Financial Times,* October 4, 1994, and W. Dawkins, "Tokyo to Lift Veil on Currency Risks," *Financial Times,* October 5, 1994. Reprinted with permission.

2 For a good general introduction to the foreign exchange market, see R. Weisweiller, *How the Foreign Exchange Market Works* (New York: New York Institute of Finance, 1990). A detailed description of the economics of foreign exchange markets can be found in P. R. Krugman and M. Obstfeld, *International Economics: Theory and Policy* (New York: HarperCollins, 1994).

3 C. Forman, "Allied-Lyons to Post $269 Million Loss from Foreign Exchange as Dollar Soars," *The Wall Street Journal,* March 20, 1991, p. A17.

4 P. Harverson, "Billion Dollar Man the Money Markets Fear," *Financial Times,* September 30, 1994, p. 10; "A Quantum Dive," *The Economist,* March 15, 1994, pp. 83–84; B. J. Javetski, "Europe's Money Mess," *Business Week,* September 28, 1992, pp. 30–31; "Meltdown," *The Economist,* September 19, 1992, p. 69; and T. L. Friedman, "Mahathri's Wrath," *New York Times,* December 18, 1997, p. 27.

5 Data from Bank for International Settlements, *Central Bank Survey of Foreign Exchange and Derivatives Market Activity, 1998* (Basle: BIS, May 1999).

6 Ibid.

7 Ibid.

8 For a recent comprehensive review, see M. Taylor, "The Economics of Exchange Rates," *Journal of Economic Literature* 33 (1995), pp. 13–47.

9 Krugman and Obstfeld, *International Economics: Theory and Policy.*

10 M. Friedman, *Studies in the Quantity Theory of Money* (Chicago: University of Chicago Press, 1956). For an accessible explanation, see M. Friedman and R. Friedman, *Free to Choose* (London: Penguin Books, 1979), chap. 9.

11 Juan-Antino Morales, "Inflation Stabilization in Bolivia," in *Inflation Stabilization: The Experience of Israel, Argentina, Brazil, Bolivia, and Mexico,* ed. Michael Bruno et al. (Cambridge, MA: MIT Press, 1988), and The Economist, *World Book of Vital Statistics* (New York: Random House, 1990).

12 For reviews and recent articles, see L. H. Officer, "The Purchasing Parity Theory of Exchange Rates: A Review Article," *International Monetary Fund Staff Papers,* March 1976, pp. 1–60; M. Taylor, "The Economics of Exchange Rates," *Journal of Economic Literature* 33 (1995), pp. 13–47; H. J. Edison, J. E. Gagnon, and W. R. Melick, "Understanding the Empirical Literature on Purchasing Power Parity," *Journal of International Money and Finance* 16 (February 1997), pp. 1–18; J. R. Edison, "Multi-Country Evidence on the Behavior of Purchasing Power Parity under the Current Float," *Journal of International Money and Finance* 16 (February 1997), pp. 19–36; and K. Rogoff, "The Purchasing Power Parity Puzzle," *Journal of Economic Literature,* 34 (1996), pp. 647–68.

13 For a summary of the evidence, see the survey by Taylor, "The Economics of Exchange Rates.

14 R. E. Cumby and M. Obstfeld, "A Note on Exchange Rate Expectations and Nominal Interest Differentials: A Test of the Fisher Hypothesis," *Journal of Finance,* June 1981, pp. 697–703.

15 Taylor, "The Economics of Exchange Rates."

16 See H. L. Allen and M. P. Taylor, "Charts, Noise, and Fundamentals in the Foreign Exchange Market," *Economic Journal* 100 (1990), pp. 49–59, and T. Ito, "Foreign Exchange Rate Expectations: Micro Survey Data," *American Economic Review* 80 (1990), pp. 434–49.

17 For example, see E. Fama, "Forward Rates as Predictors of Future Spot Rates," *Journal of Financial Economics,* October 1976, pp. 361–77.

18 R. M. Levich, "The Efficiency of Markets for Foreign Exchange," in *International Finance,* ed.

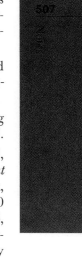
G. D. Gay and R. W. Kold (Richmond, VA: Robert F. Dane, Inc., 1983).

19 J. Williamson, *The Exchange Rate System* (Washington, DC: Institute for International Economics, 1983).

20 J. Burton, and G. Baker, "The Country That Invested Its Way into Trouble," *Financial Times,* January 15, 1998, p. 8; J. Burton, "South Korea's Credit Rating Is Lowered," *Financial Times,* October 25, 1997, p. 3; J. Burton, "Currency Losses Hit Samsung Electronics," *Financial Times,* March 20, 1998, p. 24; and "Korean Firms' Foreign Exchange Losses Exceed US $15 billion," *Business Korea,* February 1998, p. 55.

21 R. M. Levich, "Currency Forecasters Lose Their Way," *Euromoney,* August 1983, p. 140.

22 Rogoff, "The Purchasing Power Parity Puzzle."

23 C. Engel and J. D. Hamilton, "Long Swings in the Dollar: Are They in the Data and Do Markets Know It?" *American Economic Review,* September 1990, pp. 689–713.

24 J. R. Carter and J. Gagne, "The Do's and Don'ts of International Countertrade," *Sloan Management Review,* Spring 1988, pp. 31–37.

25 D. S. Levine, "Got a Spare Destroyer Lying Around?" *World Trade* 10 (June 1997), pp. 34–35.

26 "Bitter Pill for the Thais," *Straits Times,* July 5, 1997, p. 46; World Bank, *1997 World Development Report.* Table 2 (Washington, DC: World Bank, 1997); T. Bardacke, "Somprasong Defaults on $80 Million Eurobond," *Financial Times,* February 6, 1997, p. 25; and T. Bardacke, "The Day the Miracle Came to an End," *Financial Times,* January 12, 1998, pp. 6–7.

Chapter 9

1 G. Fossedal, "The IMF's Role in Zaire's Decline," *The Wall Street Journal,* May 15, 1997, p. 22; J. Burns and M. Holman, "Mobutu Built a Fortune of $4 Billion from Looted Aid," *Financial Times,* May 12, 1997, p. 1; J. D. Sachs and R. I. Rotberg, "Help Congo Now," *New York Times,* May 29, 1997, p. 21; H. Dunphy, "IMF, World Bank Now Make Political Judgements," *Journal of Commerce,* August 21, 1997, p. 3A; and *The World Factbook* (Washington, DC: CIA, 1998).

2 D. Driscoll, *What Is the International Monetary Fund?* (Washington, DC: IMF, July 1997).

3 The argument goes back to 18th century philosopher David Hume. See D. Hume, "On the Balance of Trade," reprinted in *The Gold Standard in Theory and in History,* ed. B. Eichengreen (London: Methuen, 1985).

4 R. Solomon, *The International Monetary System, 1945–1981* (New York: Harper & Row, 1982).

5 International Monetary Fund, *World Economic Outlook, 1998* (Washington, DC: IMF, May 1998).

6 For an extended discussion of the dollar exchange rate in the 1980s, see B. D. Pauls, "U.S. Exchange Rate Policy: Bretton Woods to the Present," *Federal Reserve Bulletin,* November 1990, pp. 891–908.

7 S. Brittan, "Tragi-comedy of the Rising Yen," *Financial Times,* March 3, 1994, p. 16; G. Baker, "Stay-at-home Investors Drive the Yen's Rise," *Financial Times,* April 21, 1995, p. 5; "Dial C for Chaos," *The Economist,* March 11, 1995, pp. 69–70; and P. Abrahams, "Dreaming of a Way to Curb Slide," *Financial Times,* June 5, 1998, p. 2.

8 For a feel for the issues contained in this debate, see P. Krugman, *Has the Adjustment Process Worked?* (Washington, DC: Institute for International Economics, 1991); "Time to Tether Currencies," *The Economist,* January 6, 1990, pp. 15–16; P. R. Krugman and M. Obstfeld, *International Economics: Theory and Policy* (New York: Harper Collins, 1994); J. Shelton, *Money Meltdown* (New York: Free Press, 1994); and S. Edwards, "Exchange Rates and the Political Economy of Macroeconomic Discipline," *American Economic Review,* 86, no. 2 (May 1996), pp. 159–63.

9 The argument is made by several prominent economists, particularly Stanford's Robert McKinnon. See R. McKinnon, "An International Standard for Monetary Stabilization," *Policy Analyses in International Economics* 8 (1984). The details of this argument are beyond the scope of this book. For a relatively accessible exposition, see P. Krugman, *The Age of Diminished Expectations* (Cambridge, MA: MIT Press, 1990).

10 A. R. Ghosh and A. M. Gulde, "Does the Exchange Rate Regime Matter for Inflation and Growth?" *Economic Issues,* no. 2 (1997).

11 "The ABC of Currency Boards," *The Economist,* November 1, 1997, p. 80.

12 International Monetary Fund, *World Economic Outlook, 1998* (Washington, DC: IMF, May 1998).

13 Ibid.

14 J. Darling and D. Nauss, "Stall in the Fast Lane," *Los Angeles Times,* February 19, 1995, p. 1; "Mexico Drops Efforts to Prop up Peso," *The Wall Street Journal,* December 23, 1994, p. A3; and R. Dornbusch, "We Have Salinas to Thank for the Peso Debacle," *Business Week,* January 16, 1995, p. 20.

15 See P. Carroll and C. Torres, "Mexico Unveils Program of Harsh Fiscal Medicine," *The Wall Street Journal,* March 10, 1995, pp. A1, A6, and "Putting Mexico Together Again," *The Economist,* February 4, 1995, p. 65.

16 S. Erlanger, "Russia Will Test a Trading Band for the Ruble," *New York Times,* July 7, 1995, p. 1; C. Freeland, "Russian to Introduce a Trading Band for Ruble against Dollar," *Financial Times,* July 7, 1995, p. 1; J. Thornhill, "Russians Bemused by 'Black Tuesday,'" *Financial Times,* October 12, 1994, p. 4; R. Sikorski, "Mirage of Numbers," *The Wall Street Journal,* May 18, 1994, p. 14; "Can Russia Fight Back?" *The Economist,* June 6, 1998, pp. 47–48; and J. Thornhill, "Russia's Shrinking Options," *Financial Times,* August 19, 1998, p. 19.

17 World Trade Organization, *Annual Report, 1997,* vol. II, table III.69.

18 J. Ridding and J. Kynge, "Complacency Gives Way to Contagion," *Financial Times,* January 13, 1998, p. 8.

19 J. Burton and G. Baker, "The Country That Invested Its Way into Trouble," *Financial Times,* January 15, 1998, p. 8.

20 P. Shenon, "The Suharto Billions," *New York Times,* January 16, 1998, p. 1.

21 World Bank, *1997 World Development Report,* table 11.

22 Ridding and Kynge, "Complacency Gives Way to Contagion."

23 Burton and Baker, "The Country That Invested Its Way into Trouble."

24 "Bitter Pill for the Thais," *The Straits Times,* July 5, 1997, p. 46.

25 World Bank, *1997 World Development Report,* table 2.

26 International Monetary Fund, press release no. 97/37, August 20, 1997.

27 T. S. Shorrock, "Korea Starts Overhaul; IMF Aid Hits $60 Billion," *Journal of Commerce,* December 8, 1997, p. 3A.

28 See J. Sachs, "Economic Transition and Exchange Rate Regime," *American Economic Review* 86, no. 92 (May 1996), pp. 147–52, J. Sachs, "Power unto Itself," *Financial Times,* December 11, 1997, p. 11.

29 Sachs, "Power unto Itself."

30 Martin Wolf, "Same Old IMF Medicine," *Financial Times,* December 9, 1997, p. 12.

31 Sachs, "Power unto Itself."

32 P. Gumbel and B. Coleman, "Daimler Warns of Severe 95 Loss Due to Strong Mark," *New York Times,* June 29, 1995, pp. 1, 10, and M. Wolf, "Daimler-Benz Announces Major Losses," *Financial Times,* June 29, 1995, p. 1.

33 R. S. Eckley, "Caterpillar's Ordeal: Foreign Competition in Capital Goods," *Business Horizons,* March–April 1989, pp. 80–86; H. S. Byrne, "Track of the Cat: Caterpillar Is Bulldozing Its Way Back to Higher Profits," *Barron's,* April 6, 1987, pp. 13, 70–71; R. Henkoff, "This Cat Is Acting Like a Tiger," *Fortune,* December 19, 1988, pp. 71–76; and "Caterpillar and Komatsu," in *Transnational Management: Text, Cases, and Readings in Cross-Border Management,* ed. C. A. Bartlett and S. Ghoshal (Homewood, IL: Richard D. Irwin, 1992).

Chapter 10

1 R. Blumenstein, "GM Is Building Plants in Developing Nations to Woo New Markets," *The Wall Street Journal,* August 4, 1997, p. A1; Haig Simonian, "GM Hopes to Turn Corner with New Astra," *Financial Times,* November 29, 1997, p. 15; and D. Howes, "GM, Ford Play for Keeps Abroad," *Detroit News,* March 8, 1998, p. D1.

2 M. E. Porter, *Competitive Strategy* (New York: Free Press, 1980).

3 M. E. Porter, *Competitive Advantage* (New York: Free Press, 1985).

4 Empirical evidence seems to indicate that, on average, international expansion is linked to greater firm profitability. For some recent exam-

ples see M. A. Hitt, R. E. Hoskisson, and H. Kim, "International Diversification, Effects on Innovation and Firm Performance," *Academy of Management Journal* 40, no. 4 (1997), pp. 767–98, and S. Tallman and J. Li, "Effects of International Diversity and Product Diversity on the Performance of Multinational Firms," *Academy of Management Journal* 39, no. 1 (1996), pp. 179–96.

5 This concept has been popularized by G. Hamel and C. K. Prahalad, *Competing for the Future* (Boston: Harvard Business School Press, 1994). The concept is grounded in the resource-based view of the firm. For a summary, see J. B. Barney, "Firm Resources and Sustained Competitive Advantage," *Journal of Management* 17 (1991), p. 99–120, and K. R. Conner, "A Historical Comparison of Resource Based Theory and Five Schools of Thought within Industrial Organization Economics: Do We Have a New Theory of the Firm?" *Journal of Management* 17 (1991), pp. 121–54.

6 Based on C. S. Trager, "Enter the Mini-Multinational," *Northeast International Business,* March 1989, pp. 13–14.

7 J. P. Womack, D. T. Jones, and D. Roos, *The Machine that Changed the World* (New York: Rawson Associates, 1990).

8 M. E. Porter, *The Competitive Advantage of Nations* (New York: Free Press, 1990).

9 R. B. Reich, *The Work of Nations* (New York: Alfred A. Knopf, 1991).

10 Kathleen Deveny et al., "McWorld?" *Business Week,* October 13, 1986, pp. 78–86; "Slow Food," *The Economist,* February 3, 1990, p. 64; Harlan S. Byrne, "Welcome to McWorld," *Barron's,* August 29, 1994, pp. 25–28; and Andrew E. Serwer, "McDonald's Conquers the World," *Fortune,* October 17, 1994, pp. 103–16.

11 G. Hall and S. Howell, "The Experience Curve from an Economist's Perspective," *Strategic Management Journal* 6 (1985), pp. 197–212.

12 A. A. Alchain, "Reliability of Progress Curves in Airframe Production," *Econometrica* 31 (1963), pp. 693–97.

13 Hall and Howell, "The Experience Curve from an Economist's Perspective."

14 For a full discussion of the source of scale economies see D. Besanko, D. Dranove, and M. Shanley, *Economics of Strategy* (New York: Wiley & Sons, 1996).

15 J. Main, "How to Go Global—and Why," *Fortune,* August 28, 1989, pp. 70–76.

16 "Matsushita Electrical Industrial in 1987," in *Transnational Management,* ed C. A. Bartlett and S. Ghoshal (Homewood, IL: Richard D. Irwin, 1992).

17 C. K. Prahalad and Yves L. Doz, *The Multinational Mission: Balancing Local Demands and Global Vision* (New York: Free Press, 1987). Prahalad and Doz talk about local responsiveness rather than local customization.

18 "The Tire Industry's Costly Obsession with Size," *The Economist,* June 8, 1993, pp. 65–66.

19 T. Levitt, "The Globalization of Markets," *Harvard Business Review,* May–June 1983, pp. 92–102.

20 C. A. Bartlett and S. Ghoshal, *Managing across Borders: The Transnational Solution* (Boston: Harvard Business School Press, 1989).

21 C. J. Chipello, "Local Presence Is Key to European Deals," *The Wall Street Journal,* June 30, 1998, p. A15.

22 This section is based on Bartlett and Ghoshal, *Managing across Borders.*

23 Guy de Jonquieres and C. Bobinski, "Wash and Get into a Lather in Poland," *Financial Times,* May 28, 1989, p. 2; "Perestroika in Soapland," *The Economist,* June 10, 1989, pp. 69–71; "After Early Stumbles P&G Is Making Inroads Overseas," *The Wall Street Journal,* February 6, 1989, p. B1; and Bartlett and Ghoshal, *Managing across Borders.*

24 Bartlett and Ghoshal, *Managing across Borders.*

25 A recent empirical study seems to confirm this hypothesis. See J. Birkinshaw, N. Hood, and S. Jonsson, "Building Firm Specific Advantages in Multinational Corporations: The Role of Subsidiary Initiative," *Strategic Management Journal* 19 (1998), pp. 221–41.

26 See P. Marsh and S. Wagstyle, "The Hungry Caterpillar," *Financial Times,* December 2, 1997, p. 22, and T. Hout, M. E. Porter, and E. Rudden, "How Global Firms Win Out," *Harvard Business Review,* September–October 1982, pp. 98–108.

27 Guy de Jonquieres, "Unilever Adopts a Clean Sheet Approach," *Financial Times,* October 21, 1991, p. 13.

28 See K. Ohmae, "The Global Logic of Strategic Alliances," *Harvard Business Review,* March–April 1989, pp. 143–54; G. Hamel, Y. L. Doz,

and C. K. Prahalad, "Collaborate with Competitors and Win!" *Harvard Business Review,* January–February 1989, pp. 133–39; and W. Burgers, C. W. L. Hill, and W. C. Kim, "Alliances in the Global Auto Industry," *Strategic Management Journal* 14 (1993), pp. 419–32.

29 "Asia Beckons," *The Economist,* May 30, 1992, pp. 63–64.

30 P. M. Reilly, "Sony's Digital Audio Format Pulls Ahead of Philips's, *The Wall Street Journal,* August 6, 1993, p. B1.

31 R. B. Reich and E. D. Mankin, "Joint Ventures with Japan Give Away Our Future," *Harvard Business Review,* March–April 1986, pp. 78–90.

32 J. Bleeke and D. Ernst, "The Way to Win in Cross-Border Alliances," *Harvard Business Review,* November–December 1991, pp. 127–35.

33 D. Darlin, "Daewoo Will Pay GM $170 Million for Venture Stake," *The Wall Street Journal,* November 11, 1992, p. A6, and D. Darlin and J. B. White, "Failed Marriage," *The Wall Street Journal,* January 16, 1992, p. A1.

34 W. Roehl and J. F. Truitt, "Stormy Open Marriages Are Better," *Columbia Journal of World Business,* Summer 1987, pp. 87–95.

35 K. McQuade and B. Gomes-Casseres, "Xerox and Fuji-Xerox," Harvard Business School Case #9-391-156.

36 T. Khanna, R. Gulati, and N. Nohria, "The Dynamics of Learning Alliances: Competition, Cooperation, and Relative Scope," *Strategic Management Journal* 19 (1998), pp. 193–210.

37 Hamel, Doz, and Prahalad, "Collaborate with Competitors."

38 B. Wysocki, "Cross-Border Alliances Become Favorite Way to Crack New Markets," *The Wall Street Journal,* March 4, 1990, p. A1.

39 Hamel, Doz, and Prahalad, "Collaborate with Competitors," p. 138.

40 Furnishing the World, *The Economist,* November 19, 1994, pp. 79–80; H. Carnegy, "Struggle to Save the Soul of IKEA," *Financial Times,* March 27, 1995, p. 12; J. Flynn and L. Bongiorno," IKEA's new game plan," *Business Week,* October 6, 1997, pp. 99–102; and IKEA's website at www.ikea.com.

Chapter 11

1 Japan's Big Bang. Enter Merrill, *The Economist,* January 3, 1998, p. 72; J. P. Donlon, "Merrill Cinch," *Chief Executive,* March 1998, pp. 28–32; D. Holley, "Merrill Lynch to Open 31 Offices throughout Japan," *Los Angeles Times,* February 13, 1998, p. D1; and A. Rowley, "Merrill Thunders into Japan," *The Banker,* March 1998, p. 6.

2 This can be reconceptualized as the resource base of the entrant, relative to indigenous competitors. For work that focuses on this issue see W. C. Bogenr, H. Thomas, and J. McGee, "A Longitudinal Study of the Competitive Positions and Entry Paths of European Firms in the U.S. Pharmaceutical Market," *Strategic Management Journal* 17 (1996), pp. 85–107; D. Collis, "A Resource Based Analysis of Global Competition," *Strategic Management Journal* 12 (1991), pp. 49–68; and S. Tallman, "Strategic Management Models and Resource Based Strategies among MNEs in a Host Market," *Strategic Management Journal* 12 (1991), pp. 69–82.

3 For a discussion of first-mover advantages see M. Liberman and D. Montgomery, "First Mover Advantages," *Strategic Management Journal* 9 (Summer Special Issue 1988), pp. 41–58.

4 J. M. Shaver, W. Mitchell, and B. Yeung, "The Effect of Own Firm and Other Firm Experience on Foreign Direct Investment Survival in the United States, 1987–92," *Strategic Management Journal* 18 (1997), pp. 811–24.

5 S. Zaheer and E. Mosakowski, "The Dynamics of the Liability of Foreignness: A Global Study of Survival in the Financial Services Industry," *Strategic Management Journal* 18 (1997), pp. 439–64.

6 Shaver, Mitchell, and Yeung, "The Effect of Own Firm and Other Firm Experience on Foreign Direct Investment Survival in the United States, 1987–92."

7 P. Ghemawat, *Commitment: The Dynamics of Strategy* (New York: Free Press, 1991).

8 L. Pappas, "Amway Sells Itself in China," *St. Petersburg Times,* March 15, 1998, p. 1H; M. Farley, "Avon and Amway Repoen in China," *Los Angeles Times,* July 25, 1998, p. D1; and Associated Press, "China Gives Amway Sales OK," *Minneapolis Star Tribune,* July 22, 1998, p. 3D.

9 R. Luecke, *Scuttle Your Ships before Advancing* (Oxford: Oxford University Press, 1994).

10 This section draws on several studies including: C. W. L. Hill, P. Hwang, and W. C. Kim, "An Eclectic Theory of the Choice of International Entry Mode," *Strategic Management Journal* 11 (1990), pp. 117–28; C. W. L. Hill and W. C. Kim, "Searching for a Dynamic Theory of the Multinational Enterprise: A Transaction Cost Model," *Strategic Management Journal* 9 (Special Issue on Strategy Content; 1988), pp. 93–104; E. Anderson and H. Gatignon, "Modes of Foreign Entry: A Transaction Cost Analysis and Propositions," *Journal of International Business Studies* 17 (1986), pp. 1–26; F. R. Root, *Entry Strategies for International Markets* (Lexington, MA: D. C. Heath, 1980); and A. Madhok, "Cost, Value and Foreign Market Entry: The Transaction and the Firm," *Strategic Management Journal* 18 (1997), pp. 39–61.

11 For a general discussion of licensing, see F. J. Contractor, "The Role of Licensing in International Strategy," *Columbia Journal of World Business,* Winter 1982, pp. 73–83.

12 See E. Terazono and C. Lorenz, "An Angry Young Warrior," *Financial Times,* September 19, 1994, p. 11, and K. McQuade and B. Gomes-Casseres, "Xerox and Fuji-Xerox," Harvard Business School Case #9-391-156.

13 O. E. Williamson, *The Economic Institutions of Capitalism* (New York: Free Press, 1985).

14 R. Howard, "The CEO as Organizational Architect," *Harvard Business Review,* September–October 1992, pp. 106–23; D. Kearns, "Leadership Through Quality," *Academy of Management Executive* 4 (1990), pp. 86–89; McQuade and Gomes-Casseres, "Xerox and Fuji-Xerox"; and Terazono and Lorenz, "An Angry Young Warrior."

15 J. H. Dunning and M. McQueen, "The Eclectic Theory of International Production: A Case Study of the International Hotel Industry," *Managerial and Decision Economics* 2 (1981), pp. 197–210.

16 Andrew E. Serwer, "McDonald's Conquers the World," *Fortune,* October 17, 1994, pp. 103–16.

17 For an excellent review of the literature of joint ventures, see B. Kogut, "Joint Ventures: Theoretical and Empirical Perspectives," *Strategic Management Journal* 9 (1988), pp. 319–32.

18 D. G. Bradley, "Managing against Expropriation," *Harvard Business Review,* July–August 1977, pp. 78–90.

19 Speech given by Tony Kobayashi at the University of Washington Business School, October 1992.

20 A. C. Inkpen and P. W. Beamish, "Knowledge, Bargaining Power, and the Instability of International Joint Ventures," *Academy of Management Review* 22 (1997), pp. 177–202, and S. H. Park and G. R. Ungson, "The Effect of National Culture, Organizational Complementarity, and Economic Motivation on Joint Venture Dissolution," *Academy of Management Journal* 40 (1997), pp. 279–307.

21 Inkpen and Beamish, "Knowledge, Bargaining Power, and the Instability of International Joint Ventures."

22 For a review of the kinds of problems encountered when making acquisitions, see Chapter 9 in C. W. L. Hill and G. R. Jones, *Strategic Management Theory* (Boston: Houghton-Mifflin, 1995).

23 This section draws on Hill, Hwang, and Kim, "An Eclectic Theory of the Choice of International Entry Mode."

24 C. W. L. Hill, "Strategies for Exploiting Technological Innovations: When and When Not to License," *Organization Science* 3 (1992), pp. 428–41.

25 S. T. Cavusgil, "Global Dimensions of Marketing," in P. E. Murphy and B. M. Enis, *Marketing* (Glenview, IL: Scott, Foresman, 1985), pp. 577–99.

26 S. M. Mehta, "Enterprise: Small Companies Look to Cultivate Foreign Business," *The Wall Street Journal,* July 7, 1994, p. B2.

27 W. Pavord and R. Bogart, "The Dynamics of the Decision to Export," *Akron Business and Economic Review,* 1975, pp. 6–11.

28 J. Norman, "Small Businesses Have Big Role in Export Field," *Orange County Register,* April 27, 1998, p. D15.

29 A. O. Ogbuehi and T. A. Longfellow, "Perceptions of U.S. Manufacturing Companies Concerning Exporting," *Journal of Small Business Management,* October 1994, pp. 37–59.

30 R. W. Haigh, "Thinking of Exporting?" *Columbia Journal of World Business,* 29 (December 1994), pp. 66–86.

31 F. Williams, "The Quest for More Efficient Commerce," *Financial Times,* October 13, 1994, p. 7.

32 L. W. Tuller, *Going Global* (Homewood, IL: Business One Irwin, 1991).

33 Haigh, "Thinking of Exporting?"

34 R. L. Rose and C. Quintanilla, "More Small U.S. Firms Take up Exporting: With Much Success," *The Wall Street Journal,* December 20, 1996, pp. A1, A10, and interview with Bryan Williams of Red Spot Paint.

35 Case written by Mureen Kibelsted and Charles Hill from original research by Mureen Kibelsted.

Chapter 12

1 Guy de Jonquieres and C. Bobinski, "Wash and Get into a Lather in Poland," *Financial Times,* May 28, 1992, pp. 2; "Perestroika in Soapland," *The Economist,* June 10, 1989, pp. 69–71; "After Early Stumbles P&G Is Making Inroads Overseas," *The Wall Street Journal,* February 6, 1989, p. B1; C. A. Bartlett and S. Ghoshal, *Managing across Borders: The Transnational Solution* (Boston: Harvard Business School Press, 1989); and N. Shirouzu, "P&G's Joy Makes an Unlikely Splash in Japan," *The Wall Street Journal,* December 10, 1997, p. B1.

2 See R. W. Ruekert and O. C. Walker, "Interactions between Marketing and R&D Departments in Implementing Different Business-Level Strategies," *Strategic Management Journal* 8 (1987), pp. 233–48, and K. B. Clark and S. C. Wheelwright, *Managing New Product and Process Development* (New York: Free Press, 1993).

3 T. Levitt, "The Globalization of Markets," *Harvard Business Review,* May–June 1983, pp. 92–102.

4 For example, see S. P. Douglas and Y. Wind, "The Myth of Globalization," *Columbia Journal of World Business,* Winter 1987, pp. 19–29, and Bartlett and Ghoshal, *Managing across Borders.*

5 S. Tully, "Teens: The Most Global Market of All," *Fortune,* May 16, 1994, pp. 90–97; M. Robichaux, "Leave It to Beavis," *The Wall Street Journal,* February 8, 1995, p. A1; A. Rawsthorn, "MTV Makes the Big Record Groups Dance to its Tune," *Financial Times,* July 7, 1995, p. 17; M. Cox, "Global Entertainment: We Are the World," *The Wall Street Journal,* March 26, 1993, p. 17; and information posted on Viacom website at www.viacom.com.

6 "Slow Food," *The Economist,* February 3, 1990, p. 64.

7 J. T. Landry, "Emerging Markets: Are Chinese Consumers Coming of Age," *Harvard Business Review,* May–June 1998, pp. 17–20.

8 C. Miller, "Teens Seen as the First Truly Global Consumers," *Marketing News,* March 27, 1995, p. 9.

9 This approach was originally developed in K. Lancaster, "A New Approach to Demand Theory," *Journal of Political Economy* 74 (1965), pp. 132–57.

10 V. R. Alden, "Who Says You Can't Crack Japanese Markets?" *Harvard Business Review,* January–February 1987, pp. 52–56.

11 T. Parker-Pope, "Custom Made," *The Wall Street Journal,* September 26, 1996, p. 22.

12 A. Rawthorn, "A Bumpy Ride over Europe's Traditions," *Financial Times,* October 31, 1988, p. 5.

13 "RCA's New Vista: The Bottom Line," *Business Week,* July 4, 1987, p. 44.

14 N. Gross and K. Rebello, "Apple? Japan Can't Say No," *Business Week,* June 29, 1992, pp. 32–33.

15 "After Early Stumbles P&G Is Making Inroads Overseas."

16 "Advertising in a Single Market," *The Economist,* March 24, 1990, p. 64.

17 D. Waller, "Charged Up over Competition Law," *Financial Times,* June 23, 1994, p. 14.

18 Kamran Kashani, "Beware the Pitfalls of Global Marketing," *Harvard Business Review,* September–October 1989, pp. 91–98.

19 J. Lumbin, "Advertising: Tina Turner Helps Pepsi's Global Effort," *New York Times,* March 10, 1986, p. D13.

20 These allegations were made on a PBS "Frontline" documentary telecast in the United States in May 1992.

21 G. Smith and B. Wolverton, "A Dark Moment for Kodak," *Business Week,* August 4, 1997, pp. 30–31.

22 R. Narisette and J. Friedland, "Disposal Income: Diaper Wars of P&G and Kimberly-Clark Now Heat up in Brazil," *The Wall Street Journal,* June 4, 1997, p A1.

23 "Printers Reflect Pattern of Trade Rows," *Financial Times,* December 20, 1988, p. 3.

24 J. F. Pickering, *Industrial Structure and Market Conduct* (London: Martin Robertson, 1974).

25 V. Mallet, "Climbing the Slippery Slope," *Financial Times,* July 28, 1994, p. 7, and A. Bolger, "Growth by Successful Targeting," *Financial Times,* June 21, 1994, p. 27.

26 The phrase was first used by economist Joseph Schumpeter in *Capitalism, Socialism, and Democracy* (New York: Harper Brothers, 1942).

27 See D. C. Mowery and N. Rosenberg, *Technology and the Pursuit of Economic Growth* (Cambridge: Cambridge University Press, 1989), and M. E. Porter, *The Competitive Advantage of Nations* (New York: The Free Press, 1990).

28 C. Farrell, "Industrial Policy," *Business Week,* April 6, 1992, pp. 70–75.

29 W. Kuemmerle, "Building Effective R&D Capabilities Abroad," *Harvard Business Review,* March–April 1997, pp. 61–70.

30 "When the Corporate Lab Goes to Japan," *New York Times,* April 28, 1991, sec. 3, p. 1.

31 D. Shapley, "Globalization Prompts Exodus," *Financial Times,* March 17, 1994, p. 10.

32 E. Mansfield, "How Economists See R&D," *Harvard Business Review,* November–December 1981, pp. 98–106.

33 Ibid.

34 Booz, Allen & Hamilton, "New Products Management for the 1980's," privately published research report, 1982.

35 A. L. Page, "PDMA's New Product Development Practices Survey: Performance and Best Practices," PDMA 15th Annual International Conference, Boston, MA, October 16, 1991.

36 K. B. Clark and S. C. Wheelwright, *Managing New Product and Process Development* (New York: Free Press, 1993), and M. A. Shilling and Charles W. L. Hill, "Managing the New Product Development Process," *Academy of Management Executive* 12, no. 3 (1998), pp. 67–81.

37 O. Port, "Moving Past the Assembly Line," *Business Week Special Issue. Reinventing America,* 1992, pp. 177–80.

38 K. B. Clark and T. Fujimoto, "The Power of Product Integrity," *Harvard Business Review,* November–December 1990, pp. 107–18; Clark and Wheelwright, *Managing New Product and Process Development;* S. L. Brown and K. M. Eisenhardt, "Product Development: Past Research, Present Findings, and Future Directions," *Academy of Management Review,* 20 (1995), pp. 343–78; and G. Stalk and T. M. Hout, *Competing against Time* (New York: Free Press, 1990).

39 Shilling and Hill, "Managing the New Product Development Process."

40 C. Christensen, "Quantum Corporation–Business and Product Teams," Harvard Business School Case #9-692-023.

41 Information comes from the company's website, and from K. Ferdows, "Making the Most of Foreign Factories," *Harvard Business Review,* March–April 1997, pp. 73–88.

42 M. Sawyer, "Fashion: It's Not Working Out," *The Observer,* May 3, 1998, p. 12; P. Vallely, "Saturday Story," *The Independent,* December 6, 1997, p. 19; and N. Robinson, "Nike Just Does It in Bad Taste," *The Guardian,* November 26, 1996, p. 22.

Chapter 13

1 J. Margretta, "Fast, Global, and Entrepreneurial: Supply Chain Management Hong Kong Style," *Harvard Business Review,* September–October 1998, pp. 102–14; J. Ridding, "A Multinational Trading Group with Chinese Characteristics," *Financial Times,* November 7, 1997, p. 16; J. Ridding, "The Family in the Frame," *Financial Times,* October 28, 1996, p. 12; and J. Lo, "Second Half Doubts Shadow Li & Fung Strength in Interims," *South China Morning Post,* August 27, 1998, p. 3.

2 B. C. Arntzen, G. G. Brown, T. P. Harrison, and L. L. Trafton, "Global Supply Chain Management at Digital Equipment Corporation, "*Interfaces,* 25 (1995), pp. 69–93.

3 D. A. Garvin, "What Does Product Quality Really Mean," *Sloan Management Review* 26 (Fall 1984), pp. 25–44.

4 For general background information, see "How to Build Quality," *The Economist,* September 23, 1989, pp. 91–92; A. Gabor, *The Man Who Discovered Quality* (New York: Penguin, 1990); and P. B. Crosby, *Quality Is Free* (New York: Mentor, 1980).

5 M. Saunders, "US Firms Doing Business in Europe Have Options in Registering for ISO 9000 Quality Standards," *Business America,* June 14, 1993, p.7

6 G. Stalk and T. M. Hout, *Competing Against Time* (New York: Free Press, 1990).

7 M. A. Cohen and H. L. Lee, "Resource Deployment Analysis of Global Manufacturing and Distribution Networks," *Journal of Manufacturing and Operations Management* 2 (1989), pp. 81–104.

8 For a review of the technical arguments, see D. A. Hay and D. J. Morris, *Industrial Economics: Theory and Evidence* (Oxford: Oxford University Press, 1979). See also C. W. L. Hill and G. R. Jones, *Strategic Management: An Integrated Approach* (Boston: Houghton Mifflin, 1995).

9 See P. Nemetz and L. Fry, "Flexible Manufacturing Organizations: Implications for Strategy Formulation," *Academy of Management Review,* 13 (1988), pp. 627–38; N. Greenwood, *Implementing Flexible Manufacturing Systems* (New York: Halstead Press, 1986); and J. P. Womack, D. T. Jones, and D. Roos, *The Machine That Changed the World* (New York: Rawson Associates, 1990).

10 J. H. Gilmore and B. J. Pine II, "The Four Faces of Mass Customization," *Harvard Business Review,* January–February 1997, pp. 91–101.

11 Womack, Jones, and Roos, *The Machine That Changed the World.*

12 M. A. Cusumano, *The Japanese Automobile Industry* (Cambridge, MA: Harvard University Press, 1989); Taiichi Ohno, *Toyota Production System* (Cambridge, MA: Productivity Press, 1990); and Womack, Jones, and Roos, *The Machine That Changed the World.*

13 J. D. Goldhar and D. Lei, "The Shape of Twenty-First Century Global Manufacturing," *Journal of Business Strategy,* March/April, 1991, pp. 37–41; "Factories That Turn Nuts into Bolts," *U.S. News and World Reports,* July 14, 1986, pp. 44–45; and J. Kotkin, "The Great American Revival," *Inc.,* February 1988, pp. 52–63.

14 K. Ferdows, "Making the Most of Foreign Factories," *Harvard Business Review,* March–April 1997, pp. 73–88.

15 This argument represents a simple extension of the dynamic capabilities research stream in the strategic management literature. See D. J. Teece, G. Pisano, and A. Shuen, "Dynamic Capabilities and Strategic Management," *Strategic Management Journal* 18 (1997), pp. 509–33.

16 Ferdows, "Making the Most of Foreign Factories," and "Hewlett-Packard: Singapore," Harvard Business School case #694-035.

17 Based on interviews between Charles Hill and senior management personnel at Boeing.

18 For a review of the evidence, see O. E. Williamson, *The Economic Institutions of Capitalism* (New York: The Free Press, 1985).

19 A. D. Chandler, *The Visible Hand* (Cambridge, MA: Harvard University Press, 1977).

20 For a review of these arguments, see C. W. L. Hill and R. E. Hoskisson, "Strategy and Structure in the Multiproduct Firm," *Academy of Management Review* 12 (1987), pp. 331–41.

21 C. W. L. Hill, "Cooperation, Opportunism, and the Invisible Hand," *Academy of Management Review* 15 (1990), pp. 500–13.

22 See R. Narasimhan and J. R. Carter, "Organization, Communication and Coordination of International Sourcing," *International Marketing Review* 7 (1990), pp. 6–20, and B. C. Arntzen, G. G. Brown, T. P. Harrison, and L. L. Trafton, "Global Supply Chain Management at Digital Equipment Corporation," *Interfaces* 25 (1995), pp. 69–93.

23 H. F. Busch, "Integrated Materials Management," *IJPD & MM* 18 (1990), pp. 28–39.

24 P. Bradley, "Global Sourcing Takes Split Second Timing," *Purchasing,* July 20, 1989, pp. 52–58, and S. Greenblat, "Continuous Improvement in Supply Chain Management," *Chief Executive,* June 1993, pp. 40–44.

25 P. Buxbaum, "Timberland's New Spin on Global Logistics," *Distribution,* May 1994, pp. 33–36; A. E. Serwer, "Will Timberland Grow Up?" *Fortune,* May 29, 1995, p. 24; M. Tedeschi, "Timberland Vows to Get on the Ball," *Footwear News,* May 22, 1995, p. 2; and *Timberland Annual Report, 1997.*

Chapter 14

1 D. A. Amfuso, "HR Unites the World of Coca-Cola," *Personnel Journal,* November 1994, pp. 112–20, and S. Foley, "Internationalizing the Cola Wars," Harvard Business School Case #9-794-146.

2 P. J. Dowling and R. S. Schuler, *International Dimensions of Human Resource Management* (Boston: PSW-Kent, 1990).

3 J. Millman, M. A. von Glinow, and M. Nathan, "Organizational Life Cycles and Strategic International Human Resource Management in Multinational Companies," *Academy of Management Review* 16 (1991), pp. 318–39.

4 E. H. Schein, *Organizational Culture and Leadership* (San Francisco: Jossey-Bass, 1985).

5 H. V. Perlmutter, "The Tortuous Evolution of the Multinational Corporation," *Columbia Journal of World Business* 4 (1969), pp. 9–18; D. A. Heenan and H. V. Perlmutter, *Multinational Organizational Development* (Reading, MA: Addison-Wesley, 1979); and D. A. Ondrack, "International Human Resources Management in European and North American Firms," *International Studies of Management and Organization* 15 (1985), pp. 6–32.

6 V. Reitman and M. Schuman, "Men's Club: Japanese and Korean Companies Rarely Look Outside for People to Run Their Overseas Operations," *The Wall Street Journal,* September 26, 1996, p. 17.

7 S. Beechler and J. Z. Yang, "The Transfer of Japanese Style Management to American Subsidiaries," *Journal of International Business Studies* 25 (1994), pp. 467–91.

8 Reitman and Schuman, "Men's Club: Japanese and Korean Companies Rarely Look Outside for People to Run Their Overseas Operations."

9 C. A. Bartlett and S. Ghoshal, *Managing across Borders: The Transnational Solution* (Boston: Harvard Business School Press, 1989).

10 S. J. Kobrin, "Geocentric Mindset and Multinational Strategy," *Journal of International Business Studies* 25 (1994), pp. 493–511.

11 P. M. Rosenzweig and N. Nohria, "Influences on Human Resource Management Practices in Multinational Corporations," *Journal of International Business Studies* 25 (1994), pp. 229–51.

12 Kobrin, "Geocentric Mindset and Multinational Strategy."

13 J. S. Black, M. Mendenhall, and G. Oddou, "Towards a Comprehensive Model of International Adjustment," *Academy of Management Review* 16 (1991), pp. 291–317, and J. Shay and T. J. Bruce, "Expatriate Managers," *Cornell Hotel & Resturant Administration Quarterly,* February 1997, pp. 30–40.

14 M. G. Harvey, "The Multinational Corporation's Expatriate Problem: An Application of Murphy's Law," *Business Horizons* 26 (1983), pp. 71–78.

15 Shay and Bruce, "Expatriate Managers."

16 S. Caudron, "Training Ensures Overseas Success," *Personnel Journal,* December 1991, p. 27.

17 Black, Mendenhall, and Oddou, "Towards a Comprehensive Model of International Adjustment.

18 R. L. Tung, "Selection and Training Procedures of U.S., European, and Japanese Multinationals," *California Management Review* 25 (1982), pp. 57–71.

19 C. M. Salomon, "Success Abroad Depends upon More Than Job Skills," *Personnel Journal,* April 1994, pp. 51–58.

20 Ibid.

21 E. Smockum, "Don't Forget the Trailing Spouse," *Financial Times,* May 6, 1998, p. 22; V. Frazee, "Tearing Down Roadblocks," *Workforce,* 77, no. 2 (1998), pp. 50–54; and C. Sievers, "Expatriate Management," *HR Focus* 7593 (1998), pp. 75–76.

22 M. Harvey, "Addressing the Dual Career Expatriation Dilemma," *Human Resource Planning* 19, no. 4 (1996), pp. 18–32.

23 M. Mendenhall and G. Oddou, "The Dimensions of Expatriate Acculturation: A Review," *Academy of Management Review* 10 (1985), pp. 39–47.

24 I. Torbiorin, *Living Abroad: Personal Adjustment and Personnel Policy in the Overseas Setting* (New York: John Wiley, 1982).

25 R. L. Tung, "Selection and Training of Personnel for Overseas Assignments," *Columbia Journal of World Business* 16 (1981), pp. 68–78.

26 Salomon, "Success Abroad Depends upon More Than Job Skills."

27 S. Ronen, "Training and International Assignee," in *Training and Career Development,* ed. I.

Goldstein (San Francisco: Jossey-Bass, 1985), and Tung, "Selection and Training of Personnel for Overseas Assignments.

28 Salomon, "Success Abroad Depends upon More Than Job Skills."

29 Harvey, "Addressing the Dual Career Expatriation Dilemma," and J. W. Hunt, "The Perils of Foreign Postings for Two," *Financial Times,* May 6, 1998, p. 22.

30 Dowling and Schuler, *International Dimensions of Human Resource Management.*

31 Ibid.

32 G. Baliga and J. C. Baker, "Multinational Corporate Policies for Expatriate Managers: Selection, Training, and Evaluation," *Advanced Management Journal,* Autumn 1985, pp. 31–38.

33 C. Rapoport, "A Tough Swede Invades the U.S.," *Fortune,* June 20, 1992, pp. 67–70.

34 J. C. Baker, "Foreign Language and Departure Training in U.S. Multinational Firms," *Personnel Administrator,* July 1984, pp. 68–70.

35 A 1997 study by the Conference Board looked at this. For a summary, see L. Grant, "That Overseas Job Could Derail Your Career," *Fortune,* April 14, 1997, p. 166.

36 J. S. Black and M. E. Mendenhall, *Global Assignments: Successfully Expatriating and Repatriating International Managers* (San Francisco: Jossey-Bass, 1992).

37 Ibid.

38 Grant, "That Overseas Job Could Derail Your Career.

39 C. M. Salomon, "Repatriation: Up, Down, or Out?" *Personnel Journal,* January 1995, pp. 28–34.

40 S. C. Schneider, "National v. Corporate Culture: Implications for Human Resource Management," *Human Resource Management* 27 (Summer 1988), pp. 231–46.

41 Bartlett and Ghoshal, *Managing across Borders.*

42 G. Oddou and M. Mendenhall, "Expatriate Performance Appraisal: Problems and Solutions," in *International Human Resource Management,* ed. Mendenhall and Oddou (Boston: PWS-Kent, 1991); Dowling and Schuler, *International Dimensions*; R. S. Schuler and G. W. Florkowski, "International Human Resource Management," in

B. J. Punnett and O. Shenkar, *Handbook for International Management Research* (Oxford: Blackwell, 1996); and K. Roth and S. O'Donnell, "Foreign Subsidiary Compensation Strategy: An Agency Theory Perspective," *Academy of Management Journal* 39, no. 3 (1996) pp. 678–703.

43 Oddou and Mendenhall, "Expatriate Performance Appraisal."

44 "Expatriates Often See Little Benefit to Careers in Foreign Stints, Indifference at Home," *The Wall Street Journal,* December 11, 1989, p. B1.

45 Oddou and Mendenhall, "Expatriate Performance Appraisal," and Schuler and Florkowski, "International Human Resource Management."

46 R. C. Longworth, "US Executives Sit on Top of the World," *Chicago Tribune,* May 31, 1998, p. C1.

47 A. Bennett, "Executive Pay: What's an Expatriate?" *The Wall Street Journal,* April 21, 1994, p. A5, and J. Flynn, "Continental Divide over Executive Pay," *Business Week,* July 3, 1995, pp. 40–41.

48 C. Reynolds, "Compensation of Overseas Personnel," in *Handbook of Human Resource Administration,* ed. J. J. Famularo (New York: McGraw-Hill, 1986).

49 M. Helms, "International Executive Compensation Practices," in *International Human Resource Management,* ed. M. Mendenhall and G. Oddou (Boston: PWS-Kent, 1991).

50 G. W. Latta, "Expatriate Incentives," *HR Focus,* March 1998, p. S3.

51 C. K. Prahalad and Y. L. Doz, *The Multinational Mission* (New York: The Free Press, 1987).

52 Ibid.

53 Schuler and Florkowski, "International Human Resource Management."

54 J. P. Womack, D. T. Jones, and D. Roos, *The Machine That Changed the World* (New York: Rawson Associates, 1990).

55 J. S. Lublin, "Managing Globally: Younger Managers Learn Global Skills," *The Wall Street Journal,* March 31, 1992, p. B1; B. Hagerty, "Companies in Europe Seeking Executives Who Can Cross Borders in a Single Bound," *The Wall Street Journal,* January 25, 1991, p. B1; and C. M. Solomon, "Global Operations Demand That HR Re-think Diversity," *Personnel Journal,* 73 (1994), pp. 40–50.

Name Index

Subject Index

P

X

Y

Z